Lecture Notes in Computer Science　13322

More information about this series at https://link.springer.com/bookseries/558

Marcelo M. Soares · Elizabeth Rosenzweig ·
Aaron Marcus (Eds.)

Design, User Experience, and Usability

Design for Emotion, Well-being and Health, Learning, and Culture

11th International Conference, DUXU 2022
Held as Part of the 24th HCI International Conference, HCII 2022
Virtual Event, June 26 – July 1, 2022
Proceedings, Part II

 Springer

Editors
Marcelo M. Soares
Southern University of Science
and Technology – SUSTech
Shenzhen, China

Elizabeth Rosenzweig
World Usability Day and Bubble Mountain
Consulting
Newton Center, MA, USA

Aaron Marcus
Aaron Marcus and Associates
Berkeley, CA, USA

ISSN 0302-9743   ISSN 1611-3349 (electronic)
Lecture Notes in Computer Science
ISBN 978-3-031-05899-8   ISBN 978-3-031-05900-1 (eBook)
https://doi.org/10.1007/978-3-031-05900-1

This Springer imprint is published by the registered company Springer Nature Switzerland AG
The registered company address is: Gewerbestrasse 11, 6330 Cham, Switzerland

Foreword

Human-computer interaction (HCI) is acquiring an ever-increasing scientific and industrial importance, as well as having more impact on people's everyday life, as an ever-growing number of human activities are progressively moving from the physical to the digital world. This process, which has been ongoing for some time now, has been dramatically accelerated by the COVID-19 pandemic. The HCI International (HCII) conference series, held yearly, aims to respond to the compelling need to advance the exchange of knowledge and research and development efforts on the human aspects of design and use of computing systems.

The 24th International Conference on Human-Computer Interaction, HCI International 2022 (HCII 2022), was planned to be held at the Gothia Towers Hotel and Swedish Exhibition & Congress Centre, Göteborg, Sweden, during June 26 to July 1, 2022. Due to the COVID-19 pandemic and with everyone's health and safety in mind, HCII 2022 was organized and run as a virtual conference. It incorporated the 21 thematic areas and affiliated conferences listed on the following page.

A total of 5583 individuals from academia, research institutes, industry, and governmental agencies from 88 countries submitted contributions, and 1276 papers and 275 posters were included in the proceedings to appear just before the start of the conference. The contributions thoroughly cover the entire field of human-computer interaction, addressing major advances in knowledge and effective use of computers in a variety of application areas. These papers provide academics, researchers, engineers, scientists, practitioners, and students with state-of-the-art information on the most recent advances in HCI. The volumes constituting the set of proceedings to appear before the start of the conference are listed in the following pages.

The HCI International (HCII) conference also offers the option of 'Late Breaking Work' which applies both for papers and posters, and the corresponding volume(s) of the proceedings will appear after the conference. Full papers will be included in the 'HCII 2022 - Late Breaking Papers' volumes of the proceedings to be published in the Springer LNCS series, while 'Poster Extended Abstracts' will be included as short research papers in the 'HCII 2022 - Late Breaking Posters' volumes to be published in the Springer CCIS series.

I would like to thank the Program Board Chairs and the members of the Program Boards of all thematic areas and affiliated conferences for their contribution and support towards the highest scientific quality and overall success of the HCI International 2022 conference; they have helped in so many ways, including session organization, paper reviewing (single-blind review process, with a minimum of two reviews per submission) and, more generally, acting as goodwill ambassadors for the HCII conference.

This conference would not have been possible without the continuous and unwavering support and advice of Gavriel Salvendy, founder, General Chair Emeritus, and Scientific Advisor. For his outstanding efforts, I would like to express my appreciation to Abbas Moallem, Communications Chair and Editor of HCI International News.

June 2022   Constantine Stephanidis

HCI International 2022 Thematic Areas and Affiliated Conferences

Thematic Areas

- HCI: Human-Computer Interaction
- HIMI: Human Interface and the Management of Information

Affiliated Conferences

- EPCE: 19th International Conference on Engineering Psychology and Cognitive Ergonomics
- AC: 16th International Conference on Augmented Cognition
- UAHCI: 16th International Conference on Universal Access in Human-Computer Interaction
- CCD: 14th International Conference on Cross-Cultural Design
- SCSM: 14th International Conference on Social Computing and Social Media
- VAMR: 14th International Conference on Virtual, Augmented and Mixed Reality
- DHM: 13th International Conference on Digital Human Modeling and Applications in Health, Safety, Ergonomics and Risk Management
- DUXU: 11th International Conference on Design, User Experience and Usability
- C&C: 10th International Conference on Culture and Computing
- DAPI: 10th International Conference on Distributed, Ambient and Pervasive Interactions
- HCIBGO: 9th International Conference on HCI in Business, Government and Organizations
- LCT: 9th International Conference on Learning and Collaboration Technologies
- ITAP: 8th International Conference on Human Aspects of IT for the Aged Population
- AIS: 4th International Conference on Adaptive Instructional Systems
- HCI-CPT: 4th International Conference on HCI for Cybersecurity, Privacy and Trust
- HCI-Games: 4th International Conference on HCI in Games
- MobiTAS: 4th International Conference on HCI in Mobility, Transport and Automotive Systems
- AI-HCI: 3rd International Conference on Artificial Intelligence in HCI
- MOBILE: 3rd International Conference on Design, Operation and Evaluation of Mobile Communications

List of Conference Proceedings Volumes Appearing Before the Conference

39. CCIS 1582, HCI International 2022 Posters - Part III, edited by Constantine Stephanidis, Margherita Antona and Stavroula Ntoa
40. CCIS 1583, HCI International 2022 Posters - Part IV, edited by Constantine Stephanidis, Margherita Antona and Stavroula Ntoa

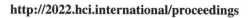

http://2022.hci.international/proceedings

Preface

User experience (UX) refers to a person's thoughts, feelings, and behavior when using interactive systems. UX design becomes fundamentally important for new and emerging mobile, ubiquitous, and omnipresent computer-based contexts. The scope of design, user experience and usability (DUXU) extends to all aspects of the user's interaction with a product or service, how it is perceived, learned, and used. DUXU also addresses design knowledge, methods and practices, with a focus on deeply human-centered processes. Usability, usefulness, and appeal are fundamental requirements for effective user-experience design.

The 11th Design, User Experience, and Usability (DUXU) Conference 2022, an affiliated conference of the HCI International Conference, encouraged papers from professionals, academics, and researchers that report results and cover a broad range of research and development activities on a variety of related topics. Professionals include designers, software engineers, scientists, marketers, business leaders, and practitioners in fields such as AI, architecture, financial and wealth management, game design, graphic design, finance, healthcare, industrial design, mobile, psychology, travel, and vehicles.

This year's submissions covered a wide range of content across the spectrum of design, user-experience, and usability. The latest trends and technologies are represented, as well as contributions from professionals, academics, and researchers across the globe. The breadth of their work is indicated in the following topics covered in the proceedings.

Three volumes of the HCII 2022 proceedings are dedicated to this year's edition of the DUXU Conference:

- Design, User Experience, and Usability: UX Research, Design, and Assessment (Part I), which addresses topics related to processes, methods, and tools for UX design and evaluation; user requirements, preferences and UX influential factors; as well as usability, acceptance, and user experience assessment.
- Design, User Experience, and Usability: Design for Emotion, Well-being and Health, Learning, and Culture (Part II), which addresses topics related to emotion, motivation, and persuasion design; design for well-being and health; learning experience-design; as well as globalization, localization, and culture issues.
- Design, User Experience, and Usability: Design Thinking and Practice in Contemporary and Emerging Technologies (Part III), which addresses topics related to design thinking and philosophy, analysis of case studies, as well as design and user experience in emerging technologies.

Papers of these volumes are included for publication after a minimum of two single–blind reviews from the members of the DUXU Program Board or, in some cases, from members of the Program Boards of other affiliated conferences. We would like to thank all of them for their invaluable contribution, support, and efforts.

June 2022   Marcelo M. Soares
                                                   Elizabeth Rosenzweig
                                                   Aaron Marcus

11th International Conference on Design, User Experience and Usability (DUXU 2022)

Program Board Chairs: **Marcelo M. Soares**, Southern University of Science and Technology – SUSTech, China, **Elizabeth Rosenzweig**, World Usability Day and Bubble Mountain Consulting, USA, and **Aaron Marcus**, Aaron Marcus and Associates, USA

- Sisira Adikari, University of Canberra, Australia
- Ahmad Alhuwwari, Orange Jordan, Jordan
- Claire Ancient, University of Winchester, UK
- Roger Ball, Georgia Institute of Technology, USA
- Eric Brangier, Université de Lorraine, France
- Tian Cao, Nanjing University of Science & Technology, China
- Silvia De los Rios, Indra, Spain
- Romi Dey, Solved By Design, India
- Marc Fabri, Leeds Beckett University, UK
- Wei Liu, Beijing Normal University, China
- Zhen Liu, South China University of Technology, China
- Martin Maguire, Loughborough University, UK
- Judith Moldenhauer, Wayne State University, USA
- Gunther Paul, James Cook University, Australia
- Francisco Rebelo, University of Lisbon, Portugal
- Christine Riedmann-Streitz, MarkenFactory GmbH, Germany
- Patricia Search, Rensselaer Polytechnic Institute, USA
- Dorothy Shamonsky, Brandeis University, USA
- David Sless, Communication Research Institute, Australia
- Elisangela Vilar, Universidade de Lisboa, Portugal
- Wei Wang, Hunan University, China
- Haining Wang, Hunan University, China

The full list with the Program Board Chairs and the members of the Program Boards of all thematic areas and affiliated conferences is available online at

http://www.hci.international/board-members-2022.php

HCI International 2023

The 25th International Conference on Human-Computer Interaction, HCI International 2023, will be held jointly with the affiliated conferences at the AC Bella Sky Hotel and Bella Center, Copenhagen, Denmark, 23–28 July 2023. It will cover a broad spectrum of themes related to human-computer interaction, including theoretical issues, methods, tools, processes, and case studies in HCI design, as well as novel interaction techniques, interfaces, and applications. The proceedings will be published by Springer. More information will be available on the conference website: http://2023.hci.international/.

General Chair
Constantine Stephanidis
University of Crete and ICS-FORTH
Heraklion, Crete, Greece
Email: general_chair@hcii2023.org

http://2023.hci.international/

Contents – Part II

Learning Experience Design

Globalization, Localization, and Culture Issues

Emotion, Motivation, and Persuasion Design

Research on Museum Online User Classification and Evaluation Model Based on the Fogg's Behavior Model

Hanwen Du[✉], Meiyu Zhou, and Yihui Li

East China University of Science and Technology, Shanghai, China
soarmrd@163.com

Abstract. The main purpose of this paper is to construct the evaluation index of the system and study the degree of influence of the main factors affecting the design of mobile music app from the perspective of user experience. By means of literature research and questionnaire survey, the index system of influencing factors of user experience was established, and the fuzzy DEMATEL model was established. This paper constructs an index system of influencing factors of mobile phone music app user experience, which includes five dimensions (reliability, usability, ease of use, interaction, security) and 19 influencing factors. The 10 key factors affecting the mobile music App user experience were identified, namely, music richness, personalized service, listening function, copyright information protection, interpersonal interaction, system performance, personal information protection, audio quality, interface design and payment protection. Finally, the index system of influencing factors of mobile music App user experience is constructed, and the importance of influencing factors of mobile music App user experience is analyzed.

Keywords: Fogg's behavior model · User type evaluation · Cultural and creative product design

1 Introduction

In the period of rapid development of internet, the concept of "intelligent earth" and "intelligent city" has been widely accepted by society. In this trend of digitization, intelligencing and networking, museums, which are cultural landmarks in urban centers, are playing a new role by creatively integrating the link between people and the internet.

From the theme of International Museum Day—"Hyperlinked Museums: A New Approach, a New Public," to "Equality Museums: Diversity and Inclusion" [1], we can see that museums, as social actors, have become involved in the political and cultural issues of modern society in a very constructive way, which shows the increasingly close mutually empowering relationship between museums and society.

As museums grow in popularity, new museum concepts are popping up that rely on digital virtual reality, the Internet of Things, 3D modeling, big data, cloud computing, 5G and more. For example, the Museum of Digital Culture, the Virtual Museum, the Museum

M. M. Soares et al. (Eds.): HCII 2022, LNCS 13322, pp. 3–20, 2022.
https://doi.org/10.1007/978-3-031-05900-1_1

of New Media Art, the Pan-Museum, the Museum of Smart Cities, etc. [2]. In particular, the development of digital museums, which transform objects into numbers, has greatly enhanced their vitality and interaction, expanded time and space, and communicated information to the museum public in a more direct and efficient way. With the widespread adoption of new technologies such as the Internet of Things, the advanced phase of digital museums, the "human-centric" museum, has come to the museum public.

Museums have seen a global "collective wave" of online visits, according to the 2019 Museums Venture Market Data Report, published jointly by Tsinghua University's Institute of Cultural Economics and Tmall [3]. At present, museums' online and online Venture shopping platforms have received more attention for their convenience and freedom, and major museum websites have sprung up over the same period.

In terms of overall size, the market size of cultural and creative products tripled in 2019 compared to 2017, the report noted. It can be seen that China's cultural innovation market economy, especially in the field of cultural museums, has developed rapidly in recent years, and the online museum market has also risen and developed rapidly. The resulting museum creations are also hugely popular among contemporary youth, especially on online e-commerce platforms.

Arguably the modern museum's precious resource is no longer just its digital collection, but also its online users, who are not to be trifled with and cannot be ignored in the modern online world [4]. These user resources bring the unique gifts of the new information technology era, making modern museums function under the change of the new era. The digitization of museums is one of the means to realize the fundamental goal of serving society and developing museums [2]. We are ushering in and creating the era of the new museum in all its fullness.

However, with the development of the new craze, "single product type", "lack of interactive engagement sense", "lack of user motivation", "repetitive venture-based merchandise sales' 'and other problems seriously affect the user participation experience, which leads to low user retention rate of museum platforms, low repurchase rate of online venture-based products and lack of freshness. Therefore, it is practical to study the user behavior of online platforms of museums.

This paper conducts a questionnaire survey on the users of the museum online platform, and forms a 33-member panel of experts, uses fuzzy comprehensive evaluation model to analyze the relationship between quantitative ability and motivation factors to influence the behavior of museum online users, puts forward online user type evaluation model, and enriches the theoretical and practical research of Fogg's behavior model.

2 Fogg's Behavior Model

According to Fogg's behavior model, human behavior is the product of three factors: motivation, ability, and trigger [5]. There are three types of triggers, according to their different roles: facilitator, sign, and sparks. Therefore, an individual must have sufficient motivation at the same time to perform his or her targeted behavior; sufficient ability to perform his or her targeted behavior; and prompt a successful trigger behavior.

As Fogg's behavior model becomes more widely used in the study of user behavior, more and more research has been done on it. For example, Johannes Zachrisson Daae [6] selected design strategies from the Fogg Behavioral Grid to combine with insights to further study guidelines for different types of design strategies. However, Fogg's behavior model does not have a clear operating standard, so it makes sense to integrate appropriate simulation modeling practices through ancillary integration when using it. Therefore, a corresponding study of specific simulated modeling practices and mathematics has been carried out: Fernando et al. [7] proposed an Fogg's behavior model-based modeling framework for persuasion techniques that adds data and practical methodological support to their conceptual theory. Also in view of the lack of data information in the model, Marcus Guimaraes et al. [8] proposed a threshold line dynamic behavior based on the Kolmogorov mean of the dataset to identify trigger positions, providing theoretical support for the technical evaluation process of the model. It is also used as a behavioral design model for online social network users [9]. In addition, Yansen Theopilus et al. [10] combine FBM with universal design, analyze user experience, and finally develop a new product design approach that is suitable for creating persuasive universal products that generate positive user experiences that lead to desired behavior.

Fogg's behavior model can be used in marketing, healthcare, environmental advocacy, organizational management, and social affairs [11, 12]. For example, it has been applied to product design, and many product managers often use it at work. [13] These fields are just a few examples of the application of behavioral design. With the development of science and technology and the importance and practice of behavioral design, behavioral design has influenced more fields, and the Fogg's behavior model is bound to mature.

By using the deep analysis and application of Fogg's behavior model on the Internet, we can influence online users from the behavioral level, and even merge user goals and museum service goals to achieve user-centered goals and develop more efficient design strategies.

Researcher Pedro et al. looked at how Facebook, the world's largest social network, uses the FBM model [14]. The study shows that all the principles of the Computer Persuasion Tool category (with the exception of self-monitoring) can be implemented on social networks. It also explains what each principle does and how it affects the interactions of social network users. The findings suggest that social network users can be divided into three profiles: content producers (users who create and post content on the network), participants (whose primary characteristics are through likes and comments), and then finally viewers (users whose primary behavior is watching content posted on the social network), suggesting that some persuasive principles affect users differently based on their personal information, suggesting that the effectiveness of some principles is related to this online behavior. It also proves the feasibility of Fogg's behavior model in the analysis of Internet user behavior.

All in all, the mathematical modeling and practice of Fogg's behavior model is a further exploration of Fogg's theory. These studies provide practical guidance for the further practical operation of Fogg's behavior model, such as the research direction and method of Fogg's behavior model, especially how to observe the definition of Fogg's behavior model motivation and ability, and how to adapt the classification of triggers to the user.

3 Online Museum User Classification Based on Fogg Behavior Model

If the user's use of the museum's online platform is to be considered a complete act, the occurrence of such an act necessarily requires sufficient motivation, ability, and adaptive cue triggers. If users are willing to use different modules of the museum's website, will the factors influencing this behavior have the same effect? Or will the user's position on the Fogg's behavior model 2D coordinate axis remain the same when using the operation? If the location is the same, can this provide different design method information for the cultural product module of this design practice? In order to solve this problem and explore its practical significance, this paper, based on the investigation of the user behavior environment of "Heritage Plus" App, a typical representative museum platform, examines the relationship between user behavior and the three elements of Fogg's behavior model from a macroscopic perspective, and qualitatively analyzes the composition of Fogg behavior model elements when users use platform adaptation modules, so as to obtain their impact on cultural and creative product design.

According to Fogg's behavior model's three-element theory of motivation, competence and cues, the core influencing factors of motivation depend on three variables: feelings, expectations and social belonging. Similarly, there should be five relative variables of ability: money, time, physical effort, brain cycles and routine.

In the model, the validity of behavior is correlated with an individual's motivation and ability level before a given task, suggesting persuasion can be obtained from trigger intervention. So we propose the basic framework of reasoning rules for the relationship between competence and motivation and triggers, first selecting the trigger category and then selecting the trigger cue, like Table 1.

Table 1. Based on the summary of fogg's behavior model three-factor

Motivation and competency levels	Triggers
Low motivation, low ability	N/A
Low motivation, average ability	Sparks
Low motivation, high ability	Sparks
Average motivation, low ability	Facilitator
Average motivation, average ability	Sign
Average motivation, high ability	Sparks
High motivation, low ability	Facilitator
High motivation, average ability	Facilitator
High motivation, high ability	Sign

The premise of using the above framework rules is that designers or platforms need to judge the motivation and ability of online users first. According to the characteristics of online users, the typical corresponding user motivation and ability level of three typical triggers are analyzed as shown in Table 2.

Table 2. Three typical user models

Triggers	Motivation and competency levels
Sparks	Low motivation, high ability
Facilitator	High motivation, low ability
Sign	High motivation, high ability

4   Online User Type Evaluation Model

4.1   Sample Data

A questionnaire of museum website users was conducted between 2020-09-01 and 2020-09-30 (the questionnaire collected 300 responses, but excluded 83 responses from respondents who chose not to trust the museum online, as well as 4 invalid questionnaires with time factors, and 213 valid questionnaires). Table 3 shows a preliminary selection of 178 subjects with experience using the online platform and further analysis based on professional, cultural background, age group, etc. (two subjects chose to keep their gender confidential).

Table 3. Basic information about the users interviewed.

	Classification	Number of people	Proportion
Gender	Male	72	40.45%
	Female	104	58.43%
Occupation	Researcher	23	12.92%
	Art lovers	78	43.82%
	Artist	8	4.49%
	Art students	30	16.85%
	Literature and history students	17	9.55%
	Museum staff	2	1.12%
	Teacher	2	1.12%
	Other	18	10.11%
Degree of artistic literacy	Experts	33	18.54%

(*continued*)

Table 3. (*continued*)

	Classification	Number of people	Proportion
	In process of learning	130	73.03%
	Little or no dabbling	15	8.43%
Age	20–24	55	30.90%
	25–34	92	51.69%
	35–39	31	17.41%

In the process of analytic hierarchy process (AHP) index construction, 33 experts with senior experience in the questionnaire were invited to carry out the questionnaire, and the significance of each index was compared by following the scale 1–9. First, collect the scores and count the number of times each indicator is scored on the scale of importance. Examples of motivational factors are given in Table 4 below, frequency statistics are shown in Table 5, and the total frequency of each indicator is equal to the number of experiencers interviewed (33); then, after several rounds of feedback exchanges, an agreement is reached and each indicator is assigned a separate value based on the results.

Table 4. Questionnaire of level 2 motivation indicators

Level 1 indicators	Level 2 indicators	Equally important		Slightly important		More important		Quite important		Most important
		1	2	3	4	5	6	7	8	9
Motivation (P1)	Pleasure (C6)				✓					
	Hope (C7)					✓				
	Social acceptance (C8)			✓						

In this paper, 6 users were randomly selected from 178 target users as sample data. The sample users were evaluated by the model, and the validity, scientificity and accuracy of the fuzzy user evaluation model were verified by the sample.

4.2 Construction of the Model

Based on the Fogg's behavior model reference to the suitability of triggers, this paper further breaks them down into three typical user profiles based on user behavior factors: M type user-high motivation and low ability, B type user-low motivation and high ability, P type user-high motivation and high ability.

Table 5. Score frequency statistics of level 2 motivation indicators

Level 1 indicators	Level 2 indicators	Equally important		Slightly important		More important		Quite important		Most important
		1	2	3	4	5	6	7	8	9
Motivation (P1)	Pleasure (C6)	0	0	1	3	5	6	9	6	3
	Hope (C7)	1	2	5	7	6	5	3	4	2
	Social acceptance (C8)	0	1	4	9	10	4	4	1	0

Because the boundaries of the various influencing factors in Fogg's behavior model are not clear, it is difficult to know how much of an impact each has on ability and motivation. Therefore, this paper uses fuzzy comprehensive judgment theory to classify and evaluate users.

Constructing Fuzzy Comprehensive Evaluation Index System. The selection of multi-level fuzzy comprehensive evaluation index directly influences the accuracy of the evaluation results. This paper constructs fuzzy comprehensive evaluation index by AHP, then establishes factor set, evaluation set and weight set according to the characteristics of the evaluation index.

Based on the Fogg's behavioral model theory, this paper summarizes the factors of ability and motivation indicators. The ability factors include time, money, physical effort, brain cycles and routine. Motivation factors include pleasure, hope, and social acceptance three subfactors. Ability score = [time, money, physical effort, brain cycles, routine]; motivation score = [pleasure, hope, social acceptance].

Dividing Factor Set. Factor set $U = \{u_1, u_2, \ldots, u_n\}$ is divided into groups $U = \{u_1, u_2, \ldots, u_k\}$ based on correlation.

$$U = U_{i=1}^k U_1 \text{ and } U_i \cap U_j = \emptyset (i \neq j) \tag{1}$$

U is primary factor and U_i is secondary factor.

The factor set in this paper is U = {ability, motivation}, divided to $U_1 = \{$time $u_1^{(1)}$, money $u_2^{(1)}$, physical effort $u_3^{(1)}$, brain cycles $u_4^{(1)}$, routine $u_5^{(1)}\}$, $U_2 = \{$pleasure $u_1^{(2)}$, hope $u_2^{(2)}$, social acceptance $u_3^{(2)}\}$, U_1: ability, U_2: motivation.

Constructing Evaluation Set. Determine the evaluation set $V = \{V_1, V_2, \ldots, V_m\}$. Determine the evaluation set V = {Type M, Type B, Type P} for the three main groups of subjects studied in this paper: type M user with high motivation and low ability, type B user with low motivation and high ability, type P user with high motivation and high ability. Type M user is the motivational behavior user, type B user is the energy behavior user, and type P user is the trigger user.

Determine the Weight of Each Factor. This paper constructs weight vectors by analytic hierarchy process (AHP), evaluates the weight of two indexes in the same level group {time, money, physical effort, brain cycles, routine, pleasure, hope, social acceptance}, evaluates the structure of judgment matrix in two comparison, and evaluates the order and consistency of the hierarchy to obtain the weight results of each index system. $A = \{a_1, a_2, ..., a_n\}$, in which a_i is the weight of factor i and satisfies $\sum_{i=1}^{n} a_i = 1$.

The weight structure process of AHP to study the influence of target ability and motivation on online user classification is as follows:

The First Step is to Establish a Hierarchical Model. Based on the in-depth analysis of user behavior influencing factors in Fogg's behavior model, this paper divides users into several hierarchies according to the objective of the decision to be made: categorize users into typical, ability and motivation factors and the affiliation of decision making objects, as shown in Fig. 1 and Fig. 2.

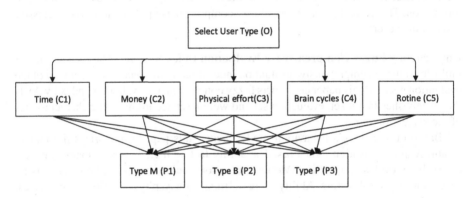

Fig. 1. Structure hierarchies of ability influencing factors

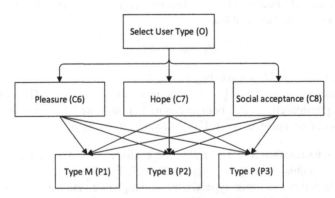

Fig. 2. Structure hierarchies of motivation influencing factors

The Second Step is to Establish Pairwise Judgment Matrix. The judgment matrix represents a comparison of the relative importance of this level with the corresponding upper level elements. The matrix element a_{ij} is the result of comparing the importance of factor i with factor j. The pairwise judgment matrices follow the scale 1–9 method, as Table 6 below:

Table 6. The scale of the nine-point system and its definition

Quantized value	Definition
1	Factor i is as important as factor j
3	Factor i is slightly more important than factor j
5	Factor i is more important than factor j
7	Factor i is significantly more important than factor j
9	Factor i is totally more important than factor j
2, 4, 6, 8	The relative importance scale is in the middle of the aforementioned adjacent scale
1, 1/2, …, 1/9	Factor i vs factor j: $a_{ij} = 1/a_{ij}$

Based on Fogg's behavior model research and questionnaires, the scores of 33 people with senior experience of online museum platforms were selected to obtain the following judgment matrix, as shown in Table 7.

Table 7. Ability influencing factors judgment matrix O-C

O	C1	C2	C3	C4	C5
C1	1	2	4	5	6
C2	1/2	1	3	4	5
C3	1/4	1/3	1	2	3
C4	1/5	1/4	1/2	1	3
C5	1/5	1/5	1/3	1/3	1

$$A1 = \begin{bmatrix} 1 & 2 & 4 & 5 & 6 \\ 1/2 & 1 & 3 & 4 & 5 \\ 1/4 & 1/3 & 1 & 2 & 3 \\ 1/5 & 1/4 & 1/2 & 1 & 3 \\ 1/5 & 1/5 & 1/3 & 1/3 & 1 \end{bmatrix}$$

Before weight is calculated, the matrix is checked for consistency. Calculate consistency indicator CI first.

$$CI = \frac{\lambda_{max} - n}{n - 1} \qquad (2)$$

Bringing data into calculations yields CI = 0.0552.

Calculate consistency ratio CR,

$$CR = \frac{CI}{RI} \qquad (3)$$

Bringing in data calculated RI = 1.12, CR = 0.0493.

Since CR < 0.10, the consistency of the judgment matrix A is acceptable, and then the next weighting step is done, first normalizing matrix A1 to get matrix W1.

$$W1 = \begin{bmatrix} 0.4651 & 0.5286 & 0.4528 & 0.4054 & 0.3333 \\ 0.2381 & 0.2643 & 0.3396 & 0.0324 & 0.2778 \\ 0.1163 & 0.0881 & 0.1132 & 0.1622 & 0.1667 \\ 0.0930 & 0.0661 & 0.0566 & 0.0811 & 0.1667 \\ 0.0930 & 0.0529 & 0.0377 & 0.0270 & 0.0556 \end{bmatrix}$$

Then, add the normalized columns. Finally, divide each element of the added vector by n to get the weighted vector W_i.

$$W_i = \frac{1}{n} \sum_{j=1}^{n} \frac{a_{ij}}{\sum_{k=1}^{n} a_{kj}} (i = 1, 2, \ldots, n) \qquad (4)$$

Enter the above formula and calculate the corresponding weight vector of the index of judgment matrix A1.

$$W1 = \begin{pmatrix} 0.4371 & 0.2877 & 0.1293 & 0.0927 & 0.0532 \end{pmatrix}^{T}$$

W1 measures the weight of ability factors: time, money, physical effort, brain cycles and routine (Table 8).

Table 8. Motivation influencing factors judgment matrix O-C

O	C6	C7	C8
C6	1	3	7
C7	1/3	1	5
C8	1/7	1/5	1

Calculate matrix A2 from motivation influencing factors judgment matrix O-C,

$$A2 = \begin{bmatrix} 1 & 3 & 7 \\ 1/3 & 1 & 5 \\ 1/7 & 1/5 & 1 \end{bmatrix}$$

Check the consistency of the matrix. Calculate consistency indicator CI by the formula (2), calculate consistency ratio CR by the formula (3).

$$CI = 0.0324; \quad CR = 0.0624$$

Since CR < 0.10, the consistency of the judgment matrix A2 is acceptable, and then the next weighting step is done, first normalizing matrix A2 to get matrix W2.

$$W2 = \begin{bmatrix} 0.6774 & 0.7143 & 0.5385 \\ 0.2258 & 0.2381 & 0.3846 \\ 0.0968 & 0.0476 & 0.0769 \end{bmatrix}$$

Next, add the normalized columns, and finally, divide each element of the added vector by n, get the weight vector W_i according to the formula (4), and substitute the data to calculate the corresponding weight vector W2 for the indicator of the A2 judgment matrix.

$$W2 = \begin{pmatrix} 0.6434 & 0.2828 & 0.0738 \end{pmatrix}^T$$

The vector W2 is the weight corresponding to the motivational indicator {pleasure, hope, social acceptance}.

Using the same computational steps and using software MATLAB to calculate judgement consistency, the following matrices were obtained for the judgment matrices of 8 subfactors (5 ability subfactors: C1–C5; 3 motivational subfactors: C6–C8) and three user types (P1–P3) (Tables 9, 10, 11, 12, 13, 14, 15 and 16).

Table 9. Judgment matrix C1-P

C1	P1	P2	P3	W
P1	1	1/7	1/8	0.0616
P2	7	1	1/2	0.3545
P3	8	2	1	0.5839

$\lambda_{max} = 3.0349; CR = 0.0336 < 0.1$

Table 10. Judgment matrix C2-P

C2	P1	P2	P3	W
P1	1	1/6	1/9	0.0598
P2	6	1	1/3	0.2819
P3	9	3	1	0.6583

$\lambda_{max} = 3.0536; CR = 0.0516 < 0.1$

Table 11. Judgment matrix C3-P

C3	P1	P2	P3	W
P1	1	1/5	1/8	0.0683
P2	5	1	1/3	0.2746
P3	8	3	1	0.6557

$\lambda_{max} = 3.0441$; CR $= 0.0424 < 0.1$

Table 12. Judgment matrix C4-P

C4	P1	P2	P3	W
P1	1	1/6	1/7	0.0703
P2	6	1	1/2	0.3496
P3	7	2	1	0.5801

$\lambda_{max} = 3.0324$; CR $= 0.0311 < 0.1$

Table 13. Judgment matrix C5-P

C5	P1	P2	P3	W
P1	1	1/6	1/6	0.0769
P2	6	1	1	0.4615
P3	6	1	1	0.4615

$\lambda_{max} = 3.0000$; CR $= -4.2701e{-}16 < 0.1$

Table 14. Judgment matrix C6-P

C6	P1	P2	P3	W
P1	1	4	1/3	0.2842
P2	6	1	1/3	0.0964
P3	9	3	1	0.6194

$\lambda_{max} = 3.0858$; CR $= 0.0825 < 0.1$

Table 15. Judgment matrix C7-P

C7	P1	P2	P3	W
P1	1	7	1	0.5105
P2	1/7	1	1/3	0.1001
P3	1	3	1	0.3893

$\lambda_{max} = 3.0803$; CR $= 0.0772 < 0.1$

Table 16. Judgment matrix C8-P

C8	P1	P2	P3	W
P1	1	5	1/2	0.3258
P2	1/5	1	1/8	0.0703
P3	2	8	1	0.6039

$\lambda_{max} = 3.0055$; CR $= 0.0053 < 0.1$

Table 17. Weight matrix scores C-P-1

	Indicator weights	P1	P2	P3
C1	0.4371	0.0616	0.3545	0.5839
C2	0.2877	0.0598	0.2819	0.6583
C3	0.1293	0.0683	0.2746	0.6571
C4	0.0927	0.0703	0.3496	0.5801
C5	0.0532	0.4615	0.4615	0.4615

Table 18. Weight matrix scores C-P-2

	Indicator weights	P1	P2	P3
C6	0.6434	0.2842	0.0964	0.6194
C7	0.2828	0.5105	0.1001	0.3893
C8	0.0738	0.3258	0.0703	0.6039

Third, Calculate the Weight of Each Element. The results as shown in Table 17 and Table 18.

Based on the weight matrix, the weight of {Type M, Type B, Type P} - W3 is obtained under the ability index.

$$W3 = \begin{pmatrix} 0.0636 & 0.3285 & 0.6079 \end{pmatrix}^T$$

The weight of {Type M, Type B, Type P} - W4 under the motivation index.

$$W4 = \begin{pmatrix} 0.3513 & 0.0955 & 0.5532 \end{pmatrix}^T$$

The CR values of the above judgment matrices are all less than 0.1, which indicates that the judgment matrices are consistent and can be used to quantitatively describe weights.

According to W1, the time factor has the biggest influence on ability factor, followed by money, physical effort and brain cycles factors, and the routine factor has the least weight. According to W2, pleasure factor has the greatest weight for motivation factor, followed by hope factor, and the least weight for social acceptance factor, indicating that the user's level of motivation is most influenced by pleasure, followed by expectation, and the least by the user's desire to share. According to W3 and W4, the weight of the Type-P user is the maximum; the Type-M user weight is the smallest in the capability factor and the largest in the motivation factor; and the Type-B user weight is larger in the capability factor and smaller in the motivation factor.

The weight of each factor is calculated by analytic hierarchy process (AHP), and the rationality and feasibility of user classification for Fogg's behavior model are verified.

Constructing Fuzzy Comprehensive Judgment Matrix. Firstly, the fuzzy comprehensive evaluation matrix R is obtained by evaluating the second level factor set $U_i = \left\{ u_1^{(i)}, u_2^{(i)}, \ldots, u_{n_i}^{(i)} \right\}$. Once again, 33 experts were invited to make a comprehensive evaluation of the user's u, and the evaluation data were statistically and collated according to the recovered expert questionnaire to construct fuzzy matrix R.

$$R_i = \begin{bmatrix} r_{11}^{(i)} & r_{12}^{(i)} & \cdots & r_{1m}^{(i)} \\ r_{21}^{(i)} & r_{22}^{(i)} & \cdots & r_{2m}^{(i)} \\ \vdots & \vdots & \ddots & \vdots \\ r_{n_i 1}^{(i)} & r_{n_i 2}^{(i)} & \cdots & r_{n_i m}^{(i)} \end{bmatrix}$$

If the weight of $U_i = \left\{ u_1^{(i)}, u_2^{(i)}, \ldots, u_{n_i}^{(i)} \right\}$ is $A_i = \left\{ a_1^{(i)}, a_2^{(i)}, \ldots, a_{n_i}^{(i)} \right\}$, the overall judgment is Q_i. Q_i denotes U_i's affiliation with each element in the review set.

$$Q_i = A_i \cdot R_i (i = 1, 2, \ldots, k) \tag{5}$$

The second level factor weight A_i corresponds to W2 in the previous section, k = 2, Q1: U1 - ability for each element in the evaluation set V = {Type M, Type B, Type P}. Q2: U2 Motivation's membership of each element in the evaluation set V = {Type M, Type B, Type P}.

Then, based on the combined assessment of factor $U = \{U_1, U_2, \ldots, U_k\}$ of the first order by 33 experts, the weight is $A = \{a_1, a_2, \ldots, a_k\}$, in this case U = {ability, motivation}, and the weight W1.

$$R = (Q_1, Q_2, \ldots, Q_k)^T$$

Conducting Integrated Evaluations

$$Q = A \cdot R \tag{6}$$

Finally, the maximum membership principle is used to determine which type of user to belong to.

The online user evaluation and selection model is based on the classification of user groups in the intelligent museum system, so we can identify the online user types scientifically and rationally, get the appropriate trigger, and promote the occurrence of target behavior. According to Fogg's behavior model principle, M-type user adaption "Facilitator", B-type user adaption "Spark", P-type user adaption "Sign".

4.3 Verification of the Model

In this section, we will first select a sample for model validation and describe the fuzzy evaluation process in detail, then compare the results of the overall validation of the diverse data.

Secondary indicators for sample 1 were evaluated as shown in Table 19 and Table 20.

Table 19. Results of the ability factor evaluation of sample 1

Average number of selections	P1	P2	P3
Time u_1	2	14	17
Money u_2	1	10	22
Physical effort u_3	1	13	19
Brain cycles u_4	2	14	17
Routine u_5	4	16	13

Table 20. Results of the motivation factor evaluation of sample 1

Average number of selections	P1	P2	P3
Pleasure u_1	2	14	17
Hope u_2	1	10	22
Social acceptance u_5	1	13	19

Sample 1 was evaluated in a multi-level synthesis below, using fuzzy statistical method to organize 33 experts to evaluate the sample synthetically, and the data were collected and collated to obtain fuzzy matrix R1 based on the recovered expert questionnaire.

$$R1 = \begin{bmatrix} 0.06 & 0.42 & 0.52 \\ 0.03 & 0.30 & 0.67 \\ 0.03 & 0.39 & 0.58 \\ 0.06 & 0.30 & 0.67 \\ 0.12 & 0.48 & 0.40 \end{bmatrix}$$

The weight is $A1(W1) = \begin{pmatrix} 0.4371 & 0.2877 & 0.1293 & 0.0927 & 0.0532 \end{pmatrix}^{T}$. Matrix synthesis operations are performed according to the formula (6), and the composite judgment is

$$Q1 = A1 \cdot R1$$

$$= \begin{pmatrix} 0.4371 & 0.2877 & 0.1293 & 0.0927 & 0.0532 \end{pmatrix} \cdot \begin{bmatrix} 0.06 & 0.42 & 0.52 \\ 0.03 & 0.30 & 0.67 \\ 0.03 & 0.39 & 0.58 \\ 0.06 & 0.30 & 0.67 \\ 0.12 & 0.48 & 0.40 \end{bmatrix}$$

$$= \begin{pmatrix} 0.05 & 0.37 & 0.58 \end{pmatrix}$$

Similarly, we get fuzzy matrix R2.

$$R2 = \begin{bmatrix} 0.36 & 0.12 & 0.52 \\ 0.52 & 0.12 & 0.36 \\ 0.30 & 0.06 & 0.64 \end{bmatrix}$$

The weight is $A2(W2) = \begin{pmatrix} 0.6434 & 0.2828 & 0.0738 \end{pmatrix}^T$. Matrix synthesis operations are performed according to the formula (6), and the composite judgment is

$$Q2 = A2 \cdot R2$$

$$= \begin{pmatrix} 0.6434 & 0.2828 & 0.0738 \end{pmatrix} \cdot \begin{bmatrix} 0.36 & 0.12 & 0.52 \\ 0.52 & 0.12 & 0.36 \\ 0.30 & 0.06 & 0.64 \end{bmatrix}$$

$$= \begin{pmatrix} 0.40 & 0.12 & 0.48 \end{pmatrix}$$

The U = {ability, motivation} of Sample 1 was then comprehensively evaluated based on 33 experts, and the first-order weight A5 = (0.33, 0.66) was obtained by the same fuzzy statistical method, and

$$R = \begin{bmatrix} 0.05 & 0.37 & 0.58 \\ 0.40 & 0.12 & 0.48 \end{bmatrix}$$

We got a comprehensive evaluation based on the formula (6):

$$Q = A5 \cdot R = \begin{pmatrix} 0.2805 & 0.2013 & 0.5082 \end{pmatrix}$$

Finally, in accordance with the principle of maximum affiliation, the Type-P corresponding to the composite evaluation result value of 0.5082 is the user type of Sample 1. Namely, the sample 1 user is a high-capacity, high-motivator online user type, combined with the typical user model of Table 2 in the previous section, namely, output signal type prompt.

This paper constructs a user type evaluation model, analyzes the online museum users by using the user's operational behavior data, achieves the purpose of classifying and adapting corresponding prompts respectively, and promotes the successful trigger of online user behavior.

5   Conclusion

This paper simply defines three user types, in order to further subdivide user types, uses more scientific judgment to study ability and motivation factors, and uses analytic hierarchy process to analyze the weight and affiliation of each of the user behavior subfactors to its corresponding principal factor ability or motivation. In addition, this paper applies the comprehensive fuzzy evaluation to study the influencing factors of different user behavior and classifies them separately.

Secondly, a user behavior evaluation model is established, which reflects the relationship between the subfactors of user ability and motivation and three user types. Furthermore, in discussing the analytical role of the Fogg's behavioral model for online users, the ability and motivation of users are emphasized, and the influence of other sub-factors on user behavior is highlighted.

Smart Museum - new development trend of Digital Museum.

The online user evaluation model of intelligent museum provides a user screening and classification mechanism for constructing parametric product design framework, which is oriented from the perspective of online user behavior, and studies different factors affecting online user behavior. It is possible to combine the self-creation, behavioral Big Data and cultural and creative products of online users to perfect the process framework of the new cultural and creative products product design.

References

1. Duan, Y.: On the diversity and inclusion of museums. Chin. Mus. **02**, 11–14 (2020)
2. Chen, G.: Smart museum - new development trend of digital museum. Chin. Mus. **04**, 2–9 (2013)
3. Institute of Cultural Economics: 2019 Museum Cultural and creative products market data report. Tsinghua University, Beijing (2019)
4. Marty, P.F.: Museum websites and museum visitors: before and after the museum visit. Mus. Manag. Curator **22**(4), 337–360 (2007)
5. Fogg, B.J.: A behavior model for persuasive design. In: Proceedings of the 4th International Conference on Persuasive Technology (2009). Article 40
6. Daae, J.Z., Boks, C.: Reinforcing preliminary design strategy selection guidelines with insight from Fogg's behavior grid. In: 6th International Conference on Persuasive Technology, Ohio, USA, pp. 1–7. Association for Computing Machinery (2011)
7. de Toledo, F.P., Devincenzi, S., Kwecko, V., Mota, F.P., Botelho, S.S.C.: A framework for modeling persuasive technologies based on the Fogg behavior model. In: 48th Annual Frontiers in Education (FIE) Conference, San Jose, CA, USA, pp.1–5. IEEE Press (2018)
8. Guimaraes, M., Emmendorfer, L., Adamatti, D.: Persuasive agent based simulation for evaluation of the dynamic threshold line and trigger classification from the Fogg behavior model. Simul. Model. Pract. Theor. **83**, 18–35 (2018)
9. da Silveira, P.H.B.R., et al.: Behavioral model of online social network users: an adaptation of Fogg's Behavior Model. In: 15th Brazilian Symposium on Human Factors in Computing Systems, Horizonte, Brazil, pp.1–4. Association for Computing Machinery (2016)
10. Theopilus, Y., et al.: Persuasive-universal design model for creating user experience in product to solve behavior problems. AIP Conf. Proc. **1977**, 030009 (2018)
11. Oinas-Kukkonen, H., Harjumaa, M.: Persuasive systems design: key issues, process model, and system features. Commun. Assoc. Inf. **24**(1), 28 (2009)
12. Toledo, F. P., et al.: A framework for modeling persuasive technologies based on the Fogg behavior model. In: 2018 IEEE Frontiers in Education Conference (FIE), San Jose, CA, USA, pp. 1–5. IEEE Press (2018)

13. Fogg, B.J., Euchner, J.: Designing for behavior change—new models and moral issues: an interview with B.J. Fogg. Res. Technol. Manage. **62**(5), 14–19 (2019)
14. da Silveira, P.H.B.R., et al.: A Influência das estratégias persuasivas no comportamento dos usuários no Facebook. In: 13th Brazilian Symposium on Human Factors in Computing Systems, Brazil, pp. 255–264. Association for Computing Machinery (2014)

Emotional Design and Research of Children's Picnic Tableware

Yuan Feng, Yadie Rao, and RongRong Fu[✉]

College of Art Design and Media, East China University of Science and Technology,
Shanghai, China
1048874974@qq.com

Abstract. At present, the design of children's tableware has become a hot spot
in children's product design. But designers lack attention to special usage scenarios of children's tableware (picnic scene) as well as children's emotional needs
for picnic tableware. This paper uses Muse experiment and pictorial Likert scale
questionnaires to objectively obtain children's perceptual preferences for shapes,
decorative patterns and colors of picnic tableware to solve the problem that children's picnic tableware lack emotional attention to users. Then locates the picnic
tableware design forms that meet the emotional needs of children and assists the
subsequent design practice of children's picnic tableware. Finally, it is verified
that the method can effectively improve users' satisfaction with children's picnic
tableware in the design effectiveness evaluation part. And it provides a method for
the application of emotional factors in the design of children's picnic tableware.

Keywords: Children · Picnic tableware · Emotional design · Muse experiment

1 Introduction

With the development of economy, parents pay more and more attention to every aspect
of children's growth and life. Family spending on children's products has increased
rapidly. The data of the Chinese Children's Industry Center in 2019 shows that the
consumption of children in 80% of the households accounts for 30%–50% of the total
household consumption. The annual consumption of children in the country is about 3.9
trillion–5.9 trillion Yuan, and the market potential of children's products is huge [1].
The optimized three-child policy promulgated in June 2021 indicates that the market
share of children will continue to grow [2]. The growth of market demand has spawned
the emergence of a series of children's products. And the market of children's tableware
has also received more and more attention. But there is still a lack of attention to special use scenarios - picnic scenes. Infancy and preschool are important periods for the
development of children's cognition and habitual character. At these stages, children's
psychology and physiology are growing rapidly [3]. However, the current design of children's tableware is relatively lacking in emotional factors and fun, which will lead to
problems such as low tableware usage and inattention when children are eating that is
not conducive to children's growth [4]. The changeable external environmental factors

M. M. Soares et al. (Eds.): HCII 2022, LNCS 13322, pp. 21–36, 2022.
https://doi.org/10.1007/978-3-031-05900-1_2

will make children more easily distracted by external information and exacerbate various problems of eating behaviors such as long eating time, inattentive eating, and less eating when children go out on a picnic. This paper takes preschool children aged 1–6 as target users and uses the Muse experiment to explore users' preference for appearances of children's tableware from a more objective physiological perspective with the help of related concepts in emotional design. Accordingly, locates design forms of picnic tableware that meet children's emotional needs and arouse their interest in eating, and then assists the emotional design practice of children's picnic tableware.

2   Emotional Design of Children's Picnic Tableware

2.1   Overview of Emotional Design

In the process of product design evolution, the focus of design begins to turn from products to users, from technology to experience. Emotional design becomes more and more important. The "three-level theory" (instinctive layer, behavioral layer, and reflection layer) proposed by American cognitive psychologist Donald Norman is widely used in emotional design and has a directive function in product design [5]. Among them, the instinctive layer is to design the appearance of products. The more the appearance of the product conforms to users' instinctive perception, the easier it is for users to like and accept the product. Add to this, appearance elements such as shapes, colors and materials often impress users firstly [6]. The users' instinctive layer is reflected in the product's shapes, colors, materials, decorative patterns and other design elements for the design of children's picnic tableware.

2.2   Acquisition of Perceptual Evaluation Vocabularies of Children's Picnic Tableware

We obtained the frequency statistics of relevant comment words on a shopping website to dig the users' concerns by digital ways to understand consumers' concerns about children's picnic tableware. The entire program is mainly implemented by Python language, and the data science production tool JupyterLab is used to write the debugger.

This paper conducted words frequency statistics on 7,500 comments about children's picnic tableware on the shopping website and finally obtained the word frequency statistics of meaningful adjectives for further research. The data are shown in Table 1.

Table 1. Statistics of adjective frequency in consumer comments.

Number	Word	Word frequency
1	Good	3550
2	Insulted	1836
3	Right	1605
4	Good-looking	698

(continued)

Table 1. (*continued*)

Number	Word	Word frequency
5	Satisfied	649
6	Convenient	635
7	Level of appearance	578
8	Material	436
9	Color	435
10	Appearance	429
11	Small	428
12	Tall	417
13	Praise	353
14	Worth	323
15	Pretty	312
16	Appropriate	295
17	Practical	283
18	Recommend	238
19	Price	219
20	Lovely	218

The research results for the classification of adjective properties are shown in Table 2.

Words with repeated meanings were removed from the perceptual evaluation vocabulary of appearance and function categories, and six perceptual evaluation words of "pretty, lovely, insulted, convenient, practical, and satisfied" were obtained. Investigating the emotional preferences of the target user group for the appearance design of picnic tableware from the shapes, colors, materials, and decorative patterns of the tableware by taking 6 evaluation degrees above as standards which can measure the user's emotional preference. Then locate the design form of picnic tableware in line with user preferences to assist subsequent design practices.

Table 2. Classification of adjectives in consumer comments.

Classification	Adjective	Frequency
Appearance	Pretty, appearance, color, level of appearance, pretty, lovely…	2862
Function	Insulted, convenient, material, appropriate, practical, thick…	4381
Price	Cost performance, cheap, high quality and inexpensive, price…	675
Broad	Good, right, satisfied, price, recommend, perfect…	6755

3 User Preference Acquisition Experiment of Children's Picnic Tableware Based on Muse Equipment

3.1 Identify Target User Groups

Human childhood is a very long age span covering the 12 years of a newborn's growth. Childhood stage is divided into infancy (less than 1-year-old), early childhood (1–3 years old), preschool age (4–6 years old), school-age (7–12 years old) although Freud's theory of psychological development and Erikson's theory of social cognitive development have small differences in the division of them. Children cannot eat independently before the age of one, and they are usually assisted by guardians. However, the early childhood and preschool years are critical periods for children to improve their hands-on ability and coordination ability in all aspects of life. According to surveys, children aged 1–6 have various eating behavior problems such as less eating, inattentive eating, long eating time, poor appetite, picky eaters, and refusal to try new foods [7]. The interference of external environmental factors will aggravate children's eating behavior problems when going out on a picnic. Therefore, it is necessary to attract children's attention through the emotional design of picnic tableware, increase children's interest in eating, and improve their eating conditions during picnics. Thus this paper sets the target user group of picnic tableware as children aged 1–6.

3.2 Collection and Determination of Product Samples

We have extensively collected 100 sample pictures of children's picnic tableware products from product manuals, magazines, books, e-commerce platforms, and social networks to form a library of sample pictures. Then summarize the design elements of children's picnic tableware into four types: shape, color, material, and decorative pattern through the analysis of these samples. The material is set as the control variable due to the surface material is mostly plastic. And it is determined as polypropylene plastic according to relevant literature [8]. The design forms contained in the shape can be divided into cylindrical, square, special-shaped according to the morphological analysis method of product design [9]. Color can be divided into warm color, cool color, and colorless. Decorative patterns can be divided into printed patterns, concave-convex patterns, and no patterns. Grayscale images were used in Muse experiments to avoid the interference caused by color. So color was not considered when selecting experimental samples (Table 3). Arranging and combining the obtained design forms to get representative samples of children's picnic tableware (Table 4).

Table 3. Design elements and forms of children's picnic tableware.

Design element	Shape A			Decorative pattern B		
Design form	Cylinder	Square	Special-shaped	Printing	Concave-convex	No pattern
Number	A_1	A_2	A_3	B_1	B_2	B_3

Table 4. Samples of children's picnic tableware.

Number	Sample image	Design form	Number	Sample image	Design form
1		A_1B_1	6		A_2B_3
2		A_1B_2	7		A_3B_1
3		A_1B_3	8		A_2B_2
4		A_2B_1	9		A_3B_3
5		A_2B_2			

Nine children's tableware samples were divided into six groups according to six design forms of shapes and decorative patterns with three samples in each group in the muse experiment. Each group of pictures adopted the same precision, size, and white background effect. The experimental materials are as follows (Table 5).

Table 5. Experimental materials.

Number	Sample image
Group A_1	
Group A_2	
Group A_3	
Group B_1	
Group B_2	
Group B_3	

3.3 Experimental Procedure

The experimental instruction told the subjects to make an overall perception of pictures of children's picnic tableware appeared on the screen. A white screen for 1000 ms will first appear in the center of the computer screen, then the first set of tableware samples will be displayed for 1 min followed by a white screen of 1000 ms, and then the second set of tableware samples will be displayed for one minute until the 6 sets of samples are presented. The experimental process is as follows (Fig. 1).

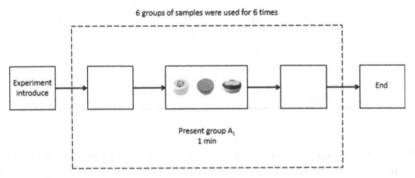

Fig. 1. Flow chart of EEG Muse experiment.

3.4 EEG Experiment

The muse experiment is used to objectively obtain the target users' preference for the appearances of children's picnic tableware and as a guide to record the EEG data. Then analyze users' preference on the shape and decorative patterns of children's picnic tableware through the data.

Experimental Equipment. Muse 2, iPad, Muse: Meditation & Sleep app.

Experimental Participants. 15 children aged 4–6 years were invited to be the research participants due to the incomplete head development and weak communication abilities of children aged 1–3 years. All research subjects participated in the experiment voluntarily and ensured that they had good rest, physical and mental health, good mental state, and normal vision or corrected vision before the experiment. Subjects were instructed to wash their hair and don't makeup before the experiment to rule out distractions.

Experimental Environment. The experiment was carried out in a laboratory with functions such as light and sound insulation. In the course of the experiment, there is no interference from others except the main test and the subjects.

Experimental Indexes. The experiment uses three data to represent the activity of the brain in the Muse app which are Active, Neutral, and Calm as experimental indexes. The higher the Active value, the stronger the sample stimulus to the subject, the higher the degree of arousal, and the more interested the subject is. On the contrary, the higher the Neutral and Calm value, the weaker the sample stimulus to the subject, the lower the degree of arousal, and the less interested the subject is.

3.5 Questionnaires

This paper added a questionnaire based on the Muse experiment to conduct a subjective test in order to obtain the picnic tableware preferences of 4–6 years old users more comprehensively. And parents of children aged 1–3 were selected to conduct a questionnaire survey to obtain the preferences of children aged 1–3 on picnic tableware who lack communication skills. Combining the 6 users' perceptual evaluation indicators on tableware obtained through data collation of an e-commerce website with 9 tableware samples, a questionnaire was made according to the Likert five-level scale method. To obtain the user's preference for color, the option of product color is added to the questionnaire.

15 subjects in the Muse experiment and 20 parents of children aged 1–3 conducted this investigation, and 35 valid questionnaires were collected. The schematic diagram of the users' preference measurement table is shown in Table 6.

Table 6. User preference subscale.

Sample	User preference evaluation index					
	Pretty	1	2	3	4	5
	Lovely	1	2	3	4	5
	Insulted	1	2	3	4	5
	Convenient	1	2	3	4	5
	Practical	1	2	3	4	5
	satisfied	1	2	3	4	5
	Color selection					

Calculate the data of the 6 perceptual evaluation words corresponding to each sample first. Then calculate the user preferences evaluation index score corresponding to every design form based on the results above. The calculation method is as follows formulas (1)–(6).

$$A_1 = \text{User preference value (sample1 + sample2 + sample3)}/3 \qquad (1)$$

$$A_2 = \text{User preference value (sample4 + sample5 + sample6)}/3 \qquad (2)$$

$$A_3 = \text{User preference value (sample7 + sample8 + sample9)}/3 \qquad (3)$$

$$B_1 = \text{User preference value (sample1 + sample4 + sample7)}/3 \qquad (4)$$

$$B_2 = \text{User preference value (sample2 + sample5 + sample8)}/3 \qquad (5)$$

$$B_3 = \text{User preference value (sample3 + sample6 + sample9)}/3 \qquad (6)$$

4 Result

4.1 Result of Muse Experiment

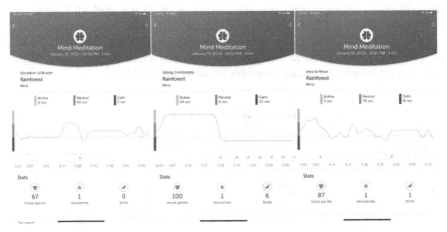

Fig. 2. Data diagram of mind mediation app.

Count the Muse index data of the 6 groups of samples in the statistical experiment and calculated the average value of each group respectively. The results are shown in Table 7. It can be seen from Table 7 that the design elements with the highest average active Muse index of users are the A_3 special-shaped and the B_1 printing pattern respectively, and the design elements with the lowest average neutral index are the A_3 special-shaped and B_1 printing pattern respectively, the design elements with lowest average calm index were the A_1 cylinder and B_1 printed patterns. Therefore the special-shaped combined with the printed pattern-A_3B_1 is the best combination of design elements based on the results of Muse data analysis (Fig. 2).

4.2 Result of Questionnaires

The above experiment conducted a questionnaire survey on the parents of children aged 1–3 years and obtained 20 valid questionnaires. The Muse experiment on children aged 4–6 years was combined with the questionnaire survey and obtained 15 valid questionnaires.

Table 7. Mean value of user Muse experimental indexes in six design forms.

Design form	Muse index		
	Active (sec)	Neutral (sec)	Calm (sec)
A_1 cylinder	3	33.87	19.2
A_2 square	1.13	36.07	22.8
A_3 special-shaped	3.07	28.33	28.6
B_1 printed pattern	4.33	35.13	20.53
B_2 concave-convex pattern	2.27	37.07	20.67
B_3 no pattern	2.47	35.2	22.33

The preference evaluation average value of the 6 indicators corresponding to each design form in the questionnaires filled in by parents and children is calculated by processing the questionnaire data. The results are shown in Tables 8 and 9.

The results of the questionnaire data from parents show that the most pretty design form in the users' perceptual preference is A_3B_2, the most lovely design form is A_3B_1, the design form with the best thermal insulation performance is A_2B_3, the most convenient design form is A_1B_2, and the most practical design form is A_1B_3 and the most satisfying design form is A_2B_2. The results of children's questionnaire data show that A_3B_1 is the most pretty and lovely design form among users' perceptual preferences, A_2B_3 is the design form with the best thermal insulation performance, and the two most convenient design forms are A_2B_2 and A_2B_3. The most practical design form is A_2B_3, and the most satisfying design form is A_2B_2. Combining the questionnaire data of parents and children, it can be concluded that the design form with higher user preference in appearance is A_3B_1, the design form with higher user preference in thermal insulation performance is A_2B_3, and the design form with higher user preference of convenience are A_1B_3, A_2B_2, and A_2B_3. The design forms with higher user preference in terms of practicality are A_1B_3 and A_2B_3, and the design form with higher user preference in terms of satisfaction is A_2B_2.

Table 8. User perceptual preference data sheet - Parents.

User perceptual preference	Design form					
	A_1	A_2	A_3	B_1	B_2	B_3
Pretty	3.78	3.83	3.95	3.9	3.93	3.73
Lovely	3.8	3.91	4.03	4.08	3.92	3.75
Insulated	4	4.11	3.82	3.95	3.92	4.07
Convenient	4.12	4.07	3.67	3.93	3.97	3.95
Practical	4.07	4.05	3.73	3.9	3.97	3.98
Satisfied	3.95	4.07	3.8	3.95	3.95	3.92

Table 9. User perceptual preference data sheet - Children.

User perceptual preference	Design form					
	A_1	A_2	A_3	B_1	B_2	B_3
Pretty	3.65	3.75	3.84	4.25	3.75	3.23
Lovely	3.33	3.84	3.92	4.17	3.73	3.19
Insulated	3.47	3.52	3.24	3.4	3.31	3.47
Convenient	3.36	3.42	3.09	3.24	3.31	3.31
Practical	3.55	3.71	3.36	3.51	3.55	3.56
Satisfied	3.29	3.51	3.18	3.29	3.49	3.2

The color preference of users is investigated separately in the questionnaire. The data processing results of color preference of parents and children are shown in Table 10 and Table 11. In the questionnaire data of parents, the average selection rate of warm-colored products is 63%, and the average selection rate of warm-colored products in the questionnaire data of children is 54%. It can be concluded that users have a higher color preference for warm-colored children's picnic tableware.

Table 10. User color preference data sheet - Parents.

Color classification	Sample number									Mean value
	1	2	3	4	5	6	7	8	9	
Warm	0.65	0.6	0.7	0.45	0.55	0.55	0.8	0.65	0.7	0.63
Grey	0.2	0.15	0.05	0	0.05	0.05	0	0	0.15	0.07
Cool	0.25	0.25	0.25	0.55	0.4	0.4	0.2	0.35	0.15	0.31

Table 11. User color preference data sheet - Children.

Color classification	Sample number									Mean value
	1	2	3	4	5	6	7	8	9	
Warm	0.56	0.5	0.44	0.375	0.56	0.5	0.75	0.56	0.625	0.54
Grey	0.25	0.19	0.06	0.25	0	0.06	0.125	0.06	0.1875	0.13
Cool	0.19	0.31	0.5	0.375	0.44	0.44	0.125	0.38	0.1875	0.33

5   Design Practice of Children's Picnic Tableware Based on User's Perceptual Preference

5.1   Design Scheme

Apply the design forms with the highest user preference obtained from the above experiments such as special-shaped, printed patterns, warm color, and plastic material to the overall design of children's picnic tableware. The shape and habits of rabbits are used as inspiration sources. The design process is as follows (Fig. 3).

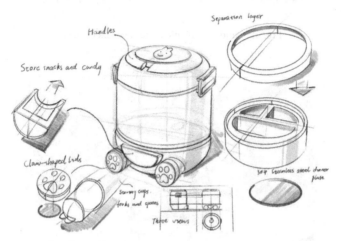

Fig. 3. Design sketch of children's picnic tableware.

Design Description

Appearance. The shape adopts a special-shaped design form and abstractly expresses the shape of the rabbit which not only presents the cute posture of the rabbit sitting on the side but also has a sense of simplicity. The color caters to users' preference for warm colors. The overall color tone is mainly pink with white accents which increase the affinity of the product color. Chooses a printed pattern as the decorative pattern, and prints the smiling face of a white rabbit on the top of the product to increase the fun and attractiveness of the tableware (Fig. 4 and Fig. 5). The three views and dimensions of the product are as follows (Fig. 6).

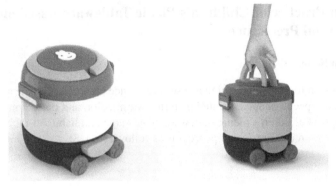

Fig. 4. Children's picnic tableware renderings.

Fig. 5. Scene map of children's picnic tableware.

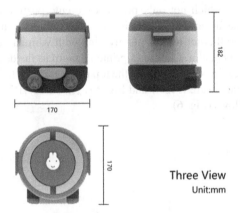

Fig. 6. Three views of children's picnic tableware.

Structure. In the form of a combined design, the tableware consists of ① handles, ② safety locks, ③ covers, ④ separation layer, ⑤ 304 stainless steel dinner plate, ⑥ polypropylene plastic housing, ⑦ storage slot, ⑧ water cup, ⑨ cup lid, ⑩ spoon, ⑪ fork, and ⑫ claw-shaped lid. And it adopts a modular design method so that each part can be used separately or combined into a whole, which is convenient for storage (Fig. 7).

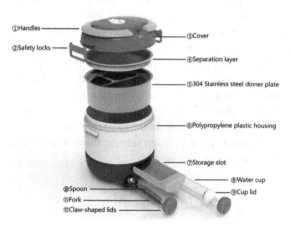

Fig. 7. Exploded view of children's picnic tableware.

Function. In terms of convenience, the portability of the tableware is increased by the design of the ① handles on the ③ cover. In terms of heat preservation function, the interior of the ⑤ 304 stainless steel dinner plate is vacuumed to effectively block the heat source, and the use of the ④ partition layer achieves a more heat preservation effect. In terms of practicability, the design of ② safety locks and ⑫ claw-shaped lids more effectively ensures the integrity of the tableware and effectively prevents the falling off of each part when the product moves as a whole. The part that touches the mouth and grasps of ⑩ spoon and ⑪ fork are designed with smooth chamfering to ensure that no sharp parts of the product will harm children. ④ Separation layer can carry snacks, fruits, etc. ⑤ Stainless steel dinner plate with a capacity of about 550 ml is used to pack food. ⑦ Storage slot can store candy, snacks, etc. conveniently. ⑧ Cup can be used to carry various drinks, ensuring 1–6 years old children's needs for food variety and capacity at different stages.

Material. The product is made of high-safety polypropylene plastic and stainless steel. Polypropylene plastic has high chemical stability and good hygienic properties and is odorless, non-toxic. It can withstand temperatures of −20 to 120 °C. In addition, it also has the advantages of being lightweight, drop resistant, and easy to process. Stainless steel material is applied to the dinner plate and the parts that touch the mouth of forks and spoons to increase the safety of the product.

6 Design Evaluation

Comparing the final design scheme with the three samples A_1B_1, A_2B_1, and A_2B_2 which have higher average user evaluations in results of the questionnaire, and design a satisfaction questionnaire based on the seven-level Likert scale to verify whether the design scheme conforms to users' perceptual preferences. In design evaluation, we selected 15 children aged 4–6 and 15 parents whose children aged 1–3 for investigation. The design scheme is compared with the three samples on the left side of the questionnaire. The questionnaire design is shown in Fig. 8 below. According to the scoring principle of the scale, the higher the users' preference for the final design scheme, the more the score approaches 1 point. The higher the user's preference for the sample, the more the score approaches 7 points. It means that the user's preference for the final design scheme and the sample is the same or similar if the score is 4 points or close to 4 points. The average values of user preferences obtained after processing the questionnaire data are as shown in Table 12 and Table 13. It can be seen from the two tables that both parents and children have much higher preferences for the design scheme than samples in the comparison of the design scheme with the three samples.

⁎ 1. Please carefully observe and compare the children's tableware in the following two pictures, and evaluate it according to your preferences.

	Left and its conformity	The left side fits very well	The left side is more consistent	Both sides are equally consistent	The right side is more consistent	The right side fits very well	Right and its conformity
Score	1	2	3	4	5	6	7
Pretty	○	○	○	○	○	○	○
Lovely	○	○	○	○	○	○	○
Insulated	○	○	○	○	○	○	○
Convenient	○	○	○	○	○	○	○
Practical	○	○	○	○	○	○	○
Satisfied	○	○	○	○	○	○	○

Fig. 8. Questionnaire design combined with Likert seven-point scale.

Table 12. User perceptual design evaluation data sheet - Parents.

User perceptual preference	Sample for comparison		
	A_1B_1	A_2B_1	A_2B_2
Pretty	2.13	2.6	2.27
Lovely	2.53	2.67	2.53
Insulted	2.2	2.33	2.07
Convenient	2.87	3.07	2.6
Practical	2.2	2.47	2
Satisfied	2.13	2.67	2.33
Mean value	2.34	2.63	2.3

Table 13. User perceptual design evaluation data sheet - Children.

User perceptual preference	Sample for comparison		
	A_1B_1	A_2B_1	A_2B_2
Pretty	2.47	3	3.2
Lovely	3.33	3.27	4.47
Insulted	1.8	2.07	2.4
Convenient	1.93	3.47	3.8
Practical	2.4	2.93	2.87
Satisfied	2.33	2.6	2.87
Mean value	2.38	2.89	3.27

7 Conclusion

This paper proposes a method to assist the emotional design of children's picnic tableware by using Muse experiments and questionnaires based on the in-depth analysis of users' preferences for products' shapes, colors, and decorative patterns in the design of children's picnic tableware. Finally, the design evaluation verifies that the method can effectively improve the user satisfaction of children's picnic tableware design. A design method for the emotional design of picnic tableware for children aged 1–6 years is proposed in this paper, hoping to meet children's emotional needs for picnic tableware as well as increase children's interest in eating during picnics, and then improve the situation when children eating out. It is also hoped that this design method can provide a reference for the application of emotional factors in the design of children's picnic tableware.

References

1. Huang, S.: How can the children's meal market "grow up"? People's Wkly. **12**, 50–51 (2019)
2. Xu, H.: The three-child policy is good, and the compliance of children's products must rely on high standards. Chin. Fiber Inspection **07**, 29–31 (2021)
3. Zhang, C.: Research on the Interesting Design of Children's Tableware. China University of Mining and Technology (2016)
4. Zhang, H., Zhang, W.: Research on the innovative design of children's tableware oriented by perceptual elements. Packag. Eng. **42**(20), 202–209 (2021)
5. Donald, A.: Design Psychology—Emotional Design. CITIC Publishing Group, Beijing (2016)
6. Li, S., Yi, S., Zheng, R., Jia, Y.: Research on the emotional design of cultural and creative products in museums. Packag. Eng. **2**(09), 1–13 (2022)
7. Liu, P., Peng, N., Huang, Z., Zeng, T., Zhang, Y., Wei, L.: Analysis of 1720 children's eating behavior problems aged 1 to 6. J. Youjiang Med. Coll. Nationalities **37**(06), 828–830 (2015)
8. Kang, Z., Yang, H.: Safety analysis of plastic food packaging in my country. Chin. Plast. **32**(10), 13–19 (2018)
9. Li, D.: Introduction of morphological analysis in product design. Tianjin Text. Sci. Technol. **02**, 26–28+62 (2003)

How Architectural Forms Can Influence Emotional Reactions: An Exploratory Study

Bárbara Formiga[1,2](✉), Francisco Rebelo[1,2,3,4], Jorge Cruz Pinto[1,2], and Emerson Gomes[1,2]

[1] CIAUD, ergoUX, Faculdade de Arquitetura, Universidade de Lisboa, Rua Sá Nogueira, Lisboa, Portugal
barbaranevesf@gmail.com
[2] Pólo Universitário, Alto da Ajuda, 1349-063 Lisboa, Portugal
[3] ITI/LARSsys Universidade de Lisboa, Rua Sá Nogueira, Lisboa, Portugal
[4] Polo Universitário, Alto da Ajuda, 1349-055 Lisbon, Portugal

Abstract. Emotional reactions are important in people's lives and can be positively or negatively affected by the architectural environment in which they find themselves. This study aims to understand how architectural forms, whether curved or straight, can influence emotional reactions, through an objective (biosensors) and subjective (questionnaires) evaluation of two apartments. Most of the studies carried out with biosensors and subjective techniques we analyzed do not present any context and isolate the stimuli from the experiences (static situations) in such a way that they become unreal in the face of the environments that people experience in their daily lives. In this study, we designed two similar apartments, with only formal architectural variations, one with curved shapes and the other with rectilinear shapes. The methodology applied is based on subjective techniques, depending on the opinion of the participants (Self-assessment Manikin), and also on objective techniques, which use physiological measurements obtained by biosensors (Electrical Dermal Activity, Electrocardiogram, Respiratory Frequency and Amplitude). A narrative was used to give the same context to all participants and give them freedom to explore the space during the visit to the apartments. The objective results showed that the curvilinear apartment provoked less activation than the rectilinear apartment, which may mean that the participants were more relaxed or calm in this apartment. Regarding the subjective results, the participants reported feeling more pleasure in the curvilinear apartment, also perceiving a greater activation (excitement) than in the straight apartment. This last result is not in agreement with the objective evaluation, probably because the sample is made up of design students who have a more refined critical spirit, or simply because they took the questionnaire moments after the virtual experience and now have some difficulty in accessing their memory and emotions. The results obtained with the objective evaluation are in agreement with the data reported in the literature, carried out in studies with static experiences, which means that the methodology proposed in this article proved to be effective. This discovery may motivate future studies to use this methodology, in which the interaction with space is more natural.

Keywords: Architectural form · Architectural Design Process · Emotional reactions · Virtual reality · Biosensors

© The Author(s), under exclusive license to Springer Nature Switzerland AG 2022
M. M. Soares et al. (Eds.): HCII 2022, LNCS 13322, pp. 37–55, 2022.
https://doi.org/10.1007/978-3-031-05900-1_3

1   Introduction

1.1   The Importance of Form for Architecture

Geometry has always played a very important role in architecture, singularly present in the proportions of the Pantheon, in the design of churches and convents in the Middle Ages, and even in modern single-family dwellings, where the "invisible" matrices and layouts revealed the canonical-geometries of the built space [1]. This means that the spatial quality is affected not only by the air quality and ventilation of a space, but also by other characteristics, such as the geometric shape (Fig. 1) [2].

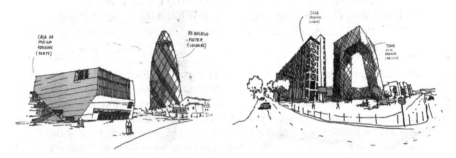

Fig. 1. The different formal geometries of buildings.

Haberakn et al. state that "it is hard to separate the human behavior and the form of spaces that human lives in" [2]. The form is not reduced to the visible configuration of the content, described by the painter Bem Shahn [3], nor to the appearance, the structure, the physical limits that surround the body, or the practical function of things. In all its configurations, the form retains "the visual qualities such as roundness or sharpness, strength or fragility, harmony or discord." [3] the form guides, leads and excites users who travel through the space. Arnheim mentions as an example that: "the entire passage from a corridor to the sudden expansion of a room enhances the visitor's experience with a small visual shock" [4].

In Baroque architecture, for example, form was worked as a sculpture and as an artistic setting, buildings were adorned and decorated by superimposing curved and rectilinear shapes, which created complex geometries. In contrast, in modern architecture, "one lives in effective cohabitation with the pure forms of geometry." [5] that not only brought a new meaning to man on a cultural and psychic level, with the machinist (rationalist) idea, but also had an impact on the emotional reactions transmitted through these pure forms.

Le Corbusier believed that one of the goals of architecture was in the architectural form and in the way of life of the occupants of the houses, he defended geometry as: "a decisive gesture in the process of architecture, as a basis for the creation and ordering of forms, generating harmony and satisfaction, and, at the same time, a coherent and creative organism" [6]. Around us, everything is geometry, everything is form [6], "we are surrounded by buildings every hour of the day. Our built environment is revealed to us visually through constructed architectural forms, and the visible has always played a prime role in transmitting information to us about our surroundings" [7], especially interior spaces [8].

The form thus acquires (consciously and unconsciously) an extremely important role in the users' perception and emotional reactions and depending on its combination with other characteristics of the space (light, color, materiality, scale), it can be more protagonist or more underhanded. In this sense, it will be relevant for the architect to know the emotional reactions associated with the various types, or combinations of shapes, to design the space according to what he intends to convey to users.

1.2 The Importance of Measuring How Shape Influences People

For Le Corbusier, the primordial meaning of the "machine to inhabit" was to thrill, "the lines, angles, walls, openings, etc., had the basic purpose of reaching emotion and the senses." [6] although architects are aware that architecture impacts the senses and emotions of users [7], the challenge remains to capture it's psychological [9] and emotional effect. In fact, this information has always been subjective and inconsistent/different from architect to architect. For this reason, in addition to the architect's own intuition and feelings, there is a need to measure or quantify the influence of architectural space, with the help of other areas and new complementary tools. As reported by Elbaiuomy et al. [10]: "This may support architects and designers in identifying appropriate geometric forms to meet the required uses and functions that need particular consciousness statuses."

1.3 Studies Carried Out on the Form

The studies found so far show that the geometric shape is one of the architectural features that influence people's emotional reactions, with curved shapes being more pleasant than rectilinear or angular shapes [8, 10–22]. "Curves, especially the large ones, produce warm- or light- aroused feelings, whereas sharp angles create a perception of roughness [20]" [8].

Studies carried out by Silvia and Barona [11] revealed that there is a perceptual difference between design experts and non-experts, with non-experts preferring curved shapes to simple angular shapes (circles or hexagons), and experts with more knowledge they prefer more complex shapes and angular spaces [14].

The authors Banei et al. [8] carried out a pilot study with EEG and Virtual Reality (HMD-VR), in which various aspects of shape (type, geometry, angle, scale and location) were tested about 3 emotional reactions dimensions (pleasure, arousal and dominance), with an emphasis on individual personality differences. The results showed that curved geometry had a greater pleasure effect and rectilinear geometry caused less pleasure in participants with low openness to experience, as well as in participants with low neuroticism [8]. Regarding arousal emotion, curvilinear geometries had a greater arousal effect in participants with high pleasantness and rectilinear geometries had a lesser arousal effect in participants with low pleasantness.

Another study [10] of biogeometry, using the CST Microwave.

The analyzed studies consider in their experiences "simplified" or abstract spaces [10, 14], without framing or location [10, 14], some without materials [8, 14], offering a static experience in space [8, 10], without natural lighting and shadows [8, 10, 14], and none of them presents a context or a narrative to the participants. The spaces are isolated and without a predetermined function.

On the one hand, these approaches have a high level of control, on the other hand, they do not reproduce the real experience of the user with the architectural space, a fundamental aspect linked to the architectural project and which distinguishes it from sculpture or an artistic installation. As Arnheim [4] says, "the visual form of a building cannot be understood if we do not take into account its function (…) and therefore there is nothing symbolic about a set of steps or stairs as long as they are seen as a mere geometric configuration" [4].

As mentioned above, in most studies the experience of space is static [8, 10], which makes it possible to control the experience more easily. However, the world is not perceived as static, it is rather a succession of planes interrelated by the movement of the gaze (exploration of visual fields): "Since architectural experience cannot be captured from a mere snapshot in time, continuous assessment is important in capturing the overall experience" [9], similar to what happens in a movie.

1.4 The Purpose of This Study

This study aims to evaluate the architectural environment of two apartments that vary only in their shape (curvilinear and rectilinear), through objective information (biosensors – Electrocardiogram (ECG), Galvanic Skin Response (GSR), Respiratory Rate (RESP)), that operates with the unconscious side of the human being, and subjective information (Self-assessment Manikin (SAM)), conducted by the conscious side.

2 Method

2.1 Materials

2.1.1 Apartment Design Sketches

The project started with the study of architectural form through sketches, with the exploration of various design hypotheses, both for the curvilinear form and for the rectilinear form. We opted for the project of two apartments that fit into a housing tower located in the city, which will then be compatible with the context narrative that is shown to the participant, before entering the apartments. The sketches of the project were all drawn by hand raised on a roll of tracing paper, which followed the evolution of the project ideas. The chosen hypotheses have a similar basis, with the same spatial arrangement, lighting, scale and materials, varying only in their shape, more rectilinear, or more curved, as we can see in Fig. 2.

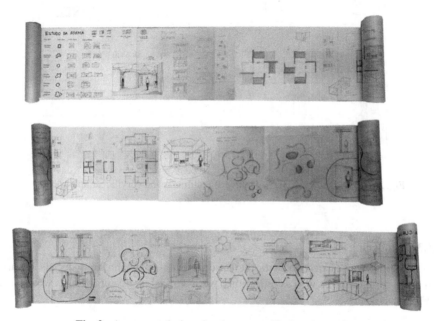

Fig. 2. Apartment design sketches on a roll of tracing paper.

2.1.2 Modeling (2D, 3D)

After the development of the two design hypotheses (curvilinear and rectilinear shape), these were passed to rigorous design in Autocad (2D) and later a 3D model of the hypotheses was created in Sketchup (Fig. 3), where the materials were applied.

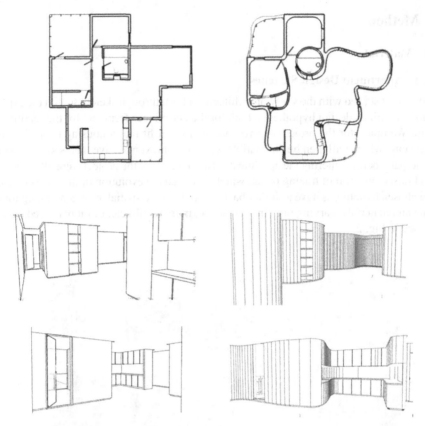

Fig. 3. 2D Drawing and 3D Modeling of rectilinear and curvilinear apartments.

2.1.3   Rendering

The rendering was carried out with the Enscape Plug-in, where the materials, natural and artificial lighting, as well as reflections, were worked in greater detail as we can see in Fig. 4.

Fig. 4. Final images of the two apartments. The straight one on the left and the curvilinear one on the right.

2.1.4 Movie Storyboard with Context

To contextualize the participant and make the experience more realistic, a film was developed (Fig. 5), all of it drawn, similar to a comic strip that interacts with the participant. The narrative shows the participant that he has received a new job and that the company is offering an apartment near the office space to employees who live far from the city, as is his case. Since this company cares about the well-being of its employees, it gives them the possibility to choose between two apartments, according to the one where they feel better. Through this narrative, the participant is led to arrive at the building of his future home and visit the two apartments.

Fig. 5. Frames of the film are presented as a context narrative of the experience.

2.2 Instruments

2.2.1 Objective Assessment – Biosensors

To carry out this experiment we used three types of biosensors: EDA; ECG; RESP. The first (EDA), to measure the variation of the electrical conductivity of the skin caused by the different sensations, the second (ECG), to measure the variation of the heart rate, and the last (RESP), to measure the variation of the respiratory rate.

2.2.2 Subjective Assessment – SAM

The Self-Assessment Mannequin (SAM) is a pictorial assessment technique, without the use of verbal language, to measure the level of pleasure and arousal/activation, related to the affective reaction of the participants to the presented stimuli.

This type of questionnaire was used to obtain the users' conscious perception of the emotions they felt. Perception was measured with two scales from 1 to 9: one for valence (unpleasant = 1/pleasant = 9) and another for arousal (calm = 1/excited = 9).

2.2.3 Computer

The computer was used to connect the biosensors to a collection platform (viewing the context film and visiting the two apartments) and data processing (application of filters) [23].

2.3 Sample

The sample was carried out with only 6 participants, from different nationalities (Portugal, São Tomé, Angola, China and Peru), all of them Design students. However, the first participant was not considered in the sample, as it served to perform the pre-tests. 50% of the participants were men and the other 50% were women, aged between 18 and 65 years.

2.4 Protocol

1. The participant was informed about the objectives of the study and that the information collected was completely confidential;
2. The participant signed the document in which he agreed to participate in the study;
3. It was explained how to place the EDA, ECG, RESP biosensors;
4. The participant placed the biosensors on himself, and the EDA was placed on the left hand if the person was right-handed and on the right hand if the person was left-handed;
5. The participant was placed in front of the computer, and he was explained and indicated which computer keys he would have to handle during the experiment;
6. The participant underwent a three-minute relaxation period to obtain the resting baseline, while listening to "melody-of-nature-main-6672" music.
7. The participant watched a two-minute movie that showed the context narrative of the experience.
8. The participant visited virtually in the rectilinear apartment (5 min).
9. The participant virtually visited the curvilinear apartment (5 min).
10. After visiting both apartments, the participant chose his/her preference.
11. A SAM questionnaire was carried out for the experience of the straight apartment and the curvilinear apartment, and the participant answered taking into account their valence (unpleasure/pleasure) and arousal (calm/excited) level.
12. At the end, an open interview was carried out, where considerations were obtained from the participant's perception of their preference, as well as what they liked most and least about each apartment.

3 Results and Discussion

Before any discussion, it is important to mention that all the results take into account the baseline measure (resting state) collected at the beginning of the experiment, to the sound of a chosen music song lasting 3 min.

Figure 6 shows three graphs corresponding to the EDA values of a participant. The first graph shows baseline data, with a decline over time. The second graph shows the

EDA – 3rd participant

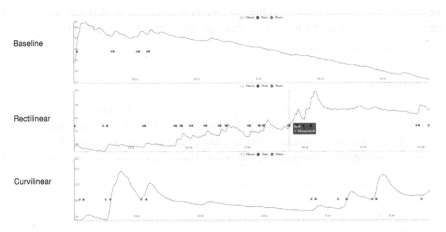

Baseline

Rectilinear

Curvilinear

Fig. 6. EDA graphs for one of the participants show the data collected at rest (baseline), the data acquired during the rectilinear apartment experience and during the curvilinear apartment experience, respectively.

data related to the visit of the rectilinear apartment. Note that there was an increase in activation over time and then a stabilization. In turn, the third graph, corresponding to the curvilinear apartment, shows an increase in activation at the beginning of the visit and soon after a fall and stabilization, increasing again in the final part.

Table 1 reveals the EDA values of each graph. The first column corresponds to the baseline data (minimum value), the second and third correspond to the activation peaks (maximum value), respectively for the straight and curvilinear flat. The fourth and fifth

Table 1. EDA values and respective percentages of all participants.

EDA	Baseline	Rectilinear apartment	Curvilinear apartment	Rectilinear shape activation (%)	Curvilinear shape activation(%)
P6	50	128	48	156%	-4%
P5	310	360	370	16.1%	19.4%
P4	70	86	71	22.9%	1.4%
P3	110	200	236	81.8%	114.5%
P2	106	160	140	50.9%	33.1%
Average	-	-	-	65.6%	12.6%

columns correspond to the positive and negative percentage values in relation to the baseline value (minimum value). The last row of the table shows the average value of the percentages of the last two columns. It is verified that the rectilinear apartment caused an activation increment of 65.6% in relation to the baseline, while the curvilinear apartment proved to have an activation increment of 12.6%. We can then deduce that the curvilinear flat caused less activation, that is, it made the participants more relaxed.

Figure 7 also shows three graphs, corresponding to the variation in heart rate (HRV), measured from the ECG. The first graph shows the values relative to the baseline, which remained with few oscillations over the time the participants listened to the music. However, in the second graph, referring to the rectilinear apartment, we can observe a variation and amplitude of the oscillations much higher than the baseline values. In the third graph, referring to the curvilinear flat, we can continue to observe amplitude oscillations greater than those of the baseline, but with less frequency than those of the second graph. The variations in heart rate, referring to the frequency of oscillations, are lower in the curvilinear apartment, which contributes to the participant's state of relaxation and confirms the trend found in the EDA.

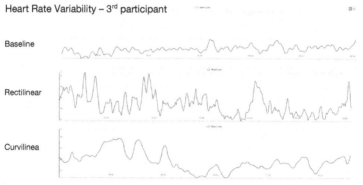

Fig. 7. HRV graphs of one of the participants show data collected in the resting state (baseline), during the rectilinear apartment experience, and during the curvilinear apartment experience, respectively.

Table 2 refers to the mean values of the HRV for the three conditions (baseline, rectilinear and curvilinear apartments). The last two lines show the mean and standard deviation values of the results. It is verified that the mean values of heart rate are lower during the baseline state. However, with the average heart rate being 70.1 beats per second, it indicates that the participants were not that relaxed or in a natural resting state. These results can be explained by the fact that the participants were being monitored with the biosensors, a situation that is not normal in their daily lives and that can cause some anxiety or stress. It is also verified that the average heart rate was 71.5 in the straight apartment and 69.7 in the curvilinear apartment. It should also be noted that the standard deviation of the heart rate data is very similar in the two apartments (8.8 for the straight and 8.2 for the curvilinear). In summary, the average heart rate of sample participants was lower in the curvy apartment, although the differences are minimal.

Table 2. Mean and standard deviation table for the HRV values of all participants.

HRV	Baseline	Rectilinear apartment	Curvilinear Apartment
P6	76,2	76,4	74,8
P5	54,6	63,2	62,4
P4	86,6	83,3	79,7
P3	63,4	62,6	60,03
P2	69,5	71,9	71,3
Average	70,1	71,5	69,7
S desviation	12,2	8,8	8,2

Respiratory Rate Variability – 3rd participant

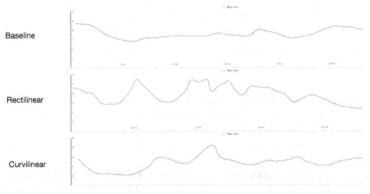

Baseline

Rectilinear

Curvilinear

Fig. 8. RRV graphs of one of the participants show data collected at rest (baseline), during the rectilinear apartment experience, and during the curvilinear apartment experience, respectively.

Figure 8 shows the three graphs corresponding to the variation in respiratory rate (VFR). The baseline measurement was very stable over time, with a low amplitude and frequency of oscillation. In the second graph, there is an increase in the amplitude and frequency of oscillation of the RRV. Regarding the third graph, there is a decrease in frequency and amplitude, when compared to the previous graph. If there are smaller variations in respiratory amplitude and frequency, this may be related to less activation and more relaxation. These data confirm the results obtained in the EDA and HRV.

In summary, regarding the architectural form, we can observe that, similar to the results presented by other authors [9, 14, 21], this study showed that the curved form caused greater relaxation and the rectilinear form greater activation.

3.1 Activation Peaks Depending on Architectural Experience

The highest peaks of each graph (EDA, HRV, RRV) reveal the moments of greatest activation of the participants in relation to the architectural experience. Next, some examples are presented to illustrate that these moments of activation are associated with the participant's experience with other characteristics of the space, in addition to form. This means that the images corresponding to these activation peaks can be related to other properties, such as light, the size of the window openings, the framing, the landscape, or the materials. These characteristics, when combined with the architectural form, provoke unconscious reactions in the participants (autonomic nervous system).

In the case of Electral Dermal Activity (EDA), Fig. 9 shows two images related to the moments of greatest activation of one of the participants, according to what he was

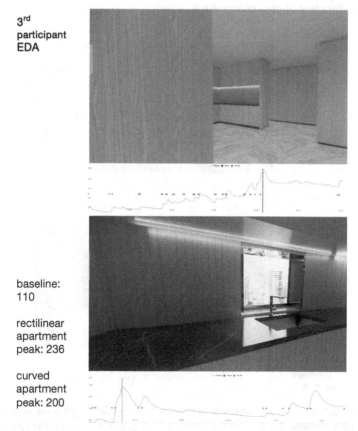

Fig. 9. EDA activation peaks, illustrated by the images corresponding to what the participant was observing at that moment. The top image is about the EDA graph of the rectilinear apartment, and the bottom image is about the EDA graph of the curvilinear apartment.

observing at that moment. The top image shows the peak moment for the rectilinear apartment, while the bottom image shows the peak moment for the curvilinear one. In the rectilinear apartment. The activation peak occurs in the space dedicated to the living room, with a point of view towards a part of the kitchen and the entrance area, as half of the shot appears hidden, it can create a moment of expectation for the observer. On the other hand, in the curvilinear apartment, the peak of activation takes place in the kitchen, looking at a small window that is above the sink and which frames the urban landscape in the background. In this case, the combination of the curved shape underlying the entire space, together with the rectangular "frame" of the window, the natural light combined with the artificial light, as well as the landscape, produces a greater activation in the participant.

The first image of Fig. 10 shows the HRV activation peak, corresponding to the rectilinear apartment. There was an increase in the HRV when entering the apartment (hall), which shows the perspective of the living room, with several planes at different distances and with a large window in the background that accentuates the depth of the look. In this case, the form and the distance relation of the walls, the natural light, the materiality and the framing that come from the observer's perspective are the characteristics that promote this moment of greater activation.

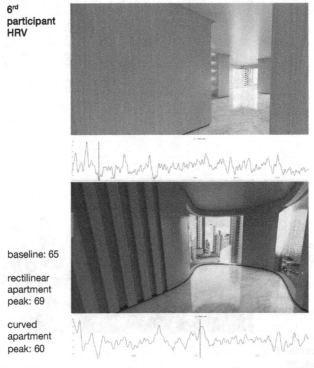

Fig. 10. RRV activation peaks, illustrated by images corresponding to what the participant was observing at that moment. The top image is about the RRV graph of the rectilinear apartment, and the bottom image, is about the RRV graph of the curvilinear apartment.

The second image in Fig. 10, corresponding to the curvilinear apartment, shows that the peak of greater HRV activation was at the moment of the living room, closer to the windows and the urban landscape. Here, the most striking architectural features are the curved shape together with the urban landscape framed by the large spans. In addition, the effect of natural lighting produces reflections on the materials and expands the space vertically.

In the case of Respiratory Frequency Variation (RRV), the first image of Fig. 11 shows that an oscillation and a peak occurred when the participant has his back to the kitchen, towards the bifurcation between the living room space and the circulation space of the bedrooms, in which the built-in furniture appears illuminated, as a prominent element. The double choice of path to take may have caused the oscillation.

In the second image of Fig. 11, the moment of greatest activation of the curvilinear apartment appears, in this case, it is fundamentally the urban landscape that overlaps any other features present in the image. This peak may have occurred, for example, due to the reaction to the height of the building in which the participant is located, as well as the permeability with the outside through the large glazing.

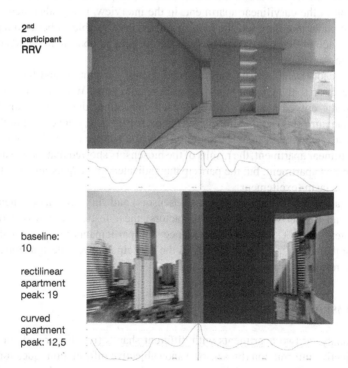

Fig. 11. HRV activation peaks, illustrated by images corresponding to what the participant was observing at that moment. The top image is about the HRV graph of the rectilinear apartment, and the bottom image, is about the HRV graph of the curvilinear apartment.

3.2 Participant Preference (Subjective Data)

Eighty percent of the participants chose the apartment with curvilinear shapes and twenty percent of the participants chose the rectilinear shape. In the interview, the participants who chose the curvilinear shape justified their choice with the argument that they would feel better in that space, however, they were reticent about how they would furnish the space. Participants who chose the flat with rectilinear shapes justified this preference with the argument that the space would be more functional and easier to furnish.

3.3 SAM Questionnaire (Self-assessment Manikin)

Regarding the valence scale (pleasure scale 1 to 9), the results of the SAM questionnaire showed an average value of 6.25 for the rectilinear apartment and 8.25 for the curvilinear apartment. On the arousal scale (activation scale 1 to 9), the results of the SAM questionnaire showed a mean value of 5 for the straight apartment and 6.25 for the curvilinear apartment.

In terms of valence and arousal, it was found that the participants felt more pleasure and activation in the curvilinear apartment. In the interview, it was also mentioned by all the participants that they felt the lack of furniture to be able to better imagine the future experience of that space, especially in the curvilinear apartment, which could be a challenge in that sense.

The biosensors data indicate that the participants' perception and the organism's automatic reaction to the presented stimuli were not the same. While the biosensor data showed that the curved shape conveyed greater relaxation, the data acquired by the SAM questionnaire showed that the curved shape, on average, conveyed a higher level of excitement (excitement) than relaxation. The same happens with the data obtained from the rectilinear apartment, the results of the biosensors showed that there was greater activation in this apartment, but the participants indicated in the questionnaire that they felt less enthusiasm (excitement).

This variation between the objective (biosensors) and subjective assessment (questionnaires) can be derived from several factors: the questionnaire was carried out moments later, and not during the experience; the participants had greater difficulty in accessing their emotions; the fact that all the participants were design students who have a more refined critical spirit about space.

4 Conclusions

The study analyzed two apartments with different shapes (rectilinear and curvilinear) through objective information (biosensors) and subjective information (questionnaires), which according to Shemesh et al. is the most complete way to obtain better results: "We believe that successful results can be achieved by combining qualitative and quantitative research" [14].

The results obtained are in agreement with previous studies that also used biosensors [9, 14, 21], demonstrating that the curved shape transmits a state of greater relaxation than the rectilinear shape. This result may have an association impregnated in the collective memory of the human being, since the first ways of inhabiting and organizing space were organic, with curved or circular limits: the grotto, prehistoric constructions (Stonehenge, Cromeleque dos Almendres, etc.) and indigenous, the igloo, and at the limit, the maternal uterus.

Regarding the subjective results, we found that there is no direct correspondence with the results of the biosensors. This can be explained by the fact that our sample is made up of design students who have a more refined critical spirit about space, or simply because they took the questionnaire moments after the virtual experience and now have some difficulty in accessing their memory and emotions.

This article was a novelty in this field by filling three gaps found in previous studies, which only use static analyzes (images or VR with no possibility of displacement). These differences can be presented on three levels: (1) it presents a more realistic experience of the space, (2) it presents a narrative that contextualizes the participant's experience, (3) it allows free exploration of the space in the visit to the apartments (ecological experience). Regarding the latter, although there is less control over the variables, we consider that the simulated architectural space should not be read as a static plane, but rather as a moving experience that reveals the interaction between several planes, as happens in normal daily life [24].

We already know that architecture evokes certain emotional states, whether we are aware of it or not. People choose the space consciously and unconsciously, according to what their body needs at any given moment (balance, concentration, relaxation). That's why we go to watch the sea when we want to calm our minds, we choose a secluded corner of the library when we want to concentrate or we go to big show arenas when we want to have fun. In this context, if the participants of this study are at a stage in their lives where they are looking for more activation than relaxation, it is justified that their choice falls on the architectural form that most conveys this sensation to them, the rectilinear one. This can somehow explain why 20% of the participants chose the rectilinear apartment and the physiological results of these participants indicate greater activation in the rectilinear than in the curvilinear.

It is important to bear in mind that people's state of mind and life dynamics are constantly changing, as are the needs of each individual. In this sense, the subjective (conscious) results obtained in this study may be different in another phase of the life of the same participants. On the other hand, it is likely that the physiological results measured with the biosensors, in the same simulated environment, may remain more stable over time.

The patterns created by combining the characteristic of form with other characteristics of space, provide unconscious data communicated by the body itself through peaks of activation and relaxation. The decoding of these patterns through this methodology will be useful for architecture, to make the project more conscious and intentional in relation to the target audience.

During the investigation, several limitations were found. Firstly, we consider that the sample of this study was too small, not allowing the generalization of the results obtained. Another limitation found was the presence of the researcher guiding the participant during the experiment, which may also influence the reactions of the individual's autonomic nervous system.

Finally, in future studies, the use of Virtual Reality is considered, to make the experience more immersive and realistic, to understand if the results obtained by the biosensors would be the same. From this study, we understand that through an ecological approach, that is, a free exploration of space when the participant visits the apartment, we obtained the same results/trends in relation to the laboratory experiments (static) carried out by the other studies [9, 14, 21], which means that the methodology proposed in this article proved to be effective. This discovery may motivate future studies to use this methodology, in which the interaction with space is more natural.

It is essential that from now on a more complete investigation is carried out in this area, and the present study can be replicated starting from the exploration of other characteristics of space, such as color, light or materiality.

Acknowledgements. This work is financed by national funds through FCT - Fundação para a Ciência e a Tecnologia, I.P., under the Projects with the references "UID/EAT/04008/2020" and "2021.05015.BD". Research funded by CIAUD, (Project UID/EAT/4008/2020) and ITI -LARSyS, (Project - UIDB/50009/2020).

References

1. Cruz Pinto, J.: A CAIXA, Metáfora e Arquitetura, Volume I. Colecção Arquitectura e Urbanismo, Faculdade de Arquitetura de Lisboa (2007)
2. Elbaiuomy, E., Hegazy, I., Sheta, S.: The impact of architectural spaces' geometric forms and construction materials on the users' brainwaves and consciousness status. Int. J. Low-Carbon Technol. **14**, 326–327 (2017)
3. Arnheim, R.: Arte & Percepção Visual - Uma Psicologia da Visão Criadora, pp. 89–90. Pioneira Thomson Learning, São Paulo (2005)
4. Arnheim, R.: A Dinâmica da Forma Arquitectónica, p. 13, 132, 173. Editorial Presença (1977)
5. Corbusier, L.: El Espíritu Nuevo en Arquitectura, p. 34. Colegio Oficial de Aparejadores y Arquitectos Técnicos de Madrid, Madrid (1983)
6. Simões Da Silva, A.C.: A Casa do Homem - A Máquina de Habitar na Arquitetura de Le Corbusier. Dissertação de Mestrado Integrado em Arquitetura, FAUP, p. 33, 35, 43 (2014)
7. Salameh, Z.: Aesthetics of Architecture - An Empirical Study of Proportion in Perceived Architectural Facades. Dissertation submitted at the Welsh School of Architecture. p. 4, 52 (2011)
8. Banaei, M., Ahmadi, A., Gramann, K., Hatami, J.: Emotional evaluation of architectural interior forms based on Personality differences using virtual reality. Front. Archit. Res. **9**, 139, 144 (2019)
9. Balakrishnan, B., Kalisperis, L.N., Sundar, S.S.: Capturing affect in architectural visualization - a case for integrating 3-dimensional visualization and psychophysiology. eCAADe **24**, 664 (2006)
10. Elbaiuomy, E., Hegazy, I., Sheta, S.: The impact of architectural spaces' geometric forms and construction materials on the users' brainwaves and consciousness status. Int. J. Low-Carbon Technol. **14**(3), 327 (2017)
11. Silvia, P., Barona, C.: Do people prefer curved objects? Angularity, expertise, and aesthetic preference. Empir. Stud. Arts **27**(1), 25–42 (2009)
12. Bar, M., Neta, M.: Humans prefer curved visual objects. Psychol. Sci. **17**(8), 645–648 (2006)
13. Leder, H., Tinio, P.P.L., Bar, M.: Emotional valence modulates the preference for curved objects. Perception **40**(6), 649–655 (2011)

14. Shemesh, A., Talmon, R., Karp, O., Amir, I., Bar, M., Grobman, Y.J.: Affective response to architecture – investigating human reaction to spaces with different geometry. Archit. Sci. Rev. **60**(2), 116–125 (2016)
15. Bertamini, M., Palumbo, L., Gheorghes, T.N., Galatsidas, M.: Do observers like curvature or do they dislike angularity? Br. J. Psychol. **107**, 154–178 (2016)
16. Cotter, K.N., Silvia, P.J., Bertamini, M., Palumbo, L., Vartanian, O.: Curve appeal: exploring individual differences in preference for curved versus angular objects. i-Perception **8**(2), 204166951769302 (2017)
17. Dazkir, S.S., Read, M.A.: Furniture forms and their influence on our emotional responses toward interior environments. Environ. Behav. **44**, 722–732 (2011)
18. Madani Nejad, K.: Curvilinearity in Architecture - Emotional Effect of Curvilinear Forms in Interior Design. Texas A&M University, Texas, TX (2007)
19. Vartanian, O., et al.: Preference for curvilinear contour in interior architectural spaces: evidence from experts and nonexperts. Psychol. Aesthet. Creativity Arts **13**(1), 110–116 (2019)
20. Poffenberger, A.T., Barrows, B.: The feeling value of lines. J. Appl. Psychol. **8**, 187e205 (1924)
21. Banaei, M., Hatami, J., Yazdanfar, A., Gramann, K.: Walking through architectural spaces: the impact of interior forms on human brain dynamics. Front. Hum. Neurosci. **11**, 477 (2017)
22. Lundholm, H.: The affective tone of lines - experimental researches. Psychol. Rev. **28**, 43e60 (1921)
23. BrainAnswer website. www.brainanswer.com
24. Tschumi, B.: The Manhattan Transcripts. Academy Editions (1994)

Research on the Gamification Design of Reading App Based on PAD Emotion Model

Chen Jiang[✉] and Yongyan Guo

East China University of Science and Technology, Shanghai 200237, China
2017441483@qq.com

Abstract. Objective: To investigate the influence of reading APP gamification design elements on users' emotional experience and the correlation between such emotional experience and users' usage behavior, so as to provide some reference opinions for reading APP to overcome its homogenization problem and gamification design solutions. Methods: Taking WeChat Reading App as an example, based on the GAMEX game experience evaluation scale, the gamification design elements of reading app are classified into three categories: achievement and progress-oriented elements, social-oriented elements and immersion-oriented elements, and the statistical methods of PAD emotion model and questionnaire are used. Different gamification design elements produce different user emotional experiences, and all of them have influence on user behavior. The influence is in the order of achievement and progress-oriented, immersion-oriented and social-oriented elements. Conclusion: For the gamification design of reading APP, we can increase or decrease the design proportion and content of related elements according to the influence degree of each element on user behavior and the positive or negative degree of emotional experience, so that the reading APP can give users better emotional experience and participation behavior and improve the overall use value of the product.

Keywords: Gamification design · PAD emotion model · Reading app

1 Gamification Design and User Experience

1.1 Gamification Design

In 2010, Jane McGonigal, a famous game designer, gave a speech called "Gaming can make a better world", explaining the benefits of games and advocating the use of game thinking to solve real-life problems [1]. Since then, the term "gamification" has been active in the public eye.

The term "gamification" refers to "the application of game design elements in non-game situations" [2], which emphasizes the use of game design methods to solve problems in non-game areas. With the development of Internet technology, gamification design elements are now embodied in various mobile applications, using gamification design elements to make the product better meet user needs to achieve user value, so that they get a better interactive experience, and then enhance user motivation and improve

M. M. Soares et al. (Eds.): HCII 2022, LNCS 13322, pp. 56–71, 2022.
https://doi.org/10.1007/978-3-031-05900-1_4

user participation [3]. For Internet products, whether gamification design encourages users to actively participate and bring positive emotional and interactive experiences, and promotes positive user behavior, is the core issue related to the success of its product design [4]. That is to say, the game experience brought by gamification design is the key to determine whether the product is engaging or not.

1.2 Game Experience and Design Elements

In his book "Emotional Design", Donald Norman divided user experience into three levels, namely, instinctive level, behavioral level, and reflective level [5]. Among them, the reflective layer focuses on the higher level of feeling such as the inner consciousness and emotion of users, which is the resonance between products or services and users' emotion. In the human-centered design principle, the focus on the reflective layer and the user's emotional experience has increased and deepened in the gamification design.

For the user experience generated by gamification design, Koivisto and Hamari define it as a gaming experience in a non-gaming environment, i.e., the positive emotions and willingness to engage that users have when using a gamified application [6]. It presents a multidimensional structure with certain specific emotions and various sub-dimensions. When evaluating its user experience, it is necessary to divide its specific gamification elements and then measure them because it is in a non-gamification scenario.

In other words, the user experience of gamification design is closely related to the gamification design elements [7], which are the basis of gamification design and the relevant elements to capture the user's game experience.

Table 1. GAMEX game experience evaluation scale

Category	Design elements
Achievement and progress-oriented elements	Scores, challenges, badges, leaderboards, levels, performance stats, progress, quizzes, timers, difficulty increases
Socially oriented elements	Social networking features, cooperation, competition, peer rating, customization, multiplayer, group voting
Immersion-oriented elements	Incarnation, narrative, virtual worlds, game rewards, role-playing
Non-numeric elements	Real world/economic rewards, check-ins, motion tracking, physics cards, physics game board, real world interactive objects, physics objects as game resources, physics dice
Other miscellaneous	Full game, assistance, virtual currency, reminders, retries, boarding, adaptive difficulty, game rounds, warnings, penalties, game slogans, funny movies, virtual pets, trading, making suggestions, virtual objects as augmented reality

Among them, PBL elements are the most common elements used in gamification design, including points, badges and leaderboards, but they are only the special typical elements of gamification design elements [8]. In this paper, the GAMEX scale (Table 1) proposed by Koivisto and Hamari is used to classify gamification design elements [6]. It classifies gamification design elements into five categories, including achievement and social-oriented elements, social-oriented elements, immersion-oriented elements, non-digital elements, and other miscellaneous elements. Basically, all the existing elements of gamification design elements are included.

1.3 Reading App

With the popularization of mobile Internet technology, electronic reading has become more and more common, giving rise to a series of electronic reading apps, which have rapidly occupied half of the book reading market with the advantages of massive reading resources and portable and ready-to-view. However, the emergence of a large number of products has also caused the phenomenon of homogenization of reading apps [9]: (1) homogenization of basic reading functions: although all kinds of products have their own advantages in visual display, the basic functions are e-book shelves, font adjustment, progress display, etc., and there is no distinct difference in the feeling of use. (2) Homogenization of user operating system: The operation logic of reading apps is similar, with the interface tab bar, three modules of book city, book library and personal center, and the content difference is small. (3) Homogenization of promotion method: the product promotion method is still not directly oriented to the user's promotion method, and the actual click rate of users is low. WeChat Reading, on the other hand, adopts user sharing mechanism based on WeChat friends to upgrade product promotion strategy and enhance user experience in order to increase product stickiness. Moreover, nowadays, mobile application products are emerging, such as short videos, social media platforms, games and other leisure and entertainment products to increase the attractiveness of users, how to enhance the existing user stickiness and activity at the same time, and constantly improve the user experience and increase the retention of new users is also one of the market challenges facing reading APPs today.

1.4 Reading App Gamification Design

Compared with traditional paper reading, users have a more intuitive feeling of the overall overview of reading books and stronger correlation between users. At present, in order to overcome the homogenization of reading APPs and low user activity, existing reading APP products, such as "WeChat Reading", "QQ Reading", "Palm Reader iReader "WeChat Reading", "QQ Reading", "Palm Reader iReader", "NetEase Cloud Reading" and other products, all set reading progress bar, reading ranking, cooperative team, playing cards and other gamification design elements to enhance user motivation to improve the use of the product. And gamification design elements are becoming more and more common on mobile applications [10].

However, whether these gamification design elements bring positive user experience, what direct emotional experience they bring to users, and what kind of elements can better promote users' usage behavior are the focal points of gamification design for reading apps. Therefore, this paper focuses on WeChat reading in reading APP, and explores the impact of reading APP gamification design elements on users' emotional experience and their reactions on user behavior with the help of PAD emotion model, so as to provide some reference significance for reading APP design and development.

2   User Emotional Experience Measurement

2.1   PAD Emotion Model

The PAD affective model is a common method used to measure and evaluate users' affective experience, which can make a qualitative analysis and quantitative expression of users' affective tendencies when using a product or service [11]. The PAD affective model contains three independent dimensions of Pleasure, Arousal, and Dominance [12].

Among them, Pleasure indicates the degree of positive or negative user emotion, such as happy, joyful or sad. A high state of pleasantness, i.e., when the P value is positive, indicates that the product has good usability and friendliness, and the user is able to complete the required requirements clearly and comfortably.

Arousal is the degree of individual neurophysiological activation, which indicates the user's alertness strength and excitement level, such as boredom, calmness, surprise, etc. When the user is activated or excited, i.e. when the A-value is positive, the user is highly concentrated and easily attracted to the product and interested in it. Therefore, a moderate short-term activation level is more helpful for users' emotional experience.

The degree of dominance indicates how much control the individual has over the external scene or others, i.e. whether the user's emotional experience is autonomous or passively influenced by the external environment, such as fear, resentment, or compliance. When the dominance is higher, i.e., the D value is positive, the stronger the user's control over the product, the lower the user's cognitive load and learning cost, and the higher the ease of use of the product.

The PAD affective model effectively establishes a three-dimensional affective space [13] (see Fig. 1), and different affective states can be put into this three-dimensional affective space to find their corresponding positions, which can provide a more intuitive understanding and performance of individual affective experience.

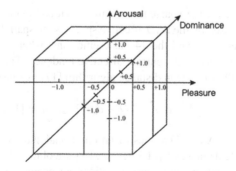

Fig. 1. PAD three-dimensional emotional model

2.2 PAD Emotion Scale and Tendencies

Based on the PAD emotion model, Mehrabian et al. developed the PAD emotion scale [14] for measuring emotion values. Thereafter, the Institute of Psychology of the Chinese Academy of Sciences developed the PAD emotion scale [15] (Table 2) and PAD values for 14 basic emotions [16] (Table 3) based on this scale applicable to Chinese contexts.

The emotion scale is a nine-point semantic scale with 12 groups of emotion words, each group rated from −4 to 4 nine, with a score of 0 indicating neutrality and the more polarized, the stronger the corresponding degree of emotion. The final P, A, and D values were calculated based on the normalized metric (Table 2) and derived by taking the mean value of each sample. With the values of each emotion dimension, the user's emotion type and tendency can be calculated based on the 14 basic emotion PAD values.

Table 2. Chinese version of PAD emotional scale and normalized publicity

Emotional dimension	Corresponding vocabulary	Normalization formula
Pleasure (P)	P1: Angry - Interested	P = P1 − P2 + P3 − P4
	P2: Friendly - Dismissive	
	P3: Painful - Pleasant	
	P4: Excited - Irritated	
Arousal (A)	A1: Sober - Sleepy	A = −A1 + A2 − A3 + A4
	A2: Calm - Excited	
	A3: interested - Relaxed	
	A4: Restrained - Surprised	
Dominance (D)	D1: Controlled - Master Controlled	D = D1 − D2 + D3 − D4
	D2: Dominant - Submissive	
	D3: Humble - Condescending	
	D4: Influenced - Influenced	

Emotional Tendencies, the sparseness of an individual's emotion to the 14 basic emotions, can be expressed on the PAD affective space as the spatial coordinate distance between the current emotion and the 14 basic emotions, where the smallest distance between the two is the individual's current affective tendency. The coordinate distance L can be obtained by the Euclidean distance algorithm [17] as follows.

$$L = \left[(P - p_n)^2 + (A - a_n)^2 + (D - d_n)^2 \right]^{1/2}, \quad n = [1, 14], \quad n \in Z \quad (1)$$

That is, when the P, A and D values of an emotional state are brought in, the 14 basic spatial coordinate distances $L_1, L_2, L_3, \ldots, L_{14}$ are obtained, where the minimum distance $L_{min} = L_n$, then one of the 14 basic emotions corresponding to n is the emotional tendency of the current emotional state. For example, when the minimum value of n is 5, it corresponds to the user's current emotional tendency of "Mild".

Table 3. Reference table of PAD values of 14 basic emotions

Number	Emotional type	P-value	A-value	D-value
1	Joy	2.77	1.21	1.42
2	Optimistic	2.48	1.05	1.75
3	Relaxation	2.19	−0.66	1.05
4	Surprised	1.72	1.71	0.22
5	Mild	1.57	−0.79	0.38
6	Dependence	0.39	−0.81	−1.48
7	Boring	−0.53	−1.25	−0.84
8	Sadness	−0.89	0.17	−0.70
9	Fear	−0.93	1.30	−0.64
10	Anxiety	−0.95	0.32	−0.63
11	Contempt	−1.58	0.32	1.02
12	Disgust	−1.80	0.40	0.67
13	Resentment	−1.98	1.10	0.60
14	Hostility	−2.08	1.00	1.12

3 Research Process

3.1 Research Background

At present, WeChat Reading is unique in the reading APP market with the concept of "social + reading" [18]. This paper focuses on WeChat Reading APP, compares the gamification design elements, and evaluates and measures the user emotional experience brought by various gamification design elements and their impact on user behavior.

WeChat Reading App is divided into four main functional areas, namely Reading, Bookshelf, Discovery and My. The reading page is mainly for book recommendation, including: book classification, book list recommendation, friends reading, today's reading, as well as book reading, book squad, etc. Built-in likes, shares, comments on book content, mutual relations, private messages, formation, etc. The bookshelf page is for recently read books and book lists, which involves less gamification design elements. The discovery page is mainly social, including friends' ideas, small circles, subscribed public numbers, free books, welfare factory, paper book specials, WeChat listening books, etc. Users can like, comment and forward them. My page mainly includes personal information, my home page, account, monthly card, shopping cart, order, reading list, concern, notes, read books, subscription, and private message and notification message, etc.

The above functional sections and elements involved in WeChat Reading were organized and analyzed, and eight typical gamification design elements were selected from them, namely, reading leaderboard, reading progress bar, reading time accumulation, friends' ideas, small circle, book squad, profile, book coins\infinite card rewards, which were classified according to the GAMEX Gamification Design Element Scale into three major categories of achievement and progress-oriented elements, social-oriented elements, and immersion-oriented elements (Table 4), and each typical element was marked in the screenshot of the interface (Fig. 2) to give the subjects a clearer understanding of each type of element afterwards.

Table 4. Classification of WeChat reading game design elements

Category	Design elements	APP display form
Achievement and progress-oriented elements	Leaderboards, progress bars, time accumulation, badges, challenges	Reading ranking, reading progress bar, reading time accumulation
Socially oriented elements	Teamwork, social networking, multiplayer games	Friends' ideas, cliques, book squads
Immersion-oriented elements	Game rewards, personal data, role-playing	Personal information, book coins\infinite card rewards

Achievement and progress-oriented elements (reading ranking, reading progress bar, reading time accumulation)   Socially oriented elements (ideas for friends, cliques, reading squads)   Immersion-oriented elements (profile, book coins/infinite card rewards)

Fig. 2. Extraction and division of game design elements

3.2 Questionnaire Design and Variable Measurement

The study was mainly in the form of a self-report questionnaire, and the framework was integrated using existing scales [3, 7, 11] to ensure the accuracy of the post-measurement data.

The questionnaire study variables are mainly user sentiment experience scores of PAD regarding achievement and progress-oriented, social-oriented, and immersion-oriented gamification design elements, and their user behaviors regarding willingness to use, word-of-mouth, and evaluation of the WeChat Reading App. Among them, the emotional experience scores of gamified design elements are measured by a nine-point Likert scale of PAD; the overall usage behavior of WeChat Reader is measured by a 7-point Likert scale, from 1 = "strongly disagree/strongly dissatisfy" to 7 = "strongly agree/strongly satisfied". Finally, the study included several other control variables: gender, age, experience, and time per use.

3.3 Data Collection

The questionnaire participants were limited to those who had used the WeChat Book App within one year, and after excluding 13 participants who did not meet the requirements of the questionnaire or did not complete the whole questionnaire, the final sample consisted of 142 people. The users who met the usage profile were further screened (Table 5) to count whether the subjects had used all the eight extracted gamification design elements, i.e., the functions of the area marked in Fig. 2, of which 63 users indicated that they had used all three types of gamification design elements, 54% were female and 46% were male (Table 6).

Table 5. Usage of gamification design elements of WeChat reading app

Statistical characteristics	Use category	Number of people	Frequency (%)
Achievement and progress oriented gamification design elements	Yes	118	83.10
	No	24	16.90
Socially oriented gamification design elements	Yes	85	59.86
	No	57	40.14
Immersion-oriented gamification design elements	Yes	104	73.24
	No	38	26.76

4 Data Analysis and Results

A total of 63 valid questionnaires were collected, each containing 12 PAD emotional ratings of three types of gamification design elements and 5 ratings on user behavior, and finally 2583 data were obtained, and the research data were analyzed using Excel and SPSS 26 data processing software.

4.1 Common Method Deviation Test

In this paper, the self-report questionnaire method was mainly used, and the main variables were all from the same respondents, which may lead to the problem of common method bias. The Harman one-way test was used to determine whether the correspondence between the measured factors and the measured scale items remained consistent with the predictions.

The data obtained from the measurement were all imported into SPSS for analysis, and the final results showed that: the common factor with eigenvalues greater than 1, the variance explained by the first factor was 23.60%, which was less than 40%, and the common method bias was not serious, so the data did not have a single factor explaining most of the variance, that is, few people scored all 1 or 7 and other extreme bias values, indicating that there was no serious common method bias problem, and the scale measurement data are usable.

Table 6. Basic information statistics of the questionnaire survey

Statistical characteristics	Category	Number of people	Frequency (%)
Gender	Male	29	46.03
	Female	34	53.97
Age	Under 18 years old	3	4.76
	18–35 years old	52	82.54
	35–55 years old	7	11.11
	56 years old and above	1	1.59
Education	Junior high school	2	3.17
	High school	6	9.52
	Specialized	7	11.11
	Bachelor's degree	29	46.03
	Postgraduate	19	30.16
Length of time used	1–3 months	23	36.51
	3–6 months	8	12.70
	6–12 months	12	19.05
	More than one year	20	31.75
Length of single use	15 min or less	26	41.27
	15–30 min	17	26.98
	30–60 min	13	20.63
	More than an hour	7	11.11

4.2 Reliability and Validity Analysis

Reliability is used to measure the reliability, stability and consistency of the questionnaire. In this paper, two indicators, Cronbach's Alpha (CA) and Composite Reliability (CR), were chosen to test the reliability of the questionnaire. The study shows that when both CA and CR are greater than 0.7, it indicates a good internal consistency. The CA and CR of each latent variable in this paper exceeded 0.7 (Table 7), indicating that the questionnaire has high reliability.

Validity is used to measure the degree of validity of the measurement results. The validity of the data was tested by KMO and Bartlett and convergent validity of the questionnaire. The results showed that the KMO coefficient was greater than 0.5, the significance p-value was less than 0.05 (Table 8), and the standardized factor loading values of each variable were greater than 0.7, and the average variance extracted value AVE was greater than 0.5 (Table 7), indicating that the questionnaire had good validity.

Table 7. Standard load, Cronbach's α, CR and AVE values of each factor

Observation variables standard			Standard load	Cronbach's α	CR	AVE
Pleasure (P)	Achievement and progress oriented elements	P1	0.736	0.874	0.8562	0.6661
	Socially oriented elements	P2	0.878			
	Immersion-oriented elements	P3	0.828			
Arousal (A)	Achievement and progress oriented elements	A1	0.740	0.845	0.779	0.5403
	Socially oriented elements	A2	0.742			
	Immersion-oriented elements	D3	0.723			
Dominance (D)	Achievement and progress oriented elements	D1	0.717	0.813	0.8332	0.6263
	Socially oriented elements	D2	0.773			
	Immersion-oriented elements	D3	0.876			
User behavior (U)	Willingness to use	W1	0.894	0.921	0.9385	0.754
		W2	0.915			
	Word of mouth	K1	0.888			
		K2	0.877			
	Rating	R1	0.759			

Table 8. KMO and Bartlett test

KMO Sampling suitability quantity		.820
Bartlett's sphericity test	Approximate cardinality	660.087
	Degree of freedom	91
	Significance	.000

4.3 Variable Description Analysis

The raw data of the PAD sentiment scores of the three gamified design elements of WeChat Reading were imported into Excel, and after conversion according to the normalized PAD value metric, the data of all subjects were averaged to derive the P, A, and D values corresponding to each item (Table 9). The obtained values were brought into the affective tendency calculation metric, and the minimum values corresponding to each item were marked to obtain the affective spatial distance and affective tendency of the 14 basic emotions of the three gamified design elements (Table 10). The emotional tendency of the achievement and progress-oriented elements is "Joy"; the emotional tendency of the social-oriented and immersion-oriented elements is "Relaxation".

Table 9. PAD sentiment values of three types of gamification design elements

Gamification design elements	P-value	A-value	D-value
Achievement and progress oriented elements	4.27	0.02	0.48
Socially oriented elements	2.02	−0.19	0.78
Immersion-oriented elements	3.14	0.10	0.63

Table 10. The emotional spatial distance between the PAD value of gamification design elements and the 14 basic emotional types

Number	Emotional Type	Achievement-oriented elements	Socially oriented elements	Immersion-oriented elements
1	Joy	**2.14***	1.72	1.41
2	Optimistic	2.43	1.64	1.61
3	Relaxation	2.26	**0.57***	**1.28***
4	Surprised	3.07	2.00	2.19
5	Mild	4.21	0.85	1.82
6	Dependence	4.42	2.85	3.59
7	Boring	5.14	3.20	4.18
8	Sadness	5.29	3.28	4.25
9	Fear	5.47	3.59	4.43
10	Anxiety	6.87	3.32	4.29
11	Contempt	5.88	3.64	4.74
12	Disgust	6.09	3.86	4.95
13	Resentment	6.34	4.20	5.22
14	Hostility	6.46	4.28	5.32

Note: * is the minimum value of the corresponding emotional space of the item, which is its emotional tendency

4.4 Related Analysis

Pearson correlation analysis was conducted among the variables to test whether the emotional tendencies generated by various types of gamification design elements on users were related to user behavior, in order to better verify the enhancement value of the overall product after the application of various types of gamification design elements. The test results are shown in Table 11, where P1, P2, P3 and U are all influential to each other, i.e., the pleasantness of all three types of gamification design elements have significant correlation with user behavior.

Table 11. Pearson correlation and significance level among various variables

	P1	P2	P3	A1	A2	A3	D1	D2	D3	U
P1	1.00									
P2	.46**	1.00								
P3	.39**	.37**	1.00							
A1	0.14	.30*	.44**	1.00						
A2	−0.04	0.20	0.07	.40**	1.00					
A3	0.10	0.01	.37**	0.06	−0.07	1.00				
D1	0.05	−0.13	−0.04	−0.10	−0.04	−0.04	1.00			
D2	0.01	0.20	0.23	0.01	0.04	−0.21	.32**	1.00		
D3	0.05	0.03	0.10	−0.02	−0.18	−0.14	0.12	0.03	1.00	
U	.35**	.29*	.30*	0.17	−0.08	0.10	−0.21	0.01	0.02	1.00

** Significant correlation at the 0.01 level (two-tailed).
* At the 0.05 level (two-tailed), the correlation is significant.

4.5 Regression Analysis

Based on the results of the correlation analysis, there is an influence relationship between the pleasantness generated by the three types of gamification design elements and user behavior. Following that, regression analysis is used to test how the three elements affect user behavior, i.e., how much weight the three elements have on user behavior. The results of the test are shown in Table 12, where each variable satisfies a VIF value less than 5, there is no multicollinearity, and the residual values obey a normal distribution (Fig. 3), indicating that the results of this regression analysis are reliable. The results show that the significance level of P1 and P3 is less than 0.05, and P1 is positively correlated with user behavior, P3 is negatively correlated with user behavior, while the significance level between P2 and user behavior is not high, so the level of influence of the pleasure generated by gamification design elements and user behavior is P1, P3 and P2 in order.

Table 12. Results of linear regression analysis of pleasure and user behavior

Factor[a]					t	Significance	Covariance statistics	
Models		Unstandardized coefficient		Standardization factor				
		B	Standard error	Beta			Tolerances	VIF
1	(Constant)	1.967	.175		11.245	.000		
	P1	.069	.031	.329	2.190	.032	.674	1.484
	P2	−.004	.029	−.017	−.130	.897	.850	1.176
	P3	−.076	.035	−.310	−2.177	.034	.750	1.334

a. Dependent variable: user behavior.

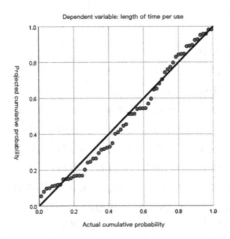

Dependent variable: length of time per use

Fig. 3. The normal P-P plot of the regression standardized residuals

5   Data Analysis Summary

According to the above statistics, different gamification design elements produce different user emotional experiences, and all three types of elements have an impact on user behavior.

The PAD value of achievement and progress-oriented gamification design elements is (4.27, 0.02, 0.48), and the emotional tendency is "Joy". The P, A and D values are all positive, which means that the usability, user activation and ease of use of these elements are good, and users are able to adapt to these functions when using the reading list, reading progress bar and viewing the accumulated reading time. And regression analysis shows that the degree of pleasure generated by achievement and progress orientation has the greatest influence on user behavior, and there is a positive relationship between the two, when the higher the degree of pleasure, the more user behavior feedback, that is, the higher the user's willingness to use, word-of-mouth dissemination of the product, and evaluation. Therefore, when designing the interactive elements of reading app, we can focus on the achievement and progress-oriented gamification design elements, such as setting scores, leaderboards, challenges, badges, levels, performance statistics, progress feedback or display, quizzes, timers, increasing difficulty and other functions.

The PAD value of socially oriented gamification elements is $(2.02, -0.19, 0.78)$, and the sentiment tendency is "Relaxation". The P and D values are positive, indicating that the usability and ease of use of socially oriented gamification design elements are good, and users can use the product directly and independently, but the A value is negative and the activation degree is low, and this type of element is not very attractive and active to users. It also verifies that the socially oriented gamification design elements of reading APP are not highly attractive and usable to users, and some users will not use this type of function, and the socially oriented has the lowest influence on user behavior, and users are more interested in achieving an independent personal reading experience, with low participation in the social part of reading, so in terms of reading APP design, it is possible to Appropriately delete the setting of this type of element function, such as social network function, cooperation, competition, multiplayer games, collective voting, etc.

The PAD value of immersion-oriented gamification design elements is $(3.14, 0.10, 0.63)$, and the emotional tendency is "Relaxation". The P, A and D values are all positive, which are similar to the user experience of achievement and progress-oriented gamified social elements, but their emotional tendency is more "relaxed", and users are more calm and natural when using the product, and their influence on user behavior is in the middle value, so their design elements can be increased appropriately, such as incarnation settings, narrative stories, virtual worlds, voting, etc. Narrative stories, virtual worlds, game rewards, role-playing, etc.

And for reading APPs, when most similar APPs set the achievement and progress-oriented elements of "PBL trinity" (points, badges and rankings), to overcome this homogeneity, we can start with immersion-oriented elements and strengthen the design of personalized user performance and role-playing. For example, setting up a user virtual image, when the user has read the book or part of the content, the virtual image can add part of the energy enrichment, or change the internal and external performance image to improve the user experience such as user attraction and immersion, to break through the homogeneity while creating its own characteristics and improve the user's usage and willingness to participate, in order to improve the overall value of the product.

6 Conclusion

Therefore, as far as the gamification design of WeChat Reading APP is concerned, different gamification design elements will cause different emotional experiences for users, and such emotions will directly act on user behavior, which will in turn affect the use of the whole product. However, this paper mainly analyzes a single reading APP of WeChat Reading, although the eight gamification design elements selected have certain typicality, the overall coverage represented by them may be insufficient, and subsequent research can select multiple reading APPs for research and analysis, so as to explore more deeply the user emotional experience and its influence on user behavior.

To sum up, this paper takes WeChat Reading APP as a mapping point, makes an objective analysis and comparison of the role and proportion of gamification design elements set in reading APPs, and puts forward certain reference opinions. Achievement and progress-oriented gamification design elements have the greatest impact on user behavior, and their user emotional experience is better, so they can be placed among the design priorities; social-oriented gamification design elements are less attractive to users and have less impact on users' active participation behavior, so they can be set with less relevant functions; immersion-oriented elements have better impact on both user emotional experience and user behavior, and now reading class APP, there is not much focus on this, so it can be used as a breakthrough point or distinctive point of design. These systematic analysis of gamification design will better support the further development of reading APP gamification design, and provide some theoretical support and guidance for its improvement of user emotional experience and user participation and other behaviors.

References

1. Mcgonigal, J.: Gaming can make a better world. Pub. Manage. **96**, 5 (2010)
2. Qin, X.: Study on the application strategy of gamification design in health behavior promotion. Jiangnan University (2017)
3. Bitrián, P., Buil, I., Catalán, S.: Enhancing user engagement: the role of gamification in mobile apps. J. Bus. Res. **132**, 170–185 (2021)
4. Ha, T., Lee, S.: User behavior model based on affordances and emotions: a new approach for an optimal use method in product-user interactions. Int. J. Hum. Comput. Interact. **31**(6), 371–384 (2015)
5. Norman, D.A.: Design Psychology 3-Emotional Design. CITIC Press, Beijing (2015). Translated by Xiaomei He and Qiuxing Ou
6. Eppmann, R., Bekk, M., Klein, K.: Gameful experience in gamification: construction and validation of a gameful experience scale [GAMEX]. J. Interact. Mark. **43**, 98–115 (2018)
7. Qin, Y.: Attractiveness of game elements, presence, and enjoyment of mobile augmented reality games: the case of Pokémon Go. Telematics Inform. **62**, 101620 (2021)
8. Nasirzadeh, E., Fathian, M.: Investigating the effect of gamification elements on bank customers to personalize gamified systems. Int. J. Hum. Comput. Stud. **143**, 102469 (2020)
9. Xing, C.: Research on the social reading phenomenon of WeChat reading community. Henan University (2020)
10. Koivisto, J., Hamari, J.: The rise of motivational information systems: a review of gamification research. Int. J. Inf. Manage. **45**, 191–210 (2019)
11. Yan, G.: A study of user information behavior in social Q&A communities based on PAD sentiment model. Southwest University of Science and Technology (2020)
12. Mehrabian, A.: Pleasure-arousal-dominance: a general framework for describing and measuring individual differences in Temperament. Curr. Psychol. **14**(4), 261–292 (1996)
13. Xinyan, W., Dawei, W.: Research on the influence of perceptual fluency on users' emotional experience during package opening. Packaging Engineering, pp. 1–8 (2020)
14. Mehrabian, A., Wihardja, C., Ljunggren, E.: Emotional correlates of preferences for situation-activity combinations in everyday life. Genet. Soc. Gen. Psychol. Monogr. **123**(4), 461–477 (1997)
15. Xiaoming, L., Xiaolan, F., Guofeng, D.: A preliminary trial of the simplified Chinese version of the PAD emotion scale among college students in Beijing. Chin. J. Ment. Health **05**, 327–329 (2008)

16. Xiaoming, L.: The PAD three-dimensional emotion model, 29 January 2007
17. Ni, J., Ran, L., Chunyao, L.: The application of PAD emotion model in user emotion experience evaluation. Packaging Engineering, pp. 1–9 (2020)
18. Nan, Z.: Research on user motivation of WeChat reading app. Yunnan University of Finance and Economics (2021)

In Sync! Design for Social Connection

Satu Jumisko-Pyykkö[1](✉) and Gail Kenning[2]

[1] Häme University of Applied Sciences, Vankanlähde 9, 13100 Hämeenlinna, Finland
satu.jumisko-pyykko@iki.fi
[2] fEEL (felt Experience and Empathy Lab), University of New South Wales, Sydney, Australia
gail.kenning@unsw.edu.au

Abstract. Participatory approaches are increasingly used in solving complex design challenges. Workshop facilitation is a key aspect of many co-design projects bringing together heterogeneous groups of people to connect share and co-create. Developing high quality social connections across the group and recognizing when they occur can be highly beneficial to workshop engagements and outcomes. Such connections between people are often established through temporal aspects of non-verbal communication, known as behavioral synchrony. The aim of this study was to examine whether high quality connections could be facilitated in dyads engaged in set-tasks that involved 'doing' and 'making' activities. The results showed that all activities evoked behavioral synchrony, high-quality connections, and positive emotions, but the extent and type of connection differed according to the activity. This paper proposes that non-verbal communication and behavioral synchrony should be considered in designing for social connection between co-design participants and suggests a framework for its use in design and evaluation.

Keywords: Non-verbal communication · Design tasks · Quality of connection · Emotion · Design research · Systems intelligence

1 Introduction

Participatory approaches are increasingly being used to solve pressing and complex design challenges. This often means that interdisciplinary teams and stakeholders, not familiar with design processes, are invited to co-design, co-create, and co-produce outputs and outcomes. When taking on complex design challenges such as new services, systems, experiences, sustainability, and transformation, designers collaborate with a wide range of stakeholders including end-user groups, decision makers, other designers, and developers. Participants may be required to engage with people with significantly different world views when it comes to the design challenge being addressed, the language used, and the approaches and methods they use. This is apparent, for example, in projects that address health matters which may involve designers, technologists, clinical and medical staff and patients—each with different experiences and agendas. The success of participatory projects often rests on how well projects participants work together, communicate agreements and differences, and trust each other. Therefore, workshops, often the mainstay of participatory engagements, need to be carefully facilitated to overcome

© The Author(s), under exclusive license to Springer Nature Switzerland AG 2022
M. M. Soares et al. (Eds.): HCII 2022, LNCS 13322, pp. 72–91, 2022.
https://doi.org/10.1007/978-3-031-05900-1_5

the many differences, and build a sense of connection and trust. Thus, building social connection is an essential aspect in systemic, human-centred and empathic co-design.

To understand how social connection can be supported it is necessary to understand the needs and wants of stakeholders and the relational dynamics, and so designers need to be attuned to the sensitivities of participants, how they collaborate, and see themselves being a part of the system [1, 2]. Recent research has proposed systemic approaches to support these designers' practices underlining the need for new frameworks, processes, methods, and tools [2]. The quality of social connections can be understood by looking at interpersonal behavioural synchrony; by observing nonverbal communication. Behavioural timing including rhythm, pausing, simultaneity, turn-taking conveys important information about connection between people independently of the content of their conversation or mode of engagement [3]. This non-verbal and implicit communication is unconscious, emotional, and is visible in gaze, facial expressions, speech, spatial orientation, touch, self-touch, and posture [4]. People can experience being "in synch" with each other, reporting a higher level of empathy and affect a greater sense of co-operation, social cohesion, liking, a sense of similarity, and a feeling of trust [5]. This can be observed as people tend to coordinate their movements with others both in small and larger groups [5]. From a design perspective, establishing behavioural synchrony can promote collaboration, creativity, impact quality of outcome, and can potentially support greater degrees of success in participatory projects with people with differing motivations. A goal of this study is to explore how different types of design activities can impact the building of social connection.

2 Context for Connection in Codesign

Participatory approaches, such as co-design, co-creation, co-production, have developed in a range of ways, depending on where they occur (taking different trajectories, for example, in the US and Europe). They also manifest differently according to the design challenge being addressed, the designers background and experience, the stakeholders involved and the desired outcomes [6]. These practices have brought about a shift in understandings of the role of the user and who the user(s) is/are. While user-centred practices positioned the user as subject, providing feedback on concepts developed by others, participatory approaches position the user in an active role as partner in co-creating outcomes [6–8]. A further shift has occurred as designers, increasingly aiming for meaningful design practices and outcomes, take on the challenges of working in and for real world contexts using living labs and co-production methods [6–9]. Operating in the messiness of the real-world means working with people who are not designers or familiar with the design process and entering dynamic social spaces impacted by legacies, sometimes contradictory stakeholder needs, and often competing relationships. It becomes increasingly apparent that there is usually no one user, but multiple shareholders invested in the success of any design challenge. However, while many may be invested in design challenges and in producing or improving artefacts, services, systems and processes, stakeholders frequently do not have a shared language, approach, practice or method. They may harbor mistrust, be subject to power relations that prevent their airing their views, or simply not able to sufficiently articulate their response to proposed developments.

This has many implications for designers. Understanding the context of a design challenge, the intricacies of relational dynamics and user(s) needs—beyond simply providing feedback to questions or relying on what they say. As Dervin and Foreman-Wernet [10] suggest we need to pay attention to the "hows" of communicating "to understand how we communicate [and] to intervene, change and improve these practices". To this end workshops, as a methodology, have become a mainstay of participatory approaches providing creative ways for participants to explore what they think and feel, what others think and feel, and what they think and feel in response to what others think and feel [10]. The complex dynamics of real-world environments and relationships can impact how people respond so, for people to fully participate in workshops, they need to be a safe environment where they can trust that they can share their thoughts and concerns without judgement.

Workshops need to be carefully facilitated to build trust between participants, between researchers/designers and participants, and in the desired design outcomes. In addition, reciprocal approaches are needed that build empathy and move beyond cognitive decision-making processes, to engage with affective responses, to recognize and attune to the thoughts, feelings and actions of others [11, 12]. In short, the workshop environment would ideally be a 'safe' social space that resists judgement [13]. However, this does not always occur, so activities are often designed as 'ice breakers' to encourage social interaction and build social connections. But not everyone is comfortable engaging in icebreaker activities and some participants need more time to build up trust and connect to others.

Recently, Systems Intelligence (SI) has introduced factors and tactics to deepen designers' understanding of the relational complexities and to support empathy in co-design [2]. It is characterised by the primacy of the whole, acknowledging interconnectivity, interdependence, systemic feedback, viewing system inside-out, action-orientation, and optimism [2]. It has eight key factors (systemic perception, attunement, positive attitude, spirited discovery, reflection, wise action, positive engagement, effective responsiveness) and 32 tactics. For example, designing for attunement and positive engagement pays attention to the quality of interaction between actors in co-design processes. The tactics offer guidance for approaching people with warmth and acceptance, taking into account others' thoughts about situation, contributing shared atmosphere, and bringing out the best in others. They underline that "empathy is built before and during interactions, is heavily impacted by nonverbal communications alongside verbal communication, and that the process is reciprocal in nature [2]". So, in co-design, we are engaged in designing ourselves, people, and the world around us in an ongoing process [14].

In this paper, we explore how social connections can be recognized and developed in workshops, that are a typical co-design practice, by focusing on dyads working together in small workshop environment to build high quality social connections through interaction. We asked participants to engage in three different activities with a partner allocated to them. We wanted to know whether some activities had more impact in building social connection, and to what extent and quality this social connection could be observed. To do this we began by reviewing how social connection is built based on behavioral synchrony as a base for a growing sense of connection and how positive emotions are associated to connection.

3 Social Connection

3.1 Behavioral Synchrony

The quality of social connection can be determined by interpersonal behavioural synchrony of nonverbal communication. Behavioral synchrony refers to the unconscious coordination of movement between individuals both timing and form during interpersonal interaction [15]. Behavioural timing such as rhythm, pausing, simultaneity, turn-taking conveys critical information about connection between partners independently of the content of conversation or modality [3]. This appears in gestures, postures, facial expression, gazing, touch, spatial orientation, vocal and emotions and is also known as entrainment, mimicry, mirroring and joint attention [4, 16]. It is also unconscious and emotional [4]. Behavioral synchrony is closely related to the early development of relationship between infant and caregiver, language acquisition, and rapport [e.g., 16–18]. People tend to coordinate their movements with others as demonstrated in various tasks such as in rocking in rocking chair, hand waving and drumming [5, 19–21, 51]. People also tend to react favorably to those with whom they move synchronously as well as those who mimic their actions [20, 22]. When people experience being "in synch" they also report a higher level of empathy and affect, sense greater co-operation, social cohesion, liking, similarity and trust [3, 5, 25, 27, 53].

Behavioral synchrony might play important role in the evolution of synchronized movements in humans and other species. For example, impairments in coordination of behavior may be linked to physical separation for pair-bonded animals [23]. Similarly, it has been argued that humans who experience social synchrony might be likely to experience significant social benefits, such as marriage or safety [24]. Furthermore, this would increase the probability for reproduction and decrease social predispositions [24].

Behavioral synchrony promotes co-operation [22, 25, 26]. It cultivates social cohesion such as the commitment to the group, greater feelings of liking, similarity and trust [22, 27]. Behavioral synchrony also builds sense of "oneness" or "we" through rich and common rhythms e.g. in the rituals in sport teams, religious singing and dancing activities, and military drilling [28]. It can also support behaviors that normally would be contrary to individuals' beliefs [29]. Relation between behavioral synchrony and co-operation has been confirmed in several studies carried out in both controlled and natural settings as well as with diverse cultural groups [30–32]. Synchrony detection seems be one of the earliest mechanisms for establishing intergroup boundaries and for creating intergroup bias in human-to-human communication [33]. Furthermore, it has been reported that people have enhanced memory and higher pain tolerance, indicated by endorphin activity, related to the behavior synchrony [20, 30, 34]. Taken together, these studies have shown tight connections between synchronous action and building of co-operation.

3.2 High-Quality Connection

"High-quality connections (HQCs) are short-term, dyadic interactions that are positive in terms of the subjective experience of the connected individuals and the structural features of the connection [35]". HQC have positive impacts to affective, cognitive, physiological and behavioral processes [35]. For example, interaction can improve cognitive processing speed and working memory performance of the dyad [36]. In work and organisational research, HQC contributes positively to psychological safety and trust which can further increase collaboration and trustworthiness [37]. HQC is composed of three attributes of experiences; 1) Feelings of vitality and aliveness describing positive arousal and a heightened sense of positive energy [38], 2) Felt mutuality captures the sense that both people experience full participation and engagement in the connection [39], and 3) Positive regard which is a feeling of being known, loved, or of being respected and cared for in the connection [35].

4 Positive Emotion

Emotions, also called affects, are multisystem responses to some change in the way people interpret their current circumstances [e.g., 40, 41]. They contain an individual's assessment of personal meaning of circumstances, occupy the foreground of consciousness, unfold over relatively short timespans, create action tendencies, and physiological changes [41, 42]. Positive emotions have different action tendencies than negative emotions. While positive emotions facilitate actions without momentary benefit (e.g., approach behavior and continued action) negative emotions narrows down the behavioral options calling for an urge to act to gain a momentary benefit (e.g. fear-escape; anger-attack) [41]. Positive emotions often occur without external physical sensations making the difference to the concept of sensory pleasure as automatic fulfillment of bodily needs (e.g., eating, stimulating body) [40, 41]. Ten typical positive emotions are joy, gratitude, serenity, interests, hope, pride, amusement, inspiration, awe and love [overview, 40, 41]. Each of these emotions has their own appraisal theme, way they broaden through-action tendency, and build resources. For example, joy includes appraisal of safe and familiar unexpectedly good, evokes though-action tendencies of play and get involves and accrue resources as skills gained via experiential learning [40].

The broaden-and-build theory describes functions of positive emotions to broaden people's momentary thought-action repertoires and their function in building enduring personal resources [43]. According to theory, positive emotions have two broadening functions. Firstly, positive emotions widen the array of thoughts, action urges, and percepts that spontaneously come to mind (relative to negative emotions and neutral states) [43]. People experiencing positive emotions show patterns of thought that are notably unusual, flexible and inclusive, creative, integrative, open to information, forward-looking and high-level and efficient [see overview, 40]. Positive emotions also extend visual, semantic, and social awareness, and physical posture [44–47]. Secondly, positive emotions undo lingering negative emotions as they clean or 'loosen the hold' of the after-effects of negative emotions and undo the preparations for specific response actions [43].

Positive emotions build human well-being in three ways. 1) They fuel psychological resiliency [43]. People who experience and express positive emotions more frequently than others are more resilient, resourceful, socially connected, and more likely to function at optimal levels [overview, 40]. People can improve their psychological and physical well-being by cultivating experiences of positive emotions at opportune moments to cope with negative emotions [40, 43]. 2) Positive emotions over time build psychological resources [43]. Momentary positive emotions accumulate over time and incrementally build people's enduring resources [40]. For example, daily experience of positive emotions predicts increases over time in trait resilience which is associated with improved life satisfaction [40]. Within intimate relationship positive emotional exchanges between partners predict increases in relational resources [48]. 3) Positive emotions trigger upward spirals toward improved emotional well-being [43]. Experiences of positive emotions forecast in multiple ways personal resources and these personal resources reciprocally forecast increases over time in positive emotions [40]. This mutual influence represents upward spiral that leads to higher levels of well-being and functioning over time. The spiral dynamics between positive emotions and personal, social and physiological resources in several recent longitudinal studies [40, 49, 50].

Love, as a positive emotion, is an interpersonally situated experience and a micro-moment positivity resonance [40, 51]. This resonance is not limited to interaction between two people, but it can include more people, groups, networks and crowds and therefore represents early phase of building social relationship [51]. As Fredrickson [40] describes: "Within moments of interpersonal connection resource building resonates between and among people and this back-and-worth reverberation of positive emotional energy sustains itself and can even grow stronger until the momentary connection inevitably wanes ". The positivity resonance marked by momentary increase in shared positive emotions, biobehavioral synchrony, and mutual care [40]. Biobehavioral synchrony refers to the mirroring across people's behaviors, bodies, and brains that each moment of shared positive emotional connection creates (e.g. nonverbal behavioral synchrony, oxytocin between caregiver and child, brain coupling between speaker and listener) [40]. For example, research have shown that behavioral synchrony influences on self-disclosure on the development of embodied rapport [52]. Mutual care as continuous investment to other person represents the motivated action of action-tendency of love as positive emotion [51]. The momentary experience of love brings an urge to focus on the other person, holistically, with care and concern for his or her well-being, a motive that momentarily eclipses any tendency toward self-absorption [51]. Perception of safety and true sensorial as co-presence of bodies and temporal connection are the requirements for positivity resonance [51].

In sum, we suggest that facilitating social connection is an essential skill that can support versatile co-design practices such as workshops. When approaching these practices from a systemic perspective, we should pay attention to the qualities of interaction such as attunement, positive engagement, reciprocity, and empathy alongside the functional goals of the design practices. The quality of social connection can be determined by observing interpersonal behavioral synchrony; the timing and form of nonverbal communication. When people experience being "in synch" they report a higher level of empathy, affect, sense greater co-operation, social cohesion, liking, similarity and trust. This can also foster a building of high-quality connection between actors which contributes positively to psychological safety, trust, increased collaboration and trustworthiness. This interpersonally situated experience can also enable micro-moments of positivity resonance between actors increasing shared positive emotions. These short-term positive emotions have capability to broaden people's momentary thought-action repertoires and build enduring personal resources. These broadened repertoires are visible as a widened array of thoughts, action urges, percepts that spontaneously come to mind. They manifest as increased flexibility, creativity, forward-lookingness and higher quality thinking. Taken together, design for social connection is about creating circumstances where behavioral synchrony, high-quality connection and positive emotions can occur, impacting the quality of outcome in the co-design practice. Therefore, a goal of this study was to explore how different design activities of 'making' and 'doing' together can impact the building of social connection and foster better participatory design outcomes.

5   Research Method

5.1   Participants

Eight participants took part in the study (1 male, 7 female; Mean age: 25.1). We organized two workshops each with two dyads. All participants were from a design background. The participants knew their partner in passing but they had not collaborated or worked together in anyway beforehand. Each participant was given 10€ for taking part.

5.2   Procedure

Participants completed demographic questionnaires and consent forms. Each pair was asked to engage in three design tasks (20 min) (See Table 1). During this task they could engage directly with each other in the moment but were not allowed to make notes or record their thoughts in anyway. This was followed by a short period where they captured their ideas in written form (5 min). Each of the design activities involved active problem solving with an emphasis on visual, motor-skills and verbal engagement and design. Each task encouraged embodied expression between participants and directly drew on Fredrickson's theories of micro moments and resonance in the design of the set-tasks [51]. The order of the tasks during the first workshop was from one to three and reversed for the second workshop.

5.3   Questionnaires and Observation

Data-collection focused on behavioral synchrony, high-quality connection and emotion during the design tasks. After each task the participants filled the self-reporting questionnaires. The questionnaires included:

- Inclusion-of-other in self as a 7-point single-item scale that visually depicts increasingly overlapping "self" and "partner" circles [54].

Table 1. Overview of tasks, focus, rational, and intended engagement

Task	Focus	Rationale	Task	Intended engagement
Task 1 Character	Design a cartoon character for a children's television show	Visual focus, light-hearted to promote a sense of fun	Develop an animated character for a children's show. Describe the character, where it lives, give it a name, and show how children from 3–6 might engage or respond to it	Create micro-moments of play, through eye contact, physical contact and to promote laughter
Task 2 Bricks	Build a Lego artefact (from instructions – without seeing the finished image first	Motor-skills, task-oriented and involves physical making	Build a pre-designed object using Lego® bricks according to the given instructions and then develop the object further through sketching	Create a "parallel" activity, that is a shared activity, but where little focus was placed on the other
Task 3 Project	Design a social project in an area that has special significance for you	Verbal engagement to promote meaningful discussion and allow for self-disclosure	Focus on an area of disadvantage or perceived disability and develop a product or service to make a positive contribution to this sector	Create micro moments of sincerity and meaningful engagement, focusing on issues important to one or both participants

- High-quality connections assessments which are based on short-term, interactions in which both people experience vitality, positive regard and mutuality [39]. Three theoretically-derived subscales are combined ($\alpha = .92$) and scores are standardized from each subscale and aggregated for each pair.
- Modified Differential Emotions Scale (mDES) to examine participants' emotional response. They rated 20 categories of emotions, on a 5-point scale, to indicate the intensity they felt during the interaction [55].
- Emotion-action urges were measured using a thought-listing task [44]. Participants were asked not to focus on the specifics of the workshop but, to more generally record the strongest emotion they had experienced during the interaction. They were then required to focus on a situation where this particular emotion may arise and respond to this feeling by listing all the things they would like to do 'right now'. They were given a form with 60 blank lines that began with "I would like to _____." Participants

were instructed to write as many things as possible within a minute. This an index of each individual breadth of thought-action repertoire.

The workshop sessions were audio and video recorded using two cameras set at opposite ends of the room and each at 45 degrees to the participants ensuring all angles of any engagement were captured. At the end of the session, participants were asked to complete six open-ended questions about the relationship and their feelings towards their partner; the tasks; the workshop; and their feelings about their and their partner's role in completing tasks. During the workshop, two researchers individually took notes focusing on emotions, non-verbal communication, and level of connection perceived during the design tasks.

5.4 Methods of Analysis

Questionnaire data was analyzed using Friedman's test and Wilcoxon matched-pair signed-ranks test as the presumption of parametric methods (normality) was not met (Kolmogorov-Smirnow $p < .05$) and a small sample size was used [56]. Friedman's test measures differences between several data sets and Wilcoxon's between two related and ordinal datasets [56].

Video recordings were analysed by two trained coders independently. The videos were watched on VLC player with the audio muted and coded into a pre-formatted excel coding sheet. The video observation analysed every second minute resulting in a total of 15 values being coded for each pair per task. Analysis of one minute 'slices' over the length of a video has been shown to be representative [57]. Increasing the duration of each slice or the number of slices has been shown to have minimal impact on the predictive validity in interaction research [57]. For each minute of video three aspects of behavioral synchrony were coded using a 9-point semantic differential scale [58]. These were simultaneous movement (nonconcurrent-simultaneous), tempo similarity (dissimilar-similar), and coordination and smoothness (uneasy-smooth) [58]. By carrying out the analysis using the video muted behavioral synchrony could be observed as a purely physical phenomenon [59]. The inter-rater reliability between the two researchers was high (Cohen's Kappa $\alpha = .88$). The two coders' behavioral synchrony rating was averaged to obtain a final behavioral synchrony score for each pair. The final value of synchrony combined three aspects of synchrony ($\alpha = .94$).

Observation notes and emotion-action urges followed the principles of Grounded Theory [60]. All research material was transcribed to text, meaningful sentences were extracted and open-coded for creating concepts. All concepts were organized into subcategories and the further organized under main categories. Several mentions of the same concept by the same participant were recorded only once. All phases were carried out independently by two researchers, combined and agreed by two researchers.

6 Results

The results showed that tasks impacted on social connection in terms of behavioral synchrony, high-quality connection, and positive emotions. There were significant differences between the tasks.

6.1 Behavioral Synchrony (Dyads)

Video Analysis. Based on video analysis, all tasks had significant influence on the synchrony of the pairs ($F_R = 18.5$, df = 2, p < .001; Fig. 1). The greatest synchrony was observed in Task 2 (Brick) followed by Task 1 (Character), movements of the pair were performed simultaneously, their tempo was similar and their coordination was smooth. In Task 3 (Project) synchrony was less noticeable (p < .05).

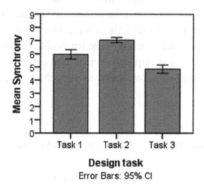

Fig. 1. Influence of design tasks on behavioral synchrony

Qualitative Analysis. Based on observation and notes the design tasks varied in their non-verbal behavior, emotion and nature of collaboration (Table 2). Task 1 (Character) - Both verbal and visual communication channels were used. The participants were seated face-to-face, physically in a close position and maintained active eye-contact. They expressed large movements in their upper-body and hands to share and clarify ideas and express the nature of the character they were designing together. Mirroring of each other's gestures was visible during the character design process. Co-operative connection between participants was created actively by nodding, smiling, eye-to-eye contact, movements of upper-body and laughing. Most of these actions were reciprocated as pairs frequently copied each other's actions. Frequency and intensity of the gestures increased towards the end of the task. For example, in celebration of their achievements, at the end of the tasks some of the pairs shook hands. The emotional atmosphere was excited through this design task.

Task 2 (Bricks) – The verbal communication channel was highlighted as participants maintained little eye-contact. Participants were seated very close together, and side-by-side rather than face-to-face. They expressed only small movements of their upper-body and hands. Such movements were largely guided by the task. Pairs leaned into each other and signs of similar body movements could be observed as pairs dipped forward or sat back at the same time. Progress and achievements were celebrated with applause or 'high-fives' when for example the bricks were found. The participants shared, and changed, responsibilities during the task. For example, one searched the blocks and checked the instructions while the other took responsibility for assembling the bricks. Participants were comfortable in touching each other's hand when, for example, the 'searcher' gave the building blocks to the 'builder'. Participants expressed most excitement while completing this task, with excitement aroused quickly at the beginning of the task and staying until the end. The participants also recovered very fast from any errors to continue building.

Task 3 (Project) and Task 1 (Character), both used verbal and visual communication channels. Participants were seated face-to-face and closeby. They used mainly small torso and hand movements when explaining ideas. Some larger movements were also used, but they were rather controlled movements in Task 3 compared to the open spontaneous movements in Task 1 (Character). Task 1 elicited lots of nodding, turn taking and observed cooperative behaviors. Connections were in evidence in the synchronisation of behaviors as for example both touching face for prolonged period and then stopping at the same time (P5, P6). The participants overall took a more serious approach to Task 3 manifesting as calm discussion, low speed of speech, and low levels of energy and excitement.

Table 2. Characteristics of difference design tasks based on observation

Characteristics	Task1 (Character)	Task 2 (Lego)	Task 3 (Project)
Non-verbal behavior			
Communication channels	Verbal and visual	Verbal mainly	Verbal and visual
Eye-contact	Strong most of the time	Very little	Strong most of the time
Upper-body	Large movements	Small movements	Small, few large movements
Hands	Large movements	Small movements, touches each other's hands during giving objects	Small, few large movements, lack of spontaneous movements
Use of gestures	To share and clarify ideas and character using upper-body and hands, shake hands after task finished Copy other's gestures	To celebrate progress 'high-fives' using hands, applauding Copy of other' gestures	To explain ideas using hand or upper body Coping and synchronizing gestures
	Frequency, intensity of gestures increased towards to the end		
Posture	Face-to-face, Physically close, upper-body straightened up	Side-to-side, lean forward Physically very close	Close, slightly turned to each other, lean backward or straightened up
Connection	Nodding, smiling, laughing, eye-contact	Smiling, laughing	Nodding, eye-contact

(*continued*)

Table 2. (*continued*)

Characteristics	Task 1 (Character)	Task 2 (Lego)	Task 3 (Project)
Emotions	High-level of excitement	The highest level of excitement; Quick and fast start of task	Calm discussion, serious, less excitement, less gestures
Collaboration	Active, no shared responsibilities	Active, shared responsibilities: one searched for blocks, check building, other build	Active, no shared responsibilities
		Changing responsibilities during task	

6.2 High Quality Connections

Each task had a different impact on the development of high-quality connections ($F_R = 8.65$, df = 2, p < .05). High quality connections are investigated by assessing 'Feelings of Vitality and Aliveness', 'Felt Mutuality', and 'Positive Regard'. Feelings of vitality and aliveness reflect a heightened sense of positive arousal and positive energy [38]. The levels of vitality and aliveness were reportedly higher after Tasks 1 (Character) and Task 2 (Bricks) ($F_R = 35.6$, df = 2, p < .001; pairwise comparisons p < .001; Fig. 2). Felt mutuality captures the sense that both people in a connection were engaged and actively participating [39]. This was higher overall after Task 2 (Bricks) ($F_R = 9.83$, df = 2, p < .001; pairwise comparisons p < .05; Fig. 3). Positive regard refers to the feeling of being known and loved or respected and cared for [35]. A heightened sense of positive regard was reportedly experienced particularly in relation to Task 2 (Bricks) ($F_R = 7.2$, df = 2, p < .05; difference to Task 2 p < .05; Fig. 3).

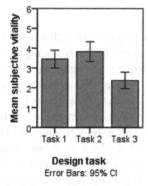

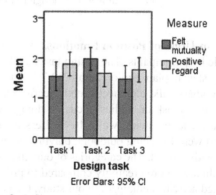

Fig. 2. Influence of design tasks on subjective vitality

Fig. 3. Influence of design tasks on felt mutuality and positive regard in high quality connections.

Inclusion-of-Other in Self (Dyads). In all tasks, the participants experienced only moderate levels of overlap between self and other (Fig. 4) and there did not seem any significant influence on the inclusion of other in self ($F_R = 3.5$, df = 2, p = 1.74, ns). Although Task 2 (Bricks) shows a slightly higher tendency for self-other inclusivity.

6.3 Positive Emotions

All design tasks provided at least moderate level of positive emotions (Fig. 5). Both Task 1 (Character) and Task 2 (Bricks) evoked both positive emotions and synchrony of movement. The analysis of mDes shows they had significant influence on positive emotions ($F_R = 20.2$, df = 2, p < .001; Fig. 5). There was no significant impact on negative emotions ($F_R = 0.6$, df = 2, p = .76, ns) for these tasks. Task 1 (Character) and Task 2 (Bricks) evoked more positive emotions than Task 3 (Project) (pairwise comparisons p < .05). Task 1 (Character) evoked "quite a bit" or "extremely" responses in relation to emotions of joy, interest, inspiration, amusement and proudness and produced only moderately negative feelings of stress (Fig. 6). Task 2 (Bricks) was experienced as joyful, interesting, inspiring and amusing. Task 3 (Project) reached "moderate" to "quite a bit" levels of positive emotions, and was labelled as being interesting, curious, promoting serenity, proud, inspiration and joyfulness.

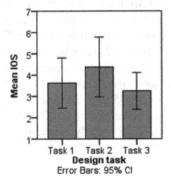

Fig. 4. Influence of design tasks on inclusion-of-other in self

Action-Urges of Position Emotions. A total of 111 descriptions of action urges were made by participants. The design tasks evoked mostly interests towards being creative (e.g., sketch, plan, explore, draft; 38.7% of mentions), social (e.g. engage in interaction with others, talk, e.g. meet friends, learn to know other people; 18%), engage in doing (e.g. finish task or studies, focus on doing, prioritize; 14%) or doing sports (e.g. run, release energy, swim, walk; 10%). Less mentioned activities (below 6% of all mentions) were for being outdoors, playing, eating or drinking, resting, reading and being in positive mood. The categories of our study were mainly similar to [44], but our study highlighted more creativity compared to previous studies where more school or work-related activities emerged. In our study, the task types did not have any influence on the number of mentions about action urges ($F_R = 3.23$, df = 2, p = .20, ns).

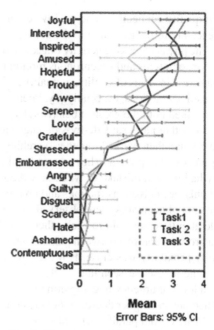

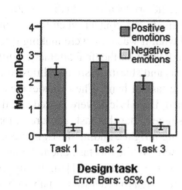

Fig. 5. Influence of design tasks on positive and negative emotions

Fig. 6. Emotions evoked by different tasks

7 Discussion

Design methodologies, methods, approaches, processes and ways of thinking are increasingly used by cross-disciplinary and interdisciplinary teams to bring about understanding and transformation of complex dynamic social challenges. Participatory approaches aim to facilitate the exchange of ideas, thoughts, feeling, reservations, wants, needs and desires of individual participants, representing themselves and/or other stakeholders without judgement, to build connections, foster understanding and cultivate empathy, to tackle the challenges at hand. The challenge for designers as facilitators using workshop as a methodology is to evaluate the success or otherwise of an engagement. Interest in workshop evaluation is growing with the development frameworks to evaluate artefacts produced, and levels of interaction [61]. Contributing to understandings of what can happen in workshop engagements we have focused on exploring the types of activities that encourage social connection between workshop participants.

We wanted to find out to what extent the growth of social connection could be identified and explore whether high quality connections could be established and observed in dyads engaged in shared set-tasks. The tasks engaged the participants in 'doing' and 'making' activities. Two tasks required participants to engage in a creative design activity without any physical material support (i.e., no drawing, writing, or audio recording etc.), and a third task involved hand-use in a physical making activity where participants worked in parallel. The results showed that all activities evoked behavioral synchrony, high-quality connections and positive emotions but there were differences between the levels and profile according to the activities undertaken.

The physical making activity (Task 2, Bricks) was the most powerful in eliciting connection, emotions and synchronous motion in dyads. It evoked high levels of immediate connection in terms of vitality, mutuality and positive regards. It aroused moderate levels of positive emotions, especially joy, interests, inspiration, amusement and proudness. It also evoked both the greatest behavioral synchrony and differences in behaviors. It was observed that pairs sat side-by-side engaged in the task, not engaging with each other one minute, then worked together searching out specific bricks and mutually constructing parts of the project. They shared laughter and made eye contact when they found they had made a mistake or when they recognized what it was they were making (they had only been given instructions and no image of indication of the final artefact). While elements of teamwork were observed, in taking turns and sharing responsibilities, very little attention was paid to each other outside of the task at hand. There was evidence of a growing comfort between pairs as hands touched, Lego bricks were passed and the bodily proximity was close. However, we might suggest that this task appeared more outcome focused as seen in the celebration of 'getting it right', finding the right pieces, and a level of urgency in completing the Lego structure. While this task elicited a more immediate and higher degree of quality connection than Fredrickson [51] might suggest would arise from parallel activities, there is further research to be carried out about how these responses develop over longer time periods or repetition of this type of task.

Creative design activity (Task 1, Character) was the second most effective in eliciting connection, emotions and synchronous behavior. This activity was designed to be playful and fun, light-hearted and to engage imagination and allow for free-thinking. It evoked high-quality connection through subjective vitality and positive regards in dyads. The task also elicited moderate levels of positive emotions, especially joy, curiosity, interests and amusement. Behavioral synchrony was observable as simultaneous, being in same tempo and smooth. There were higher levels of performance during this task as demonstrated by large hand and body movements. A degree of playfulness could be observed in exchanges with a high degree of copying, frequency and intensity of gestures. Throughout the tasks participants engaged in frequent eye to eye contact, gesturing directly to each other, and face-pulling. Participants demonstrated a high level of satisfaction in completing the task and seemingly in how the relationship developed. These findings support ongoing research with regard to the importance of playfulness, and fun in developing and sustaining relationships and growth [40, 62].

The design activity (Task 3, Project) provided significantly lower levels of connection, emotions and synchronous behaviors than other activities. The task was selected to promote meaningful engagement by encouraging participants to engage in designing for a cause that was of special interest or concern to one or both partners, or to think about how they may use a design approach to contribute. Although it initiated relatively high-level connection it initiated less subjective vitality and aliveness than other activities. It evoked positive emotions, such as interests, curious, serenity, proud, inspiration, joyfulness. Compared to other activities, the dyads acted in less synchronous manner. Participants were noticeably earnest in their discussion of ideas and their engagement with each other. Non-verbal communication was observed as offering encouragement as ideas developed through nodding, smiling (rather than laughter as had been frequent in Task 1) and smaller hand and body movements. An underlying seriousness could be observed throughout the task and the duration of turn taking seemingly increased length of time listening/watching the other before talking/gesturing in response.

The findings indicate that by exploring behavioral synchrony, positive emotions and high quality connections in relation to making and doing activities we can gain insights into the types of activities that are likely to promote and support the creation of meaningful connection and build relationships. While this was a limited study the findings suggest that participants experienced positive resonance in their communication with one another. In addition, the findings suggest that the type of activity undertaken had an influence on emotions, behavioral synchrony and the depth of the collaborative experience.

The implications for design practice and research is that by understanding the nature of behavioral synchronism, design tasks can be created to specifically promote social co-operation, positive emotions and impact on well-being. For example, Task 2 (Bricks) type activities, that require parallel rather than face to face engagement and focus on motor-skills rather than personal disclosure, may be an ideal first approach in workshops to bring people together in ways that are safe and not challenging and introduce excitement and a sense of achievement. Task 1 (Character), while fun needed participants to 'warm' to each other. In our study each of the pairs enjoyed the task and had fun, but careful consideration needs to be given in introducing the task. The pairs in Task 3 (Project) were more subdued and some were hesitant to fully engage and talk about their interests. It offered a meaningful engagement that though slower to develop revealed possibilities for longer term engagement in this way. Being attuned to behavioral synchrony is key for workshop facilitators/designers using participatory approaches providing early insights into the success of the workshop engagement.

This research contributes new understanding on recently introduced Systems Intelligent (SI) approach to empathic design and tangible tools for designers [2]. As a key aspect, we looked at the relational dynamics, or systems of interaction, rather than focusing on individual contributions. Design for attunement of SI pays attention for example to engaging intersubjectivity, being present, and situationally sensitive. As a tactic for a designer, it proposes approaching people with warmth and acceptance being at the heart of affective empathy and focusing on interactive process as nonverbal intersubjectivity and dyads. Our design and structure of activities presents a novel way to facilitate this non-verbal intersubjectivity. It enables experience of being in synch and further empowers high-quality connections and experiences of positive emotions. These together have capability to build psychological safety, trust, increased collaboration and trustworthiness [37]—which is at the heart of human-to-human collaboration, and impact the quality of outcome in the co-design practice. Within SI, when designing for positive engagement, attention is paid to contribution of shared atmosphere in group situation. Here, designer/facilitator is in responsible for fostering connection through different facilitation methods and techniques to create a sense of togetherness, respect, trust, and confidentiality from the beginning [63]. Our design and structure of activities gives a new approach to this facilitation.

7.1 Limitations and Further Work

Further work is needed to go beyond limitations of this study. The main limitations were the use of only three different design activities, a relatively small sample size and focus on the dyads. Future work is needed to explore different types of connection promoting design activities to build broader understanding on their efficiency in use for designers. Further work also needs to address different sizes of heterogeneous groups when designing for social connection to be able to respond to the modern needs of co-design and co-creation with different stakeholders with very different experiences, world view-points and interests. From the systemic perspective, further work is needed to explore the relation of good design for social connection to the success of whole design project.

7.2 Conclusions

The goal of this study was to explore how different design activities influence the building of social connection. The results showed that all activities impacted social connection. They evoked synchrony, high-quality connection, and positive emotions, but the extent and type of connection differed between activities. This paper proposes that non-verbal communication needs to be a key focus in designing activities for social connection and suggests a framework for designing and evaluating it. Further work is needed to explore the range of connection promoting activities and the applicability to participatory design process and practices.

Acknowledgements. We thank Jenny and Antti Wihuri Foundation, ESR funded project "Change driver" and our participants.

References

1. Mattelmäki, T., Vaajakallio, K., Koskinen, I.: What happened to empathic design? Design Issues **30**(1), 67–77 (2014)
2. Jumisko-Pyykkö, S., Viita-aho, T., Tiilikainen, E., Saarinen, E.: Towards systems intelligent approach in empathic design. Proc. Acad. Mindtrek **2021**, 197–209 (2021). https://doi.org/10.1145/3464327.3464370
3. Beebe, B., Lachmann, F.M.: Infant Research and Adult Treatment: Coconstructing Interactions. Analytic Press (2002)
4. Beebe, B., Knoblauch, S., Rustin, J., Sorter, D.: Introduction a systems view. Symposium on intersubjectivity in infant research and its implications for adult treatment. Psychoanal. Dial. **13**(6), 743–841 (2003)
5. Valdesolo, P., Ouyang, J., DeSteno, D.: The rhythm of joint action: synchrony promotes cooperative ability. J. Exp. Soc. Psychol. **46**, 693–695 (2010)
6. Sanders, E.B.N., Stappers, P.J.: Co-creation and the new landscapes of design. CoDesign **4**(1), 5–18 (2008). https://doi.org/10.1080/15710880701875068
7. Papanek, V.J.: Design for the Real World (Third edition. Paperback edition). Thames and Hudson, London (2019)
8. Krippendorff, K.: The Semantic Turn: A New Foundation for Design. CRC/Taylor & Francis, Boca Raton (2006)

9. Brankaert, R., Ouden, E.D.: The design-driven living lab: a new approach to exploring solutions to complex societal challenges. Technol. Innov. Manag. Rev. (2017). https://timreview.ca/article/1049

10. Dervin, B., Foreman-Wernet, L.: Sense-making methodology as an approach to understanding and designing for campaign audiences: a turn to communicating communicatively. In: Rice, R.E., Atkin, C.K. (eds.) Public Communication Campaigns. Sage, London (2013)

11. Kenning, G.: Reciprocal design. In: Brankaert, R., Kenning, G. (eds.) HCI and Design in the Context of Dementia. HIS, pp. 17–32. Springer, Cham (2020). https://doi.org/10.1007/978-3-030-32835-1_2

12. Smeenk, W., Sturm, J., Eggen, B.: A comparison of existing frameworks leading to an empathic formation compass for co-design. Int. J. Design **13**(3), 53–68 (2019)

13. Lewin, K.: Experiments in social space (1939). Reflections (Cambridge, Mass.) **1**(1), 7–13 (1999). https://doi.org/10.1162/152417399570241

14. Akama, Y., Prendiville, A.: Embodying, enacting and entangling, a phenomenological view to co-designing services. Swedish Design Res. J. **13**(1), 29–40 (2013)

15. Kimura, M., Daibo, I.: Interactional synchrony in conversations about emotional episodes: a measurement by "the between-participants pseudosynchrony experimental paradigm." J. Nonverb. Behav. **30**, 115–126 (2006)

16. Tickle-Degnen, L., Rosenthal, R.: Group rapport and nonverbal behavior. Rev. Personal. Soc. Psychol. **9**, 113–136 (1987)

17. Condon, W.S., Sander, L.W.: Synchrony demonstrated between movements of the neonate and adult speech. Child Dev. **45**, 456–462 (1974)

18. Wylie, L.: Language learning and communication. Fr. Rev. **53**, 777–785 (1985)

19. Richardson et al. 2007; Kirschner, S., Tomasello, M.: Joint drumming: social context facilitates synchronization in pre-school children. J. Exp. Child Psychol. **102**, 299–314 (2009)

20. Macrae, C.N., Duffy, O.K., Miles, L.K., Lawrence, J.: A case of hand waving: action synchrony and person perception. Cognition **109**, 152–156 (1985)

21. Kirschner, S., Tomasello, M.: Joint drumming: social context facilitates synchronization in pre-school children. J. Exp. Child Psychol. **102**, 299–314 (2009)

22. Wiltermuth, S.S., Heath, C.: Synchrony and cooperation. Psychol. Sci. **20**, 1–5 (2009)

23. Dunbar, R.I.M., Shultz, S.: Bondedness and sociality. Behaviour **7**, 775–803 (2010)

24. Haidt, J., Seder, J.P., Kesebir, S.: Hive psychology, happiness, and public policy. J. Legal Stud. **37**, 133-S156 (2008)

25. Miles, L.K., Nind, L.K., Macrae, C.N.: The rhythm of rapport: interpersonal synchrony and socialperception. J. Exp. Soc. Psychol. **45**, 585–589 (2009)

26. Valdesolo, P., Ouyang, J., DeSteno, D.: The rhythm of joint action: synchrony promotes cooperative ability. J. Exp. Soc. Psychol. **46**, 693–695 (2010)

27. Lakens, D.: Movement synchrony and perceived entitativity. J. Exp. Soc. Psychol. **46**(5), 701–770 (2010)

28. McNeill, W.H.: Keeping Together in Time: Dance and Drill in Human History. Harvard University Press, Cambridge (1995)

29. Bock, E.R.: Common Ground: A Look at Entrainment in Romantic Relationships, Ph.D. thesis (2012)

30. Cohen, E., Mundry, R., Kirschner, S.: Religion, synchrony, and cooperation. Religion Brain Behav. **4**, 1–11 (2013)

31. Cohen, E.E.A., Ejsmond-Frey, R., Knight, N., Dunbar, R.I.M.: Rowers' high: behavioural synchrony is correlated with elevated pain thresholds. Biol. Lett. **6**, 106–108 (2010)

32. Fischer, R., Callander, R., Reddish, P., Bulbulia, J.: How do rituals affect cooperation? Hum. Nat. **24**, 115–125 (2013)

33. Baimel, A., Severson, R.L., Baron, A.S., Birch, S.A.J.: Enhancing 'theory of mind' through synchrony. Front. Psychol. **6**, 870 (2015)

34. Sullivan, P., Rickers, K.: The effect of behavioral synchrony in groups of teammates and strangers. Int. J. Sport Exerc. Psychol. **3**, 286–291 (2013)
35. Stephens, J.P., Heapy, E., Dutton, J.: High quality connections. In: Spreitzer, G.M., Cameron, K.S. (eds.) The Oxford Handbook of Positive Organizational Scholarship (2012)
36. Ybarra, O., et al.: Mental exercising through simple socializing: social inter-action promotes general cognitive functioning. Pers. Soc. Psychol. Bull. **34**(2), 248–259 (2008)
37. Ferrin, D.L., Bligh, M.C., Kohles, J.C.: It takes two to tango: an inter-dependence analysis of the spiraling of perceived trustworthiness and cooperation in interpersonal and intergroup relations. Organ. Behav. Hum. Decis. Process. **107**, 161–178 (2008)
38. Quinn, R., Dutton, J.: Coordination as energy in conversation: a process theory of organizing. Acad. Manag. Rev. **30**(1), 38–57 (2005)
39. Dutton, J.E., Heaphy, E.D.: The power of high-quality connections. In: Cameron, K., Dutton, J. (eds.) Positive Organizational Scholarship: Foundations of a New Discipline, pp. 262–278, Berrett-Koehler Publishers (2003)
40. Fredrickson, B.L.: Positive emotions broaden and build. Adv. Exp. Soc. Psychol. **47**, 1–53 (2013)
41. Fredrickson, B.L.: The broaden-and-build theory of positive emotions. Phil. Trans. R. Soc. Lind. **359**, 1376–1377 (2004)
42. Oatley, K., Jenkins, J.M.: Understanding Emotions. Blackwell Publishing, Oxford (2003)
43. Fredrickson, B.L.: The role of positive emotions in positive psychology: the broaden-and-build theory of positive emotions. Am. Psychol. **56**, 218–226 (2001)
44. Fredrickson, B.L., Branigan, C.: Positive emotions broaden the scope of attention and thought-action repertoires. Cognit. Emot. **19**(3), 313–332 (2005)
45. Gasper, K., Clore, G.L.: Attending to the big picture: mood and global versus local processing of visual information. Psychol. Sci. **13**(1), 34–40 (2002)
46. Dunn, J.R., Schweitzer, M.E.: Feeling and believing: the influence of emotion on trust. J. Pers. Soc. Psychol. **88**(5), 736–748 (2005)
47. Gross, M.M., Crane, E.A., Fredrickson, B.L.: Effort-shape and kinematic assessment of bodily expression of emotion during gait. Hum. Mov. Sci. **31**(1), 202–221 (2012)
48. Gable, S.L., Gonzaga, G.C., Strachman, A.: Will you be there for me when things go right? Supportive responses to positive event disclosures. J. Pers. Soc. Psychol. **91**(5), 904–917 (2006)
49. Salanova, M., Bakker, A.B., Llorens, S.: Flow at work: evidence for an upward spiral of personal and organizational resources. J. Happiness Stud. **7**(1), 1–22 (2006)
50. Kok, B.E., Fredrickson, B.L.: Upward spirals of the heart: autonomic flexibility, as indexed by vagal tone, reciprocally and prospectively predicts positive emotions and social connectedness. Biol. Psychol. **85**(3), 432–436 (2010)
51. Fredrickson, B.L.: Love 2.0. Hudson Street Press, New York (2013)
52. Vacharkulksemsek, T., Fredrickson, B.L.: Strangers in sync: achieving embodied rapport through shared movements. J. Exp. Soc. Psychol. **48**, 399–402 (2012)
53. Wiltermuth, S.S., Heath, C.: Synchrony and cooperation. Psychol. Sci. **20**, 1–5 (2009)
54. Aron, A., Aron, E.N., Smollan, D.: Inclusion of other in the self scale and the structure of interpersonal closeness. J. Pers. Soc. Psychol. **63**, 596–612 (1992)
55. Fredrickson, B.L., Tugade, M.M., Waugh, C.E., Larkin, G.R.: What good are positive emotions in crisis? A prospective study of resilience and emotions following the terrorist attacks on the United States on September 11th, 2001. J. Pers. Soc. Psychol. **4**, 365–376 (2003)
56. Coolican, H.: Research Methods and Statistics in Psychology, 4th edn. J. W. Arrowsmith, London (2004)
57. Bernieri, J.F.: The expression of Rapport. In: Manusov, V.L. (ed.) The Sourcebook of Nonverbal Measures: Going Beyond Words, vol. 552. Psychology Press (2004)

58. Bernieri, F.J., Reznick, J.S., Rosenthal, R.: Synchrony, pseudosynchrony, and dissynchrony: measuring the entrainment process in mother-infant interactions. J. Pers. Soc. Psychol. **54**, 243–253 (1998)
59. Vacharkulksemsuk, T., Fredrickson, B.L.: Strangers in sync: achieving embodied rapport through shared movements. J. Exp. Soc. Psychol. **48**(1), 399–402 (2012)
60. Strauss, A., Corbin, J.: Basics of Qualitative Research: Techniques and Procedures for Developing Grounded Theory, 2nd edn. Sage, Thousand Oaks (1998)
61. Thoring, K., Mueller, R.M., Badke-Schaub, P.: Workshops as a research method: guidelines for designing and evaluating artifacts through workshops. Paper Presented at the International Conference on System Sciences, Hawaii (2020)
62. Rogerseon, R., Treadaway, C., Lorimer, H., Billington, J., Fyfe, H.: Permission to play: taking play seriously in adulthood. Paper Presented at the AHRC Connected Communities, Swindon (2013)
63. Soto, M.: Emotional skills for service designers in co-creation practices. Ph.D. thesis. Acta Electronica Universitatis Lapponiensis (2021)

Research on the Emotional Expression Design of Robots for Human-Robot Interaction

Zaixing Liu[1,2](✉)

[1] School of Art and Design, The Wuhan University of Technology, Wuhan, Hubei,
People's Republic of China
392641@qq.com
[2] Guangzhou Academy of Fine Arts, Guangzhou, Guangdong, People's Republic of China

Abstract. Due to the continuous development of intelligent technology, the form of active interaction appears in the working mode of smart products. With this change of human-computer interaction mode, the concept of human-computer interaction is gradually migrating to human-computer collaboration. One of the idiosyncrasies of the human-computer synergy process is the active nature of the intelligent system in the interaction process, and therefore the design of the emotional expression of the intelligent terminal becomes a key factor affecting the user experience. In this regard, this paper focuses on the use and experiential effects of active interactive feedback in outdoor, indoor, and self-driving service scenarios, as well as the differences in user experience in terms of action attraction, action empathy, and trust conveyed by different behavior patterns, ability expressions and image forms for users in these scenarios. The analysis summarizes the key factors affecting user experience during the active interaction of intelligent devices and provides a reference for the design of interaction forms for intelligent service robots.

Keywords: Human-computer interaction · Human-machine collaboration ·
Artificial emotional expression · User experience

1 Introduction

Today's society is in the era of diversified smart scenarios, and the public's demand for smart technology. At the same time, they are also very concerned about the experience in the use of smart products. Service robots have broad application prospects in areas such as health care, nursing, home services, entertainment, education, biotechnology, and disaster relief [1]. In 2015, Nestle placed 1,000 Pepper robots in Japanese appliance stores to help customers find Nespresso coffee machines. In 2019, robots for making salads, pizzas, hamburgers, and even cocktails have emerged in Britain and America. In 2019, China launched a robot restaurant for Chinese food, which not only uses chef robots to make various complex Chinese dishes but also includes food delivery robots, welcoming robots, and so on.

With the popularization of Smart Products, the mode of human-computer interaction has changed. After 2017, researchers began to pay attention to the user experience

M. M. Soares et al. (Eds.): HCII 2022, LNCS 13322, pp. 92–103, 2022.
https://doi.org/10.1007/978-3-031-05900-1_6

of smart products, such as acceptance, cognitive architecture, perception, and other topics [2]. In the research field of active interaction, compared with the interaction form in the field of "explicit interaction", Wendy JU and Leifer, doctoral tutors of Cornell University, put forward the definition of "implicit interaction" theory from a deeper level, and explained how to create similar interaction behaviors with implicit interaction framework, which can further increase the user's affection for non-social bots [3]. For example, if the user is in a coffee shop, the waiter will refill the coffee for him because of the user's request, which is the feedback to the user's explicit request. However, if the waiter immediately fills the user's cup when he sees it empty, this interaction constitutes an implicit condition. The latter interaction behavior leads to a higher level of user goodwill, and the approach-ability of the information conveyed is key to this type of interaction design. Leila Takayama and others once said in the research that the affinity of interactive communication is particularly important when people accidentally use non-anthropomorphic devices such as automatic doors and vending machines. Here, the attention of user experience is very high. If this kind of system does not convey a sense of welcome to passers-by and attract them to engage in interactive tasks, then the subsequent design of the system cannot be further completed [4].

Due to the widespread use of artificial intelligence capabilities, users are more likely to face a thinking subject when interacting with these smart devices. The essence of this phenomenon is that the media of human-computer interaction has undergone a fundamental change: from the current hardware-based on-screen feedback to personified virtual roles. The interaction model has also changed from the "input-output" model in which the user initiates the product operation instruction to the "man-machine cooperation" mode in which the user interferes with the automatic operation of the product to a limited extent. In the process of this kind of collaborative interaction, the main difference is that the smart terminals can also be the ones that ask for interaction. The emotional expression of the smart terminal is one of the key points that cause the difference in user experience. In the daily communication between people, emotional expression is mainly accomplished by language, expression, and body movements. The process of human-computer cooperation mainly depends on the intention generated by nonverbal behavior to express emotions, different attitudes, and complete cooperative tasks. Therefore, this paper hopes to focus on discussing which modeling and behavioral factors will affect the user experience under the active interaction mode of smart products and the degree of influence.

2   Related Work

2.1   Active Interaction in Human-Computer Collaboration

From a psychological point of view, effective communication starts with a cue, then attraction, and finally an empathy-building that plays an effective role in guiding the subsequent communication, a process that goes on and on, with stage changes in the user's emotions being key to enhancing the user's communication experience. Therefore, non-verbal behavior in conveying specific information and expressing emotional intent is equally key in the human-computer interaction experience. The process by which a machine can trigger effective communication when it senses a person lies in:

catching the eye, making the user perceive that it is coming towards them, arousing their curiosity or speculation, and then showing further interaction intentions by conveying friendly gestures. By looking at human-computer interaction from the perspective of human-smart device synergy, the psychological corollary of human-computer interaction can be extended to human-computer interaction, where the emotions conveyed by interpersonal behavior often apply to the interaction between smart devices and people. For example, handshakes and high-fives are important in situations where cooperation is required, and many studies of interpersonal relationships have found that appropriate, interaction behavioral mimicry with others has a positive impact on interpersonal interactions [5]. As with interpersonal communication, physical contact enhances trust in the other person, and a non-humanoid device that moderately mimics human behavior is also more attractive than a humanoid device with only mechanical panning movements. As shown in Fig. 1, a better explanation of the changing focus of interaction design is due to the active interaction of smart terminals in the process of human-intelligent system collaboration.

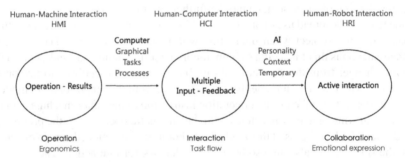

Fig. 1. The evolution of interaction design across different terminals

In the process of active interaction with smart terminals, emotional expression is the focus of interaction design. There are three important factors for further research on how to achieve a harmonious interaction experience between humans and smart terminals. They are **action attraction**, is defined as "Behavior that is noticed"; **action empathy**, is defined as "the ability to understand the other person's state appropriately through the other person's behavior"; **communicating of trust**, is defined as "expressing the clarity of the task and both parties."

2.2 Elements of Emotional Expression in Active Interaction

Elements that Influence Attractiveness. Professor Hoffman et al. suggest that robots that are carefully designed to resemble animated movements may be more engaging to human users and trigger more effective active communication [6]. Thus, incorporating expressive behavior into actions can help guide the interaction while making participants feel equal. Having robots perform expressive actions can greatly influence how users perceive interactions. Loffler et al. use rapid rotation and circular movements to allow the ground robot to express a happy welcome, slow rotation away from the user to express sadness, jumping movement away from the user to express fear, and rocking movement to express anger [7]. Guy Hoffman, Wendy Ju et al. found that scenario-based studies showing similarities in human actions to complete the same task in different scenarios can also be generalized to robot interaction behavior [8]. Yamaji et al. found that a machine bin could more effectively motivate the probability of a user to actively pick up litter by moving towards the litter rather than towards the user, i.e. the act of moving quickly towards the target was more likely to provoke user attention and perception [9]. Heather Knight et al. found that under conditions of low device speed, users were more willing to interrupt the robot's task and that the speed of the robot's movement could affect the efficiency of task completion as well as serve the purpose of engaging interaction [10].

Empathic Perception of Boundaries of Competence. Auriel Washburn, in his study, gave different subjects different descriptions of the boundaries of the robot's capabilities to give them different levels of expectation, and then asked the subjects and the robot to complete the same collaborative task, testing their feelings with a questionnaire during the process, and found that the robot was rated higher when the user expected that the robot would make a mistake [11]. Maartje de Graaf et al. show that users' expectations exceeding the robot's actual capabilities may lead to over-reliance and disappointment when the robot's actual capability boundaries are known. Elisa Prati et al. incorporate experience design tools such as user research, user journey mapping, and user interviews into the collaborative development of human-intelligent robots, examining the user's task completion, time spent, and feelings in a set number of tasks [12].

Communication of Trust. Trust is one of the most important conditions for people to deal with social interactions. Trust is the degree to which the subject trusts the object, so there is a great deal of subjectivity and probability. One can only give oneself sufficient security if one holds control of anything in one's hands or is familiar with the entire flow of events. The opposite is true of driverless news, which leaves all operational actions to the control of an artificial intelligence system. When people assess whether an automated system is trustworthy or not, they usually evaluate it based on how well it performs its tasks. People will distrust an automated system when they perceive that it performs tasks less well, is less reliable than a human operator, or has unclear feedback on task completion. Conversely, people will rely on an automated system if they perceive it to be very good and reliable.

2.3   Interpret-Ability of Emotional Expressions in Human-Computer Interaction and the Elements that Influence the Experience

The Advantages of Ultra-Realistic Human Figures. In human-computer interaction, the emotional communication of an interactive interface is undoubtedly determined first and foremost by its styling (or graphical interface) design. Mireia Ribera delineates interpretability at three levels: developer, expert user, and end-user, proposing that user-directed interpretable AIares to be interpreted in the context in which the user is placed, rather than creating a context that requires interpretation to explain the intelligent system

[13]. Avi Rosenfeld, on the other hand, analyses the degree of intelligibility and authenticity of interpretability [14]. Jacob Haspiel points out that explaining the machine before it reacts will dramatically increase human trust [15]. Hancock et al. point out that a person's dependence on an intelligent robot is the most critical factor influencing their trust in it. Auriel Washburn, in his research, points out that the trustworthiness correction of a bot should be in line with the actual boundaries of the bot's capabilities [16]. Sungwoo Choi et al. studied how customers responded and felt differently when faced with the same words from a human waiter, a humanoid robot, and a computerized help desk, with the human service receiving better ratings than the humanoid robot in all situation tests, but the computerized help desk also performed better than the human in some situations [17]. Jakub Złotowski et al. used the Wizard of Oz method to investigate the role of the appearance of hyper-animated and generic humanoid robots on human perception and showed that hyper-animated robots outperformed generic humanoid robots in terms of emotional communication and trustworthiness [18].

Establishing a Narrative Context. Another important factor that affects the communication of emotions in smart terminals is the ability of both parties to establish a shared perception of the narrative context at the beginning of establishing communication. During human-to-human communication, misunderstandings are often caused by deviations in the understanding of the narrative context. It can discuss extensively how narrative contexts can be effectively established during human-machine collaboration, and for this reason, the scope of this paper is limited to a few typical contexts in which humans communicate with driving assistants in autonomous driving scenarios. Florian Eyben et al. at the Institute for Human-Computer Interaction at the Technical University of Munich with a simulated virtual car to simulate the efficiency of a driving assistant in assisting a virtual driver in a simulation while completing multiple tasks. Kenton J. Williams, Joshua C. Peters, and Cynthia L. Breazeal, MIT Media Lab, tested the AIDA Intelligent Driving Assistant against a mobile device in a simulated driving task. Paul Bucci, Lotus Zhang, Xi Laura Can, and Karon E. MacLean, Columbia University, UK, investigated a theory of robot mind in which interactors build multiple interactions with the robot in a narrative context generating emotional understanding and a theory of mind that emotional interactions need to be based on the meaning and purpose of the behavior. Tests have found that physical driving assistants have the potential to better assist drivers in driving tasks than a smart smartphone that driving assistants as socially attuned robots in the in-car space can improve social skills and influence the driver's expression as a static. The design concepts and operational experiences of existing physical driving assistants are analyzed, based on the concepts of technological visitation and emotional design. It is argued that future human-machine interaction will be integrated into multilevel and multidimensional interactions, and that future research on the design of emotional interaction experiences in cars should focus on simplifying tasks and conveying trust and emotion.

Perception of Competence Boundaries. As mentioned earlier, in the design of human-computer interaction between humans and intelligent terminals, the expression of the boundaries of the intelligent terminal's capabilities is an important factor affecting the user experience. In their study, Gagan Bansal et al. categorize the error boundaries of robots into three dimensions and investigate how these three dimensions affect the human mental model, and show that different error boundaries for the same performance of intelligent systems have an impact on the efficiency of human-robot collaboration in completing tasks [19]. Auriel Washburn et al. showed that robot errors are inevitable in the process of human-robot collaboration, and they studied the changes in the impressions and experiences of experimenters and robots with different expectations when they performed the same task and the robot made the same error [20]. In testing the service and experience, Samantha Reig found that the appearance of the bot could cause subjects to misunderstand the boundaries of its capabilities, leading to easily reached capability boundaries and affecting the user experience [21].

3 Materials and Methods

3.1 Research Questions

For the above proposed key elements of emotion expression in the active interaction mode of smart terminals: action attraction, action empathy, and trust conveyance, this paper conducts an experimental study on the differences in different behavioral patterns, ability expressions, and image forms in three scenarios: outdoor, indoor and autopilot. To summarize the experimental content of these elements within the different scenarios is shown in Table 1.

Table 1. Experimental contents

Scenes	Description	Emotional expression	IV	DV
Outdoor service	Community service robot meets pedestrians	Acting attraction	Can it attract users to interact further	Moving speed
				Physical tendency
				Interactive height
Indoor service	The dining robot in the restaurant completes the meal delivery service	Acting empathy	Meal delivery task completion (system usability)	Eye contact assistance
				Movement assistance
				Voice assistance
Autonomous driving	Interaction with passengers during autopilot	Communicating of trust	Evaluation of the ride experience in various traffic conditions	Screen assistant
				Entity assistant
				Holographic assistant

In the experiment, participants (n = 20) were given a questionnaire to test the effect of different independent variables on the dependent variable by viewing an immersive virtual scene and interacting with a smart terminal within the scene without completing a set of experiments.

For the outdoor service smart terminal scenario, subjects were arranged to watch three sets of video clips depicting three interactive actions actively displayed by the non-anthropomorphic device while walking forward from the subject's perspective: speed, physical inclination, and interaction height. The user experience was analyzed for changes in performance under different behavioral weights. Based on the user questionnaire responses, it was determined whether the behavioral attractiveness of the different behavioral weights could increase the willingness of the user experience to interact further.

For the indoor service IWT scenario, the subjects were shown 4 sets of programs containing interactable scenarios. The scenarios are virtual restaurant scenarios with several tables and chairs and an abstract restaurant environment. The 4 groups of experiments are progressive, with the robot gradually increasing the variety and richness of the interaction forms. Interaction form A: smiling expressions without movement and no physical activity; interaction form B: changing expressions but no physical activity, socially competent interaction form expected. C: changing expressions + physical activity; D: changing expressions + physical activity + continuous voice reminders. The completion and efficiency of the task are recorded to determine the impact of various behavioral capabilities of the intelligent terminal on the completion of the food delivery task.

For the self-driving smart terminal scenario, the subjects were arranged to watch three video clips, namely the on-screen assistant, the physician assistant, and the holographic projection assistant. Three common road conditions were designed in the test experiment: driving, traffic jam, and smooth driving, to test how users in the Self-driving vehicles react to and emotionally perceive the use of the driving assistant in different scenarios. A questionnaire will be used to assess the emotional perception of the user and the ride experience.

3.2 Research Questions

In the experiment, 24 cognitively normal users of different professions were randomly recruited and met the following two criteria: (1) mentally and physically healthy users who had been aware of intelligent robotic devices but had not specifically used them in their lives. (2) Twelve adult users of each gender, 24 in total, ranging in age from 23 to 26 years, with an average age of 24 years. The experimenters were broadly informed of the scope of the experiment before participating and were not allowed to talk about relevant experiences.

3.3 Variable Settings

A mixed design of 2 (attractiveness weights) × 3 (behavioral weights) was used in this experiment. Where the behavioral weights are the within-subject variables. The behavioral weights were divided in a modified way based on the findings of the literature on the communication of relevant behavioral emotions by extracting the degree of attractiveness, trust, and empathy construction brought about by different behavioral moves and dividing the behavioral weights into 3 levels.

Experimental Procedure

The interactive experiment was conducted using an interactive program based on Unity3D. The experimental site was converted into a studio where the subjects sat at a table in front of a huge display to create an immersive experience. The questionnaire was completed alone as much as possible during the experiment. Participants were informed of the experiment beforehand and were not allowed to share their past experiences. After each group, each user was given a questionnaire containing six closed-ended questions and two open-ended questions. This is shown in Fig. 2.

Fig. 2. Middle left and right show the experimental process for outdoor, indoor, and autopilot scenarios respectively

4 Results and Discussion

4.1 Experimental Results

The results of the experiment corroborate our findings that action attraction, action empathy, and trust communication are, to some extent, elements that influence the user experience during human-smart device interaction, and in addition, the results of the experiment show some specific valuable information:

Behaviors that Are Suggestive Increase Action Attraction. In behavioral experiments with action attraction, the machine travels along a route at a constant speed without sensing a person, and by, turning its head from side to side to convey the act of active seeking, it can make the user feel that the machine is actively moving towards them.

Head Movements have a Stronger Expression of Interactive Intent. In the body tilt experiment of action attraction, the subjects expected that the combination of head actions on top of "body tendencies" would improve the user's understanding of the task. The clarity of task expression in smart terminals can further build trust in the interaction.

Voice Interaction is the Most Helpful Way to Communicate with a Smart Device.
The interaction gradient setting of the experiment appeared to have little effect on user task completion in the four sets of experiments for action empathy. In the choice of factors that influenced task completion, subjects all overwhelmingly chose voice, followed by action, with expressions scoring the lowest. The statistical results are shown in Fig. 3.

Physical Intelligent Terminals Feel a Greater Degree of Understanding of Emotional Changes and Driving Status than the Messages (Expressions, Texts) in Screen Assistants and Holographic Projections. In terms of the image of the driving assistant product, people trust the information conveyed by the screen assistant and the physician assistant more than the holographic projection assistant. The three types of intelligent terminals were used in order of satisfaction: physical assistant, holographic projection assistant, and screen assistant. The statistical results are shown in Fig. 4.

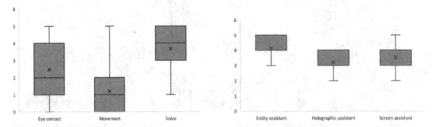

Fig. 3. Statistics on influencing factors affecting task completion

Fig. 4. Satisfaction statistics for three types of smart terminals

In the experimental study of movement attraction, subjects showed significant uniformity in their interpretation of the behavior of non-anthropomorphic robotic devices, with participants perceiving these movements as expressions of emotions with human or pet-like characteristics, for example, the expressed intentions of attraction and empathy at the behavioral level. Research has shown that machine movements can convey a sense of proactivity and friendliness and approachability, even in non-humanoid machines. However, the degree of outward expression of perceptual emotions needs to be refined more through later practice with different behavioral iterations.

In the action empathy experiment, Group A had the fewest actions, with subjects giving a rather negative response to the question on re-experiencing, with an average score of 1, and all choosing to expect very rich features in the question on what kind of robot service to expect. Group D was the group with the richest set of interactions, with the highest score of 4.5 for the whether to experience it again section after removing one special value, and all of the subjects chose to expect richer features. On the question of re-experiencing, one participant responded: "Although the robot's performance was below my expectations, I still have a good feeling about it and would like to experience it again", which indicates that for the participant the robot's performance met his needs and provided a good experience.

The results of the trust communication experiments show that the driving assistant products in the driverless service scenario have obvious value needs in the mobile space. The existing driving assistants have physical assistants as carriers to convey emotions that can make users perceive, trust, affinity and approve of their information delivery methods, and it can be considered that the novel technology similar to holographic projection and the intuitive combination of text and expressions can meet the preferences of different users.

4.2 Experimental Limitations

This experiment was carried out with a virtual image, which may have some differences in perception compared to a real robot service experience, and could be carried out in a real restaurant in the future to more realistically record the impact of different interaction expressions on the user's perception. The majority of the subjects in the experiment were young people of the same age group, and it would be worthwhile to conduct further experiments on the perception of these robots by a wider age group. In a real environment, there may be situations where multiple types of robots work in tandem when task and non-task attributes intermingle and become more difficult to handle. Within the category of robotic services, there are more typical examples that deserve to be explored, such as usher robots, welcome robots, etc. How great are the task and non-task attributes of these robots? What are the areas of concern for users? What are the incremental designs to be made for their design and manufacture? These are all questions that future researchers can go on to delve into.

4.3 Discuss

Get the User's Attention Naturally. Regarding the importance of non-verbal communication during human-computer interaction, the author has extracted some of the behavioral elements that bring associativity to the interaction from the interpersonal process, prompting the realization of devices that further express emotions and intentions in active interaction, completing the experimental and validation methods. In the experiments of this study, it was shown that the closeness of the behavioral mix of the smart device to the user's everyday communicative behavior constitutes a key element in improving the user experience. When the subject was in the background of attention, the actions of the smart device were appropriately triggered, creating a simpler and more comfortable human-computer interaction process than the mere output of specific commands. With more diverse application scenarios for smart technologies in the future, it is important to re-examine the task role robots take on in human-robot collaboration and how they can be a functional design element for ways to engage users in further interaction.

Appropriate Behavioral Expressions Increase the Efficiency of Interactions. Robots are not as attractive to people as they could be, for example, if they are too visible and customers want to watch them in action. In this case, too much localized human traffic in a restaurant can cause congestion and affect restaurant service, thus reducing overall customer satisfaction. At this point, comprehensive testing should be done in the future in actual robot development to ensure that the attractiveness of the robot to people does not interfere with the robot's ability to fulfill its function. In our field interviews with some of the robot restaurants, some operators informed us that the welcome robot in front of the restaurant had broken the robot's arm when a customer mistakenly thought it could do a handshake by mistake. In such cases, we should re-examine the role and user expectations of such robots, and then redefine their form and interaction.

Different Styles of Interactive Performance Depending on the Scene-Setting. In this experiment, it appears that the robot's movements became progressively 'larger' or 'jumpy', due to the increase of the robot's ability to perform. The same level of intelligence can also be demonstrated in the form of 'quieter' and 'more active' expressions. In previous research, researchers have addressed the issue of the conversational style of intelligent voice assistants, where the impact on the user of the same response differs between a straightforward answer and a polite one. Based on the present research, it is possible to further explore the nuances of interaction presentation styles within the context of appropriate interactions, which could be of great benefit to practical bot development.

5 Conclusions

Unlike the interaction of non-intelligent terminals, the behavior of the systems in this study attempts to present a partially anthropomorphic or animated emotional nature, just as interactive doors and vending machines in convenience stores, which can use emotionally charged interactive behaviors to attract attention, the smart devices in question attempt to convey fixed emotional perceptions and intentions. Whether the emotionally oriented expressions of the intent of smart terminals meet human psychological needs is the focus of the interaction design of artificial intelligence terminals at the level of emotional expression.

In future human-machine interaction experiences, if designers can communicate a variety of 'command messages' within a more restricted space, then in future design, it is also possible to continue to think about new types of human-machine interaction, in addition to voice and screen forms, and to communicate non-verbal cues in both directions between human-machine interaction information with rich emotion to improve the quality of the human-intelligent system interaction experience. The main purpose of this paper is to investigate the use and experiential effects of active interactive feedback in outdoor, indoor, and self-driving service scenarios, and the differences in user experience between different behavior all patterns, expressions of competence, and image forms in these scenarios in terms of action attraction, action empathy, and trust conveyance. The analysis summarizes the key factors affecting user experience during the active interaction of intelligent devices and provides a reference for the design of interaction forms for intelligent service robots.

References

1. Yunhui, Y., Jing, X., Zhiguo, L., Kechen, S., Bohang, L.: Development and research status of humanoid service. ROBOT **39**(04), 551–564 (2017)

2. Liang, C., Yue, H., Huai-yu, L.: Review on service robots based on bibliometric analysis. Packag. Eng. **42**(08), 12-19+35 (2021)
3. Ju, W.: The design of implicit interactions. Synth. Lect. Hum. Center. Inf. **8**(2), 1–93 (2015)
4. Ju, W., Takayama, L.: Approachability: how people interpret automatic door movement as gesture. Int. J. Design **3**(2) (2009)
5. Gallace, A., Spence, C.: The science of interpersonal touch: an overview. Neurosci. Biobehav. Rev. **34**(2), 246–259 (2010)
6. Hoffman, G., Ju, W.: Designing robots with movement in mind. J. Hum. Robot Interact. **3**(1), 91–122 (2014)
7. Nakata, T., Sato, T., Mori, T., Mizoguchi, H.: Expression of emotion and intention by robot body movement. In: Intelligent Autonomous Systems 5 (IAS-5), pp. 352–359 (1998)
8. Mok, B., Yang, S., Sirkin, D., Ju, W.: Empathy: interactions with emotive robotic drawers. In: 2014 9th ACM/IEEE International Conference on Human-Robot Interaction (HRI), pp. 250–251. IEEE, New York (2014)
9. Fischer, K., Yang, S., Mok, B., Maheshwari, R., Sirkin, D., Ju, W.: Initiating interactions and negotiating approach: a robotic trash can in the field. In: AAAI Symposium on Turn-taking and Coordination in Human- Machine Interaction, pp. 10–16, AAAI Press, New York (2015)
10. Knight, H., Veloso, M., Simmons, R.: Taking candy from a robot: speed features and candy accessibility predict human response. In: 2015 24th IEEE International Symposium on Robot and Human Interactive Communication, pp. 355–362, IEEE, Roman (2015)
11. Kwon, M., Huang, S., Dragan, A.: Expressing robot incapability. In: Proceedings of the 2018 ACM/IEEE International Conference on Human-Robot, pp. 87–95. IEEE, New York (2018)
12. Prati, E., Peruzzini, M., Pellicciari, M., Raffaeli, R.: How to include user eXperience in the design of human-robot interaction. Robot. Comput. Integrat. Manufact. **68**, 102072 (2021)
13. Rueben, M., Tang, M., Rothberg, E., Matarić, M.: Helping users develop accurate mental models of robots' perceptual capabilities: a first approach. In: Workshop on Trust, Acceptance and Social Cues in Robot Interaction (SCRITA), Roman (2019)
14. Rosenfeld, A., Richardson, A.: Explainability in human-agent systems. Autonom. Agents MultiAgent Syst. **33**(6), 673–705 (2019)
15. Haspiel, J., et al.: Explanations and expectations: trust building in automated vehicles. In: Companion of the 2018 ACM/IEEE International Conference on Human-Robot Interaction, pp. 119–120. IEEE, New York (2018)
16. Washburn, A., Adeleye, A., An, T., Riek, L.: Robot errors in proximate HRI: how functionality framing affects perceived reliability and trust. ACM Trans. Human-Robot Interact. **9**(3), 1–21 (2020)
17. Choi, S., Liu, S.Q., Mattila, A.: "How may i help you?" Says a robot: examining language styles in the service encounter. Int. J. Hosp. Manag. **82**, 32–38 (2019)
18. Złotowski, J., Sumioka, H., Nishio, S., Glas, D.F., Bartneck, C., Ishiguro, H.: Appearance of a robot affects the impact of its behaviour on perceived trustworthiness and empathy. J. Behav. Robot. **7**(1) (2016)
19. Bansal, G., Nushi, B., Kamar, E., Lasecki, W., Weld, D., Horvitz, E.: Beyond accuracy: The role of mental models in human-AI team performance. In: Proceedings of the AAAI Conference on Human Computation and Crowdsourcing, vol. 7, no. 1, pp. 2–11 (2019)
20. Prati, E., Peruzzini, M., Pellicciari, M., Raffaeli, R.: How to include user eXperience in the design of human-robot interaction. Robot. Comput. Integrat. Manuf. **68**, 102072 (2021)
21. Reig, S., et al.: Not some random agent: multi-person interaction with a personalizing service robot. In: Proceedings of the 2020 ACM/IEEE International Conference on Human-Robot Interaction, pp. 289–297 (2020)

Design for Well-being and Health

Designing a Digital Mental Health App for Opioid Use Disorder Using the UX Design Thinking Framework

Kajia Coziahr[1]([✉]), Laura Stanley[1], Angelica Perez-Litwin[2],
Camille Lundberg[3], and Alain Litwin[3]

[1] Montana State University, Bozeman, MT 59715, USA
kajia.coziahr@student.montana.edu
[2] Clemson University, Clemson, SC 29634, USA
[3] Prisma Health Department of Medicine, Greenville, SC 29605, USA

Abstract. The opioid crisis persists in shattering lives and devastating families across the US with nearly 38 opioid-related deaths per day in 2019. Mobile health applications, commonly known as mhealth apps, have shown potential in improving interventions in addictive disorders and are increasing in popularity as smartphone technology becomes more affordable and accessible. Although thousands of mhealth apps are available, several reviews have noted gaps in assessing the efficacy of these apps. Specifically, many of these apps lack evidence-based strategies and do not implement a user experience (UX) design approach. UX design thinking seeks to optimize the success of a product and provides critical insights into user needs and preferences. In this work, we provide a case study that follows the UX design framework, empathizing, defining, ideating, prototyping, testing, to guide the development of a mhealth app focused on managing cravings related to Opioid Use Disorder (OUD). We empathized with 11 adults diagnosed with OUD through semi-structured interviews and performed heuristic evaluation with three experts on a low-fidelity prototype. In conjunction with literature review findings, the interview results reveal a need for evidence-based remote interventions and providing an appropriate level of care congruent to individual recovery progress. We identified through literature investigation and consultation of a licensed clinical psychologist that cognitive behavioral therapy videos and biofeedback breathing interventions are efficacious strategies for managing cravings caused by OUD. Therefore, we implemented these features into a high-fidelity prototype influenced by findings from the literature, our target population, and heuristic evaluation.

Keywords: Digital health · mHealth app · Opioid use disorder · User experience UX

1 Introduction

Continued widespread misuse of prescription and non-prescription opioids remains a national public health emergency [48]. The Coronavirus Disease of

© The Author(s), under exclusive license to Springer Nature Switzerland AG 2022
M. M. Soares et al. (Eds.): HCII 2022, LNCS 13322, pp. 107–129, 2022.
https://doi.org/10.1007/978-3-031-05900-1_7

2019 (COVID-19) has exacerbated the situation, causing isolation, disruption to treatment, and an increased risk of life-threatening illness to those who suffer from opioid use disorder (OUD) [12]. An unprecedented rise in fatal overdoses was also observed in 2019, where opioid misuse was responsible for more than 70% of the 71,000 total drug overdose deaths [16]. Diminished quality of life, productivity, significant healthcare, and criminal justice costs are additional by-products of the opioid epidemic [37]. The US economic burden caused by these repercussions and opioid overdose deaths was estimated to be $1.02 trillion in 2017 alone [18].

Although safe and effective evidence-based treatments for OUD exist, less than 10% of people who need help receive care for this dependence [53]. The stigma associated with substance use disorders and limited access to care are major factors for the few people undergoing treatment [13]. Furthermore, negative public and healthcare professional attitudes might discourage individuals from seeking therapy, causing patients to experience discrimination during their visits and leading to poor treatment outcomes [43]. Similarly, travel barriers in rural areas, financial instability, and outdated policies constrict the accessibility of treatment [38]. Despite the growing concerns surrounding the current opioid crisis, remote craving, recovery, and relapse management techniques fail to address the situation properly. There is a need to design an easily accessible, discreet, and efficacious remote intervention to support those who suffer from OUD.

Rapid technological advancements have prompted developers and practitioners to seek digital solutions for the management of OUD and other substance use disorders. Mobile technologies show promise because of their potential to deliver "just-in-time" interventions capable of adapting to an individual's unique needs, both internally and externally [36]. Smartphone applications' cost-effectiveness, anonymity, and customizability add to their appeal [23]. Our solution to support OUD sufferers involves developing a mobile health application, commonly known as a mhealth app, utilizing the UX design thinking framework to help mitigate cravings associated with OUD.

UX design thinking is an ideology that begins with an empathizing process to identify users' needs, preferences, and mental models [28]. After empathizing, a specific problem statement is defined, followed by ideation, prototyping, and testing [39] (See Fig. 1). It is essential that this process is integrated into the development of mhealth apps to improve user engagement [15], trust [8,36], and retention [4,8,51]. Conducting in user testing early in the design process can also help developers save time and money [44]. For these reasons, we provide a case study that applies the UX design framework to create an efficacious mhealth prototype as an adjunct therapy for OUD craving management. This work will greatly benefit individuals who struggle with opioid addiction and provide an asset for developers, physicians, and therapists for developing innovative treatment approaches.

2   Background

There are currently over 100,000 mhealth applications available [54]. Mhealth applications target many psychological and physical disorders, some of which focus on substance cessation [30,49] and craving management [11,31,49]. Several reviews have noted gaps in the assessment of the efficacy of mhealth apps [22,27,29,40], and it has been found that there is little documentation or evidence of clinical validation in addition to concerns about privacy [41,46]. Despite the abundance of existing applications in mhealth, very few focus specifically on OUD [40]. Furthermore, many mhealth apps do not offer evidence-based strategies, lack personalization, and do not follow the proper UX design thinking approach during development [3,27].

The UX design thinking framework has six phases, as shown in Fig. 1. This non-linear and iterative process allows developers and researchers to traverse through stages as needed.

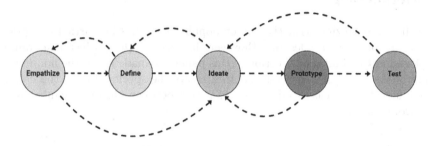

Fig. 1. A generic design thinking process.

The empathize and define stages often entail a literature review, interviews with focus groups, and empathy mapping. In tandem with the literature review, empathy maps can reveal gaps in the research, reduce bias, and gain knowledge on motivations for user behaviors [45]. From that insight emerges a powerful tool known as persona generation that allows UX researchers, designers, and software developers to tailor their designs for a specific type of user. User personas can provide a shared understanding of the target population, which improves communication and expectations throughout the team and thus facilitates collaboration during the development of an app [9]. Ideation can take on many forms, including, but not limited to, mind mapping, brainstorming, and sketching, to provide potential suggestions for the problem at hand [14]. The proposed ideas can be transformed into tangible solutions by creating diagrams and low/high-fidelity prototypes that describe the system. The prototyping phase exposes the feasibility of the intended features and provides a means to test ideas [10]. Usability testing can assess the efficiency, effectiveness, and desirability of the application and plays an integral role in the design process [7]. Heuristic testing is another UX method of evaluation in which experts compare the prototype or product's user interface to recognize usability principles of design and identify violations [24]. Insights from testing can be implemented into an improved design.

Although it has been noted that UX design thinking is lacking in the mhealth space, some research in other areas employ this framework within their case studies [35,42,47]. A recent study used the UX design approach to redesign the main menu of a Peruvian Bank's ATM interface and discovered that the new design allowed the user greater freedom and enjoyment when withdrawing money and engaging with the main menu interface [35]. Another study was able to confirm that using a design thinking approach improved an e-learning system prototype to better accommodate user needs [42]. Similarly, developers minimized task completion time and errors and increased user satisfaction for an enterprise resource planning system by utilizing this framework [47]. These studies indicate that the UX design thinking framework is efficacious in improving product designs that better accommodate the users that engage with them.

3   Methodology

Typically, empathizing with the target population would be carried out prior to creating preliminary designs. However, because of the project constraints mentioned in the limitations section of this paper, we made use of the non-linear nature of the UX design process. Figure 2 shows the specific flow of the design process used for this case study. Each transition between phases is numbered in order from one to 10.

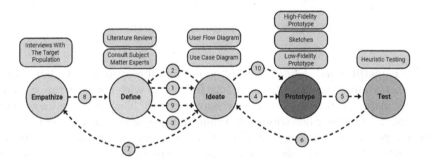

Fig. 2. The design thinking process for this case study.

3.1   Define the Problem: Literature Review and Expert Consultation

Initially, we performed a systematic literature review in the space of OUD and mhealth applications. However, due to the lack of studies focusing specifically on OUD, we extended our search to include digital interventions for substance use disorders and associated cravings. We determined the following efficacious features in mitigating substance use disorders; Cognitive Behavioral Therapy (CBT) [3,34,46], biofeedback exercises [5,17], community integration [6,20], gamification strategies [1,3,52], visual progress tracking [2], goal entry [2,50,51], and privacy transparency [3,41,46]. In addition to wearable devices [19], immersive technology can be an excellent tool for practicing new treatment strategies in recovery [21]. To further guide our preliminary designs and define our problem statement, we consulted subject matter experts, including licensed clinical psychologists and other mental health experts.

3.2   Ideation Through Diagram Creation

We created a use case diagram using the Unified Modeling Language (UML) [33] to describe the interaction between our users and the system. We first recognized two subsystems: the mhealth smartphone application, and the wearable device needed to collect physiological data for the biofeedback breathing intervention. Next, we identified external entities, otherwise known as actors, within our design. Each actor's role was defined as it pertains to their relationship with the application and wearable device as shown in Table 1. Subsequently, we constructed use cases to represent each feature and determined the associations needed for the system to function. Features were chosen based on findings from the literature and input from subject matter experts.

Table 1. Use case diagram actors and roles.

Actor	Role
User	Users initiate the interaction with the mhealth application. They may log in, take a brief survey, and engage in various interventions/features of the app to help reduce craving intensity
Recommender	The recommender system takes input data from the user responses to the survey questions. This information is used to recommend a CBT video or biofeedback intervention
Server	The server accesses, stores, and transfers data files containing saved app information (i.e. username, password, email address, gender, survey responses, etc....)

A user flow diagram was created to supplement the use case diagram and provide a high-level view of the path the user will take to complete the CBT video or biofeedback breathing interventions. Similarly, this diagram was created using UML [33]. These two features were prioritized based on findings from the literature, expert opinion, and the project completion timeline.

3.3 Low-Fidelity Prototype Development

A preliminary prototype design was created using a touchscreen tablet and version 0.7.2.0 of Miro's visual collaboration software/online sketching template [1]. The prototype was derived from the previously constructed user flow diagram and each screen of the smartphone application was hand-drawn to represent the skeletal framework of the user interface. After experimenting with several user flow variants, the hand-drawn prototype was converted into a low-fidelity wireframe using Adobe XD version 47.1.22.

3.4 Heuristic Evaluation

For this study, three UX experts formerly trained in UX research and design heuristic evaluation were consulted to capture usability problems and optimal benefits to cost ratio [24].

Procedure. The three experts were sent an evaluation template to ensure consistency and asked to evaluate the low-fidelity Adobe XD wireframe using Jakob Nielsen's 10 usability heuristics for user interface design [26]. The template contained a list of tasks, a link to the Adobe XD wireframe prototype, and space to record observations. For each recognized usability principle violation, the evaluators recorded: 1.) the identified problem, 2.) a brief description that explains the problem, 3.) the specific heuristic that was violated, and 4.) the location within the wireframe prototype where the violation was found. Each expert was required to complete the evaluation twice for a thorough investigation. Once expert responses were received, a comprehensive list of all usability problems found in the low-fidelity wireframe was compiled and returned. The evaluators provided a severity rating from 0–4 to capture the frequency, impact, and persistence of each identified problem [25]. Finally, the average severity rating was computed for each violation and potential solutions were brainstormed in a team meeting.

3.5 Interviews with the Target Population

Participants. A total of 11 participants (5 M, 5 F, 1 Non-binary, mean age 40.27, SD 8.13) completed the in-depth qualitative interviews. We selected individuals who met the following inclusion criteria: 1.) adults 18–75 years, 2.) diagnosed with opioid use disorder and have participated in medication-assisted treatment through the Prisma Health Recovery Clinic, 3.) own a smartphone, 4.) consent to participate in the study. Most participants were between 36 to 45 years old (72.73%), high school graduates or GED equivalent (54.55%), unemployed (54.55%), and rent their homes (63.64%). Nearly half of the participants receive healthcare funding through a hospital sponsorship (45.45%).

---

[1] The online sketching template can be found on miro.com.

Procedure. Qualitative data was collected through in-depth, semi-structured moderated interviews. The interview questions were constructed with the guidance of a licensed clinical psychologist to explore the overall experiences of the participants' lives, daily living, smartphone usage, cravings, interventions, and sociodemographic information. Interviews were conducted either remotely via an online meeting tool or in person at the Prisma Health Recovery Clinic. The audio was recorded for every interview, while video was recorded when possible.

Data Analysis. The audio-recorded interviews were transcribed and coded in NVIVO 12, a qualitative data analysis program, employing a coding scheme focused on smartphone usage, triggers, happiness, craving and relapse prevention, therapy and interventions, and views on immersive technology and wearable devices. Empathy maps for each of the 11 participants were created using Miro to identify what the users say, do, think, and feel as they go through their recovery. Two personas were generated in tandem with user scenarios to provide a comprehensive understanding of the user's needs and pain points. Word frequency queries were carried out to reveal trends in craving triggers, phone usage, and preferences.

3.6 High-Fidelity Prototype Development

A high-fidelity prototype was developed using Adobe XD. This iteration of the design implemented learnings from the literature review, heuristic evaluation, and user interviews. Interactive elements were incorporated to provide a true representation of the interface that users will interact with for the purpose of optimizing future usability testing efforts.

4   Results

4.1   Diagrams

The use case and user flow diagrams produced in the preliminary ideation phase are shown in Figs. 3 and 4, respectfully.

Our use case diagram provides a high-level overview of the interactions between the user, mobile application, wearable device, recommender system, and server. The user can log in, take the survey, and participate in a variety of OUD interventions determined to be efficacious through the literature review. The server and recommender system communicate with the wearable device and the application. More specifically, the recommender system obtains input from the survey to recommend an intervention. The server collects and stores key metrics. This stage in the UX design process was not limited by constricting factors such as cost, time, or other obstacles and serves as a preliminary investigation into potential implementations of the app design.

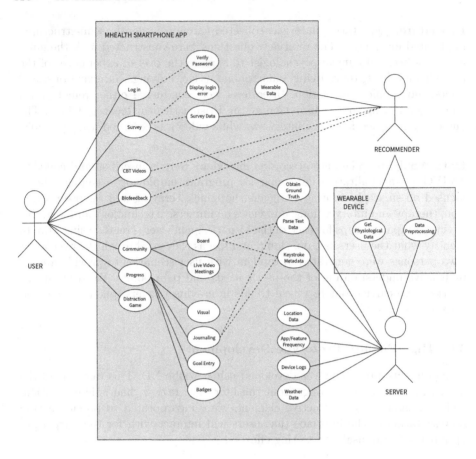

Fig. 3. Use case diagram.

This use case diagram was presented in a stakeholder meeting to provide clarification on the scope of our project and initiate discussion on the system functionality. Feedback from the licensed clinical psychologist and app developers on the team suggested that cognitive behavioral videos and biofeedback breathing interventions should be prioritized and the number of features should be reduced. The proceeding user flow diagram visually represents the path the user will take to participate in the cognitive behavioral therapy videos or biofeedback breathing exercises from start to finish.

The user initiates interaction with the application upon the onset of a craving. They can either log in or create an account and are prompted to take a survey to assess their current cravings and triggers. Based on their survey responses, the recommender system will suggest an intervention, either CBT videos or the biofeedback breathing exercise, that will aid them in their current situation. If the user chooses not to take the survey, they can still access the biofeedback breathing intervention from the homepage. A wearable wrist device is needed

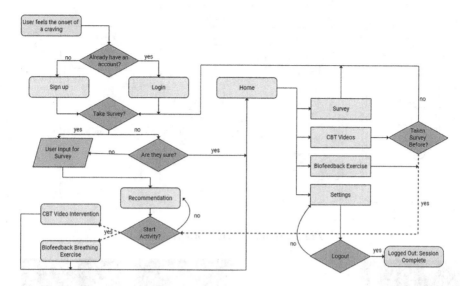

Fig. 4. User flow diagram.

to collect physiological data for this type of intervention. However, the user can only watch CBT videos that the recommender suggests, and therefore must complete the survey prior to participating in this intervention. Once the user has completed their recommended intervention, they can either repeat the activity or return to the home screen. The user can log out of the application by navigating to settings at any time during engagement with the application.

4.2   Low-Fidelity Prototypes

A sample of the hand-drawn sketches and low-fidelity prototype can be found in Figs. 5 and 6. These visualizations showcase four screens that the user will interact with when using the app. The first page on the left is the login/sign up page, which takes the user to either a survey check-in or onboarding process depending on if it is the user's first time using the app. The user is prompted to take the survey in screen two, and the confirmation page of the survey is shown directly after. The completed survey page displays the intervention recommended by the system based on survey data. The final page portrays an example of a CBT video screen.

4.3   Heuristic Evaluation

A total of 20 problems were identified through the heuristic evaluation process. Visibility of System Status and Consistency & Standards were the two heuristics with the most violations and highest severity ratings. The evaluators found that it was difficult to tell where the user was within the system and that knowing

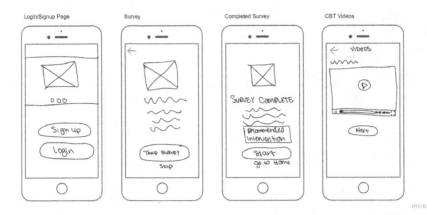

Fig. 5. Hand-drawn prototype.

Fig. 6. Low-Fidelity wireframe prototype.

how to return to the homepage after entering an intervention was unclear. Some areas of the application contained acronyms (e.g. CBT) while others provided the full word. It was also noted that several pages contained text blocks that were too verbose, while others did not contain enough information for the user to understand the purpose of the page content. Additionally, there were light and dark themes mixed throughout the prototype and buttons that were inconsistent in both color and size. Some pages used back arrows located on the top left corner of the screen, but other pages contained a cross in the top right corner of the screen. Another glaring issue with the first iteration of the wireframe was aesthetic appeal. The background colors are mostly dark with vibrant buttons and writing, which was determined to be ill-suited for our target population. Moreover, it was challenging to distinguish text from the background color of the buttons.

4.4   Qualitative Interviews

Smartphone Usage. Over half of the participants use their phones more than 15 times per day, with 72.73% of them owning Android phones. The most used smartphone applications among these users are YouTube and Facebook, though several participants mentioned playing games, checking the weather, monitoring their bank accounts, and responding to emails on their phones as well.

Triggers. The importance of each trigger mentioned in the interviews is depicted by the font size and color of the word cloud shown in Fig. 7. A number of internal and external triggers were reported to provoke cravings, notably anxiety, pain, people, and arguments. Physical withdrawal symptoms have a major influence on cravings, as well as seeing or talking about substance use. Other factors, such as hunger, lack of sleep, sickness, boredom, and stress also make it difficult for people recovering from OUD to refrain from using opioids.

Fig. 7. Word cloud of triggers.

"When I get high anxiety, that is a big trigger."

"If there wasn't no withdrawal, if you didn't have no physical withdrawals, I mean, I might be different than everybody else, but to me it'd be a lot easier not to do it."

Happiness. More than 80% of the participants mentioned friends, family, kids, and connection when asked what makes them most happy in life. The remaining participants spoke of sobriety, freedom, and being "normal." The direct quotes below further exemplify the importance of these life aspects and contribute to a better understanding of the participants.

"It's when I can find a way to interact with the people that I care about in a meaningful way."

"Being normal. Not taking any drugs, you know, and living a normal life where you're not having to look for drugs or do drugs or whatever to be happy."

Craving and Relapse Prevention. Participants were asked how they prevent and deal with cravings. The compiled list of mentioned activities is shown in Table 2, followed by source quotes for responses to questions regarding craving and relapse prevention.

Table 2. Activities to prevent cravings and relapse.

Tend to the garden	Take a walk	Visit with neighbors	Fantasy football
Teach yoga	Play guitar	Have a discussion with their partner	Take a hot bath/shower
Play Pickleball	Watch TV	Help others	Cook
Take Suboxone	Watch movies	Stay active in the recovery community	Get a massage
Exercise	Watch YouTube videos	Spend time with pets	Meditate
Get fresh air	Play games on their phone	Call and talk with someone over the phone	Have an internal conversation and think about the consequences of using
Go Fishing	Listen to podcasts	Woodworking	Removal from the situation or environment
Listen to nature	Talk about their substance use disorder	Make furniture	Journaling

"Block it out, think about something else, do something else. Only thing that somewhat helps."

"I don't have anything. I don't have any tools right now to prevent cravings."

"Find something else to do, honestly. The craving will go away in under 15 min if you just distract yourself."

"Helping out other people. I think that's probably the single most important thing that I've found in my recovery."

Therapy and Interventions. Only two participants claim to have tried CBT. One reported that it was helpful, while the other thought that they did not have experience with it early enough in their recovery. All 11 participants have had a counseling experience and 90% of them stated that it was helpful. However, two participants disclosed that they felt unprepared for the level of counseling that they experienced.

"I would say [counseling is] helpful, but probably not the right therapist at the right time. And by that, I mean I felt like when I was in early recovery, I was with a therapist who was trying to do the deep stuff and what I really needed was someone to just help me get through the day. And then later I had a different therapist, and I was working with her for a couple of months, and I just felt like alright when are we going to like dig in and do the deep stuff?"

Most users (73%) have tried some form of meditation and 75% of these users perceive it to be helpful. Those who have not tried meditation are willing to try it. The participants who declared that it was somewhat helpful or not helpful report feelings of anxiety and worry about doing it incorrectly.

"It [meditation] does not relax me. I just focus on my breathing and then I just get anxious about not doing it right."

Immersive Technology and Wearable Devices. Over half (54.5%) of the participants have used virtual reality (VR). Mixed responses were given when asked about their experiences. Exactly half had positive attitudes towards the technology, while the other 50% had negative recounts. Those who noted a negative experience have only been exposed to VR games involving roller coasters, race cars, "moving stuff," and haunted houses. However, once an intervention using immersive technologies was described to the user in the context of recovery, an overwhelmingly positive response was received. One-hundred percent of the participants expressed a willingness to try a recovery intervention using immersive technology in combination with a smartphone app and wearable device.

Empathy Maps and Personas. A total of 12 empathy maps were created; one for each user, and one to capture the main themes found between all users. Two fictional characters were generated from the interview findings and themes identified in empathy mapping to represent user demographics, motivations, frustrations, and mental models (Figs. 8 and 9).

About Ryan. Ryan has a disability that makes it tough to find a full-time job that's right for him. Instead, he works part-time as a mechanic and cuts grass to pay his rent. He listens to music and makes furniture in his time off, though he often finds himself not having enough to do. He says that having too much time is a killer, especially after starting his opioid use recovery journey. He loves the outdoors and the mountains and hopes to take his new girlfriend to Alaska someday to explore. They have been dating for a couple months now and feel

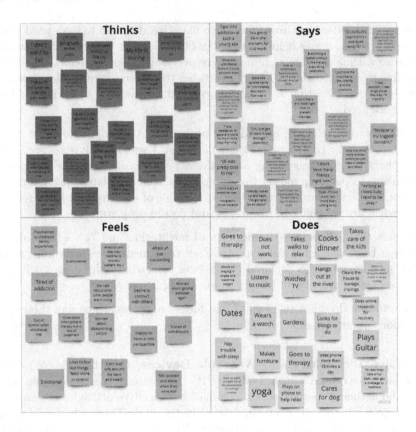

Fig. 8. Empathy map representing all 11 participants.

like things could start to get serious. He says he is very appreciative of her and all she does to help out his parents. His father recently had a stroke, so they've been over at his parents' house often to help out with chores (Fig. 10).

Use Case Scenario. Ryan was working at the mechanic shop one Friday afternoon when the manager approached him. He told Ryan that he has been working hard and should take the remainder of the afternoon off to get an early start on his weekend. Ryan finds himself with a few extra hours to kill before going out to dinner with his girlfriend. While trying to figure out how to spend his time, Ryan starts to notice oncoming withdrawal symptoms and begins experiencing a strong sense of anxiety. He recognizes these feelings as an opioid craving. To help him manage this craving, he takes his phone out of his pocket and opens the mhealth application. He completes a short survey and is redirected to a page that recommends that he participate in a biofeedback breathing exercise. He makes sure that his watch is on and presses the 'start activity' button. The application coaches him to inhale as a ring on the screen expands and to exhale

Fig. 9. User persona 1: Ryan Jones.

👍 **Motivations**

Helping other people with their recovery through group counseling.

Wanting to make his friends and family proud.

Using wood working as a distraction tool during withdrawal. He likes having a nice end result.

👎 **Frustrations**

Transportation is an issue. It makes it very difficult to make it to therapy meetings and appointments on time.

Ryan doesn't have any tools to help him prevent cravings right now.

Physical withdrawal symptoms make it very difficult to stay away from opioid use.

Fig. 10. Ryan's motivations and frustrations with recovery.

as it contracts. Ryan feels the craving start to subside as the intervention comes to an end. He closes the app and is able to go about his day (Fig. 11).

About Natalie. Natalie has overcome many hardships. She was homeless for about two months, where her drug use was at an all-time high. She overdosed and was hospitalized for some time, but is thankful that she is still able to be here for her son and her family. She has taken this recent tragedy and has turned it into an opportunity to become the best version of herself. She moved in with her mother and has been studying to get her GED, going to therapy, and exercising. She says some days are very trying and she sometimes has issues getting out of bed, but as long as she doesn't get too far off track, she is happy with her

Fig. 11. User persona 2: Natalie Williams hugging her son.

progress. She has found new hobbies, including making her own bath products, listening to podcasts, and playing Play-Doh with her son (Fig. 12).

Use Case Scenario. Natalie finds herself in a state of worry as she studies for her GED. She is frustrated because she doesn't understand a concept and is growing tired of reading the same paragraph over and over again. As her anxiety rises, her mind begins to wander and she thinks about how nice it would be to use opioids to help her deal with the overwhelming combination of feelings. She quickly pulls herself out of her daydream because she knows that if she doesn't do something to distract herself, she'll give in. She opens her mhealth application and completes the survey. The recommender system suggests that she should participate in watching a short series of videos to address her craving. She watches three videos, each only about two minutes long, and finds that her craving weakens. She puts her phone away and is able to continue her studies.

High-Fidelity Prototype. The prototype in Fig. 13 shows an updated and improved version of the preliminary hand-drawn sketches and low-fidelity prototype. User interviews revealed several pain points experienced throughout recovery, the most prominent being the sense of anxiety that coincides with cravings. Keeping this in mind, along with lack of consistency discovered in heuristic testing, the decision was made to make each page in the prototype light with soft colors. This design choice was intended to evoke a welcoming and calm sensation for our users. We also added graphics in attempts to increase aesthetic appeal. To improve visibility of system status, progress bars were included in the onboarding and survey sections of the application so that users had a visual representation of how many pages remained. Numbers signifying both the page the

👍 **Motivations**	👎 **Frustrations**
Being there for her son and family.	Being stuck on medicine the rest of her life because of a mistake.
Getting healthy and staying in shape to feel better.	Gets anxious when she tries breathing exercises or meditation.
Finding joy in life again.	
Learning; getting her GED.	Wrong therapist at the wrong time in her recovery.

Fig. 12. Natalie's motivations and frustrations with recovery

Fig. 13. High-fidelity prototype.

user is on and the total number of pages for the section are also displayed above the progress bar for further clarification. A navigation bar was added on pages succeeding account setup to allow users access to the homepage, interventions, and settings for more control over the system. Acronyms were removed except when explicit definitions were provided and text blocks were refined to provide appropriate levels of information. All back arrows were replaced by crosses in the top right corner of the screen and main buttons were adapted to be the same color, shape, and size for consistency and coherence.

5 Discussion

The purpose of this study was to utilize UX design thinking to develop an easily accessible and discrete mhealth app prototype to help mitigate cravings associated with OUD. We received valuable insight through literature investigation, heuristic evaluation, and user interviews to help guide us in the design of our mhealth app. Key findings include realizing a lack of validated remote mhealth apps specifically tailored for OUD and a need for user-centered development in this space. Useful interventions and strategies, namely CBT and biofeedback breathing exercises, were determined and implemented into an early prototype design. Expert review influenced the user interface such that coherence with recognized usability principles was improved. Most importantly, we gained a better understanding of user motivations, frustrations, and behaviors.

Congruent to literature findings [13,38], we determined through user interviews that transportation and access to care are pain points for people in recovery. Smartphone usage is not restricted to a specific place or time of day. This flexibility offers users the ability to receive additional care when they are unable to physically attend a meeting session or experience a craving at a time when other resources are unavailable. This type of intervention is sensible for those in recovery because they can control when they use the app and who knows about it [32,36]. By creating a remote mhealth intervention to mitigate cravings, we are progressing towards facilitating accessibility of recovery resources.

The heuristic investigation noted several problems with our preliminary design. This evaluation was a rapid and cost-friendly method to find early usability problems. Detecting these problems early in the development process minimized design deficiencies prior to spending valuable resources on coding and implementation. Further, the severity ratings helped prioritize usability problems. We were able to make adjustments to the design based on expert feedback that improved clarity and consistency. This is likely to increase usability, utility, and user satisfaction in future usability testing with the target population.

The most profound learnings came directly from our target population. We learned through moderated interviews that the most influential triggers to craving for these individuals are anxiety, pain, people, and arguments. This insight can change the way we approach intervention delivery and tailor messages the users will assimilate. We also discovered that most participants either don't know what CBT is or have never tried it. Given that CBT is efficacious in mitigating substance use disorder, it is essential that people in recovery become exposed and educated in this intervention strategy. No two people experience recovery in the same way or at the same pace, resulting in a need for an appropriate level of care congruent to the individual's unique stage in recovery. This consideration could potentially make the user more comfortable attending therapy or counseling sessions, thus improving recovery retention and progress. Further speculation on the activities people partake in to prevent a craving suggests that the two most valuable strategies are finding healthy distractions while continuing medication-assisted treatment. We were also able to confirm our belief that there is a demand for remote support interventions because all users expressed optimism and a willingness to try a smartphone intervention in the context of OUD management. Further, we were able to refine our efforts to Android development because more users within our target population own this type of phone.

Additionally, Android development is cost efficient and easy to use, which better accommodates the team's timeline and resources for the project. Speaking with the participants gave us an opportunity to see life from their perspective and effectively communicate their needs to the entire team.

The high-fidelity prototype was devised from implementations of our findings and captures the main interactions in our system. The early sketches and low-fidelity prototype do not meet the necessary standards and expectations as defined by usability principles of design [26]. However, improvement can be seen when compared to the high-fidelity prototype. Because the only approach to lessen the danger of relapse and overdose is to establish effective tactics and interventions, it is critical that the prototype is appealing and captures users' needs. More studies need to follow a UX design thinking approach, starting with user interviews, to tackle the opioid crisis head-on and support substance use remission.

6   Limitations

User interviews are meant to be conducted prior to prototype creation and heuristic evaluation. As noted in the methodology section of this study, we were unable to carry out those efforts before constructing preliminary diagrams and prototypes. This limitation was introduced by a combination of project time constraints and delayed Institutional Review Board approval. Further limitations include the small number of app developers on the team, which pushed us to prioritize CBT videos, and biofeedback breathing exercises to keep pace with the project timeline.

7   Conclusion and Future Directions

In this paper, we investigate the unmet needs of people who suffer from opioid use disorder and integrate interventions to reduce craving in an early mobile smartphone prototype. Based on qualitative analysis of user recovery perspectives, it can be concluded that smartphone technology, in combination with CBT and biofeedback breathing exercises, has potential to increase accessibility and provide additional discreet support for craving management. Practitioners should consider the following in future development of mhealth applications to address OUD: Follow a user-centric UX design thinking framework. Consult experts in addiction psychology, UX design, and development. Base interventions in cognitive behavioral therapy. Utilize diagrams, personas, and wireframes to establish a shared understanding of project aims throughout a team. In future iterations of this project, we will develop a functioning version of the Android app, conduct usability testing with the target population, and measure the efficacy of the app to fill the gaps associated with mhealth technologies for OUD.

Acknowledgements. This project is sponsored by the National Institutes of Health and The National Science Foundation. In addition, Montana State University, Clemson University, and Prisma Health are partnered for this study. We thank Karrissa

Rabideaux, Vishnunarayan Girishan Prabhu, Ranjana Mehta, Asaduzzaman Noor, Apostolos Kalatzis, Ruth Striegel Weissman, and Matt Kuntz for their contributions to the project, insightful feedback, and attentive reading of our paper.

References

1. Ahmed, M., et al.: Game on? the gamification of mHealth apps in the context of smoking cessation (2015). https://doi.org/10.2196/games.5678
2. Attwood, S., Parke, H., Larsen, J., Morton, K.L.: Using a mobile health application to reduce alcohol consumption: a mixed-methods evaluation of the drinkaware track & calculate units application. BMC Publ. Health **17**(1), 1–21 (2017)
3. Bakker, D., Kazantzis, N., Rickwood, D., Rickard, N.: Mental health smartphone apps: Review and evidence-based recommendations for future developments. JMIR Mental Health **3**(1) (2016). https://doi.org/10.2196/mental.4984
4. Bauer, A.M., et al.: Acceptability of mHealth augmentation of collaborative care: a mixed methods pilot study. Gen. Hosp. Psychiatry **51**, 22–29 (2018)
5. Beckjord, E., Shiffman, S.: Background for real-time monitoring and intervention related to alcohol use. Alcohol Res. Curr. Rev. **36**(1), 9 (2014)
6. Bergman, B.G., Kelly, N.W., Hoeppner, B.B., Vilsaint, C.L., Kelly, J.F.: Digital recovery management: characterizing recovery-specific social network site participation and perceived benefit. Psychol. Addict. Behav. **31**(4), 506 (2017)
7. Bevan, N., Carter, J., Earthy, J., Geis, T., Harker, S.: New ISO standards for usability, usability reports and usability measures. In: Kurosu, M. (ed.) HCI 2016. LNCS, vol. 9731, pp. 268–278. Springer, Cham (2016). https://doi.org/10.1007/978-3-319-39510-4_25
8. Bilgihan, A.: Gen y customer loyalty in online shopping: an integrated model of trust, user experience and branding. Comput. Hum. Behav. **61**, 103–113 (2016)
9. Blanco, E., Pourroy, F., Arikoglu, S.: Role of personas and scenarios in creating shared understanding of functional requirements: an empirical study. In: Gero, J.S. (ed.) Design Computing and Cognition '12, pp. 61–78. Springer, Dordrecht (2014). https://doi.org/10.1007/978-94-017-9112-0_4
10. Brenner, W., Uebernickel, F., Abrell, T.: Design thinking as mindset, process, and toolbox. In: Brenner, W., Uebernickel, F. (eds.) Design Thinking for Innovation, pp. 3–21. Springer, Cham (2016). https://doi.org/10.1007/978-3-319-26100-3_1
11. Carreiro, S., Newcomb, M., Leach, R., Ostrowski, S., Boudreaux, E.D., Amante, D.: Current reporting of usability and impact of mHealth interventions for substance use disorder: a systematic review. Drug Alcohol Depend. **215** (2020)
12. Centers for Disease Control and Prevention. Covid-19 and people at increased risk (2021). https://www.cdc.gov/drugoverdose/resources/covid-drugs-QA.html
13. Corso, C., Townley, C.: Intervention, treatment, and prevention strategies to address opioid use disorders in rural areas: a primer on opportunities for medicaid-safety net collaboration (2016). https://www.nashp.org/wp-content/uploads/2016/09/Rural-Opioid-Primer.pdf
14. Daly, S.R., Seifert, C.M., Yilmaz, S., Gonzalez, R.: Comparing ideation techniques for beginning designers. J. Mech. Design **138**(10) (2016). https://doi.org/10.1115/1.4034087
15. Dirin, A., Laine, T.H.: User experience in mobile augmented reality: emotions, challenges, opportunities and best practices. Computers **7**(2) (2018). https://doi.org/10.3390/computers7020033

16. Centers for Disease Control. Prevention: CDC's efforts to prevent opioid overdoses and other opioid-related harms (2021). https://www.cdc.gov/opioids/framework/index.html

17. Ferreri, F., Bourla, A., Mouchabac, S., Karila, L.: e-Addictology: an overview of new technologies for assessing and intervening in addictive behaviors. Front. Psychiatry 51 (2018)

18. Florence, C., Luo, F., Rice, K.: The economic burden of opioid use disorder and fatal opioid overdose in the united states. Drug Alcohol Depend. **218** (2021). https://doi.org/10.1016/j.drugalcdep.2020.108350

19. Goldfine, C., Lai, J.T., Lucey, E., Newcomb, M., Carreiro, S.: Wearable and wireless mHealth technologies for substance use disorder. Curr. Addict. Rep. 1–10 (2020)

20. Hartzler, A.L., BlueSpruce, J., Catz, S.L., McClure, J.B.: Prioritizing the mHealth design space: a mixed-methods analysis of smokers' perspectives. JMIR mHealth uHealth **4**(3), e5742 (2016)

21. Hone-Blanchet, A., Wensing, T., Fecteau, S.: The use of virtual reality in craving assessment and cue-exposure therapy in substance use disorders. Front. Human Neurosci **8**, 844 (2014)

22. Maramba, I., Arunangsu Chatterjee, C.N.: Methods of usability testing in the development of ehealth applications: a scoping review. Int. J. Med. Inf. **126**(10), 95–104 (2019). https://doi.org/10.1016/j.ijmedinf.2019.03.018

23. Isaac Vaghefi, B.T.: The continued use of mobile health apps: insights from a longitudinal study. Ann. Behav. Med. **7** (2019). https://doi.org/10.2196/12983

24. Nielsen, J.: How to conduct a heuristic evaluation (1994). https://www.nngroup.com/articles/how-to-conduct-a-heuristic-evaluation/

25. Nielsen, J.: Severity ratings for usability problems (1994). https://www.nngroup.com/articles/how-to-rate-the-severity-of-usability-problems/

26. Nielsen, J.: 10 usability heuristics for user interface design (2020). https://www.nngroup.com/articles/ten-usability-heuristics/

27. Wang, K., Varma, D.S., Prosperi, M.: A systematic review of the effectiveness of mobile apps for monitoring and management of mental health symptoms or disorders. JMIR Mhealth Uhealth **7**(4) (2019). https://doi.org/10.2196/11831

28. Lin, Y.-T., Hertzum, M.: How do designers make user-experience design decisions? In: Marcus, A., Rosenzweig, E. (eds.) HCII 2020. LNCS, vol. 12200, pp. 188–198. Springer, Cham (2020). https://doi.org/10.1007/978-3-030-49713-2_13

29. Marcolino, M.S., Oliveira, J.A.Q., D'Agostino, M., Ribeiro, A.L., Alkmim, M.B.M., Novillo-Ortiz, D.: The impact of mhealth interventions: systematic review of systematic reviews. JMIR mHealth uHealth **6**(1), e8873 (2018). https://doi.org/10.2196/mhealth.8873

30. Marcolino, M.S., Oliveira, J.A., D'Agostino, M., Ribeiro, A.L., Alkmim, M.B., Novillo-Ortiz, D.: The impact of mhealth interventions: Systematic review of systematic reviews. JMIR mHealth uHealth **6**(1) (2018). https://doi.org/10.2196/mhealth.8873

31. Marsch, L.A.: Digital health and addiction. Curr. Opin. Syst. Biol. **20**, 1–7 (2020)

32. Messner, E.M., Probst, T., O'Rourke, T., Stoyanov, S., Baumeister, H.: Mhealth applications: potentials, limitations, current quality and future directions. Stud. Neurosci. Psychol. Behav. Econ. 235–248 (2019). https://doi.org/10.1007/978-3-030-31620-4_15

33. Miles, R., Hamilton, K.: Learning UML 2.0: A Pragmatic Introduction to UML. O'Reilly Media (2006)

34. Moore, B.A., et al.: Cognitive behavioral therapy improves treatment outcomes for prescription opioid users in primary care buprenorphine treatment. J. Substan. Abuse Treat. **71**, 54–57 (2016). https://doi.org/10.1016/j.jsat.2016.08.016

35. Moquillaza, A., Falconi, F., Paz, F.: Redesigning a main menu ATM interface using a user-centered design approach aligned to design thinking: a case study. In: Marcus, A., Wang, W. (eds.) HCII 2019. LNCS, vol. 11586, pp. 522–532. Springer, Cham (2019). https://doi.org/10.1007/978-3-030-23535-2_38

36. Nahum-Shani, I., et al.: Just-in-time adaptive interventions (JITAIS) in mobile health: key components and design principles for ongoing health behavior support. Ann. Behav. Med. **52**(6), 446–462 (2017). https://doi.org/10.1007/s12160-016-9830-8

37. National Institute of Drug Abuse. Opioid overdose crisis (2021). https://nida.nih.gov/drug-topics/opioids/opioid-overdose-crisis

38. Nguyen, C., Chernew, M., Ostrer, I., Beaulieu, N.: Comparison of healthcare delivery systems in low-and high-income communities. Am. J. Account. Care **7**(4), 11–8 (2019)

39. Nielsen Norman Group. Design thinking 101 (2016). https://www.nngroup.com/articles/design-thinking/

40. Nuamah, J., Mehta, R., Sasangohar, F.: Technologies for opioid use disorder management: mobile app search and scoping review. JMIR Mhealth Uhealth **8** (2020). https://doi.org/10.2196/15752

41. Nurgalieva, L., O'Callaghan, D., Doherty, G.: Security and privacy of mHealth applications: a scoping review. IEEE Access **8**, 104247–104268 (2020)

42. Ostrowski, S., Rolczyński, R., Pniewska, J., Garnik, I.: User-friendly e-learning platform: a case study of a design thinking approach use. Assoc. Comput. Mach. (2015). https://doi.org/10.1145/2814464.2814483

43. Patel, K., Bunachita, S., Agarwal, A.A., Lyon, A., Patel, U.K.: Opioid use disorder: treatments and barriers. Cureus (2021). https://doi.org/10.7759/cureus.13173

44. Roberts, J.C., Headleand, C., Ritsos, P.D.: Sketching designs using the five design-sheet methodology. IEEE Trans. Visual. Comput. Graph. **22**(1), 419–428 (2016). https://doi.org/10.1109/TVCG.2015.2467271

45. Siricharoen, W.V.: Using empathy mapping in design thinking process for personas discovering. In: Vinh, P.C., Rakib, A. (eds.) ICCASA/ICTCC -2020. LNICST, vol. 343, pp. 182–191. Springer, Cham (2021). https://doi.org/10.1007/978-3-030-67101-3_15

46. Stawarz, K., Preist, C., Tallon, D., Wiles, N., Coyle, D.: User experience of cognitive behavioral therapy apps for depression: an analysis of app functionality and user reviews. J. Med. Internet Res. **20**(6) (2018)

47. Suzianti, A., Arrafah, G.: User interface redesign of dental clinic ERP system using design thinking: a case study, pp. 193–197. Association for Computing Machinery (2019). https://doi.org/10.1145/3364335.3364369

48. The Secretary of Health and Human Services. Renewal of determination that a public health emergency exists (2018). https://www.cms.gov/About-CMS/Agency-Information/Emergency/Downloads/PHE-Declaration-USVI-Maria-9-11-2018.pdf

49. Tofighi, B., Chemi, C., Ruiz-Valcarcel, J., Hein, P., Hu, L.: Smartphone apps targeting alcohol and illicit substance use: Systematic search in in commercial app stores and critical content analysis. JMIR Mhealth Uhealth **7**(4) (2019). https://doi.org/10.2196/11831

50. Tofighi, B., Chemi, C., Ruiz-Valcarcel, J., Hein, P., Hu, L.: Smartphone apps targeting alcohol and illicit substance use: systematic search in in commercial app stores and critical content analysis. JMIR mHealth uHealth **7**(4), e11831 (2019)
51. Vaghefi, I., Tulu, B.: The continued use of mobile health apps: insights from a longitudinal study. JMIR Mhealth Uhealth **7**(8), e12983 (2019). https://doi.org/10.2196/12983
52. Wang, T., et al.: The impact of gamification-induced users' feelings on the continued use of mHealth apps: a structural equation model with the self-determination theory approach. J. Med. Internet Res. **23**(8), e24546 (2021). https://doi.org/10.2196/24546
53. World Health Organization. Opioid overdose (2021). https://www.who.int/newsroom/fact-sheets/detail/opioid-overdose
54. Xu, W., Liu, Y.: mHealthapps: a repository and database of mobile health apps. JMIR mHealth uHealth **3**(1), e28 (2015). https://doi.org/10.2196/mhealth.4026

Experiences in the Design of Localized eHealth Tools for Users Facing Inequality of Access to Healthcare

Juan Jimenez Garcia[1]([⊠]), Carlos Castilla[2], Javier Aguirre[2], Juan Pablo Martinez[3], and Wei Liu[4]

[1] School of Industrial Design, Carleton University, Ottawa K1S5B6, Canada
juanjimenezgarcia@cunet.carleton.ca
[2] Department of Design and Innovation, Universidad ICESI, 760031 Cali, Colombia
{carlosco96,jaaguirre}@icesi.edu.co
[3] Fundación Valle del Lili, 760026 Cali, Colombia
[4] Beijing Normal University, Beijing 100875, China
wei.liu@bnu.edu.cn

Abstract. In Colombia, making healthcare accessible to all as a basic human right poses a myriad of challenges. The rising prevalence of chronic non-communicable conditions in the growing population of elderly patients, have led to a healthcare paradigm where home-based care and self-management have become cornerstones. At the same time, as a geographically diverse and tropical country with a high prevalence of vector-borne and infectious diseases, there's a large amount of population at risk that still faces access barriers to healthcare. Thus, Colombia's health profile encompasses a series of scenarios in need of innovative solutions to deliver healthcare to its population regardless of access, literacy and/or economic barriers. New approaches such as Human-Computer Interaction for Development (HCI4D), have highlighted the need for a localized way of building digital solutions to properly function in a resource constrained context. This paper focuses on sharing reflections on the design methodology and implementation of two eHealth prototypes in different settings within Colombia using a localized approach and user-centered analysis of patient's context in urban and rural settings. We have identified that although a highly situated analysis is a valuable design practice for health technologies for the Global South, there should be also considered how contextual and individual factors are intertwined to maximize the use of human resources, relationships and social structures in the communities that the technologies are intended to serve. We aim to extend the limited body of knowledge about the in-the-wild development of patient-centric personal health technologies for vulnerable communities in Latin America.

Keywords: HCI4D · Patient-driven design · eHealth · Localized design

1 Introduction and Motivation

Providing accessible healthcare as a right for Colombia's population faces a diverse set of challenges, especially in its ongoing process of changing trends between disease

M. M. Soares et al. (Eds.): HCII 2022, LNCS 13322, pp. 130–148, 2022.
https://doi.org/10.1007/978-3-031-05900-1_8

and mortality patterns. The past 50 years have shown a rise of an active population (15 to 64 years), leading us to think that life expectancy will continue rising, following same trends it has for the last half a century [1]. Therefore, prevalence of chronic non-communicable diseases on the adult population has risen to the point that when "analyzing general morbidity in Colombia, they occupy the first place as main causes of health services use" [2]. At the same time, while this holds true, it is important to note the fact that "given the geographical location of Colombia and the characteristics of a tropical country, Colombia has a high prevalence of vector-borne diseases" [2]. Hence, according to Padilla et al. [3], the magnitude of this type of diseases turns them into a primary concern for public health in urban and rural areas, where nearly 12 million people live near endemic zones.

Both scenarios are just a part of the myriad of situations that constitute Colombia's health profile, making it a deeply diverse one. Therefore, it encompasses a series of situations from urban to rural settings in geographically diverse territories, where violence, gaps in access to healthcare and inequality are still present [1]. Hence, Colombia's profile could benefit from the development of innovative solutions to deliver healthcare regardless of access, literacy and/or economic barriers elderly, impoverished and vulnerable populations might face.

In this light, trends in healthcare have highlighted how digital technologies have proven to be effective at "disease control, telemedicine, improving doctors' efficiency, offering low-cost diagnostics, improving data collection, and providing patient management tools" [4]. Therefore, a plausible way forward to improve healthcare in Global South countries, such as Colombia, is to "encourage the development and use of health technologies that can benefit the poorest people in the world" [5]. Nevertheless, previous efforts in the implementation of health technologies in the Global South "falter due to simplistic assumptions about end user preferences and activities, or because large-scale implementations are far more complex" [6]. Even though digital technologies are useful in alleviating these issues, it still begs the question of how implementations are perceived useful and used by users in context within Colombia's most vulnerable populations living in resource-constrained settings.

When it comes to the adaptation of technical systems that have been initially developed in and for different contexts than those of the Global South, there is a need for a deep understanding of the user, his experiences, and his context so the risk of implementation failure is lessened [7]. As cases of donation of second-hand or surplus devices have shown, in low income countries technologies from high-income countries are often deployed in these settings without enough thought of the consequences, and such technologies might rapidly become useless [5].

As is currently happening within countries in the Global South, experiencing an ever-growing technological penetration, technical and cultural factors have raised questions about Human-Computer Interaction (HCI) research practices [7–9]. Global South approaches to technology development such as Human-Computer Interaction for Development (HCI4D), deeply embedded in the principles of socially situatedness carried around by a third wave of HCI [10], emphasizes the phenomenological dimensions of its practice calling for an understanding of "the situated cultures and contexts in which people give meaning to and adopt practices with digital technologies as part of their everyday lives" [11]. Therefore, this indicates the need for localization for health technologies to properly fit and function in cultural and social contexts that differ from the Global North. Hence, the need for a localized and user-centered analysis of patient's context, in urban and rural settings, are in principle key scopes for health technology design for the Global South in resource constrained settings.

This paper focuses on sharing our experiences, challenges, and limitations gathered from two case studies where initial prototypes were created for a vulnerable urban and rural communities experiencing inequality of access to healthcare in Colombia. For each case study, we describe the specific motivations, the elements of the design process, the functional features of the prototypes, and the experiences with the initial attempts at deployment.

The first case study describes the development of RIHAG, a system to empower Total Hip Replacement (THR) patients in post-surgical rehabilitation process living in slums in Cali, Colombia; the second describes CURACAO, a system for supporting adherence to an antiparasitic medication for Cutaneous Leishmaniasis (CL) patients in Tumaco, Nariño, a common infection in the tropical areas, including the coastal regions of Colombia. Based on the experiences gained with these two projects, we acknowledge that effective solutions for the Global South necessitate a contextualized approach, however for vulnerable, low socioeconomical status communities, the perceived usefulness and use value of digital solutions are highly related to the challenges they confront within their structural social and economic inequalities. In line with [12], these challenges hinder their motivation and experiences towards digital solutions since their priorities are determined by the demands of their daily life and the characteristics of the community, such as low level of employment, low literacy, very low penetration of technology, and lack of safety—that present important (and difficult) constraints for the development, implementation and use of technological health solutions. We aim to extend the lack of body of knowledge for Latin American countries, about the development of localized, in-the-wild health informatics for vulnerable communities.

2 RIHAG: Personal Informatics as a Tool for Empowerment in Elderly Vulnerable Patients

Improvements in the medical field have provided a way to transition acute diseases into chronic conditions, increasing the amount of elderly and chronic patients in systems around the world, thereby privileging a patient-driven approach [13] since the type of care for this population "is now one that requires long term, low intensity, continual care". This is consistent with a trend where practices such as early discharge and shorter hospitalization are strategies that have been adopted to solve the high demand for hospitalization [14] and bed overcrowding [15]. This shift, deeply impacts the type of care that will be required to better patient's quality of life, provide a safe and successful recovery and protect patient's emotional wellness.

As these practices become more commonplace, barriers arise where poor data recollection, doctor-patient communication and clinical assistance continuity seem jeopardized, resulting in a lesser quality of patient control [19]. Even though they seem like an ideal solution for the recovery process of patients and the increasing demand for health-care systems, meant to reduce the cost of hospitalizations as well as improve quality of life and recovery by allowing patients to live more independently with less risk of infections [20, 21], this situation has given rise to increasing number of patients in charge of their rehabilitation processes. In turn, affecting patient's emotional and physical well-being by creating an emotional load due to the incredible amount of responsibility the patient must assume on his behalf [14].

With this in mind, there is a "worldwide trend to move patients out of clinical set-tings for them to self-manage health conditions at home with medical technology" [21]. Therefore, digital technologies have emerged as a plausible way forward that can provide support to home-based care issues derived from early discharge scenarios. For instance, Personal Informatics (PI) have demonstrated to be useful as a tool that, through self-reflection and data collection [22], have proven to be useful to promote empowerment [23], therapy adherence [13] and behavioral change [24].

2.1 Motivation

The rising population of elderly citizens (50 years and up) seems to be a trend in Latin American countries [16]. In Colombia's case, for example, $10'913.693$ (22%) of its citizens are now 50 years or older and 7.037.283 (14%) surpasses the 65-year-old mark [17]. The ageing of the population and increasing prevalence of disability and chronic illness in the elderly population will translate in a higher rate of hospitalization of elderly population and elder abandonment representing higher healthcare spending for the Colombian health system [1, 18]. This also has a deep impact in the rise of trends in patient-driven healthcare, in the light of the inherent challenges to a system where there's a rising demand for care of patients suffering from chronic conditions. Hence, the country is no exception when it comes to be a part of this epidemiological transition where home-based care, self-management and early discharge will become regular.

In a recent study [43], it is concluded that despite Colombian's improvements in healthcare insurance programs, an equal provision of healthcare to older adults is still not guaranteed and it poses a particular challenge, especially for preventive and out-patient care. The digital barrier for elderly population, where learning how technology works and how to use it implies a big challenge for this population [44]. Although Colombia has improved the internet penetration [45], in rural areas and low socioeco-nomic communities, access remains challenging. With the aforementioned challenges, a team of interaction design researchers from Universidad Icesi and health practition-ers from the Orthopaedic Department of the Fundación Valle del Lili, formed a 1-year research project to explore design opportunities of technology-based solutions for urban communities facing inequality of access to healthcare.

2.2 Case Study: Total Hip and Knee Replacement Recovery Process

The goal of this study was to explore strategies to empower urban, Low Socioeconomic Status (Low SES) elderly patients to self-manage the recovery process of Total Hip (THR) and Knee Replacement (TKR) surgeries. THR and TKR procedures are becoming more commonplace in developing countries, as the population of elders grows and there are improvements in medical care [25], in Colombia THR and TKR surgeries are being performed at a rate of up to 10.000 per year [26]. This trend raises concerns regarding the need for self-management of the rehabilitation process in an ongoing shift to a patient-driven paradigm where early discharge scenarios and ambulatory surgery are also becoming more relevant, especially in patients that face economic and access barriers. Considering how difficult and scarce are the opportunities for such patients to schedule appointments with physicians and begin physical therapy right after surgery, there's a need to address the in-home rehabilitation process.

2.3 Methodological Approach

The design of an assistive tool for this target population is challenging from the technological and design perspective in terms of understanding and identifying the complexity of patients' sociocultural context. It is worth nothing that all participants came from low socioeconomic statuses, unemployed, and faced access and economic barriers; also, some of them being illiterate and with little to no access to digital technology. A user-centered and "design in the wild" approaches [46] were taken to address this challenging context. The methods implemented comprised in-depth interviews, contextual inquiry, Wizard of Oz, roleplay and performance ethnography.

As highlighted by Toyama [27], as do ICT4D projects, the first phase involved an ethnographic work due to the deep analysis of meaning, motivation, and overall situated lived experiences of THR and TKR patients. An initial phase of context understanding was carried out using in-depth interviews (n = 4, >45 min each) with volunteer elderly patients (65+, 2 males, 2 females) residing in urban marginalized neighborhoods, living in a single-family home, unemployed, who were under rehabilitation process; and semi-structured interviews with surgeons (n = 2, >30 min each) and physiotherapists (n = 2, >30 min each). With the goal in mind of creating a prototype that fitted not just the user's needs, but that also was usable under a specific social and cultural context, the user relationship with technology was also explored (see Fig. 1). In this case, a contextual inquiry (n = 4, >320 min each) was further needed to become familiar with the user's device ecology and their familiarity with digital and analog technologies. This was especially useful in the sense that addressed the fact that the patients where technologically illiterate. All interviews were audio recorded and transcribed. This data was coded and analyzed using Grounded Theory techniques. This information was later complemented with the qualitative material collected by the contextual inquiry method.

2.4 Design Development

One of the most valuable insight gathered through interviews and contextual inquiry, suggested that elderly' preferences towards technology are close related to the analog radio, the TV's remote control and the landline telephone, pieces of technology commonly used and known by all these users (see Fig. 2). Therefore, the team used the morphological characteristics of these devices as a design principle for the prototypes' interface and form factor. The team developed in total three prototypes: two low-resolution design concepts that were iteratively tested with two elderly patients (65+, 2 males), and one fully-functional prototype tested in the field with three elderly THR and TKR patients

(65+, 2 males, 1 female) for five days immediately after hospital discharge. These patients were volunteers recruited by the Ortopheadic Department of Fundación Valle del Lili.

Fig. 1. Early field work in patient's homes.

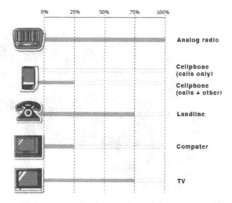

Fig. 2. Percentages corresponding to the presence of devices in patients' homes.

Methods such as Wizard of Oz and roleplay were used to validate the sequence of use for the two initial design iterations. However, the team found out that these methods fell short to introduce digital devices for users that don't own or have previous experience using digital technology since their previous relation with technological devices is little to none. Therefore, following the work of Medhi and Toyama [29], when designing for first time and semiliterate users, the use of full context videos of the use of the prototypes in a real-life situation was presented similarly manner to a Latino soap opera; a largely common and familiar format to this user segment. Additionally, in-depth interviews were performed for each design iteration to collect data about users' opinions and experiences after using the prototypes.

Within the qualitative information collected from the specialists, it was informed that there is a lack of tools to understand patients' recovery process beyond the functional progress, making it a blind spot for practitioners to know the patients' emotional experiences of recovery, especially when this process happens far away from the hospital. As stated by [47], here is limited time for clinicians to educate patients and to follow-up their progress during the early stages of recovery. This adds an extra load to the psychological and emotional state of patients creating an environment of fear and uncertainty for the patients who might forget or misunderstand spoken information, or they might not get all their questions answered. Then, the research team defined that facilitating self-collection of emotional experiences and self-management of potential questions risen during recovery are two functional aspects of the proposed solution.

RIHAG is an informative tool that aims to empower elderly patients to self-manage their recovery process by providing timely, on spot information when questions and concerns regarding the rehabilitation process are prompted by the patient (see Fig. 3). This tool uses a familiar interface for reliable and easy information retrieval, using metaphor analog elements such as knobs, dials, color codes and number pads for selecting emotional states and question navigation. Without the need for an internet connection, such questions are retrieved from an in-built pool of a pre-defined questions drawn by patients (n = 2) and validated by experienced specialists (n = 3) and physiotherapists (n = 2). In total 45 recurrent questions were categorized in 5 dimensions: Diagnosis – Rehabilitation – Physical restrictions – Social life – Surgery procedure.

Fig. 3. RIHAG. Left, 3D modeling. Right, functional prototype.

RIHAG's interface performs a linear sequence of steps where, through questions and prompts, the device asks about the user's emotional states at fixed hours (8:00 h, 12:00 h, 16:00 h and 20:00 h). Then, the device collects data about four pre-defined emotional states [23]. Since all participants resided in single-family homes and lived with at least one caregiver, this data was used as a part of a family informatics strategy [27], where the caregiver, and later with the physician, have access to this information. This provides a way to collectively engage in sense-making of patterns to change habits and improve overall patient's wellbeing despite physical presence. To achieve this, a mobile application was developed to pair RIHAG with the caregiver's and physician's smartphones. Due to reasons of low presence of Wi-Fi accessibility in patients' home, the device needs to be plugged into a device connected to the internet network. When RIHAG is connected the application displays detailed information about the patient's emotional journey and questions made to the device.

2.5 Evaluation, Encountered Challenges and Opportunities

The design development involved usability tests (n = 3) carried out in low fidelity prototypes, seeking out to establish a consensus with the patients about the interface and the usage (see Fig. 4). The final stage of this testing process was carried out in a fully-functional 3D printed prototype that used Arduino and several components for the patients to interact and register data. The entire evaluation process faced several challenges due to the socio-economic characteristics of these communities, since access to patients and their homes was difficult due to safety concerns, especially in some neighborhoods where crime rates are high.

Fig. 4. User testing with early RIHAG concepts.

Also, ethical concerns, availability, and willingness of patients played a big part in the difficulties in testing the prototypes. It was found that building a common space of mutuality is an important aspect for researchers to engage with participants. With a sense of empathy and active listening, the researchers spent days building enough trust: *"I don't believe the healthcare provided is making efforts to help people like me... Are you one of them?"* [P2]. However, once this trust was built researchers found participants very engaged with the study. This is because elderly patients and caregivers were curious about this technology: *"I want to see what kind of apparatus you will bring next week"* [Caregiver1]. Most of the patients expressed concerns regarding their participation in the study. They felt that by participating (sharing their opinions and experiences), retaliations would come and affect the limited healthcare service they receive: *"If I sign up this consent, they will come later and cancel my appointments"* [P3].

Nonetheless, the final test was carried on three THR and TKR patients. They used the device for five consecutive days, where a SD card registered data entry in a CSV file for later analysis. For this test, the prototype needed to be plugged into an electrical socket. This led the patients to plug and unplug the device several times causing problems within the system. Nevertheless, tests showed that patients understood the interface and were able to use the device. For example, one prototype recorded the emotion "anger" while registering a pre-recorded question asked, followed next day by more positive self-reported emotions such as "calm": *"How long will the pain from the surgery last?"* [P2]. Another prototype registered a sequence of negative self-reported emotions, while the questions made were about pain and healing the wound: *"How long will the wound take to heal?"* [P1]. The value of the device was expressed by two of the participants

[P1, P2], when they found useful information regarding their recovery process: *"Does the weather affect my pain?"* [P1]; *"What is a hip replacement?"* [P2].

In particular, one of the participants [P3] was very skeptical and critical about the device. His attitude towards the recovery was more about his social role as a male, leaving behind the need for a technology device to assist his process. Caregivers, most of them patients' sons and grandchildren, played an active role during the test of RIHAG. They encouraged patients to know more about their process by presenting the data through the mobile application. As a younger generation, their inherent curiosity in technology catalyzed the use of this family informatic device.

While the trial time with the device was short, and not all the functionalities were tested, such as presenting the data to the medical team, the collected information through user feedback showed that patients understood the interface and some patients made active use of the device. By a using a contextualized approach, elderly and technological illiterate patients were able to use the interface successfully with minimum training. Therefore, this suggest an opportunity for empowerment, possibly alleviating barriers in access to information about good practices in their rehabilitation. Additionally, there is important data that indicates a correlation between emotional states and questions asked. As a prototype in its early stage, much research is needed to perform longer trials and tests, leading to future iterations.

3 CURACAO: A Tool for Patients to Self-Manage the Treatment of Leishmaniasis in Low Access Areas

Leishmaniasis is a parasitic disease transmitted through the bites of infected female phlebotomine sandflies, which feed on blood to produce eggs [48]. The different forms of Leishmaniasis are a widespread public health problem in the Americas due to their high prevalence, mainly affecting those who face economic and access barriers to health care. As a group of tropical diseases, Leishmaniasis has several clinical manifestations, being Cutaneous Leishmaniasis (CL) the most frequent form of this disease accounting for 98% of the 10,743 newly registered cases of Leishmaniasis in 2016 [33]. It causes skin lesions, mainly ulcers, on exposed parts of the body, leaving life-long scars and serious disability or stigma [48].

As a high burden and endemic vector-borne disease, Leishmaniasis poses an inherent challenge to public health, especially to rural vulnerable populations facing access and economic barriers. This is in line with the fact that low socioeconomic status, malnutrition, and population mobility are major risk factors [34]; where poor housing and domestic sanitary conditions are present factors that may increase sand-fly breeding. This seems to be consistent with statistics revealed by Colombia's National Institute of Health (INS) on the 2018 report on leishmaniasis [35], showing how 65% (4151) of registered cases of CL were patients that belonged to the subsidized regime and 79,2% (5010) came from rural areas.

3.1 Motivation

In Colombia, the incidence of Leishmaniasis is high and exceeds 12,000 cases per year [30], showing a growing tendency until 2016 when it plateaued [31], in 2018 there was a decrease of 18% (1377) in cases contrast with the year prior (6319) [32]. According to Colombia's Ministry of Health [32], Leishmaniasis is an endemic pathology in almost all the country where an estimated 11 million people are at risk of transmission; especially those living in rural areas. There is a high prevalence of CL in the pacific coast areas of Colombia (see Fig. 5) in the south and mid-western regions of the country [35]. This part of the country comprehends a "highly contrasting region that evidences challenging gaps arising or deriving from armed conflict, low education and health coverage, inadequate infrastructure, insecurity, and unemployment" [36]. This makes the region more vulnerable to vector-borne diseases and highlights how the high mortality and mobility rates due to vector-borne diseases are aggravated due by social, political, and economic factors, such as deficient living conditions, malnourishment, and poor vector control, as is the case with the department of Chocó [37].

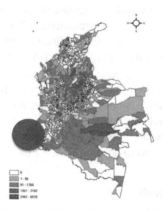

Fig. 5. Cutenous Leismaniasis cases in Colombia.

Paired with the socioeconomic factors surrounding Leishmaniasis, the detection and treatment of LC also become a challenge in these areas. Even though 90% of the population living on the pacific coast is affiliated under Colombia's general health programs, there are barriers impeding effective access to healthcare such as a "lack of health centers, human resources, resources for transfer patients from rural areas, amongst other" [38]. The challenge is bigger considering that the recommended treatments for LC cause adherence problems since they are expensive, have long durations, cardiotoxic, hepatoxic, and can also cause pancreatitis, leukopenia, thrombocytopenia, arthralgia, and myalgia [39]. Therefore, for patients to access treatment administered by a professional represents costs and time that impair the patient to seek treatment and complete successful treatment. Thus, this situation could benefit from innovative solutions that can help patient's adherence with treatment, regardless of the access barriers that they must face in order to access health care services.

Our team partnered up with Centro Internacional de Investigaciones Médicas (CIDEIM) and took the vulnerable populations suffering from LC living in the area of Tumaco, Nariño as a case study. Specifically, this area is classified ecologically as a humid tropical rain forest where most human residences are constructed on wooden platforms with wooden walls and zinc or thatch roofs, being an active CL transmission zone that has been the site of multidisciplinary research by the CIDEIM [40].

Access to treatment faces multiple barriers. Being the application of Glucantime® or pentavalent antimonials the first line of treatment recommended by health authorities [39], this approach requires a health professional in order to apply an injection for up to 20 days. Thus, patients living in nearby areas must travel to the health center in order to seek a complete treatment. This situation poses a myriad of problems to poor villagers who can't afford the expenses of accommodations and travel in order to complete their treatment successfully.

With this in mind, CIDEIM has pursued a strategy where the use of Miltefosine®, an oral medication, has been considered as an alternative strategy to the treatments mentioned above. By suggesting a strategy known as DOTS (Directly Observed Treatment, Short-course), proven useful in the treatment of tuberculosis and HIV treatment [41], coupled with this treatment, they seek to alleviate the access barriers. As this new approach requires major cooperation with the treatment, calling for the daily intake of a pill for 28 days, and the DOTS strategies calls for direct observation of patients, CIDEIM trained members of the community appointing them as community leaders. Since there are no medical centers near the area, these leaders serve as accountability partners, monitoring the patients' progress. This strategy allows the community to be more connected to health centers in urban Tumaco, since CIDEIM have provided the community leaders with smartphones and resources to travel and pick up medicine for the treatment and bring skin samples from patients. Even though there's no stable access to an internet connection, there are future plans to develop tools for the diagnostic of Leishmaniasis.

3.2 Methodological Approach

Due to safety concerns, the geographical location of the rural communities, and ethical considerations when directly assessing patients, a decision was made in order to collect qualitative information from community leaders in urban Tumaco. Using semi-structured interviews (n = 8, female), our team was able to gather information about the affected communities, knowledge about lived experiences of patients, and the leaders' experiences within the training program provided by CIDEIM. Additionally, the team was immersed in the training program, insights were gained in how the sample collection process was carried out and the tools that they already used for overseeing patients' progress (see Fig. 6). During 3 days, our team was able to talk and get to know their stories and the actual situation of guerrilla warfare in the communities they lived and visited. This information was later turned into insights for the design process using Grounded Theory, which revealed valuable insights about perceptions, feelings, myths, prejudices of patients toward LC and the treatment. Last, but not least, our team enquired about the use of technology and access to energy, phone, internet, and weather conditions, in order to gather design parameters for the proposed solution.

Fig. 6. 3-Day immersion with community leaders in CIDEIM training sessions.

3.3 Design Development

Considering the data collected in the fieldwork, where constraints regarding the limited to nonexistent access to energy supply, internet, and digital technology, the design was oriented in order for the prototype to be nondependent of any existing energy network, digital or analog technology in the area. Also, the materials used for the final prototype had to be durable due to humid weather, and light in order for the prototype to be easily carried around. These determinants lead lto five design iterations where different form factors were considered for the solution to effectively store the dose of Miltefosine®, easily remind the patient of its daily intake, give the ability to report contingencies, give feedback to patients and inform of their progress to the community leaders and CIDEIM. These design iterations were discussed with epidemiologists (n = 2) from CIDEM and community leaders (n = 2) through semi-structured interviews.

After these concepts were assessed and qualified, an initial prototype was built and tested with urban patients under treatment with poly medication (n = 2; 1 male, 1 female), with a similar pill intake routine. They used the prototype for five consecutive days. This decision was taken to facilitate the users' recruitment and avoid risky traveling, as we were alerted by possible public disorder in rural areas in Tumaco. Later, a workshop with 17 specialists from CIDEIM with high experience in field research, was organized to discuss and debate the functional and non-functional characteristics of the prototype. The final prototype, CURACAO (see Fig. 7), is a medication kit backpack that seeks to ease patients' adherence process to the Miltefosine® treatment by simplifying the monitoring and self-administered drug intake process of patients suffering from CL in scattered rural settlements. As a backpack, it aims to enable its portability when community leaders are delivering this device to the patients' homes. Once the patient receives it, he/she has the possibility of hanging out the backpack to the palafito's structure (stilt houses), since these constructions lack clean and clear horizontal surfaces. Three main columns representing morning, afternoon, and night doses, contain small plastic containers, each one storing one single dose. The containers can be removed and opened for immediate consumption or transported in the pocket for later intake outside the home.

The form factor is inspired by the shape of a Cocoa pod and a Cununo, both a typical fruit and instrument used locally in the Pacific Coast of Colombia (see Fig. 8). This particular shape aims to bring familiar features such as the way to open it, collect pills as seeds, and the way the fruit hang on the tree.

Fig. 7. Left, backpack prototype. Center, afternoon doses column. Right-top, collecting a single dose. Right-center, storing empty container. Right-bottom, self-reporting adverse side-effects.

CURACAO is based on the DOTS strategy, helping the community leader to better oversee the treatment progress. As such, the approach used by this tool leverages the potential of human infrastructures [42] such as the communal leader in order for the tool to function within the context of the community. Thus, it allows both the patient, communal leader, and CIDEIM to share information about how the patient treatment was carried out.

Fig. 8. CURACAO form factor concept, modeled after a Cocoa pod and a Cununo.

While this tool seeks to help the patient adherence to treatment, it also serves the purpose of making easier the data collection process regarding the patient's treatment. Therefore, this prototype uses an Arduino mini pro, a speaker, a digital clock, a Micro SD reader, and an RFID sensor that collects information about the patient schedule for using the treatment, possible adverse effects, and function as an alarm that reminds the patient when to take the medicine. With the RFID sensor placed in the back pocket, where the empty containers are stored, the RFID tags placed under the containers are detected and they register the ID for the patient, timestamp, and possible adverse effects. By means of using electronic components, that did not depend on an internet connection, the process of overseeing should become easier and more reliable than existing forms used currently by community leaders to register the patient progress. The results are automatically stored in a micro SD chip that codifies the data in a CSV for later analysis.

3.4 Evaluation, Encountered Challenges and Opportunities

Costs, system reliability, access, and availability of patients were major setbacks for the trials. Additionally, the team found frequent safety concerns about the armed actors in the territory making this task a very difficult one. The situation regarding the law in these communities is one where armed conflict is still happening in their territories, and so a feasible way to interact with these populations is through the community leader.

In total three tests were carried out with CURACAO. Initial eligibility for this study required that participants be <35, low SES, living in rural areas, and starting a LC treatment with Miltefosine®. However, due to limited access to the area and time constraints, only P1 (male, rural) was diagnosed with LC, while P2 (male, urban) with Lupus and P3 (female, urban) with depression were available for the study. Nonetheless, all three participants shared the same important characteristics: being under a long-term regime of dose intake, poor adaptation or irregularity to the treatment, and the need for the medication to improve their health. Each prototype was delivered to the patient's home, introduced, explained (10 min), and obtained consent. The study was designed to collect a total of 75 days of tests (P1 = 25, P2 = 25, P3 = 25), however, it was possible to collect only 14 days with P1 due to a technical failure and the time spent in delivering and returning the prototype from Tumaco. After the tests were completed, semi-structured interviews were conducted and recorded. The interviews consisted of questions regarding usability, durability, and usefulness. The SD cards were extracted and analyzed to find insights about data entry, system stability, data retrieval, dose intake behavior, and treatment adherence. For the purpose and extension of this paper, here we will focus on the qualitative dimensions of implementing this solution in the field and the user experience with the prototype.

At the introductory session, all participants welcomed the prototypes expressing positive compliance with the study. However, [P1] seemed to be particularly neutral with the study itself (noted that this participant is the one who fulfills entirely the target user: *"Ok... I have other priorities... but, let's see what do I have to do"*. Findings from the exit interviews provided insights on how participants experienced the system. All participants commented that CURACAO is intuitive, easy to use. The way the prototype arranges the plastic pill containers in morning/afternoon/night doses was a design factor valued by the participants: *"How to go wrong? Each column is a moment in the day and each container has a sticker with a symbol"* [P3]. Participants stated that sound reminders made it easier for them to comply with daily doses. However, technical failures occurred due to battery life and RFID reader, affected this feedback and consequently, affecting participants' behavior pattern. Early data analysis corroborates this behavior, particularly during the initial 6 days: *"Just right before going to bed, I noticed...no pills today. Later, I realized it was (the prototype) not making any sound"* [P3]; *"The bag stopped working... next day I said: did I take the pill?"* [P2]. Several technical failures with the prototype designated to P1 resulted in an incomplete data set. We infer that transportation and/or humid climate affected the data logging. Interestingly, P1, who initially showed low interest in the prototype, stated that its presence at home, size, and color, helped him to remember to take the pill. However, he was not fully aware of what dose was already taken and what follows: *"... too big (the prototype), somehow cumbersome, but it helped me to remember"* [P1].

Since access was limited due to geographical limitations and different technical issues were presented during the tests, longer trials are needed to collect more quantitative and qualitative data. Nevertheless, findings from the exit interviews provided insights on how participants experience the system and to what extend technical and design limitations affect the overall experience. This early work helped our team to envision opportunities where health technologies can alleviate the access gap to healthcare that these isolated communities face. Also, to consider that this tool could be helpful in the treatment of other diseases where patients need self-management afar from health centers and medical practitioners.

4 Discussion

RIHAG and CURACAO shed light on how electronic health solutions can be useful and powerful tools to empower patients facing socioeconomic barriers and limited access to timely healthcare services. Additionally, both case studies presented in this paper provided a view of the challenges to executing technology design projects in resource-constrained settings. As suggested by Best and Smyth [7] and Chetty and Grinter [8], both research and design experiences showed the imperative need for a situated analysis of the research methods and design process in the Global South. Building health technology through a localized approach rather than a universal one means that both the patient and his context should be true at the center of the design process. The patient was thought of as embedded in his context, and not detached from it at any time. Therefore, a situated analysis of the user in context was a useful and key asset in the design of prototypes that considered cultural, social, and other contextual factors.

As highlighted by Sambasivan and Smyth [42], the identification of human infrastructures and intermediated interaction was crucial for both the design and implementation of CURACAO and RIHAG. Therefore, communities and families were not overlooked, understanding the role that they have in the use of technology in developing regions. The development of both prototypes served as a vehicle to understand how, in resource constrained settings, communities and families become cornerstones playing a big role in the final solution.

Based on our experience, we identified that the characteristics of the end-user influence the deployment of design methods in the field. For instance, the design process of RIHAG involved the use of culturally adapted research methods to engage with patients and to facilitate a better understanding of usability and interactions. In line with Chavan [49], our work required researchers' sensitivity to identify the triggers that enable communication within the community. Latin American soap-operas (telenovelas) are a fundamental part of the local elderly's daily life, and for this reason, several videos using a telenovela's storyline were used in the field with the end-user. We also identified that the contextual factors shape and determined usability and form factors. The design of CURACAO responded to where and how the end-user lives. For instance, hanging the prototype on the palafito's wooden structure, the way of collecting and picking up pill doses are based on the shape of cacao fruit, design strategies to enrich the user's engagement with the device.

In the middle of the epidemiological and demographic shift of Colombia, electronic health devices can become tools for bridging the access gap for patients living in resource-constrained settings. Future projects alongside communities and families have the potential to alleviate inequalities that are inherent threats to patient's access to healthcare. Thus, technology design projects for Colombia's vulnerable and sensitive population should use a localized lens, where, by examining contextual and cultural factors, accessible and usable solutions can potentially improve the lives of patients and their communities. However, given the challenges of designing for the communities described in this work, the limitations related to access and fielding of the prototypes provided us with several reflections. One important question might be: How solutions for low-SES communities need to be developed?

The design process of digital healthcare solutions and its fieldwork alongside should strive for highly contextualized, unique solutions that best match the community's characteristics. But this approach should go beyond this. We argue that what researchers should be aiming for is not so much to solely develop individual solutions for different communities, but also to empower communities to design their own solutions. This approach introduces a shift where the "design for the user" had to be expanded and include a larger view into the "design with the user". The role of the researchers then becomes to train community members to devise their own solutions using the full range of community resources. Although such an approach has been implemented in other contexts, we acknowledge that a participatory-oriented approach with remote, high-sensitive, low-SES communities demands an acute revision on time constraints, limited resources, safety issues, and field-work logistics. The development of more holistic approaches towards ways of intertwining context, user participation, and technology design, becomes even more relevant in these communities because the socioeconomic context influences any design action or research decision.

Beyond the technical issues, one of the biggest challenges of deploying a longitudinal study with RIHAG and CURACAO in the field was to provide motivational mechanisms to keep participants active over time. Although both prototypes were welcomed by patients, interviews showed that after the first days, participants perceived pressure to use the devices. As mentioned by [50], "people simply stop using technologies that do not correspond in any way with their daily lives, habits, or rituals. In the end, the use of new technologies appears to be time-consuming and frustrating for all those involved" Therefore, one more question risen: How can we provide sustained usefulness for these kinds of technology-oriented solutions?

The results to date provided evidence that RIHAG and CURACAO match participants' sociodemographic characteristics. Both case studies provide knowledge that uncovers the interdependencies between the user's context, design, and research processes, where socioeconomic characteristics play a determinant factor in the design of solutions that fulfills user's needs. However, this might be only the first step towards a more integrated approach for designing for sensitive, low-SES communities. It is necessary to account for deeper aspects, such as agency, individual motivations, family values, psychological resources, and cultural norms. These aspects are fundamental settings for sustained and scalable digital design interventions. An integrated approach for low-SES communities should consider the interplay between socioeconomic and individual characteristics.

Future work includes the need for reducing production costs and more iterations and testing. Since both projects were just prototypes, the production costs were high, and in an implementation scenario that would not be feasible. Also, the need for further research and longer tests are required in order to obtain results that can be compared. Nevertheless, these experiences suggest the potential and benefit that localized solutions can bring. Even though these projects just addressed the adherence to treatment and the rehabilitation processes of TKR and THR, these experiences suggest that there is a need for further research addressing other health conditions where this type of tool could potentially empower users to improve their wellbeing.

5   Conclusion

This paper aims to share the experiences around the design and development of two prototypes addressing two important healthcare scenarios for sensitive patients in low socioeconomic status. We describe that research methods need to be adapted to the user's socioeconomic and cultural characteristics, and these same characteristics, influence the usability and form factor of proposed solutions. Based on the fieldwork, we state that effective solutions for the Global South necessitate highly contextualized, participatory-based, and value-oriented designs that consider the full range of constraints and resources in individual communities. Our next step is to fully implement and test these prototypes with the goal of alleviating and empowering patients in post-surgery rehabilitation and therapy adherence processes. Thereby, we aim to extend the body of knowledge in HCI about the development of personal health technologies for sensitive communities living in resource-constrained settings.

Acknowledgements. We want to thank the students and institutions involved in these two projects, K. Urango, D. Arenas, A. Quintero, and L. Ruiz; CIDEIM and Fundación Valle del Lili.

References

1. MINSALUD. Encuesta Nacional de Salud y Demografía (ENDS). National Survey of Health and Demography (2017)
2. World Health Organization (WHO). Primary Health Care Systems (PRIMASYS) (2017)
3. Padilla, J.C., Lizarazo, F.E., Murillo, O.L., Mendigaña, F.A., Pachón, E., Vera, M.J.: Epidemiología de las principales enfermedades transmitidas por vectores en Colombia, 1990–2016. Rev. Inst. Nacl. Salud. **37** (2017)
4. Bewer, E., et al.: The case for technology in developing regions. Computer **38**(6), 25–38 (2005)
5. Howitt, P., et al.: Technologies for global health. Lancet **380**(9840), 447–536 (2012)
6. Holeman, I., Kane, D.: Human-centered design for global health equity. Inf.. Technol. Develop. **26**(3), 477–505 (2019)

7. Best, M.L., Smyth, T.N.: Global/Local Usability: Locally Contextualized Usability in the Global South in Global Usability, pp. 9–22. Springer, London (2011). https://doi.org/10.1007/978-0-85729-304-6_2

8. Chetty, M., Grinter, R.E.: HCI4D: HCI challenges in the global south. In: Proceedings of the CHI 2007 Extended Abstracts on Human Factors in Computing Systems (CHI EA 2007), pp. 2327–2332 (2007)

9. Kumar, N., Dell, N.: The ins and outs of HCI for development. Proceedings of the 2016 CHI Conference on Human Factors in Computing Systems (CHI 2016), pp. 2220–2232 (2016)

10. Filimowicz, M., Tzankova, V.: Introduction: new directions in third wave HCI. In: New Directions in Third Wave Human-Computer Interaction, vol. 2, Methodologies, pp. 1–10 (2018)

11. Lupton, D.: 3D printing technologies: a third wave perspective. In: New Directions in Third Wave Human-Computer Interaction, vol. 1, Technologies, pp. 89–104 (2018)

12. van Dijk, J.: The Network Society: Social Aspects of New Media, 2nd edn. SAGE, London (2016)

13. Den Blanken, F.: Exploring interaction styles: tailored reflection & interaction for different patient profiles (2014)

14. Herrera, N., Jimenez, J., Keyson, D., Havinga, P.: THR Patient's Emotional and Physical Assessment After Early Hospital Discharge, RCHD: Creación y Pensamiento, pp. 1–9 (2018)

15. Sánchez, M.A., Fuentes, G.P.: Gestión clínica de programas de cuidado domiciliario. Manag. Clin. Home Care Program. CES Salud Públ. 7(2), 7–18 (2016)

16. CEPAL.   https://www.cepal.org/socinfo/noticias/paginas/3/44733/newsletter12.pdf. Accessed 27 Dec 2020

17. Orjuela, A., et al.: Artículo de revisión II Consenso Colombiano para el Manejo de la Osteoporosis Posmenopáusica, Revista Colombiana de Reumatologia (2018)

18. Prada, S.: Costs of health care in the last-year-of-life in Colombia: evidence from two contributive regime health plans. Rev. Fac. Med. Univ. Nac. Colomb. 66, 601–604 (2018)

19. Lugo, Y., Núñez Viloria, S., Barros Díaz, C., Cardona Peña, J.: Seguimiento de pacientes en estado postoperatorio de cirugías ambulatorias a través de la Web. Salud Uninorte 29(3), 384–393 (2013)

20. Frederico-Avendaño, C.: El reto de la cirugía ambulatoria; tendencias actuales. Rev. Mexican. Anestesiol. 36(1), 167–168 (2013)

21. O'Kane, A.A.: Using a Third-Wave HCI Approach for Researching Mobile Medical Devices (2014)

22. Li, I., Dey, A., Forlizzi, J.: A stage-based model of personal informatics systems. Proceedings of the SIGCHI Conference on Human Factors in Computing Systems (CHI 2010), pp. 557–566 (2010)

23. Jiménez García, J.C.: Beyond the Numbers: A User-Centered Design Approach for Personal Reflective Healthcare Technologies, Delft (2014)

24. Murnane, E.L., Walker, T.G., Tench, B., Voida, S., Snyder, J.: Personal informatics in interpersonal contexts: towards the design of technology that supports the social ecologies of long-term mental health management. In: Proceedings of the ACM on Human-Computer Interaction, vol. 2, no. CSCW, p. 127 (2018)

25. Holzwarth, U., Cotogno, G.: Institute for Health and Consumer Protection, Total Hip Arthroplasty: State of the Art, Challenges and Prospects, Luxembourg (2012)

26. El Espectador. https://www.elespectador.com/noticias/salud/articulo114216-colombia-se-rea lizan-10000-reemplazos-de-cadera-o-rodilla-al-ano. Accessed 01 Sept 2020

27. Pina, L.R., et al.: From personal informatics to family informatics: understanding family practices around health monitoring. Proceedings of the 2017 ACM Conference on Computer Supported Cooperative Work and Social Computing (CSCW 2017), pp. 2300–2315 (2007)

28. Toyama, K.: Human–Computer Interaction and Global Development, Foundations and Trends in Human-Computer Interaction, vol. 4, no. 1 (2010)
29. Medhi, I., Toyama, K.: Full-context videos for first-time, non-literate PC users. In: Information and Communication Technologies and Development (2007)
30. Picón-Jaimes, Y.A., Ruíz-Rodríguez, J., Jiménez-Peña, O.M.: Comportamiento epidemiológico de la Leishmaniasis cutánea en Boyacá 2012–2015, Revista Investigación en Salud Universidad de Boyacá, vol. 4, no. 1 (2017)
31. Padilla, J.C., Lizarazo, F.E., Murillo, O.L., Mendigaña, F.A., Pachón, E., Vera, M.J.: Epidemiología de las principales enfermedades transmitidas por vectores en Colombia, 1990–2016, Suplemento 2, Entomología médica, vol. 37 (2017)
32. Ministerio de Salud y Protección Social. Lineamientos Para la Atención Clínica Integral de Leishmaniasis en Colombia, Bogotá D.C. (2018)
33. Patino, L.H., et al.: Spatial distribution, Leishmania species and clinical traits of Cutaneous Leishmaniasis cases in the Colombian army (2017)
34. World Health Organization (WHO). https://www.who.int/news-room/fact-sheets/detail/leishmaniasis. Accessed 01 June 2020
35. Instituto Nacional de Salud (INS), Ministerio de Salud (MINSALUD). Leishmaniasis cutanea, mucosa y visceral, Colombia (2018)
36. Propacífico. https://propacifico.org/en/about-us/region-pacifico. Accessed 01 Aug 2020
37. Carrillo-Bonilla, L.M., Trujillo, J.J., Álvarez-Salas, L., Vélez-Bernal, I.D.: Estudio de los conocimientos, actitudes y prácticas de la leishmaniasis: evidencias del olvido estatal en el Darién Colombiano. Cadern. Saúd. Públ. 30(10), 2134–2144 (2014)
38. Universidad de los Andes. https://uniandes.edu.co/es/noticias/salud-y-medicina/el-pacifico-con-oportunidades-para-mejorar-en-salud. Accessed 01 Oct 2010
39. Lopez, L., Robayo, M., Vargas, M., Vélez, I.: Thermotherapy. An alternative for the treatment of American cutaneous leishmaniasis. Trials 13(58) (2012)
40. Rojas, C.A., Weigle, K.A., Tovar, R., Morales, A.L., Alexander, B.: A multifaceted intervention to prevent American cutaneous leishmaniasis in Colombia: results of a group-randomized trial. Biomedica 26(1), 152–166 (2006)
41. Out, A.A.: Is the directly observed therapy short course (DOTS) an effective strategy for tuberculosis control in a developing country? Asian Pacific J. Trop. Dis. 3(3), 227–231 (2013)
42. Sambasivan, N., Smyth, T.: The human infrastructure of ICTD. In: Proceedings of the 4th ACM/IEEE International Conference on Information and Communication Technologies and Development (ICTD 2010), no. 40, pp. 1–9 (2010)
43. Garcia-Ramirez, J., Nikoloski, Z., Mossialos, E.: Inequality in healthcare use among older people in Colombia. Int. J. Equity Health 19, 168 (2020)
44. Iancu, I., Iancu, B.: Elderly in the digital era. Theoretical perspectives on assistive technologies. Technologies 5, 60 (2017)
45. Colombiatic. https://colombiatic.mintic.gov.co/679/w3-article-80413.html. Accessed 02 Dec 2020
46. Rogers, Y.: Interaction Design Gone Wild: Striving for Wild Theory in Interactions 11 July–August 2011, pp. 58–62. ACM (2011)
47. Jimenez Garcia, J., Romero, N.A., Boerema, S.T., Keyson, D., Havinga, P.J.M.: ESTHER: a portable sensor toolkit to collect and monitor total hip replacement patient data. In: Proceedings of the 3rd ACM MobiHoc Workshop on Pervasive Wireless Healthcare, MobileHealth 2013, pp. 7–12. Association for Computing Machinery (2013)
48. World Health Organization. https://www.who.int/news-room/fact-sheets/detail/leishmaniasis. Accessed 29 Dec 2020
49. Chavan, A.: Around the World with 14 Methods Innovation and Culture (2009)
50. van Gemert-Pijnen, J.E., et al.: A holistic framework to improve the uptake and impact of eHealth technologies. J. Med. Internet Res. 13(4), e111 (2011)

Visualizing Tacit Knowledge in Cardiac Operating Room: A Need-Finding Study

Soo Jin Kang[✉], Cecilia Xi Wang, Tjorvi Perry, Stephen Richardson, and Lisa Miller

University of Minnesota, Twin Cities, MN 55455, USA
kangx770@umn.edu

Abstract. Fluent team communications in the 'Cardiac operating room (cOR) require significant preparation between a team of multiple disciplines. One of the key elements in effective communication during complex tasks such as those found in the cOR is tacit knowledge. Unlike other knowledge, tacit knowledge is not written, and is generally learned through experience. Our research tries to define tacit knowledge by establishing the needs of each discipline in the cOR, as follows: (i) define team communications among cOR team members, including surgeons, anesthesiologists, nurses, a perfusionist and technicians, and (ii) define what tacit knowledge-based tools can improve team communications. This need-finding study included a co-creation workshop to identify categories of needs, and in-depth interviews to better understand those categories. Our results highlight the need for (i) standardization of pre and post-operative processes, (ii) reliable tracking methods for supplies/equipment, (iii) adaptive training for new staff, (iv) physical layouts minimizing wasted movements, and (v) noise reduction. To further investigate our findings, we developed a team communication diagram for delineating tacit knowledge gaps of team communications among team members during pre-op-procedure. Of the tacit knowledge found in our studies, half are not addressed in the existing OR team training, motivating new design directions.

Keywords: OR team communication · Tacit knowledge · Need finding

1 Introduction

1.1 Cardiac Operating Room Team Communication

Cardiac operating room (cOR) teams caring for complex, high-risk cardiac surgical patients require close teamwork and precise communication [1]. Team members include surgeons, anesthesiologists, nurses, a perfusionist, and technicians. Each team member is highly trained in discipline-specific technical skills and is expected to collaborate closely with team members from other disciplines [2]. To optimize efficiency and ensure patient safety, clear and uninterrupted communication is of utmost importance as [3] the quality of communication within and between disciplines in the cOR correlates directly with surgical performance and patient safety [1]. Counterintuitively, a large proportion of communications in the cOR relies on implicit knowledge and cannot be found in written policy, instructions, or manuals [4]. Implicit knowledge, also known as tacit knowledge,

© The Author(s), under exclusive license to Springer Nature Switzerland AG 2022
M. M. Soares et al. (Eds.): HCII 2022, LNCS 13322, pp. 149–161, 2022.
https://doi.org/10.1007/978-3-031-05900-1_9

is learned during long-term collaboration and experiences. As it is not uncommon for team members in the cOR to frequently change, the need for an extended learning process may result in medical errors in the cOR [5].

1.2 Tacit Knowledge in cOR

Both tacit and objective knowledge are important for effective and efficient communication. Objective knowledge can be documented, explained, understood, and shared [6]. Tacit knowledge has the opposite attributes to objective knowledge [7]. Polanyi who first introduced the term described the tacit knowledge as follows: 'I shall reconsider human knowledge by starting from the fact that we can know more than we can tell' [8]. Tacit knowledge is, therefore, hard to be documented and explained [7]. Even people who fluently use tacit knowledge find it difficult to articulate their reason behind decision-making in the situation [9, 10]. Finally, tacit knowledge is context-specific, acquired while performing a task in a specific situation, and continued to evolve through practice [7, 9, 10, 12]. Nonaka explains, 'tacit knowledge is...deeply rooted in action and in an individual's commitment to a specific context – a craft or a profession, a particular technology or product market, or the activities of a workgroup or team' [10]. Thus, tacit knowledge is personal, procedural, and contextual to people and the organization to which these people belong [11, 13, 14].

Tacit knowledge is difficult to mimic or emulate by people outside of an organization or team precisely because tacit knowledge has been experientially cultivated between members of a specific team [6]. Tacit knowledge is commonly used during many types of team communication and can be especially useful when acuity and complexity are high, such as in the cOR, where information often needs to be conveyed in a succinct and timely manner [1, 5]. Without tacit knowledge, communication can be interrupted, resulting in task failure [15]. To date, little is understood about how tacit knowledge is learned and effectively used [12, 15, 16]. Herein, we describe communication patterns between disciplines in the cOR of a large academic medical center in an effort to better understand how tacit knowledge can play a role in effective and efficient communication, and how we might expedite communication training for new members of a team.

There are five distinct disciplines in a cOR team: a cardiac surgeon, a technician, a circulating nurse, a perfusionist, and an anesthesiologist, and all five disciplines should share one or more mental models through effective communication at various times during a procedure to ensure surgical success and patient safety [2, 3]. Current training strategies, however, exist in isolation, i.e., each member learns their role in the absence of team members from other disciplines [4, 14, 17, 18]. While training in isolation can be ideal for learning explicit knowledge by allowing members to focus on their own tasks [18]. It does not provide a contextual understanding of collaborative tasks. Alternatively, training programs may offer an opportunity whereby a number of experiences can be lived together by the entire team [3, 15]. Unfortunately, these types of training programs require prohibitively laborious and costly sessions, e.g., training with all possible combinations of other team members to handle various cases [13]. Instead, we suggest converting tacit knowledge into explicit knowledge by further characterizing challenging situations for each role.

1.3 Need-Finding of cOR Team Members

In this study, tacit knowledge for cOR teams was investigated through need-finding of all team members. Need-finding is a human-centered design approach for understanding users' unmet needs and identifying their latent challenges [19, 20]. Through direct observation and in-depth interviews where researchers empathize and immerse themselves in team members' perspectives, we are able to gain a deep understanding of their actual behavior, an approach that often reveals users' internalized intention behind behaviors [19, 21, 22]. As such, a need-finding approach can be useful to investigate internalized information such as tacit knowledge. Observing team communication and listening to individual team members' stories provides clues on the unconscious process of the cOR team's tacit knowledge use (e.g., picking up the right idea from a simple gesture) [7, 15].

2 Methods

The primary aim of this study was to delineate tacit knowledge gaps in team communication via need-finding of five team members: cardiac surgeon, technician, circulating nurse, perfusionist, and anesthesiologist in the cOR. We performed a qualitative cOR team communication need-finding study to learn: (i) what communication support each member of the cOR team wants, and (ii) what spectrum of tacit knowledge is needed to support effective team communication. Our investigation included: 1) co-creation workshops to identify categories of needs, and 2) structured in-depth interviews of individual team members to better understand those categories. In the formative co-creation workshops and structured in-depth interviews, team members were asked to list their roles, identify problem areas and brainstorm ways of improvements that they would like to implement.

2.1 Co-creation Workshops

We carried out a co-creation design thinking workshop with key team members to define the current status of cOR team communication. The team synthesized their observations about team communication from the empathize stage. The workshop activities included, 1) Ice Breaker: Identify your skill and superpower, 2) Identifying: List relevant stakeholders, 3) Mapping: Importance/Influence Stakeholder Matrix, 4) Analyzing: Empathy Mapping, 5) Defining: Point Of View – Problem Statement, 6) Discussion: Next Steps. The co-creation workshop tools included stakeholder matrix, empathy mapping, and point of view (POV) (see Fig. 1). Workshop participants were asked to make importance versus influence map as a team member to team communication-at-stake matrix to generate insights on the importance and influence of each team member in relation to the cOR team communication. Then, the participants generated an empathic map of what each team member says, does, thinks, and feels. At the end of the co-creation workshop, participants defined a research problem statement using the point of view (POV) tool as follows:

The cOR team communication is highly complex and personal. Currently, there is anxiety and confusion for key team members regarding conceptual wayfinding and decision making. Current explicit knowledge for team communication does not meet this challenge.

The overarching objective of this project is to develop a tacit knowledge-sharing toolkit with a focus on communication that will allow the cOR team to understand how to make decisions that will result in improved team performance and ensure patient safety.

Fig. 1. Scenes of the problem framing workshop: cOR team members are working on stakeholder matrix and empathy map by describing their roles and skills and their relation to those of other team members. *(Photo courtesy of cOR cardiac research team at University of Minnesota)*

2.2   Structured In-Depth Interviews

We conducted structured interviews with key team members of the cOR team at M Health Fairview University of Minnesota Medical Center. The interview questionnaire consisted of open-ended questions to foster the sharing of unanticipated information. Each interview started with an introduction and a brief explanation of the study being conducted. Team members were then asked about their general roles, their responsibility during a procedure, team communication challenges, and ideas for changes that they thought would improve OR communication. We also asked team members to create a user journey map to identify their communication needs during a procedure. Interviews were conducted either in cardiac operating rooms (see Fig. 2) or using audio-visual conferencing. The average length of interviews was 55 min, ranging from 25 min to 100 min; due to the time constraint of team members, two interviews were done in 30 min. We recorded all interviews with the permission of team members. Video data was auto-transcribed by the audio-visual conferencing software used for interviews and the transcribed data were manually compared to the original audio by authors to ensure its accuracy.

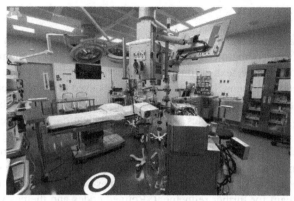

Fig. 2. A panorama view of cOR: the structured in-depth interviews were conducted in a cardiac operating room in order to effectively capture and elicit the OR team member's challenges and needs by walking through their workflow side by side. (*Photo courtesy of cOR cardiac OR research team at University of Minnesota*).

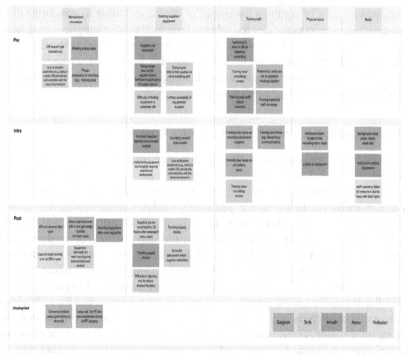

Fig. 3. Affinity diagram created in Mural app: each digital post-it contains short phrases, labels, and keywords identified by open coding from transcribed interview data. Total 17 themes emerged, and they were narrowed down to five key themes by additional axial coding and further categorized by three operative phases; preoperative phase, intraoperative phase, and postoperative phase. (*Diagram courtesy of authors*)

2.3 Data Analysis

We transcribed a total of 5.5 h of audio recordings. First, we used open-coding for all transcripts. An open coding method was utilized to identify labels, themes, keywords, and interpretations of the text, artifacts, or other relevant data without the use of a predetermined coding scheme [23]. Open-coding was used to identify relevant phrases or short descriptive sentences thought to potentially reveal new insights. Codes were transferred into digital post-it notes via the web application Mural (see Fig. 3). We then conducted a thematic analysis on the digitized notes by grouping related codes into themes. As a part of the thematic analysis, axial coding was performed to form a hierarchy of themes, requiring several rounds of grouping notes, creating keywords, and summarizing each group [23]. The codes and themes were regularly presented to the entire research team for further refinement. Refined codes and themes were inspected by the second author separately for validity and reliability.

3 OR Team Communication Needs

From a directed content analysis conducted on transcribed interviews and workshops, we developed a series of common categories of needs, including a) standardization of pre-and postoperative processes, b) reliable tracking methods for supplies/equipment, c) adaptive training for new staff, d) physical layouts to minimize wasted movements, and e) noise reduction. These categories of findings are visualized on a team communication diagram, providing a comprehensive understanding of both team member-specific as well as shared tacit knowledge gaps of the team.

3.1 Standardization of Pre and Post Operative Procedure

cOR team members suggested missing procedure steps or required supplies as a reason for surgical case delay. Less common during the intraoperative phase, missed procedure steps or missing supplies occur more often during the pre and postoperative phases, especially if team members do not have a well-established procedure routine. For example, a cardiac surgeon suggested that because many people from different domains work on different parts of a procedure simultaneously, some steps become discordant, causing incomplete or incorrect task completion, and delays (e.g., spending extra time to correct the issue). Circulating nurses and technicians use surgeons' preference cards as a guide to ensure steps are not missed and/or supplies are available. The preference cards include a list of required steps, supplies, and equipment per procedure for each surgeon. Accurate preference cards are essential to ensure efficiency and avoid incomplete or inaccurate information. Delays due to incomplete or inaccurate information due to inaccurate preference cards can be a source of poor communication between team members, especially during the preoperative phase. Team members also explained that maintaining up-to-date preference cards was challenging due to time constraints and inadequate resources. In an effort to maintain up-to-date preference cards, team members suggested developing and maintaining a comprehensive case guide for comparing supplies used from one case to another. Such a case guide might enable team members to interactively and automatically discover common and uncommon supplies and resources used from one surgical case to the next and facilitate accurate and up-to-date preference cards.

The majority of team members (4/6) expressed a strong desire to develop and maintain a comprehensive guide for pre/post-operative procedures. They were curious about capturing recurring steps required for setting up and cleaning up before and after routine procedures. Because recurring steps indicate refactoring opportunities to standardize its process and how to perform them appropriately. For instance, although surgeons and anesthesiologists share a common goal of working efficiently, medical errors and adverse patient outcomes are still possible. To meet these needs, we plan to create a virtual coaching tool that allows different team members to seamlessly collaborate as an integrated team.

"There are many steps that need to take place. From coming in the physical door of the operating room. And I don't know if you guys have watched Formula One car racing. That process should be like a formula and car pit stop. Like every person in the operating room should have a list of tasks and know exactly when and how to do those things." [Cardiac surgeon]

3.2 Reliable Tracking Methods for Supplies/Equipment

Currently, the organization of the cOR supply cabinets lacks standardization. The majority of team members complained that time and energy are wasted searching for appropriate supplies before and during an operation. Many team members suggested a universal standard to organize commonly used supplies and equipment across all cOR cabinets; case-specific sections within each cabinet can be reserved to accommodate special needs and to more easily track and maintain needed supplies and resources.

Team members mentioned that a lack of consistency in organizing supplies and equipment causes major delays during the entire operative phases. Past efforts to improve the layout and processes to restock supply cabinets have not been successful, and team members who are not regularly in the cOR's have significant challenges locating supplies. Team members suggested developing a tool to more effectively communicate the organizing system with team members who are less frequent in OR to improve consistency and reduce errors among all team members. In particular, an anesthesiologist and a scrub nurse suggested developing an organizing system based on its usage patterns because such a system would be more likely to fit the existing mental model of the team members, regardless of their level of experience.

While studying usage patterns, error-inducing events and recurring human mistakes can be also identified. The new system design should implement mechanisms targeting such recurring challenges. This calls for OR cabinet design in order to appeal to the existing mental model of team members, to prevent errors, to reduce delays due to searching for supplies, and to ultimately reduce ambiguity in team communication.

"So one of the reasons why we redesigned this cabinet is because the person from the head of supply chain came in and said, this is where these things fit. I can lay this out in this order and all my bins fit properly…But the problem is, if you need a syringe and a needle, you have to go to two cabinets. So we said no, we don't want

that. We would like you to put the syringes and needles together…because you want to be efficient with your movement and spend the least amount of energy gathering things. So we had them readjusted…one issue that we are still having with this is, when you're having supply people, they are only followed by a number…So, if this number (numbers on supply package) doesn't match what they see on that shelf. They may not know what substitute to put in it. Or they may bring a substitute because it looks similar, but it doesn't function the same." [Scrub technician]

3.3 Updated Training for Staff

There were two types of issues caused by training moments. First, training moments burden experienced team members with repetitive teaching, especially about basic tasks common for routine procedures (e.g., setting up patient posture on OR bed, setting up surgical tray). Second, training moments often emerge during stressful events. For instance, a surgeon mentioned that teaching moments can be easily turned into heated conversations with training staff in the process of resolving pressing or critical issues. Anesthesiologists also pointed out that they have to spend a considerable amount of their time teaching and correcting new staff about routine procedures, and it becomes a challenge as such lessons should be provided on a daily basis. Interestingly, one experienced nurse gathered existing preference cards/procedure protocol and created libraries (e.g., printouts organized in a 3-ring binder) for new staff, so they can review and follow required steps/supplies for both common and special procedures without requiring repetitive/unexpected training moments. Such libraries are useful, yet it is difficult to keep them updated with changes of each procedure and individual surgeon's preferences. Therefore, it may be beneficial to design a new interactive channel that allows OR team members to communicate and be trained about changes in supply requirements and procedure updates in real-time. It may also be beneficial to transfer existing libraries in an electronic format to account for enhanced editing capability.

All OR team members wished to gather several major clues to understand experienced team members' training needs, including the intent of using a teaching moment, how the moment was discovered, what steps it took to train unfamiliar information, how long it took, where new trainees often make mistakes. By understanding the details of such training needs, inconsistent expectations between experienced staff and new staff can be identified, and teaching methods/training tools can be enhanced to reduce such confusion and learning barriers.

"I asked her (new trainee) what we're doing. Do you understand it, you know, you don't understand what you do or what surgery. So, kind of hope she did as well…if she doesn't know what it is we'll look at this (three-ring binder), look and see if I have something." [Experienced nurse]

The experienced nurse said teaching procedures before cases and watching her trainee over their shoulders helped her understand what the trainee was familiar with, what was misunderstood, and what they had not learned yet. Several participating team members mentioned that they could get a sense of where they are not on the same page with their trainees by asking questions of them before a procedure, to anticipate training needs that will come next. However, it is not an additional simple task (besides clinical tasks) to comprehensively plan every single teaching moment ahead in an attempt to optimize team communication in OR.

3.4 Physical Layouts Minimizing Wasted Movements

Team members mentioned that they also pointed out the layout of sterile trays that could be simplified to minimize footsteps and simplify team communication, shortening surgery time. For example, a cardiac surgeon said the current layout required a scrub technician to travel between the tray location and the end of the patient bed numerous times to deliver requested surgical instruments to the surgeon. To increase team communication by protecting them from physical and mental fatigue, team members underscored their needs for optimized physical layouts of furniture and equipment in the OR. To address such an issue, it would be beneficial to analyze the architectural flow (e.g., arrangement of equipment) during different operative phases and redesign based on naturally emerged patterns of team members' movement [24].

3.5 Noise Reduction

Noise in a cardiac operating room was manifested in several ways. First, there were multiple equipment and devices simultaneously generating similar tones of alarms to alert team members, so team members must investigate which devices caused which alarms. In addition, one device might produce different alarms in different contexts, making it hard to distinguish the root cause of the alarm without additional efforts to investigate. Such ambiguity caused by alarms and alerts fueled frustration among team members and delayed surgery time. Second, noise can be generated by humans. A leading cardiac surgeon stated that sometimes it is hard to communicate his directions to team members because they are in the middle of a different conversation or the volume of the radio was set too high. Systematically reducing the noise level of the OR is challenging in various aspects, since it requires redesigning of alarm systems as well as analyzing team dynamics. Thus, implementing techniques and strategies that can effectively streamline the chain of team communication in noisy environments is much needed.

4 Discussion

cOR teams including surgeons, anesthesiologists, nurses, a perfusionist, and technicians caring for complex, high-risk cardiac surgical patients require close teamwork and precise communication. Teams leverage both tacit and objective knowledge to learn how to optimally communicate and perform. Tacit knowledge (insight and intuition) can be especially useful when acuity and complexity are high, such as in the cOR, where information often needs to be conveyed in a succinct and timely manner. Without tacit knowledge, communication can be interrupted, resulting in task failure. In this study, tacit knowledge for cOR teams was investigated through need-finding, a human-centered design approach for understanding team members' unmet needs and identifying their latent challenges. From the directed content analysis conducted using transcribed interviews and workshops with team members from each discipline in the cOR, we identified a series of common categories of needs. These included a) standardization of pre and post-operative processes, b) reliable tracking methods for supplies/equipment, c) adaptive training for new staff, d) physical layouts minimizing wasted movements, and e) noise reduction.

During the interviews, most team members touched upon the tension that emerges during team communications. The tension often came from the fact that one team member made certain implicit decisions and tradeoffs that were not articulated. The complexity of tasks/steps increases exponentially as the number of team members increases (see Fig. 4). While teaching tacit knowledge can improve communications, there are still several challenges of tacit knowledge training.

- First, it is challenging to keep tacit knowledge between team members up-to-date due to time constraints and inadequate resources.
- Second, it was also difficult to track most tacit knowledge use cases in team communication and include them in training.
- Third, team members were concerned about the applicability of tacit knowledge if the training contents become overly extensive (e.g., covering every single skill and know-how of each team member in performing every operative task/step), and it would take a long time to be studied and mastered.

Hence, team members are in need of not only tool support for identifying use cases of tacit knowledge in team communication but also a new toolkit for effectively disseminating identified tacit knowledge among the team. Identifying commonly shared categories for knowledge gaps between team members in the cOR is an initial step toward understanding how tacit knowledge contributes to these gaps, and how this investigatory team can design programs to facilitate communication and performance through tacit knowledge.

We recognize several limitations to the study design that led to our stated outcomes. Firstly, this study was completed in a single academic, tertiary care hospital, and we are unlikely to be able to extrapolate our findings to other institutions. Furthermore, while we made every effort to target a representative group of team members, we did not speak to every member of the cOR team. Future work will include a multi-institutional effort as well as increasing the number of team members with whom we interview. Finally, knowledge acquisition is complex, and while the focus of this research has been on tacit knowledge, our findings must be understood within the context of many types of knowledge acquisition.

	PRE	INTRA	POST
Team communication needs	Standardization of Pre-op procedure Reliable tracking system for supplies Updated training tools for staff	Effient physical layout of OR Noise reduction in communication Updated training tools for staff	Standardization of post-op procedure Reliable tracking system for supplies Updated training tools for staff
Surgeon	Check lab results Examine/talk to patient Discuss plan	Perform/lead procedure — Receive sterile itnstruments — Receive patient status updates	Preparing next case
Scrub Technician	Receive/set up sterile instruments Perform counts	Receive sterile itnstruments Perform counts	Preparing patient for transporting Returning supplies/equitments
Circulating Nurse	Set up and hand in supplies Record counts	Hand in sterile insturments Record counts	Preparing patient for transporting Returning supplies/equitments
Anesthesiologist	Select/hand in supplies Position line Probe placement	Running patient on equipment Monitoring patient status	Weaning patient Preparing patient for transporting Rebuild equipment
Perfusionist	Select/hand in supplies Set up equipment	Running patient on equipment Monitoring patient status	Returning blood Preparing patient for transfering Rebuild equipment

Fig. 4. Team communication diagram. This diagram illustrates the level of complexity of cOR team communication and those of emerging needs. In the first row, team communication needs are organized by three operative phases (pre, intra, and post). The following rows represent simplified instances of team communication-based tasks per team member. *(Diagram courtesy of authors)*

5 Conclusion

The cOR is a complex system that requires effective and efficient communication to optimize team performance. To date, little has been done to measure and describe how tacit knowledge can be leveraged to optimize communication and performance in the cOR. Herein, we describe five gaps in knowledge that may lead to or be caused by poor communication and sub-optimal performance: a) standardization of pres and post-operative processes, b) reliable tracking methods for supplies/equipment, c) adaptive training for new staff, d) physical layouts to minimize wasted movements, and e) noise reduction. Future work will be directed at building programs that invoke tacit knowledge to bridge these knowledge gaps with and between team members of the cOR. Future work will be directed at building programs that invoke tacit knowledge to bridge these knowledge gaps between team members of the cOR. The potential programs could include VR technology-supported interactive team training toolkits that allow them to walk through other team members' tacit knowledge (e.g., know-how and skills) by emulating them in virtual reality. Such VR team training toolkits would promote sharing tacit knowledge among team members, honing team communication and performance, and ultimately ensuring patient safety.

References

1. Wahr, J.A., et al.: Patient safety in the cardiac operating room. Hum. Factors Teamwork Circ. **128**, 1139–1169 (2013). https://doi.org/10.1161/CIR.0b013e3182a38efa
2. Gurses, A.P., et al.: Identifying and categorising patient safety hazards in cardiovascular operating rooms using an interdisciplinary approach: a multisite study. BMJ Qual. Saf. **21**, 810–818 (2012). https://doi.org/10.1136/bmjqs-2011-000625
3. Brown, E.K.H., et al.: Identifying variability in mental models within and between disciplines caring for the cardiac surgical patient. Anesth. Analg. **125**, 29–37 (2017). https://doi.org/10.1213/ANE.0000000000002087
4. Paige, J.T., et al.: Getting a head start: high-fidelity, simulation-based operating room team training of interprofessional students. J. Am. Coll. Surg. **218**, 140–149 (2014). https://doi.org/10.1016/j.jamcollsurg.2013.09.006
5. Paige, J., Garbee, D., Bonanno, L., Kerdolff, K.: Qualitative analysis of effective teamwork in the operating room (OR). J. Surg. Educ. **78**, 967–979 (2021). https://doi.org/10.1016/j.jsurg.2020.09.019
6. Sobol, M.G., Lei, D.: Environment, manufacturing technology, and embedded knowledge. Int. J. Hum. Factors Manuf. **4**, 167–189 (1994). https://doi.org/10.1002/hfm.4530040205
7. Ambrosini, V., Bowman, C.: Tacit knowledge: some suggestions for operationalization. J. Manag. Stud. **38**, 811–829 (2001). https://doi.org/10.1111/1467-6486.00260
8. Polanyi, M.: Tacit knowing: its bearing on some problems of philosophy. Rev. Mod. Phys. **34**, 601–616 (1962). https://doi.org/10.1103/RevModPhys.34.601
9. Sternberg, R.J., Wagner, R.K.: Tacit knowledge: an unspoken key to managerial success. Creat. Innov. Manag. **1**, 5–13 (1992). https://doi.org/10.1111/j.1467-8691.1992.tb00016.x
10. Nonaka, I.: The knowledge-creating company. In: The Economic Impact of Knowledge, pp. 175–187. Elsevier (1998). https://doi.org/10.1016/B978-0-7506-7009-8.50016-1
11. Winter, S.G., Nelson, R.R.: An Evolutionary Theory of Economic Change. Social Science Research Network, Rochester, NY (1982)
12. Leonard, D., Sensiper, S.: The role of tacit knowledge in group innovation. Calif. Manage. Rev. **40**, 112–132 (1998). https://doi.org/10.2307/41165946
13. Eraut, M.: Non-formal learning and tacit knowledge in professional work. Br. J. Educ. Psychol. **70**, 113–136 (2000). https://doi.org/10.1348/000709900158001
14. Kothari, A.R., Bickford, J.J., Edwards, N., Dobbins, M.J., Meyer, M.: Uncovering tacit knowledge: a pilot study to broaden the concept of knowledge in knowledge translation. BMC Health Serv. Res. **11**, 198 (2011). https://doi.org/10.1186/1472-6963-11-198
15. Bennet, D., Bennet, A.: Engaging tacit knowledge in support of organizational learning. VINE **38**, 72–94 (2008). https://doi.org/10.1108/03055720810870905
16. Andrews, M., Smits, S.: Using tacit knowledge exchanges to improve teamwork. ISM J. Int. Bus. **3**, 15–23 (2019)
17. Cumin, D., Boyd, M.J., Webster, C.S., Weller, J.M.: A systematic review of simulation for multidisciplinary team training in operating rooms. Simul. Healthcare **8**, 171–179 (2013). https://doi.org/10.1097/SIH.0b013e31827e2f4c
18. Fleetwood, V.A., Veenstra, B., Wojtowicz, A., Kerchberger, J., Velasco, J.: Communication through simulation: developing a curriculum to teach interpersonal skills. Surgery **164**, 802–809 (2018). https://doi.org/10.1016/j.surg.2018.05.037

19. Schaffhausen, C.R., Kowalewski, T.M.: Large-scale needfinding: methods of increasing user-generated needs from large populations. J. Mech. Des. **137**, 071403 (2015). https://doi.org/10.1115/1.4030161
20. Rous, B.S., Nash, J.B.: Visual communication as knowledge management in design thinking. In: The Handbook of Applied Communication Research, pp. 233–248. Wiley (2020). https://doi.org/10.1002/9781119399926.ch14
21. Patnaik, D., Becker, R.: Needfinding: the why and how of uncovering people's needs. Des. Manag. J. Former Ser. **10**, 37–43 (1999). https://doi.org/10.1111/j.1948-7169.1999.tb00250.x
22. Blindheim, J., Wulvik, A., Steinert, M.: Using secondary video material for user observation in the needfinding process for new product development and design. In: 84 Proceedings of Design 2016 14th International Design Conference, pp. 1845–1854 (2016)
23. Williams, M., Moser, T.: The art of coding and thematic exploration in qualitative research. Int. Manag. Rev. **15**, 45–72 (2019)
24. Palmer, G., et al.: Realizing Improved Patient Care through Human-centered Operating Room Design | Anesthesiology | American Society of Anesthesiologists. https://pubs.asahq.org/anesthesiology/article/119/5/1066/13663/Realizing-Improved-Patient-Care-through-Human. Accessed 4 Oct 2021

Experimental Research on Anthropomorphic Design in Interactive Sleep Persuasion Interface

Ying Li[1], Yanfei Zhu[2], Boqian He[1], Jinlai Liu[1], and Junliang Zhou[1]([✉])

[1] Beijing University of Chemical Technology, Changping, Beijing, China
zhoujl@mail.buct.cn
[2] Southeast University, Nanjing, Jiangsu, China

Abstract. Sleep deprivation is a public health problem, and the increase in interactive entertainment products and the stress of daytime life and work have led to sleep disorders in young people. In this study, a 2 anthropomorphic (anthropomorphic vs. non-anthropomorphic) $\times$ 2 information framing (positive vs. negative) intergroup experiment was conducted to investigate effective combinations of interactive persuasive interface design, aiming at how to design visual information for health persuasion during entertainment interactions for young users. The results showed that anthropomorphism and information framing both had positive effects on the behavioral intention for healthy sleep. When anthropomorphism was combined with negative framing descriptions, they were more effective in persuading young users to sleep healthily.

Keywords: Sleep health · Persuasive technology · Anthropomorphism · Message frame

1 Introduction

Sleep is an important bodily function that is vital to human health. It benefits not only our brain and mental health but also our cardiovascular and immune systems (Stern 2021). To draw attention to the importance of sleep and sleep quality, the International Foundation for Mental Health and Neuroscience launched World Sleep Day as a global event in 2001. In 2003, the Chinese Sleep Research Society (CSRS) introduced "World Sleep Day" to China, which has drawn attention to the importance of sleep at home and abroad. However, at present, human sleep problems are still serious, as shown in the "White Paper on Exercise and Sleep 2021" published by the Chinese Sleep Research Society (CSRS), which indicates that over 300 million people in China currently suffer from sleep disorders; foreign studies have also shown that people who do not get enough sleep are more likely to experience negative emotions (Dinges et al. 1997), inefficiency (Killgore et al. 2006), lack of creativity (Harrison and Horne 1999), and obesity (Taheri et al. 2004), sleep deprivation is becoming a serious health risk (Godsell and White 2019).

Sleep is influenced by multiple factors, and the inconsistency between the structure of people's time allocation and healthy sleep patterns can lead to unhealthy sleep (Barnes and Drake 2015). According to the National Bureau of Statistics' 2018 National Time Use Survey Bulletin, residents spent 2 h and 28 min more time using the Internet in 2018 compared to 2008, making the Internet the biggest factor changing the allocation of time for the nation (National Bureau of Statistics 2019). The popularity of the Internet has contributed to the rapid development of urbanization, and technological progress and social development have brought about a dramatic change in the lifestyle of the youth group and provided them with more interactive products to choose from for entertainment and leisure, and stress relief. In addition, the high-pressure work content during the day and the behavior of staying at home at night make young users more inclined to choose interactive entertainment products to release their stress after work. However, there is substantial evidence (Schweizer et al. 2017) that the shortened continuous sleep time and delayed bedtime at night caused by interactive entertainment products such as TV, computers, and cell phones can lead to sleep disorders.

In summary, the increase in interactive entertainment products and the increased stress of daytime work life have led to sleep disorders in young people. Specifically, the richness of the interface design of entertainment products often leads users to delay or shorten their normal sleep time indefinitely due to over-indulgence in the content, which directly leads to criticisms such as disrupted physiological circulation and mental work anxiety the next day. Over time, long-term sleep deprivation can bring about serious consequences such as excessive daytime sleepiness, poor concentration, impaired emotional regulation, and increased risk-taking behavior (Hayley et al. 2015; Owens 2014), seriously endangering the health of our youth. So, how to effectively prevent addiction? Currently, moderated entertainment information persuasion in interactive product design has become an important issue to be addressed at the intersection of design and public health.

This study proposes to investigate how effective combinations of interactive persuasive interface design, through analytic experiments, can aim to design visual messages for health persuasion during recreational interactions for young users. In previous health intervention/persuasion message design studies, risk perception and behavioral intention have been identified as important factors in implementing/influencing protective behaviors (Rogers et al. 1983; Ajzen and Fishbein 2000; Guan and So 2020). Health behavior theory (Rogers 1975; Witte 1992) conceptualizes risk perception as a favorable predictor of protective behavior, i.e., when individuals perceive themselves to be vulnerable to serious threats, they are likely to take action (Rogers et al. 1983). Anthropomorphism as a descriptive device is widely used in persuasive behaviors. Robbins and Niederdeppe (2015) demonstrated that descriptive norms have a positive predictive effect on behavioral intentions and are an effective information strategy for healthy sleep behavior. In addition to this, Steinmetz et al. (2016) and Branscum et al. (2020) also suggested that healthy sleep behavior intention interventions should take the form of providing information (advantages/disadvantages of obtaining healthy sleep), persuasion, and social encouragement. Therefore, this experiment hopes that the risk perception and behavioral intention to persuade young users about healthy sleep behaviors can be enhanced by the anthropomorphic design of visual information.

Specifically, a 2×2 between-group experiment was conducted with four prototype product persuasion interface animations designed based on anthropomorphic graphics and positively and negatively framed Chinese descriptive information in the visual elements of the interface. The dependent variables were measured by two subjective behavioral Likert scales, risk perception, and behavioral intention, to investigate the differential effects of a two-by-two design approach of anthropomorphic graphics (anthropomorphic/non-anthropomorphic) and linguistic framing effects (positive framing/negative framing) on the unhealthy sleep behavior of young users who sleep late.

2 Literature Review

2.1 Anthropomorphism

Anthropomorphism has been defined as the tendency to attribute human-like characteristics, intentions, and behaviors to inanimate objects (Epley et al. 2007; Epley et al. 2008; Kim and McGill 2011; Duffy 2003). Over the past few decades, anthropomorphism has attracted the attention of sociologists, philosophers, and psychologists, and most anthropomorphic research has focused on three areas: business, human-computer interaction, and law (Yue et al. 2021). While previous research has focused more on when and what people anthropomorphize (Epley et al. 2008; Epley et al. 2007; Kim and McGill 2011), more recent research has focused more on how anthropomorphism affects people's judgments and behaviors, and much of the literature suggests that anthropomorphism has a positive impact on judgments and behaviors. Sinha et al. (2020) illustrated the positive impact of anthropomorphism on employees' behavioral intentions to accept robots in the workplace. Lee and Lai (2021) showed that anthropomorphized pet emotions had a significant positive impact on behavioral intentions in pet hotels. Yue et al. (2021) primarily examined the positive effects of anthropomorphism on wildlife conservation, and the experimental results indicated that anthropomorphic strategies would help increase public support for wildlife conservation. However, Kim and McGill's (2011) study on how anthropomorphism affects perceptions and behaviors showed that risk perceptions were influenced by anthropomorphism with a sense of social power, while anthropomorphism had no main effect on risk perceptions. Therefore, we make the following hypothesis.

H1: Anthropomorphism in persuasive animation had a positive effect on participants' behavioral intention to sleep healthily.

2.2 Message Framing

Prospect theory describes the nonlinear relationship between gains and losses in objective outcomes and viewers' subjective responses (Tversky and Kahneman 1981; Toll et al. 2008), and the theory has been applied in many contexts, particularly in designing persuasive health behavior messages (Cho et al. 2018). In the past decades, prospect theory-based message frameworks have been one of the most widely adopted health behavior persuasion strategies (Liu and Yang 2020; Chang and Lee 2009; De et al. 2010;

Gerend and Cullen 2008; Krishnamurthy et al. 2001; Levin et al. 1998). When using an informational frame to communicate health issues, the positive frame emphasizes the potential benefits of performing health behaviors, compared to the negative frame that highlights the negative outcomes of not performing health behaviors (Huang et al. 2019; Liu and Yang 2020).

Previous research has found that discussing different health behaviors makes gaining and losing framing information differentially persuasive (Rothman and Salovey 1997). Specifically, positive framing information is more persuasive when the outcome of the behavior has little to no associated risk (prevention of health problems) compared to negative framing information (running activity, Cho et al. 2018; sunscreen, Detweiler et al. 1999). When the outcome of the behavior leads to a high level of risk (detection of disease) compared to positive framing information, negative framing information is more convincing (breast cancer, Schneider et al. 2001). Since unhealthy sleep is risky behavior, in promoting healthy sleep as a behavior, we make the hypothesis that:

H2: Participants who viewed negatively framed messages had a higher intention to engage in healthy sleep behavior than those who viewed positively framed messages.

2.3 Anthropomorphism and Its Joint Effect with Message Framing

Information frames are significant predictors of perceived risk (Mitchell et al. 2015), and risk perception variables and self-other risk perception gaps are significant predictors of behavioral intention to facilitate (Huang et al. 2019). Significant interactions between information framing and other factors on risk perception were found in previous studies, e.g. Huang et al. (2019) examined the effects of information framing, reference points, and modality in a recall promotion scenario and found that loss framing messages were more effective in increasing risk perception than gain framing messages only when paired with infographics and other reference points. Ma and Nan (2019) explored moderating role of information framing in narrative persuasion in the context of smoking cessation promotion, showing a significant interaction between information framing and type of evidence (narrative vs. non-narrative) on smoking-related risk perceptions.

However, the literature exploring the interaction between anthropomorphism and information framing in risk perception is less extensive, with only Karpinska et al. (2020) examining how information framing and anthropomorphism interact to promote environmental intentions and finding that negative messages were more effective in promoting green intentions when they were combined with anthropomorphic cues. In summary, we predict that.

H3: Anthropomorphism and positive and negative framing interact on participants' health risk perceptions during healthy sleep persuasion animations.

H3a: Participants showed stronger risk perceptions when viewing anthropomorphic animations matched with negative frames rather than positive frames. H3b: Anthropomorphism showed higher risk perceptions than non-anthropomorphism when viewing negative framing animations.

3   Methodology

The experimental design used a 2 (anthropomorphic: anthropomorphic vs. non-anthropomorphic) × 2 (information frame: positive depiction of healthy sleep vs. negative depiction of unhealthy sleep) between-group experiment to explore the main and interaction effects between the two variables of anthropomorphic, positive/negative frames. A total of four persuasive interface animations were also designed as experimental stimuli based on the anthropomorphic graphics and positive/negative framed Chinese character's information in the visual elements of the interface.

3.1   Stimulus Materials

The experimental stimuli for this study took the form of animations. Four different animation (Anthropomorphic × Positive frame; Anthropomorphic × Negative frame; Non-anthropomorphic × Positive frame; Non-anthropomorphic × Negative frame) were used to explore the differential effects of a two-by-two design approach of anthropomorphic graphics (anthropomorphic/non-anthropomorphic) and verbal framing effects (positive/negative frames) on the unhealthy sleep behavior of young users who sleep late.

Regarding the design of information frames, each animation was modified in a way that included the relevant frames. Specifically, in the animations involving negative frames, we inform about negative consequences (e.g., "lack of sleep is harmful to physical and mental health"); similarly, in the animations involving positive frames, the structure of the message is the same but indicates positive outcomes of adopting healthy behaviors (e.g., "good sleep is good for your health"). In summary, negative frames contain negative words and negative outcomes, while positive frames contain positive descriptions and positive outcomes.

Regarding the anthropomorphic design, we drew on previous studies that have used primarily face features to induce anthropomorphic thinking (Earth, Karpinska et al. 2020; Mr. Potato, Shao et al. 2020; Stomach, Newton et al. 2017). Thus, facial features (eyes and expressions) can serve as an adequate cue to give inanimate objects human-like qualities (Karpinska et al. 2020). Thus, we depicted the alarm clock and the moon as forms with eyes and expressions in the anthropomorphic condition, and without eyes and expressions in the nonanthropomorphic condition. To further enhance the anthropomorphic perception, human-like features were added in the anthropomorphic condition (e.g., "alarm clock's stretched hands", "sleeping symbol: ZZZ", "dizzy-eyed symbol", and the sleeping cap of the moon).

In addition to this, to ensure that our study is more in line with the interaction scenario, we designed the stimuli to be more like the pop-up animations of the interactive product. However, to avoid factors other than information framing and anthropomorphism in the persuasion animations from interfering with participants' judgments, we designed all four sets of animations to be as simple as possible, e.g., each animation consists of four interfaces that are visually close together in a natural way.

3.2 Procedure and Measures

By distributing a questionnaire, we invited 56 subjects to participate in an online experiment, and after reading the participant informed consent form, they were randomly assigned to one of four groups. First, participants were asked to watch a minimum of 11 s of persuasive animation. Second, they were asked to answer a series of items on a manipulation check, dependent variable test. Specifically, participants were asked to answer (1) anthropomorphic manipulation check (2) positive and negative framing manipulation check (3) risk perception scale (4) behavioral intention scale, four sets of questions. To ensure validity and reliability, we based these questions on the manipulation check measure from previous studies, slightly modified for the context of this study. Six items on assessing anthropomorphism and four items on positive and negative framing were used in this study. To examine manipulations of anthropomorphism, six items were selected from Newton et al.'s (2017) study, for example, "Alarm clock/moon seems to have emotions and feelings," measured using a 7-point Likert scale (1 = strongly disagree; 7 = strongly agree). To examine the manipulation of the positive and negative frames, four items were selected from the study of Boster et al. (2008). For the examination of positive framing, two items were used. For example, "This animation focuses on the benefits of healthy sleep." For the negatively framed examination, two items were used. For example, "This animation focuses on the disadvantages of sleep deprivation" was given on a five-point Likert scale of 1 (strongly disagree) to 5 (strongly agree).

Risk perception is mainly measured through two dimensions, perceived susceptibility, and perceived severity, and the six items of the risk perception scale are taken from the studies of Witte et al. (1996) and Guan and So (2020), with minor modifications. Perceived susceptibility was measured by three items, such as "I am at risk for sleep deprivation", "I am likely to experience health problems related to sleep deprivation", and "I am likely to develop health problems related to sleep deprivation". Perceived severity was measured by three items, such as "I think the health problems caused by lack of sleep are serious", "I think the health problems caused by lack of sleep are serious", and "I think the health problems caused by lack of sleep is significant". A seven-point Likert scale (1 = strongly disagree; 7 = strongly agree) was used for all six questions. The results reported the good agreement ($\alpha = 0.715$). Regarding the measurement of behavioral intentions, two items were selected from previous related studies (Robbins and Niederdeppe 2019; Ajzen and Fishbein 1980). To assess intention for healthy sleep behavior, viewers were asked to answer the questions "I intend to sleep 8–9 h most nights of the week" and "I will sleep 8–9 h most nights of the week" on a seven-point Likert scale (1 = strongly disagree; 7 = strongly agree). "two questions, the Healthy Sleep Behavior Intentions Scale also reported the good agreement ($\alpha = 0.835$). Finally, participants were asked to respond to demographic information for descriptive statistics.

4 Results

4.1 Sample Description

A total of 56 questionnaires were distributed in the experiment, and 52 valid questionnaires were returned. About 60% of the participants were between the ages of 18 and 25, 45% were male, 55% were female, and 75% had a bachelor's degree or higher.

4.2 Manipulation Checks

To check whether the independent variables were treated correctly, we conducted separate independent samples t-tests for each of the two independent variables (anthropomorphism and information framing). The results showed that subjects who watched interface animations that included anthropomorphic factors (e.g., eyes, expressions) perceived anthropomorphism ($M_{anth} = 5.29$) more than subjects who watched interface animations without anthropomorphic factors ($M_{non} = 4.21$) ($t[52] = 2.121$; $p < 0.05$). Subjects who viewed the positive frame were more concerned with the positive effects of healthy sleep ($M_1 = 4.385$; $M_2 = 4.039$; $p < 0.05$), while those who viewed the negative frame were more concerned with the negative effects of unhealthy sleep ($M_1 = 5.347$; $M_2 = 4.942$; $p < 0.05$). In conclusion, the results of the manipulation examination confirm the validity of both manipulations, indicating that they can be used as subjects for this experiment.

4.3 Hypothesis Testing

To test the proposed hypothesis, a two-factor ANOVA, i.e., 2 (anthropomorphic vs. non-anthropomorphic) × 2 (gain vs. loss) between-subjects ANOVA was conducted. Hypothesis 1 hypothesized that anthropomorphism in the persuasive animation would have a positive effect on participants' intention to engage in healthy sleep behaviors. Results indicated a significant main effect of anthropomorphism on healthy sleep behavioral intentions ($F[1,48] = 36.678$; $p < .001$). Therefore, hypothesis 1 is supported: anthropomorphic animation is more likely to have outcomes that persuade viewers to sleep healthily compared to non-anthropomorphic animation.

Hypothesis 2 proposed that participants who viewed negatively framed messages had higher behavioral intention to sleep healthily than those who viewed positively framed messages. The results indicated a significant main effect of positive and negative framing on the behavioral intention for healthy sleep ($F[1,48] = 4.678$; $p < 0.05$). Therefore, hypothesis 2 was supported: negative framing was more effective in persuading participants' behavioral intention to sleep healthily with positive framing.

In hypothesis 3, we hypothesized that (a) participants showed stronger risk perceptions when viewing anthropomorphic animations matched with negative frames rather than positive frames (b) anthropomorphic people showed higher risk perceptions than non-anthropomorphic people when viewing negative frame animations. The results indicated a significant two-way interaction between positive and negative frames and anthropomorphism on viewers' risk perceptions of sleep deprivation ($F[1,48] = 14.085$; $p < .001$). Follow-up simple effects showed no difference in risk perception between anthropomorphism and non-anthropomorphism for positive frames. However, participants viewing the negative frame reported higher anthropomorphic risk perceptions than non-anthropomorphic ($F[1,48] = 10.992$; $p = .002$). For non-anthropomorphic, there was no difference in risk perceptions between positive and negative frames, however, participants viewing anthropomorphs reported higher risk perceptions for negative frames than positive frames ($F[1,48] = 15.937$; $p < .001$). This provides support for Hypothesis 3 (see Table 1 for relevant data).

Table 1. Interaction and simple effects result in anthropomorphism and frame

		SS	df	MS	F	P
Anthropomorphism × Message frame		8.368	1	8.368	14.085**	0.000
Message frame	Positive frame	2.358	1	2.358	3.969	0.052
	Negative frame	6.530	1	6.530	10.992*	0.002
Anthropomorphism	Anthropomorphism	9.468	1	9.468	15.937**	0.000
	Non-anthropomorphism	1.028	1	1.028	1.730	0.195

Note. Dependent variable: Risk Perception; * $p < .05$ ** $p < .001$

5 Discussion

The purpose of the current study was to investigate the role of anthropomorphic design in an interactive sleep persuasion interface. We, therefore, designed a two-factor between-subjects experiment with 2 anthropomorphic (anthropomorphic/non-anthropomorphic) × 2 information frames (positive frame/negative frame) to explore the differential effects of their two-two combination design approach on the unhealthy sleep behavior of young users sleeping late, with the dependent variables assessed mainly through the perceived risk of sleep deprivation and behavioral intention to sleep healthily. The experimental results showed that (i) anthropomorphism had a significant main effect in persuading young users' behavioral intention to sleep healthily and played a direct effect on healthy sleep; (ii) the framing effect had a main effect in persuading young users' behavioral intention to sleep healthily; (iii) there was an interaction between anthropomorphism and positive and negative framing on risk perception, and anthropomorphism played a moderating role in the effect of positive and negative framing on risk perception (anthropomorphic negative framing > non-anthropomorphic positive framing > non-anthropomorphic negative frame > anthropomorphic positive frame). Thus, our study provides several important contributions to the public health domain literature and health information design.

First, this study has some theoretical implications for anthropomorphism research. Previous research has demonstrated that anthropomorphism has a significant role in several domains. In the hospitality industry, Sinha et al.'s (2020) study demonstrated that anthropomorphism positively influenced employees' behavioral intentions to accept robots in the workplace; in the field of nature conservation, Yue et al.'s (2021) experimental results suggested that anthropomorphic strategies would help increase public support for wildlife conservation; in the field of health persuasion, Newton et al.'s (2017) study demonstrated that elements of self-anthropomorphism may represent a new way to motivate behavior change. Similarly, our experimental results validate the role of anthropomorphic design in persuasion as previously discussed, i.e., anthropomorphism had a positive effect on healthy sleep behavior of young users, and anthropomorphism moderated the role of positive and negative frames in risk perception. Interestingly, we found that the matching of anthropomorphic and positive frames in the interaction between anthropomorphic and informational frames resulted in the least risk perception, probably because when the positive effects of healthy sleep are shown in anthropomorphic design it creates a sense of security for the viewer, which reduces the perception of risk; while when the negative outcomes of sleep deprivation are shown in the anthropomorphic design, it gives the viewer a sense of vicariousness, which enhances the perception of risk.

Second, framing effects have often been used in past research to explore interactions with other factors, yet few studies have examined the combined effects of anthropomorphism and information framing. Even fewer studies have demonstrated the role of anthropomorphism and information framing in health behavior persuasion. In our study, the interaction between anthropomorphism and information framing in persuading young users to sleep healthily was demonstrated, enriching the application of framing effects in the health domain.

Finally, this study also provides some practical implications for industries related to health persuasion product design, providing crude support for future health product design. Our study is the first to experiment with the introduction of anthropomorphic design into the field of health persuasion product design, and the experimental results show that the combination of anthropomorphic graphics (with human-like characteristics) and negative framing text (describing the negative consequences of unhealthy behaviors) can serve the purpose of persuading young users to behave healthily. Specifically, the use of anthropomorphic graphics and negatively framed text can be tried in the design of health persuasion products. However, the persuasive message design in our current experiments is based on the cell phone's interactive interface animation, and the presentation of the combination of anthropomorphic and message frames will have to change when the message medium changes in the future.

6 Conclusion

This study is the first empirical study of the interaction effects between anthropomorphism and information frames in the health persuasion domain. We manipulated anthropomorphism and information frames in our experiments using persuasive interactive interface animations. The results show that anthropomorphism and information frames have a positive effect on young users' healthy sleep behavior and that the combination of anthropomorphism and information frames has a significant persuasive effect. Thus, our study enriches anthropomorphic design theory and frame effect theory, and also provides rough support for future healthy product design.

References

Ajzen, I., Fishbein, M.: Attitudes and the attitude-behavior relation: reasoned and automatic processes. Eur. Rev. Soc. Psychol. **11**, 1–33 (2000)

Barber, L.K., Munz, D.C.: Consistent-sufficient sleep predicts improvement in self-regulatory performance and psychology strain. Stress Health **27**, 314–324 (2001)

Barnes, C.M., Drake, C.L.: Prioritizing sleep health: public health policy recommendations. Perspect. Psychol. Sci. **10**(6), 733–737 (2015)

Branscum, P., Fay, K.Q., Senkowski, V.: Do different factors predict the adoption and maintenance of healthy sleep behaviors? A reasoned action approach. Transl. Behav. Med. **10**(1), 78–86 (2020)

Chang, C.T., Lee, Y.K.: Framing charity advertising: influences of message framing, image valence, and temporal framing on a charitable appeal. J. Appl. Soc. Psychol. **39**(12), 2910–2935 (2009)

Chinese Sleep Research Society (2021). 3.21 World Sleep Day China theme conference and largescale science popularization event launched in Beijing. In: 2021 White Paper on Exercise and Sleep, Released (2021). http://www.zgsmyjh.org/

Cho, J., Chun, J., Lee, M.J.: Impacts of message framing and social distance in health campaign for promoting regular physical exercise. J. Health Commun. **23**(9), 824–835 (2018)

de Bruijn, G.J., Spaans, P., Jansen, B., et al.: Testing the effects of a message framing intervention on intentions towards hearing loss prevention in adolescents. Health Educ. Res. **31**(2), 161–170 (2016)

De Velde, L.V., Verbeke, W., Popp, M., Huylenbroeck, G.V.: The importance of message framing for providing information about sustainability and environmental aspects of energy. Energy Policy **38**(10), 5541–5549 (2010)

Detweiler, J.B., Bedell, B.T., Salovey, P., Pronin, E., Rothman, A.J.: Message framing and sunscreen use: gain-framed messages motivate beach-goers. Health Psychol. **18**(2), 189–196 (1999)

Witte, K.: Predicting risk behaviors: development and validation of a diagnostic scale. J. Health Commun. **1**(4), 317–342 (2010). https://doi.org/10.1080/108107396127988

Dinges, D.F., et al.: Cumulative sleepiness, mood disturbance, and psychomotor vigilance performance decrements during a week of sleep restricted to 4–5 hours per night. Sleep **20**, 267–277 (1997)

Duffy, B.R.: Anthropomorphism and the social robot. Rob. Auton. Syst. **42**(3–4), 177–190 (2003)

Epley, N., Waytz, A., Cacioppo, J.T.: On seeing human: a three-factor theory of anthropomorphism. Psychol. Rev. **114**(4), 864–886 (2007)

Epley, N., Waytz, A., Akalis, S., Cacioppo, J.T.: When we need a human: motivational determinants of anthropomorphism. Soc. Cogn. **26**(2), 143–155 (2008)

Gallagher, K.M., Updegraff, J.A.: Health message framing effects on attitudes, intentions, and behaviour: a meta-analytic review. Ann. Behav. Med. **43**, 101–116 (2012)

Gerend, M.A., Cullen, M.: Effects of message framing and temporal context on college student drinking behavior. J. Exp. Soc. Psychol. **44**(4), 67–73 (2008)

Godsell, S., White, J.: Adolescent perceptions of sleep and influences on sleep behaviour: a qualitative study. J. Adolesc. **73**, 18–25 (2019)

Guan, M., So, J.: Tailoring temporal message frames to individuals' time orientation strengthens the relationship between risk perception and behavioral intention. J. Health Commun. **25**(12), 971–981 (2020)

Harrison, Y., Horne, J.A.: One night of sleep loss impairs innovative thinking and flexible decision making. Organ. Behav. Hum. Decis. Process. **78**, 128–145 (1999)

Hayley, A.C., Skogen, J.C., Øverland, S., Wold, B., Williams, L.J., Kennedy, G.A., et al.: Trajectories and stability of self-reported short sleep duration from adolescence to adulthood. J. Sleep Res. **24**(6), 621–628 (2015)

Huang, G., Li, K., Li, H.: Show, not tell the contingency role of infographics versus text in the differential effects of message strategies on optimistic bias. Sci. Commun. **41**(6), 732–760 (2019)

Karpinska-Krakowiak, M., Skowron, L., Ivanov, L.: "I will start saving natural resources, only when you show me the planet as a person in danger": the effects of message framing and anthropomorphism on pro-environmental behaviors that are viewed as effortful. Sustainability **12**(14), 5524 (2020)

Killgore, W.D.S., Balkin, T.J., Wesensten, N.J.: Impaired decision making following 49 h of sleep deprivation. J. Sleep Res. **15**, 7–13 (2006)

Kim, S., McGill, A.L.: Gaming with Mr. Slot or gaming the slot machine? Power, anthropomorphism, and risk perception. J. Consum. Res. **38**(1), 94–107 (2011)

Krishnamurthy, P., Carter, P., Blair, E.: Attribute framing and goal framing effects in health decisions. Organ. Behav. Hum. Decis. Process. **85**(2), 382–399 (2001)

Lee, Y.H., Lai, C.M.: The pet affection scale development, validation, and influence on consumers' behavior of pet hotels. Mathematics **9**(15), 1772 (2021)

Levin, I.P., Schneider, S.L., Gaeth, G.J.: All frames are not created equal: a typology and critical analysis of framing effects. Organ. Behav. Hum. Decis. Process. **76**(2), 149–188 (1998)

Louzada, F.M., da Silva, A.G.T., Peixoto, C.A.T., Menna Barreto, L.: The adolescence sleep phase delay: causes, consequences, and possible interventions. Sleep Sci. **1**, 49–53 (2008)

Ma, Z., Nan, X.: Positive facts, negative stories: message framing as a moderator of narrative persuasion in antismoking communication. Health Commun. **34**(12), 1454–1460 (2019)

Mitchell, V.W., Bakewell, C., Jackson, P.R., et al.: How message framing affects consumer attitudes in food crises. Br. Food J. **117**(8), 2200–2211 (2015)

National Bureau of Statistics. 2018 National Time Use Survey Bulletin (2019). http://www.stats.gov.cn/tjsj/zxfb/201901/t20190125_1646796.html

Newton, F.J., Newton, J.D., Wong, J.: This is your stomach speaking: anthropomorphized health messages reduce portion size preferences among the powerless. J. Bus. Res. **75**, 229–239 (2017)

Owens, J.: Insufficient sleep in adolescents and young adults: an update on causes and consequences. Pediatrics **134**(3), e921–e932 (2014)

Robbins, R., Niederdeppe, J.: Testing the role of narrative and gain-loss framing in messages to promote sleep hygiene among high school students. J. Health Commun. **24**(1), 84–93 (2019)

Rogers, R.W.: A protection motivation theory of fear appeals and attitude change. J. Psychol. **91**(1), 93–114 (1975). https://doi.org/10.1080/00223980.1975.9915803

Rogers, R.W.: Cognitive and physiological processes in fear appeals and attitude change: a revised theory of protection motivation. In: Cacioppo, J.T., Petty, R.E. (eds.) Social Psychophysiology: A Sourcebook, pp. 153–176. Guilford Press, New York (1983)

Rosenstock, I.M.: Why people use health services. Milbank Mem. Fund Q. **44**(3), 94 (1966). https://doi.org/10.2307/3348967

Rothman, A., Salovey, P.: Shaping perceptions to motivate healthy behaviour: the role of message framing. Psychol. Bull. **121**, 3–19 (1997)

Schneider, T.R., Salovey, P., Apanovitch, A.M., Pizarro, J., McCarthy, D., Zullo, J., et al.: The effects of message framing and ethnic targeting on mammography use among lowincome women. Health Psychol. **20**, 256–266 (2001)

Schweizer, A., Berchtold, A., Barrense-Dias, Y., et al.: Adolescents with a smartphone sleep less than their peers. Eur. J. Pediatr. **176**(1), 131–136 (2017)

Shao, X., Jeong, E.H., Jang, S.C.S., et al.: Mr. Potato Head fights food waste: the effect of anthropomorphism in promoting ugly food. Int. J. Hospitality Manage. **89**, 102521 (2020)

Sinha, N., Singh, P., Gupta, M., et al.: Robotics at workplace: an integrated Twitter analytics–SEM based approach for behavioral intention to accept. Int. J. Inf. Manage. **55**, 102210 (2020)

Steinmetz, H., Knappstein, M., Ajzen, I., Schmidt, P., Kabst, R.: How effective are behavior change interventions based on the theory of planned behavior? A three-level meta-analysis. Z Psychol. **224**(3), 216 (2016)

Stern, P.: The many benefits of healthy sleep. Science **374**(6567), 550–551 (2021)

Taheri, S., Lin, L., Austin, D., Young, T., Mignot, E.: Short sleep duration is associated with reduced leptin, elevated ghrelin, and increased body mass index. PLoS Med. **1**, 210–217 (2004)

Tversky, A., Kahneman, D.: The framing of decisions and the psychology of choice. Science **211**, 453–458 (1981)

Witte, K.: Putting the fear back into fear appeals: the extended parallel process model. Commun. Monogr. **59**(4), 329–349 (1992). https://doi.org/10.1080/03637759209376276

Witte, K., Cameron, K.A., McKeon, J.K., Berkowitz, J.M.: Predicting risk behaviors: development and validation of a diagnostic scale. J. Health Commun. **1**(4), 317–341 (1996)

Yue, D., Tong, Z., Tian, J., et al.: Anthropomorphic strategies promote wildlife conservation through empathy: the moderation role of the public epidemic situation. Int. J. Environ. Res. Public Health **18**(7), 3565 (2021)

Health Knowledge Visualization for the Elderly

Manhai Li[(✉)], Lang Luo, Sijian Chen, and Xingyi Zhou

Chongqing University of Posts and Telecommunications, Chongqing 400065, China
limh@cqupt.edu.cn

Abstract. Aiming at the problem of cognitive mismatch between the knowledge structure of the ordinary elderly and medical professionals, health knowledge visualization is used to help the elderly understand vague medical information clearly. Based on the literature research of domestic senile diseases, a study of optimizing medical report of urine testing was conducted, and the information display interface before and after the redesign is compared. The new medical treatment can make the people of ordinary elderly know their physical conditions more intuitively and comprehensively by health knowledge visualization, like providing the cartoon diagram and the color expression in accordance with cognitive limitations of the elderly. The user interface of new medical report can also effectively provide the elderly immediate precautions according to their actual needs of health supervision. The goal is to improve the efficiency and quality of decision-sharing for the elderly and to improve the therapeutic experience.

Keywords: Knowledge visualization · Health supervision · Urine test · The elderly

1 Introduction

1.1 Knowledge Visualization

Knowledge can be defined as a clear and certain perception of a subject or object, and/or the understanding of certain facts. In essence, it is the content that resides in our minds. The process of acquiring knowledge is therefore through our interpretation of information. Some would consider information and knowledge interchangeable, but this is true only to certain extent. This is true when the same content occupies more than one space. For example, information content of a communication email also becomes knowledge of the reader once it is read. However, information is by no means equal to knowledge particularly deep knowledge. The process of information-knowledge transformation is through learning and human interpretation; and the process of knowledge-information transformation is achieved by communication of what is known amongst people. Process of knowledge is dependent on the person that knows or the cognitive ability of the subject, as well as on the abilities of the person to assimilate symbolic knowledge. The purpose of knowledge is to guide the exchange of knowledge between people and assist decision-making.

M. M. Soares et al. (Eds.): HCII 2022, LNCS 13322, pp. 174–184, 2022.
https://doi.org/10.1007/978-3-031-05900-1_11

Knowledge visualization is a context-based and continuous active inquiry process. It uses collaborative creation, abductive reasoning methods and various visualization methods to assist individuals in interactive memory systems, share mental models, transform uncertain situations into controlled contexts, and finally arrive at "founded judgments." As an emerging discipline, knowledge visualization was first proposed by Professor Martin and Professor Bucard in 2004. They believe that knowledge visualization is to use visual representation to improve the creation and dissemination of knowledge between at least two people. Furthermore, the definition of knowledge visualization was also proposed, which clarifies the research content, objects, and representation methods of knowledge visualization. The purpose is to enhance the dissemination and creation of knowledge among the crowd by giving people rich means of expressing what they know [1]. In the field of management and education, there have been many research on knowledge visualization, for example, visualizing professional medical knowledge into universal knowledge that can be understood by the public [2]. Using three-dimensional visualization technology to improve students' understanding of concepts, so as to improve the effectiveness of teaching methods [3].

1.2 Health Knowledge Visualization

In the era of big data, research on knowledge visualization is being carried out in various fields, which has attracted more and more attention. In the medical field, there have been some studies on using knowledge visualization method to convert clinical medical data into useful knowledge [4–6], but few applications of medical knowledge visualization based on real scene. In fact, patients do not understand the professional knowledge of medical treatment, which leads to the inability to understand the meaning of doctors, especially elderly patients. When using visual methods, human beings have a stronger ability to receive information [7]. Therefore, it is necessary to carry out research on health knowledge visualization for the elderly.

Many studies have shown that the design related to the medical and health field can improve the doctor-patient relationship from multiple angles, improve the treatment effect of patients and reduce the occurrence of medical accidents [8]. Arturo Gonzalez conducted relevant research, using visual aid, manuals, and handouts to test the effect of patient disease and nursing knowledge education on the disease improvement. The results confirmed that this education can reduce the recurrence rate of venous ulcer [9]. If the test results are visualized and the opinions and predictions of medical staff are directly reflected on the test result table, it will be more conducive to the patient's understanding of the test results. Research shows that age-related memory loss may be related to changes in visual exploration, and the memory mode of the elderly depends on what they see [10].

2 Cognitive Difficulties of Health Knowledge

According to a research report, in 2001, China's population over the age of 65 accounted for more than 7%, which means that it has begun to enter an aging society; in 2019, China's old people over 65 accounted for 12% of the total population. The social health problems brought by aging have also attracted extensive attention. The health of the elderly has become a serious social problem.

With the growth of age, the physical function of the elderly continues to deteriorate, and the trouble caused by diseases is increasing. Common diseases of the elderly are diabetes, hypertension, vaginitis, prostatitis, urinary tract infection and chronic kidney disease. According to the survey report in 2019, the elderly disease rate of people over 45 years old in China is on the rise. The report shows that the incidence rate of diabetes is 26% [11]. The prevalence of hypertension was 34.38% [12]; The prevalence of vaginitis was 21.33%; The incidence rate of chronic prostatitis is 6%–32.9% [13]. The incidence rate of male urinary tract infection was 380.8/100000, and the incidence rate of female urinary tract infection was 2812.3/100000 [14]. The prevalence of chronic kidney disease in China is 10.8% [15]. It must be mentioned that these common senile diseases can be quantified and evaluated by urine test. In my research, the health knowledge visualization for elderly is also based on urine detection technology.

2.1 Common Senile Diseases of the Elderly

Routine urine examination can be used to diagnose the following six common elderly diseases, such as diabetes, nephropathy, urinary tract infection, vaginitis, and hypertension, prostatitis, etc. According to the research report, the routine urine test results of diabetic patients are basically the same with clinical diagnosis data [16, 17].

The first one is diabetes. Diabetes is a chronic and long-lasting health condition that affects how your body turns food into energy, which is one of the most common geriatric diseases. Diabetes can cause serious health problems, such as heart disease, vision loss, and kidney disease.

The second one is nephropathy. Nephropathy is a broad medical term used to denote disease or damage of the kidney, which can eventually result in kidney failure. The primary and most obvious functions of the kidney are to excrete any waste products and regulate the water and acid-base balance of the body. Kidney disease means your kidneys are damaged and can't filter blood the way they should. Loss of kidney function is a potentially fatal condition. Nephropathy is considered a progressive illness, including acute kidney injury, kidney cysts, kidney stones, and kidney infections. Routine urine examination can be used to diagnose kidney diseases. The third one is Urinary Tract Infection (UTI), which is an infection in any part of your urinary system — your kidneys, ureters, bladder, and urethra. Most infections involve the lower urinary tract — the bladder and the urethra. Women are at greater risk of developing a UTI than are men. An infection limited to your bladder can be painful and annoying. However, serious consequences can occur if a UTI spreads to your kidneys.

The fourth one is Vaginitis, which is an inflammation of the vagina that can result in discharge, itching and pain. The cause is usually a change in the normal balance of vaginal bacteria or an infection. Due to the deterioration of physiological function of elderly women, the resistance of vaginal natural defense system decreases, and candida vaginitis often occurs. Reduced estrogen levels after menopause and some skin disorders can also cause vaginitis.

The fifth one is Hypertension, which is called a "silent killer". Most people with hypertension are unaware of the problem because it may have no warning signs or symptoms. Hypertension is the most common senile disease at present. When symptoms do occur, they can include early morning headaches, nosebleeds, irregular heart rhythms, vision changes, and buzzing in the ears. Severe hypertension can cause fatigue, nausea, vomiting, confusion, anxiety, chest pain, and muscle tremors. Different kidney diseases are often accompanied by hypertension.

The sixth one is Prostatitis, which is swelling and inflammation of the prostate gland. Prostatitis often causes painful or difficult urination. Other symptoms include pain in the groin, pelvic area or genitals and sometimes flu-like symptoms.

2.2 Difficulties in Understanding Medical Terminology

From the description of these geriatric diseases, we can see that only medical professionals can understand each key point. In fact, every medical staff in the hospital must undergo many years of professional training to understand and master this professional knowledge. People with different knowledge backgrounds have different understandings of information. It means that it is difficult for the ordinary elderly to understand the information in a professional urine test report, as shown in Fig. 1.

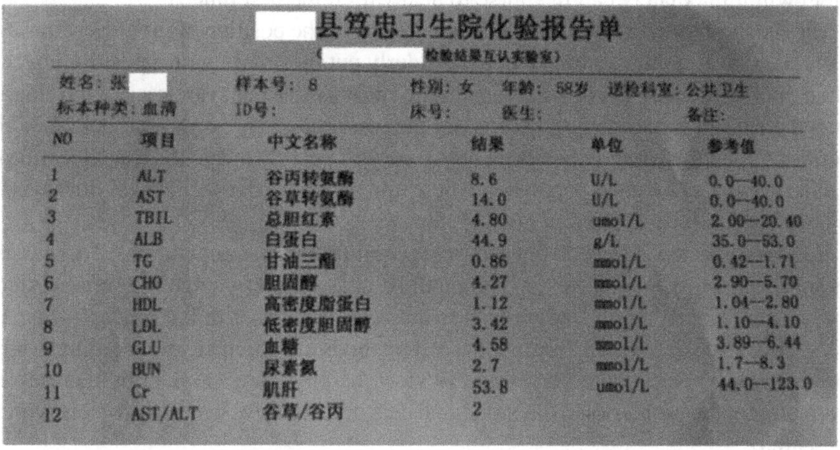

Fig. 1. Incomprehensible urine test report. Photo by the author.

It is difficult for the elderly to understand the medical terminology in the urine test report and find out whether the value of each item is in the normal range. The elderly must take the urine test report to medical staff to get useful information.

This method has two shortcomings: one is that there are only a few tests closely related to the elderly in the report, while it needs to spend the elderly extra time to make an appointment with the medical staff. It is widely known that making an appointment is a boring thing, because the medical staff are busy and the medical procedures are cumbersome [18]; On the other hand, even with the help of medical staff, many useful information in the inspection report will be omitted, because the concerns of medical staff and the elderly are different. The elderly are concerned about whether they have diabetes or hypertension, rather than learning to understand the meaning of detection items.

2.3 Technological Approach

Health is the prerequisite and core foundation for the comprehensive development of human beings and the coordinated development of society and economy. The improvement of the national health level indicates that the country is prosperous and prosperous, and it is also the united aspiration of citizens of all walks of life. In China, many medical equipment manufacturers have developed digital health management systems, hoping to help the elderly realize personal health management through intelligent technical means. Here are some examples.

The first example is the real-time monitoring of physiological indicators of the elderly through smart watches. The elderly only need to wear a smart watch on their wrist without complex interface operation. The health management system automatically detects the physiological data through the chip, then remotely analyzes the physiological data through Internet technology, and then notifies the relevant people of the processing results in the simplest way. For example, once cardiac arrest is detected, the health management system will immediately call the nurse to deal with it the first time.

The second example is the real-time monitoring of the position of the elderly through the wireless positioning system. When the elderly put the device with a positioning chip in their pocket, the wireless positioning system can draw the behavior track of the elderly. When the elderly is in a state of emergency, he just needs to press the call button on the equipment, then the wireless positioning system will quickly locate the exact location of the elderly and call medical personnel to help him get out of danger. The product system has been successfully applied in nursing homes.

In these cases, the elderly do not need to do complex interface operations. This passive way solves the problem of the elderly's cognition of health knowledge to a certain extent. However, the elderly prefer individuals to actively participate in the process of health care, such as choosing which exercise and rest methods to participate in according to their own health data. Once the elderly want to view the physiological data by themselves, how to present the professional physiological data in a cognitive way is a problem worthy of research.

3   The Practice of Health Knowledge Visualization

Knowledge visualization tools include heuristic sketches that can find new ideas for decision makers; conceptual maps that can structure decision content; visual metaphors that connect the role of knowledge domains; and dynamic, interactive knowledge animation. The knowledge visualization framework includes collaborative activities that identify needs, identify gaps in knowledge, complete through interactive memory systems and shared mental models, and create new knowledge and accurate visual representations through these activities, leading to (decision-making) behavior. Subsequently, the author defines in detail the mechanism and process of knowledge visualization based on shared decision-making in medical scenarios.

3.1 Reduce Cognitive Complexity of Health Knowledge

Let's take diabetes as an example. To accurately evaluate the health status of the elderly, traditionally, hospitals need to detect more than 10 physiological indicators of the elderly, including blood pressure, liver, and kidney function. Different test items need different test equipment, and the test frequency of different items is also different. For example, blood pressure needs to be detected every day, and liver and kidney function needs to be detected every six months. These testing items are very cumbersome as shown in Fig. 2. The elderly spend a lot of time on these items, while they have no perception of the whole process, which is a very bad medical experience, because they don't understand the meaning of these tests at all.

糖尿病的检查项目对比			
	检测项目	检测频率	检查设备
常规方式	身高、体重、腹围	经常	
	血压	经常	血压检测仪
	空腹血糖、餐后血糖、随机血糖	经常、必要时随机查	血糖仪
	糖化血红蛋白	至少每3~4个月查一次	糖化血红蛋白检测仪
	肝肾功能	至少每半年复查一次	全自动生化分析仪
	胆固醇、甘油三酯	至少每半年复查一次	全自动生化分析仪
	高密度脂蛋白、低密度脂蛋白	至少每年复查一次	全自动生化分析仪
	眼、神经、足部检查	至少每年复查一次	裂隙灯等
	胸片、心电图	至少每年复查一次或必要时	心率检测仪
	血管检测	至少每4年复查一次或必要时	血管检测仪
新的方式	十四项尿检指标	每天一次或必要时	智能马桶

Fig. 2. Comparison of diabetes checklist. List made by the author.

According to the previous medical literature analysis, diabetes can be detected and evaluated by urine test technology. So, in my design practice, the urine detection function is integrated into the toilet used by the elderly every day. The smart toilet combing with urine detection can detect 14 medical indicators such as protein, glucose, PH, occult blood, white blood cells, and ketones at one time. This method of inspection is very suitable for the elderly. It not only avoids queuing at the hospital, but also avoids being unable to know how to perform the inspection due to the complexity of the inspection process, which greatly improves efficiency in terms of time. Even if it is tested once a day, it will not feel complicated. At the same time, the test once a day allows the results to be more accurate and to respond to possible conditions in a timely manner. It is useful for detecting chronic kidney disease, vaginitis, diabetes, and other diseases. Through intelligent analysis and risk prediction, potential patients are kept away from disease risks.

3.2 Propose a New Technical Solution

Deepening the improvement of the medical service system is a core part of medical strategy. The extensive application of science and technology in daily life is the performance of social progress, but it also brings many troubles to the daily life of the elderly. Because the elderly have cognitive barriers to their understanding of new technologies and equipment, the elderly cannot enjoy the convenience brought by intelligent services. It is worth mentioning that the Chinese government has vigorously advocated solutions in this regard. For example, on November 15, 2020, the general office of the State Council issued an implementation plan to solve the technical problems of the elderly using intelligent devices. New technology and equipment can hand over some cumbersome manual operations to machines, to reduce people's cognitive thresholds. To enable the ordinary elderly to understand the contents of medical reports, new technical solutions can be introduced and developed. The product concept of integrating urine detection technology with toilets is shown in Fig. 3.

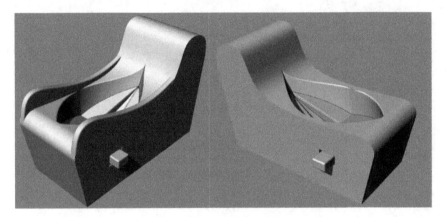

Fig. 3. Comprehensible urine test report. Photos made by the author.

The new intelligent toilet can automatically complete the detection of 14 urine indicators. The detection process is impossible without any manual operation. The elderly only need to use the toilet as usual, such as detection, analysis, report, and other operations are handed over to the machine to complete automatically. This solution is an important step of health knowledge visualization, especially suitable for the elderly.

3.3 Make Urine Test Report Comprehensible

Knowledge visualization is the visualization of an important part of information to be transmitted, to realize the knowledge transmission between two or more people. The content of knowledge visualization includes not only data, but also insights, expectations, and forecasts for the future. For the elderly, some visual images may be easier to understand and remember than the professional data results on the checklist. Displaying clinical trial data to the elderly through visualization methods such as images can make it easier to accept this information.

The improvement of the efficiency and quality of medical decision-making cannot separate from doctor-patient communication. The core goal of doctor-patient communication is to achieve knowledge sharing and make high-quality medical decisions through communication. Researchers have found that collaborative creative activities have a stable role in the current visual selection of means of knowledge exchange. Visualizing the knowledge of urine test reports is a kind of communication, which can make it comprehensible for the elderly to understand the test results.

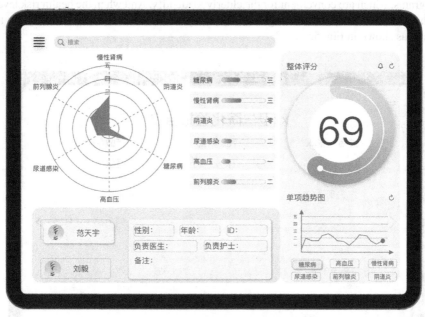

Fig. 4. Comprehensible urine test report. Photos made by the author. (Color figure online)

As shown in the upper left corner of Fig. 4 the six common senile diseases most concerned with the elderly are visually identified in the user interface. They are diabetes, nephropathy, urinary tract infection, vaginitis, hypertension, prostatitis, etc. The risk probability of six common senile diseases is divided into 1–5 levels, and the value of the level is determined according to the comprehensive analysis results of multiple urine detection indicators. The higher the level, the higher the risk of corresponding geriatric diseases. To facilitate the elderly to easily identify and understand, low values are represented in green and high values are represented in red. From the human-computer interface, the elderly can intuitively know that their health risk level of diabetes and chronic kidney disease is three, the health risk level of prostatitis and urinary tract infection is two, the health risk level of hypertension is grade one, and the health risk level of vaginitis is zero, indicating that it is healthy. As shown in the upper right corner of Fig. 4, the overall health status of the elderly is scored by quantitative values from 0 to 100. The elderly can understand their physiological status, which is easy to compare with the past state, and it is also convenient to set health goals. In the lower left corner of Fig. 4, the name, gender, and other basic information of the elderly are displayed, and the information of the responsible doctor and nurse of the elderly is also displayed to facilitate rapid contact. In the lower right corner of Fig. 4 is the trend of six common senile diseases. The elderly can intuitively select one of them and see whether it is getting better or worse over a period.

In addition to ensuring that the man-machine interface should convey information intuitively and accurately, good knowledge visualization also needs to provide constructive opinions to users. The common senile diseases are intuitively presented by organ diagrams, which are convenient for the elderly to identify. And when the health risk level of hypertension in the elderly is grade two, the system should remind the elderly not to drink, as shown in Fig. 5.

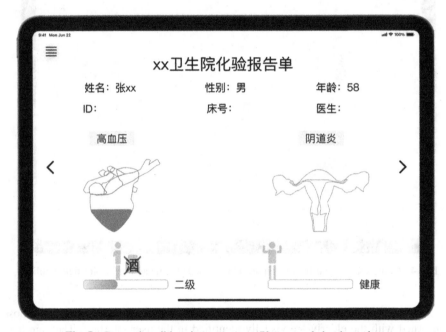

Fig. 5. Comprehensible urine test report. Photos made by the author.

For the elderly, providing them with targeted guidance is the most important value embodiment of the health management system, rather than presenting them with a pile of indicators and data that are difficult to understand. For example, when the elderly suffer from chronic kidney disease, the system should not only accurately display the current risk level, but also remind a reasonable work and rest schedule; When the elderly are suffering from diabetes, the system should remind them of what kind of adjuvant therapy is needed, including proper physical exercise. If the system can achieve this degree of intelligence, then the health management system is humanized.

Making urine test reports comprehensible is not easy, but it is essential. This is not only to facilitate the elderly and doctors, but also to improve the trust relationship between doctors and patients. The goal of health knowledge visualization is to help the elderly recover their health. Although the number of face-to-face meetings between the elderly and doctors has been reduced, in fact, the effectiveness of online interaction between doctors and the elderly has increased.

4 Conclusion

Health priority, reform, innovation, scientific development and fairness and justice are the strategic themes for promoting healthy China. The development of the country is not only for the new generation, but also for the life of the old generation. The problem of aging has been paid more and more attention in China. To pay attention to the problem of aging, we should pay attention to the health care of the elderly. The health knowledge visualization for the elderly is to help the elderly recover their health by making the physiological state and health knowledge comprehensible.

Routine urine examination can be used to diagnose the following six common elderly diseases, such as diabetes, nephropathy, urinary tract infection, vaginitis, and hypertension, prostatitis, etc. To enable the ordinary elderly to understand the contents of medical reports, Intelligent toilet integrating urine detection technology was proposed, which is an important step of health knowledge visualization. The elderly only need to use the toilet as usual, such as detection, analysis, report, and other operations are handed over to the machine to complete automatically.

The content of knowledge visualization includes not only data, but also insights, expectations, and forecasts for the future. The new medical treatment can make the people of ordinary elderly know their physical conditions more intuitively and comprehensively by health knowledge visualization, like providing the cartoon diagram and the color expression in accordance with cognitive limitations of the elderly. Displaying clinical trial data to the elderly through visualization methods such as images can make it easier to accept this information.

The user interface of new medical reports can also effectively provide the elderly with immediate precautions according to their actual needs of health supervision. The goal is to improve the efficiency and quality of decision-sharing for the elderly and to improve the therapeutic experience. In my study, common senile diseases are intuitively presented by organ diagrams, which is convenient for the elderly to identify. And when the health risk level of hypertension in the elderly is high, the system should remind the elderly not to drink.

Acknowledgments. This work was supported by Doctoral startup fund and talent introduction fund project of Chongqing University of Posts and Telecommunications – Research on the cost and benefit distribution of big data productization (K2020-201) and Chongqing educational science planning project – Research on the talent training system of "social theme" in Colleges and Universities (2020-GX-284) and Research Center for network social development of Chongqing University of Posts and Telecommunications – Research on the cost of network big data production (2020SKJD06).

References

1. Eppler, M.J., Burkhard, R.A.: Knowledge visualization: towards a new discipline and its fields of application. University of Lugano. In: Schwartz, D.G. (ed.) Encyclopedia of Knowledge Management (2004)
2. Jahn, F., Höffner, K., Schneider, B.: The SnIK graph: visualization of a medical informatics ontology. Stud. Health Technol. Inform. **264**, 1941–1942 (2019)
3. Hanson, J., Andersen, P., Dunn, P.K.: Effectiveness of three-dimensional visualization on undergraduate nursing and midwifery students' knowledge and achievement in pharmacology: a mixed methods study. Nurse Educ. Today **81**, 19–25 (2019)
4. Copeland, A.D., Mangoubi, R.S., Desai, M.N.: Spatio-temporal data fusion for 3D+T image reconstruction in cerebral angiography. IEEE Trans. Med. Imaging **29**(6), 1238–1251 (2010)
5. Ruedinger, K.L., Schafer, S., Speidel, M.A.: 4D-DSA: development and current neurovascular applications. Am. J. Neuroradiol. **42**(2), 214–220 (2021)
6. Chen, S., Huang, T., Wen, T.: MutScan: fast detection and visualization of target mutations by scanning FASTQ data. BMC Bioinform. **19**(1), 16 (2018)
7. Miller, G.A.: The magical number seven, plus or minus two: some limits on our capacity for processing information. Cornell Hotel Restaurant Adm. Q. **1956**(6), 81–97 (1956)
8. C, M.S.F.: Obstacles and Solutions. Healthcare Design (2010)
9. Gonzalez, A.: The effect of a patient education intervention on knowledge and venous ulcer recurrence: results of a prospective intervention and retrospective analysis. Ostomy Wound Manage. **63**(6), 16–28 (2017)
10. Wynn, J.S., Amer, T., Schacter, D.L.: How older adults remember the world depends on how they see it. Trends Cogn. Sci. **24**(11), 858–861 (2020)
11. Yang, W.: epidemiology and trends in diabetes in China. Scientia Sinica (Vitae) **48**(8), 812–819 (2018)
12. Yuan, J., Wu, Q., Lei, S.: The prevalence of hypertension and its influencing factors in middle-aged and elderly people in China. Chin. Gen. Pract. **23**(34), 4337–4341 (2020)
13. Li, J., Wei, Y., Song, G.: Research progress in traditional Chinese medicine constitution of prostate disease. China Mod. Med. **28**(04), 23–26 (2021)
14. Yuan, S., Shi, Y., Li, M., Hu, X., Bai, R.: Trends in incidence of urinary tract infection in mainland China from 1990 to 2019. Int. J. Gen. Med. **14**, 1413–1420 (2021)
15. Yano, Y., Fujimoto, S., Asahi, K., Watanabe, T.: Prevalence of chronic kidney disease in China. Lancet **380**(9838), 213–214 (2012)
16. Liu, X.: The Value of routine urine test in the diagnosis of urinary tract infection and its influence on prognostic efficacy and satisfaction. China Pract. Med. **16**(8), 2019–2021 (2021)
17. Zhang, H.: Clinical significance of urinalysis in elderly patients with candida vaginitis. Chin. J. Mod. Appl. **14**(21), 43–45 (2020)
18. Qiu, M., Lv, J., Liu, T.: Discussion on the process of outpatient treatment under the support of information technology. China Digital Med. **15**(12), 2018–2020 (2020)
19. Wang, X.: Research on Knowledge Visualization in Healthcare Shared Decision-making. Jiangnan University (2018)
20. Wang, X., Xin, X.: Influence of information and knowledge visualization medical marking. Packag. Eng. **36**, 20 (2015)
21. Liao, Y.: Epidemiology and research advances in diabetes mellitus in China. J. Chongqing Med. Univ. **40**(7), 1042–1045 (2015)

Visualizing the Electroencephalography Signal Discrepancy When Maintaining Social Distancing: EEG-Based Interactive Moiré Patterns

Jingjing Li[1(✉)] [iD], Ye Yang[2] [iD], Zhexin Zhang[1], Yinan Zhao[1], Vargas Meza Xanat[1], and Yoichi Ochiai[1]

[1] Research and Development Center for Digital Nature, University of Tsukuba, Tsukuba, Japan
li@digitalnature.slis.tsukuba.ac.jp
[2] College of Design and Innovation, Tongji University, Shanghai, China

Abstract. In the context of the COIVD-19 pandemic, everyone must maintain social distances in public. Our ability to perceive each other through "distances" in public places has been compromised. However, "distance" is an essential factor in communication that cannot be ignored, like "facial expressions" and "body movements". This paper reflects on the current fixed "social distancing" in the context of the current viral pandemic. The innovative point of our research is to detect and calculate the differences of brainwave signal data between two people and visualize the differences through programmed 2D moving images. In terms of the research process, first, we explored a new way of interaction, using brainwave signals to express "distances" and moiré patterns as visual representations. Then we wrote an algorithm to generate the dynamic responses of the moiré patterns to different stimuli in real-time to represent the concepts of distances and visualize people's reactions. Finally, we developed an interactive device to imagine "electroencephalography (EEG) signal discrepancy" to perceive the "distances" in social situations. Nowadays, online meetings, classes, etc., are becoming more and more popular, and the distances between people in virtual spaces will be more ambiguous. In light of this, we plan to explore the visualization of electroencephalography (EEG) signal discrepancy in remote communication to enhance people's perceptions of each other in the future.

Keywords: COVID-19 · Social distancing · Visualization · Electroencephalography (EEG) · Moiré patterns · Generative art

1 Introduction

1.1 Social Distancing Under the COVID-19 Pandemic

In the area of public health, social distancing is also called physical distancing [1–3]. Physical distancing is the practice of staying at least 6 feet away from others to avoid

---

J. Li and Y. Yang—The first two authors contributed equally to this work.

© The Author(s), under exclusive license to Springer Nature Switzerland AG 2022
M. M. Soares et al. (Eds.): HCII 2022, LNCS 13322, pp. 185–197, 2022.
https://doi.org/10.1007/978-3-031-05900-1_12

catching a disease such as COVID-19. It is a set of non-pharmaceutical interventions or measures designed to prevent the spread of infectious diseases by maintaining physical distances among people and reducing the number of times people come into close contact [1, 4]. It usually involves keeping a certain distance from others (the prescribed distance varies from country to country and can be modified over time) and avoiding gathering in large groups [5, 6].

Physical distance always maps the psychological distance between individuals, reflecting the degree of intimacy of the human relationship. However, the relationship mapping is disrupted in the context of the COVID-19 pandemic. Keeping social distance has become a new rule, which protects us from viral influences from others. In this way, the language of physical distance is becoming ambiguous and turning into an indeterminate situation [7], as the traditional specific meanings conveyed through physical distances have been disrupted [8]. The idea for the "6 Foot Cover" campaign, spreading on social media in 2020, came about when designers Paco Conde and Beto Fernandez were on lockdown in Los Angeles. They changed the characters' positions on classic record covers, pulling people apart from each other [9]. The overall atmosphere of each redesigned image turns cold due to the physical distances of the characters. Arguably one of the most iconic album covers, The Beatles' Abbey Road, sees the band spread out down the road rather than information on the legendary crossing. While two men who once appeared destined to meet on the front of Oasis' (What is The Story) Morning Glory cover, now are passing on opposite sides of the street [10] (see Fig. 1).

Fig. 1. This picture is taken from Four Redesigned Music Covers from the "6 Foot Cover" Campaign. The Four Original Music Covers Are, The Beatles - Abbey Road, Oasis - (What's The Story) Morning Glory!, Blondie - Blondie, The Freewheelin' Bob Dylan [10]

1.2 Personal Space Theory in the Context of the COVID-19 Pandemic

Each of us has an invisible bubble, and we are enveloped by four different sizes of bubbles, each of which applies to a different potential interloper. This phenomenon is evidenced in American anthropologist Edward Hall's Personal Space Theory [11]. There are four kinds of personal space distances. Within 0.45 m is intimate distance, often occurring between love, family and friends. 0.45–1.2 m belong to the personal distance, suitable for familiar people, and can be cordial handshake and conversation. 1.2–3.6 m are social distances, often occurring in workplaces and public places. More significant than 3.7 m is designated as the public distance, such as the distance maintained with the audience during speeches, lectures, theatrical performances and movie screenings in the Assembly Hall (see Fig. 2).

However, during the COVID-19 Pandemic, people are asked to keep at least 6 feet from each other to avoid spreading the virus. This situation meant that the categories of distances between people were diminished, losing the "intimate distance", "personal distance", and part of the "social distance". In light of this, the definition of Personal Space Theory has been changed.

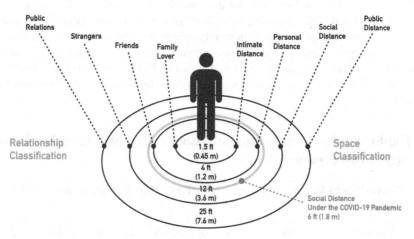

Fig. 2. Classifications of personal spaces and relationships under the COVID-19 pandemic (©Jingjing Li, 2022)

1.3 A New Era of "Distance Crisis"

More importantly, online communication is turning into a new normal, e.g., online class, online meeting, online negotiation, which accelerates online communications and interactions more and more popular and even becomes a necessity for everybody. The network makes it possible to chat across time and space and seems to make the distance disappear. However, something inherently embedded in the virtual world blocks actual soul communications, which is unreal, distorted and false (e.g., AI-facilitated chatting tool [12]). Overall, we face the reality of uncertain and confused distances both in the physical and virtual worlds, bringing us into a new era of "distance crisis".

1.4 A New Form of Distance Expression Under "Distance Crisis" Era

As mentioned above, we are in a "distance crisis" era. In this context, our research question is how could we truly see and understand the "distances" in this new era of "distance crisis"? The purpose of this study is to find a new method to express "distances" to help people judge relationships between each other while maintaining social distances. More importantly, we try to explore "distances" that are intuitive and spontaneous psychological distances between individuals, mainly reflecting on the gaps of preferences, knowledge, emotions and values towards the same matters.

The object of our research is a new way of expressing distance in the era of "distance crisis". This new form of distance expression needs to be visualized to help people judge "distances" more easily. Data visualization of various information has always been an effective way to transform abstract data and concepts into clearly understandable images [13]. The visualization of "distances" can enhance the perception of human interactions.

Since people's physiological signal data are closely related to their emotional and physical states and reactions, we aim to express the "distances" between people by visualizing physiological signals. Among physiological signals, brainwave signals come from voltage fluctuations caused by ionic currents within brain neurons [14] and have been shown to represent macroscopic activity in the surface layers of the brain. Therefore, our study explores new physical distance expressions through differences between EEG signals.

2 Exploring the Visualization of "Electroencephalography (EEG) Signal Discrepancy"

2.1 Converting "Electroencephalography (EEG) Signal Discrepancy" into Moiré Patterns

Illusory patterns always appear like water ripples when shooting a screen with digital devices. This kind of pattern is named moiré, which is accidental, transient and fluid, easy to be ignored but contains variable visual forms. moiré patterns can be traced back to the 10th century BC; they were applied on silk fabrics to present rippled and glittering textures [28]. From the 17th to the 20th century, moiré patterns were gradually discovered and explored in mathematics, physics, and art. They were defined as interference images produced by more than two similar fence-like stripes overlapping [29]. In physics, their manifestations are wave interferences and co-frequency resonances such as rainbow phenomena on bubble films, double silt experiments, or the sand patterns generated by beating in acoustics. Wave interferences can be divided into two categories (see Fig. 3). One is constructive interference generated when two waves are in Phase, and the other is destructive interference produced by two waves out of Phase.

The operating principle of EEG is to detect and record brainwave signals in real-time. When we attempted to communicate the relationships between two brainwave images, we automatically associated them with moiré patterns. They have a lot in common, not only in principles behind but also in visual properties. On account of it, we applied moiré patterns to visualize EEG signal discrepancies to make an analogy in this way: when the two brainwaves were in Phase and got more similar, the generated moiré patterns

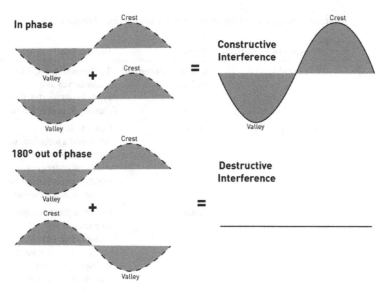

Fig. 3. Demonstration of the principle for constructive and destructive interferences (©Ye Yang, 2022)

would have a smaller size with shorter diameters, echoing constructive interferences and shorter "distances" between the two participants, and vice versa.

2.2 Related Work

According to the research objective of exploring the visualization of "Electroencephalography (EEG) Signal Discrepancy". We investigated two main areas:

- Current Applications of EEG Signals in Human-Computer Interaction
- Visualization of EEG Signals

Talking about current applications, with the emergence of headset-based non-invasive EEG signal detection devices, research on human-computer interaction based on EEG signals are increasing. These studies are divided into two main areas, "interaction art" and "interaction product". Table 1 shows representative examples and descriptions of the content of these studies.

Table 1. Representative cases of human-computer interactions based on EEG signals

Fields	Transformation methods	Examples	Descriptions	Ref.
Interactive Art	Visualization	Interface generation graphics	The brain scanning EEG reader serves as a symbolic data-extracting channel from one's mind	[15]
	Audibility	Music	Grace Leslie has developed a technique to use her brain and body as a musical instrument, which converts them into flowing waves of sounds	[16]
	Tactile	Water	Lisa Park has developed an interactive performance and installation that attempts to display invisible human emotions and physiological changes as auditory and tactile representations	[17]
Interactive Product	Manipulability	Drones	A University of Florida research team has developed a drone controlled by brain waves. Furthermore, the first time using BCI software to control a group of DJI Phantom drones	[18]
		Wheelchairs	Anton Lodder et al. have developed a real-time brain-computer interface. Moreover, they used these commands to control a wheelchair	[19]
		Vehicles	Teng Teng et al. have developed a new approach of detecting emergency braking intention for brain-controlled vehicles by interpreting drivers' electroencephalography (EEG) signals	[20]

There are two main categories for visualizing EEG signals: the 2D model presentation and the 3D model presentation. These two models are divided into static and dynamic display methods separately, so there are four display methods in total. Table 2 summarizes the representative cases of these four visualization methods and descriptions of the work contents.

Table 2. Summaries of the four primary EEG signal visualization representative cases

Visualization methods	Examples	Descriptions	Ref.
2D scalp model visualization	Tracking of EEG activity	This study aimed to identify the dominant topographic components of electroencephalographs (EEG). And their behaviour during the wake-sleep transition	[21–23]
Dynamic 2D scalp model visualization	Evaluation of signal quality and usability	The overall goal of this study was to understand the overall usability and signal quality of a dry EEG headset in an unrestricted environment compared to a conventional gel-based system	[24]
3D Scalp model visualization	Implementing 3D visualizations	This method uses OpenGL to construct an artificial spatial, spectral representation of EEG data. Moreover, they provide several examples of the implementation of this method in OpenGL visualization	[25]
Dynamic 3D scalp model visualization	From EEG signals to sound and visual textures	They proposed this method in generating visual textures from EEG by mapping alpha, beta and theta band energy mapping to RGB values to generate texture generation	[26]

3 Research Process

3.1 Experiments

We conducted two phases of experiments. The first stage was to detect the differences between brainwave signals, and we built a platform to calculate the differences in real-time (see Fig. 4). The second stage was to visualize and transform the signal differences. Throughout the experiment, we used an EPOCX headset-based brainwave signal detection device, developed by EMOTIV, which was used to collect the EEG signals from the users. In addition, the software EMOTIVPRO 3.0, developed by EMOTIV, was used to obtain the raw EEG data [27] (see Fig. 5). Before starting the experiment, the researchers explained the purpose of the procedures and helped the participants wear the EPOCX devices to ensure their comfort.

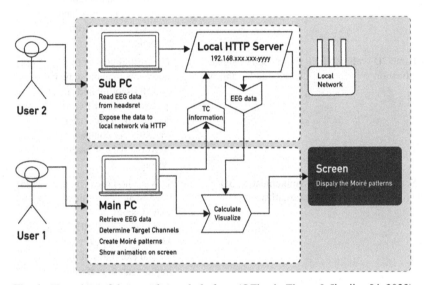

Fig. 4. Flow chart of the experimental platform (©Zhexin Zhang & Jingjing Li, 2022)

3.2 Transferring EEG Signals to Moiré Patterns

Target Channels. EEG signals are usually unstable and intensely influenced by multiple factors. We tried to exclude some typical factors, for instance, unconscious activities of facial muscles.

Fig. 5. EEG signal detection equipment EPOCX and Software EMOTIVPRO 3.0, manufactured and developed by the company EMOTIV [27].

Hence, in our approach, we selected to measure the critical channels, which varied more obviously in a given time. These chosen channels are called target channels, or TCs.

Regarding the Stability of the Moiré Patterns in Our Experiments. Although the signal differences between TCs could be recorded into a vector of variable lengths, we had one more factor that must be considered: the stability regarding the moiré patterns. Since we were collecting data at a rate of 144 Hz, it was a very high flicker frequency for human eyes. In this case, it could make the user feel dizzy and might even cause photosensitive epilepsy. In order to avoid the uncomfortable visual effects, it was necessary to ensure the stability of moiré patterns so that they would not have instantaneous and significant changes.

The general moiré patterns are formed by various waves interfering under certain conditions. In addition, three parameters are needed to define a wave: Amplitude (also referred to as intensity), Wavelength and Phase.

Moiré patterns are usually generated by two waves with the same amplitude and wavelength but different phases. The phase differences may vary over time, leading to a change in the interference pattern. Considering that we measured an EEG signal that rises or falls slowly, unlike the usual physical processes, the difference we measured may change abruptly. Besides, the differences may be unusually significant for other reasons because we used non-invasive EEG monitoring instruments during our experiments. The degree of instrument adaptation may vary from person to person, with different baselines (e.g., when one EEG signal is at a low level and the other is at a high level). Suppose we were to control the EEG waves' amplitude to avoid the problems caused by such different baselines. In that case, this could lead to very weak EEG wave amplitudes that would eventually lead to undetectable changes in the moiré patterns. Since our ultimate goal is to ensure that participants can all perform the experiment without differences and contribute equally through the EEG signal, we need to address the problem of brainwave signal differences through appropriate methods.

In addition, this is also true for wavelengths, so we addressed the problem of wavelength instability. If the wavelength is very short, the variation produced in the moiré patterns is negligible. However, the opposite is if the wavelength is very long, making it difficult to be rendered intact on the screen.

Our Approach of Calculating Distance. In order to solve the problems mentioned above, we chose to vary the phase with only the mutable variable difference in the final experiment to ensure a stable and smooth change of the moiré pattern.

Our purpose is to map the differences between two vectors into a single value. In the first stage of the experiment, we used a simple method: Euclid Distance, or ED. We measured the Euclid Distance between two vectors, took ED's square root, and multiplied it by a shrinking factor. The result is used as the difference of Phase of the two waves.

3.3   Generation and Interaction Methods

At present, the first-stage method of measuring the difference between 2 EEG signals is to calculate the square root of ED between EEG signals. However, EEG signals have a varying baseline from person to person. We do not wish to ignore the difference, for the users are individuals and should have differences in mind. However, we need to figure out a method to treat the users' EEG signals equally.

The method we are using to generate moiré patterns now includes three methods to handle the EEG signals:

- We move the wave source rather than shifting the Phase directly, so it is easy to feel that it creates two equal people.
- We keep the two wave sources centrosymmetric to make the view balanced.
- We make the two wave sources spin by a randomly changing angular speed within a fixed range to make the view lively.

Suppose both people get into a mentally stable situation. In that case, the EEG signal will also stabilize, and therefore, the difference will be relatively stable, which will be reflected in the moiré animation (see Fig. 6).

In an identical situation, the EEG activity was stable in both individuals. The animation should be a gently spinning wave interfering pattern (see Fig. 7).

Fig. 6. The Figure Shows the Moiré Animation Effect in the Steady-State EEG Signal of Two Participants (©Jingjing Li, 2022)

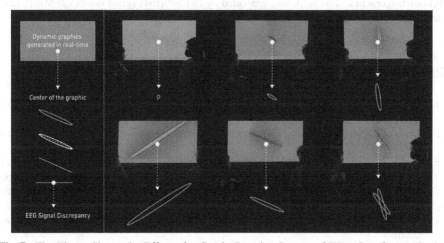

Fig. 7. The Figure Shows the Effect of a Gently Rotating Pattern of Wave Interference in the Unstable State of the EEG Signal for Both Participants (©Jingjing Li, 2022)

4   Conclusion and Future Work

Conclusion of Research. Our study provides a new way of "distance expression" based mainly on visualizing participants' EEG signals generated through dynamic programmed moiré patterns. This new visual representation varies in real-time based on EEG signals depending on participants' EEG activity states. Changes in EEG activity states reflect people's responses to different things (e.g., music, movies, topics of conversations, etc.).

The new "distance expression" explored in our study has many similarities with Edward Hall's Personal Space Theory [11], divided into two main aspects.

- Both are based on real-time distance judgements according to relationships among people.
- Both can be distinguished visually by the differences in distances.

However, there are still some shortcomings in our current approach, mainly in the way we present it, as participants need to look at the screen to understand each other's distance status during the "distance expression" process. This situation has a certain degree of impact on the smoothness of communications between participants.

Future Work. We plan to explore more visual presentations to help participants easily and quickly see the differences in EEG signals, that is, the differences in their states while communicating with each other. The brainwave form reflects "the psychological distance," mapping the distance between people in different spaces and enhancing empathy between people.

Acknowledgements. This work was supported by JST SPRING (grant number JPMJSP2124) and CREST (grant number JPMJCR19F2).

References

1. Harris, M., et al.: Costas (2020–03–20). "COVID-19" (PDF). World Health Organization. Archived (PDF) from the original on 2020–03–25. Accessed 29 March 2020
2. Hensley, L.: Social distancing is out; physical distancing is in–here's how to do it. Global News (2020)
3. Venske, R., Schwyzer, A. (ed.): "Die Wirkung von Sprache in Krisenzeiten" [The effect of language in times of crisis] (Interview). NDR Kultur (in German). Norddeutscher Rundfunk. Archived from the Original on 27 March 2020 (2020). Accessed 27 Mar 2020. (NB. Regula Venske is president of the PEN Centre Germany.)
4. Post, W.: Social distancing could buy US valuable time against coronavirus. Washington Post (2020)
5. Pearce, K.: What is Social Distancing, and How Can It Slow the Spread of COVID-19. Johns Hopkins University, The Hub (2020)
6. Risk Assessment and Management. Centres for Disease Control and Prevention. 2020–03–22. Archived from the original on 2020–03–04. Accessed 29 Mar 2020
7. Dewey, J.: Logic-The theory of inquiry. Read Books Ltd. (2018)
8. Hall, E.T.: The Hidden Dimension, vol. 609. Doubleday, Garden City, NY (1966)
9. Double, J.: Music Reads. Features page. https://www.abc.net.au/doublej/music-reads/features/classic-album-covers-reimagined-for-the-age-of-social-distancing/12193624
10. 6FeetCovers. ActivistaLA. https://6feetcovers.wixsite.com/6feetcovers

11. Hall, E.T.: The Hidden Dimension. Anchor Books, Garden City, NY (1966)
12. Sheth, A., Yip, H.Y., Iyengar, A., Tepper, P.: Cognitive services and intelligent chatbots: current perspectives and special issue introduction. IEEE Internet Comput. **23**(2), 6–12 (2019)
13. WIKIPEDIA, Visualization (graphics) Page. https://en.wikipedia.org/wiki/Visualization(graphics)
14. Niedermeyer, E., Da Silva, F.L.: Electroencephalography-Basic Principles, Clinical Applications, and Related Fields. Urban & Schwarzenberg, Munich (2020)
15. Demarest, L.: Ornamental. In: ACM SIGGRAPH 2020 Art Gallery, pp. 470–470 (2020)
16. Georgia Institute of Technology. School of Music College of Design. Grace Leslie (2020). https://music.gatech.edu/grace-leslie
17. Lisa Park. Eunoia II Page (2014). https://www.thelisapark.com/work/eunoia2
18. YouTube. University of Florida Official Account. Controlling Drones With Your Mind (2015–2016). https://www.youtube.com/watch?v=hLjxMjBlB9k
19. Razvi, A.L.S.D.Z.: EEG-controlled wheelchair - McMaster University 2012. https://sites.google.com/site/engfinalprojects/
20. Teng, T., Bi, L., Liu, Y.: EEG-based detection of driver emergency braking intention for brain-controlled vehicles. IEEE Trans. Intell. Transp. Syst. **19**(6), 1766–1773 (2017)
21. Hooi, L.S., Nisar, H., Voon, Y.V.: Tracking of EEG activity using topographic maps. In: 2015 IEEE International Conference on Signal and Image Processing Applications (ICSIPA), (pp. 287–291). IEEE (October 2015)
22. Duffy, F. H. (Ed.): Topographic mapping of brain electrical activity. Butterworth-Heinemann, Boston (2013)
23. Tanaka, H., Hayashi, M., Hori, T.: Topographical characteristics and principal component structure of the hypnagogic EEG. Sleep **20**(7), 523–534 (1997)
24. Cruz-Garza, J.G., et al.: Deployment of mobile EEG technology in an art museum setting: Evaluation of signal quality and usability. Front. Hum. Neurosci. **11**, 527 (2017)
25. Christopher, K.R., Kapur, A., Carnegie, D.A., Grimshaw, G.M.: Implementing 3D visualizations of EEG signals in artistic applications. In: 2013 28th International Conference on Image and Vision Computing New Zealand (IVCNZ 2013), (pp. 364–369). IEEE November 2013
26. Filatriau, J.J., Lehembre, R., Macq, B., Brouse, A., Miranda, E.R.: From EEG signals to a world of sound and visual textures. In: Submitted to ICASSP07 Conference (2007)
27. EMOTIV. EPOC X. Product information page. https://www.emotiv.com/epoc-x/
28. Spillmann, L.: The perception of movement and depth in moiré patterns. Perception **22**(3), 287–308 (1993)
29. Isaac, A.: The Theory of the Moiré phenomenon, pp. 1–8. Kluwer Academic press, Dordrecht (2000)

Service Design of Clinical Infusion Monitoring System

Manhai Li[✉], Sijian Chen, Lang Luo, Yujiao You, and Chenguang Ma

Chongqing University of Posts and Telecommunications, Chongqing 400065, China
limh@cqupt.edu.cn

Abstract. The clinical infusion is an important service touch point between patients and medical staff in medical services, which directly affects the satisfaction of patients with medical treatment. It's necessary to analyze the complex process by using the methods of service design such as the service blueprint and the experience journey, find out the potential problems, and put forward improvement measures. In this study, the different demands of patients and medical staff in the infusion process were analyzed through the service blueprint, and the key factors affecting the patient experience were obtained through the refinement of the experience of journey. Based on these analyses, the common demand of patients, medical staff and medical institutions was illustrated, which was automatic monitoring of infusion process. Furthermore, a product prototype was designed by using Internet of Things technology. The research results show that the clinical infusion monitoring system was verified to be effective, which not only reduced the work intensity of medical staff, but also improved the clinical treatment experience of patients.

Keywords: Service design · Clinical infusion monitor · Service blueprint · Experience journey

1 Introduction to Service Design

Service design refers to the product design in service marketing, that is, the strategic thinking and plan made by enterprises on service items, service personnel, service process, service environment, service style and service communication in the process of providing services to customers. Service design is an overall business behavior, which can help enterprises comprehensively and empathically understand user needs [1], explore different contact points of user journey [2], and find opportunities to jointly create value. From the perspective of users, service design aims to focus on comprehensive customer feelings, including the experience before, during and after service contact, design useful, available, easy-to-use, and desired services, and assist enterprises or organizations to design effective, unique, efficient, attractive and customer expected services from the perspective of service providers [3]. Service design was proposed and concerned by scholars in the 1980s. The methods of service design were usually applied to the fields of economics and management. This study mainly uses two tools: service blueprint and experience journey, which are briefly introduced as follows.

M. M. Soares et al. (Eds.): HCII 2022, LNCS 13322, pp. 198–208, 2022.
https://doi.org/10.1007/978-3-031-05900-1_13

Service blueprint is a tool of service design to accurately describe the service system, which is more precise than verbal definitions and less subject to misinterpretation. With the help of flow charts in the process design, it visually shows the service by continuously describing the service provision process, the service encounter, the roles of employees and customers, and the tangible evidence of the service. The behavior analysis of service blueprint and service design scheme must establish a model and express it in visual form. Just like traditional product design, drawing design must be clearly expressed according to certain concepts, such as simultaneous interpretation of language, vision, and perception. The establishment of service blueprint depends on the study of human behavior attributes. Understanding and applying the technologies and methods of the service blueprint is the key to service design [4]. Using the tool of service blueprint, the service not only is reasonably decomposed into the steps, tasks, and methods in the process of service provision, but more importantly, the contact points between enterprises and customers are identified, so that the quality of service can be improved according to these contact points. The service blueprint can clearly describe the structure of the service system in the clinical infusion, find the disadvantages of the existing infusion process, design systematic infusion monitoring products, and realize the optimal experience of various stakeholders. Therefore, it is necessary to apply the method of service blueprint to form a better clinical infusion experience.

Experience journey is the progression of users across touchpoints, and identifying a journey allows it to be analyzed to uncover critical obstacles and opportunities. This information offers a roadmap to plan for investment in your products and services in the future. Experience journey mapping, which is also called user journey mapping, is the process of building a customer journey map, a visual story of your customers' interactions with your brand. This activity enables businesses to see their business from the customer's perspective and step into their customer's shoes and. It helps you to gain insights into common customer pain points and how to improve them. The data which is collected on the journey can be analyzed to provide insights into your current customers' current opportunities, obstacles, and market segmentation. Experience journey mapping is crucial because it is a strategic approach to improve understanding expectations and is important for optimizing the experience. Journey mapping is not only crucial for small and medium-sized companies but is also necessary for larger companies. Different businesses require different customer expectations, regardless of size-customers demand an omnichannel approach to marketing, sales, and customer service. Experience journey mapping training is crucial because it is a strategic approach to improve understanding customer expectations and is important to optimize the customer experience [5].

With the rapid development of the medical service quality, the concept of service design has gradually sprouted in leading hospitals to make the diagnosis and treatment experience more humanized and personalized. Some scholars applied the ISO 9001 process approach and service blueprint to hospital management systems [6]. The methodology in the field of service design is used to guide how to better serve the medical field, aiming at providing solutions to meet and beyond the expectations of patients for medical service.

2 Problems of Clinical Infusion Service

With the continuous promotion of medical reform, information system has been widely used in medical treatment, making the medical process more friendly. It not only breaks through the limitations of traditional medical conditions such as region and time, but also effectively solves the sharing of medical resources and information transmission between regions and hospitals. But so far, the information system has not completely solved the convenience problem of clinical infusion in hospital. With the improvement of people's living standards, the quality of medical service has been paid more and more attention. Most patients hope to have better medical service and experience in the process of diagnosis and treatment, which has also attracted the attention of medical institutions.

As we know, the clinical infusion is an important service touch point between patients and medical staff in medical services, which can easily lead to a bad medical experience without special attention [7]. In fact, many medical experience issues in the clinical infusion are discussed and researched. Here are some examples. The intelligent infusion monitoring system design based on service and experience was proposed by Dong after analyzing the feasibility of the solution [8]. The various infusion auxiliary products and nursing assistant devices were designed and researched by scholars in order to improve the intelligence of the equipment [9–13]. The application and development of Internet of things in medical service is the general trend. Actually, there are many studies on infusion monitoring using Internet of things technology [14].

2.1 Strenuous Service of Clinical Infusion

The medical staff need to master more than 30 skills to meet the professional requirements of nursing work. In addition, they should also have to spend their time in dealing with non-medical nursing affairs, which requires the meticulous attitude of medical staff. The number of patients per day has exceeded the medical capacity load in most hospitals. Due to the contradiction between limited medical resources and the large amount of infusion, the medical staff in the infusion department of medical institutions have been under great pressure every day [15]. It is difficult for medical staff to ensure every patient can get complete service. In a strenuous medical environment, the management of medical service is very complex. Unfortunately some medical accidents occurred in the process of clinical infusion, which inevitably aggravates the tension between patients and medical staff, bringing bad clinical experience to patients [16]. Therefore, improving patient experience, reducing management costs, reducing medical accidents, and improving nursing efficiency have become the most important objectives of digital wise hospitals.

The complexity of the infusion process can be illustrated by the service blueprint tool. There are nearly 20 steps in the infusion process, and most of the service touch points are directly related to the medical staff, as shown in Fig. 1.

At present, the upper second-class hospitals and the upper first-class hospitals already use this infusion process to carry out their work. In this management mode, each medical staff is responsible for at least nine patients. The huge workload may lead to confusion in the management. For example, the medical staff cannot change the patient's clothes in time, and repeatedly verify the drug information or patient's identity. Although Personal

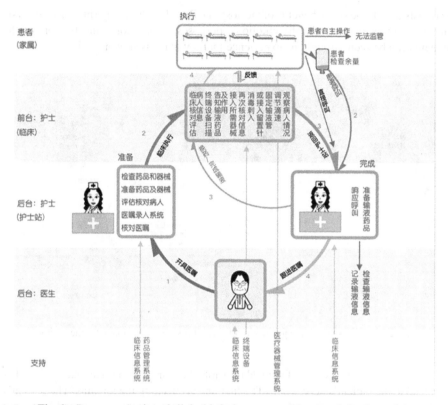

Fig. 1. Strenuous service of clinical infusion process. Photo made by the author.

Digital Assistant equipment alleviates some pressure of the medical staff, accidents cannot be completely avoided.

Here is a scenario example. During the infusion process, the patients need to call the medical staff when they observe the medicine bottles are about to empty. And then the medical staff need to take the rest of the medicine to the patient's ward after answering their call. It is worth mentioning that the medical staff may need to respond to multiple calls at the same time. After the clinical infusion, the medical staff need to take them some extra time to record the infusion information manually. All these steps require manual operation, which will lead to potential hazards of human error.

2.2 Tedious Experience Journey of Clinical Infusion

The experience journey of clinical infusion can help us interpret the patient's experience at all stages of the infusion process [17]. According to related literature reports, more than 90% of hospitalized patients need to receive infusion therapy, and an infusion experience journey can reach 20 steps or more. In the tedious infusion process, patients are easily prone to have strong bad emotions, which can lead to conflict between patients and doctors. The incidence of doctor-patient disputes ranges from 7.5% to 43.3%, which seriously affects the social benefits of the hospital. Based on the service blueprint analysis and user interview analysis, the emotions, purposes, interactions, and barriers of the patients can be seen through the experience journey map, as shown in Fig. 2.

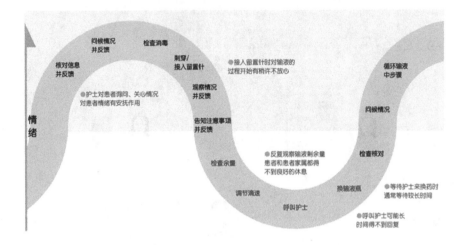

Fig. 2. Tedious experience journey of clinical infusion. Photo made by the author.

During the whole process of clinical infusion, there are four service touch points that can lead to the patient's depression. The first one is checking the remains. The patient's family or the patient needs to check whether the infusion is coming to an end from time to time, which means they must keep eyes on the process instead of having a good rest. The second one is adjusting dropping speed. The depressed mood may make the patient impatient. As a result, the patient may speed up the drip without authorization and put himself in a dangerous situation. The third one is calling the medical staff. When the infusion is about to be completed, the patient needs to press the button to call the medical staff. Due to the busy work, it is difficult for the medical staff to respond in time. The waiting time may not be long, but this kind of waiting will make the nerves that were originally in a tense state more nervous. The fourth one is changing infusion bottle. Changing infusion bottles is an easy thing for medical staff, but it is also a professional thing, which needs to be handled by nurses themselves. It means another anxious waiting moment. These four service touch points that cause patients to be in a bad mood are also easy to trigger medical accidents.

3 The Design of Clinical Infusion Monitoring System

Clinical infusion process is easy to produce some medical accidents, causing unnecessary harm to patients. For example, after the infusion, if the bottle is not changed or the needle is not pulled out in time, it is easy to return blood. In the process of infusion, the infusion dropping speed may be too fast, too slow, or even abnormal stop.

Clinical infusion monitoring system refers to the automatic monitoring of clinical infusion process through Internet of Things technology, optimizing infusion process and improving medical quality and safety. From the perspective of patients, the needle pulling time can be predicted in advance. If the infusion dropping speed is abnormal, the system will send an alarm to remind nurses to deal with it. From the perspective of medical staff, they can not only remotely control the infusion situation of all patients, but also know well according to monitoring information and professional judgment, scientifically arrange work priorities, reduce frequent and ineffective rush, and improve their work efficiency.

3.1 Analysis of Influencing Factors

The experience of patients is affected and restricted by many factors. Problems in the clinical infusion process can be found out by the service design tools, such as Experience Journey and Service Blueprint. The list of improvement opportunities of service touch points is shown in the Table 1.

Table 1. The list of improvement opportunities of service touch points

Service touch points	Affected objects	Design tools	Improvement opportunities
Calling the medical staff	The patients	Experience Journey	Calling autonomously
Checking the remains	The patients	Experience Journey	Checking autonomously
Adjusting dropping speed	The patients	Experience Journey	Adjusting under monitor in time
Changing infusion bottle	The patients	Experience Journey	Changing autonomously
Managing nine patients	The medical staff	Service Blueprint	Managing more than nine patients
Answering the calling	The medical staff	Service Blueprint	Answering autonomously
Recording information	The medical staff	Service Blueprint	Recording autonomously

Totally there are seven items in the table. The first four service touch points in the table are as follows: calling the medical staff, checking the remains, adjusting dropping speed, and changing infusion bottle. The affected objects of these four service touch points are patients. And their improvement opportunities can be found out through the Experience Journey, which is one of the Service Design tools. The last three service touch points in the table are as follows: managing nine patients, answering the calling, and recording information. The affected objects of these three service touch points are patients. And their improvement opportunities can be found out through the Service Blueprint, which is another one of the Service Design tools.

Through the research results, it is found that the core factor affecting the clinical experience of patients is that patients need to spend a long time to check the infusion process. If a kind of clinical infusion monitor can be added into the medical service and be integrated into the medical information system, the clinical experience of patients will be greatly improved. It means that the supervision of clinical infusion is automatic rather than manual. The common demand of the medical staff and patients is to have a set of infusion monitoring system, fully considering the experience of patients and medical staff, and building an efficient and humanized medical environment.

As an important equipment for medical service management, infusion monitoring system can provide safer and more efficient guarantee for inpatients and medical staff. With the help of the automatic operation of the infusion monitor system, patients can take an easy rest instead of observing the infusion progress by themselves. The infusion monitor system will automatically check the data and transmit it to the clinical information system in real time. It can also directly remind and call the medical staff in time if the patient operates the infusion equipment abnormally. In addition, the infusion monitor system can also help medical staff automatically complete the reconciliation of drugs.

3.2 Optimize Clinical Infusion Process

To make patients get good medical experience, it is necessary to keep the clinical infusion process consistent with the original. The infusion process is suitable for minor addition and modification rather than major changes. The purpose of the infusion monitoring system is to solve the problems of patients and medical staff in the infusion process by the Internet of Things technology and information technology, to make the medical service smoother.

For example, the medical staff stays at the nurse station as usual in the preparation stage. After the medicine and equipment are prepared, the medical staff stops charging the infusion monitor, and pairs with RFID device of the infusion bottle, and then inserts the ID card into the infusion bottle. The infusion drug information and patient information are recorded automatically in the instrument. What the medical staff need to do is to check whether the process is abnormal at the nurse station.

When the medical staff approaches the drug to the patient's RFID device, the infusion monitoring system can automatically read the drug related information and associate it with the patient. Therefore, the medical staff can remotely check whether the patient's identity matches the drug at the nurse station. The system can further reduce the incidence of medical accidents in the process of clinical infusion.

During the infusion process, patients do not need to care about the infusion state, because the infusion monitoring system will automatically check the remaining amount of liquid medicine and transmit it to the clinical information system in real time. When the amount of remaining liquid is insufficient, the infusion monitoring system will automatically remind nurses to adjust in time. If the patient operates the infusion equipment by himself, the infusion monitoring system will call the nurse directly.

When the patient's infusion is completed, the information of drug recorded in the infusion ring will be automatically read and transmitted into the information system. What the medical staff need to do is to remove the infusion ring manually, supplement relevant information of medical equipment and check whether the infusion information is correct. The whole infusion process is shown in Fig. 3.

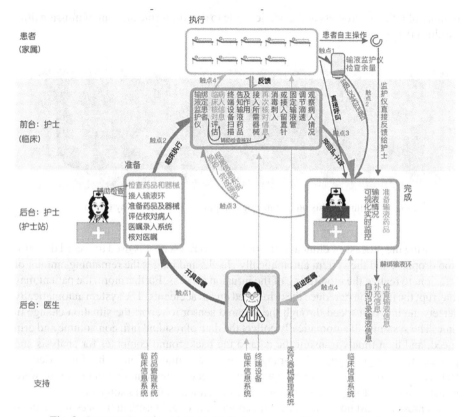

Fig. 3. Improved service of clinical infusion process. Photo made by the author.

3.3 The Design of Clinical Infusion Monitor

Among the related technologies of clinical infusion monitoring, infrared technology is a relatively mature scheme, which is usually used to monitor the liquid level of infusion drugs. There are two types of monitoring equipment using infrared technology. One is pipe clamp infusion alarm, which is usually clamped on the infusion pipe. When the liquid level is lower than a certain position, the alarm will give a violent alarm sound. Because the alarm can only work once, it is very inflexible and cannot monitor the infusion process at any time. The other is the weighing infusion alarm. Although it can monitor the process, it is not an ideal scheme because of too many mis-operations. Both devices can only achieve basic infusion monitoring function and cannot give patients a complete infusion service experience.

In the past few years, the development of Internet of Things technology has made many operating scenarios automated and programmed, to a certain extent, to solve the problem of staff shortage in various industries, its technology can also be used in the field of medical treatment [18]. Infrared level monitoring technology can also achieve droplet speed monitoring, infrared monitoring device placed at the drip pot, the use of infrared technology to achieve the monitoring of the infusion process, by estimating the number of infusion droplets in the whole bottle to determine the amount of infusion drug surplus [19], as shown in Fig. 4.

Fig. 4. Clinical infusion monitoring equipment. Photo made by the author.

During the process of clinical infusion, the infrared sensor is used to record the infusion droplets, and the system automatically checks and judges the remaining amount of infusion, to realize the monitoring of the infusion process. Furthermore, the patient may interrupt the infusion or reduce the drip speed due to accidents. The system automatically detects the infusion speed through the infrared sensor to report the situation change in time. The system will automatically collect the data of residual infusion volume and drip speed, and then timely transmit the data to the background computer for analysis and processing through ZigBee short-range wireless communication technology. Medical staff can view the intuitive visual data chart, to realize the remote monitoring of ward infusion and effectively reduce the pressure of medical staff infusion care.

At present, most hospitals are equipped with handheld terminal devices for medical staff and frequency identification wristbands for patients. These devices can help the medical staff quickly input and check patient information. With the increasing popularity of wireless radio wristbands in hospitals, the clinical infusion monitoring system can also integrate these devices. For example, when starting infusion, it can automatically read the personal information of the patient's radio identification wristband. When the infusion monitoring equipment is bound with the patient's identity, it means that each patient has a unique identification number, which not only facilitates the medical staff to accurately view the information, but also avoids data confusion.

As shown in Fig. 5, the medical staff can view the clinical infusion monitoring data of multiple patients under their responsibility through the handheld terminal device. Because the equipment adopts the Internet of things technology, all clinical infusion monitoring data are collected, transmitted, and processed in real time, medical staff can master the clinical infusion situation of patients globally, including the remaining amount of liquid medicine and the dropping speed of liquid medicine, etc. More interestingly, when the clinical infusion monitoring system is integrated with the existing information system of the hospital, the medical staff can more comprehensively understand the heartbeat, body temperature and other information of each patient on the handheld terminal device. This information helps the hospital to bring better medical experience to patients.

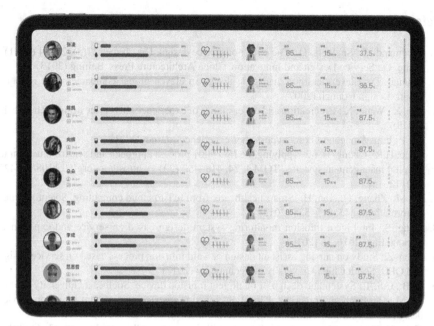

Fig. 5. User interface of clinical infusion monitoring system. Photo made by the author.

4   Conclusion

The clinical infusion is an important service touch point between patients and medical staff in medical services. During the process of clinical infusion, the high-intensity work pressure of medical staff and poor experience of patients were illustrated by the service design methods such as Service Blueprint and Experience Journey. To solve these problems, a set of clinical infusion monitoring system was proposed. The clinical infusion monitoring system refers to the automatic monitoring of clinical infusion process through Internet of Things technology, optimizing infusion process and improving medical quality and safety. The research results show that the system was verified to be effective, which not only reduced the work intensity of medical staff, but also improved the clinical treatment experience of patients.

During the period of COVID-19, it is difficult to study and investigate in the hospital for a long time, so the design details of the clinical infusion monitoring system need to be further improved. At present, the prototype of the system has been designed, but the system still needs to be tested and iterated in the actual environment.

Acknowledgments. This work was supported by Doctoral startup fund and talent introduction fund project of Chongqing University of Posts and Telecommunications – Research on the cost and benefit distribution of big data productization (K2020-201) and Chongqing educational science planning project – Research on the talent training system of "social theme" in Colleges and Universities (2020-GX-284) and Research Center for network social development of Chongqing University of Posts and Telecommunications – Research on the cost of network big data production (2020SKJD06).

References

1. Secomandi, F., Snelders, D.: The object of service design. Des. Issues **27**(3), 20–34 (2011)
2. Wang, G.: Service Design and Innovation. China Architecture Press, Beijing (2013)
3. Council, D.: Eleven lessons: managing design in eleven global companies-desk research report. Design Council (2007)
4. Xin, X., Wang, X.: Co-creation and uncertainties of experiences in service design. Zhuangshi (2018)
5. Le, P.: https://magenest.com/en/customer-experience-journey/2021
6. Chen, H.R., Cheng, B.W.: Applying the ISO 9001 process approach and service blueprint to hospital management systems. TQM J. **24**, 418–432 (2012). https://doi.org/10.1108/175427 31211261575
7. Ni, M., Zhang, Q., Tan, H.: Smart healthcare: from IoT to cloud computing. Scientia Sinica (Informationis) **43**, 515–528 (2013)
8. Dong, S.: Intelligent infusion monitoring system design based on service and experience. Packag. Eng. **2016**, 18 (2016)
9. Chen, Z.: Study on nursing assistant design of ward infusion process based on service design and QFD. South China University of Technology (2017)
10. Ji, B., Cui, T.: Systematic design of intelligent infusion device. Southeast University (2017)
11. Li, M.: Research and practice of inpatient infusion management system based on service design concept. South China University of Technology, vol. 124 (2018)
12. Yang, F.: Design and research of infusion auxiliary products. China Packag. **39**, 42–44 (2019)
13. Gong, Q., Chen, H.: On the intelligent design of medical products-taking the design of 'fly' intelligent infusion set for an example **34**, 134–136 (2021)
14. Wang, Z., Ran, P., Chen, Q.: Application and development of Internet of Things in medical service. Chin. J. Internet Things **2**, 1–10 (2018). https://doi.org/10.11959/j.issn.2096-3750. 2018.00058
15. Chen, Q., Meng, K., Liu, X.: Analysis on research status of job burnout among Chinese medical staffs based on bibliometric method. Chin. J. Health Educ. **33**, 346–353 (2017)
16. Gao, M.: Application of nurses' work stress management in clinical nursing management. J. Clin. Psychosom. Dis. **21**, 360 (2015)
17. Xin, X.: Interaction design: from logic of things to logic of behaviors. Zhuangshi **1**, 58–62 (2015). https://doi.org/10.16272/j.cnki.cn11-1392/j.2015.01.012
18. Dai, D.: Using information and communication technologies to consult with patients in primary care: the views of Shanghai family doctors. Fudan University (2014)
19. Xu, Y., Song, R.: Designation of infusion monitor. China Med. Device Inf. **23**, 91–93 (2017). https://doi.org/10.15971/j.cnki.cmdi.2017.07.026

Exploring the Potential Causes of Picky Eating and Relationship Between Experiences and Behaviors for Mental Model of Contemporary Young Adult

Zhen Liu[1] and Luanyin Huang[2(✉)]

[1] School of Design, South China University of Technology,
Guangzhou 510006, People's Republic of China
[2] School of Visual Arts, New York, NY 10010, USA
1178645023@qq.com

Abstract. Human being has food they do not like. It may be caused by personal experience or genetics. The unlike food that is singled out can cause food waste. Recently a number of countries have issued policies and regulations to curb food waste. The economic issue and environmental impact caused by wasted food are incalculable. Picky eating itself may put the individuals into embarrassing situations in social situations as well, which mostly be exposed from experiences and behaviors of young adults. Young adults are an essential product and consuming force in society, who play a decisive role in the development of society. But picky eating can cause unnecessary awkwardness in serious social situations, affecting an individual's mood and even overall decision-making. Understanding the potential causes of picky eating and the relationship between experiences and behaviors for the mental model of contemporary young adults is essential. Most of the current research on picky eating are focusing on children. There is a lack of research on the relationship between the causes of picky eating and mental models that determine behavior that is related to experience. The problem cannot be solved without exploring the relationship between picky eating and mental models. Therefore, this paper explores the relationship between the potential causes and mental models of young adult's picky eating. This paper conducts a questionnaire and followed by PEESTL analysis for developing a picky eating behavior model of young adults. The results show that there are two key aspects, namely technology and social interaction, might help people with overcoming picky eating. Since, Young people are curious, eager, and yearning for technology, as such they may tend to try new technology enhanced products, which the technology may has impact on the picky eating behavior of young adult. Further, young adults on different social occasions react differently to picky food. In real world situations, such as important social events and parties, young adults may eat foods they dislike for social needs. In virtual world, such as internet, young adults may hide their picky eating behavior to present a relatively perfect image to others.

Keywords: Experience behavior · Picky eating · Social interaction · Technology · Young adult · Mental model · Questionnaires

M. M. Soares et al. (Eds.): HCII 2022, LNCS 13322, pp. 209–222, 2022.
https://doi.org/10.1007/978-3-031-05900-1_14

1 Introduction

The pandemic and climate change exacerbate the food crisis. At present, the environmental and economic losses caused by the massive amount of food wasted every year have drawn people's attention. According to the Food and Agriculture Organization of the United Nations (FAO), 931 million tons of food are wasted every year [1], as UNESCO Country Director Dr. Kozue Kay Nagata said in her speech. It is estimated that 8–10% of global greenhouse gas emissions are related to uneaten food [1]. Such a large amount of food waste creates incalculable negative impacts on the economy and environment. These negative impacts make reducing food waste an urgent need.

As a populous country globally, China needs a large amount of grain every year. At the same time, China also faces the problem of how to reduce food waste, slow climate change, and use resources efficiently. The results show that the consumption waste of major grains in China in 2010 was about 628.18 million kg, accounting for 14.5% of China's total grain production. Food waste causes a lot of water loss and greenhouse gas emissions. Among them, 60,502 mm (3) of water resources were lost, more than 10% of the country's total water consumption, and 608,500 tons of carbon emissions [2]. The food and resource and environmental crises caused by food waste must be solved. Wasted food may come from spoiled food improperly stored during transportation or leftover food that consumers cannot finish. There are different reasons for leftovers. It could be that consumers order too much food to finish or they do not like certain foods resulting in singling out. As such, this paper focuses on picky eating behavior, and analyzes the underlying causes among young adults and the relationship between their psychological models and behaviors.

2 Picky Eating and Behavior

2.1 Picky Eating in Young People

There is no widely accepted single definition of picky eating. Usually, picky eaters are characterized by being picky about certain foods or eating only a few foods they like [3]. Severe eating disorders are also included in the definition of picky eating [4, 5]. This paper mainly discusses the common and non-extreme picky eaters.

In the past, the theme of picky eating research was mainly focused on issues of children, such as weight [6–9], disease [4, 5], parent [3, 5, 10, 11], taste [12], nutrition [13–15], and gene [16], and adult regarding body mass index [17] and psychosocial and nutritional [18]. and picky eating behavior in young adults has been ignored, as shown in Fig. 1. However, young adults are an essential productivity and consumption force in society. They play an essential role in the development of society. Young adults are more independent and objective than infants and minors. Economically, they have achieved fundamental independence and can choose the food they like to eat. Ideologically, young adults are more aware of the stakes between picky eating and health. Compared with infants and minors, young adults are more likely to try foods they do not like because of their interests. Young adults are the most dynamic and influential group in society. They are about to train the next generation and support the previous generation. The change of their habits will affect three generations. It is precise because of the particularity of young adults and their importance to social development that the research on picky eating behavior among young adults has become inevitable.

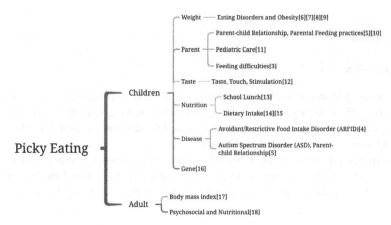

Fig. 1. The current study about picky eating.

2.2 Risks Caused by Picky Eating

For individuals, long-term picky eating may lead to nutritional imbalance, which further leads to physical and mental health problems. Picky eating is an essential factor causing obesity, hyperlipidemia, and other diseases. Research shows that vitamins are essential elements of human health. Lack of vitamins will make body's metabolism out of balance and reduce immunity. As such, various diseases and viruses will take advantage of it [19]. Some studies have also shown that picky eating is closely related to individual psychological and social functions. Picky eaters are more likely to show anxiety, avoidance, and isolation in social interaction [17, 18].

2.3 Explore the Potential Causes of Picky Eating

Many factors cause picky eating. The growth environment of picky eaters, their personality, personal experience, the surrounding environment during eating, and the impact of society are all potential incentives for picky eaters. The picky eating habits of most young adults are formed in infancy [18]. This kind of picky eaters usually cannot tell the specific reasons why they do not eat this kind of food. They stress that they do not like this kind of food since they have memory or were young. The formation of this kind of habit is closely related to the environment in which picky eaters grow up or their parents' attitude towards picky eaters [20]. A situation corresponding to this kind of picky eaters is that picky eaters can recall the events that led to their picky eating. This event often forms a kind of stress or psychological hint to remind or prevent picky eaters from eating the food. Some studies have shown that some picky eating behaviors may be related to genes. Researchers at the University of Illinois suggest that mutations in TAS2R38 (rs713598) and CA6 (rs2274327) genes may be related to children's picky eating. This paper is aiming to explore the potential relationship between psychological influence and picky eating [16].

3 Method

3.1 Questionnaire

Based on the fast and effective data collection and the convenience of easy statistics and analysis of the survey results, the semi-structured online questionnaire is used as the primary way of this survey. The survey investigated the reasons, emotions, and behaviors of young adults picky eating, as shown in Fig. 2.

The questionnaire has been uploaded to www.wjx.com.cn and sent to the working group of young adults through WeChat, China's most popular social media platform. Within one week, 74 completed questionnaires were collected and analyzed.

3.2 PESTLE Analysis

PESTLE analysis method is employed to divide the collected data into six aspects: policy, economy, environment, society, technology, and law [21]. In this analysis method, it is easier for researchers to pay attention to the overall picture of the macro background and understand the relationship between different aspects. It will also have a deeper understanding of the behavior and psychology of the micro-analyzed object.

3.3 Behavior Model

This paper uses the Fogg behavior model to construct young adults' picky eating behavior psychology. This behavior model is straightforward and contains only three basic elements: Motivation (M), Ability (A), and a Prompt (P), as below conditions [22]:

$$B = MAP$$

The data analyzed and collected by micro (questionnaire) and macro (PESTLE) are helping with constructing a picky eating behavior model of young adults.

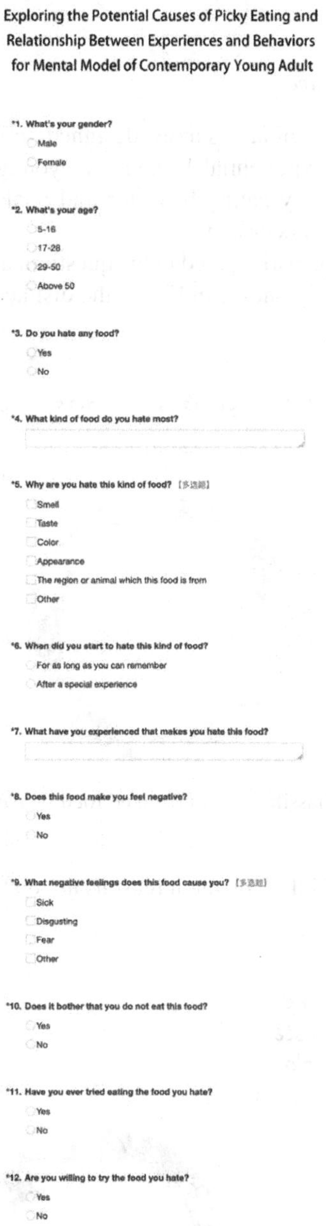

Exploring the Potential Causes of Picky Eating and
Relationship Between Experiences and Behaviors
for Mental Model of Contemporary Young Adult

*1. What's your gender?
  ○ Male
  ○ Female

*2. What's your age?
  ○ 5-16
  ○ 17-28
  ○ 29-50
  ○ Above 50

*3. Do you hate any food?
  ○ Yes
  ○ No

*4. What kind of food do you hate most?
  [   ]

*5. Why are you hate this kind of food? [多选题]
  ☐ Smell
  ☐ Taste
  ☐ Color
  ☐ Appearance
  ☐ The region or animal which this food is from
  ☐ Other

*6. When did you start to hate this kind of food?
  ○ For as long as you can remember
  ○ After a special experience

*7. What have you experienced that makes you hate this food?
  [   ]

*8. Does this food make you feel negative?
  ○ Yes
  ○ No

*9. What negative feelings does this food cause you? [多选题]
  ☐ Sick
  ☐ Disgusting
  ☐ Fear
  ☐ Other

*10. Does it bother that you do not eat this food?
  ○ Yes
  ○ No

*11. Have you ever tried eating the food you hate?
  ○ Yes
  ○ No

*12. Are you willing to try the food you hate?
  ○ Yes
  ○ No

Fig. 2. The structure and questions of a semi-structure questionnaire for exploring the reasons, emotions, and behaviors of young adults picky eating.

4   Results

4.1   Results of Questionnaire

This questionnaire is a preliminary survey designed to investigate the relationship between picky eating and experiential behavior in young adults. The purpose is to summarize the causes of picky eating behavior and analyze young adults' behavior on annoying food on different occasions.

A total of 72 young adults participated in the questionnaire, of which 69 participants had foods they did not like. As shown in Fig. 3, the disliked food are meat, vegetables, fruits, and other foods.

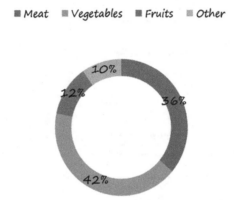

Fig. 3. Classification of disliked food by participants.

The participants believed that the main reasons are the taste and smell, as shown in Fig. 4.

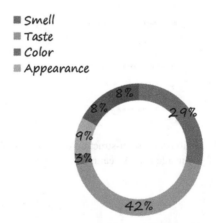

Fig. 4. Reasons for disliked food by participants.

60 participants pointed out that the moment caused their picky eating since they had memory, as shown in Fig. 5. Additionally, the 12 participants stressed that they did not have picky eating until they had experienced special events, which are bad memories to them.

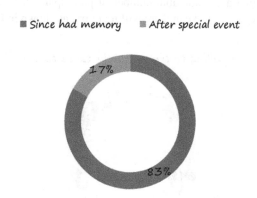

Fig. 5. The moment caused picky eating by participants.

Interestingly, 41 participants thought that the food they disliked did not create negative emotions to them. In the contrast, 31 participants said that annoying food could lead to negative emotions. The negative emotions generated by these foods are usually manifested as nausea and disgust, as shown in Fig. 6.

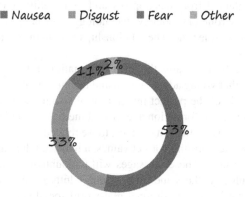

Fig. 6. The negative emotions when the participants see their disliked food.

In the absence of specific scenarios, 70 participants believed that without eating their disliked food would not bother them. 58 participants even had tried these foods they disliked. Interestingly, 26 participants expressed their willingness to try foods they did not like in the absence of specific scenarios. 46 participants stressed reluctance to try. It can be seen that a considerable number of participants have a positive attitude towards the food they do not like and are willing to try, as shown in Fig. 7.

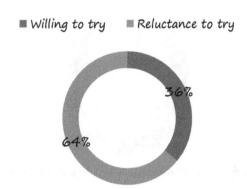

Fig. 7. The participants' attitudes towards trying disliked food.

4.2   PESTLE Analysis Method and Online Desktop Research

The information obtained from desktop research is roughly divided into six aspects: policy, economy, environment, society, technology, and law, most of which involve different aspects at the same time. The relationships among the six aspects are illustrated in Fig. 8.

As shown in Fig. 8, it contains the most information in terms of society and technology. This means that young adults' social and technology impact is the greatest. The Internet is an example of the perfect integration of social and technology. At present, the world has entered the information age. Social media and messages surround young adults from all directions. In these messages, those related to food and picky eating call for reducing food waste, forming correct values, a balanced diet, and many meaningful things to the environment. These messages will undoubtedly imperceptibly affect the mind of young adults. At the same time, young adults must face a variety of social occasions. Whether it is more traditional real-world social occasions or virtual world social occasions, picky eating behavior could cause social embarrassment. Therefore, the scenario can be further divided into the impact of social relations on picky eating in the real world and in the virtual world, as shown in Fig. 9 and Fig. 10.

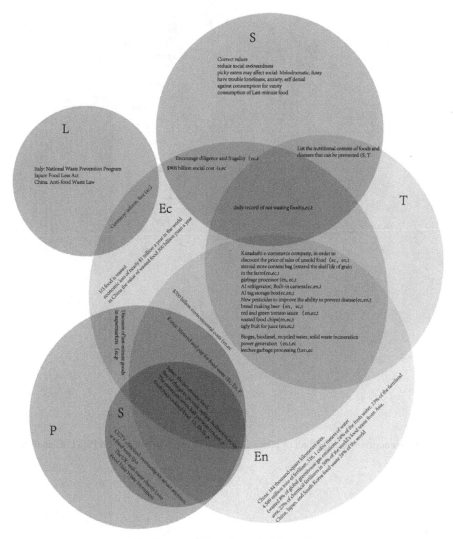

Fig. 8. PESTLE analyze of picky eating.

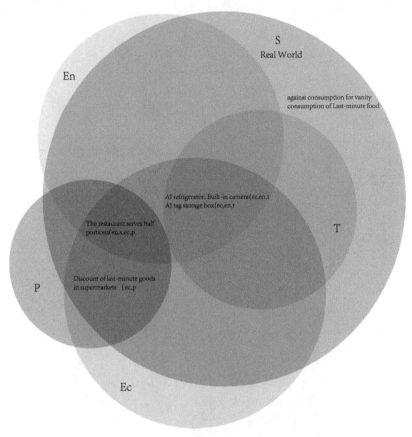

Fig. 9. Scenario of social effect of picky eating in the real world based on PESTLE analyze.

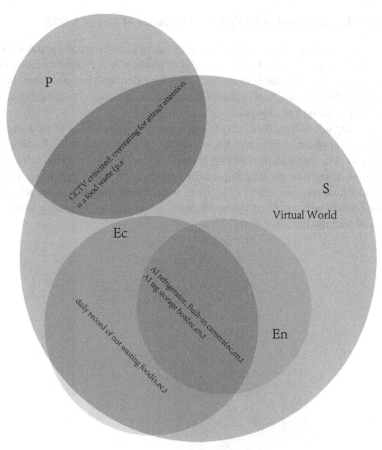

Fig. 10. Scenario of social effect of picky eating in the virtual world based on PESTLE analyze.

4.3 Psychological Model of Picky Eating Behavior of Young Adults

According to the data analyzed and collected by micro (questionnaire) and macro (PES-TLE) methods, a picky eating behavior model of young adults is constructed in Fig. 11. There are three kinds of methods to make it easier for individuals to realize their behavior, i.e. improving the motivation of use, improving the ability of use (reducing the difficulty of use), and providing use channels.

Since young adults have the ability to eat, improving the usability or reducing the use difficulty is not applicable. However, improving the use of motivation is a feasible method in this model. The motivation could be promoting the nutritional value or re-package disliked food. These new positive impressions conflict with the negative impressions of food in individual memory. The two kinds of impressions integrate with each other, so that young adults will not resist trying the food. Alternatively, the young adult may be curious and take the initiative to try.

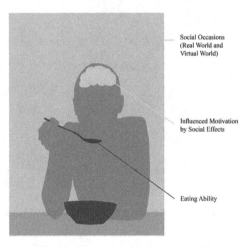

Fig. 11. Picky eating behavior model.

The trigger condition is a relatively accidental situation. In the model of picky eating behavior of young adults, the trigger condition is often the scene and surroundings, for example, a severe social engagement or dinner party. It is not in line with typical social etiquette to be picky about food on solemn social occasions. This picky eating behavior itself may cause the attention of other individuals, resulting in social embarrassment. Seriousness may cause dissatisfaction of the partners, thus damaging the benefit of picky eaters. So on this occasion, picky eaters often choose to eat the food they do not like.

There must be stronger trigger conditions if the motivation is not strong enough. Similarly, if the trigger conditions are not strong enough, stronger motivation must be. If the motivation and trigger conditions both are not strong enough, picky eaters will not eat food that they dislike.

5   Discussion and Conclusion

The results in this paper indicate that 16.22% of the participants did not like to eat some kinds of food after experiencing special events. These participants can recall detail in the events. 43.24% of the participants believed that the food they hated would negatively affect them. They subconsciously associate the events in their memory with food, resulting in resistance and refusing to eat the food. This situation is consistent with the more isolated anxiety of picky eaters in previous studies [14, 16]. In the analysis of PESTLE, it can be concluded that social and technological factors significantly impact young adults. The social impact can not be ignored. Positive effects can help young adults with correcting values and developing good eating habits. Such healthy eating behavior undoubtedly dramatically reduces the possibility of social embarrassment.

A picky eating behavior model of young adults is constructed through the micro (questionnaire) and macro (PESTLE) analysis. As long as there is a subtle motivational influence on the individual and triggered on the right occasion, picky eaters of young adults will make the behavior of eating food they do not like.

This paper connects the questionnaire with PESTLE analysis and Fogg behavior model, preliminarily exploring the causes of contemporary young people's picky eating and the relationship between their related experience behavior, and concludes that most picky eating is closely related to psychology. All the practices discussed in this paper that may improve picky eating behavior are based on the psychological impact of picky eaters. However, whether picky eaters of young adults want to overcome picky eating, it is largely depends on the subjective consciousness of them. If they think that picky eating does not cause trouble, there is no way to force them to eat food they do not like. To some extent, this paper is a wake-up call for picky eaters of young adults to remind waste food and provide an idea that may overcome pickiness.

Acknowledgements. The authors wish to thank all the people who provided their time and efforts for the investigation. This research was supported by Guangdong Province Education Science Planning Project, "Research on Youth Psychological/Mind Models and Art Therapy Strategies: Taking Greater Bay Area University as an Example", grant number 2019GXJK196.

References

1. Forbes, H., Quested, T., O'Connor, C.: UNEP Food Waste Index Report 2021, 1st edn. (2021)
2. Lu, Y., et al.: Reports from Northwest A&F University Provide New Insights into Greenhouse Gases (Impacts of food wastage on water resources and environment in China). Food Weekly News, p. 464. NewsRX LLC, Atlanta (2018)
3. Taylor, C., Wernimont, S., Northstone, K., Emmett, P.: Picky/fussy eating in children: review of definitions, assessment, prevalence and dietary intakes. Appetite **95**, 349–359 (2015)
4. Dovey, T., Kumari, V., Blissett, J.: Eating behaviour, behavioural problems and sensory profiles of children with avoidant/restrictive food intake disorder (ARFID), autistic spectrum disorders or picky eating: same or different? Eur. Psychiatry **61**, 56–62 (2019)
5. Rogers, L., Magill-Evans, J., Rempel, G.: Mothers' challenges in feeding their children with autism spectrum disorder—managing more than just picky eating. J. Dev. Phys. Disabil. **1**(24), 19–33 (2012)

6. Antoniou, E., et al.: Picky eating and child weight status development: a longitudinal study. J. Hum. Nutr. Diet. 3(29), 298–307 (2016)
7. Viljakainen, H., Figueiredo, R., Rounge, T., Weiderpass, E.: Picky eating - a risk factor for underweight in Finnish preadolescents. Appetite 133, 107–114 (2019)
8. Sandvik, P., Ek, A., Eli, K., Somaraki, M., Bottai, M., Nowicka, P.: Picky eating in an obesity intervention for preschool-aged children - what role does it play, and does the measurement instrument matter? Int. J. Behav. Nutr. Phys. Act. 1(16), 76–85 (2019)
9. Sandvik, P., Ek, A., Somaraki, M., Hammer, U., Eli, K., Nowicka, P.: Picky eating in Swedish preschoolers of different weight status: application of two new screening cut-offs. Int. J. Behav. Nutr. Phys. Act. 1(15), 74–85 (2018)
10. Walton, K., Kuczynski, L., Haycraft, E., Breen, A., Haines, J.: Time to re-think picky eating?: a relational approach to understanding picky eating. Int. J. Behav. Nutr. Phys. Act. 1(14), 62 (2017)
11. Parker, S., Zuckerman, B., Augustyn, M.: Developmental and Behavioral Pediatrics: A Handbook for Primary Care, 2nd edn. Wolters Kluwer, Philadelphia (2004)
12. Nederkoorn, C., Jansen, A., Havermans, R.C.: Feel your food: the influence of tactile sensitivity on picky eating in children. Appetite 1(84), 07–10 (2015)
13. Gan, K., Tithecott, C., Neilson, L., Seabrook, J., Dworatzek, P.: Picky eating is associated with lower nutrient intakes from children's home-packed school lunches. Nutrients 6(13), 1759–1774 (2021)
14. Volger, S., Sheng, X., Tong, L., Zhao, D., Fan, T.: Nutrient intake and dietary patterns in children 2.5–5 years of age with picky eating behaviours and low weight-for-height. Asia Pac. J. Clin. Nutr. 1(26), 104–109 (2017)
15. Kwon, K., Shim, J., Kang, M., Hee-Young, P.: Association between picky eating behaviors and nutritional status in early childhood: performance of a picky eating behavior questionnaire. Nutrients 5(9), 463–477 (2017)
16. Cole, N., Wang, A., Donovan, S., Lee, S., Teran-Garcia, M.: Supplementary Material for: Variants in Chemosensory Genes are Associated with Picky Eating Behavior in Preschool-Age Children. Karger Publishers, Basel (2017)
17. Ellis, J., Zickgraf, H., Galloway, A., Essayli, J., Whited, M.: A functional description of adult picky eating using latent profile analysis. Int. J. Behav. Nutr. Phys. Act. 1(15), 109 (2018)
18. Chiu, J.: Adult picky eating behaviors: impact of psychosocial and nutritional factors. Ohio (2015)
19. Calder, P., Field, C., Gill, H.: Nutrition and Immune Function: Frontiers in Nutritional Science. 1st edn., no. 1. CABI, Egham (2002)
20. Brown, C.L., Perrin, E.M.: Defining picky eating and its relationship to feeding behaviors and weight status. J. Behav. Med. 43(4), 587–595 (2019). https://doi.org/10.1007/s10865-019-00081-w
21. Cullinane, K.: Identifying the main opportunities and challenges from the implementation of a port energy management system: a SWOT/PESTLE analysis. Sustainability 11(21), 6046 (2019)
22. Fogg, B.: Designing for behavior change-new models and moral issues: an interview with B.J. Fogg: B.J. Fogg talks with Jim Euchner about persuasive technology and Behavior Design. Res. Technol. Manag. 5(62), 14–14 (2019)

Can Electromyography and Subjective Metrics Work Better Together? Exploring Dynamic Muscle Fatigue to Promote the Design of Health and Fitness Technology

Lanyun Zhang[1]([⊠]), Yan He[1], and Haiou Zhu[2]

[1] Nanjing University of Aeronautics and Astronautics, 29 Yudao Street, Nanjing 210016, People's Republic of China
lanyunzhang@nuaa.edu.cn
[2] Loughborough University, Epinal Way, Loughborough L11 3TU, UK

Abstract. The assessment of local muscle fatigue during dynamic exercises is viewed as essential, since people tend to maximise effective muscle training and minimise harmful muscle injuries. This study aims to investigate how surface electromyography (sEMG) and subjective metrics together can play a role in dynamic muscle fatigue prediction during exercises to promote the design of health and fitness technology. 20 healthy male participants were recruited in the experiment, and sEMG and self-reported data were collected. Features in temporal and spatial domain were extracted from sEMG data, such as RMS (root mean square) and FI_{nsm5} (spectral parameter proposed by Dimitrov). Our results showed that some sEMG features indicated directional changes with the increase of dynamic muscle fatigue. Spearman correlation analysis indicated that Borg ratings had strong correlations with RMS and FI_{nsm5} (spectral parameter proposed by Dimitrov) slopes. Then this paper discusses how to use sEMG and Borg data to evaluate muscle fatigue during exercises. A framework is proposed based on the joint analysis of spectra and amplitudes across RMS and FI_{nsm5} slopes. This paper further discusses how to design health and fitness technology for the benefits and the limitations of the study.

Keywords: Subjective metrics · Electromyography · Muscle fatigue · Design · Fitness technology

1 Introduction

Muscle fatigue describes a decrease in the ability of a muscle to contract and exert force, and it develops gradually from the start of a contraction [1]. In muscle strength training, muscle fatigue could be beneficial in muscle growth while it can also be harmful if the fatigue level is high for too long [2]. Apart from the physiological aspect of fatigue, the psychological aspect also plays an important role. People may perceive and sense fatigue differently, and it, in turn, can affect people's physiological performance [3]. Therefore,

© The Author(s), under exclusive license to Springer Nature Switzerland AG 2022
M. M. Soares et al. (Eds.): HCII 2022, LNCS 13322, pp. 223–237, 2022.
https://doi.org/10.1007/978-3-031-05900-1_15

it is important to explore the relationships between the physiological measurements and psychological aspects of fatigue.

Currently, existing health and fitness technologies on the market are mostly limited to monitoring heart rate, counting the number of steps, and they require users to manually select specific sports for recording purposes. Very few intelligent products can monitor and evaluate muscle fatigue. Since excessive muscle fatigue can lead to muscle injuries during resistance training, a research gap, as well as a business opportunity, exists in innovating wearable devices for monitoring muscle fatigue in-situ.

Generally, there are two approaches to measure and assess individuals' degree of muscle fatigue. The first approach is to collect people's physiological data such as surface electromyography (sEMG). sEMG electrodes can be easily placed on different muscle parts on the surface of the body. Most of the research makes use of sEMG to obtain objective data that can reflect muscle fatigue. However, it is complicated to collect suitable physiological data and translate it into individuals' degree of muscle fatigue. The second approach is to collect people's subjective fatigue, where self-reported data are collected during or after each repetition of a workout. Currently, the most widely used subjective measure is the Borg scale CR10 [4].

This study aims to explore how sEMG data and subjective metrics can be combined to assess dynamic muscle fatigue during exercises. We intended to initiate discussions for the purpose of designing new health and fitness interactions to help people monitor muscle fatigue during muscle training. The objectives of this study include:

- To understand how sEMG features and subjective metrics change with the increase of muscle fatigue.
- To explore how to combine sEMG data and subjective metrics to evaluate dynamic muscle fatigue.

2   Background and Related Work

This section introduces related work in three parts: (1) muscle fatigue assessment via sEMG, (2) fatigue assessment via subjective metrics, and (3) challenges of evaluating muscle fatigue in the fitness context.

2.1   Muscle Fatigue Assessment via sEMG

sEMG is a non-invasive approach that is widely used for muscle fatigue monitoring. There are a variety of articles discussing static and dynamic muscle fatigue detection by analysing sEMG data, such as exploiting and comparing sEMG features in temporal and spatial domain methods. Strimpakos et al. [8] explored neck muscle fatigue, using two features of sEMG data: normalised median frequency (MDF) and root mean square (RMS). Al-Mulla et al. [6] required participants to perform a static biceps curl activity and sEMG signals were successfully utilised to predict muscle fatigue. However, during the dynamic muscle fatigue monitoring, some changes, such as changes in muscle force, changes in muscle length, and muscle fibre conduction velocity, may increase the non-stationarity of the sEMG signals [17]. This study intends to focus on exploring how to evaluate dynamic muscle fatigue using sEMG, for the purposes of eliciting design ideas to promote the user experience of health and fitness technologies.

To evaluate dynamic muscle fatigue, features in the spatial domain are mostly used. Cruz-Montecinos et al. [18] asked participants to perform five sets of leg presses and found that the Dimitrov spectral index of muscle fatigue (FI_{nsm5}) was significantly relevant to local muscle fatigue during a high-loading fatiguing task. Chang et al. [13] found that the regression line of median frequency (MDF) decreased with the increase of dynamic fatigue, where their experimental tasks required participants to run on a pedalled-multifunctional elliptical trainer for approximately 30 min at different loading levels. However, Jesus et al. [14] found that when muscular loads are at a low level, mean frequency (MNF) and MDF will be less effective to measure fatigue level. As for temporal domain features, the amplitude of sEMG features is rarely used as an independent indicator to assess muscle fatigue [17]. There is a controversy among researchers regarding reproducibility [10], and amplitude might be significantly influenced by muscle force level [11]. While in assessing static muscle fatigue, temporal features are often used in combination with other indicators, such as the Joint Analysis of EMG Spectrum and Amplitude (JASA) [12]. In JASA, four different categories of muscle performance can be distinguished based on the sEMG features, such as muscle fatigue and recovery.

Classification of dynamic muscle fatigue can be approached via various methods. Different machine learning algorithms can predict muscle fatigue by utilising sEMG features, but there is not a widely agreed mechanism that can evaluate muscle fatigue effectively and efficiently across all contexts. Papakostas et al. [15] proposed a postprocessing mechanism that has improved the classification accuracy combining both subjective reports and sEMG signals. For repeated isokinetic dumbbell curl exercise, Hwang et al. [5] proposed an algorithm to predict dynamic muscle force and fatigue level based on integrated values and slopes of sEMG features. For example, frequency and amplitude of certain sEMG features are influenced by both the degree of muscle force and fatigue. Yet, most studies focus on physiological data such as sEMG, while subjective reports by users are often ignored.

2.2 Fatigue Assessment via Subjective Metrics

Muscle fatigue can also be evaluated via psychological approaches. There are three types of subjective rating scales that are mostly used to evaluate fatigue [9]: (1) visual analogue scales (continuous scale); (2) Borg scale (12 points with detailed descriptions); and (3) Likert scale. Grant et al. [9] found that compared with visual analogue scales and Likert Scales, Borg scales had a higher sensitivity for general fatigue during submaximal exercises.

Borg's ratings of perceived exertion (RPE) (6–20 Borg) and Category-Ratio (CR10) scales were developed to rate the level of perceived exertion regarding cardiovascular (e.g., increased heart rate and breathing difficulty) and muscular (e.g., muscle exertion and pain) loads during physical activity [4]. The 6–20 Borg scale ranges from "6" (no exertion) to "20" (maximal exertion), while the CR10 scale ranges from "0" (no exertion) to "10" (maximal exertion) [4]. Borg ratings were coincidental with decreases in muscle's power output [8], while an increase in the RPE value using CR10 is correlated with a reduction in maximal voluntary muscle force [18]. Research has found that the ratings of perceived fatigue are related to muscle fatigue, and the ratings can be measured physiologically. However, existing literatures lack the knowledge about how Borg ratings and physiological data can together play a role in muscle fatigue assessment.

Some studies have analysed the correlation between self-reported data and physiological data. For example, Öberg et al. [7] found that when assessing shoulder muscle fatigue, a statistically significant correlation was shown between Borg scores and mean power frequency (MPF) values of sEMG at high load level, but no significant correlation at low load level. Some studies used subjective reports as labels for fatigue assessment to train and test the machine learning algorithms. Elshafei et al. [19] mark the fatigue level as high when reported Borg values are greater than 16, using the RPE scale, for algorithm development. However, subjective data can be more than the labels in machine learning algorithms. This study intends to explore the combination of subjective fatigue and physiological data for dynamic muscle fatigue assessment.

2.3 Challenges of Evaluating Muscle Fatigue in Fitness Context

To collect sEMG signals in the fitness and exercise context, one of the obstacles is that most movements of strength training are dynamic and complex, so the sEMG signals may be interfered with because of the constant moving. Meanwhile, it is normal for people to change the parameters during a training session. The parameters include the choices of weight in dumbbell workouts, the rest time length between sets and repetitions, etc. It is important that the sEMG signals can capture these changes of choices so that further analysis can evaluate muscle fatigue accordingly.

Collecting users' subjective perceptions of the feeling of fatigue in the process of strength training is also a challenge. Firstly, people's perception of muscle fatigue varies between individuals. Similar to people's perceptions of pain, psychological factors such as situational and emotional factors can profoundly alter the strength of people's perceptions of muscle fatigue. Secondly, the timing of collecting subjective perceptions of fatigue is also very important. It is an intrusive method to assess fatigue levels, as data are collected during exercise sets or between sets. The question that whether or not the collection of subjective data would disturb the exercise process needs careful consideration.

Since the scale and sampling frequency of subjective reports are different from the scale and sampling frequency of sEMG data, it requires more work to explore how to combine these two metrics to evaluate muscle fatigue. Subjective reports can act as labels of fatigue level, but they can also be viewed as an input variable of a fatigue evaluation mechanism. Thus, one of the goals of this study is to explore how to combine subjective metrics and sEMG data in a framework to assess muscle fatigue, to further elicit design ideas for health and fitness interactions and technologies.

3   Method

3.1   Study Design and Procedure

To simulate strength training scenarios, participants were asked to complete at least five sets of seated isolated dumbbell curls, 12 repetitions in each set. A warm-up session was required at the beginning. To suit the participants with different muscle strengths, we provided three weights of dumbbells (5 kg, 8.5 kg, or 10 kg) that allowed the participants to select freely according to their individual abilities. To include different resting settings between repetitions, two exercise patterns were designed (see Fig. 1), and half of the participants were required to follow pattern 1 and the remaining to follow pattern 2.

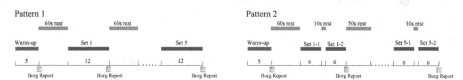

Fig. 1. Exercise pattern 1: 60 s rest between sets, Exercise pattern 2: 10 s rest in the middle of each set and 50 s rest between sets.

The procedure of the experiment included:

Step 1: After reading the information sheet and signing the consent form, participants were asked to choose a weight of the dumbbell that fit their ability best and were informed of the given exercise pattern. After a warm-up of the biceps brachii (using a 2 kg dumbbell), the participants were asked to sit down and wear the wireless sEMG device until the end of the whole procedure. Alcohol pads were used to clean the skin surface before putting the sEMG nodes on.

Step 2: The participants were required to complete the second warm-up of seated isolated dumbbell curls, using the dumbbell that they chose (5 kg, 8.5 kg, or 10 kg). Then, the participants could officially start their sets. We asked them to complete at least five sets with 12 repetitions in each set. The participants were instructed to continue the sets until they felt extreme fatigue, but they could stop at any fatigue level. The fatigue levels were also measured through subjective metrics right after each set (see Fig. 1). The participants needed to report their subjective feeling of fatigue (Borg scale). Table 1 shows the details of the subjective metrics, where Borg's CR10 was adopted and adapted. Without explanation, the participants might rate their fatigue level differently based on their own feeling of exhaustion, which would lead them to report their levels of exertion inaccurately. To address this, we provided them with a few brief explanations. For example, '3' indicates that the muscle starts to ache and '10' indicates a status of the arm that is unable to lift the dumbbell at all. Not all points from 0 to 10 were explained since it was hard to specify, and it might be sensible to give the participants some room.

Step 3: After completing the workout, the participants were asked to answer semi-structured questions about the whole experience, involving the time of rest between sets and the pattern of their daily exercises.

Table 1. Borg's CR10 scale

To what extent do you feel tired or exhausted?			
Point	Level	Note	Explanation
0	Nothing at all		
0.5	Extremely weak	(Just noticeable)	
1	Very weak		
2	Weak	(Light)	
3	Moderate		Muscle starts to ache
4			
5	Strong	(Heavy)	
6			
7	Very strong		
8			Lifting dumbbell is very difficult
9			
10	Extremely Strong	(Almost max)	Arm is unable to lift the dumbbell at all

3.2 Participants and Data Collection

20 healthy male participants were recruited for the experiment, Table 2 shows the participant information and their choices of dumbbell weights with the given exercise patterns. Raw sEMG signals were collected through wireless 8-channel biosignals Plux HUB, a sampling rate at 1000 Hz. Body mass index (BMI) was measured (shown in Table 2) that indicates body fat based on height and weight.

Table 2. Participant information.

Number	BMI	Dumbbell weight (kg)	Exercise pattern
1	30.86	5	Pattern 1
2	20.76	5	Pattern 1
3	20.76	5	Pattern 2
4	23.66	5	Pattern 1
5	25.95	5	Pattern 2
6	23.39	5	Pattern 1
7	22.2	5	Pattern 2
8	21.97	5	Pattern 1

(continued)

Table 2. (*continued*)

Number	BMI	Dumbbell weight (kg)	Exercise pattern
9	23.14	5	Pattern 2
10	22.4	5	Pattern 1
11	22.49	10	Pattern 2
12	23.06	8.5	Pattern 1
13	22.86	8.5	Pattern 2
14	22.20	8.5	Pattern 2
15	23.05	8.5	Pattern 2
16	21.60	8.5	Pattern 1
17	23.12	10	Pattern 2
18	21.38	8.5	Pattern 1
19	23.14	10	Pattern 1
20	25.95	10	Pattern 2

3.3 SEMG Signal Processing

The sEMG signals were sampled at 1000 Hz and a bandpass filter was applied to cut off the frequencies between 20–500 Hz. The muscles were intermittently activated during the dumbbell curls. Teager-Kaiser Energy Operator (TKEO) was used to detect muscle activation. Then, six features were extracted in this study through python. The details of the six features are deliberated as follows:

(1) Mean absolute value (MAV)

For amplitude features, two indicators were extracted: mean absolute value (MAV) and root mean square (RMS) value. They are defined by the following equations:

$$MAV = \frac{1}{N} \sum_{i=1}^{N} |x_i| \tag{1}$$

where x_i is the ith sample of a signal and N is the number of samples in the epoch.

(2) Root mean square (RMS)

$$RMS = \sqrt{\frac{1}{N} \sum_{i=1}^{N} |x_i|} \tag{2}$$

where x_i is the ith sample of a signal and N is the number of samples in the epoch.

(3) Zero crossing rate (ZCR)

$$ZCR = \frac{1}{N-1} \sum_{n=1}^{N-1} (sig(x_t) - sig(x_{t-1})) \tag{3}$$

where $sig(x) = \begin{cases} 1 & \text{if } x > 0 \\ 0 & \text{if } x = 0 \\ -1 & \text{if } x < 0 \end{cases}$ and N is the number of samples in the epoch.

ZCR indicates the rate of sign-changes of the signal during the duration of a particular frame.

(4) Mean power frequency (MPF)

$$MPF = \frac{\int_{f_1}^{f_2} f \cdot P(f) df}{\int_{f_1}^{f_2} P(f) df} \tag{4}$$

where f = frequency, $P(f)$ is the power spectral density of the signal. $f_1 = 20$ Hz and $f_2 = 500$ Hz are determined for the bandwidth of the surface electromyography.

(5) Median frequency (MDF)

$$\int_{f_1}^{f_{med}} P(f) df = \int_{f_{med}}^{f_2} P(f) df \tag{5}$$

where f_{med} is the median frequency, f_s is the sampling frequency, and $P(f)$ is the power spectral density of the signal, and $f_1 = 20$ Hz and $f_2 = 500$ Hz.

(6) The new frequency parameter proposed by Dimitrov (FI_{nsm5}) is defined as:

$$FI_{nsm5} = \frac{\int_{f_1}^{f_2} f^{-1} \cdot P(f) df}{\int_{f_1}^{f_2} f^5 \cdot P(f) df} \tag{6}$$

where $P(f)$ is the power spectral density of the signal, and $f_1 = 20$ Hz and $f_2 = 500$ Hz.

3.4 Data Analysis

To explore how sEMG features and subjective metrics change with the increase of muscle fatigue, descriptive analysis and statistical analysis were employed via SPSS. All the sEMG features were firstly normalized. Then, the features were independently compared via a one-way analysis of variance. When a significant F-value was achieved, Sheffé post hoc procedures were performed to locate the pairwise differences between the means. At last, correlation analysis was conducted to analyse the correlation among the sEMG features and the correlation between sEMG features and subjective metrics. The results of the semi-structured interview data are not reported in this paper due to the limitation of paper length.

4 Results

4.1 Results of the Descriptive and Statistical Analysis

As shown in Fig. 2, the sEMG features in the time-domain (RMS, ZCR, MAV) and frequency-domain (MDF, FInsm5, MPF) indicate directional changes with the increase of dynamic muscle fatigue.

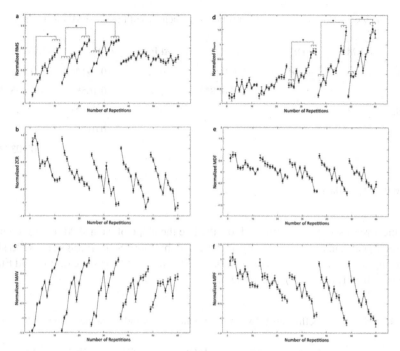

Fig. 2. Changes of sEMG features (mean ± SD). (a) RMS, (b) ZCR, (c) MAV, (d) FI_{nsm5}, (e) MDF, (f) MPF.

ANOVA tests and post hoc procedures on RMS and FInsm5 respectively showed that: (1) among the first three sets, RMS recorded during the first four repetitions was significantly lower ($p < 0.05$) than the recorded during the last four repetitions; (2) among the last three sets, FI_{nsm5} recorded during the first three repetitions was significantly higher ($p < 0.05$) than the recorded during the last three repetitions.

4.2 Results of the Correlation Analysis

Spearman correlation analysis revealed that among the six extracted sEMG features, MDF and FI_{nsm5} showed strong correlation ($r = -0.608$, $p < 0.01$), followed by RMS and MAV ($r = 0.313$, $p < 0.01$), while the others showed either weak or very weak correlation (Table 3).

Table 3. Correlation coefficients between each two of the six sEMG features

	RMS	MDF	FI$_{nsm5}$	MPF	ZCR	MAV
RMS		−0.059**	0.090**	−0.029	−0.091**	0.313**
MDF			−0.608**	0.025	0.165**	−0.175**
FInsm5				−0.036	−0.206**	0.208**
MPF					0.018	−0.02
ZCR						−0.103**
MAV						

*p < 0.05, **p < 0.01

Linear regression was employed to calculate the slope of each sEMG feature within each set. Spearman correlation analysis indicated that Borg Scale ratings and RMS slope had strong correlation ($r = -0.638$, $p < 0.01$), followed by Borg Scale ratings and FI$_{nsm5}$ slope ($r = 0.531$, $p < 0.01$), see Table 4.

Table 4. Correlation coefficients between Borg scale ratings and the slope of six sEMG features

	RMS	FI$_{nsm5}$	MDF	MPF	ZCR	MAV
Borg Scale ratings	−0.638**	0.531**	−0.360**	−0.415**	−0.193	−0.504**

*p < 0.05, **p < 0.01

5 Discussion

This section discusses the findings from this study, including theoretical contributions and practical implications. Theoretical contributions mainly focus on explaining a framework structured by sEMG features, proposed to assess dynamic muscle fatigue. Practical implications cover a range of design considerations that might elicit design ideas for future research and the development of health and fitness technologies.

5.1 Theoretical Contributions

Existing research showed that an increase in the sEMG amplitude is highly related to muscular force [12] and a shift in the frequency spectrum is a typical sign of muscle fatigue [16]. We found that in the first three sets, RMS significantly increased with the increase of muscular force, and there was no obvious change in the remaining two sets. On the other hand, FI$_{nsm5}$ significantly increased in the last three sets, which is considered to be highly related to the increase of fatigue. Compared with other sEMG features, the slope of RMS and FI$_{nsm5}$ of each set has a higher correlation with Borg scale ratings. Therefore, a joint analysis of the spectra and amplitudes across RMS and

FI_{nsm5} was applied. Three fatigue states were proposed: Muscle Activation, Transition to Fatigue, and Fatigue to Exhaustion. A framework was proposed to assess the muscle fatigue level shown in Fig. 3.

(1) Muscle activation (RMS slope > 0.1 and FI_{nsm5} < 0.15), in this stage muscular force increases without fatigue.
(2) Transition to fatigue (RMS slope > 0.1 and FI_{nsm5} > 0.15), in this stage muscular force increases and fatigue increases. Fatigue to exhaustion (RMS slope < 0.1 and FI_{nsm5} > 0.15), in this stage muscular force decreases and fatigue increases.

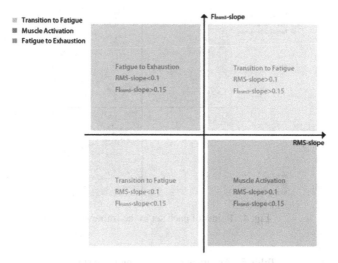

Fig. 3. Framework of fatigue assessment with RMS and FInsm5 slopes

As shown in Fig. 3, the x axis represents the RMS slope of each set, and the y axis represents the FI_{nsm5} slope of each set. For example, if RMS slope is greater than 0.1 and FI_{nsm5} slope is less than 0.15, the framework would decide that the muscle state of this set is Muscle Activation.

The threshold shown in the framework is adjustable according to inter-person and intra-person performances. Based on the data we collected, we found that the sets with Borg scale ratings between 0 and 3, their RMS slopes were mostly greater than 0.1; the sets with Borg ratings greater than 7, their RMS slopes were mostly less than 0.1. Then we decided to set 0.1 as the threshold of the x axis (RMS axis). The determination of the threshold of FI_{nsm5} axis was similar. Overall, the thresholds should be able to self-adjust according to different users and different user performances. In practical scenarios, with the increase of one user using fitness product, a large amount of data will be collected about this user. Therefore, the data should be able to support self-adjustment. To test our framework, we use Borg scale ratings as labels. According to the Borg scale ratings, we defined 0–3 as Muscle Activation, 4–6 as Transition to Fatigue and 7–10 as Fatigue to Exhaustion. In Fig. 4, dots with three different colours represent different ranges of

Borg scale ratings. We took our experimental data into this framework and each dot in the axis represents the subjective fatigue level about one set. The accuracy rate is calculated by dividing the number of dots falling in the corresponding colour area by the total number of dots. The results are shown in Table 5. 64.29% of the least fatigue Borg ratings were identified as Muscle Activation; 55.56% of the medium fatigue Borg ratings were identified as Transition to Fatigue; while 61.29% of the most fatigue Borg ratings were identified as Fatigue to Exhaustion. The accuracy can be further tested with different approaches, e.g., alternative mechanisms or machine learning algorithms. On the other hand, subjective feelings (i.e., Borg ratings) can also play a role in setting the thresholds in the framework rather than labels. The next section will elaborate in detail.

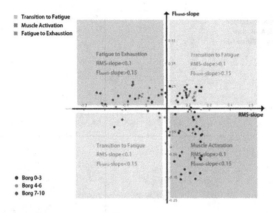

Fig. 4. Points of each set in the framework

Table 5. Accuracy of identifying three states.

	Identified as muscle activation	Identified as transition to fatigue	Identified as fatigue to exhaustion
Borg 0–3	64.29%	30.95%	4.8%
Borg 4–6	22.22%	55.56%	22.22%
Borg 7–10	9.7%	29.03%	61.29%

5.2 Practical Implications

Our framework is proposed to assess fatigue in the context of strength training. This framework can help understand people's muscle conditions by analysing sEMG signals. The state of Muscle Activation can be used to help users understand whether the warm-up is sufficient and the state of Fatigue to Exhaustion can be used to prevent excessive fatigue. In practical applications, the thresholds can be determined by the data collected from a user's first two to three workout repetitions. And with the increase of the user's muscle activation, muscular force, and fatigue level, the thresholds in the framework should be able to adjust accordingly. Furthermore, we identified different ways to utilise subjective data. Two approaches are discussed in this section in terms of how to integrate users' subjective feedback into the proposed framework:

1. Subjective reports as labels to adjust the framework and influence the fatigue assessment outcome indirectly. The thresholds that distinguish the three fatigue states are not fixed across different user segments. For example, according to a user's subjective report, when the accuracy of the mechanism is lower than a certain value, the framework will need to update its thresholds to improve the accuracy. In this case, the subjective data needs to be collected repeatedly, that the sampling frequency can be varied according to the user's degree of change in muscular force and fatigue.
2. Subjective reports as input and influence the fatigue assessment outcome directly. Feedback from subjective metrics can be used to make corrections to the results of the framework. In other words, results from subjective reports do not play a role in the adjustment of the framework for fatigue assessment, rather they adjust the outcome from the framework directly. For example, if the framework determines that a user's current state is Muscle Activation, while the user's subjective metric keeps reporting high fatigue ratings, then the result that given back to the user might be adjusted to Transition to Fatigue or even Fatigue to Exhaustion.

In real case scenarios, these two approaches can co-exist at the same time to suit different user segments. Based on the previous discussions, the requirements about designing fitness products for monitoring muscle fatigue are considered: (1) the product should be able to collect the sEMG signals of a designated muscle that is expected to be strengthened via specific workouts. sEMG sensors need to be attached to the targeted muscle, so wearable fabrics with sEMG sensors might be a good choice. (2) The product should be able to record users' subjective reports and make full use of them. A user can inform the device about his/her subjective fatigue feelings through voice or manual input, where subjective data should be collected with a certain regular pattern for him/her. (3) The product should be able to give feedback to the users about the degree of their muscle fatigue. To complete a full interaction between the users and the device, the device should be able to push the information back to the users as notifications. A portable and wearable device with a display function might be an option. The form of the notification can use voice, visual, or vibration alerts. The product could also show the users about the changes in their muscle status during strength training.

6 Conclusions, Limitations and Future Work

6.1 Conclusions

This study reveals the changes and speed of changes in which different sEMG features respond to dynamic muscle contractions in the context of strength training. Spearman correlation analysis indicated that Borg Scale ratings had strong correlations with RMS slope and FI_{nsm5} slope, which indicates that sEMG and subjective metrics could be used to predict muscle fatigue during dynamic exercises.

Practically, this study discussed two pairs of dimensions that can be put to design practices either separately or simultaneously: (1) RMS and FI_{nsm5} complement each other during the fatigue process and a framework based on RMS and FI_{nsm5} slopes is proposed. (2) sEMG data and Borg ratings can be utilised to assess muscle fatigue, and subjective metrics can either be a direct input that supports user interaction or be viewed as labels to adjust the framework structured by sEMG.

6.2 Limitations and Future Work

Firstly, this study only investigated two exercise patterns and their impacts on sEMG and subjective metrics, while there are more diverse patterns in daily fitness scenarios. Secondly, in our framework, the thresholds that distinguish the three fatigue states are determined based on the relatively small samples in this study and were classified manually. To adapt to individual users, the thresholds should be able to adjust automatically. Thirdly, in the last two sets, some participants' postures were getting poorer and improper due to fatigue, which may lead to the inaccuracy of the sEMG signals about the measured muscle. Future work could focus on exploring new mechanisms that can detect postures.

Acknowledgements. This work is supported by Shuangchuang Programme of Jiangsu Province for the Grant JSSCBS20210190 and Nanjing University of Aeronautics and Astronautics for the Grant 1005/56YAH20099.

References

1. Søgaard, K., Gandevia, S.C., Todd, G., Petersen, N.T., Taylor, J.L.: The effect of sustained low-intensity contractions on supraspinal fatigue in human elbow flexor muscles. J. Physiol. **573**(2), 511–523 (2006)
2. Garrett, W.E.: Muscle strain injuries: clinical and basic aspects. Med. Sci. Sports Exerc. **22**(4), 436–443 (1990)
3. Cutsem, J.V., Van Marcora, S., Pauw, K.D., Bailey, S., Meeusen, R., Roelands, B.: The effects of mental fatigue on physical performance: a systematic review. Sports Med. **47**(8), 1569–1588 (2017)
4. Borg, G.: Psychophysical scaling with applications in physical work and the perception of exertion. Scand. J. Work **16**(1), 55–58 (1990)
5. Hwang, H.-J., Chung, W.-H., Song, J.-H., Lim, J.-K., Kim, H.-S.: Prediction of biceps muscle fatigue and force using electromyography signal analysis for repeated isokinetic dumbbell curl exercise. J. Mech. Sci. Technol. **30**(11), 5329–5336 (2016). https://doi.org/10.1007/s12 206-016-1053-1
6. Al-Mulla, M.R., Sepulveda, F., Colley, M.: An autonomous wearable system for predicting and detecting localised muscle fatigue. Sensors **11**(2), 1542–1557 (2011)
7. Öberg, T., Sandsjö, L., Kadefors, R.: Subjective and objective evaluation of shoulder muscle fatigue. Ergonomics **37**(8), 1323–1333 (1994)
8. Strimpakos, N., Georgios, G., Eleni, K., Vasilios, K., Jacqueline, O.: Issues in relation to the repeatability of and correlation between EMG and Borg scale assessments of neck muscle fatigue. J. Electromyogr. Kinesiol. **15**(5), 452–465 (2005)

9. Grant, S., et al.: A comparison of the reproducibility and the sensitivity to change of visual analogue scales, Borg scales, and Likert scales in normal subjects during submaximal exercise. Chest **116**(5), 1208–1217 (1999)

10. Koumantakis, G.A., Arall, F., Cooper, R.G., Oldham, J.A.: Paraspinal muscle EMG fatigue testing with two methods in healthy volunteers. Reliability in the context of clinical applications. Clin. Biomech. **16**(3), 263–266 (2001)

11. Chang, J., Chablat, D., Bennis, F., Ma, L.: Estimating the EMG response exclusively to fatigue during sustained static maximum voluntary contraction. Adv. Phys. Ergon. Hum. Factors **489**, 29–39 (2016)

12. Luttmann, A., Jäger, M., Sökeland, J., Laurig, W.: Electromyographical study on surgeons in urology. II. Determination of muscular fatigue. Ergonomics **39**(2), 298–313 (1996)

13. Chang, K.M., Liu, S.H., Wu, X.H.: A wireless sEMG recording system and its application to muscle fatigue detection. Sensors **12**(1), 489–499 (2012)

14. Jesus, I.R., Mello, R.G., Nadal, J.: Muscle fatigue assessment during cycle ergometer exercise using principal component analysis of electromyogram power spectra. J. Appl. Biomech. **32**(6), 593–598 (2016)

15. Papakostas, M., Kanal, V., Abujelala, M., Tsiakas, K., Makedon, F.: Physical fatigue detection through EMG wearables and subjective user reports - a machine learning approach towards adaptive rehabilitation. In: Proceedings of the 12th ACM International Conference on Pervasive Technologies Related to Assistive Environments, pp. 475–481. Association for Computing Machinery, New York (2019)

16. Dimitrov, G.V., Arabadzhiev, T.I., Mileva, K.N., Bowtell, J.L., Crichton, N., Dimitrova, N.A.: Muscle fatigue during dynamic contractions assessed by new spectral indices. Med. Sci. Sports Exerc. **38**(11), 1971–1979 (2006)

17. Farina, D.: Interpretation of the surface electromyogram in dynamic contractions. Exerc. Sport Sci. Rev. **34**(3), 121–127 (2006)

18. Cruz-Montecinos, C., et al.: Perceived physical exertion is a good indicator of neuromuscular fatigue for the core muscles. J. Electromyogr. Kinesiol. **49**, 102360 (2019)

19. Elshafei, M., Costa, D.E., Shihab, E.: On the impact of biceps muscle fatigue in human activity recognition. Sensors **21**(4), 1070 (2021)

Learning Experience Design

Utilization of Digital Fabrication Technology in Hybrid Courses for Industrial Design Education During the COVID-19 Pandemic

Jaime Alvarez[1](✉) and Usuke Tomida[2]

[1] Department of Design, Faculty of Engineering, Takushoku University, Tatemachi 815-1, Hachioji-shi, Tokyo 193-0985, Japan
a-jaime@id.takushoku-u.ac.jp

[2] Fab Design Association, Industry-Academia Collaboration Center, Takushoku University, Tokyo, Japan

Abstract. Due to COVID-19 pandemic. Education systems all around the world had been forced to migrate from face-to-face education to online format by using digital platforms. In Japan, the shift to distance education was particularly challenging across the higher education sector due to lack of experience in conducting classes online, as well as the slow pace of the country education system to take up digital technology.

The scope of the field of industrial design has been increasingly widening, including non-tangible products such as services, interfaces and experiences, among others. Additionally, CAD technology facilitates design distance learning. However, the core of industrial design remains in the development of proposals of physical products, especially in Japan where there is a very strong culture of *monozukuri* or "making of things". Since the practice of industrial design cannot be taught solely by remote classes, this paper documents the attempt to carry out two hybrid courses with face-to-face lessons for physically building design proposals. In order to adapt to the academic conditions in the pandemic context, digital fabrication technology was utilized, specifically laser cutting machines. By using online communication platform students attended lectures, submitted design ideas, received professor feedback and built necessary data. During face-to-face lessons, students used laser cutting machine to make parts, built prototypes and received feedback. Surveys were applied at the end of each course, showing high level of satisfaction among students. This research aims to contribute to finding the most optimum balance point between online and face-to-face lessons for industrial design courses towards the "new normal" reality.

Keywords: Industrial design · Laser cutting machine · Hybrid course

1 Introduction

Traditionally, the main core of the industrial design discipline is the material embodiment of physical products [1]. However, as a strategic problem-solving process it is building

© The Author(s), under exclusive license to Springer Nature Switzerland AG 2022
M. M. Soares et al. (Eds.): HCII 2022, LNCS 13322, pp. 241–255, 2022.
https://doi.org/10.1007/978-3-031-05900-1_16

new bridges and getting connected to all kind of industries. Moreover, products are becoming more physically and technologically complex, and the definition of "product" itself is evolving to include dimensions that are not physical, such as digital and virtual.

In the highly dynamic context of an evolving discipline, the COVID-19 pandemic appeared and have forced the whole world to shift the education system from face-to-face to online lessons. Computers, internet and learning platforms for online learning are highly compatible with industrial design tools such as 3D CAD software, so building digital models of design proposals has been a central practice for industrial design education during the pandemic, especially for the cases in which is not possible to access campus facilities. The condition of the pandemic is continuously changing, and Japanese universities are considering having a limited number of face-to-face lessons. As design educators, how can we make the most of face-to-face lessons while being restricted to limited time and other issues? This paper attempts to contribute to answering this question by documenting the exploration of using digital fabrication technology -specifically laser cutting machine- during two consecutive product design courses that were carried out in a hybrid format, with a combination of online and face-to-face lessons.

Due to the COVID-19 pandemic changing conditions, university procedures to deal with them, such as duration of academic semester, campus access and face-to-face lessons time extension -among others- were not the same. Therefore, this paper does not aim to provide an extensive and detailed pedagogic documentation of the two courses. Rather, it is intended to contribute to find strategies for -in one way- making the most of face-to-face lessons time while -on the other way- allow students to materialize their design proposals.

2   Evolving Industrial Design Education

One of the most acknowledged definitions of industrial design comes from John Heskett's book "Industrial Design": Industrial design is a process of design applied to physical products that are to be manufactured by mass production [2] However, the meaning of "physical products" is rapidly changing, and at the same time, the scope of industrial design discipline is widening and producing non-physical outcomes, such as services and experiences, within a context of quickly evolving technology. This paper identified three trends that are shaping industrial design education.

2.1   Expansion of Design Discipline

As Willis [3] stated, "We design our world, while our world acts back on us and designs us". This continuous and reciprocal interaction between humans and artefacts leads to its increasing complexity. Moreover, increasingly technical, and structural complexity of physical products makes them even difficult to categorize them. Dinar et al. [4] illustrate this complexity by asserting that modern products are becoming "cyberphysical systems". Bhise [5] asserts that the complexity of physical products can be attributed to several factors such as an increasing number of parts; number of product's internal systems as well as external systems affecting it; types of technologies associated with the systems; number of variables associated with the systems; number and type of users and number of specialized fields required to address then, among others. Another source of increasing complexity is the integration between products, services and systems, which has been labelled using the concept of "product-service system" (PSS) [6]. Additionally, when complex systems are composed of elements that are themselves complex, it has been defined as "systems of systems" (SoS) [7]. Meyer and Norman [8] asses that, although designers face increasingly complex and impactful challenges, many design programs focus on transferring knowledge and skills that are too often related to outdated process and working methods. Among the new skills required to address the increasing complexity of a world in which the boundaries of systems, products and services are becoming fuzzy, they propose systems thinking as a key element to enhance design education.

2.2 Increasing Complexity of Physical Products

Together with artefacts increasing complexity, design discipline has been expanding continuously [9]. One direction of this expansion extends from physical products to non-tangible artefacts, such as interactions, services and systems [10], thus pushing integration with other disciplines from natural and social sciences as well as humanities [11]. One example is the way design thinking has become an important trend in areas that are considered distant from arts and design, such as banking and financial services [12]. Values, knowledge and methods from the industrial design discipline are being adopted in other fields, aiming disruptive and human-centered solutions that can add new value to business and solve environmental and social issues. Ekert [13] notes that due to the discipline expansion, design education is not limited to design schools and design became a profession not exclusively limited to designers anymore.

   Another example of the expansion of the industrial design discipline is the emerging of different subjects of design, different that physical products. Nowadays, several universities worldwide offer industrial design curriculums that include topics such as brand design, service design, system design and experience design, among others. Here it is worth to mention that, although industrial design and product design has been conceived as synonyms [14], the meaning of "product design" is changing rapidly and is gradually encompassing the design of interphases, experiences and other elements of digital applications (digital products). Furthermore, it is not difficult to find design websites on the subject of "product design" that completely exclude physical products and focus only in digital products [15, 16]. Contents related to digital products interaction design such as User Interface (UI) and User Experience (UX) are being increasingly included within industrial design curriculums [17].

2.3 Adoption of Virtual Technology

Virtual Reality (VR) -including Augmented Reality (AR) and Mixed Reality (MR)- applications are being introduced as tools for the education of industrial designers. Increasing processing capability of personal computers, the developing of technology that allows real time interaction -such as sensors and displays- and (relatively) affordable prices of devices and applications have brought VR technology into design classrooms for purposes such as simulation, sketching, 3D modeling and design evaluation. In a extensive literature review regarding VR and industrial design, Hamurcu, Timur and Rizvanoglu [18] revealed that, although studies of virtual reality focused in industrial design were initially performed for professional practice, since year 2015 studies for educational practice started increasing significantly. Years ago, industrial design students started owning digital tablets or pen tablets for sketching and modeling. In the same way, presently, it is relatively common to find industrial design students owning VR headset devices such as HTC Vive Pro Eye, Oculus Quest and Sony Playstation VR.

2.4   Japanese Culture of Monozukuri or "Making of Things"

Monozukuri (also spelled as Monozukuri) literally means 'making of things' in Japanese. Also it can also be translated as 'manufacturing', its meaning encompasses the spirit of Japanese character of 'spirit' towards craftmanship, design, engineering and manufacturing [19–21]. Although the world monozukuri has come into use since the end of 20th century, it has long been the source of Japan's international competitiveness [22]. Japan's manufacturing industry is the driving force that has supported the Japanese economy to the extent that it became the third-largest economy in terms of GDP and is known as one of the "Manufacturing Superpowers". It accounted for about 20% of the total GDP in FY 2019–20, led by automobile, robotics and many other players [23].

Presently, monozukuri has become a buzz word that is being extensively promoted by the Japanese government, as a key advantage for realizing Society 5.0 through the country excellence in the manufacture of things [24]. In this vision, Japanese universities play a fundamental role of cultivating technology by boosting science, technology and innovation [25, 26], and industrial design has been recognized as a powerful level for rating new value by connecting them [27]. Although -as previously stated- industrial design is a field in which some objects of design are produced in digital forms and virtual environments, fostering values of monozukuri in universities require to pay attention on producing physical things.

3   Laser Cutting-Based Task During Hybrid Course

3.1   COVID-19 and Japanese Universities

The COVID-19 pandemic has resulted in schools shut all across the world. Practically the whole national education system (from elementary schools to universities) were closed during spring of 2020 [28]. Most of the schools that had been temporarily closed reopened during May. However, higher education institutions remained closed and switched their courses to online formats by using digital platforms. In Japan, despite having its image of a futuristic country due to the production of robots and high technology, the shift from face-to-face to online education was particularly challenging across universities, due to lack of experience in conducting distance learning classes before the pandemic crisis [29], as well as the slow pace of universities, lecturers and students to take up digital technology for online learning [30, 31].

Additionally, access to campus in Japanese universities, particularly in metropolitan areas, has been changing during the pandemic. During the first state of emergency in spring of 2020 and in the following months, access to students was not allowed or several access restrictions were applied [32]. The level of strictness of access restrictions has been going back and forth, since four states of emergency [33] (as well quasi-states of emergency [34]) as have been declared in several prefectures.

3.2   Experience in Product Design Course at Takushoku University

The Design Department of Takushoku University belongs to the faculty of engineering, and it is composed by five majors, which are chosen by students after completing their first year: product design, lifestyle design, emotional design, web design and social innovation. The pillars of product design major are Product Design Studio and Design Project, which are taught during 2nd and 3rd year (see Fig. 1). In the 4th year students work in their graduation research project.

1st year	2nd year		3rd year		4th year
	COVID-19 Pandemic in Japan ➡				
	Academic year 2020		Academic year 2021		
	Spring	Autumn	Spring	Autumn	
Design basics	Product Design Studio 1	Product Design Studio 2	Product Design Studio 3	Design Project	Graduation Research Project

Fig. 1. Design studio courses of Product Design major during the COVID-19 pandemic.

3.3   Experiences in Design Studio Classes

In order to switch classes to online format, the start of academic year 2020 in Takushoku University was delayed two weeks in order to give more time for preparation to students and faculty, and spring semester was carried out in a full online format. During Autumn 2020 and Spring 2021, online classes continued but it was possible to have face-to-face lessons during limited number of times. In the faculty of engineering some courses required face-to-face sessions for activities such as applying exams, conducting laboratory experiments -or as in the design department- for making models. Additionally, face-to-face lessons allowed to test different procedures and equipment for virus spread prevention, such as face masks, temperature check, cleaning and disinfection, air cleaners and circulators, and physical distancing, among others.

3.4   Product Design Studio 1

Product Design Studio 1 course focused on concept development, ideation by drawing and making rough models with cardboard and blue foam and presentation model making using chemical wood (see Fig. 2).

Fig. 2. Examples of rough models (left) and presentation models (right) for vegetables peelers built in the Design Studio I course before pandemic.

The Product Design Studio I course was carried out at the beginning of the pandemic in Japan. The course was taught completely online in a synchronous (real-time) format using Microsoft Teams. The task of the course was the design of a remote control for a robot being developed in the university [35]. The course started during the country first state of emergency for COVID-19 pandemic in Japan, so students were not allowed to come to university and had to build their models at home. Additionally, since it was highly encouraged to stay at home, all kinds of material (available at home or bought online) were accepted for model making.

Despite students' models of design proposals were built at their homes while having limitations of materials, equipment and tools, there were interesting design proposals and models with very good quality (see Fig. 3). However, on the other side, since there were no restrictions regarding material and tools, some students were not able to make or finish their models properly. After checking students background, it was revealed that the majority of students who submitted good quality work came from technical high schools or pursued design-related courses, thus having some knowledge, skills and tools that helped them to achieve good results.

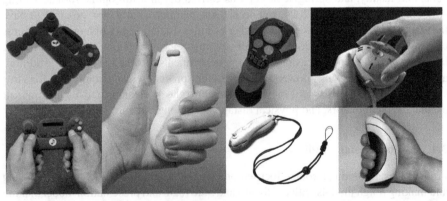

Fig. 3. Examples of presentation models with good quality that were built in the Design Studio I course during pandemic.

3.5   Product Design Studio 2 and 3

Although during the spring semester of the academic year 2020 access to campus was highly restricted, for autumn 2020 and spring 2021 the university authorities allowed students of online classes to have a limited number of face-to-face lessons. Professors interested in having online lessons had to complete an application process. Professors in charge of Product Design major decided to use these sessions for model making work, so three activities were evaluated (see Table 1): (1) Manual modeling making (as in Product Design Studio 1), (2) CAD and 3D printing and (3) using laser cutting machine.

Table 1. Evaluation of options for model making during face-to-face lessons.

	Model producing time	Required finishing work	Required time for online check	Available facilities and equipment
Manual work	Long	Sanding, priming and painting	Short	Workshop, painting room
CAD and 3D printing	Parts printing takes several hours	Sanding, priming and painting	Medium	Workshop, painting room, 3D printers (3)
Lasser cutting machine	Parts cutting and engraving takes less than 1 hour	Sanding	Short	Workshop, painting room, Laser cutting machines (2)

Since face-to-face lessons time was limited, we evaluated which activity could make the most of available time, and the use of laser cutting machine was selected (see Table 2). Manual work requires long time for model making, and also takes time preparing material (cutting block for each student) and cleaning after sanding work. 3D printing is faster than manual model making, however printing a model use to take several hours, and if there is a fail during printing must be done again. In order to finish the model, manual work and 3D printing requires sanding, priming and painting work, while engraved and cut parts with laser machine require just light sanding to remove staining caused by the process. Additionally, due to limited for face-to-face lessons, check of student progress before the lesson had to be done. For manual work check can be done by submitting pictures and showing the model on camera. For CAD models, digital files must be open and reviewed, which takes longer time. For laser cutting machine, data is usually built in Adobe Illustrator format and is easier to check. Available facilities and equipment were also considered and, despite having only two laser cutting machines-production time is much shorter that the one of 3D printers.

As stated above, the evaluation resulted in selecting the use of laser cutting machine for working in the design assignment during the face-to-face lessons. Additionally, it was decided to divide the course in two assignments, one to be tackled by using CAD (without 3D printing) and the other one by using laser cutting machines (See Fig. 4). Each semester is composed of 15 lessons, and every weekly lesson takes 3 h. It was authorized to carry out five face-to-face lessons (hence 10 lessons to be done by online format).

Table 2. Overall structure of Product Design Studio 2 and 3 courses.

Number of sessions	Contents	Format
1	Course guidance	Online (synchronic)
7	CAD assignment	
7	Lasser cutter assigment	Hybrid -Online -Face-to-face

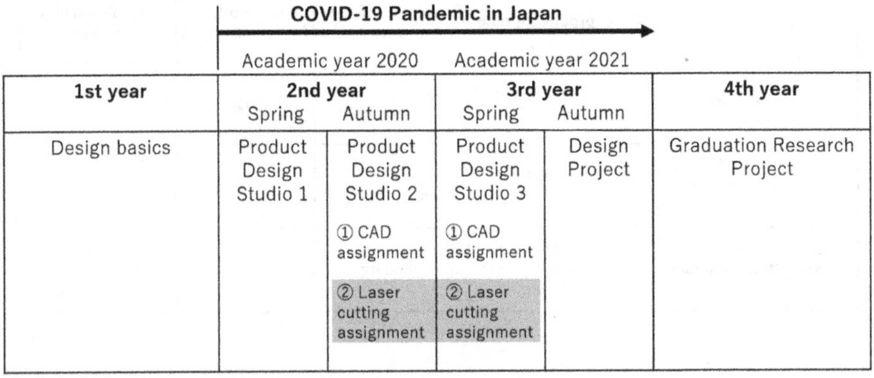

	COVID-19 Pandemic in Japan				
	Academic year 2020		Academic year 2021		
1st year	**2nd year**		**3rd year**		**4th year**
	Spring	Autumn	Spring	Autumn	
Design basics	Product Design Studio 1	Product Design Studio 2 ① CAD assignment ② Laser cutting assignment	Product Design Studio 3 ① CAD assignment ② Laser cutting assignment	Design Project	Graduation Research Project

Fig. 4. Laser cutting Assignments for Product Design Studio courses during the COVID-19 pandemic.

The switch to online learning also affected student location, and hence their availability to attend face-to-face courses. Students coming from distant cities usually rent a place close to university. However, since semester of spring 2020 started fully online, several students canceled their rent contract and stayed at their hometown. Therefore, few students were able to enroll in the courses (8 students for Product Design Studio 2 and 7 students for Product Design Studio 3, out of a total of 21 students). Although higher numbers of students were desirable for pedagogic purposes, the fact of having few students in each course was useful for the application of face-to-face courses, because at that time the university (as well as other institutions in Japan) was reluctant to carry out activities gathering larger number of students to avoid risk of cluster infections.

Product Design Studio 2 was carried out in semester autumn 2020. The second assignment, intended for a hybrid mix of online and face-to-face lessons, was to design a wall clock that can be built with parts cut and engraved by laser cutting machine. The clock movement was provided and one important requirement was to design proposals having some volume, thus avoiding designs having a simple and flat clock face. During the first face-to-face lesson, basic operation of the laser cutting machine was explained. In the following lessons, design proposals were presented and students got feedback from professors, and rough and final models were built by using laser cutting machine (see Fig. 5). Each weekly lesson time (180 min) was sufficient for cutting students parts, and the students who made mistakes or wanted to improve a part were able to do it during the lesson. One key point that helped to make the most of each face-to-face lesson time was that students were asked to submit their design and data few days before the lesson, so professors were able to give feedback regarding design and check the data to avoid waste of material and time during face-to-face lessons.

Fig. 5. Aspects of face-to-face lesson during Design Studio 2 course [(a) Overall aspect, (b) Concept presentation, (c) Parts making, (d) Assembly and validation].

By improving design proposal and preparing date as assignments, students could further develop their ideas, allowing them to produce clocks with some level of elaboration, as well as working with other different materials different than plywood, such as acrylic, Japanese paper and metallic finish laminate. By quickly modifying data and cutting a new part, students were able to try different structures, shapes and ways of assembly (see Fig. 6).

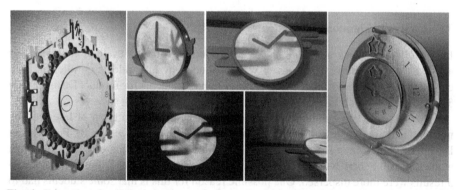

Fig. 6. Examples of wall clock design proposals made with laser cutting machine in Design Studio 2 course.

Product Design Studio 3 was carried out in the semester spring 2021. As in Studio Design 2 course, the second assignment, intended for both online and face-to-face lessons, was to design a toy for children of any age. Some students taking this course were also enrolled in Product Design Studio 2 course the previous semester, but other students used laser cutting machine for the first time, so it was necessary to lecture about laser cutting machine and its operation. Since toys require being manipulated, assignment required students to think about a sturdy and safe structure for each proposal. As in the previous course, students submitted design ideas or data, and obtained feedback by professors by using the online platform, so the time of face-to-face lessons was mostly used for producing the parts with the laser cutting machine, assemble prototypes and get feedback from professors. Since some students improved their proficiency of Adobe Illustrator software, in this assignment the graphic part of the design proposals tended to be more elaborated (see Fig. 7). Since it was not possible to paint parts due to required time for drying, some students added colors by cutting colored paper and attached them by spray glue.

Fig. 7. Examples of toy design proposals made with laser cutting machine in Design Studio 3 course.

3.6 Course Evaluations by Students

In the following week after the end of each course, an online evaluation survey was applied for each course. The survey was responded by all students enrolled in each course (8 students for Product Design Studio 1 and 7 students for Product Design Study 3). This section presents and compares the main findings of each survey.

The survey asked opinion about perceived difficulty of operation of laser cutting machine and about using Adobe Illustrator for creating data (See Fig. 8). For Product Design Studio 2, more students perceived operation as "somewhat difficult", although at the same time there where students who perceived as "very easy". For Design Studio 3 results were more dispersed. One possible reason for this is that some students had to adjust machine power and speed in a trial-and-error way because they wanted to achieve specific darkness of laser engraving. Regarding difficulty of using Adobe Illustrator, data shows that overall perception changed towards less difficult, possibly due that students became more proficient in using the software.

Regarding difficulty of combining online and face-to-face format, for both courses the majority of students did not found particular problem, while some students perceived some difficulty (See Fig. 9). Regarding perception of each course design assignment, in both courses most of students found assignments interesting. The assignment for Product Design Studio 3 (toy design) was better evaluated, perhaps because there was more freedom for conceiving the design concept than in the wall clock assignment.

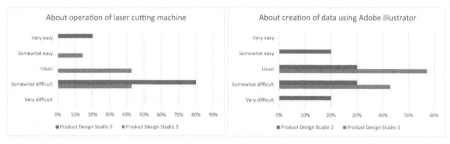

Fig. 8. Opinion about operation of laser cutting machine (left) and creation of data using Adobe Illustrator software (right).

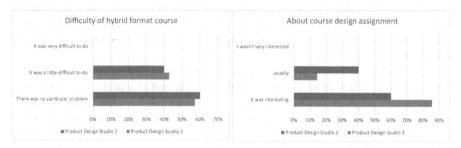

Fig. 9. Opinion about difficulty of hybrid format course (left) and design assignment (right).

Concerning overall satisfaction, both courses were positively evaluated with no neutral or negative opinion (see Fig. 10). Open-ended question regarding course opinion registered positive comments for Product Design Studio 2 such as "by actually going to school and operating laser machine myself I learned more than just making data at home", "I was happy that I managed to bring my project to completion" and "I think I can use the laser machine in future tasks". For Product Design Studio 3 there were opinions such as "It as a little hard to complete assignments for online and face-to-face lessons, but I am glad that I was able to complete the work as a result", "at first I was worried because other students had previous experience using laser machine, but it was a very good experience to be able to make a prototype with this technology", "I had to decide the design by my own, so I was able to create my own design by exploring various ideas and receiving advice". It seems that in both courses the students experienced a sense of accomplishment, but perhaps it was somewhat stronger for Product Design Studio 3 because the toy design assignment was not narrowed down as wall clock, so students had to generate their own design concepts.

Regarding comments of aspects that need to be improved, in Product Design Studio 2 one student expressed that "at the beginning of the course, even though that professor told us the clock movement dimensions, it was difficult to think and verify initial ideas without it". In this case it would have been useful to ask students to make a cardboard model of the clock movement, so they could have a better image of size and volume. For Product Design Studio 3, one student expressed having difficulties for working in the course due to technical problems with personal computer. Even in a hybrid format, the

Fig. 10. Opinion regarding overall course satisfaction.

course required intensive use of computer for working in both CAD and laser cutting machine assignments, as well as for online interaction. The university can lend laptops in case of broken computer; however, student must install 2D graphics and 3D CAD software by his or her own.

Finally, although having online classes may be convenient to students in several ways, some comments showed appreciation of the attempt of introducing face-to-face lessons during semester in which the great majority of courses were imparted online. Examples of those opinions are "I would like to thank the professors for setting up the lecture in this situation. It was a very fulfilling lecture."; "Setting the laser cutting machine was difficult, but I received kind and accurate advice, so the course was fun. I', glad I took this course"; "I would like to make use of what I learned in this class in subsequent classes and outside university. Thank you very much!" and "Thank you for completing the class under difficult circumstances".

4   Conclusions and Reflections

This paper documents the introduction of face-to-face lessons during few weeks in two product design courses that were carried out mainly online. The main aim of this experimental attempt was to give the students the opportunity to physically build, evaluate and present their design proposals. Because of limited number of face-to-face lessons, it was decided to tackle design assignment using laser cutting machine, aiming to make the most of its capability of producing parts in shorter time than manual work or 3D printing. The assignment for Product Design Studio 2 was to design and build a wall clock, and for Product Design Studio 3 was to design and build a toy proposal. Professors lectured and students presented their concepts and designs during online lessons, so face-to-face lessons were mainly used for producing parts, assemble design proposals and review them together with professors. Students worked at home improving their designs and preparing data, and improved parts were produced and assembled during face-to-face lessons. This dynamic proved to be highly efficient and allowed students to fix errors, improve parts and try new ideas. Evaluation surveys were applied in both courses, showing overall positive appraisal towards use of laser cutting machines, design assignments and hybrid course format. Overall level of satisfaction was also high, and the attempt try a hybrid format course during the pandemic was also valued.

Finally, several practice-based reflections emerged. These reflections will support the development of future models of hybrid education of product design that combines both online and face-to-face interaction in Takushoku University, especially in the Product Design major. Additionally, the following reflections may be useful for design education practitioners in other design fields and contexts:

- Narrowness of design assignment theme: Design assignments with a narrower theme are more suitable for groups that are using laser cutting machines for the first time, because they can spend more time in designing the structure and parts detailed aspects, rather than thinking on new and more ambiguous design concepts.
- Alternation of online and face-to-face lessons: Although face-to-face lessons were carried out during the second half of each course, they were not done all consecutively. It is important to alternate them with online lessons, in order to give students more time for developing their ideas, as well as for preparing data. In some cases, it may also help giving more time for looking and buying new materials.
- Feedback: During online interaction, although professors must review sketches, rough models and prototypes just by watching their pictures of videos, without physically manipulating them, using an online education platform, it offers several advantages to the student's side. For example. Professor can digitally draw or take notes over the pictures; all students can see and listen more clearly and resulting images or video recording can be stored and shared.
- Materials and samples: In order to help students to take decisions regarding material, colors and dimensions, it is important to have a collection of different materials and samples. Even waste material can be used for this purpose.
- Management of design complexity: In the cases reported in this paper, it was noticed that in a group having students that have used laser cutting machine and students that are using it for the first time, some students that are familiar with the technology tended to propose ideas with more complex structure or with higher number of parts. In some cases, those characteristics may be justified, but in other cases it seemed that the student wanted to express in his or her design that he or she is not a beginner. For such cases, it is better to encourage students to try using new materials.
- 2D graphics software literacy: One key point for working with laser cutting machine is the use of 2D graphics. Having proficiency on this type of software can help designing parts that are cut and engraved with higher levels of completeness, and data production work can be done with more efficiency.

References

1. Greet, G.: Elements of Design: Rowena Reed Kostellow and the Structure of Visual Relationships. Princeton Architectural Press, New York (2002)
2. Heskett, J.: Industrial Design. Oxford University Press, Oxford (1980)
3. Willis, A.M.: Onthological design: laying the ground. Des. Philos. Pap. 4(2), 69–92 (2006)
4. Dinar, M., Summers, J.D., Shah, J., Park, Y.-S.: Evaluation of empirical design studies and metrics. In: Cash, P., Stankovic, T., Štorga, M. (eds.) Experimental design research, pp. 13–39. Springer, Cham (2016). https://doi.org/10.1007/978-3-319-33781-4_2

5. Bhise, V.D.: Designing Complex Products with Systems Engineering Processes and Techniques, pp. 21–22. CRC Press (2014)
6. Sakao, T., Lindahl, M. (eds.): Introduction to Product/Service-System Design. Springer, London (2009). https://doi.org/10.1007/978-1-84882-909-1
7. Jamshidi, M. (ed.): System of Systems Engineering: Innovations for the 21st Century. Wiley, New Jersey (2011)
8. Meyer, M.W., Norman, D.: Changing design education for the 21st century. She Ji J. Des. Econ. Innov. 6(1), 13–49 (2020)
9. Alvarez, J., Nishimura, H.: Revisiting the concept of 'function': a conceptual expansion for product, service and system innovation. In: 5th International Service Innovation Design Conference (ISIDC), pp. 201–208 (2018)
10. Why Transdisciplinary Design? https://medium.com/sunnyminds/why-transdisciplinary-design-99577199cc4a. Accessed 28 Feb 2018
11. Expanding orders of design. http://www.ac4d.com/2014/11/expanding-orders-of-design/. Accessed 3 Mar 2018
12. Design Thinking: The Hottest New Trend in Banking. https://medium.com/GuilhermeCuri/why-transdisciplinary-design-99577199cc4a. Accessed 13 Dec 2021
13. Eckert, J.: Why design schools should take the lead in design education. In: Perspective on Design, pp. 3–15. Springer, Cham (2020). https://doi.org/10.1007/978-3-030-32415-5_1
14. Evans, M., Pei, E., Chesire, D., Graham, I.: Digital sketching and haptic sketch modelling during product design and development. Int. J. Prod. Dev. 20(3), 239–263 (2015)
15. Product Design guide Part 2: Research, Analysis, Ideation. https://xd.adobe.com/ideas/guides/comprehensive-guide-product-design-research-user-analysis-ideation-part-2/. Accessed 14 June 2021
16. What Skills You Need To Be A Good Product Designer? https://think360studio.com/blog/what-skills-you-need-to-be-a-good-product-designer. Accessed 14 June 2021
17. Morris, J.A.: Enhancing industrial design education with user experience design. In: Education Papers, Industrial Designers Society of America. https://www.idsa.org/sites/default/files/Enhancing%20ID%20Education.pdf. Accessed 12 Oct 2021
18. Ahmet, H., Timur, Ş., Rızvanoğlu, K.: An overview of virtual reality within industrial design education. J. Eng. Des. Technol. 18(6) (2020). https://doi.org/10.1108/JEDT-02-2020-0048
19. Hiraoka, M.: Traditional images of Japan as a Monozukuri country, with special reference to education in Japan and Cool Japan abroad. In: 2009 IEEE International Professional Communication Conference, pp. 1–6. IEEE, July 2009. https://doi.org/10.1109/IPCC.2009.5208712
20. Japan's culture of Craftmanship. https://www.businesstoday.in/magazine/features/story/what-indian-manufacturing-can-learn-from-monozukuri-63994-2016-04-02. Accessed 10 July 2021
21. Monozukuri — another look at a key Japanese principle. https://japanintercultural.com/free-resources/articles/monozukuri-another-look-at-a-key-japanese-principle/. Accessed 13 July 2021
22. Japan, the World's Leading "Robot Nation". https://www.u-tokyo.ac.jp/en/whyutokyo/wj_003.html. Accessed 2 Aug 2021
23. The Japanese manufacturing industry is expanding with the promotion of digitalization. https://www.jetro.go.jp/en/invest/attractive_sectors/manufacturing/overview.html#:~:text=Japan's%20manufacturing%20industry%20is%20the,automobile%20and%20many%20other%20players%20. Accessed 6 Aug 2021
24. Realizing Society 5.0. https://www.japan.go.jp/abenomics/_userdata/abenomics/pdf/society_5.0.pdf. Accessed 27 Aug 2021
25. Fukuda, K.: Science, technology and innovation ecosystem transformation toward society 5.0. Int. J. Prod. Econ. 220, 107460 (2020). https://doi.org/10.1016/j.ijpe.2019.07.033

26. Harayama, Y.: A living concept "Society 5.0" and the role of universities. In: Council for Science, Technology and Innovation (2017). https://okm.fi/documents/1410845/5310220/Harayama+Society5+Finland.pdf/70f24ddc-8ab1-47d7-8583-12934bbbd3eb/Harayama+Society5+Finland.pdf.pdf. Accessed 22 Aug 2021

27. Kang, M.: Industrial design policies: a review of selected countries. In: OECD Directorate for Science, Technology and Innovation. DSTI/IND, vol. 9 (2014)

28. Information on MEXT's measures against COVID-19. https://www.mext.go.jp/en/mext_0 0006.html. Accessed 7 Sept 2021

29. Japan Univ. lecturers worry over crumbling class quality as virus forces courses online. https://mainichi.jp/english/articles/20200509/p2a/00m/0na/002000c. Accessed 16 Sept 2021

30. Nae, N.: Online learning during the pandemic: where does Japan stand? Euromentor J. **11**(2), 7–24 (2020)

31. Sugino, C.: Student perceptions of a synchronous online cooperative learning course in a Japanese women's university during the COVID-19 pandemic. Educ. Sci. **11**, 231 (2021). https://doi.org/10.3390/educsci11050231

32. Measures at Hiyoshi Campus relating to the "Use of campus facilities (from the Fall Semester)". https://www.hc.keio.ac.jp/corona/hiyoshi_en_reopening.pdf. Accessed 18 Sept 2021

33. Japan has expanded its 4th state of emergency again as medical system is overwhelmed. https://www3.nhk.or.jp/nhkworld/en/news/backstories/1746/. Accessed 25 Sept 2021

34. Japan's COVID-19 state of emergency lifted as infections decline - Nikkei Asia. https://asia.nikkei.com/Spotlight/Coronavirus/Japan-s-COVID-19-state-of-emergency-lifted-as-infections-decline. Accessed 1 Oct 2021

35. Alvarez, J., Hara, E., Koyama, T., Adachi, K., Kagawa, Y.: Design of form and motion of a robot aimed to provide emotional support for pediatric walking rehabilitation. In: Soares, M.M., Rosenzweig, E., Marcus, A. (eds.) HCII 2021. LNCS, vol. 12780, pp. 403–419. Springer, Cham (2021). https://doi.org/10.1007/978-3-030-78224-5_28

Characteristics of Interaction Design and Advantages of Network Teaching

Qian Cao[1](✉) and Xiandong Cheng[2]

[1] Central Academy of Fine Arts, No. 8 Hua Jia Di Nan Street, Chao Yang District, Beijing, China
caoqian@cafa.edu.cn
[2] Beijing City University, No. 269 Bei Si Huan Zhong Lu, Hai Dian District, Beijing, China

Abstract. With the popularization of computer and Internet and the increasing demand for experiential consumption, interactive design came into being and has become a popular subject in college design teaching in recent years. Because interactive design was born in the Internet era, and has the characteristics of fast alternation speed, multi domain intersection, strong technical support and user-centered, the traditional "professor" teaching mode cannot fully adapt to it. In contrast, network teaching shows various advantages in the teaching of interactive design. Based on the subject characteristics of interactive design, this paper analyzes the advantages of interactive design network teaching.

Keywords: Interaction design · Network teaching · Internet

1 Overview of Interaction Design Discipline

1.1 Generation Background

The concept of "interaction design" dates back to the last century. The emergence of interaction design relies on the birth and popularization of personal computers and the Internet. The spread of personal computers enabled users to interact more with the content entered into the computer. At the same time, the Internet has realized the openness of communication between people across time and space constraints. The growing use of personal computers and the Internet has made the emergence of interactive media and digital interactive consumer products a trend of the last decade. Trend watchers have noticed for more than a decade that people are more and more inclined to experience consumption rather than material consumption. Experience economy research experts Joseph Pine II, James Gilmore and William Gilmore declared in the book "Experience Economy" in 1998: "After the product economy and the service economy, the experience economy era has arrived. The 21st century has Enter the era of the experience economy". Nowadays, the crux of the business is no longer the product but the experience. Based on the above conditions, the concept of interaction design became popular in the Internet environment in the last century and attracted the common interest of the two disciplines of design and engineering, thus forming a new and popular discipline (Fig. 1).

M. M. Soares et al. (Eds.): HCII 2022, LNCS 13322, pp. 256–264, 2022.
https://doi.org/10.1007/978-3-031-05900-1_17

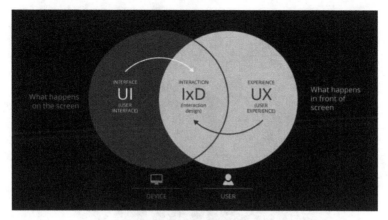

Fig. 1. UI/IxD/UX

1.2 Subject Content

The book "Principles of Interaction Design" by Lisa Graham, an associate professor at the University of Texas at Arlington, has gained widespread recognition in the interaction design community. In her book, she identifies interaction design as a user-oriented discipline devoted to meaningful media communication through cyclical and collaborative processes between humans and technology [2]. "Interaction design is the creation of a dialogue between people and products, systems, services. This dialogue is both physical and emotional in nature. At the same time, it manifests itself in form, function and technology over time interaction between them" [3].

At present, the branches of interaction design mainly include web design, game design, interactive device, APP design, etc. Graham breaks down successful interaction design into building content, planning, flowcharts, storyboards, creating example layouts, determining navigation, prototyping, usability testing, and mastering. Based on this, the teaching stage of interaction design is adjusted and modified according to the actual situation, and integrated into basic theoretical learning, case analysis, programming learning, scheme sketches, prototype design, and final APP or web design (Fig. 2).

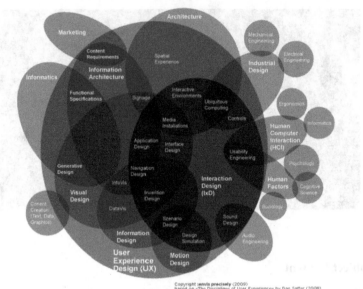

Fig. 2. About interaction design (IxD). From: www.kickerstudio.com

2 Disciplinary Characteristics of Interaction Design

Interaction design is a new design discipline arising from the development of scientific and technological means and the rise of consumer experience [2]. The following four characteristics can be summarized from its background and subject content.

2.1 Fast Change Speed

Compared with traditional design disciplines, the discipline of interaction design has a relatively short history. Emerging disciplines are characterized by rapid changes. On the one hand, interaction design was born in the Internet era, which means that its development relies on the iteration of hardware such as computers and the update of related software. These technologies are all fields of rapid development and change, and related new technologies and new theories are also constantly emerging and updated. On the other hand, the discipline of interaction design is in a phase of rapid development and constant adaptation to new situations. The corresponding teaching is also in the stage of exploration and construction, and a systematic and perfect model has not yet been formed.

2.2 Multi-domain Intersectionality

The innovative potential of interaction design lies in bringing together almost all forms of media and information delivery. Interaction design is the meaningful arrangement of graphics, text, video, photos, illustrations, sound, animation, and 3D images. Each of these elements may involve a more specialized field [2]. Interaction design involves a wide range of disciplines, and the intersection between multiple fields is very complex. Therefore, in the current teaching of colleges and universities, interaction design courses will have teachers from different professional backgrounds, covering psychology, industrial design, graphic design, computer science, art and so on. At the same time, a variety of inter-professional courses will be arranged to meet the multi-domain intersection of interaction design (Fig. 3).

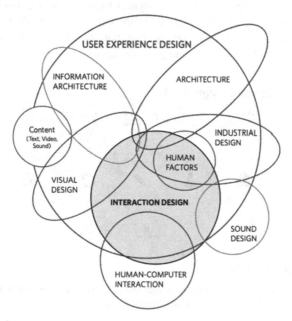

Fig. 3. Interaction design is a part of UX design. Image by Dan Saffer.

2.3 Strong Technical Support

Compared with traditional design disciplines, interaction design is particularly reliant on digital media technology and computer hardware. The core of any design discipline is the designer's thinking and creativity, but the practice of interaction design transforming thinking into objective reality must be bridged by technology. In interaction design, the level of software and hardware and the designer's thinking ability are mutually reinforcing and interacting. On the one hand, the higher the quality of hardware materials used in interaction design, the more reasonable the system operation design will be. The more skilled the designer is to master and use the technology, the higher the degree of reduction of the final design result to implement the designer's concept. On the other hand, the development and perfection of hardware and other conditions can also develop a larger thinking space for interaction designers from the technical level.

2.4 User-Centered

The goal of interaction design is to create products that enable users to achieve their needs in the best possible way. Key features of the interaction design process are the explicit inclusion of user engagement, iteration, and specific usability criteria. The early design is centered on user behavior research, and focuses on user experience in the process. The latter focus on user feedback, that is, providing interactivity by focusing on the possibilities and boundaries of human cognitive processing. According to the Interaction Design Institute, interaction designers focus on user-centered design based on an understanding of real users, including their experiences, goals, needs, and tasks. The discipline designs from a user perspective, but also strives to balance user needs with business technical capabilities and goals (Fig. 4).

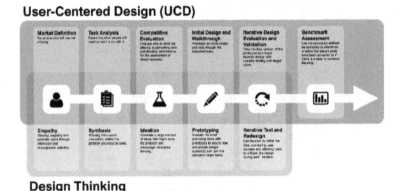

Fig. 4. The process flows of user-centered design and design thinking. Image from: user-centered design and design thinking: different origins, similar practices

3 The Characteristics of Interactive Subjects Highlight the Advantages of Online Teaching

At present, we are at the crossroads of technological update iteration and cultural collision, so the definition of the roles of designers and teachers has also changed accordingly [4]. For design to be ecologically and socially responsible, it has to be revolutionary and radical. Interaction design, as an emerging discipline, needs to improve the new educational methods to support it, and actively through the improvement, optimization and innovation of teaching models, to cultivate outstanding interaction design talents who can serve the future. The discipline of interaction design was born in the Internet era, and has the characteristics of rapid change, multi-domain intersection, technical support and user-centricity. The network teaching, which is also conceived under the background of the Internet, has shown significant advantages in the teaching of interaction design (Fig. 5).

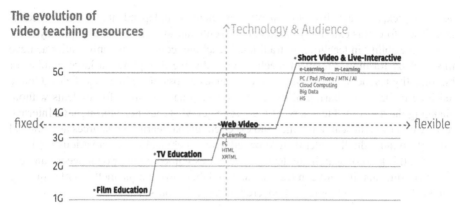

Fig. 5. The evolution of video teaching resources. Image by Xiandong Cheng

3.1 The Immediacy of Information Meets the Rapid Change of Disciplines

In the information age, the high-frequency and high-speed update and development of technology and theory is the key problem that the interaction design discipline must solve. In the past few decades, the times have developed rapidly, and the richness and update frequency of information is dizzying. This rate of change is still on the rise, leading to an unprecedented complex situation in the teaching of interaction design. In the current environment, the traditional design education model has been unable to meet the needs of interaction design, and Internet teaching is a new way and method for interaction design. On the one hand, Internet information is updated in a timely manner. Therefore, compared with the traditional teaching mode that is based on textbooks and guided by teachers' personal experience, online teaching built in the Internet environment can provide new technologies and new academic theories at the fastest speed. On the other hand, the knowledge and information transmission of the Internet can transcend the limitations of time and space, and inject fresh blood into the education of domestic colleges and universities within the maximum scope and possibility. Compared with China, the interaction design disciplines of universities in Europe and the United States were established earlier, with longer development history, richer exploration experience, and more complete teaching models. For students, the Internet's ability to transmit information across space allows them to retrieve more advanced subject knowledge and industry cases at home and abroad in real time. For teachers, they can timely refer to, learn from, and introduce the subject education methods and methods of foreign universities, and convey them to students through a more intuitive and convenient way of online teaching.

3.2 Diversified Educational Resources Meet the Intersection of Multiple Fields

Interaction design is a multi-disciplinary comprehensive design discipline, which involves a wide range of disciplines. The intersection between multiple fields is also

very complex, and each discipline involved is relatively independent and highly specialized. Therefore, it is extremely challenging to cultivate students' interdisciplinary comprehensive ability in teaching. In traditional teaching, colleges and universities achieve
this goal by forming a team of teachers with diverse disciplines, a large number of
high-quality teachers, and setting up rich courses across disciplines and fields. Online
teaching realizes the sharing of diversified educational resources for students without
changing the traditional teachers. Students can get what they need through the Internet,
relying on powerful search engines and excellent global learning resources as technical
support, to individually meet their knowledge and technical needs in various fields. In
addition, this kind of search and learning activities guided by their own needs can help
stimulate students' initiative in learning and find their own unique methods of acquiring
knowledge and expand topics not covered in research courses.

3.3 Practical Operation of Software and Hardware Promotes the Mastery of Technical Skills

The subject content of interaction design is destined to use more digital media and
computer hardware in practice. Interaction designers need to master the practical ability of software and hardware technology on the basis of building complete theoretical
knowledge. "The real transformation comes not from political innovation, but from
technological innovation, whose impact on society has become increasingly urgent. [6]"
Strengthening students' technical level in interaction design teaching is one of the core
tasks for students to keep up with the times and become excellent interaction designers.
The student's relationship with technology not only addresses specific implementation
issues in design projects at a practical level, but also involves systems development practices. Therefore, cultivating students' comprehensive software and hardware use ability
is a major focus of interaction design teaching. These competencies include modeling,
programming, and information science professional software development, as well as the
use of media tools. One of the major advantages of online teaching is that the traditional
offline teaching scenarios are moved to online platforms, and all teaching activities rely
on computers and the Internet. In such a teaching scenario, students are naturally familiar
with the operation logic and operation mode of digital media in the process of education, and the practical operation of relevant software and hardware has become more
frequent and convenient. In addition, in recent years, the operation modes of various
industries have shown the general trend of online, network, and digitalization, and the
same is true of the design industry. Interaction designer is a comprehensive role, acting
as a listener, communicator, decision maker, designer and other multiple identities in the
complete design process. At the same time, interaction design is a subject with strong
market application. Therefore, interaction designers must have the ability to communicate with people. At present, online communication has become the mainstream way
of communication, and online meetings of online teaching are one of the typical modes
of online communication. Through online teaching, students unknowingly adapt to the
development trend and the fast-paced design industry operation model in the digital age,
thus stepping into the digital age.

3.4 User-Centered

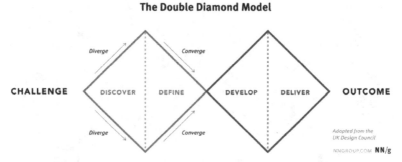

Fig. 6. The double diamond model. From: www.nngroup.com

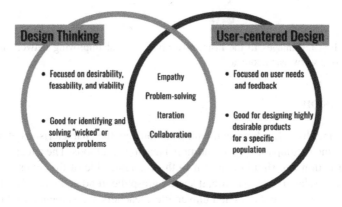

Fig. 7. Design thinking & user-centered design. From: www.careerfoundry.com

All contemporary design fields show a human-centred trend. Instead of focusing on the product itself, they focus more on the user experience. Therefore, user-centeredness has become an important concept in contemporary design, especially in interaction design. Interactivity in interaction design is not only the mutual echo of computer programs and design presentations, but should also involve more communication and response between products and users. Online teaching skillfully constructs common user usage scenarios, that is, the transmission of teaching information relies on the Internet, and the feedback from students to teachers is also presented in the form of the Internet. This process allows both teachers and students to perceive the user experience from the perspective of users and the process of building information visualization from the perspective of interaction designers. Both students and teachers experience the user experience in their teaching, so as to achieve a highly visual user experience (Figs. 6, 7 and 8).

Fig. 8. The best advantages to the instructive division what improving network in Canberra Australia. From: www.nshry.com.au

4   Conclusion

As an emerging discipline born in the information age, the characteristics of interaction design show the incompatibility of traditional teaching methods. The educational model of the information age should conform to the changing tide of the times. As a design subject closely related to human life, it should grasp the trend and take advantage of the advantages. Therefore, colleges and universities, teachers and students need to adapt to the current situation of the times, make full use of the advantages of network teaching, and cooperate with the subject characteristics of interactive design. It should be noted that online teaching is a double-edged sword. The advantages and disadvantages of this model coexist, and it should be used rationally. In this way, while adapting to the development of the times, it is possible to explore and promote the construction and improvement of the teaching mode of interaction design discipline.

References

1. Joseph Pine, B., Gilmore, J.H., William Gilmore, H.: The Experience Economy. 哈佛商学院出版社(1999)
2. Graham, L.: Principles of Interactive Design. Delmar Cengage Learning, 1 edn., p. 240 (1998)
3. Kolko, J.: Thoughts on Interaction Design (2011)
4. Papanek, V.: Design for the Real World: Human Ecology and Social Change (1973)
5. Fuller, B.: Grunch of Giants (1983)
6. O'Brian, T.: New York Times, 12 February 2006. Accessed 28 Oct 2012

Exploring Children's Behavioral Intention of Using the Expected Game-Based Learning for Protracted Waste Problem

Ima Kusumawati Hidayat[1,2]([✉]), Francisco Rebelo[1,3], and Paulo Noriega[1,3]

[1] CIAUD, Research Centre for Architecture, Urbanism and Design, Lisbon School of Architecture, Universidade de Lisboa, Lisbon, Portugal
`ima.hidayat.fs@um.ac.id, ima.hidayat@edu.ulisboa.pt`
[2] Faculty of Letters, Universitas Negeri Malang, Malang, Indonesia
[3] ITI/LARSys, Universidade de Lisboa, Rua Sá Nogueira, 1349-063 Lisboa, Portugal

Abstract. To develop a new digital game for children effectively, we must first recognize the underlying at which point the stakeholders accept to take this media. Prior research has shown that integrating games into education can lead to a more engaging way of learning. However, adding new interactions from a social problem like prolonged littering habits to game design concepts might not easily be accepted. This study attempts to examine the children's acceptance of the expected Game-Based Learning for the waste problem through interaction scenario's video using Unified Theory of Acceptance and Use of Technology 2 (UTAUT 2) approach. It is still relatively rare for other studies to apply UTAUT 2 with the young audience of primary school students, especially to find out their acceptance of a game concept. In total, 129 primary school students in Greater Malang, East Java, Indonesia was involved in this study. The result shows that the highest scores are on the Effort Expectancy (84,9%) and Hedonic Motivation (82.9%). These scores show that students are confident in the app's ease of use and enjoyment. On the other hand, the result also indicates that in order to be accepted by children, the game designer should carefully pay attention to the user's Facilitating Conditions. Further, on Behavioral Intention, although there is a perception that using the game will be easy and pleasant (Hedonic Motivation) students perceive that using the game on a more regular basis may not be their intention.

Keywords: Children's game acceptance · UTAUT 2 · Game-based learning · Waste problem

1 Introduction

Currently, Indonesia is known as one of the largest waste producers in the oceans. The Ministry of Education and Culture and The Ministry of Maritime Affairs and Investment [1] have made various efforts and committed to reducing waste by 30% and managing plastic waste by up to 70% by 2025. Additionally, Presidential regulation was issued [2] concerning the strategies is to enhance awareness by changing people's behavior

© The Author(s), under exclusive license to Springer Nature Switzerland AG 2022
M. M. Soares et al. (Eds.): HCII 2022, LNCS 13322, pp. 265–278, 2022.
https://doi.org/10.1007/978-3-031-05900-1_18

and reducing the input of land-based waste. Proper waste management behavior will occur if the citizen has good knowledge and awareness of the environment [3]. That information needs to disseminate continuously and periodically to the community [4]. Local governments have carried out several efforts to educate the Indonesian citizen [5–8]. However, the fact that there is still much waste scattered in public areas such as tourist attractions proves a need for further action.

Considering that the current demographic composition of Indonesia is dominated by the millennial generation, who make up more than 41% of Indonesia's total population, changing the younger generation's behavior is an essential goal. Thus, the government claimed that it is necessary to integrate learning about waste management in primary school education. According to Janakirman [9], children's attitudes and behaviors toward environmental sustainability can be changed through the use of games. Game-Based Learning (GBL) provides learners with a secure environment in which they can experiment with their environmental-related behaviors without the fear of being wrong. They can also acquire new behaviors in the process [10]. With the advancement of today's educational media, games have the ability to engage students and motivate them to study more [11]. As a result, games have long been used as a form of education.

Students in primary school who are between the ages of 6 and 12 are known as Generation Alpha because of their reliance on digital technology in many aspects of daily life, including education. The Alpha's generation typically have an innate ability to master technology, as if it were created just for them [12]. Building on insights from previous research, we believe that learning about waste problem would be more effective if children have the opportunity to experience, as in the actual world, through interactive and engaging support like GBL.

Game designers might have the idea to enhance children's learning experience with more playful approach, but without the user's point of view, the game could have less value to the society. This research aims to explore the children's acceptance of the expected DGBL for protracted waste problem. Conditionally, the expected GBL is not available yet and there are no students who would have habitual use of them. For this reason, we create an interaction scenario's video to give the student's better idea about the interaction and the gameplay concept before fill out the online form. The Unified Theory of Acceptance and Use of Technology 2 (UTAUT 2) approach is employed for our questionnaire to investigated the correlation of Performance Expectancy (PE), Effort Expectancy (EE), Social Influence (SI), Facilitating Conditions (FC), and Hedonic Motivation (HM) toward users Behavioral Intention (BI) to use this expected Game-Based Learning.

2 Literature Review

2.1 Game-Based Learning

Games-to-learn is founded on a inquiry learning model articulated by John Dewey [13]. For Dewey, learning is triggered by an interruption to meaningful activity in a person's lifeworld. As the concept of games-to-learn is evolving, it's been called by many different names, including gameful learning, game-based-learning, educational game, and gamification. Although definitions are also evolving, there are a few differences in broad terms. For example, GBL is "simply learning through games," while gamification is "the application of game-like mechanics to non-game entities to encourage a certain type of behavior" [14]. GBL is unique in that the goal of facilitating learning creates tension in the design process that requires careful balancing of the need to cover the subject matter and the desire to promote gameplay [15]. If the emphasis is too much on gameplay, characteristics that promote playfulness may restrict learning. On the other hand, the inclusion of educational content in the game can detract from their interest. At certain point, Egenfeldt-Nielsen [16] and Kirriemuir [17] argued that GBL is either being designed with a focus on pedagogy, leading to games that are educational but not engaging, or GBL being designed with a focus on entertainment, leading to exciting and immersive games that lack in educational impact.

As a result, Plass [15] addressed that the design process must carefully balance how much each of these two design aims, learning outcomes vs. fun, should affect individual design decisions. The playful game, which incorporates elements of the actual world, may entice the user to in meaningful play [18]. According to Bogost [19], in response to the actions of the players, a good game should give clear, consistent, and meaningful feedback. More specifically, games should encourage the player to take action and then witness the impact of their action on the systems at play [20].

Despite the numerous prior studies aimed at improving the learning process through digital games, the necessity to broaden the scope of the research remains intriguing. Previous studies have been proven that integrating games into education has the potential to create new and more powerful ways to learn in schools [11, 16, 21–23].

2.2 The Protracted Waste Problem

Indonesia's fast population growth leads to diverse social challenges, with a population of 278 million in 2022 [24]. The rapid population growth is bringing to various social problems such as waste and filthy water. The community has known that environmental and health issues arise from urban waste [5]. According to United Nations Environment Programme [25], Indonesia generates the highest quantity of municipal waste. Yet, it is agonizing that many Indonesian people still ignore their solid waste in the environment. The low expertise and limited budget available are two classic problems that force the local governments to struggle to provide minimum waste management [26]. Previous research [3, 4, 27] showed that the main factors that influence poor waste management in Indonesia are lack of eco-literacy about handling the waste. The provision of trash bins with a garbage classification system is often ineffective because many residents still mix all their garbage.

2.3 UTAUT 2

The Unified Theory of Acceptance and Use of Technology (UTAUT) is one of the most comprehensive theories of technology acceptance. It incorporates eight prominent theories, including the Theory of Planned Behaviour (TPB) [28] and the Technology Acceptance Model (TAM) [29]. UTAUT assumes that an individual's Behavioral Intention to use a technology is influenced by performance expectancy (the extent to which technology is believed to be useful), effort expectancy (the extent to which using the technology is perceived to be easy to use), social influence (the extent to which an individual's use of technology is valued in his or her social network), and facilitating conditions (the extent to which the individual believes he or she has the resources to exploit the technology) [30, 31]. Recently, the UTAUT framework has been revised in order to more accurately predict IT usage within the consumer context, resulting in the extended UTAUT 2. The recent UTAUT2 asserts that the purpose to make use of the technology is impacted by hedonic motivation (the extent to which technology is perceived as enjoyable), price value (the cognitive trade-off between perceived benefits and monetary costs of using technology) and habit (defined as the amount of time that has passed from the first use of the technology) [32].

The UTAUT 2 was chosen in the present study because, despite its comprehensiveness and high explanatory power [33], the extention variable Hedonic Motivation is a significant positive predictor of Behavioral Intention. It is implying that individuals who perceive the expected GBL for waste problem as enjoyable are more likely to intend to use the game in the future. Therefore, in this current investigation, we did not examine the influence of price value or habit on Behavioral Intention, given the fact that the game is not available yet.

Moreover, based on our short exploration, we only found one study that use UTAUT with children as the audience. Camilleri and Camilleri [34] argued that their study might were the pioneer research about primary school acceptance in educational game. They claimed that there is no other study in academia that has explored the technology acceptance of digital games in primary education. Their study took place in small European state with 3rd grade student age 8–9 years old. The objectives of their research is to explore the primary school students' perceptions and motivations toward educational games. They did not intend to design a new game, but to investigate the students prior experience with GBL at school and home. We agree with Camilleri and Camilleri statement, since we only found that other studies related to the student's acceptance of GBL are mostly for higher education [35–38].

3 Methodology

3.1 Sample

The population of this research is primary school students from East Java province, Indonesia. In total, 129 students fill out the questionnaire with the specification, 12 1st grader students, 12 2nd grader students, 11 3rd grade students, 25 4th grade students, 20 5th grade students, and 45 6th grade students with their age range is 6–13 years old. Four students did not answer "What grade are you?" but they mention their age, in which we do not want to guess or estimate the grade. The participant's gender of this study consisted of 64 girls (50%) and 64 boys (50%) since one student left this answer blank, so that this made the two gender balance in number. We used all of the data even though 4 students did not finish the personal detail completely, since we agreed that it is a minor default. In addition, we did not require students who take part in the survey to have any prior gaming experience.

3.2   Instrument

We adopt UTAUT 2 construct for the questions with some modifications to adjust in our study. Initially, we created 25 questions from six variables, totaling 35 questions including the personal data question. However, considering our target is young student, there were several questions that needed to be eliminated since they were too similar and might confusing the children. Despite our initiation to use other survey tools that have better visual and interactivity, so that those who take the survey can have a little game experience, we decided to use Google Form as the survey platform because new software may prevent us from obtaining the data we need. Regarding the children's respondent, the questions was simple, straightforward, interesting, and easy to read so that we avoided the use of complex, vague language, slang and technical terms. Before published it to the wider audience, we did a pre-test survey to 6 children from 3 different school. We kindly asked their parents to accompany them throughout the form-filling session, and gave us the reports of any difficulties they might encountered. Of the six students who took the pre-test, three parents asked if their child should write their full names on the demographic info. Hence, we eliminated the question about students' names since we wanted respondents to have no reservations about supporting our research and answering the survey honestly. Following that, we have 13 final questions for students, which can be seen in the Table 1.

Table 1. Questions based on the UTAUT 2 variable.

Variable	Observed variable (questions)	
Performance Expectancy (PE)	I think this game can help me to learn about the environmental issue better	PE 1
	I think this game can increase my contribution to environmental cleanliness	PE 2
Effort Expectancy (EE)	I think that learning how to use this game will be easy for me	EE 1
	I think the interaction between the digital and real world in this game will be easy to understand	EE 2
Social Influence (SI)	I think my family (parents and siblings) will allow me to play this game	SI 1
	I think my teachers at school will allow me to play this game	SI 2
Facilitation Condition (FC)	I have the tools to play this game	FC 1
	I think my teacher/parents can help me if I have difficulty playing this game	FC 2

(continued)

Table 1. (continued)

Variable	Observed variable (questions)	
	I think my parents will provide enough internet quota (if needed) to play this game	FC 3
Hedonic Motivation (HM)	I think the interaction of the digital and real worlds that occur in this game will be very exciting and entertaining	HM 1
	I think that learning about the environment using this game will be very fun	HM 2
Behavioral Intention (BI)	I want to play this game immediately	BI 1
	I intend to use this game to further contribute to environmental issues in real terms	BI 2
	I intend to use this game on a regular basis	BI 3

3.3 Procedure

In this particular study, we expect to integrate online and offline meetings for data collection. However, the uncertain pandemic condition hinder our project plan, in which, all of the work has been done online. In several primary schools in the Greater Malang, East Java, Indonesia area, questionnaires were shared to teachers and parents by Whatsapp, who subsequently passed them on to the students. The data gathered, especially the demographic details, and its use for research purposes have been protected. Participants first watch a short interaction scenario's video before answering the 13 questions from seven likert scale. IBM SPSS (Statistical Package for Social Sciences) software was used to perform statistical analysis on the data.

3.4 Interaction Scenario's Video

This 3.5 min video tells the story of a child's curiosity about the garbage scattered around a tourist attraction. He wonders why people left their garbage when there is enough trash bin all over the place. His mother remarked that it probably because the people who littered is lacked sufficient understanding about garbage since childhood (Fig. 1). The child believes that he must do something positive for his community through pleasant activities. He then got his cellphone from his jeans pocket and imagined himself playing games to help clean up the environment. Several principles of interaction and gameplay, as well as the rewards that will be acquired, are explained in this scenario (Fig. 2). Because the game's premise seeks to combine the digital and actual worlds, the rewards received are related to the real world. Finally, he questioned his mother why he should study about environmental literacy from childhood and at school. Her mother responded that a knowledge of the necessity of environmental protection should be taught in schools so that children develop a sense of responsibility at a young age.

The resolution of the video is 9:16 or 1080 px by 1930 px since we expect that the respondent will use their phone to filling out the questionnaire, as well as watching the video. The lead actor is a boy age 7 who is in the 1st grade and the supporting actress is her mother who will explain any uncertainty he had. Initially, we intended for the video to be in English with Indonesian subtitles. However, we then doubted that it would impede our research procedure because not all students were comfortable reading subtitles and that it would cause the survey to take longer to complete. The whole video can be accessed on Youtube link https://www.youtube.com/watch?v=0PRvLYqj8FY.

Fig. 1. The conversation scene between the boy and his mother about the waste problem.

Fig. 2. Some of the example of the game interactions concept in the expected GBL.

4 Results

Table 2 shows the distribution of scores by percentage of participants (N = 129). The first column shows the constructs. The second column, the percentages of participants that: 1 (strongly disagree), 2 (disagree), 3 (fairly disagree). The third column, the percentage of participants that: 4 (neutral). The fifth column, the percentage of participants that: 5 (fairly agree), 6 (Agree) and 7 (strongly agree). In the questionnaire all the agreements was related with the sentences, but in the table average of the percentages are presented for each construct.

Considering our main objective, evaluate the expected students acceptance of a game for learn about environmental issues, using a scenario where a parent and a student use an app to learn to recycle, we verify in the Table 2 and Fig. 3 a distribution mainly to the right. On average, 76.1% of the participants identifies with the characters on the movie and want to try this kind of app. Concerning each construct, higher scores are on the Effort Expectancy (84,9%) and Hedonic Motivation (82.9%). Effort Expectancy is related with the effort they think they need to make to learn to play the game, thus is related with usability of app, and Hedonic Motivation is related with the UX factor of the app, thus the pleasure they expect to have when playing the game app. This higher values reflect that students think that the app will be easy to learn and play with and they will have high pleasure playing with it. The following constructs with scores slightly lower are Performance Expectancy (77.1%), Social Influence (74.8%) and Behavioral Intention (72.6%). Performance expectancy is related with the expectation students have that they will learn and apply the concepts related with the environmental issues, thus they think they will have high success in learning and applying that knowledge. Social Influence is related with the role of figures of authority like parents and teachers will have over the allowing of playing the game. Almost 75% of students think that they will be allowed to play the game. Behavioral Intention tells us about the Intention to play the game, and the value of students that manifest the Intention to play is 72.6%. Thus there is a decrease that could be explained by the Facilitating Conditions (64.1%) that are related with conditions such as having mobile, internet quota and the help parents if they don't understand to how to work with the app.

Table 2. Distribution of scores by participants for each construct.

Construct	Responses 1, 2 and 3	Responses 4	Responses 5, 6 and 7
Performance expectancy	8.1%	14.7%	77.1%
Effort expectancy	5.0%	10.1%	84.9%
Social influence	7.8%	17.4%	74.8%
Facilitating condition	16.3%	19.6%	64.1%
Hedonic motivation	4.7%	12.4%	82.9%
Behavioral intention	7.5%	19.9%	72.6%
Global average	8.2%	15.7%	76.1%

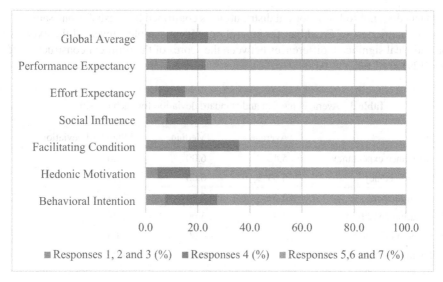

Fig. 3. Distribution of scores by participants for each construct.

In order to explore more deeply data from constructs, a transformation of the rating scale from nominal to ordinal was made. Thus the scale was transformed from 1 to 7, being 1 the Strongly Disagree and 7 the Strongly Agree. Boxplot for each construct are represented on the Fig. 4, and average, median and standard deviation values in Table 3.

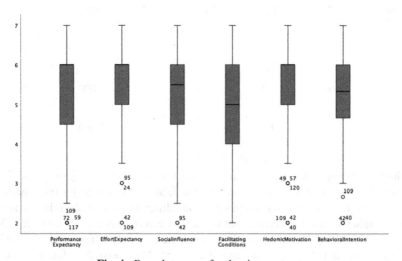

Fig. 4. Box plot scores for the six constructs

Data does not follow a normal distribution as confirmed by t-tests for one sample. A nonparametric test of Friedman for several dependent samples, revealed the existence of statistical significant differences between the scores of the different constructs $X^2(5, n = 129) = 61.64, p = 0.000$.

Table 3. Average, median and standard deviation for each construct.

Construct	Average	Median	Standard deviation
Performance expectancy	5.42	6.00	1.20
Effort expectancy	5.63	6.00	1.00
Social influence	5.32	5.50	1.14
Facilitating condition	4.97	5.00	1.29
Hedonic motivation	5.55	6.00	1.03
Behavioral intention	5.26	5.33	1.02

Post hoc Wilcoxon tests was made, and using Bonferroni Correction for the fifteen multiple comparisons (All constructs compare with all, thus 15 tests = 6 constructs * (6constructs-1)/2), differences found are highlighted in the Table 4.

Table 4. Values of significance for Wilcoxon pos hoc tests with Bonferroni correction

Construct	PE	EE	SI	FC	HM	BI
PE						
EE						
SI		.002				
FC	.000	.000	.001		.000	.038
HM						
BI		.000			.000	

The Facilitating Conditions was the construct with a lower average (X = 4.97) and median (Med = 5.0) and as can be seen in the Table 4 it is the major responsible for differences found, once it is statistical significant different from all the other constructs that have higher scores. Differences was found between Behavioral Intention (X = 5.26, Med = 5.33) and two constructs with higher scores, namely Effort Expectancy (X = 5.63, Med = 6) and Hedonic Motivation (X = 5.55, Med = 6). A difference was also found between Social Influence (X = 5.32, Med = 6) and Effort Expectancy (X = 5.63, Med = 6).

The Facilitating Conditions are the main construct responsible for the differences found. We can therefore consider that the acceptance of this new form of learning that uses game, has its greatest difficulties in the perception that students have of some difficulty in accessing technology such as smartphones and internet network infrastructure and their associated costs. The main factor that facilitates positive acceptance is the Effort Expectancy to play the recycling game which students perceive will be easy. Behavioral Intention is the second lowest value, which has to be interpreted with caution, because although there is a perception that using the game will be easy and pleasant (Hedonic Motivation) Behavioral Intention does not have the highest value. A detailed analysis of the averages per question of the behavioral intention construct shows that for question BI 3 "I intend to use this game on a regular basis" it has a lower average score ($X = 4.75$), which was responsible for lowering the average of the behavioral intention construct. Comparing this lower value with that of the other two Behavioral Intention questions (BI 1 $X = 5.60$ and BI 2 $X = 5.44$), it shows that although students want to use the game immediately and also think that it has positive effects on the environment, they perceive that using the game on a more regular basis may not be their intention.

5   Conclusion

This study seeks to find out how students accept the expected GBL about the waste problem from an interaction scenario's video. Their acceptance is critical for the long-term viability of our game design research. We employed the UTAUT 2 method, which is still used rarely to determine children's readiness to use new technologies. According to our observations, the majority of children are the end-user who are initially receptive to technology without being part in the game development.

We discover that Hedonic Motivation and Effort Expectancy are the variables that have the most impact on their acceptance of our game concept. It can be concluded that in order to be accepted by young students, the game designer should emphasis on the games that are easy yet playful. Following that are the variables of Performance Expectancy and Social Influence, which indicate that children are content if the expected GBL helps them contribute more to the environment while getting the approval from their parents and teachers to use the game.

Concerning the Facility Condition, 64% of children are convinced that they have the necessary equipment to play this game, including devices and an adequate internet capacity. There are still a significant number of children who are uncertain whether their parents or teachers at school can assist them if they are having difficulty with the expected GBL. Thus we should be careful concerning Facilitating Condition, because the use of the game concept, has its greatest difficulties in the perception that students have of some difficulty in accessing technology. This outcome is undoubtedly concerning for us as we build future games, as GBL should be enjoyed by anyone. Additionally, we see that the Behavioral Intention to use the expected GBL is really favorable, since the students eager to immediately begin playing and contributing to the environment. However, Behavioral Intention is the second lowest value in Table 2, which has to be interpreted with caution, because although there is a perception that using the game will be easy and pleasant (Hedonic Motivation) they perceive that using the game on a more regular basis may not be their intention. Thus, we have to find ways to make the intention to play this game more regular, expanding the diversity of gamification situations, using more game elements like rewards and bonus.

Certain limitations are apparent and hence, further work is suggested. The sample could be narrowed based on age levels as in children's cognitive development stages by Piaget [39]. It is apparent that the student's domicile affects the behavioral Intention to utilize the game, particularly when facilitating conditions are present. As a result, additional studies in rural areas will undoubtedly increase the sample size, especially in an island country like Indonesia with different learning facilities from the government. A deeper investigation on the UTAUT 2 variables connection will also be useful to understand the young student's acceptance.

Acknowledgments. We thank the research center CIAUD, Lisbon School of Architecture, Universidade de Lisboa, Portugal, for the publication funding, under the name CIAUD Project UID/EAT/4008/2020, and LARSyS-FCT Plurianual fundings 2020-2023 (UIDB/50009/2020). Also, this doctoral research is financially supported by Universitas Negeri Malang, Indonesia.

References

1. Kementrian Pendidikan dan Kebudayaan and Kementrian Koordinator Bidang Kemaritiman dan Investasi, Sampahku Tanggung Jawabku. Kementrian Koordinator Bidang Kemaritiman dan Investasi, Deputi Bidang Koordinasi SDM, Iptek dan Budaya Maritim, Jakarta, Indonesia (2019)
2. Presiden Republik Indonesia: Peraturan Presiden Republik Indonesia Nomor 83: Penanganan Sampah Laut. Indonesia (2018)
3. Marojahan, R.: Hubungan Pengetahuan Masyarakat Tentang Sampah Dengan Perilaku Mengelola Sampah Rumah Tangga Di Rt 02 Dan Rt 03 Kampung Garapan Desa Tanjung Pasir Kecamatan Teluk Naga Kabupaten Tangerang. In: Forum Ilmiah, vol. 12, no. 1, pp. 33–44 (2015)
4. Yulida, N., Sarto, S., Suwarni, A.: Perilaku masyarakat dalam membuang sampah di aliran sungai batang bakarek-karek Kota Padang Panjang Sumatera Barat. BKM J. Commun. Med. Public Heal. 32(10), 373–378 (2016)
5. Dethier, J.J.: Trash, cities, and politics: urban environmental problems in Indonesia. Indonesia 2017(103), 73–90 (2017). https://doi.org/10.5728/indonesia.103.0073
6. Jati, T.K.: Peran Pemerintah Boyolali Dalam Pengelolaan Sampah Lingkungan Permukiman Perkotaan. J. Wil. Lingkung. 1, 1–16 (2013)
7. Saputri, M.M., Hanafi, I., Ulum, M.C.: Evaluasi Dampak Kebijakan Pemerintah Daerah Dalam Pengelolaan Sampah Melalui Program Bank Sampah (Studi di Bank Sampah Sumber Rejeki Kelurahan Bandar Lor Kecamatan Mojoroto Kota Kediri). J. Adm. Publik 3(5), 1804–1808 (2012)
8. Wardi, I.N.: Pengelolaan Sampah Berbasis Sosial Budaya: Upaya Mengatasi Masalah Lingkungan di Bali. J. Bumi Lestari 11(1), 167–177 (2012)
9. Janakiraman, S., Watson, S.L., Watson, W.R.: Using game-based learning to facilitate attitude change for environmental sustainability. J. Educ. Sustain. Dev. 12(2), 176–185 (2018). https://doi.org/10.1177/0973408218783286
10. Janakiraman, S., Watson, S.L., Watson, W.R., Newby, T.: Effectiveness of digital games in producing environmentally friendly attitudes and behaviors: a mixed methods study. Comput. Educ. 160, 104043 (2021). https://doi.org/10.1016/j.compedu.2020.104043
11. Liu, E.Z.F., Chen, P.-K.: The effect of game-based learning on students' learning performance in science learning – a case of 'conveyance go.' Procedia Soc. Behav. Sci. 103, 1044–1051 (2013). https://doi.org/10.1016/j.sbspro.2013.10.430

12. Tootell, H., Freeman, M., Freeman, A.: Generation alpha at the intersection of technology, play and motivation. IEE Comput. Soc. (2014). https://doi.org/10.1109/HICSS.2014.19

13. Dewey, J.: Logic: Theory of Inquiry. Henry Holt and Company, Inc., New York (1938)

14. Al-Azawi, R., Al-Faliti, F., Al-Blushi, M.: Educational gamification vs. game based learning: comparative study. Int. J. Innov. Manag. Technol., 131–136 (2016). https://doi.org/10.18178/ijimt.2016.7.4.659

15. Plass, J.L., Mayer, R.E., Homer, B.D.: Handbook of Game-Based Learning. MIT Press, Cambridge (2019)

16. Egenfeldt-Nielsen, S.: Beyond Edutainment : Exploring the Educational Potential of Computer Games (2005)

17. Kirriemuir, J., McFarlane, A.: Use of computer and video games in the classroom. In: DIGRA Conference, p. 12, January 2003. http://www.digra.org/wp-content/uploads/digital-library/05150.28025.pdf, http://www.digra.org/digital-library/publications/use-of-computer-and-video-games-in-the-classroom/

18. Salen, K., Zimmerman, E.: Rules of Play: Game Design Fundamentals. The MIT Press, Massachusetts London (2004)

19. Bogost, I.: Play Anything: The Pleasure of Limits, the Uses of Boredom, and the Secret of Games, 1st edn., vol. 1. Basic Books (2016)

20. Harper, J.: Meaningful play: applying game and play design practices to promote agency in participatory performance. Int. J. Perform. Arts Digit. Media 15(3), 360–374 (2019). https://doi.org/10.1080/14794713.2019.1633148

21. Ejsing-Duun, S., Hanghøj, T.: Design thinking, game design, and school subjects: what is the connection? In: Proceedings of the European Conference on Games Based Learning, vol. 2019, pp. 201–209, October 2019. https://doi.org/10.34190/GBL.19.143

22. Dickey, M.D.: K-12 teachers encounter digital games: a qualitative investigation of teachers' perceptions of the potential of digital games for K-12 education. Interact. Learn. Environ. 23(4), 485–495 (2015). https://doi.org/10.1080/10494820.2013.788036

23. Kenny, R., Gunter, G.: Factors affecting adoption of video games in the classroom. J. Interact. Learn. Res. 22(2), 259–276 (2011)

24. Worldometer: Indonesia Population (2022) – Worldometer (2022). https://www.worldometers.info/world-population/indonesia-population/

25. Can, E., İnalhan, G.: Having a voice, having a choice: children's participation in educational space design. Des. J. 20(Suppl. 1), S3238–S3251 (2017). https://doi.org/10.1080/14606925.2017.1352829

26. Munawar, E., Yunardi, Y., Lederer, J., Fellner, J.: The development of landfill operation and management in Indonesia. J. Mater. Cycles Waste Manag. 20(2), 1128–1142 (2017). https://doi.org/10.1007/s10163-017-0676-3

27. Ashidiqy, M.R.: Analisis Faktor-Faktor yang Berhubungan Dengan Perilaku Masyarakat Dalam Membuang Sampah Rumah Tangga di Sungai Mranggen. Universitas Negeri Semarang (2009)

28. Ajzen, I.: The theory of planned behaviour: reactions and reflections. Psychol. Heal. 26(9), 1113–1127 (2011). https://doi.org/10.1080/08870446.2011.613995

29. Venkatesh, V., Davis, F.D.: A theoretical extension of the technology acceptance model: four longitudinal field studies. Manag. Sci. 46(2), 186–204 (2000)

30. Venkatesh, V., Morris, M.G., Davis, G.B., Davis, F.D.: User acceptance of information technology: toward a unified view. MIS Q. 27(3), 425–478 (2003)

31. Nordhoff, S., et al.: Using the UTAUT2 model to explain public acceptance of conditionally automated (L3) cars: a questionnaire study among 9,118 car drivers from eight European countries. Transp. Res. Part F Traffic Psychol. Behav. 74, 280–297 (2020). https://doi.org/10.1016/j.trf.2020.07.015

32. Venkatesh, V., Thong, J.Y.L., Xu, X.: Consumer acceptance and use of information technology: extending the unified theory of acceptance and use of technology. MIS Q. **36**(1), 157–178 (2012)

33. Venkatesh, V., Thong, J.Y.L., Xu, X.: Unified theory of acceptance and use of technology: a synthesis and the road ahead. J. Assoc. Inf. Syst. **17**(5), 328–376 (2016). https://doi.org/10.17705/1jais.00428

34. Camilleri, M.A., Camilleri, A.C.: The students' readiness to engage with mobile learning apps. Interact. Technol. Smart Educ. **17**(1), 28–38 (2020). https://doi.org/10.1108/ITSE-06-2019-0027

35. Bamufleh, D., Hussain, R., Sheikh, E., Khodary, K.: Students' acceptance of simulation games in management courses: evidence from Saudi Arabia. J. Educ. Learn. **9**(4), 55 (2020). https://doi.org/10.5539/jel.v9n4p55

36. Mohd, N., Mohd, N.: Determining students' behavioural intention to use animation and storytelling applying the UTAUT model: the moderating roles of gender and experience level. Int. J. Manag. Educ. **15**(3), 528–538 (2020). https://doi.org/10.1016/j.ijme.2017.10.002

37. Ibrahim, R., Jaafar, A.: User acceptance of educational games : a revised unified theory of acceptance and use. Int. J. Educ. Pedagog. Sci. **5**(5), 557–563 (2011)

38. Lawson-Body, A., Willoughby, L., Lawson-Body, L., Tamandja, E.M.: Students' acceptance of E-books: an application of UTAUT. J. Comput. Inf. Syst. **60**(3), 256–267 (2020). https://doi.org/10.1080/08874417.2018.1463577

39. Piaget, J.: The Construction of Reality in The Child. Routledge, New York (1955)

A Prototype Design and Usability Evaluation of a Chinese Educational System

Michael Li[1] and Qiping Zhang[2(✉)]

[1] Interlake High School, 16245 NE 24th Street, Bellevue, WA 98008, USA
[2] Long Island University, 720 Northern Blvd., Brookville, NY 11548, USA
Qiping.Zhang@liu.edu

Abstract. Driven by both technological advances and the onset of COVID, online resources have become ever more integrated into modern education. However, foreign language learning has been especially difficult in a virtual environment because the high degree of interactivity and adaptation necessary of language learning is often absent from online tools. Existing online resources which are popular among foreign language students – ranging from the self-study app Duolingo to the flashcard app Quizlet – all carry substantial shortfalls. Namely, these systems are individual-based and lack the collaboration between parents, students, and teachers which is often vital to student success. Utilizing relevant psychological principles, we consider the algorithmic and interface aspects of a prototype design for a Chinese learning application which can be integrated into the classroom to promote support between parents and students. We also conducted cognitive walkthrough and heuristic evaluation to assess the usability of the prototype's interface. The results found that the interface was majorly intuitive despite some minor violation of heuristic principles.

Keywords: Usability evaluation · Prototype design · Persona design · Chinese educational system · Heuristic evaluation · Cognitive walkthrough

1 Introduction

In-person instruction has long been the predominant form of education. However, due to recent technological advances and the onset of COVID, virtual classrooms have steadily gained ground and teaching has become increasingly intertwined with technology [1]. While online education is more accessible for many families, it comes with a quality tradeoff – online students often report worse content retention and understanding than their in-person counterparts [2].

Significance of Chinese as Second Language: As the world has globalized in the 20th century, the demand for foreign language instruction has risen. Especially due to China's modern rise to prominence on the global stage, there has been increasing demand for effective Chinese education [7]. From textbooks such as the *Practical Chinese Reader* in the 1980s to the development of the HSK standardized test to modern research on the influence of structuralism or other pedagogies on Chinese language learning, more and more work has been devoted to establishing effective and systematic educational support for Chinese as a second language [8].

Related Foreign Language Applications: Foreign languages have been particularly hard to learn virtually. Current language learning applications often lack adaptation and interactivity, instead providing verbatim repetition that does little to enhance students' language command beyond vocabulary memorization [3]. More importantly, such software is mostly individual based, lacking collaborative structures between students, teachers, and parents which are often important for student success.

For example, some of the most well-known applications for language learning include the flashcard app Quizlet, the language-learning app Duolingo, and the language-learning platform LingoAce. However, while they all carry benefits, they have shortfalls as well. Quizlet is a flashcard platform built to assist vocabulary memorization which does not help construct a better understanding of the language itself [4]. Duolingo has features that support students in language learning, but it is built primarily for self-study, with classroom-oriented functions premised only as additional features [5]. LingoAce is adapted for the classroom, but teachers using it must strictly follow the LingoAce curriculum, allowing little flexibility for smaller-scale or individual teachers [6].

Chinese Education System: The aforementioned virtual learning issues could be addressed by integrating online tools with regular live lessons, to maximize student engagement and retention. This paper will consider the design of such a review system, which incorporates a novel form of collaboration between parents and students which is more classroom integrated.

Objective: This paper focuses on the design and evaluation of an online tool system which helps students maximize retention and understanding of extracurricular Chinese course content. The design only concerns aspects of the system that affect parents and students, the most important stakeholders. Psychological principles such as the use of spaced repetition or gamification will be referenced. The evaluation utilizes the cognitive walkthrough and heuristic evaluation methods to identify possible avenues of improvement. This study is the first step to realizing an effective classroom design combining the merits of direct instruction and digitized resources.

2 Methodology

First, personas and scenarios in the context of this design were identified. Next, the algorithmic and interface aspects of the corresponding design were devised. Lastly, interface evaluation via cognitive walkthrough and heuristic evaluation was conducted.

Persona Design: Personas were identified for the target user groups of students and parents. Students were characterized by default lethargy and a prioritization of entertainment over academics, while parents were characterized by a busy lifestyle and wish for efficiency.

Table 1. The persona profiles for Amy and George

	Unmotivated George (student)	Busy Amy (parents)
Demography	Public elementary schooler aged 9	Software engineer aged 36 who lives in Seattle, WA, and lives with spouse and two children
Goals	(1) To have more fun when learning Chinese (2) To efficiently and effectively review lesson content (3) To perform well on tests and exams	(1) Let kids have fun and not lose interest in Chinese (2) Empower kids to do Chinese review themselves (3) Track kids' progress in Chinese school and find materials and schedules as necessary
Frustrations	(1) Homework is boring and there is a lack of motivation (2) Chinese is hard to review when there are unknown characters (3) Cannot remember the lesson content well	(1) Is busy and does not have much time to help kids review (2) Is uninformed of kids' progress (3) Tools for helping kids study are highly decentralized (3) Knows that spaced repetition is beneficial for retention, but is unable to keep up pragmatically
Skills	Has novice command of technology and limited working proficiency in the Chinese language	Has fluent command of technology and native proficiency in the Chinese language
Scenarios	(1) George's level 1 review (2) George's level 2 review (3) George's level 3 review	(4) Amy's weekly follow-up with George's Chinese school progress (5) Amy sets George's priority character list

Detailed profiles of the considered personas are presented in Table 1. The parent persona will be named Amy, while the student persona will be named George.

Scenarios: Contextualizing the above personas, George will have Chinese class every Friday, and every class, he will also take a quiz concerning the characters from previous weeks. Five scenarios were developed as follows, split roughly into 2 categories: George's weekly review and Amy's checkup on George's progress.

Scenarios 1–3 described George's review process at different proficiency levels:

1. George's level 1 review
2. George's level 2 review
3. George's level 3 review

Scenarios 4–5 regard Amy, respectively depicting a check-in on George's progress and intervention in George's study focus:

4. Amy's weekly follow-up with George's Chinese school progress
5. Amy sets George's priority character list

Prototype: A prototype was developed in alignment with the personas and scenarios presented. This prototype is detailed in Sects. 3 and 4. On both the algorithmic and interface levels, this design represents a break from existing patterns for review applications.

Cognitive Walkthrough: Cognitive walkthrough was next conducted to evaluate the action description, action availability, and action feedback for each step in the chosen scenarios regarding the prototype. Two experts conducted cognitive walkthrough evaluation. One is an app developer, and the other is a HCI scientist.

Heuristic Evaluation: Lastly, 19 heuristic questions under 7 core heuristic principles (match between system and real world, user control and freedom, consistency and standards, recognition rather than recall, flexibility and efficiency of use, aesthetic and minimalist design, and navigation) were identified to assess the prototype [9].

Two heuristic experts – an app developer and an HCI scientist – conducted a heuristic evaluation for this study, which included an individual inspection followed by a group inspection. The individual inspections were focused on allowing inspectors to get familiarized with the site design, while the group pass focused on evaluating the site interactions based on the chosen heuristic principles (Table 2).

Table 2. Heuristic principles and questions used for evaluation

Principle	Questions
(1) Match between system and real world	1.1 Are the words, phrases and concepts used familiar to the user? 1.2 Is information presented in a simple, natural, and logical order? 1.3 Are important controls represented on the screen and is there an obvious mapping between them and the real controls?
(2) User control and freedom	2.1 Are there clearly marked exits (for when the user finds themselves somewhere unexpected)? 2.2 Are facilities provided to return to the top level at any stage?
(3) Consistency and standards	3.1 Is the use of terminology, controls, graphics and menus consistent throughout the system? 3.2 Is there a consistent look and feel to the system interface? 3.3 Is the interface consistent with any platform conventions?
(4) Recognition rather than recall	4.1 Is the relationship between controls and their actions obvious? 4.2 Is it possible to search for information rather than entering the information directly?
(5) Flexibility and efficiency of use	5.1 Does the website allow for a range of user expertise? 5.2 Does the website guide novice users sufficiently? 5.3 Does the system allow for a range of user goals and interaction styles? 5.4 Does the system allow all functionality to be accessed either using function buttons or using the stylus?

(continued)

Table 2. (*continued*)

Principle	Questions
(6) Aesthetic and minimalist design	6.1 Is the design simple, intuitive, easy to learn and pleasing? 6.2 Is the website free from irrelevant, unnecessary, and distracting information? 6.3 Are icons clear and buttons labelled and is the use of graphic controls obvious? 6.4 Is the system easy to remember how to use?
(7) Navigation	7.1 Is navigational feedback provided (e.g. showing a user's current and initial states, where they've been and what options they have for where to go)?

3 Prototype Algorithm Design

The prototype consisted of a website and a corresponding mobile app based on the identified user scenarios. It targets two major user groups: students and parents.

Design Objectives
Corresponding to the user scenarios, the following two overarching design objectives are identified:

1. Students can study customized characters which appropriately challenge and prepare them for weekly written tests.
2. Parents can check in on child progress and create study plans, such as the priority character list, as necessary.

Design Rationale: Psychological principles relevant to language learning will be considered in the prototype design. Ebbinghaus's forgetting curve, the classic model of human memory deterioration from the short to long term, predicts that only about $1/3$ of learnt content is retained after 24 h under conditions of no review [10, 11].

Later developments, such as the Leitner system or Duolingo's half-life regression, proposed that spaced repetition, or regular repetition over time, can flatten Ebbinghaus's forgetting curve and commit more content into long-term memory [12, 13]. Hence, this review system is premised on spaced repetition paired with adaptive algorithms. In the rest of Sect. 3, aspects of the review system which apply to the identified scenarios will be explained.

Review System Overview: All characters learnt are categorized by the system into one of three proficiency groups: green (mastered), yellow (in progress), and red (needs work). Based on the power law of practice, students are presented most frequently with red group characters and least with green group characters.

Additionally, review exercises, categorized into three levels, becomes increasingly difficult over the week. Level one is pinyin matching, level two is phrase completion, and level three is sentence completion. Students will start at level 1 at the start of the week but will advance to higher levels as they review more. Such advancement will be premised on their cumulative weekly total score (explained below).

For each review session (other than that of the first lesson), 32 characters will be put up for review. They are selected as such:

- 16 are the new characters learnt this week
- 4 are past characters in the green group which are brought up for periodic review to prevent being forgotten
- 8 are past characters in the red group (if there are less than 8 available, as many as possible will be used)
- 4 are past characters in the yellow group (more of these characters may be utilized to make up the full 32)

This selection of characters allows students to effectively review new characters while retaining old characters in their memory.

After every review, students will be given a "score" for that review, which is added onto a "weekly total score" that allows parents and teachers to roughly gauge the student's progress. The weekly total score resets to 0 at the start of class every week. The score is calculated using the following function:

$$S(a, t) = \Sigma_{n=1}^{C}\left(\frac{20a}{t_n + a}\right)$$

The associated variables are defined as follows:

- C is the number of questions answered correctly
- t_n is the time in seconds taken to select the n th correct answer
- a is a parameter to standardize scores across different review levels; level 1 uses $a = 1$, level 2 uses $a = 2$, and level 3 uses $a = 6$

Parent Intervention: If prompted by suboptimal test results or concerning review patterns, parents can select a list of characters for their students to focus more on. These "priority characters" appear more in the student's reviews.

These priority characters selected by parents can fill up to 8 of the 16 character slots designated for review of older characters in review sessions.

4   Prototype Interface Design

Following the design process as explained above, the detailed interface design walkthrough for the 5 user scenarios will be presented.

Scenarios 1–3: George's review for Level 1 (Fri-Mon)
Step 1 - George opens the review app for students.

Fig. 1. George (student)'s review dashboard

Step 2 - George clicks on the "Review Characters" button and is prompted to begin a game of review by matching (see Fig. 1).

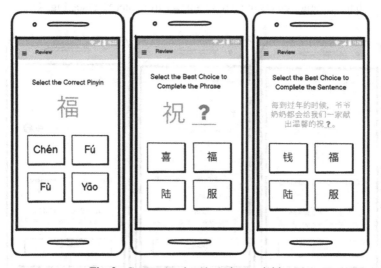

Fig. 2. George (student)'s review activities

Step 2.a – As shown in Fig. 2, for scenario 1, a new character pops up on the screen and George is prompted to select the correct pinyin for the given character. For scenario 2, new phrase pops up on the screen and George is prompted to select the best character to complete the phrase. For scenario 3, a new sentence pops up on the screen and George is prompted to select the best character to complete the sentence.

Step 2.b.i - George selects the correct answer from step 2.a (see Fig. 3).

Fig. 3. App response to correct answer by George (student)

Step 2.b.ii - George selects the wrong answer from step 2.a (see Fig. 4).

Fig. 4. App response to wrong answer by George (student)

Step 2.c - Upon clicking "continue" on the screen in steps 2.b.i or 2.b.ii, a new character appears as in step 2.a; steps 2a–2c are repeated until all 32 characters (16 new and 16 old) have been reviewed.

Step 3 - After George is done with this review, he is given a "score" based on his accuracy and speed in this review session (see Fig. 5).

Fig. 5. George (student)'s review score page

Step 4 - George clicks on the "Review Missed Characters" button to review which characters he missed, so that he may do better next time. He may click on "Try Missed" to have a practice review round with only the characters that he missed (see Fig. 6).

Fig. 6. George (student)'s missed characters

Scenario 4: Amy's Weekly Follow-Up with Chinese School Progress
Context: George has Chinese class on Fridays, and today is a Monday.
Step 1 - Amy accesses the review website's landing page (see Fig. 7).

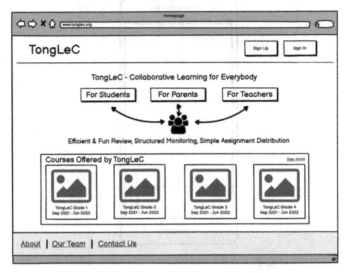

Fig. 7. Amy (parent)'s landing page

Step 2 - Amy clicks on the sign-in button and is redirected to sign in.
Step 3 - After sign-in, Amy sees a dashboard allowing her to view her children's activity (see Fig. 8).

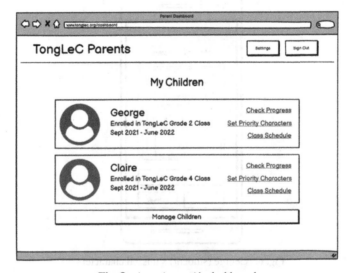

Fig. 8. Amy (parent)'s dashboard

Step 4 - Amy clicks on the "Check Progress" link next to George's name and is redirected to a page containing George's review progress (see Fig. 9).

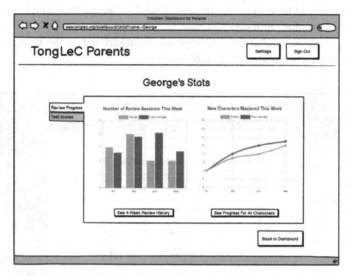

Fig. 9. Amy (parent)'s view of George (student)'s review progress

Step 5 - After looking at George's review progress, Amy clicks on the "Test Scores" tab to check in on George's recent test performance (see Fig. 10).

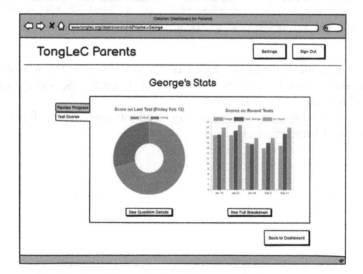

Fig. 10. Amy (parent)'s view of George (student)'s test scores

Scenario 5: Amy Sets George's Priority Character List

Context: Amy realizes George is falling behind after going through scenario 4.

Step 1 - Amy looks at George's recent scores and realizes that he is not doing as well on tests as she would have liked; for the past 2 weeks, George has scored considerably below the class average on in-class quizzes.

Step 2 - To see what characters George has been missing on the in-class quizzes, Amy clicks on the "See Question Details" button.

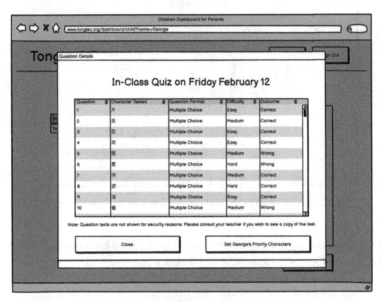

Fig. 11. Amy (parent)'s view of George (student)'s in-class quiz details

Step 3 - Amy sees a list of the characters that were tested on the quiz; she wants George to review missed characters most, so she clicks on the "Set George's Priority Characters" buttons (see Fig. 11).

Step 4 - Amy is told that she has currently no priority characters set for George, so she clicks "Add Characters to List".

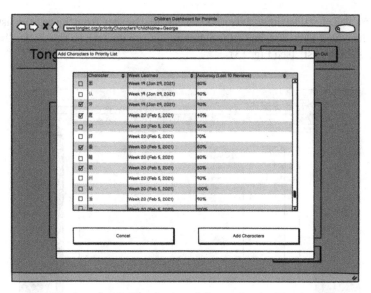

Fig. 12. Amy (parent)'s selection of George (student)'s priority list

Step 5 - A window pops up where there is a list of all characters learned so far. Amy recalls that George missed the characters 鹿, 垂, and 眠, so she quickly selects them and clicks "Add Characters"; however, she is too fast and selects the 牙 character accidentally too (see Fig. 12).

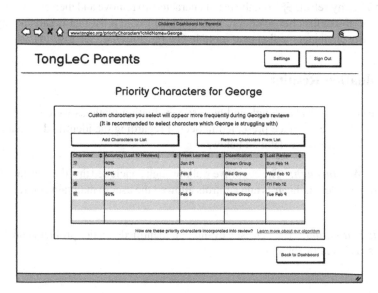

Fig. 13. Amy (parent)'s view of George (student)'s priority characters

Step 6 - The characters that Amy selected can now be seen from the priority list; Amy realizes she added 牙 by accident (it is a green group character), so she clicks "Remove Characters From List" (see Fig. 13).

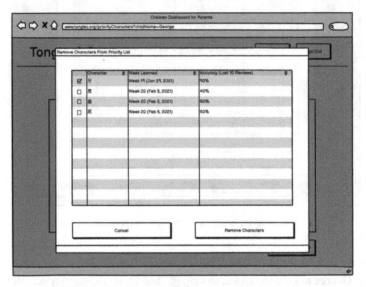

Fig. 14. Amy (parent) removing priority characters

Step 7 - Amy selects 牙 from the list of characters to remove and then clicks "Remove Characters" to confirm her selection; now she is left with a list that is satisfactory, and these priority characters will appear more in George's review (see Fig. 14).

5   Evaluation Results

Next, the cognitive walkthrough and heuristic evaluation methods were used to assess the usability of the interface presented in Sect. 4 regarding the identified scenarios and personas. The results are detailed below.

Cognitive Walkthrough: The cognitive walkthrough concluded that the interface design was intuitive – clear indicators and controls allowed the user to maintain control at every step.

Heuristic Evaluation: The heuristic evaluation identified 1 major problem and 4 minor problems, as listed in Table 3.

Table 3. Problems identified in heuristic evaluation

Major	• No clearly marked exits for mobile app
Minor	• Platform specific terminology are unfamiliar to new users (ex. "green group" and "red group") • Inconsistency between characters on tests and on the priority characters selection list • No search functions • No high-level navigational feedback

6 Conclusion and Discussion

Conclusion: From the cognitive walkthrough, it can be seen that a system supporting increased collaboration between parents and students can be readily designed to be user-friendly and usable in a flexible classroom setting. From the heuristic evaluation, avenues of improvement for the system were identified, which could be used to better the interface design before implementation.

Discussion: In the context of increasing demand for foreign language online learning resources, results from this paper can help guide the development and implementation of tooling for modern Chinese as second language classrooms. This paper also testifies to the importance of well-planned algorithms in the system design of such platforms.

In the design of the prototype, some of the most common mistakes made were:

– Inconsistency between system design and the needs of the user personas
– Unclear controls in the interface design which can possibly obfuscate users who are unfamiliar with system mechanics
– Existence of edge cases that would generate unexpected results from the algorithm and possibly crash the application
– Overcomplication of features by displaying interface components in unnecessarily elaborate configurations

The lessons learnt hence include consistency and simplicity being key to successful system design, especially for applications with a wide audience which are used in settings such as diverse classrooms.

If this prototype were to be refined or expanded upon, the role of teachers in such a system could be explicated and incorporated as well.

References

1. Bettinger, E., Loeb, S.: Promises and pitfalls of online education. Evid. Speaks Rep. **2**(15), 1–4 (2017)
2. Adnan, M., Anwar, K.: Online learning amid the COVID-19 pandemic: students' perspectives. Online Submiss. **2**(1), 45–51 (2020)
3. Yu, L.: Vocabulary recognition and memorization: a comparison of two methods (2011)

4. Quizlet. (n.d.). https://quizlet.com/. Accessed 1 Dec 2021
5. Duolingo. (n.d.). https://www.duolingo.com/. Accessed 1 Dec 2021
6. LingoAce. (n.d.). https://www.lingoace.com/. Accessed 1 Dec 2021
7. Ding, S., Saunders, R.A.: Talking up China: an analysis of China's rising cultural power and global promotion of the Chinese language. East Asia **23**(2), 3–33 (2006)
8. Zhu, Z.: A historical perspective of teaching Chinese as a second language. Teach. Learn. Chin. Issues Perspect., 33–69 (2010)
9. Brignull, H.: Home page for Heuristics interactivity (2021). http://www.id-book.com/second edition/catherb/index.htm. Accessed 25 Sept 2021
10. Murre, J.M., Dros, J.: Replication and analysis of Ebbinghaus' forgetting curve. PLoS ONE **10**(7), e0120644 (2015)
11. Newman, E.J., Loftus, E.F.: Updating Ebbinghaus on the science of memory. Eur. J. Psychol. **8**(2), 209–216 (2012)
12. Reddy, S., Labutov, I., Banerjee, S., Joachims, T.: Unbounded human learning: optimal scheduling for spaced repetition. In: Proceedings of the 22nd ACM SIGKDD International Conference on Knowledge Discovery and Data Mining, pp. 1815–1824, August 2016
13. Settles, B., Meeder, B.: A trainable spaced repetition model for language learning. In: Proceedings of the 54th Annual Meeting of the Association for Computational Linguistics (Volume 1: Long Papers), pp. 1848–1858, August 2016

A Student Experience Based Research on Brand Creation of a Private College

Bo Liu[1,2]([✉]) [iD], Zhichao Liu[1], and Chen Yang[3]

[1] Guangzhou City University of Technology, No. 1 Xuefu Road, Huadu District, Guangzhou, Guangdong, China
liubo@gcu.edu.cn
[2] University of San Carlos, P. del Rosario Street, 6000 Cebu City, Philippines
[3] South China University of Technology, No. 381 Wushan Road, Tianhe District, Guangzhou, Guangdong, China

Abstract. Private colleges participate in the fierce competition in the field of education. As a major asset, the brand is the core competitiveness of private colleges. Strengthening the brand construction can promote the sustainable development of private colleges. At present, the branding of private colleges in China is facing a great challenge. Especially under the influence of the major policy of promoting the conversion of independent colleges, for schools set up independently from their parent schools as private colleges, they face the loss of the brand aura of well-known universities, and face great challenges in sustainable development and enrollment, which are the contradictory points and blank spots in Chinese higher education at present. More importantly, as clients of private colleges, students are experiencers and beneficiaries of the school brand. The brand construction effect of private colleges can reflect real situations more objectively and scientifically through the feedback of students. From the perspective of students' experience and based on customer experience theory proposed by Schmitt, we selected Guangzhou City University of Technology as an object for case study. A questionnaire survey was conducted among 250 students at the school around the five dimensions of the school brand experience, and we received 241 valid questionnaires and analyzed the data submitted by the students. The aim was to evaluate the effectiveness of the school's branding from the perspective of the perception of the students' experience and to propose a path for the branding of private colleges.

Keywords: Customer experience · Brand creation · Student experience · Private colleges

1 Introduction

At the end of the 20th century, Chinese higher education started to expand massively and entered the stage of popularization. During this period, emerged, private colleges and universities with Chinese characteristics, and they are generally called independent colleges. Such colleges are privately-funded or fully privately-run colleges managed by private capital with the brand power of famous universities. They often take advantage of the brand reputation and brand association of a university, operate in the market through private capital, and pay "brand usage fee" to their parent college or university regularly, while the latter provides certain faculty and guidance. As an important part of higher education in China, these private colleges are rapidly emerging with the advantages of flexible mechanism, quick market response, specialties close to market demand and practical talents training [1]. As of April 3, 2020, there were 246 independent colleges in China, accounting for 9.15% of the national general colleges and universities and 56.68% of the national private colleges and universities (excluding cooperative schools) [2].

The Measures for the Establishment and Management of Independent Colleges adopted by China's Ministry of Education in February 2008 stipulates that "those who meet the criteria for the establishment of ordinary undergraduate higher education schools may apply for the conversion to private higher education schools" [3]. In May 2021, the Ministry of Education announced the revised Regulations on the Implementation of the Law on the Promotion of Private Education, which stipulates that public schools shall not be involved in the operation of private schools only in the form of brand export [4].

The historical mission of independent colleges has been completed, and the trend is to convert to private colleges [5]. The policy means that independent colleges have to be separated from their parent colleges or universities, and with the brand support of the latter, independent colleges have advantages in enrollment and employment, faculty construction and research output. Once the brand of the parent school is lost, these advantages will no longer exist [1]. Private colleges that have been converted from independent colleges have to face rebranding [6]. It is difficult to form a new school brand within a short period of time [3]. Independent colleges hold majors and teaching management homogenized with their parent schools, and their school positioning is not clear, and the society and employers hold low recognition of independent colleges [7]. Many enterprises, especially institutions and state-owned enterprises, do not hire candidates whose first degree is from independent colleges in the recruitment process; even some higher education institutions treat candidates from independent colleges differently when admitting master students [8]. Therefore, in the process of going independent, the implementation of branding strategy becomes an inevitable choice for these colleges to get rid of the status quo of running a low level of education, enrollment difficulties, and even unsustainability [1].

Branding and improvement can tap more development potential and opportunities for private colleges, which can enhance the current status of the school in the education industry and grow into a more outstanding college [9]. Branding is also becoming more and more important for private colleges. Branding is a convenient and effective way for private colleges to improve their competitiveness and gain sufficient student sources for long-term development [10].

2   Literature Review

With the orderly development of the market, more market concepts are known to the public. Higher education is also in the midst of the market where the fittest survives, and has received more attention. In the past, scholars have carried out relevant researches on customer experience, development of private colleges, and brand building of private colleges, and some research results have been achieved.

2.1 Literature Review on Experience

PINE II B J, GILMORE J H [11] clearly states that experience is distinguished from goods and services, arguing that experience is a service as a stage, a commodity as a prop to engage individual customers by creating a memorable event.

Regarding the customer experience theory, Zhen Li [12] regarded customer experience as a state, customer experience as a process and customer experience as a behavior. Customer experience includes not only cognitive understanding and reflection, but also emotional feeling and comprehension, as well as behavioral activities and practices [13]. Brand is the psychological occupancy of a company in the minds of customers. A good brand can bring a good experience to customers in the process of brand interaction through brand stimuli, which includes various factors related to the brand, such as brand logo, brand name, brand image, brand product, brand packaging, brand advertisement, brand video, brand spokesperson, etc. [14].

After the experience economy, a large number of studies on experience dimensions have emerged from the perspective of management, and the most representative results include the Strategic Experience Model ("SEM" model, sense, feel, think, act and relate) [15]. Bernd H. Schmitt [15] pointed out in 1999 that experiential marketing represents the five aspects of consumers' Sense, Feel, Think, Act, and Relate. Sense is the use of various senses to create sense experiences by appealing to the senses of sight, hearing, touch, taste and smell. Feel is to make full use of the customer's inner feelings and emotions to create a feeling experience to attract customers to make a choice decision. Thinking appeals to the intellect to create cognitive and problem-solving experiences for customers by surprising, intriguing and provoking them to think divergently and convergent. Act aims to influence physical experiences, lifestyles, and interactions with consumers. Relating appeals to the personal desire for self-improvement and wants others to feel good. Associating people with a broader social system builds personal preference for a brand while allowing people who use the brand to form a group.

2.2 Literature Review on Branding

According to David Ogilvy [16], founder of Ogilvy & Mather, "a brand is an intricate symbol and an intangible combination of attributes, name, packaging, price, history, reputation, and advertising style".

Brand experience is the subjective internal sense, feeling and cognitive reactions and external acting reactions of consumers inspired by brand design, brand recognition, packaging, communication and environment [17].

2.3 Literature Review on Brand Construction of Private Colleges and Universities

The brand of a university is a generalization of the unique visual image gradually formed in the long-term schooling practice, marked by the school's name, emblem and other symbolic signs, as well as the unique personality characteristics connoted by the school image, reputation, organizational culture, specialties and disciplines etc. [18]. Rosen [19] proposed that college branding often plays a decisive role in applicant's choice of higher education institutions to attend. They choose and eliminate schools in order based on their brand ranking. Ann Brewer [20] proposed that consumers' brand perceptions determine branding in the context of college branding, with emphasis on the students' sense of experience.

Regarding research on branding of private colleges, Bayraktar [21] pointed out that branding in public universities is more mature and has achieved some results, and that private colleges branding should follow the example of public universities. Yeravdekar [22] believes that it is important to find the variables that affect the evaluation of the private school brand and to extract them. Ermakov Yuri [23] believes that private colleges should always adapt to the market and constantly adjust their positioning. Fryges H [24] argues that the branding and formation of private colleges, like public universities, must go through the integration and rational use of the school's multifaceted excellent resources in order for them to establish an excellent brand image, which in turn will bring more and better opportunities and chances for their own development. Moffatt J [25] points out that the purpose of implementing branding strategy in private colleges is to increase awareness and reputation. He suggested that private colleges can expand their influence by marketing through experiential trials and webcast trials to motivate more students to be willing to attend.

Chinese scholars have also conducted many studies on the branding of private colleges. Wei Zhang [26] stated that with the rapid development of private higher education, the competition among domestic private colleges of the same category and level has become more and more intense, but due to their inherent weaknesses, such as short history, insufficient cultural heritage, single source of funding, and brand effect not yet formed, the competitive pressure of private colleges in the market is increasing day by day. Dan Zhang [27] pointed out that private colleges are currently ushering in an excellent period of development, but due to their short growth time, they do not have competitive advantages compared with some public schools. Private colleges can actively establish the brand banner and follow the branding development strategy by using their own flexible management mechanisms that distinguish them from public schools in order to highlight their competitiveness in the student market and employment market, and thus drive local economic development. Qiao Xu [28] argued that there are problems of weak brand awareness and unclear brand characteristics in private college brands, and proposed that the brand image management of private colleges should include four processes: brand positioning, brand planning, brand communication and brand maintenance. Xuan Su et al. [29] used Schmitt's theory to conduct an exploratory study on the brand construction of applied colleges and universities from the perspective of customer experience. Rui Zhang et al. [30] proposed a college branding model to analyze the process and method of college branding, and also to explore the cognitive composition of stakeholders. By studying the relationship between college culture and private college branding, Yinglin He and Liang Kong [31] analyzed three levels of college culture: material, physical and spiritual culture construction, and found that the cultural construction of colleges and universities has a positive boost to the branding of colleges and universities, and also plays a non-negligible influential role in promoting the healthy development of colleges and universities. Chaoran Wang [32] analyzed the brand shaping of private colleges from the perspective of elements and carried out an in-depth discussion from both explicit and invisible aspects. He believed that the name of colleges and universities, campus culture, school logo and school motto, and teaching facilities of schools are important explicit factors to promote the brand shaping of private colleges, while teaching management, faculty strength and teaching quality are important implicit factors to promote the brand shaping of colleges. Hongli He [33] analyzed the current economic environment and proposed specific measures and methods for branding universities in Jiangxi private college; she believed that private colleges should pay attention to branding awareness and atmosphere and grasp the important link of integrated communication.

However, we did not find any papers based on case studies of brand building in independent colleges converted to private colleges, nor did we find any publications using customer experience theory for brand building in private colleges.

3   Method

As the customers of private colleges, students' recognition of the school brand is the most intuitive and measurable. Students' identification with the university brand is related to the spread of university culture, the promotion of university spirit, and the functioning of the university [34].

We evaluated the effectiveness of the college's branding from the perceptive perspective of student experience based on the customer experience theory proposed by Schmitt (1999). Schmitt divided experience into five dimensions, namely, Sense, Feel, Think, Act and Relate. Taking the perspective of students' experiences into consideration, this study selected Guangzhou City University of Technology as an object for case study. Based on 250 students' brand experience from five dimensions, we carried out questionnaire surveys: the sense dimension was measured by ways for students to learn about the college, its type and its brand VI color; the feeling dimension was measured by students' reasons for applying for the college, their feeling of life and number of their new friends; the action dimension was measured by their feeling of teaching facilities, feeling of living conditions and feeling of teaching; the thinking dimension was measured by students evaluation of the students management, of the educational administration system and of the campus culture. The relating dimension was measured by students' expectation for learning, donation intention after graduation and expectation of the future impact of the college's convert. Through the survey, we hoped to further understand students' psychological, behavioral and attitudinal experience of the brand after the college's conversion.

We collected data by randomly distributing questionnaires through the Internet, and a total of 251 questionnaires were returned. Among them, there were 10 invalid questionnaires due to logical inconsistencies or incomplete answers, and 241 valid questionnaires, which were used for data analysis with an efficiency of 100%. In general, the quality of the questionnaire data is high, which is of great help to the later data analysis.

4 Result

For a more scientific analysis, we converted the text-based data collected back from the questionnaire into numerical data by using Excel and SPSS. We conducted descriptive analysis of the data of basic information and attitudes of students' experiences in the questionnaire in five aspects: valid number, minimum value, maximum value, mean value, and standard deviation, and came up with the analysis results shown in Table 1.

Table 1. Descriptive analysis

Question items		N	Minimum	Maximum	Mean	Standard deviation
Q1. Gender		241	1	2	1.43	0.496
Q2. Grade		241	1	4	2.33	0.888
Q3. Location of your home		241	1	2	1.34	0.476
Q4. Ways to learn about the college		241	1	5	2.19	1.217
Q5. Type of college		241	1	4	2.46	0.701
Q6. The VI color of the college		241	1	5	1.05	0.362
Q7. Reasons for registration		241	1	5	2.74	0.848
Q8. Life feeling		241	1	5	2.59	0.877
Q9. Number of new friends		241	1	5	2.61	0.789
Q10. Feelings of the teaching facilities		241	1	5	2.83	0.715
Q11. Feelings of living facilities		241	1	5	2.85	0.765
Q12. Feelings of teaching quality		241	1	5	2.47	0.689
Q13. Evaluation of the students' management		241	1	5	2.81	0.883
Q14. Evaluation of the teaching administration system		241	1	5	3.14	0.902
Q15. Evaluation of the campus culture		241	1	5	2.60	0.816
Q16. Learning expectations		241	1	5	3.22	1.369
Q17. Willingness to pay back to the Alma mater		241	1	5	2.32	0.876
Q18. The impact of conversion on the future of the college	q1	241	0	1	0.60	0.491
	q2	241	0	1	0.55	0.499
	q3	241	0	1	0.53	0.500
	q4	241	0	1	0.39	0.489
	q5	241	0	1	0.33	0.470
Number of effective cases (in columns)		241				

Based on the analysis of the basic statistics in Table 1, the following conclusions can be drawn.

First, from the minimum and maximum results it can be concluded that all options are within the range of reasonable options and the questionnaire data are valid.

Table 2. Sense experience

Question items	Quota	Frequency	Effective percentage
Q4. Ways to learn about the college	Through admission brochure or briefing	96	39.80%
	By listening to sb to introduce the college	55	22.80%
	From TV/ newspaper/network	43	17.80%
	Know nothing about the college	39	16.20%
	Others	8	3.30%
	Total	241	100.00%
Q5. Type of college	Research-oriented university	9	3.70%
	Applied colleges	133	55.20%
	Comprehensive universities	79	32.80%
	Others	20	8.30%
	Total	241	100.00%
Q6. The VI color of the college	Purple	235	97.50%
	Orange	3	1.20%
	Red	1	0.40%
	Blue	1	0.40%
	Green	1	0.40%
	Total	241	100.00%

Secondly, the larger the standard deviation, the less representative the mean value is, and the difference of options fluctuates around the mean value, combining the mean and standard deviation data can be concluded that Q1 Gender, Q2 Grade, Q3 location of your home, Q5 Type of college, Q6 The VI color of the college, Q7 Reasons for registration, Q8 Life feeling, Q9 Number of new friends, Q10 Feelings of the teaching facilities, Q11 Feelings of living facilities, Q12 Feelings of teaching quality, Q13 Evaluation of the students management, Q14 Evaluation of the teaching administration system, Q15 Evaluation of the campus culture, Q17 Willingness to pay back to the alma mater, Q18 The impact of conversion on the future of the college with a total of 16 variables with standard deviation less than 1, so the mean is significantly representative. From the mean value, the respondents are more male (138, 57.3%), mainly sophomore students (112, 46.5%) and junior students (61 people, 25.3%). The students are mainly from Guangdong

Province. Most students think the school is an application-oriented college, and the standard color of the school is purple. They think the school has good prospects to attract them to applied, also they feel comfortable in life and can make some new friends. At the same time, they are satisfied with the school's teaching facilities, living facilities and teaching quality. They are satisfied with students' work and campus culture. They have an average rating for the academic affairs system. They are willing to contribute to the school in the future. They envisioned that the conversion of the school would have an impact on the reputation of the college, the employment rate of students, the construction of disciplines and majors, the level of teaching and research, school-enterprise cooperation and enrollment. In addition, the standard deviations of Q4 and Q16 variables are greater than 1, so the means are not represented significantly.

We found from the survey data analysis that:

First, the findings on sense experience. The sense experience dimension was measured by ways for students to learn about the college, its type and its brand VI color. The frequencies and valid percentages of the survey data are shown in Table 2. Among them, most of the respondents learned about the school through admission brochure or briefing. As for the type of college, 55.2% of the respondents chose applied colleges. The respondents have a very high cognition of the school's standard color experience, with 97.5% of respondents choosing purple. From the analysis of sensory experience dimension, it can be concluded that the respondents have a good effect on the sensory experience of the brand, but there is still room to strengthen the education type, brand attribute awareness and brand publicity.

Second, the findings on feeling experience. The feeling experience dimension was measured by reasons for students to apply for the college, their feeling of life and number of their new friends. The frequencies and valid percentages of the survey data are shown in Table 3. Among them, regarding the reason for registration, 47.7% of the respondents were attracted by the fact that the school has better development prospects and 32.8% were attracted by the campus environment of the school. Regarding the students' feeling of life, 51.0% of the respondents thought it was average and 29.5% of them thought it were comfortable. Overall, students feel good about life. In terms of social life, 51.5% of the respondents made an average number of new friends and 34.4% of them made more friends, which shows that most students have a good social life. Analyzing from the dimension of feeling experience, most of the respondents have a good emotional life experience in general, but the social life emotion still needs to be satisfied.

Table 3. Feeling experience

Question items	Quota	Frequency	Effective percentage
Q7. Reasons for registration	The city where the school is located	13	5.39%
	Campus environment	79	32.78%
	The development prospects of the school	115	47.72%
	Professional advantages of the college	26	10.79%
	Teaching and scientific research conditions	8	3.32%
	Total	241	100.00%
Q8. Life feeling	Happy	28	11.60%
	Comfortable	71	29.50%
	Average	123	51.00%
	Boring	11	4.60%
	Gloomy	8	3.30%
	Total	241	100.00%
Q9. Number of new friends	Many	17	7.10%
	More	83	34.40%
	Average	124	51.50%
	Few	11	4.60%
	None	6	2.50%
	Total	241	100.00%

Third, the findings on action experience. The action experience dimension was measured by their feeling of teaching facilities, feeling of living conditions and feeling of teaching. The frequencies and valid percentages of the survey data are shown in Table 4. Among them, in the survey on the perception of teaching facilities experience, 56.0% of the respondents were generally satisfied and 27.4% of the respondents were relatively satisfied. In addition, 54.4% of the respondents felt generally satisfied with the living facilities. It is evident that the respondents believe that the school facilities can meet the teaching and living needs. With 49.4% of the respondents felt more satisfied with the teaching quality of the school, this shows that most of them were more satisfied with the teaching and learning facilities. Analyzed from the action experience dimension, most respondents have a high degree of action experience.

Table 4. Action experience

Question items	Quota	Frequency	Effective percentage
Q10. Feelings of the teaching facilities	Very satisfied	6	2.50%
	Relatively satisfied	66	27.40%
	Generally satisfied	135	56.00%
	Dissatisfied	32	13.30%
	Very dissatisfied	2	0.80%
	Total	241	100.00%
Q11. Feelings of living facilities	Very satisfied	5	2.10%
	Relatively satisfied	69	28.60%
	Generally satisfied	131	54.40%
	Dissatisfied	29	12.00%
	Very dissatisfied	7	2.90%
	Total	241	100.00%
Q12. Feelings of teaching quality	Very satisfied	11	4.60%
	Relatively satisfied	119	49.40%
	Generally satisfied	101	41.90%
	Dissatisfied	7	2.90%
	Very dissatisfied	3	1.20%
	Total	241	100.00%

Fourth, the findings on thinking experience. The thinking experience dimension was measured by students' evaluation of the students' management, of the educational administration system and of the campus culture. The frequencies and valid percentages of the survey data are shown in Table 5. Among them, regarding the evaluation of student management, 42.3% of the respondents were felt generally satisfied and 34.9% of them were felt relatively satisfied, which shows that most of the respondents approved of the school's student management. Regarding the evaluation of the teaching administration system, 44.4% of the respondents were generally satisfied and 25.3% were dissatisfied, which shows that the teaching administration system was complained by the majority of the respondents. Regarding the evaluation of campus culture, 43.6% of the respondents were generally satisfied and 41.1% felt relatively satisfied, which shows that most of the respondents were more satisfied with the campus culture. From the analysis of the thinking experience dimension, most of the respondents think that the feeling experience is generally above, and there is still room for further improvement in the service level and supporting and cultural atmosphere.

Table 5. Thinking experience

Question items	Quota	Frequency	Effective percentage
Q13. Evaluation of the students' management	Very satisfied	9	3.70%
	Relatively satisfied	84	34.90%
	Generally satisfied	102	42.30%
	Dissatisfied	36	14.90%
	Very dissatisfied	10	4.10%
	Total	241	100.00%
Q14. Evaluation of the teaching administration system	Very satisfied	5	2.10%
	Relatively satisfied	51	21.20%
	Generally satisfied	107	44.40%
	Dissatisfied	61	25.30%
	Very dissatisfied	17	7.10%
	Total	241	100.00%
Q15. Evaluation of the campus culture	Very satisfied	14	5.80%
	Relatively satisfied	99	41.10%
	Generally satisfied	105	43.60%
	Dissatisfied	16	6.60%
	Very dissatisfied	7	2.90%
	Total	241	100.00%

Fifth, the results of the survey on related experience. The related experience dimension was measured by students' expectation for learning, donation intention after graduation and expectation of the future impact of the college's conversion. The frequencies and valid percentages of the survey data are shown in Table 6. Among them, in the survey on study expectation, 48.1% of the respondents hope to find a satisfactory job, which shows that most students hope to acquire knowledge and skills through study in order to find a satisfactory job. In the survey on the willingness to donate to the school in the future, 49.4% of the respondents felt more willing and 14.9% felt very willing, which shows that most students have feelings for their school. Multiple choices can be selected to investigate how the conversion to a private college will affect the future development of the school. The results show that 60.2% of the respondents think it will affect the social reputation of the school, 54.8% of them think it will affect the employment rate of students, 53.1% of them think it will affect the construction of disciplines majors of the school, which shows that most students think the school should pay attention to brand building after the conversion, further improve social influence, and pay attention to the construction of disciplines, majors, teaching and research, etc. to achieve internal development.

Table 6. Related experience

Question items	Quota	Frequency	Effective percentage
Q16. Learning expectations	Studying for exams of postgraduate programs	55	22.80%
	Mastering professional skills	10	4.10%
	Graduating smoothly	31	12.90%
	Getting a satisfactory job	116	48.10%
	Opening an enterprise	29	12.00%
	Total	241	100.00%
Q17. Willingness to pay back to the alma mater	Extremely willing	36	14.90%
	Relatively willing	119	49.40%
	Average	64	26.60%
	Unwilling	18	7.50%
	Absolutely unwilling	4	1.70%
	Total	241	100.00%
Q18. The impact of convert on the future of the college	Social reputation of the college	145	60.20%
	Students employment rate	132	54.80%
	Discipline major construction	128	53.10%
	Teaching and scientific research level	94	39.00%
	College-industry cooperation	79	32.80%
	Enrollment of new students	98	40.70%

Based on the research results, this study put forward suggestions on brand construction of private colleges from the perspective of students' experience, as shown in Fig. 1.

First, the college should accurately define its brand connotation and strengthen the publicity of it, and in the process pay attention to students' perception of the experience and create the core values of the school's brand.

Second, it should develop its brand planning. We suggest designing school CI system and establishing brand building management committee with students' participation, so that students can participate in the whole process of school brand creating.

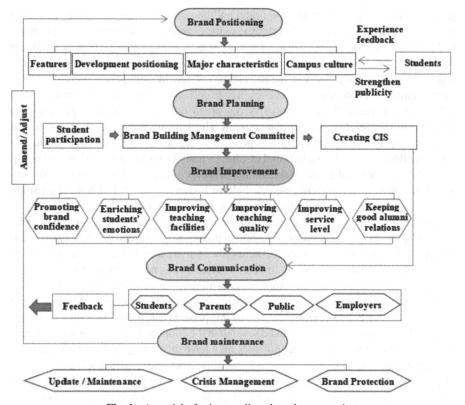

Fig. 1. A model of private college brand construction

Third, it should consolidate the good school brand image that has been established, while improving the bad brand factors. For example, by enriching students' emotional and social life, improving teaching facilities, teaching quality, service level and other measures, the college can further improve students' psychology and cognition of the college's brand experience. Also, the college should make good use of the alumni resources, and increase the source of school funds.

Fourth, it should pay attention to user participation when conducting brand communication to further enhance brand awareness and reputation. For example, establish a four-dimensional brand communication platform involving students, their parents, the public and employers, as well as establish an effective brand experience feedback mechanism.

Fifth, it should also pay attention to brand maintenance and develop a series of system for brand crisis management.

5 Discussion

This paper' contribution to the brand construction of private colleges is as follows. First, it deepens the understanding of experience theory in the study of brand building of private colleges. Previous studies on brand building of private colleges mainly focused on using theories on branding. This study uses the experience marketing theory proposed by Schmitt to conduct a case study, which expands the dimensions of brand building in private colleges. Second, this paper puts forward the brand building strategy after the independent college is transformed into a private college. In the current research results in China, almost no predecessor has chosen private colleges transformed from independent colleges as the research object to carry out brand building research. This paper can provide valuable reference for similar colleges. Third, it enriched the innovative research on the sustainable development of independent colleges after their transformation into private colleges under the background of China's transformation policy. How to develop independent colleges after the establishment of independent colleges is also the difficulty and blank point in the current research field of higher education in China. This study provides valuable reference for the sustainable development of private colleges.

However, this paper also carries certain limitations. It should be pointed out that this paper adopts the case study method. Although tracing a representative single case is beneficial to the theoretical construction, the representative case still has the particularity of the school, which makes the study limited. Therefore, it is necessary for future research to expand the sample size, for example, considering the differences between private colleges, to further refine the viewpoints of this study through multiple case studies, and improve the validity of research. The case of this paper is based on Guangzhou City University of Technology, which is ranked seventh in the country in terms of private colleges and universities. Different private colleges may have differences in brand building due to the differences of individual cases. Second, this paper only studies the brand building of private colleges from the perspective of student experience. Due to the limitation of research perspective, this study has some exploratory elements in the process of argumentation and analysis. Future research can deepen the study through the perspective of employers and social evaluation to improve the applicability and scientificity of the research results.

6 Conclusions

This paper discusses how to carry out brand building in private colleges from the perspective of student experience under the framework of Customer Experience theory proposed by Schmitt. Based on the literature review, this paper adopts an exploratory case study method to discuss, and puts forward the brand construction path of five-dimension private college. This study takes Guangzhou City University of Technology as an example, which has been converted from an independent school to a private one. From the perspective of students' experience, we analyzed students' sense experience, feeling experience, thinking experience, action experience and relating experience of the college's brand, and proposed brand building strategies for private colleges, which may provide references for other private colleges to innovate their brand building, especially for those converted from independent colleges to provide more valuable reference. Under the current background of private education in China, the findings of this paper are innovative, which can enrich the research on brand construction innovation of private colleges from the perspective of student experience, and have enlightenment significance for practice.

References

1. Zhenwu, A.: Try to discuss the construction of brand strategy of private colleges and universities. J. Henan Coll. Finance Tax. **35**(01), 29–33 (2021)
2. China Ministry of Education. http://www.Moe.gov.cn/jyb_xxgk/s5743/s5744/201906/t20190 617_386200.html2019/09/26
3. Chunmei, C., Mingkun, Q.: Attribution, status quo and suggestions of independent college convert in China. Educ. Career **24**, 34–40 (2020). https://doi.org/10.13615/j.cnki.1004-3985. 2020.24.009
4. China Ministry of Education. http://www.moe.gov.cn/jyb_sjzl/sjzl_zcfg/zcfg_jyxzfg/202 110/t20211029_575965.html
5. Xunpeng, W., Rongjun, W., Mingkun, Q.: A historical institutionalism analysis of policy changes in independent colleges. Explor. High. Educ. **10**, 111–118 (2021)
6. Haibao, Q., Ting, S.: Development strategies of independent colleges transferring under the perspective of resource dependence. J. Zhejiang Shuren Univ. **20**(04), 11–15 (2020)
7. Haidong, L.: Independent college: the development bottleneck, the opportunity of transformation and the route of transformation: a study based on Guangdong province. Educ. Teach. Forum **20**, 37–40 (2021)
8. Xiaoqing, L., Ming, F.: The logical rationality and practical direction of transformation development of independent colleges: a study based on the "k-s" combination analysis model. J. High. Educ. Manag. **12**(05), 54–61 (2018). https://doi.org/10.13316/j.cnki.jhem.201808 30.005
9. Jian, F.: A strategic review of the development of independent colleges in China. Nanjing Agricultural University, PhD dissertation (2012)
10. Chang, L.: Brand shaping of private colleges and universities--a case study of Shijiazhuang vocational college of XX. Hebei University of Geosciences, Master's thesis (2020)
11. Pine, I.B.J., Gilmore, J.H.: Welcome to the experience economy. Harv. Bus. Rev. **76**(7/8), 97–105 (1998)
12. Zhen, L.: Who creates experience - a study of three models of experience creation and their operating mechanisms? Nankai Bus. Rev. **22**(05), 178–191 (2019)
13. Pengcheng, Z., Jiafei, L.: A study of the psychological mechanism of experience. Psychol. Sci. **36**(06), 1498–1503 (2013). https://doi.org/10.16719/j.cnki.1671-6981.2013.06.037
14. Jiang, L.: Cultural branding of special town from the perspective of brand gene theory-an examination of Wuzhen as the center. J. Guizhou Univ. (Soc. Sci. Ed.) **37**(05), 83–92 (2019). https://doi.org/10.15958/j.cnki.gdxbshb.2019.05.11
15. Schmitt, B.H.: Experiential marketing. J. Mark. Manag. **15**(1), 53–67 (1999)
16. Philipp, A.R., Nina, K., Babin, B.J., Ivens, B.S.: Brand management in higher education: the University brand personality scale. J. Bus. Res. (2015)
17. Brakus, J.J., Schmitt, B.H., Zarantonello, L.: Brand experience: what is it? How is it measured? Does it affect loyalty? J. Mark. **73**(3), 52–68 (2009)
18. Hanzu, T.: On university brand strategy and its business management strategy. J. Educ. Sci. Hunan Norm. Univ. **10**(04), 39–43+47 (2011)
19. Rosen, D.E., et al: College choice in a brand elimination framework: the administrator's perspective. J. Mark. High. Educ. **8**(4), 61–81 (1998)
20. Ann, B., Jingsong, Z.: The impact of a pathway college on reputation and brand awareness for its affiliated university in Sydney. Int. J. Educ. Manag. **24**(1), 34–47 (2010)
21. Bayraktar, E., Tatoglu, E., Zaim, S.: Measuring the relative efficiency of quality management practices in Turkish public and private universities. J. Oper. Res. Soc. **64**(12), 1810–1830 (2013)

22. Yeravdekar, S.B., et al.: Bench marking model for management education in India. Bench Marking **24**(3), 666–693 (2017)
23. Ermakov, Y., Ermakova, M.Y.: Marketing orientation activity of the modern Russian University. Ann. Mark. **1** (2017)
24. Fiyges, H.: Productivity, growth, and internationalization: the case of German and British high techs. Zee Discuss. Thesis **5**(8), 9–11 (2018)
25. Moffatt, J.: An infusion approach to internationalization: drake University as a case study. Front. Interdiscip. J. Study Abroad **27** (2015)
26. Wei, Z.: An analysis of brand development strategy of private universities. Mod. Bus. Ind. **40**(1), 330–332 (2015)
27. Dan, Z.: Talking about the opportunities and threats of implementing brand strategy in private colleges and universities. Times Econ. Trade **23**(3), 439–442 (2018)
28. Qiao, X.: The study on the brand image management in private colleges and universities. High. Educ. Forum **34**, 23–25 (2019). https://doi.org/10.16400/j.cnki.kjdks.2019.12.012
29. Xuan, S., Aiying, J., Wenzhong, L.: A study on brand building of applied colleges and universities based on customer experience perspective. China Adult Educ. **15**, 12–16 (2019)
30. Rui, Z., Yi, Z.: Research on the driving mechanism and shaping method of brand formation in colleges and universities. J. Chongqing Coll. Arts Sci. (Soc. Sci. Ed.) **28**(01), 29–37 (2009). https://doi.org/10.19493/j.cnki.issn1673-8004.2009.01.007
31. Yinglin, H., Liang, K.: Campus culture construction: an important focus point for brand building of private universities. Sci. Technol. Inf. **29**, 417+434 (2009)
32. Chaoran, W.: Research on branding of private colleges and universities based on elemental analysis. Guangdong University of Technology, MA thesis (2013)
33. Hongli, H.: Research on branding image of private colleges and universities-Jiangxi College of Fashion as an example. Nanchang University, MA thesis (2012)
34. Heng, W.: Normal university students' acknowledgement of the school brand: current situation, problems and countermeasures: based on the investigation into a certain Beijing's normal university. Theory Pract. Educ. **31**(07), 35–39 (2011)

Research on Students' Learning Experience After Embedding Data Thinking into Curriculum
Take the Course "Staff Career Development" as an Example

Juan Tang(✉)

Guangzhou City University of Technology, Guangzhou 510800, Guangdong, China
710921994@qq.com

Abstract. The rapid development of Big Data provides opportunities and challenges for Higher Education. How to cultivate students' Data Analysis ability, adapt to the needs of multiple scenarios of different enterprises and cultivate integrated professionals is the main direction of Teaching Reform. The author tries to embed Data Thinking into the course module of "Employee Career Development", guides data collection, analysis, sorting and visualization, and use Technology Acceptance Model (TAM) to test students' learning effect and experience. At present, students actively support Teaching Reform, and their sense of interaction and gain are enhanced in the learning process. The practice of this teaching reform has positive significance and reference value for the teaching of other courses and the optimization of curriculum system.

Keywords: Data Thinking · Learning initiative · Learning experience · Teaching effectiveness

1 Introduction

The rapid development of the new generation of IT technology promotes the wide application of Big Data, and we are gradually transiting from the early IT era to the DT era. Under the call of a series of national policies, such as "Education Informatization, providing personalized learning conditions", Higher Education should conform to the future development trend of "combining data with education", so as to meet the needs of the era of professional and skilled personnel training. [1] Starting from a course, the author intersperses some Data analysis modules in the teaching process for Juniors and introduces data thinking to carry out teaching reform. Starting with the market demand of human resource management, the teacher guides students to learn all the knowledge of Data analysis, sorting and visualization of job demand on the recruitment website, then conducts targeted output display and training in combination with the special modules of interest to the group, and realize mutual comments, scoring, interactive Q&A to maximize students' Deep Participation in the process of classroom learning and enhance their practical application ability.

2 The Overall Design Idea

In the first class of the course, the teacher showed the complete course map, let students know how to complete the learning tasks, and the learning objectives and contents of the course. This OBE-based teaching philosophy, or results-oriented concept, allows students to focus on "what has been learned" rather than "what has been taught" in the traditional sense. [2] The ability and technology that students can substitute for the actual work post after graduation. The teaching system focuses on students' learning tasks, major Settings and career goals, and strengthens the cultivation of their comprehensive abilities. "Staff Career Development" is a professional elective course for junior students majoring in Human Resource Management. The goal of the course is to cultivate students' ability in self-career development planning and future talent development and career guidance.

2.1 The Pain Points

At present, the pain points encountered in the course teaching are as follows:

- Students have insufficient cognition of the significance of curriculum.
- Students feel that they have already learned planning courses in their freshman year and are not clear about the significance and necessity of this course;
- This course is an elective course, and students attach less importance to it than other compulsory courses.
- Lack of relevant professional course authoritative textbooks;
- There are few professional practice activities, students' social practice experience is limited, there are not enough enterprise cases in diversified scenarios, and students are not confident in the ability of theoretical practice and the transferability of learning;
- Students have not learned Data Analysis courses before and lack Data Analysis ability, which cannot be used as pre-skills to support the study of Data Analysis Module in this course.
- Traditional teaching methods can't meet the differentiated needs of students, lack of high-level ability training, and free riding behavior still exists in the process of intra group cooperation.

2.2 Teaching Reform Ideas

Based on the above analysis of learning situation, teachers adhere to the teaching philosophy of achievement oriented, project driven, heuristic teaching and "student-centered development", adopt flipped classroom in the teaching process, guide students to carry out cross group autonomous and cooperative learning, embed data thinking into some chapters of the course, and pay attention to the cultivation of students' high-level ability and the integration of interdisciplinary knowledge, reconstruct students' learning experience and enhance their sense of immersion, interaction and acquisition in the learning process.

3 Practical Application

Experiential learning needs to closely link the tasks required by the career itself, pay attention to building the learning experience into the learners' psychological structure, and support learners to obtain spiritual inspiration and knowledge sublimation. [3] Therefore, the author takes the needs of future work scenes as the starting point, carries out data analysis on the vocational skill requirements of human resources management, and guides students to start practical application and knowledge transformation on the basis of self-study video recording.

3.1 The Teacher Does Data Analysis and Display to Stimulate Students' Interest.

Taking the employment of this major as an example, teachers collect, process and analyze more than 300 recruitment postings of Human Resource Management specialty on Zhilian Recruitment Website. Among them, a complete text analysis is made for the job description in the market demand analysis, and a visual display is carried out in the form of graphics and text, which greatly stimulates the students' learning enthusiasm. They saw that all the data were displayed in the form of bubble chart, histogram, word cloud chart and so on, and showed a strong interest in learning Data Analysis. At the same time, according to the feedback of previous graduates, teachers gave feedback on the suggestions of curriculum, so that students can see the correlation between workplace needs and curriculum (Figs. 1, 2 and 3).

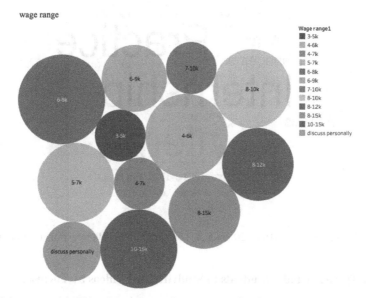

Fig. 1. Salary range bubble chart of recruitment posts in Human Resources Management (According to the original data of Zhilian recruitment website)

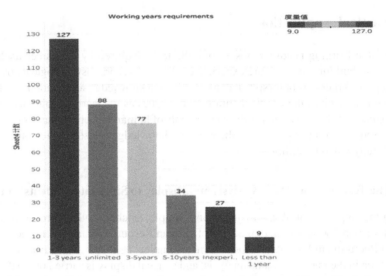

Fig. 2. Histogram of job experience requirements for recruitment posts (According to the original data of Zhilian recruitment website)

Fig. 3. Suggestions of 2016–2020 graduates on curriculum and professional skill training

3.2 The Teacher Guides Students to Study Record Videos by Themselves

The process of data crawling, processing and analysis is recorded, with a total length of 53 min. It is placed in the data area of learning pass for students to study and view at any time. They can carry out various operations such as fast forward, backward and double speed according to their own learning progress and habits, so as to meet the differentiated learning needs of students.

3.3 The Teacher Assigns Group Tasks

With the exploration of HR career direction as the theme, promote cross group cooperation, free combination between groups and independently determine the course. Perform the theme and prepare 20 min of special training materials after class.

3.4 Show What You Have Learned in Groups

Based on the data analysis knowledge learned, the group will conduct in-depth analysis and display of the topic, answer the questions of other group students, accept the comments of other group representatives, and complete the mutual evaluation between groups and within groups. The teacher will make a summary speech on the group performance and guide the students to conduct in-depth discussion and thinking.

4 Research Method and Measurement Result Display of Teaching Reform Effect

4.1 Literature Research Method

According to the research purpose and problems, the author collects, arranges and analyzes the relevant literature, and combs the existing research results in this research field. About the papers on students' learning experience, I consulted the relevant literature and had a further understanding of experiential teaching. In the 1980s, David, a professor of organizational behavior in the United States Cooper put forward the theory of experiential learning, It also summarizes the basic characteristics of experiential learning: "Experiential learning is a learning process, not a result; experiential learning is a continuous process based on experience; experiential learning is a process of resolving conflicts in a dialectical way; experiential learning is a complete process of adapting to the world; experiential learning is a process of continuous interaction between individuals and the environment; experiential learning is a process of creating knowledge." It can be seen that different from the traditional teaching which emphasizes teacher centered knowledge transmission, experiential teaching emphasizes student-centered autonomous learning, and advocates creating situations or opportunities related to the teaching content to guide students to understand and construct knowledge, develop ability, generate emotion and perceive meaning in the process of personal experience [4].

4.2 Experimental Research Method

In order to evaluate the effectiveness of data embedding in the course to improve students' learning experience and teaching effect, I mainly compare the teaching methods of two classes of different grades in different years, and reflect the differences of horizontal comparison in students' written feedback before, during and after the semester. Through the different satisfaction feedback of students, this paper reflects the different teaching effects of courses after data thinking is embedded, as well as the differences in students' learning ability and knowledge mastery and application ability.

4.3 Questionnaire Survey Method

The idea of questionnaire design is mainly based on the technology acceptance model (TAM) proposed by Davis in 1989, which is mainly used to study the acceptance and use tendency of respondents to new technologies, mainly including perceived ease of use (PEU), perceived usefulness (PU) Four research dimensions: user attitude (at) and behavioral intention (BI). Perceived ease of use refers to the ease users feel when operating new technologies; Perceived usefulness is the help of emerging technologies used by users to improve their daily life and academic performance; User attitude refers to a subjective feeling of users after using new technology, which can be like or dislike; Behavioral willingness is the urgency of users to actually use new technologies. In this study, four main research variables in the technology acceptance model are defined in order to understand the overall feeling of the research object after embedding data thinking into the curriculum and the behavioral willingness to continue to use Data analysis for professional curriculum learning: [5].

- Perceived ease of use refers to the degree of difficulty that the research object feels when using data analysis to solve problems.
- Perceived usefulness refers to the perceived degree of performance improvement and the applicability of future career needs when using data analysis.
- Use attitude refers to the degree to which the research object likes data analysis.
- Behavioral intention refers to the willingness of the research object to continuously use data analysis to solve problems.

In this paper, the students' learning experience is fed back through the questionnaire survey, to test students' perceived ease of use, perceived usefulness, use attitude and behavior intention of data analysis. The following is a screenshot of the data feedback from the questionnaire survey of the current course after the data analysis is embedded in the course teaching module (Figs. 4, 5, 6, 7 and 8):

Question 1: what is your overall satisfaction with this course. [single choice]

选项	小计	比例
A.Very satisfied	57	32.57%
B. Satisfied	101	57.71%
C.Somewhat satisfied	16	9.14%
D.Not satisfied	1	0.57%
E.Very dissatisfied	0	0%
本题有效填写人次	175	

Fig. 4. Statistical screenshot of overall satisfaction with this course

Question 2: How easy do you think this course is to master. [single choice]

选项	小计	比例
A.Easy to master	16	9.14%
B.Relatively easy	102	58.29%
C.Easy	50	28.57%
D. Difficult	6	3.43%
E.Very Difficult	1	0.57%
本题有效填写人次	175	

Fig. 5. Screenshot of feedback statistics on the difficulty of this course

Question 3: Do you want teachers to embed data analysis in future teaching? [single choice]

选项	小计	比例
A.Very much hope	75	42.86%
B.Hope	89	50.86%
C.Indifferent	9	5.14%
D.Not hope	2	1.14%
E.Really not hope	0	0%
本题有效填写人次	175	

Fig. 6. Statistical screenshot of intention value embedded in future data

Question 4: If the teacher guides you, are you willing to try to analyze the problem with data? [single choice]

选项	小计	比例
A.Very willing	73	41.71%
B.willing	94	53.71%
C.Indifferent	6	3.43%
D.Not Willing	2	1.14%
E.Very reluctant	0	0%
本题有效填写人次	175	

Fig. 7. Statistical screenshot of willingness value of future data analysis problems.

Question 5: In the following courses, which special training do you prefer to listen to in the professional module?

选项	小计	比例
A.HRBP	144	82.29%
B.Recruitment	108	61.71%
C.Human Resource Outsourcing	91	52%
D.Headhunters	82	46.86%
E.Flexible Employment	95	54.29%
F.I would like to add_____	3	1.71%
本题有效填写人次	175	

Fig. 8. Statistical screenshots of special training you want to hear in subsequent courses

Question 6: what other suggestions and feedback do you have for this course? [fill in the blanks]

According to the questionnaire survey, we can see that the vocabulary of students' feedback is mainly positive words and sentences such as "happy, excited, sense of gain, high support and hope that teachers can continue this teaching mode". Some screenshots are as follows (Fig. 9):

Fig. 9. Cloud chart of curriculum evaluation words sorted out according to the text feedback of middle school students in the questionnaire survey

5   Conclusions, Contributions and Limitations

5.1   Research Conclusion

- The embedding of data thinking provides direction for the teaching reform of professional courses.

The author adopts flipped classroom and project-based teaching mode, which makes students have a strong sense of acquisition. Through the curriculum teaching reform of data embedding, students' satisfaction, participation and interest in the curriculum have been significantly improved, and their multiple feedbacks to the curriculum are positive. They are also full of expectations for teachers to embed data thinking into other courses in the future.

- Portrait analysis of students is conducive to more targeted teaching.

Teachers' introduction of data thinking in the teaching process is equivalent to adding data-driven to the teaching reform. Teachers guide students to conduct quantitative analysis, which is a necessary supplement to the traditional qualitative analysis thinking. Teachers collect and sort out students' learning data. The accumulation in a certain period of time will be conducive to data statistics, portrait analysis of students [7], and learning prediction and intervention for different types of students, so as to make teaching more targeted, and also help to formulate the whole teaching plan and implement personalized counseling.

- The analysis and collation of data is conducive to the realization of teaching and learning.

The establishment of students' autonomous learning environment from the perspective of data-driven is conducive to further cultivate students' learning initiative and inquiry, actively respond to and feed back teachers' teaching content, and realize the purpose of teaching and learning.

- A comprehensive learning evaluation system is conducive to promoting students' learning experience.

The Teacher establishes a comprehensive student learning evaluation system, guide students to carry out student student interaction and group learning, promote students' whole process participation and cooperation, and enhance their practical ability and learning transferable ability.

5.2   Contributions

The teaching reform of this course focuses on students' experience in the learning process and emphasizes student-centered. At present, the teaching effect is good. This also provides support and reference for the construction of professional curriculum group and curriculum system in the future, and provides support for the cultivation of compound professionals.

5.3   Limitations of the Study

- At present, there are only two rounds of teaching process, so the teaching reform needs to be further explored;
- Embedding Data Analysis into the course is still the first attempt at present, which should be further promoted in the future;
- The comparative analysis between classes can only be done vertically, not horizontally, which will have a certain sample error;
- In addition to the theoretical teaching of data analysis, it also needs to be analyzed in combination with the actual cases of enterprises to meet the diversified employment needs of future students.

References

1. Shan, X.: Research on the construction and application of personalized learning environment in secondary vocational schools from the perspective of data-driven, Master's thesis of Zhejiang University of technology, pp. 1–3 (2020)
2. Feng, Q.: Research on the cultivation of applied talents under OBE education mode. J. Anhui Univ. Eng. **33**(3), 125 (2016)
3. Yang, X., Luo, J., Liu, Y., Chen, S.: Data driven teaching: a new trend of teaching paradigm in the era of big data. Journal **12**(296), 13 (2017)
4. Xing, Y., Lu, B.: Exploration of student themed experiential teaching mode - from knowledge to wisdom, research on higher engineering education. Journal **5**, 122–123 (2016)
5. Chen, J.: Research on the construction of adaptive learning framework and system design for online education, Master's thesis of Northeast Normal University, pp. 38–40 (2021)
6. Li, H.: Research on learner emotion analysis model for learning experience text. J. Distance Educ. J. **1**(261), 94–95 (2021)
7. Xia, X., Ma, Y.: Research on personalized learning guidance strategy based on student portrait. J. Heilongjiang Ecol. Eng. Vocat. Coll. **33**(3), 125–126 (2020)

How Should We Educate User Experience Designers (UXD) in Order to Design and Develop Effective Online Learning Platforms? - A Teaching and Learning Framework -

Angeiki Tevekeli(⊠) ⓘ

Royal Institute of Technology [KTH], Stockholm, Sweden
tevekeli@kth.se

Abstract. Online learning platforms are used on a daily basis by a variety of stakeholders. Students, educators, administration officers, IT departments, learning experience designers but also design and development teams are engaged with online learning platforms for a different scope and need, through a different space and individual perspective. Studies show that the effectiveness of the platforms is questioned from a pedagogical and a user experience point of view. Is it possible that the educational background of the user experience designer involved in the design process affects the effectiveness of the platform as well as the user and learning experience?

Keywords: User experience designer · UXD threshold concepts · Online learning platforms · UXD curriculum · UXD signature pedagogies · Effective online learning application design · Effective pedagogical user experience · UXD definition

1 Objective

The objective of this paper is to answer the following research question: *"How should we educate User Experience Designers in order to design and develop effective online learning platforms?"* It focuses on what effective online learning platform means to different users and examines if there is a connection between the effectiveness and the educational background of the user experience designer. It proposes a redefinition of the user experience designer's curriculum by providing a teaching and learning framework for educators and learners.

2 Introduction

User experience designers (UXD) are asked to create experiences for a variety of products and services in the industry. Designing user experience of online learning platforms requires different handling from the design and development team as well as a deeper

© The Author(s), under exclusive license to Springer Nature Switzerland AG 2022
M. M. Soares et al. (Eds.): HCII 2022, LNCS 13322, pp. 322–336, 2022.
https://doi.org/10.1007/978-3-031-05900-1_22

understanding of pedagogy starting from the user research process and moving throughout the implementation phase. *Does the education provided and obtained during the UXD field studies provide sufficient knowledge and background to support all the spectrum and variety of industry needs and demands? Are designers prepared to design effective online learning experiences?* This study proves there is need for further specialization of the user experience designers working on the design process of educational platforms and focuses on the UXD curriculum design by providing a teaching and learning framework under which educators can give a specialized learning experience to their students while on the other hand gives learners the opportunity to examine areas that are very important for their professional development.

UXD practice combines a series of disciplines as 'designers have become applied behavioral scientists' (Why Design Education Must Change - Core77 n.d.). This complexity reflects to the curriculum of future designers. Students need to understand in depth human behavior, psychology, culture, business, marketing, sales and all these in combination with excellent computational skills while at the same time educators '.. use collaborative digital communication in their teaching to mirror their professional technology environment' (Chick et al. 2012). At the same time technology evolves rapidly, devices upgrade and users adapt to these changes every day. UX designers are called to think upfront and the industry demands constant professional development. *How up to date is the curriculum in regards to the industry? Do institutes invest in updating the content of the education provided?* 'Their signature pedagogies must measure up to the standards not just of the academy, but also of the particular profession' and students must understand the discipline they will practice in depth by identifying, analyzing, criticizing, accepting and discarding knowledge (Shulman 2005). In disciplines like HCI and UX Design where there is immediate effect on humans, signature pedagogies and threshold concepts must be constantly evaluated and re-defined as there is a 'radical transformation in their identity and scope' (Mitchell et al. 2019).

During the period of the Covid-19 pandemic institutes worldwide used a variety of online learning platforms. The effectiveness of online learning platforms has been globally questioned (Progga et al. 2020; Gismalla et al. 2021; Kalansooriya and Gamage 2021). Stakeholders involved are dissatisfied with the online learning platforms and studies prove that the existing ones do not cover educational needs nor do they offer an effective online learning (Ali 2020). Therefore, the need for designing and developing new ones based on pedagogical needs is an emergency. Educating user experience designers to develop effective online learning applications is a crucial step of the process.

3   Methodology

This study has been carried out through studies of literature, qualitative and experimental methods. Qualitative methods concerned interviews with UX practitioners, HR managers and recruiters, a contextual inquiry with students and educators and an exploratory focus group. An experiment was also conducted between 6 UX designers. Empirical knowledge has also been applied as the author practices and teaches design for more than 25 years.

Context of Research

During the Covid-19 pandemic lectures in HE were given remotely. A variety of stakeholders had to use systematically the Learning Management Systems available. The use became a daily necessity and stakeholders became active users of systems they rarely used pre-pandemic. Learning experience mingled with user experience and soon many problems emerged. The author, as a user of these platforms herself but also as a UXD practitioner and researcher realized that these problems require further investigation and started this research in May 2020.

Part of this study examined Canvas, Blackboard and Moodle LMS. 'Currently, the number of LMS users worldwide is estimated at 73.8 million' with 51% of the users talking about poor user experience (*51 LMS Statistics: 2019/2020 Data, Trends & Predictions* 2020). The author explored from a User Experience Design perspective why this is happening and made a hypothesis that the educational background of the user experience designer influences the end user's experience.

4   Data Collection

4.1   Semi-structured Interviews and Discussions

36 semi-structured interviews with UXD practitioners, HR managers and recruiters, were conducted in order to better understand the status of the educational background of user experience designers in the industry as well as the job and role description of a UXD.

In specific:

20 UXD practitioners were interviewed separately through Skype, Teams and Zoom.

4 h Managers were interviewed in person.

12 recruiters were interviewed through the LinkedIn platform.

The main interview questions are listed below and further discussion was conducted when the author felt there was more information to retrieve:

a) What is the job description of a User Experience Designer?
b) According to your knowledge what is the status in 2021 in regards to the educational background of user experience designers in the industry?
c) What does the industry demand from a user experience designer in regards to their educational background?

The following question was asked only to the 20 UXD practitioners.

iv) Have you noticed a difference in the user experience design approach from practitioners coming from different educational backgrounds?

4.2 Contextual Inquiry (Educators and Students Using LMS)

In order to investigate and understand what effective online learning platform is for the stakeholders involved, the researcher conducted contextual inquiry with 4 educators and 4 students from different disciplines while using Canvas, Blackboard and Moodle. All students were in their early 20 s and belong to the 'digital natives' while on the other hand the educators were between the ages of 45–55 and belong to the 'digital immigrants' (Prensky 2001).

4.3 Experiment and Exploratory Focus Group

Experiment
Experimental research enables the identification of casual relationships. 'A hypothesis is a precise problem statement that can be tested through an empirical investigation' (Lazar 2017). The hypothesis for this research is as follows:

H0 = The educational background of the user experience designer affects the user experience and the effectiveness of online learning platforms.

H1 = The educational background of the user experience designer doesn't affect the user experience and the effectiveness of online learning platforms.

An experiment was conducted. 6 designers from different educational backgrounds, same age group (35–49), different sex, same nationality, all actively working as UX Designers in the industry were given the same brief via email. They were asked to design high-fidelity wireframes for the Home Page of a Learning Management System and the Home Page of a course within the LMS. Wireframes are fast, easy and cheap to design and they facilitate the communication between stakeholders, users and designers. The brief explained that the product would be used in Higher Education from a variety of stakeholders e.g. educators, students, administration officers even IT departments. The thematic for the landing course page was free of choice.

Control
Each individual UX designer worked alone, using their preferred tools, in their own space and time frame. As all of them are busy professionals they were kindly asked to deliver the wireframes within a months' timeframe. They had no access to the other designer's work nor did they know who the other designers were. The wireframes were printed and given to the author of this paper in a closed envelope. They were opened for the first time on the day the focus group took place. This research has no intention of diminishing or insulting any of the designer's background discipline or creativity, therefore coding using numbers has been given to each set of the wireframes e.g. Designer#1 handed in Envelope #1 which includes the wireframe set coded W#1. There was no reference on the designer's educational background or identity to any of the participants involved in the exploratory focus group.

Exploratory Focus Group
'Descriptive investigations such as focus groups focus on constructing an accurate description of what is happening' (Lazar 2017) therefore the deliverables were shown and

discussed in an exploratory focus group where 3 educators and 3 students participated. The envelopes were presented to the participants as described above. Each envelope contained 6 copies of each wireframe, one set of copies for each participant.

5 Data Analysis

The qualitative data from the interviews, discussions and contextual inquiry were analyzed via a combination of thematic analysis (Braun and Clarke 2006), In Vivo for highlighting the participants words in quotation marks, emotion and pattern coding (Saldaña 2021). For the experiment the author used a) the analytic reflection memo approach (Saldaña 2021) for the discussion and briefing of the user experience designers up to the point they handed in the wireframes and b) a combination of thematic analysis and versus coding (Saldaña 2021) for the exploratory focus group (Goodman et al. 2012).

6 Results

6.1 Semi-structured Interviews and Discussions

From the discussions and interviews with the UXD practitioners, the HR Managers and Recruiters it was obvious that there is confusion between the job descriptions and definitions of a User Experience Designer (UXD), a User Experience Researcher (UXR) and a User Interface Designer (UID). Apparently, there are companies which occupy/hire the same person for the positions of the UXR and the UXD and in some cases the same person supports the interface design (UID) as well. Most of the interviewees reported that during the past 5–7 years new job roles have arisen with no clear understanding of the job description; Product Designer, UXD Strategist, UX Lead, Content Strategist, UX Unicorn (Siang n.d.), UX Manager, UX Writer, Service Designer, Chief Experience Officer and more new titles arise constantly in the UX field. This variety of roles makes it really difficult for hiring managers to identify the proper candidate for a job. On the other hand, user experience designers looking for a job find it difficult to identify if the job offer is suitable for their skills. *Is a person educated for all these roles? Is it possible to support the job? How does a curriculum cover these demands?* Some of the UXD practitioners reported they *"never stop studying as they feel that if they do so they will stay out of market"* while others mentioned they *"feel as if they have lost their professional identity due to the confusion from the title variety, uncertain job specification and demand in the industry".*

HR managers reported that during the past few years, and especially during the burst of the Covid-19 pandemic where remote work was globally applied, a variety of already build applications and platforms were used broadly in all markets. The need for remote work and tools to support it brought a huge demand on user experience designers worldwide. Salaries varying from $16.050 to $105.122 (Fitz-Patrick n.d.) attract individuals who either seek for a career change or look for an increase in their income. A the same time, as UXD practitioners mentioned, companies who understand the importance of user experience build in-house departments sometimes using their existing stuff. Due to all of the above mentioned reasons, a frantic creation of fast online UXD courses has been globally developed from various organizations and institutes, with a fee per course, an annual subscription or company contract. These certifications are addressed to all, as there are no specifications or limitations on the background of the attendees. The result is a huge influx from various disciplines in the UXD field. *"If you own the certification you are eligible to apply for a position"* one of the HR Managers reported. Another one mentioned that *"it is highly recommended and trendy to take these courses and when finished publish them in business and employment platforms in order to be traceable by recruiters and companies seeking for personnel"*. So anyone with a certificate of this kind is considered as a UX Designer from the recruiting agencies and can proceed to an interview in companies seeking for one. *Who makes the final decision though? What happens when there are no UX experts in the company? What if the company wishes to create a new UX department? Who decides on the UX design suitability of this person in this case? What kind of portfolio do these applicants show?* This influx as well as the field background distribution and educational level percentage is depicted in Fig. 1 where 10% from field areas like Biology, Mathematics, Geology, Business and Marketing work as user experience designers. All individuals of the 10% hold certifications in UXD, UI, User Research Methods, Design Thinking and other similar online UXD courses. *Do these courses provide adequate knowledge and experience for e.g. a mathematician to be hired and considered a user experience designer?*

The forth question was only asked to the 20 UXD practitioners. 15 mentioned they have noticed a difference in the UXD software used but this is fixed by internal training, 4 mentioned they have noticed a difference in the selection of the design process e.g. Double Diamond or Google Design Sprint and this stems from the fact that the specific designers have been trained to practice these methods in *"fast food courses where you*

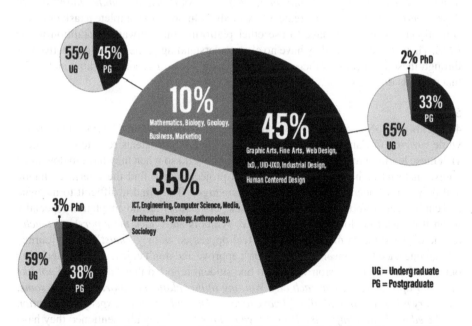

Fig. 1. Chart depicting **background field distribution** of individuals working as UXDs

become a UXD in 40 h or by taking a series of online courses". One of the UX Leads mentioned that they have recently hired a UXD who had just finished a PhD in HCI and had never worked in the industry before but found it difficult to change his mindset from academia to industry. *"We usually avoid hiring people with a PhD as we have noticed that they don't adapt easily to the fast pace of industry, especially in design"*.

6.2   Contextual Inquiry

Educators

4 educators were observed and interviewed in regards to their user and teaching experience while working in the Canvas and Blackboard LMS. The educators reported that both LMS don't satisfy their needs. They are not happy with the user experience. The interface is confusing as there is too much information that they never use. There are too many different menus and they feel insecure in navigating in all the sections as they fear that they will enter areas they are not eligible to. There is no option for personalization and adaptation. There is no live help and support. The help option provides a video course and a link to ask for help filling in an online form which they never use. The major problem is space; the design space they are offered is limited as there is so much information on the general courses and the departmental announcements. There is no clear structure on where the information they will create will appear. All 4 reported that they never use the Learning Analytics Dashboards (LAD) offered as they don't understand the visualization of the data and how to interpret it. Pedagogically these platforms don't support the way they would like to teach, *"I'd rather send all the files via e-mail to my students than use tools that none of the two sides use and understand"* one of them reported while trying to create a new module. In order to complete a task or create educational content they have to use other platforms and software in addition to the LMS. They all mentioned they have no clear understanding of the learning effectiveness through these platforms as there are no diagnostic tools or reports to show and prove that students do learn.

Students

4 students were observed and interviewed in regards to their user and learning experience while working in Canvas, Blackboard and Moodle LMS. Students reported they rarely visit these learning management systems. They only do so when they have to download course material or hand in assignments and projects. They find the interface chaotic and they don't understand the *"interface language"*. They find it difficult to navigate and can't access information easily. They lack personalization and adaptation especially when it comes to color, scheme, language, symbols and *"lack their personal touch"* as one of the students mentioned. They feel oppressed as they *"must"* take a journey into an interface they haven't chosen, don't approve and don't enjoy. A very interesting outcome from the discussion was when one student reported that *"the LMS is not like the other applications I use each day. Working in this platform is boring and tiresome, like every other learning platform I have to use"*. *Do students have a specific perception for the educational platforms? How do we change this?* They all mentioned they have the feeling that *"the teacher is not present"*, that there is no creative interactivity, no

excitement and no motivation for learning, *"this is not education; this is navigation through an impersonal platform looking for content"*. In order to complete a task or an assignment they need to use other platforms or software in addition to the LMS. They *"feel as if they aren't students"* when they log into the learning management system, *"they just feel users"* and *"it's more of an obligation than an exciting procedure"*. So how do we connect the student with the user in a creative and exciting way? How do we design effective learning experiences adapted to each end user's needs and particularities? What does *"interface language"* mean to each stakeholder involved?

The analysis of the discussion of this phase of the research provided further understanding on what effective learning means and how user experience is perceived and change depending on the lens and needs of each of the participants. The results are depicted in Table 1.

Table 1. Participant's perception of effectiveness

P#1	P#2	P#3	P#4	P#5	P#6
Ease of use	Accessible	Find information easily	Usable	Appropriate	Memorable
Freedom of choice	Technical help	Inclusive	Easy to understand	Ease of use	Autonomous
Adaptation	Appropriate	Support	Manageable	Different	Modern
Inclusive	Respect uniqueness	Personalized	Easy language	Clever	Ease of use
Memorable	Motivating	Creative solutions	Understandable symbols	Up to date	Exciting
Needed	Flexible	Empty space	Adaptable	Personalized	Inclusive

6.3   Experiment and Exploratory Focus Group

Designers

In this section the results from two different axons are presented. The first axon presents how the designers handled the project from the briefing stage to the wireframes delivery. The author kept an analytic reflection memo for the communication between the designers who participated in the experiment and her. Designer #4 and #6 requested more information about the project after the briefing document was sent and discussed. They asked for an extended analysis of the stakeholders' background, details of the course learning outcomes, learning methodology and more information on what the users find ineffective from the experiences with the LMS so far. Designer #2 and #3 were concerned about the technical aspect of the deliverables. They asked if they could use templates from an image bank and if they could only hand in the electronic version of the wireframes.

Exploratory Focus Group Findings

The second axon of this stage of the research refers to the exploratory focus group findings. The reaction to the 6 wireframe versions was different from all participants. There was a difference in the wireframe element positioning, feature choice, navigation, user journey, usability, personalization option. This triggered a variety of reactions in the focus group attendants which lead to the conclusion that indeed different educational backgrounds design user experience differently.

First of all, the participants were asked to examine each printed set of wireframes thoroughly and navigate through the printed layouts like they would if they were in front of a screen. They were then asked to add a red + (plus) symbol in the elements they found usable or a blue − (minus) symbol in elements they didn't. If the + were more than the - then a + symbol was added in Table 2. If the + and the - were equal then an asterisk * was added. This is how the participants evaluated the effectiveness of the 6 sets of wireframes.

Table 2. Wireframe effectiveness evaluation

	W1 D#1	W2 D#2	W3 D#3	W4 D#4	W5 D#5	W6 D#6
Educator #1	−	+	−	−	−	+
Educator #2	+	−	−	+	+	*
Educator #3	+	*	−	−	−	+
Student #1	−	−	−	+	−	+
Student #2	+	−	+	+	−	+
Student #3	−	+	−	+	−	+

So what makes Wireframe #6 and Wireframe #4 stand out? According to participants both wireframes were *"friendly"*, *"there was no confusion"*, *"easy navigation"*, and in W6 which was characterized as the most effective of all, *"there was space for personal touch and options to organize the space as they wished"* through personalization and adaptation in a set up page that none of the other versions had. Additionally, a profile page gave users a set of options for *"cultural adjustment"*. By cultural adjustment they referred to scheme selection, background color change, font family selection, font size selection and the option of adjusting what would appear in your home page, a selection of themes, A chat for support was always there and a custom avatar was there to accompany the learning journey by interacting with the students and helping with notifications, deadlines, links to libraries and many more options. W6 was *"creative"*, *"fresh"*, *"memorable"*, *"usable"*, *"friendly"* and *"exciting"* for all.

7 Teaching and Learning Framework

In order to develop the framework the identification of the threshold concepts through this research is of great importance. Also, defining the signature pedagogies for UXD education is also a necessity for a framework. Signature pedagogies show how students should be taught in order to be able to face the real world.

7.1 Identifying UXD Threshold Concepts and Signature Pedagogies for the Design of Effective Online Learning Platforms

The analysis from this study provided an understanding of the UXD threshold concepts, the 'building blocks' (Meyer and Land 2005) and 'action poetry' (Perkins 1999) of the education of a user experience designer as these lead to the progressive understanding of the subject through 'troublesome' (Perkins 1999) and 'transformative knowledge' (Meyer and Land 2005). These identified threshold concepts are depicted in Fig. 2. From the pattern coding of this study it is obvious that users perceive experience differently according to their needs. Notions like *"memorable"*, *"exciting"*, *"tiresome"* are repeated in different stages of this research from different participants in a different context, so for example while someone may find the experience *"exciting"* because they were offered a personalization option another one may describe the personalization experience as *"tiresome"*. This brings user experience in the intersection of the potentially troublesome and transformative threshold concepts as depicted in Fig. 2 and gives more food for thought to the designers.

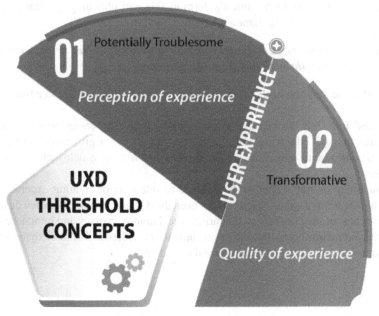

Fig. 2. UXD threshold concepts

As 'learners must cross the threshold to move their thinking in the subject area forward' (Hill 2010) threshold concept criteria play a significant role in the design of the UXD curriculum for specialization on pedagogical user experience design. While *'signature pedagogies that bridge theory and practice are never simple, and experiences of teaching and learning can influence the values, dispositions and characters of the future professional'* (Shulman 2005), reconsidering the way user experience designers are educated will determine the success and effectiveness of the product, system or service they design. Further specialization either through the field studies' curriculum or through specialized certificates is important especially when it comes to the design and development of platforms for 'key' areas like education.

7.2 Experience and Effectiveness

According to Alben (1996) the quality of experience depends on the effective design process. Even though effectiveness is one of the five criteria for usability and is described as *'the completeness and accuracy with which users achieve specified goals successfully'* (Quesenbery 2001) user experience design in the sense of a positive human computer interaction would focus on how to create outstanding quality experiences rather than merely preventing usability problems (Hassenzahl and Tractinsky 2006).

7.3 Redefining the Term User Experience Designer

The results from this study prove there is confusion of the term User Experience Designer and a misunderstanding of the description of the role in the industry therefore the author finds it important to try to redefine the term as this will play an important role in the development of the learning framework.

A user experience designer creates consciously or not perceived or imperceptible memory imprints through any form of interaction.

In a short description of this term, which I wish to further analyze in a future paper:

- **'creates'** hides all the creative thinking and creative processes which a designer acquires through education and experience, but also as a gift, as creativity is also an inherent quality and it cannot be absent from a term which includes the word designer.
- **'consciously or not'** explains the purpose or intention of creating experiences but also the creation of experiences that not even the designer thought of when designing. It describes all the phenomena that arise as technology evolves and humans change.
- **'perceived or imperceptible'** refers on how users understand or not experiences and it contains all the senses, the known and unknown.

- **'memory imprints'** refer to experiences with a broader meaning as there are no experiences without memory.
- **'any form of interaction'** refers to tangible or not, known or unknown forms of interaction.

7.4 So How Should We Educate User Experience Designers (UXD) in Order to Design and Develop Effective Online Learning Platforms? - A Teaching and Learning Framework -

The following framework depicted in Figs. 3 and 4 is a result of the analysis of the data from this research. In Fig. 3, which is based on the revised version of Bloom's taxonomy (Bloom 1956; Krathwohl 2002; Sosniak 1994), the **factual, conceptual, procedural** and **meta cognitive knowledge** (Wilson and Leslie n.d.) of the UXD curriculum is depicted.

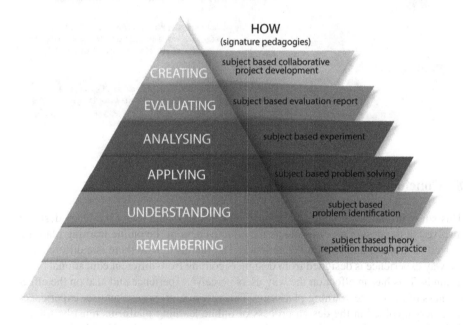

Fig. 3. Factual, conceptual, procedural and meta cognitive knowledge (Wilson and Leslie n.d.) of the UXD curriculum

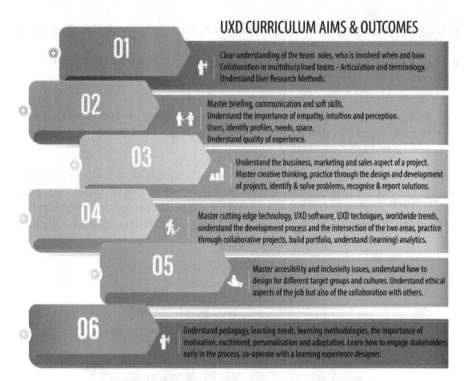

Fig. 4. UXD curriculum – Aims and Outcomes

8   Conclusion and Discussion

This study investigated if the educational background of the user experience designer involved in the design process affects the effectiveness of the online learning platform as well as the user and learning experience. The findings prove there is a difference in the way experience is designed from designers coming from different educational backgrounds. This has an effect on the way users perceive experience and also on the effectiveness of the online learning platforms. This research proposes that user experiences designers involved in the design process of online learning platforms must be trained following a specialized curriculum and proposes a teaching and learning framework for this reason.

Further studies should concern the importance of personalization and adaptation of online learning platforms as humans learn and teach in different ways and user's perception of experience varies. The development of diagnostic and evaluation frameworks for learning management systems and learning analytics dashboards is also a necessity.

Acknowledgments. I would like to thank all the participants in all the stages of this study for their time, effort and support. Their contribution is highly appreciated and valuable.

Research Ethics. For every stage of the research, informed consent was given to all the participants. The informed consent included information on:

- the study cause, description, and aim
- the stage of the study they are involved in
- their data handling and safety
- their right to withdraw and what it entails
- myself as the principal investigator and my contact details

The study was compliant with GDPR rules and COVID-19 safety measures.

References

51 LMS Statistics: 2019/2020 Data, Trends & Predictions. Research.com (2020). https://research. com/education/lms-statistics. Accessed 28 Oct 2021

Ali, W.: Online and remote learning in higher education institutes: a necessity in light of COVID-19 pandemic. High. Educ. Stud. **10**(3), 16 (2020). https://doi.org/10.5539/hes.v10n3p16

Mitchell, V., et al.: Digital touch experiences: educating the designers (2019). https://repository. lboro.ac.uk/articles/conference_contribution/Digital_touch_experiences_Educating_the_des igners/9339482/1. Accessed 20 Oct 2021

Perkins, D.: The many faces of constructivism. Educ. Leadersh. **57**(3), 6–11 (1999)

Quesenbery, W.: What Does Usability Mean: Looking Beyond "Ease of Use", p. 8 (n.d.)

Saldaña, J.: The Coding Manual for Qualitative Researchers. SAGE Publications Ltd. (2021)

Siang, T.Y.: The Ultimate Guide to Understanding UX Roles and Which One You Should Go For, The Interaction Design Foundation (n.d.). https://www.interaction-design.org/literature/article/ the-ultimate-guide-to-understanding-ux-roles-and-which-one-you-should-go-for. Accessed 27 Oct 2021

Meyer, J.H.F., Land, R.: Threshold concepts and troublesome knowledge (2): epistemological considerations and a conceptual framework for teaching and learning. High. Educ. **49**(3), 373–388 (2005). https:/doi.org/10.1007/s10734-004-6779-5

Bloom, B.: Bloom's taxonomy (1956)

Hill, S.: Troublesome knowledge: why don't they understand?. Health Inf. Libr. J. **27**(1), 80–83 (2010) https://doi.org/10.1111/j.1471-1842.2010.00880.x

Prensky, M.: Digital natives, digital immigrants part 2: do they really think differently? On the Horizon **9**(6), 1–6 (2001). https://doi.org/10.1108/10748120110424843

Alben, L.: 'Defining the Criteria for Effective Interaction Design', p. 5 (1996)

Braun, V., Clarke, V.: Using thematic analysis in psychology. Qual. Res. Psychol. **3**(2), 77–101 (2006). https://doi.org/10.1191/1478088706qp063oa

Wilson, L.O., Leslie, C.: 'Anderson and Krathwohl Bloom's Taxonomy Revised', p. 7 (n.d.)

Shulman, L.S.: Signature pedagogies in the professions. Daedalus **134**(3), 52–59 (2005). https:// doi.org/10.1162/0011526054622015

Chick, N.L., et al.: Exploring More Signature Pedagogies: Approaches to Teaching Disciplinary Habits of Mind. Stylus Publishing, LLC, Sterling (2012). http://ebookcentral.proquest.com/lib/ ucreative-ebooks/detail.action?docID=911875. Accessed 1 Nov 2020

Fitz-Patrick, M.: 10 Reasons to Become a UX Designer in 2022. The Interaction Design Foundation (n.d.). https://www.interaction-design.org/literature/article/10-reasons-to-become-a-ux-designer-in-2022. Accessed 7 Feb 2022

Sosniak, L.A.: Bloom's taxonomy. Anderson, L.W. (ed.). Univ. Chicago Press, USA (1994)

Why Design Education Must Change - Core77 (n.d.). https://www.core77.com/posts/17993/why-design-education-must-change-17993. Accessed 1 Nov 2020

Gismalla, M.D.-A., et al.: Medical students' perception towards online learning during COVID 19 pandemic in a high burden developing country. BMC Med. Educ. **21**(1), 377 (2021). https://doi.org/10.1186/s12909-021-02811-8

Goodman, E., Kuniavsky, M., Moed, A.: Analyzing qualitative data. In: Observing the User Experience. Elsevier (2012), pp. 423–451. https://doi.org/10.1016/B978-0-12-384869-7.00015-2

Hassenzahl, M., Tractinsky, N.: User experience - a research agenda. Behav. Inf. Technol. **25**(2), 91–97 (2006). https://doi.org/10.1080/01449290500330331

Kalansooriya, P., Gamage, T.: An overview on massive open online courses (MOOCs) as an online learning platform: a review (2021). https://doi.org/10.13140/RG.2.2.29201.56164

Progga, F.T., Shahria, M.D.T., Ahmed, N.: The effectiveness and acceptance of collaborative online learning in the context of Bangladesh. In: 2020 IEEE International Conference on Teaching, Assessment, and Learning for Engineering (TALE). 2020 IEEE International Conference on Teaching, Assessment, and Learning for Engineering (TALE), pp. 554–558 (2020). https://doi.org/10.1109/TALE48869.2020.9368445

Krathwohl, D.R.: A revision of bloom's taxonomy: an overview. Theory Into Pract. **41**(4), 212–218 (2002). https://doi.org/10.1207/s15430421tip4104_2

Lazar, J.: Research Methods in Human-Computer Interaction, 2nd edn. Morgan Kaufmann Publishers, Cambridge (2017)

Research on Mixed Teaching Scheme of Human Resource Management Tool Courses Based on Learning Experience

Meiying Wu[(✉)]

Guangzhou City University of Technology, No. 1 Xuefu Road, Huadu District, Guangzhou, Guangdong, China
meiying1746@163.com

Abstract. Due to the influence of COVID-19, mixed teaching has been widely carried out in various universities in China. Mixed teaching has the characteristics of convenience, exploration, interaction and individuation, which can enhance the learning effect and enhance the learning experience of students. Based on the relevant theories of learning experience and mixed teaching, this paper will sort out and analyze the research results of scholars in this field, take a human resource management tool course as an example, use the method of mixed teaching and make full use of the online teaching platform to design the teaching scheme of mixed courses in the three links before, during and after class. After the course, collect relevant data, analyze the changes of students' academic performance and students' teaching evaluation, quantitatively analyze the changes of mixed teaching design to learning experience, summarize the advantages of hybrid curriculum design of human resource management tool courses based on learning experience, and analyze the existing problems. This paper provides suggestions for further improving the learning experience from the aspects of the construction of curriculum database, the optimal design of teaching content and the transformation of students' learning concept.

Keywords: Learning experience · Mixed teaching · Human resource management tool courses

1 Introduction

In 2020, when COVID-19 suddenly broke out, the Ministry of education demanded that "suspend classes, stop learning and stop teaching", which led to the emergency reform of domestic teaching. The National University fronts organized the online teaching [1] with the largest scale, the largest number of on-line courses and the largest number of people in the shortest time.

The urgent need of teaching reform caused by force majeure poses a new challenge to the traditional teaching mode and teachers and students. A survey shows that before the epidemic, nearly 60% of students did not participate in online learning, and nearly 80% of teachers did not carry out online teaching [2].

M. M. Soares et al. (Eds.): HCII 2022, LNCS 13322, pp. 337–347, 2022.
https://doi.org/10.1007/978-3-031-05900-1_23

The traditional teaching mode is limited by time and space. It focuses on the "teaching" of teachers on the podium, supplemented by the "learning" of students on the seat. There is no personalized teaching for students' individual differences. Students' learning effects are uneven and their sense of learning experience is poor.

In the post epidemic era, hybrid teaching mode, as a more convenient, efficient and personalized teaching mode, will be accepted and adopted by teachers and students in colleges and universities on a large scale. Wu Yan, director of the Higher Education Department of the Ministry of education, pointed out at the 2020 National Conference of higher education directors and the working meeting of the Teaching Steering Committee of colleges and Universities: "we cannot and should not return to the state of teaching and learning before the outbreak of the epidemic" [3].

Different scholars have put forward their opinions on the advantages and characteristics of mixed teaching.

Tom Boyle believes that blended learning includes traditional classroom teaching learning and online learning [4].

Huang Zhen believes that hybrid teaching is a mixture of online teaching and classroom teaching. It not only makes full use of the advantages of online teaching to make online classroom an important channel for knowledge transfer, but also strengthens the face-to-face and offline classroom interaction between teachers and students, students and students, and a new teaching mode for knowledge exploration, speculation, interaction and practice [5].

Zhang Qian and others believe that the focus of hybrid teaching is not to care about the proportion of online and offline teaching, but to study how to integrate the two teaching methods and how to develop their strengths and avoid their weaknesses, so as to obtain better teaching results and promote students' learning [6].

It can be seen that the application of hybrid teaching mode can change learning from passive "subject knowledge centered" to active "student-centered learning experience". If students are in a passive state during learning, it will have an obvious negative impact on Teachers' teaching and learning effect [7]. Education should be "whole person" education, that is to promote individual "self-realization" and "self-transcendence". As the object of education, man is the unity of natural life, autonomy and creativity, and its essence is generation [8].

Hybrid teaching is a tool and a means. The purpose is to enhance students' sense of participation and experience in learning, so as to achieve the ultimate goal of education.

Many scholars have put forward their own opinions on the connotation of learning experience.

Taylor believes that curriculum learning experience refers to the experience and feelings students get around college curriculum learning inside and outside the classroom. Students' curriculum learning experience comes from their participation and investment in university curriculum teaching activities, which is the result of the interaction between teachers' teaching and students' learning [9].

Liu Bin and others believe that learning experience refers to the cognitive and emotional process and state generated in the process of learning with a certain tool or means from the perspective of learners, as well as the final cognitive and emotional results [10].

The glossary of education reform funded by the Nellie Mae Education Foundation gives a rough definition of learning experience: learning experience refers to the experience of students with courses, teaching activities, teaching interaction and learning environment in the learning process [11].

This paper will design the mixed teaching of human resource management tool courses, and analyze the influence and change of the mixed teaching mode on students' learning experience through data analysis.

2 Implementation Process of Hybrid Teaching

Human resource management tools course is a course closely combined with practice. Students learn this course well in college, which will be of great help to improve work efficiency and work quality after students enter the society. The design process of hybrid teaching scheme for human resource management tool courses is as follows (Fig. 1):

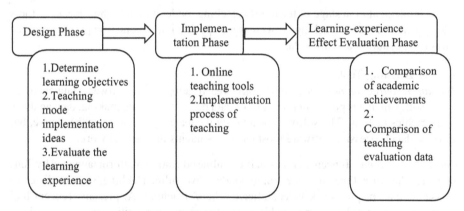

Fig. 1. A figure design process of hybrid teaching scheme

2.1 Design Phase

At this phase, we need to determine the objectives of hybrid teaching, the main implementation ideas and the methods to evaluate the learning experience.

Determine Learning Objectives
Students are the main body of cognition and the active constructors of knowledge meaning; Teachers are designers. The goal of this hybrid teaching is to build a learner centered teaching model, enhance students' learning experience and improve students' learning initiative and creativity.

Thoughts on the Implementation of Teaching Plan
During the epidemic period, online teaching was mainly used. On the basis of borrowing Internet tools, teachers designed mixed teaching according to existing resources,

and combined with the teaching mode of flipped classroom, designed teaching before, during and after class respectively. The teaching contents include: online video learning, case explanation, classroom homework, classroom discussion, question answering, after-school review, after-school interaction and other forms. Students are the main participants in all processes. Teachers are only responsible for providing video explanation, organizing discussion, answering questions and correcting homework, and returning the initiative of learning to students.

Assess Learning Experience
At the end of the course, the students' learning experience is evaluated by comparing the students' academic performance and the students' teaching evaluation results of teachers after the implementation of mixed teaching and before the implementation of mixed teaching.

2.2 Implementation Phase

In the implementation stage of the hybrid teaching mode, it mainly introduces the tools and software of online teaching, as well as the specific implementation process of three links before, during and after class.

Online Teaching Tools
Human resource management tool software. It adopts the software launched by Microsoft, which has powerful functions of data processing, table making, data analysis and graphics making. The software is not only the teaching software of the course, but also the data processing software most used by students in practical work.

Tencent classroom. Tencent classroom is an online education platform launched by Tencent. Teachers use Tencent classroom to conduct live online teaching, students listen to classes online, or play back videos after teachers' teaching. At present, Tencent hall has been widely used in online teaching in Colleges and universities. At the same time, Tencent classroom can supervise students' attendance, which can effectively make up for the disadvantage that online teaching can not supervise students.

QQ group. QQ group is a community chat software, which has the function of class group. The class group established through QQ allows teachers and students to have class discussion, answer questions, submit homework, correct homework, etc. on the group, with good interaction.

Superstar learning online learning platform. Superstar learning link software has many functions, such as course check-in, library book borrowing query, electronic resource search and download, library information browsing, video learning, live teaching, group discussion, online examination, course rush answer and so on. This teaching uses this platform for course check-in.

Implementation Process of Teaching
Based on the above internet teaching tools, the specific implementation process of hybrid teaching is as follows (Table 1):

Table 1. Implementation process of mixed teaching

Before class	Preview before class
During the class	Live video
	Interactive discussion
	Classroom Q &A
	Submit homework
After class	Review after class
	Internalized knowledge
	Learn in order to practice
	Expand and improve

Preview Before Class

Pre-class preview is an important part of mixed teaching and flipped classroom. According to their own needs and weaknesses, students learn relevant courses through online electronic resources and master relevant knowledge and skills in advance.

Learning and Interaction in Class

The teacher's explanation. For live teaching, teachers first teach the main knowledge points, supplemented by cases, so that students can be familiar with the important knowledge points in theory.

Student's practice. Give the initiative of learning to the students, and the students will complete the classroom exercises independently according to the important knowledge points explained by the teachers and the published cases.

Teacher & student interaction and discussion in class. In the process of practice, students with questions can ask questions in QQ group, be answered by teachers, or discuss with other students.

In this link, teachers can communicate with each student in real time, tutor students' existing problems, and solve students' personalized problems. At the same time, mutual discussion among students can promote the absorption and internalization of knowledge.

Consolidation After Class

Video review to consolidate review. The live video has the function of watching back. Students can watch back and review the video according to their actual needs, so as to improve the learning effect.

Internalization and promotion, learning for application. Human resources tools course is a practical course. After the course, teachers encourage students to use what they have learned in the future pre job internship and work after graduation, so as to improve work efficiency and truly apply what they have learned. At the same time, although the course is over, teachers and students keep in touch. Students can still keep in touch with teachers on practical issues of the course in the future. Teachers continue to track and coach students.

2.3 Evaluation of Learning Experience Effect

In this case, two indicators are selected as indicators to measure the effect of learning experience, namely examination results and teaching evaluation results. The survey was conducted by junior students. The number of students surveyed was 145 before the implementation of blended teaching. After the implementation of blended teaching, the number of students surveyed was 173.

The data collected are: Students' test scores and teaching evaluation results before and after the implementation of mixed teaching. Based on the above data, SPSS statistical software is used for comparison to analyze the impact of the implementation of mixed teaching on students' test scores and teaching evaluation results.

The data that can be collected are: Students' test scores and teaching evaluation before the implementation of mixed teaching, and students' test scores and teaching evaluation after the implementation of mixed teaching. Based on the collected data, SPSS statistical software is used to compare the data to analyze the impact of the implementation of mixed teaching on students' examination results and teaching evaluation results.

Comparison of Students' Examination Results

At the end of the course, students will be tested to measure the effect of learning, with a full score of 100. This paper selects two groups of data of students' test scores before and after mixed teaching, and obtains the following statistical results with the help of SPSS statistical software:

Table 2. Comparative analysis of students' scores before and after the implementation of mixed teaching.

Scores		N	Mean	Std. deviation	Std. error mean
Before Teaching	Mixed	145	82.75	15.154	1.258
After Teaching	Mixed	173	88.16	10.210	.776

It can be seen from Table 2 that after the implementation of mixed teaching, the average score of students' performance has increased by 5.41 points and the standard deviation has decreased by 4.944 points compared with that before the implementation of mixed teaching, indicating that after the implementation of mixed teaching, the average level of students' performance has improved and the gap between students' performance has narrowed.

It can be seen from Table 3, Sig < 0.05, that there are significant differences in scores after the implementation of mixed teaching and before the implementation of mixed teaching. That is, blended teaching significantly improves students' academic performance.

Table 3. Independent samples test

Scores	Levene's test for equality of variances		t-test for equality of means		
	F	Sig	t	df	Sig. (2-tailed)
Equal variances assumed	20.267	.000	−3.782	316	.000
Equal variances not assumed			−3.659	244.759	.000

Comparison of Teaching Evaluation Data

Students' teaching evaluation of teachers and courses is a more intuitive measure of learning experience. At the end of the course, students will be given an evaluation scale with 15 items. The score adopts a 5-point system, with a maximum of 5 points and a minimum of 1 point.

The contents of the evaluation are shown in the table below (Table 4):

Table 4. Teaching evaluation content

Number	Evaluation content
1	Firm political stance, love the party and patriotism, pay attention to teachers' ethics, and convey positive contents to students
2	Pay attention to teaching and educating people
3	Adequate lesson preparation, skilled lectures, reasonable teaching design and rich preparation of teaching materials
4	Rigorous teaching style and strong sense of time
5	It meets the requirements of syllabus (International) standards and has a clear teaching purpose
6	Closely follow the teaching objectives, highlight the key points and analyze the difficulties clearly
7	The regulations are clear, the logic is clear, the basic concept is analyzed, and the reasoning is correct
8	Integrate theory with practice and pay attention to the cultivation of students' speculative ability
9	Be good at inspiration and pay attention to the communication between teachers and students and the guidance of learning methods
10	Effective use of modern educational technology means to reform classroom teaching mode
11	The teaching means are reasonable, the teaching methods are properly used and the effect is good
12	The speech is standard, clear, accurate and logical

(continued)

Table 4. (*continued*)

Number	Evaluation content
13	The students listen carefully, the classroom atmosphere is harmonious, and do not do irrelevant behavior
14	Strict examination, high attendance, strict classroom discipline and high participation rate
15	Whether students master basic theories, basic skills and correct learning methods

After the course, students grade the course and teachers. The teaching evaluation of students before and after the implementation of mixed teaching is compared and analyzed. The results are as follows:

Table 5. Comparative analysis of students' teaching evaluation of the course before and after the implementation of mixed teaching

Scores of students' teaching evaluation	N	Mean	Std. deviation	Std. error mean
Before mixed teaching	141	4.799291	.2196577	.0184985
After mixed teaching	168	4.804762	.2302198	.0177618

It can be seen from Table 5 that the average value of student evaluation after mixed teaching is slightly higher than that before mixed teaching. At the same time, the standard deviation of student evaluation after mixed teaching is higher than that before mixed teaching, that is, there is a large difference in student evaluation after mixed teaching.

Table 6. Independent samples test

Scores	Levene's test for equality of variances		t-test for equality of means		
	F	Sig	t	df	Sig. (2-tailed)
Equal variances assumed	0.773	.380	−0.212	307	.832
Equal variances not assumed			−0.213	301.97	.831

It can be seen from the above Table 6 that the sig value is 0.832. There is no significant difference in student evaluation before and after mixed teaching. The reason may be that as a new teaching mode, some students are in the adaptation stage.

In the teaching scoring link, students can give comments in addition to scoring. From the students' comments, some students have a better experience (Table 7).

Table 7. Comments on students' teaching evaluation.

Students	Comments
1	This teacher really teaches very well! Deduct one point for fear of your pride. Hey!
2	Thank you for your patience in answering questions in the group
3	The teacher is very kind and knows how to get along with each other, which makes the students happy in class
4	The lecture is very good, step by step, which has benefited me a lot
5	This course is very practical

3 Conclusion

The following conclusions are found in this paper:

Through the mixed and flipped teaching design, learning can be selectively and targeted to consolidate the weak links according to their own situation, actively preview, actively participate in discussion and actively review, so as to enable students to enter the state of in-depth learning, meet their personalized needs, significantly improve their academic performance and effectively improve their learning effect.

From the statistical results of teaching evaluation, the standard deviation of students' evaluation scores is large. The reason is that different students have different degrees of acceptance of the new teaching model. At the same time, the mixed classroom gives more initiative to students, and teachers reduce the supervision and control of students. Students need to have a certain sense of self-discipline and actively participate in the classroom in order to gain something. According to the statistical results, some students who actively participate in learning have a better sense of learning experience.

4 Countermeasures and Suggestions

Based on the learning experience of Hybrid Teaching of human resource management tool courses, this paper puts forward the following suggestions:

1. Due to the epidemic, the teaching method of the course is mainly online teaching. Although the mixed classroom and flipped classroom can not be limited by time and space, the way of online communication is relatively single, and the effect of teacher-student communication will be discounted. There is no sense of on-site communication and truth. After the epidemic, students resume classes in the classroom, which can increase the proportion of offline teaching, Enhancing the experience of on-site discussion and the timeliness of information transmission can avoid the problems existing in online teaching.
2. Do a good job in students' ideological work. For a long time, most college students' learning methods are passive acceptance of knowledge and lack the habit of active thinking and active learning. Hybrid teaching and flip teaching are to break students' old learning habits and change passive into active. A large number of studies

show that active learning and cooperative learning activities are important ways of effective teaching in undergraduate education. [12] Students preview in advance, actively participate in the learning of the course, discuss the existing problems with teachers and students at any time, and review after class. Students need to adapt and be familiar with this teaching method. At the same time, teachers need to transform themselves from knowledge imparters to learning designers, take cultivating students' good learning habits as the starting point of hybrid teaching design, and take creating personalized learning experience for students and promoting students' in-depth learning as the goal of hybrid teaching design. This is also the difficulty and problem to be overcome in the smooth implementation of hybrid teaching.

3. Develop more high-quality teaching resources. An important condition for the smooth development of Hybrid Teaching and flipped classroom is the need for a large number of high-quality online teaching resources for students to preview in advance. In the future, we need to vigorously develop more high-quality teaching resources for students to choose.

The deficiency of this study is that it does not find a mature learning experience scale, but uses the test results and teaching evaluation data as the basis of learning experience evaluation, so it fails to cover many important aspects such as learning emotion, cognition, experience and so on. In the future research, it is suggested to design more perfect learning experience evaluation tools according to the characteristics of undergraduate human resource management tool courses, combined with qualitative research means such as interviews, so as to provide support and guidance for more effective implementation of Hybrid Teaching and improvement of students' learning experience.

References

1. Cao, H.Y., Sun, Y.D., Luo, Y.C., Shan, Y.G.: Thoughts on the learning design of student - centered mixed teaching curriculum in universities research. High. Eng. Educ. J. 1, 187–192 (2021)
2. Xue, C.L., Guo, Y.X.: Transformation and Countermeasures of Online Teaching Reform in Universities, Journal of East China Normal University (EDUCATIONAL SCIENCE EDITION). Journal 7, 65–74 (2020)
3. The working meeting of the national director of higher education and the Guiding Teaching Committee of universities was held in 2020. http://ctld.scnu.edu.cn/a/20200619/1189.html. 28 June 2020
4. Tom, B., Claire, B., Peter, C.: Using blended learning to improve student success rates in learning to program. J. Educ. Media, J. 2, 165–178 (2003)
5. Huang, Z.: Exploration and practice of engineering education based on mu-class and mixed teaching research on higher engineering education. Journal 4, 11–13 (2016)
6. Zhang, Q., Ma, X.P.: Construction and suggestions of mixed teaching mode in universities in the post-epidemic period. Jiangsu Higher Educ. J. 2, 93–97 (2021)
7. Gao, X.H., Zhao, J.M.: Active learning teaching method: principles, methods and suggestions. Univ. Educ. Sci., J. 1, 28–36 (2021)
8. Zhang, Z.: Reflection and correction of existential philosophy in college online teaching – based on the application of mixed teaching model. Jiangsu Higher Educ., J. 9, 62–66 (2020)

9. Taylor, R.: Basic principles of curriculum and Teaching. In: Translated by Luo Kang, Zhang Yue Beijing: China Light Industry Press, pp.55–93 (2008)

10. Liu, B., Zhang, W.L., Jiang, Y.J.: Online course learning experience: connotation. Develop. Influen. Factors, China Audio Vis. Educ., J. **10**, 90–96 (2016)

11. Nellie Mae Education Foundation: Learning Experience. http://edglossary.org/learning-exp erience/.2016/04/02

12. Sivan, A., Leung, R.W., Kember, D.: An Implementation of active learning and its effect on quality of student learning. Innov. Educ. Train. Int. J. **4**, 381–389 (2000)

Teaching a Basic Design Class for Art and Design Freshmen: Course Design and Lessons Learned

DanDan Yu[✉], LiMin Wang, WenJing Li, and HaoYue Sun

Art and Design Academy, Beijing City University, Beijing, China
diane_yu@139.com

Abstract. In Art and Design education, it is challenging to teach basic design courses for freshmen. On one hand, freshmen have a very limited knowledge base, and the transition process from high school to college education patterns may take a long time (and vary on a individual basis). On the other hand, teaching design course requires train abstract insight and design thinking and demands extensive hands-on practice. Future designers need to acquire creation in their curriculum to feel equipped to address design challenges in their career. This paper focuses course design and active learning strategies in basic design courses to increase freshmen' motivation to engage in professional learning. Different from traditional studies where the major focus is basic knowledge teaching and skill training, the course strategies follow the principle of liberal arts, thinking first, and interesting, with the aim to keep the interests of the freshmen and to avoid the creation of frustration in their early studies. The project activities were mainly performed in Art and Design department of Beijing City University. It summarizes course design strategies and share feedback from the students and lessons learned. The results highlight that designed courses increases art and design freshmen' interests in profession learning. These findings show the importance of course design model in design courses to empower future designers to address complex problems challenges through design and innovation.

Keywords: Course design · The first-year students · Basic design course · Critical thinking

1 Introduction

Freshman year is an important point in the transition from high school and university. Students' capacity to adapt to the learning style and student life at college directly affects their subsequent study of the entire university course. Specifically, adaptability not only helps students to change their way of thinking in high school, but also plays an important role in professional development. We need to address this challenge both in the curriculum and pedagogically. This paper focuses on course design and active learning strategies in basic design courses as a means to increase freshmen's motivation to engage in professional learning. In contrast with traditional studies, where the major focus is basic knowledge teaching and skill training, the course design strategies presented here

© The Author(s), under exclusive license to Springer Nature Switzerland AG 2022
M. M. Soares et al. (Eds.): HCII 2022, LNCS 13322, pp. 348–363, 2022.
https://doi.org/10.1007/978-3-031-05900-1_24

follow the principle of liberal arts, putting thinking first and ensuring they are interesting, with the aim to maintain the interests of the freshmen and avoid feelings of frustration early on in their early studies.

At present, there are many sub-design majors that come within the discipline of Chinese art design, including but not limited to environmental design, product design and fashion design. The more detailed the subdivision of the discipline, the deeper the professional level. However, the blind or poorly thought-out subdivision erects a barrier between natural self-exploration and innovation across different subjects. To address this situation, many colleges and universities specializing in art and design have adjusted their teaching systems. During their freshman year, students are required to study basic design courses, instead of engaging in professional study. The basic courses of design cover content such as the knowledge-based view, methodology, software skills, painting skills, and the materials utilized by art and design majors. However, the adjusted teaching system poses a new challenge for those professors teaching the freshman curriculum, as they need to sideline the professional knowledge, to some extent, and incorporate more general knowledge into the freshman curriculum of design. On this basis, non-professional knowledge and abilities such as critical thinking, general knowledge, and social and communication patterns need to be integrated into basic design courses to help freshmen develop comprehensive cross-professional and cross-cultural qualities.

As mentioned in the book *General Education in a Free Society, Report of the Harvard Committee,* "it is necessary to infiltrate the general knowledge into professional education as much as possible [6]". Based on the concept of general knowledge, this study endeavors to improve the curriculum system of basic education and puts forward new requirements for the teaching design of basic courses. The addition of general knowledge to basic education courses can not only improve students' thinking ability, achieving the coordinated development of quality and ability, but also realize their seamless connection with professional courses. Meanwhile, combined with efforts to address specific social problems, the design of basic teaching can improve students' ability to solve complex problems with design methods, with the purpose of cultivating students' comprehensive innovation ability.

2   Research Context and Concepts

This paper is a project on improving students' enthusiasm for further majors and learning experience through freshmen course study. Through the course, students can hone their oral and written communication skills, analytical thinking skills, and problem-solving skills. Therefore, we were the need to design a course strategy to help students complete a smooth transition from high school to a college major. During the course teaching try-out, Art and design undergraduates admitted to Beijing City University in 2021 years was selected for the study. The total number of students was more than 700. And 66 students in 2 classes of the course "Digital Life" deeply participated in the study.

2.1   Status Quo of Curriculum Setting the First year of Art and Design Majors

In recent years, many colleges and universities have taken steps to reform their teaching systems in light of new social needs. Many schools have crossed major boundaries and made significant progress in setting up design general-knowledge platforms for freshmen. However, the course content and teaching are plagued by issues, such as a lack of rationality, serious plagiarism in the curriculum system, and the blind copying of teaching content. All of these result in the design teaching system seriously lagging behind the needs of social development and discipline development. Crucially, it means that the system is not adapted to the current teaching requirements of basic courses for art design majors.

There is a widely held belief in the education profession that the scope of basic courses needs to be continually broadened; the connection between knowledge should be high-lighted and closer attention ought to be paid to the comprehensive quality of talents. However, there are different requirements for the traditional basic courses in each field of art design at present. Besides, the current basic-course teaching system cannot effec-tively be linked with other majors and cannot achieve the aim of general-knowledge design. Consequently, the overall knowledge structures of art students are not complete. Specifically, students lack basic critical thinking and social perception skills, which are crucial in the formation of self-consciousness. Due to the limitations of teachers and teaching resources, not all students will choose courses that are best suited to their future major, leading some students to feel weary or give up studying altogether. For example, students who want to study graphic design in the future believe they do not need to learn about 3D principles, whilst students who want to study environmental design do not wish to learn about trends in fashion colors.

2.2 The Teaching Situation of the First-Year Courses of University

First, the general-knowledge course at college to improve the overall quality of students is single in form and lack of practice. This teaching model does not assist students to develop a deep understanding of knowledge, nor does it foster their learning initiative, which hinders the innovation and development of the course. What's more, due to the large class sizes of general-knowledge classes, it is difficult for teachers to explore the subject in depth whilst also ensuring there are meaningful interactions between teaching and learning and maintaining classroom discipline. Students disconcertingly describe such courses as "a waste of time," or "totally irrelevant to me," even though they are choosing from a great many alternative courses within each interdisciplinary school.

This consensus has been most vividly described by Princeton University President Shirley Tilghman's metaphor comparing traditional training in science to a pyramid. In this model, students must complete a foundation of introductory science courses before they can progress to more specialized courses, more engaging scientific questions [2]. On the basis of this model, some majors will integrate professional basic skills into freshman courses using teaching methods and content that have not been adjusted to reflect the teaching objects and objectives. This leads to the situation mentioned above that some students will not choose to pursue this major in the future, or some students who want to choose this major give up studying the course due to its difficulty or for other negative reasons. It is proposed that for these courses, we move away from the pyramid model, to instead present professional design views or skills in an imaginative and insightful way along with pertinent topics, such as global climate change or the origins of the universe. This attempt to "break the pyramid" provides more possibilities for the future of students.

2.3   The Study Situation of College Students

At present, almost all Chinese college students are victims of the "theater effect" in primary and secondary education. All students will have taken after-school classes since primary school. Test scores and gaining admission to university are the ultimate goals of students. Due to these conditions, students become impetuous and utilitarian in their approach to education without the motivation and direction of learning. Based on the questionnaires on the students enrolled in the Department of Art and Design of Beijing City University in 2018 and 2020, 55.59% of them said that they were uncertain about their future majors when they entered the university, whilst 34.06% responded that they were very clear about their future majors. Among the 724 students enrolled in 2021, 61.6% of them were clear about their future development direction at the beginning of enrollment. After one semester's study, 329 of them had changed their choice of future majors, whilst 88 were still uncertain about their future major. From this, it can be seen that most students who have just gone to college either are unclear about their future majors or mistakenly think they are set on a specific major (see Fig. 1). Therefore, it is necessary to enhance students' self-cognition through the courses and course services they are exposed to in the first year of college.

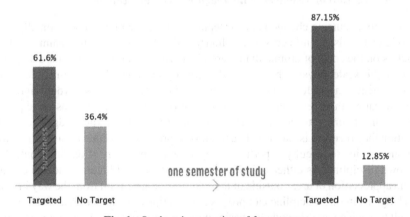

Fig. 1. Students' perception of future target

Additionally, we also surveyed the 724 students enrolled in 2021 on their aesthetic and concerns, 94.61% of whom are local students in Beijing, 87.89% of which are local students from the outer suburbs. Their preferences and interests all tended to be socially oriented, and they had not yet established their own design views and aesthetic tendencies. Their concern for the world is limited to social news, makeup, food, basketball, and other content that is promoted by social media platforms. The German art and design scholar Matthias once said: Even if higher education in China can train hundreds of thousands of designers for some time to come, it will nevertheless be difficult to change its design environment based on culture. The reason for this is that there is not a social and cultural structure conducive to basic design education. In Europe, children have received basic education of design since kindergarten, whereas Chinese children do not. The average person does not have the opportunity to understand the basic concepts of design and cannot discern what is good design or bad design, even after receiving general-knowledge education at school. It is that case that students too often think of the bachelor's degree curriculum as consisting of two largely unrelated elements: general education and the major.

The survey also showed that students believe the biggest difference between high school and college is that they have more free time and life is freer. Moreover, the learning content at college is more personalized and rich. Accordingly, students should change from the model passive learning in high school to active learning in college. This is a significant challenge for most students. Making the transition from being a high school student to a successful college student does not happen instantaneously, and it certainly does not occur passively. Therefore, the first year at college is a crucial year for the successful transition of students from high school to college. Whitehead pointed out in his book The Aims of Education that intellectual cultivation at secondary school is mainly for learning basic courses [7]. Meanwhile, at college, students need to realize that they need to overhaul their approach to learning during their first year, as failure to do so will have a serious impact on them.

2.4 The Situation of Teachers Who Teach First-Year Students

One recently occurring change is the acceptance of the idea that to be optimally effective, scientists must acquire cross-disciplinary skills. Nanoscience, the realm of 10–9 m (which is on the scale of atomic diameters), is a prime example of a cross-disciplinary forum: at this scale, physics, biology, and chemistry meet and the scientific interactions between them can produce truly novel insights [1]. Most scientists would agree that when educating their replacements, their education will have to be cross-disciplinary. However, most current teachers do not possess interdisciplinary knowledge because the education they received is exclusively a traditional professional education. Further, from the point of view of faculty expertise, many view the prospect of teaching outside of their own disciplines as either pointless or extraordinarily difficult. Students can also gain an appreciation of areas outside of the traditional curriculum from the way in which knowledge from one discipline can provoke realizations in another area. This makes it difficult to teach general-knowledge basic courses in the first year. According to the book Alternative Universities, in essence, the existence of colleges is for reshaping subjects (whether students or teachers) so that when they leave the school, they are different from who they were when they entered [3]. Therefore, by partaking in mutual communication and learning through the course, students and teachers can make progress together.

3   Course Design Strategy for College Freshman

Defining success can be an elusive proposition. Success involves all about student and is multidimensional, in that it certainly goes beyond cognitive or academic success alone.

Upcraft, Barefoot, and Gardner (2005) suggest that first-year students succeed when they make progress toward developing academic and intellectual competence, establishing and maintaining interpersonal relationships, exploring identity development, deciding on a career and lifestyle, maintaining personal health and wellness, developing civic responsibility, considering the spiritual dimensions of life, and dealing with diversity [1]. Therefore, regarding the principles of undergraduate learning, we believe that the primary way to connect students with their learning is to consider "all" of a student. In order to develop students' all-around experience, we design the learning life for freshmen to guide them to accurately study the needs of social design, strengthen their practice, and cultivate their creative thinking.

In response to this goal, our study was conducted based on the following questions.

– How incorporates innovation in teaching.
– How the develops critical and analytical thinking.
– How the develops success in the classroom and beyond.
– How fosters student involvement in the community and course.
– How develops students' personal strategies.

Based on Bloom's educational goals of cognitive goals, skill goals, and emotional goals, combined with the educational philosophy of general education, we have formed a course design strategy for the first year of college to solve the above problems (see Fig. 2). This course design strategy is based on the curriculum objectives and forms the overall learning experience of the students through the four links of Reconstruction, Practice, Theme and Evaluation. The experience includes the students' gains in cognition, knowledge, skills, emotion and so on. The first college year is not "grade 13." Incoming students, they enter a new culture. For new students, the courses will present a new norms, traditions, and rituals, and a new language and environment.

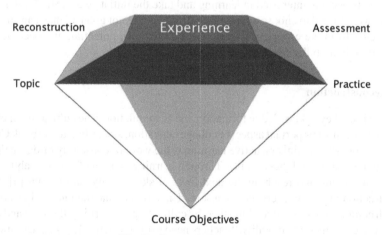

Fig. 2. Course design strategy

3.1 Course Objectives

Grammar, logic, rhetoric, arithmetic, geometry, music and astronomy were the seven skills that people needed to master at college in the Middle Ages as prerequisites for participating in civic and church life [3]. This is similar to the situation in the first year of college, where the emphasis is placed on ability rather than professional characteristics. A survey by the Association of American Universities found that students' critical thinking, clear communication and ability to solve complex problems were more important than their undergraduate major [3]. What's more, solving complex problems is one of the fundamentals of design and design thinking. Design has now moved beyond the antiquated view that it is merely decoration; design is now defined as seeking out a solution to a problem. Therefore, during their freshman year, students should master the most basic learning skills, communication skills, construction ability, thinking ability, and the ability to solve complex problems, as well as cross-culture and cross-discipline abilities. Every course should focus on these skills and abilities.

Therefore, we targeted specific goals that included the following:

- Gain academic and cognitive skills.
- Develop critical thinking.
- Build connections with faculty and peers.
- Promote in-class and out-of-class engagement.
- Exercise communication and expression skills.
- Increase preparedness for future academic coursework and academic engagement.
- Enhance sense of belonging.

Focusing on these teaching objectives can not only expand students' professional vision and humanistic qualities, construct their thinking mode, and exercise their expression, but also establish a relationship between design and life and society and people, so that students become interested in learning and take the initiative to learn. Even if some students were forced to choose courses they dislike or are not good at, they can still grow and develop from the experience, explore their unknown potential, and become more confident in their ability to complete academic work.

3.2 Reconstruction

Thinking is the key to knowledge formation and accumulation. The cultivation of critical thinking is the most important aspect of college education. According to the book Critical Thinking, for critical thinkers, active learning is the work of constantly bridging the gap between the present and the possible. Through learning, learners form the habit of continually improving and reaching the next level of skill, ability, and insight [4]. In the reconstruction phase, teachers tend to ask students to integrate the knowledge structure through communication and reading, thereby cultivating their critical thinking and establishing correct values and morality. Teachers need to design active learning activities that require students to look at multiple perspectives world and make connections between and among disciplines. Students explore the relationship between design and life, and are constantly asked to connect what they learn about themselves, others to self-assess and reflect in their writing and discussions.

In this session, teachers and students can watch movies they are interested in together. Teachers can also thought-provoking readings assigned, and students are constantly reflecting and writing. The reading the same book brings people closer together as a community by creating common ground for discussion. Teachers can dine, exercise, or build community with students, enhancing teacher-student interactions in and out of class. For the faculty and administrators who first-year programs, this emphasis on building community would made common reading especially appealing. Assigning a book or a movie before class gives incoming students, who often come from very different backgrounds, a shared experience.

3.3 Topic

In this part, the main tasks are to guide students to direct their attention to adopting a global focus, improve their cultural literacy, and acquire cross-culture abilities. According to a survey by the Association of American Universities, 76% of the respondents said it was very important for employees to understand cultures, history, values, religions and social institutions around the world [3]. At the same time, it also demonstrates the cross-culture ability to cooperate with people of different ages, from different professional backgrounds and lifestyles, with different ways of working and thinking. Therefore, students can not only improve their comprehensive quality, but also learn what they enjoy and establish the relationship between design and life by letting them explore the topics they like from culture and history to study and put them into practice. We want students to think outside the box and study for a well-paying job, a dream career, or graduate study. It is hoped that the students will want to spend time learning more about something that has always fascinated them, thus providing them with access to more valuable opportunities in life. It should be noted that this will lead to more demands being placed on teachers. In the early stage, we can adopt the following measures:

The first is to adopt the method of group teaching in which the teachers from the disciplines of design, literature, and history all participate in teaching, so as to integrate cultural cognition and thinking into basic training.

The second is to enhance the discussion and communication between teachers of different courses and jointly construct the "special-topic course group". The special topics are interrelated and the emphases of training are different. In this case, students can drill into a certain topic and think deeply about it under the condition of multiple courses sharing the same topic.

The third is to adopt online and offline teaching. The teaching parts that design teachers are not good at will be taught online. Students can learn from online resources, such as MOOCs, short videos and so on.

3.4 Practice

As a necessary part of the art design process, practice includes many aspects, such as discussion, debate, visiting, exploration, reading, games and performing except for the training of operational ability. In fact, all human activities are forms of design practice.

Therefore, practice forms are not limited to the traditional drawing, drafting, model making found in the design discipline. All of the activities mentioned above can be used as a practice form to promote and refine students' physical and mental perceptions. Especially in the basic courses for freshmen, we should blur major boundaries, break down major barriers, move beyond the narrow recognition of professional skills, and guide students to flexibly employ a variety of design languages in the course.

In the process of practice, it is not only necessary to exercise students' independent practice ability, but also to guide students to cooperate and communicate in teams. Students can learn so much from the relationships they made. From each and every person, students can learned a different thing, whether it is something from their character or culture or the way in which they view and live their life. The classroom is not the only place where learning takes place. Learn in class and out of class. In addition to the mutual communication of students in class, learning communities can be formed through the connection between classes. In learning communities, students can get in touch with more teachers, and learning communities can also become a platform for first-year students and teachers to share their achievements. Learning communities provide supportive environment to ease the transition to college for students. Teaching team can be identified early, discussed, and quickly resolved so any students' learning difficulties. Instructors also serve as learning guide for students by answering a variety of questions related to academic and college life.

3.5 Assessment

We divide the curriculum evaluation into two parts, based on three theoretical dimensions: Knowledge, Attitudes, and Behaviors (Schrader and Lawless 2004) [6]. One part is to evaluate students' learning attitude and the degree to which they are actively engaged in the curriculum. The other part evaluates students' knowledge and behavior. Although many forms of evaluation exist (i.e., oral reports, debates, essays, written reports, presentations, sketches, models, documentaries, research, information collection, etc.), writing is particularly important for design majors. For many years, it has been universally acknowledged that art and design professionals are not proficient at expression, even though they themselves think so. In fact, writing, as a process of discovery, can be a useful tool for such professionals to promote their learning, as they will gain new insights when organizing and expressing their ideas clearly. Therefore, in the future, designers should endeavor to organize their thinking and cognition through writing, and we will also encourage the inclusion of writing in the evaluation systems for freshman courses.

With regard to the assessment requirements for students in the evaluation system, the following principles should be followed:

1. There should be a greater assessment of students' comprehensive ability relating to their activities, covering their eyes, hands, body, and brain as much as possible.
2. With the orientation of thinking, there should not be an over-emphasis on students' professional skills, nor should it be unduly difficult.
3. Reduce the completion times of single tasks, as fast practice and fast iteration are more effective for thinking development and learning experience.

4. Encourage the use of a variety of design expressions, such as painting, poetry, performance, models, etc.

Based on the above principles, we hope that students will pay more attention to changing their thinking and improving their comprehensive abilities during their freshman year, so as not to let them feel daunted by the professional difficulty, let alone mistakenly focusing on professional skills and tool skills.

3.6 Experience

Many people regard college life as a journey; however, it is not a journey on which you can travel around the world with a single backpack. Even so, it is a journey that you can start whenever you want. In addition, the teacher is more like a tour guide, leading students to explore all the expertise in different fields and instructing them as to what kind of experience will allow for the realization of a more exciting and complete life journey. The so-called curriculum design is more like a kind of "experience design" based on students' spiritual growth. During the journey through the curriculum, students may experience the following feelings:

1. The topic may lead students to "want to express their views" and have something to say. The topic should not only be understood and recognized by everyone, but also have certain characteristics. If this is not the case, students will be at a loss as to what to do and find it difficult to associate the topic with their own understanding and experience.
2. Students can express their own views on the curriculum. It is important to note that there are no standard answers in the art and design curriculum. Students can start exploring different methods and show the various ways they reflect and express themselves.
3. Encourage mutual evaluation and suggestions, giving students the opportunity to express themselves and communicate with each other. Students' comments, suggestions or jokes can sometimes burst into more good ideas. As far as art or design is concerned, even laymen or ordinary people possess keen aesthetic perceptions and judgments, but teachers' tastes can easily become too narrow or rigid.
4. Teachers guide students to think more deeply by replacing comments with questions. Through questions and answers, teachers can help students to further clarify their ideas and confusion.
5. Create a barrier-free communication environment between teachers and students, so that students can always find a mentor on their journey.

In summary, the course design strategy is designed to enhance students' time management, communication, social interaction, and study skills, whilst also developing critical thinking skills based on the course target. This enables freshman year courses to serve as a bridge for students between high school to professional learning.

4 Course Design Case: Digital Life

"Digital Life" is an optional course in the enlightening module of the basic course platform, which is one of the basic courses of the art design major offered by Beijing City University's Art and Design Department. From 2018 onwards, freshmen can choose their future major during freshman year. Through practice, the department continues to explore the basic qualities of different majors and divides the freshman platform course into six modules across two semesters. One of them is the compulsory module consisting of an introduction course, history course, composition course, modeling course, and investigation and sketching. In addition, there are five other modules: design enlightening module, material design module, design performance module, skills module, and culture and trend module. Each student must choose a course in each of these five modules. "Digital Life" is one of the six courses in the design enlightening module, with a capacity for 66 students split across 2 classes. This module is provided to the freshmen group by the above majors as an enlightening course for the further study of these majors in the future.

4.1 Course Target

The original purpose of the Digital Life course is to allow students to understand the basic application scenarios and modern practice of digital design, establish the relationship between digital design and life, and develop a mode of thinking in the field of digital information design. On the basis of this curriculum goal, we apply the freshman course design strategy to redesign the course.

First of all, the course objectives are as follows:

1. Enable students to understand the form, function and scenario of digital design works in daily life.
2. Enable students to understand the frontiers and trends of digital technology.
3. Enable students to conduct a learning contextual inquiry and summarize the data.
4. Enable students to learn how to work as part of a team and expand their ideas.
5. Enable students to learn to express their views on the relationship between science, technology, and humanities using both written words and oral language.

The course is designed to "assist students in their academic and social development and in their transition to college. Is a discussion and experience-based course in which students and instructors exchange ideas and information. In most cases, there is a strong emphasis on creating community in the classroom."

4.2 Course Plan

Astin (1984) described how involvement relates to the individualization of the student. This approach assumes that there is no single approach to the subject matter, teaching, or resource allocation that is adequate for all students. Rather than adopting an all-encompassing approach to teaching and having every student immersed in the same experience, this call to action stresses the individualization of instruction and emphasizes the importance of independent study [1]. Therefore, we give full play to students' autonomy in course topics and reconstruction, and use different forms to encourage students to express their own views and those of their team. The whole course schedule is divided into three parts according to the law of students' knowledge from shallow to deep: cognition-action-reflection. The course schedule is as follows (Table 1):

Table 1. Course schedule of "Digital Life"

Stage	Theme	Reconstruction	Practice
Recognition	1. The development of information technology and key people, products and events 2. Keywords in digital design 3. The future development direction of digital technology	Discuss the pros and cons brought by digital technology to human life according to video topics or cases	Students independently look for examples of campus life that have been changed by digital technology, and take photos as records. Then they will discuss the ideas in their groups and sort out their discussions
Recognition	2021 Asian Digital Art Exhibition	Discuss the ideas that the artist wants to express based on the works of art	Visit the exhibition and choose two favorite works to talk about why students like them
Action	Digital city life	Discuss the possibility of the future of a product or service in city life. Explore how digital interaction can change people's behavior and thinking habits in their lives	Draw mind maps in the group and record videos to express their views or present the state of life in the future
Reflection	1. Digital economy 2. Digital entertainment 3. Digital creativity 4. Digital service 5. Digital education	Discuss the changes that have taken place in the industries you are interested in under the influence of digital technology	Write a short article to explain my views on the development status and future prospects of the digital industry

Through the whole curriculum, students will come to understand the impact of digital information technology on our lives, and the significance of digital design to future life. During the discussion, teachers will stimulate students' inner potential, facilitate brainstorm communication, and guide students to ask questions, thus forcing teachers to think again. Through the repeated cycle, both students and teachers can mutually grow and develop further. For example:

1. At the beginning of the course, teachers introduce the course using the latest NFT news reports to help students comprehend how their lives are slowly being changed by information technology. Teachers and students also exchange views on the Gucci-Roblox-Dionysus-bag, sold for $4,115, prompting students to consider the value of digital technology in our daily lives and the digital technology behind it.

2. Teachers and students watch the TV documentary "Big Data" to explore how big data helps primary school football coaches to train and select the most promising players. By doing so, teachers lead students to think about whether the use of visualized data of children's sports performance as the basis for selecting young players will deny some children the possibility of potential development in a certain sport and speculate on the interaction between people's natural development and the influence of data prediction.

3. Teachers guide the students to use a mind map to illustrate how their own thoughts have changed. By enabling the student group to draw a mind map collectively, teachers can trigger students' thinking from their own or other people's keywords so as to continue their development, and underscore the wisdom of the collective to the students (see Fig. 3). During this process, teachers find that most students are used to writing conclusions directly and then beautifying them through the use of illustrations.

4. Teachers guide students to arrange their views by means of language expression and writing. After visiting the exhibition, students are encouraged to analyze and think about the underpinning behind their intuitive feelings.

5. Through on-campus research, the students review their campus life from the perspective of digital networks and come to understand the technical principles behind the function. As a result, a considerable number of students will realize that not everything powered by electricity falls into the category of digital technology.

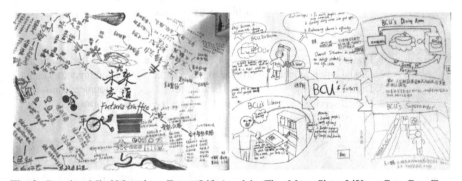

Fig. 3. Practice: Mind Map about Future Life (work by ZhanMeng Shen, LiXuan Cao, GuanTong Dong, KeXin Wang, YuXuan Lu, Bin Fang, WeiKun Lv and YuHao Xiao)

4.3 Course Assessment

The assessment of students' grades in this course is divided into three parts:

- 20% of the grade derives from teachers' subjective judgment of the students' attitude and curriculum participation. Students who actively participate in the discussion and thinking expression are encouraged to promote communication amongst students and between students and teachers.
- 40% of the grade derives from the results of drawing mind maps and presentation videos in the course. Students are encouraged to expand their thinking and give full play to their imagination.
- 40% of the grade derives from the essay at the end of the course, so as to improve students' professional vision and simultaneously enhance their narrative and expression abilities.

Each point scored on this course does not directly represent each student's overall mastery of curriculum knowledge, but only examines the student's performance in relation to a representative node during the course.

4.4 Course Summary and Reflections

This course redesigns the original course by implementing the freshman course design strategy. The emphasis is shifted from the results to instead emphasize the process and thinking. Although the students do not produce beautiful design drawings or paintings as they usually would at the end of a traditional art and design course, they are trained at the cognitive and thinking levels.

The course consistently produces a variety of positive outcomes for students:

1. Students' deep learning, as they think dialectically about the things around them.
2. Students develop strong relationships with each other through discussions, traveling to, and eating together at, the pavilion, and generally developing a deep friendship through the course.
3. Students develop strong relationships with faculty members that continue into the next semester. Some students will contact their teachers if they encounter other learning problems after the course ends, seek advice, and share successes.
4. In the field of digital information design, students broaden their horizons and provide a greater range of ideas for later professional learning.

However, there also exist the following problems in the process of curriculum implementation.

1. We should appropriately increase the arrangement of ideas and the teaching of language expression in the teaching content so as to provide students will more specifically targets and allow them to make faster progress.
2. A class size of 33 students seriously affects the frequency and quality of interaction between teachers and students, resulting in a situation in which each student does not receive sufficient attention.

3. The requirements of language expression and writing in the practical links of the course lead students to feel pressured, with some choosing to obtain information from the Internet and output the results directly without thinking.
4. Students are passively arranged to all aspects of the curriculum; the next step should be to place more emphasis on students' active participation. In the curriculum, teachers should be more encouraged to observe the students and how they go about their work.

5   Conclusion and Future Work

We have introduced the case of how it is possible to develop intercultural and critical thinking skills for freshmen of arts and design using course design strategy for the first-year college. And the six components of the model are expounded from the perspectives of principles, methods, and forms: course objectives, Reconstruction, Topic, Practice, Assessment and Experience. This allows students to transition naturally from high school to professional study at university. Including study skills, thinking mode, professional foundation, professional vision, and communication methods. Our course design strategy wishes to teach students able to solve any unexpected problem situation and who are willing to develop their full potential. During the course, we must make student an active participant in course prepared to acquire knowledge by engaging the thinking, communication and practice.

The learning that occurs in first year of Arts & Design Department at Beijing City University is deep, long lasting. The first-year course reform program continues to evolve. In few years period, by making use of best practices in the first college years, building on existing resources, and using assessment to guide change, The project has already shown some positive and transformative results. It enables students to gradually improve their cognition of themselves, of society and of learning. The next challenge was gathering information to show that students' success was connected to what we were doing. Our work is not done. We look to the future, to find better ways to meet the changing needs of students.

Acknowledgments. Many thanks to all students of the Digital Life Course and all freshmen in 2021. Their works are very essential for the paper. I am particularly grateful to Professor XianDong Cheng. He is team member of Digital Life teacher group. His suggestion has aroused my confidence in course design.

References

1. Hunter, M.S.: Peer Review Emerging trends and debates in undergraduate education, vol. 8, no. 3 pp. 4–7. A Publication of the Association of American Colleges and Universities (2006)
2. Weisler, S., Trosset, C.: Evaluating Quality of Engagement in Hampshire College's First-Year Plan, vol. 8, no. 3, pp.11–13. A Publication of the Association of American Colleges and Universities (2006)
3. Staley, D.J.: Alternative Universities: Speculative Design for Innovation in Higher Education. SDX Joint Publishing Company (August 2021)

4. Paul, R., Elder, L.: Tools for Taking Charge of Your Professional and Personal Life, 2nd edn. China RenMin University Press (November 2021)
5. Kellen, R.: Story: using involvement theory to construct a first-year seminar course for college freshmen. Ball State University (May 2012)
6. Feng, H., Huang, M., Zuo, T.: The teaching quality evaluation system and index design of general education in colleges and universities. Education Research, vol. 11 (2012)
7. Wu, L.Y.: Comparison, choice and integration: reconstruction of basic course contents for art and design majors. Chin. Acad. J. Electron. Publishing House, 1994–2021
8. Jin, S.Y.: Research and exploration on design general literacy course in art colleges under the background of new liberal arts. Chin. Acad. J. Electron. Publishing House, 1994–2021
9. Milovanovic, J., Shealy, T., Katz, A.: Higher perceived design thinking traits and active learning in design courses motivate engineering students to tackle energy sustainability in their careers. Sustainability **13**, 12570 (2021)
10. Sefton, J.E.: Reflections on the teaching of freshmen. http://www.csun.edu/afye
11. Matsuka, T., Sakamoto, Y.: A cognitive model that describes the influence of prior knowledge on concept learning. In: Marques, J., de Sá, L.A., Alexandre, W.D., Mandic, D. (eds.) Artificial Neural Networks – ICANN 2007, pp. 912–921. Springer, Heidelberg (2007). https://doi.org/10.1007/978-3-540-74695-9_93
12. First-Year Seminars Office of Undergraduate Education. https://fys.ucdavis.edu/
13. FIRSTYEAR. https://firstyear.org/

Globalization, Localization, and Culture Issues

Investigation of New Private Gardens in Yangtze River Delta and Reflection on Design Value

Tian Cao[1]([✉]) [iD] and Xinyue Wang[2] [iD]

[1] Nanjing University of Science and Technology, Xiaolingwei.200, Nanjing 210094,
Jiangsu, China
466484243@qq.com
[2] Beijing Normal University, Jinfeng Road 18, Zhuhai 519087, Guangdong, China
wangxy@bnu.edu.cn

Abstract. From the 1990s on, new private gardens are generated successively in cities in Yangtze River Delta, China. Starting from cases of new private gardens, the paper summarizes the characteristics of these gardens: Landscape design advocating nature; Combining aesthetics with practicability; Separated from but associated with modern city. Represented by new private gardens, the spontaneous transformation of the environment by urban residents reflects that the design value of contemporary dwelling environment is quietly changing. This paper discusses the change of the relationship between man and nature behind the change of design value. The new design value is different from the concept of "harmony between man and nature" embodied in the classical garden thought, and also different from the "dualism" during the process of modern industrial development. The new design value is to explore a new development path under the guidance of the strategy of common prosperity of man and nature.

Keywords: New private gardens · Design value · Relationship between man and nature

1 Introduction

From the Northern and Southern Dynasties to the Ming and Qing Dynasties, classical gardens in Yangtze River Delta had been developed for several thousand years. Most of them are "residence gardens", with residence and garden accompanying each other. Garden is not only a part of residence but also a place for the owner to relax himself. In modern and contemporary times, enormous changes have taken place in the spatial pattern of Chinese cities. Functions of different districts have become more distinct, the room for recreation in a residence area has been remarkably reduced, and people's recreational activities have been transferred to urban parks, shopping malls and playgrounds. Most ruins of classical gardens have become tourist attractions. The original dwelling function of garden has completely vanished.

From the 1990s on, new private gardens are generated successively in cities in Yangtze River Delta. The so-called new private gardens are in contrast with traditional classical gardens. Most of them are distributed in Suzhou and Yangzhou. Similar to classical gardens, most new private gardens are designed and constructed on private funds. They have different sizes, ranging from dozens of square meters to more than one hundred mu. Most gardens adjoin urban communities, and some of them are directly transformed from community residences. However, there is a great difference between new private gardens and classical gardens.

New private gardens are developing with a conspicuous speed. Within a short period of thirty years, they have grown from one or two to several hundred in number, becoming a feature of the dwelling environment of Suzhou and Yangzhou. These gardens have aroused wide attention both at home and abroad. Some have come onto the world-famous travel brochure Lonely Planet, attracting several thousand domestic and foreign visitors every day. Some have been reported in CCTV and made into feature films. The academic circle attaches great importance to these gardens. Professor Ruan Yisan, a famous scholar, calls them "new things for national rejuvenation, era progress, heritage protection and nostalgia saving". What specialties do new private gardens have? What referential value do they have to today's urban dwelling environment design? This paper attempts to make analyses from the perspective of design value.

2 New Private Gardens and Their Characteristics

New private gardens have different shapes and distinctive features. Here, we will list several classical cases:

2.1 Jingsi Garden

Located in Wujiang District, Suzhou City, Jingsi Garden was funded by private entrepreneurs. Starting from 1993, its construction lasted for a dozen years. The garden covers a floor space of several hundred mu, and its volume is at the top of the list of contemporary private gardens[1].

The pattern and elements of the garden are modeled on Suzhou Garden. Even scenic spot names such as Heting Bridge, Xiao Chuihong, Jingyuan Hall, Tianxiang Study and Pangshan Humble Cottage, are similar to those of Suzhou Garden. By imitating "Guanyun Peak" of Suzhou Lingering Garden, the owner has set "Qingyun Peak". This rockery stone from Lingbi County, Anhui Province weighs 136 tons and has a peculiar shape, thus listed in Guinness World Records (See Fig. 1).

2.2 Cui Garden

Covering a floor space of 460 m^2, Cui Garden is located in Mugu Lane, Xibei Sreet, Suzhou City and adjoins the Humble Administrator's Garden. All materials and technologies adopted by the garden are new-styled. For example, the handrail is made of cement, and coated with red paint, looking just like a wooden handrail in traditional gardens. For another example, the architectures in the garden are equipped with new-styled flush toilets and shower facilities, and so can meet the requirements of modern life.

---

[1] https://news.sina.com.cn/c/2003-09-12/1811741209s.shtml.

Fig. 1. View of Jingsi Garden[2]

2.3 Banjing Garden

Banjing Garden is locate beside Pan Gate Three Scenes of Suzhou City and at the foot of the ancient city wall near the moat. The garden is a combination of Chinese and Western elements. The outdoor landscape is an imitation of gardens in Yangtze River Delta while the indoor decoration adopts a Western style. In addition, the garden is equipped with the seventh generation of escalators imported from Britain[3].

2.4 Xianglu Garden

Built in the 1990s, Xianglu Garden is the earliest contemporary private garden in Yangzhou City. It is located in Dongguan Street of the old quarter and covers a floor space of more than 120 square meters. Though the garden has a very narrow space, it has complete elements such as pool, rockery and pavilion, almost occupying the whole yard of about 40 square meters. The garden has abundant spatial functions, not only serving as a place for the owner to appreciate flowers or the moon, but also having functions of daily life such as storage and drying clothes (See Fig. 2).

2.5 Plum Cottage Garden

Located in Dashuang Lane of the old quarter of Yangzhou City, Plum Cottage Garden got its name because the name of the garden owner contains "plum". Commenced in 2014, the garden covers a floor space of about 30 square meters and is themed with "plum". There are many landscape designs about plums. For example, a window in the shape of plum is installed in the west wall; white plums are formed by piecing together

---

[2] Suzhou Jingsi garden official website: http://www.jsycn.com.

[3] http://www.zhongpaiwang.com/tuijian/qita/226.html.

Fig. 2. View of Xianglu Garden[4]

cobblestones on the floor; rouge plums are planted in the yard; crabapple ice cracks are designed on indoor wooden doors and windows; a Guqin (a seven-stringed plucked instrument in some ways similar to the zither) named "plum language" was listed in the room (See Fig. 3).

Fig. 3. Scenery in Plum Cottage Garden[5]

---

[4] Picture source: Poetic Dwelling: One Hundred New Gardens in Yangzhou.

[5] Picture source: Poetic Dwelling: One Hundred New Gardens in Yangzhou.

3 Common Features of New Private Gardens

Through spot investigations of new private gardens, I have found that they have some common features:

3.1 Landscape Design Advocating Nature

1) **The Spatial Layout is Mainly Free-Styled.** New private gardens usually imitate nature, mainly in a free-styled layout. Architectures for the owner to relax and appreciate landscapes are usually hidden in a dense forest, far away from external noises. Main roads are usually designed as zigzag footpaths or curved bridges to increase the field depth of the garden and avoid everything being taken in a glance. In a garden with a relatively large space, rockeries are usually accompanied by pools to form a combination of hills and waters. There are even pools with islets arranged in some gardens. If the space is narrow, then only rockeries are set and water wave tiles for paving the floor are used to replace a pool. Scenic lookouts are arranged in different places of the garden so that you can appreciate landscapes beside a pool, under a tree, in a pavilion, in a room or from other angles. When you are in the garden, you seem to be in authentic nature.

   Many new private gardens are transformed from modern residences, with a large restriction in site space and miscellaneous functions of the garden space. In order to make up for the weakness of congenital conditions, designers usually set landscapes such as screens, gallery frames and plants to separate and shield the space and create a deep and serene environmental atmosphere in a restricted space.

2) **Landscape Elements Imitate Nature.** Landscape elements of new private gardens are usually inherited from classical gardens in Yangtze River Delta. Mainly imitating nature, landscape elements in a classical garden can be divided into four categories: architecture, plant, rockery and waters. It is also the same case in a new private garden. If having abundant funds and ample space, the garden owner will usually build architectures, rockeries and pools on a large scale by imitating genuine hills and waters in nature. If with a limited fund and narrow space, they will adopt micro landscapes to view nature. Take plants as an example. There is a rich variety of plants such as red maple, Chinese redbud, winter-sweet, cattail, bamboo and Chinese wistaria in a new private garden, which can imitate a forest in nature after being collocated by the garden owner. In terms of rockery and waters, they will build a pool at the corner of the yard or pile up a rockery against the yard wall to imitate hills and waters in nature.

3.2 Combining Aesthetics with Practicability

New private gardens attach importance not only to traditional aesthetics but also to comfort of modern life. They usually inherit the appearance form of a classical garden while adopting modern building materials and technologies.

The inheritance in appearance form is very evident in garden architectures. The appearance of most architecture in a new private garden will adopt an archaistic style. If a garden cannot be built largely, the appearance of modern residential buildings will be transformed and decorated in a form of "wearing clothes and hat" to create an archaistic visual effect. For example, black bricks are pasted on a cement wall to imitate a black brick wall; the flat roof of a house is bolstered by something and paved with gray tiles to imitate an archaistic gabled-roof architecture; classical garden elements such as Mei Renkao (a kind of bench seat with the building railing as a backrest) and Gua Luo (decorative components under architectural corridor frame) are set under the pergola of a yard; and so on and so forth.

As to building material and technology, common materials for a classical garden such as wood, stone and bricks usually cost too much, have to be processed in a complicated way, or are difficult to be maintained. Therefore, they can hardly meet the requirements of modern people about "simple life". On the other hand, modern materials such as concrete and steel have advantages such as low price, mature technology, durability and low maintenance cost, and so are applied to new private gardens to be "mixed" with traditional materials. This "mixture" is not casual. Sections that can be seen or touched are usually made of traditional materials such as black brick, stone and cobblestone. For example, use cobblestone to pave the floor and use stone to pile up a rockery. On the contrary, landscape structures that are "behind the scenes" and not easily observed are usually made of modern building materials such as steel and cement. For example, build a staircase with light steel, build a pavilion with reinforced concrete and pave the bottom of a pool with tiles. The renewal of building materials has caused a reform in building technology. New private gardens completely adopt modern building technologies. For example, frame structure is used to replace the traditional beam & column structure. Rockeries are not fixed and supported only with traditional technologies such as stone biting and mortar seaming. Instead, a supporting rack is erected with steel beams first. Then, stones are overlaid on the supporting rack to create different forms. It is completely a modern landscaping method.

The application of new materials and technologies makes the garden retain traditional charms and also conform more to people's demands about "economy and practicability".

3.3 Gardens Separated from but Associated with Modern City

The design of a new private garden is usually independent. Many gardens are in an unimpressive lane and look modest. So it's hard to see inside landscapes from the outside. High walls are usually set to separate the internal landscape space from the external environment so that the garden has a style of its own. The separation of the garden from the outside can make the owner able to enjoy his own landscapes alone.

However, at the same time, these private gardens are closely related to modern urban services. Many gardens are in a city center, with completed services about shopping, medicine, transportation and entertainment in the neighborhood. Some gardens are only dozens of steps away from a bus stop or a busting business street. Inside a garden architecture, modern facilities such as high-definition television and wireless network are available, so it can rival an advanced commercial residence. The owner can not only enjoy the isolated tranquility brought by the garden but also can be connected to the city at any time and synchronous with fast-paced daily life.

4 Reflection on Design Value

New private gardens are only a part of dwelling environment renewal of contemporary cities. Many urban residents have no sufficient financial or material resources to create a private garden, but will autonomously transform their dwelling environment. For example, many citizens in a high-rise residence will open a space in the balcony for planting potted flowers and creating a home environment close to nature. Neighbors in an old street of the urban area will use empty land beside the street, corner of a lane and other odd spaces to build flower beds or vegetable plots. While decorating the lanes, they have provided some exuberant scenes for the doorway (See Fig. 4, Fig. 5). Whether new private gardens or dwelling environments autonomously transformed by urban residents have reflected the quiet changes in design value of contemporary dwelling environment.

Fig. 4. Plants autonomously decorated by residents of Ren Fengli Block of Yangzhou City[6]

Let's look back to ancient times first. In the Ming and Qing Dynasties, classical gardens in Yangtze River Delta were at the height of splendor. Anything in the creation and design of classical gardens embodies the thought of "harmony between man and nature". According to the scholar Jin Xuezhi, the core concept of "harmony between man and nature" is inalienable relationship between man and nature, which is embodied in the fact that man relies on nature rather than on life. Though having the ability to adapt to and transform nature, man is eventually unified in the integrity of "nature". All landscapes in a classical garden are transformed and reconstructed according to scenes in nature so that they can be adapted to the dwelling environment. It is for being close to, perceiving and comprehending nature at any time in daily life or recreations. The design of classical gardens is condensed and solidified with man's sense of belonging and reverence to nature.

---

[6] Picture source: http://www.yznews.cn/p/691522.html.

Fig. 5. Plants autonomously decorated by residents of Ren Fengli Block of Yangzhou City[7]

From ancient Poems, we can perceive "harmony" between man and nature. For example, Yuan Mei, a poet in the Qing Dynasty, wrote *A Visit to Zhang Garden* in Essays of *Sui Garden on Poetry*:

Shielded by green poplars, a slab bridge transverses outside; the water is calm as if to welcome a boat. Flowers are sparse in the cold weather of March; rain is fresh amid heavy smoke. With feeble steps on a slim bamboo stick, I totter into a field at dusk. Don't end the banquet and hasten evening paddling; I want to drink with gulls in the wilderness.

For another example, *Record of the Old Tippler's Pavilion* written by Ouyang Xiu, a poet in the Song Dynasty:

Chuzhou is surrounded by mountains....Concerning the mists in the trees go off at sunrise and the caves grow dark at sunset when the clouds return back under the sky, this is the change from bright morning to gloomy evening in the mountains. In spring, the wild flowers bloom and send out a faint fragrance. In summer, the fine trees are very beautiful, luxuriant and shading. In autumn, the wind blowing, the frost condensing, the sky is high and clear. And In winter, water falls down and rocks appear. Those are the four seasons in the mountains. Climbing on mountain at morning and turning down at evening, the scenery of the four seasons are various and the joy is also endless. As carriers are singing on the road and pedestrians are resting under trees, the preceding people shouting and the following responding, the olds bending down and the children being held and walking to and fro ceaselessly, they are the Chuzhou's people touring about. Fishing by the stream, the stream is deep and the fish are greasy. Making wine by the spring water, the water is fragrant and the wine is crystal-clear. Delicious dishes made by the mountain specialty and the vegetables picked up from the wilderness put on the table in a jumble, that is a banquet which is held by the prefecture chief...

---

[7] Picture source: http://www.yznews.cn/p/691522.html.

The two poems chant the "harmony" between man and nature: Nature is magnificent and splendid, and will not change according to man's will. People carry out all kinds of activities such as sightseeing, singing, hunting, brewing and banqueting in response to nature. During the process of keeping on communicating with nature, we can experience the spiritual realm of "harmony between man and nature".

As large-scale industrial production gradually develops in modern times, a change has taken place in the relationship between man and nature. In order to meet the demand of a city for efficient and fast-paced production and living styles, man has changed his attitude towards nature from reliance and belonging in ancient times to conquest and utility at present. Large-scale exploitation of urban underground water, continuous acquisition of farmland, worsening of climate and decrease of animals and plants show that during the process of extorting from nature, man has separated himself from nature, thus forming a dualistic structure, in which, man is the subject and nature is the object.

In the process of industrial production, changes have taken place in design value. Just take urban landscape design as an example. In the latter half of the 20th century, many cities were filled with factories and residential buildings but lacked urban landscapes. The only natural landscapes, mostly park grasslands, street gardens and border trees, played a very limited "greening" role.

As the living standard improves, in recent years, many cities have made a renewal, building many landscapes on streets, in parks or in communities. The "landscaping" plays an active role in improving environmental quality and relieving psychological pressure. However, either the "greening" in the last century or the "landscaping" in recent years, is a separation of man from natural objects (e.g. plants, water body, hill stone, etc.), deeming natural objects as something that can be utilized and serve man as if nature was a "servant" for relieving people's urban pressure and providing leisure values. From the perspective of design value, the relationship between man and nature has broken into "two skins". The concept of "harmony between man and nature" advocated in traditional values has been ignored and weakened in contemporary urban planning and design.

5 Conclusions

In 2012, the report of the 18th National Congress of the Communist Party of China mentioned "vigorously promoting ecological civilization construction" for the first time. In 2017, the 19th National Congress of the Communist Party of China included "ecological civilization construction" into an important national strategic program. The tenet of "ecological civilization construction" is "harmonious coexistence, virtuous cycle and comprehensive development", making man and natural ecology benefit from and complement each other, forming benign interaction between man and nature.

From the macroscopic level, "ecological civilization construction" points out a direction for today's urban environmental renewal design.

Viewed from the concept of "ecological civilization", urban landscape design will lay a foundation not only for providing services about relaxation and leisure, but also for building an overall urban ecological environment. Just like numerous "roots" of nature in a city, urban landscape design constitutes an overall "urban ecosystem" with the network of artificial society. In this "urban ecosystem", people live by relying on the "root" of nature, and at the same time, actively provide nature with sustainable space so that nature can root and sprout even in a highly artificial city to form a pattern of "nature in city & city in nature".

It is a renewal of design value, that is, nature is no longer deemed as an object to be utilized but as another "subject" with equal importance as man. Man and nature rely on and complement each other, and flourish together. This new design value is different from the concept of "harmony between man and nature" embodied in the classical garden thought. The concept of "harmony between man and nature" eventually attributes "man" to "nature", stressing man's reliance on and belonging to nature, but weakening man's demands for comfort, convenience and economy. The new design value is also different from the "dualism" during the process of modern industrial development, which isolates man from nature or even makes them contradict each other. The new design value is to explore a new development path under the guidance of the strategy of common prosperity of man and nature.

At present, represented by the rise of new private gardens, urban residents start a craze for autonomously reforming their dwelling environment, which is a practice of design value renewal to some extent. However, urban residents only make reforms from the plainest demand but do not consider the significance from the height of man and nature. It seems that urban designers should be able to subtly observe the vitality behind the reform, which may bring enlightenment to urban environmental renewal in the future.

Starting from cases of new private gardens, the paper considers the changes in design value about man and nature. Construction of new private gardens and other numerous autonomous transformations of the dwelling environment are people's non-professional behaviors. Viewed from the perspective of professional design, there are many problems such as simple piling-up of natural elements and inflexible design method. With the involvement of professional design forces, these problems are believed to be solved. What is more worthy of consideration is how professional design forces can absorb nutrients from these autonomous transformations and apply them to the consideration about overall environment of a city, or even design different samples about the relationship between "man and nature" according to economic levels, regional conditions and local customs and practices of different cities. Maybe it is a research emphasis of the next stage.

Acknowledgements. This research is supported by Jiangsu Philosophy and Social Science Foundation (Research on Inheritance and Innovation of Leisure Space Design in Gardens in Yangtze River Delta for Community Pension, Project No. 19YCS009).

References

1. Peng, Y.: Analysis of Chinese Classical Gardens. China Building Industry Press, Beijing (1986)
2. Yangzhou Garden Art Seminar: Poetic Dwelling: One Hundred New Gardens in Yangzhou. Guangling Publishing House, Yangzhou (2019)
3. Pan, J.: Theoretical Construction and Practical Exploration about Ecological Civilization Construction. China Social Sciences Press, Beijing (2019)

Anthropometric Hand Dimensions of Chinese Adults Using Three-Dimensional Scanning Technique

Qi Chen, Haining Wang[(✉)], and Kexiang Liu

School of Design, Hunan University, Changsha 410082, China
haining1872@qq.com

Abstract. The purpose of this study is to represent a large-scale Chinese hand anthropometric survey. A total of 937 adults (468 males and 469 females) age between 22 and 60 years-old were involved to be measured from six main areas of China. 3D scanning technology was adopted to capture duplicated models of both left and right hands in the splayed and closed postures respectively. 10 hand dimensions were extracted from the 3D scans. Statistics including mean, standard deviation, and various percentiles were calculated. T-tests were conducted to compare the differences between left and right hands. Moreover, the differences between males and females were analyzed. The results indicate that right hands are generally thicker, broader, and shorter than left hands. Also, males have larger hand measurements than females, as expected. This study provides ergonomic indication for hand related products design.

Keywords: Hand · Anthropometric measurement · Three-dimensional scanning

1 Introduction

Most of human mechanical interactions with the surrounding world are performed by the hands [1]. There are many tools and devices which are used by hands, from everyday life (scissors, hammers, mobile phones, mouses) to areas of expertise (laparoscope, rackets, VR controllers). Extensive research has shown that hand related products and handheld devices would have a poor use experience without good ergonomic design [2–4]. Lack of ergonomic principles in these hand related products have been proved to be a contributing factor in hand diseases, such as tenosynovitis [5–7], neuropraxia [8] and etc.

Anthropometry, as an important branch of ergonomics, collects large amounts of anthropometric dimensions, analyses the measured data, and studies their relationship with the work systems, thus provide indication for the design of products and systems [9–11]. A considerable amount of literature has been published on hand anthropometry of varies countries around the world. Furthermore, different methods have been proposed to obtain hand anthropometric data. Direct measurement is the most traditional and common approach, and it is involved in hand anthropometric study of Czech population [12], Korean [13], Iranian male workers [14], Nigerian farm workers [15], northern

M. M. Soares et al. (Eds.): HCII 2022, LNCS 13322, pp. 377–387, 2022.
https://doi.org/10.1007/978-3-031-05900-1_26

Colombian [11] and Bangladeshi agricultural farm workers [16]. Except this, some researchers developed hand anthropometric database by photogrammetric technique, such as the hand anthropometry of Spain [17], and San Francisco, USA [18]. In recent years, a new progressing method to collect human dimensions data, three-dimensional scanning method, has adopted by several research. For example, the hand anthropometric examinations of Americans [19], and people from Taiwan, China [20].

The 3D scanning technology have been developing over years, which facilitates the investigation of anthropometry. Using a 3D laser or optical scanner, 3D scanning collects surface measurements including not only length and circumference but also complex geometry including shape, surface area, and volume [21–25]. Compared with direct measurement or photogrammetry, 3D scanning shows better reliability if there is good scanning quality [21–23].

On the one hand, data for hand dimensions of Chinese are scarce. On the other hand, there has been a significant rising of indigenous technological companies who have started to explore their own design, including the design of hand related products and handheld devices [26]. There is high demand for these companies to improve the ergonomics of their products to achieve good wearing comfort for hand products. Therefore, a representative and up-to-date hand anthropometric database is needed to help improve the ergonomics design of hand products. In this study, a hand anthropometry survey was created by recruiting 937 participants from 6 main geographic areas of the China (North China, Northeast China, Northwest China, Southwest China, South China, and East China). The aim of this study includes:

- To build a database including scanned hand models and hand dimensions of Chinese;
- To investigate the differences in hand dimensions between left and right hands, and between males and females;
- To compare obtained hand dimensions with corresponding dimensions from other populations.

2   Methodology

2.1   Participants

According to the procedures outlined in the *ISO 15535* [27]: *general requirements for establishing anthropometric databases*, the minimum sample size per region to build a national hand database was calculated to be 100. The accuracy of measurements depends on the sample size. In this study, a larger sample size involving 937 subjects was chosen in order to obtain sufficient data quality and generalization.

The proportional stratified random sampling method was adopted for this survey, through which the population was split into six strata. After the strata were established, a simple random sample was captured from every stratum separately according to proportion. This survey has three demographic variables: gender, age, and geographical area. With the proportional stratified random sampling method, this anthropometric survey is considered to be representative in gender, age and geographical area (Table 1).

Table 1. Basic information of all participants.

Characteristics		Amount			Percentage	
		Total	Male	Female	Male	Female
Age Group	18–29	206	108	98	11.53%	10.46%
	30–39	250	115	135	12.27%	14.41%
	40–49	229	121	108	12.91%	11.53%
	50–65	241	116	125	12.38%	13.34%
	>65	11	8	3	0.85%	0.32%
	Total	**937**	**468**	**469**	**49.95%**	**50.05%**
Living Area	North China	157	78	79	8.32%	8.43%
	Northeast China	156	78	78	8.32%	8.32%
	Northwest China	155	77	78	8.22%	8.32%
	Southwest China	156	78	78	8.32%	8.32%
	South China	156	79	77	8.43%	8.22%
	East China	157	78	79	8.23%	8.43%

2.2 Experiment

In this study, a novel 3D scanning approach was adopted after a pilot scanning trial. This trial was conducted to obtain good hand images, and avoid errors resulted from hidden hand regions and sway of the hand that were found in previous studies [24, 25, 28]. Two methods were used to improve the scanning quality. Firstly, change reflecting angle effectively to avoid the occurrence of hidden hand regions. Secondly, reduce scanning time by using Artec Eva scanner (Artec 3D, Luxembourg), which has a scanning speed with million points per second. Thirdly, enhance the proficiency of operators who were selected by the pilot hand scanning trial. In this way, the required time for scanning was shortened from 8 min to 2 min, result in the decrease of hand sway [21].

Each participant was shown a brief overview on the aim and processes before the experiment. Marking stickers ($\phi = 3$ mm, thickness $= 0.5$ mm) were attached on the hand of each participant as hand identified landmarks. Both hands were scanned in the splayed and closed postures respectively with an accuracy of up to 0.1 mm. Artec Studio 15 (Artec 3D, Luxembourg) was used as the 3D data post-processing software to export high-quality 3D hand models. Geomagic Wrap (Artec 3D, Luxembourg) were chosen to extracted measurements and features of 3D hand scans.

2.3 Measurement

Hand landmarks and dimensions were identified and extracted according to a quantity of literature [11, 13, 16, 17, 29–33]. Definition of 10 dimensions was based on ISO 7250 [32], GBT 5703 [33] and other previous studies [34], as shown in Table 2. All measurements were calculated and extracted using Geomagic Wrap.

Table 2. Definition of hand dimensions.

No	Hand dimensions	Definition
1	Palm length	The distance on the palm of the hand, from a line connecting the radial and ulnar styloid processes to the proximal finger crease of the middle finger, measured parallel to the long axis of the outstretched middle finger
2	Hand thickness	Maximum thickness of the hand, measured across the knuckles
3	Hand length	The distance from the tip of the third finger, along its long axis, to a line connecting the radial and ulnar styloid processes
4	Hand breadth	Projected distance between radial and ulnar metacarpals at the Projected distance between radial and ulnar metacarpals at the level of the metacarpal heads from the second to the fifth metacarpal, measured perpendicular to the long axis of the middle finger
5	Thumb length	Length of the thumb from the proximal thumb crease to the tip of the thumb
6	Middle finger length	The distance from the tip of the third finger to the proximal finger crease on the palm of the hand
7	Thumb breadth	Maximum breadth of the thumb in the region of the joint between the two phalanges
8	Middle finger breadth, proximal	Maximum breadth of the third finger in the region of the joint between middle and proximal phalanges
9	Wrist circumference	Minimum circumference of the wrist at the level of the radial styloid, with the hand outstretched. The tape passes just distal to the ulnar styloid
10	Hand circumference	The superficial distance around the edge of the metacarpal

2.4 Statistical Analysis

SPSS 25 (IBM Corp., Armonk, New York) was used for the statistical analysis of all dimensions for males and females respectively. Statistics like mean value, standard deviation, and various percentiles (5th, 25th, 50th, 75th and 95th) were calculated, as shown in Table 3. All hand measurements were analyzed using Kolmogorov-Smirnov test. Independent sample T-tests was conducted to compare the differences between left and right hands. Besides, to investigate the diversity between males and females, another independent sample T-tests was taken for right hand dimensions. At the aspect of ethnography, T-test were also conducted to compare the hand features from six areas of China. Moreover, differences of hand dimensions between Chinese and other populations were analyzed.

3 Result

The results of anthropometric hand dimensions of left and right including the mean and standard deviation, taken from Chinese male and female of six geographic areas, are shown in Table 3 and Table 4. These two tables also show a matched samples t-test results between left and right hands for male and female respectively. In this paper, hand dimensions comparisons mainly focus on right hands. Tables 5 and 6 lists the 5th, 25th, 50th, 75th, and 95th percentile for right hand measurements. Table 7 depicts a comparison of right hand measurements between male and female.

Table 3. Statistics of left and right hand dimensions of Chinese males.

Hand dimensions	Left hand		Right hand		% diff.	t	P
	Mean	SD	Mean	SD			
1) Palm length	113.38	5.95	113.25	6.20	0.11	0.632	0.527
2) Hand thickness	29.27	1.73	30.50	1.92	−4.21	−18.52	0.000**
3) Hand length	189.17	9.05	189.32	9.13	−0.08	−0.184	0.854
4) Hand breadth	82.46	4.09	83.58	3.89	−1.36	−10.497	0.000**
5) Thumb length	58.23	3.63	58.50	4.02	−0.45	−1.586	0.113
6) Middle finger length	78.82	4.49	78.54	4.62	0.35	2.49	0.013*
7) Thumb breadth	21.16	2.95	21.66	3.65	−2.36	−2.732	0.007*
8) Middle finger breadth, proximal	19.80	2.65	19.99	3.28	−0.97	−1.184	0.237
9) Wrist circumference	172.98	9.46	174.30	9.72	−0.76	−6.021	0.000**
10) Hand circumference	201.25	10.11	203.58	9.70	−1.16	−10.214	0.000**

% diff. = (Left hand mean-Right hand mean)/Left hand mean * 100.
*Statistically significant at $\alpha = 0.05$, ($p < 0.05$) at confidence interval percentage 95%.
**statistically significant at $\alpha = 0.001$, ($p < 0.001$).

Table 4. Statistics of left and right hand dimensions of Chinese females.

Hand dimensions	Left hand		Right hand		% diff.	t	P
	Mean	SD	Mean	SD			
1) Palm length	103.82	5.42	104.30	5.89	−0.46	−2.08	0.04*
2) Hand thickness	26.17	1.58	27.05	1.79	−3.35	−15.08	0.00**
3) Hand length	173.55	8.21	174.85	8.55	−0.75	−4.77	0.00**
4) Hand breadth	74.56	3.65	75.57	3.57	−1.36	−12.70	0.00**
5) Thumb length	54.06	3.43	54.54	3.42	−0.89	−3.09	0.00**
6) Middle finger length	73.82	3.95	73.94	4.05	−0.16	−0.85	0.40
7) Thumb breadth	18.34	3.55	19.20	2.79	−4.74	−4.14	0.00**
8) Middle finger breadth, proximal	17.56	3.38	18.05	2.54	−2.82	−2.59	0.01*
9) Wrist circumference	156.63	10.12	156.94	9.65	−0.20	−1.60	0.11
10) Hand circumference	182.46	9.68	184.61	9.60	−1.18	−12.86	0.00**

% diff. = (Left hand mean-Right hand mean)/Left hand mean.
*Statistically significant at $\alpha = 0.05$, ($p < 0.05$) at confidence interval percentage 95%.
**statistically significant at $\alpha = 0.001$, ($p < 0.001$).

Table 5. Percentiles of right hand dimensions of Chinese males.

Hand dimensions	Percentiles				
	5th	25th	50th	75th	95th
1) Palm length	103.83	108.99	112.77	117.24	123.78
2) Hand thickness	27.62	29.21	30.36	31.64	34.03
3) Hand length	175.22	182.82	189.09	195.36	204.88
4) Hand breadth	77.58	80.99	83.57	86.04	89.97
5) Thumb length	51.52	55.95	58.38	61.21	65.48
6) Middle finger length	70.83	75.58	78.55	81.65	85.53
7) Thumb breadth	19.37	21.10	22.10	23.07	24.83
8) Middle finger breadth, proximal	18.24	19.54	20.39	21.23	22.65
9) Wrist circumference	159.17	167.46	173.90	180.94	191.13
10) Hand circumference	188.43	197.00	203.69	209.88	219.21

Table 6. Percentiles of right hand dimensions of Chinese females.

Hand dimensions	Percentiles				
	5th	25th	50th	75th	95th
1) Palm length	94.65	100.40	104.20	107.70	115.31
2) Hand thickness	24.05	25.88	26.94	28.29	30.16
3) Hand length	161.84	169.07	174.32	179.84	190.33
4) Hand breadth	69.54	73.03	75.43	77.77	81.70
5) Thumb length	49.03	52.20	54.39	56.98	60.22
6) Middle finger length	67.28	71.01	74.02	76.81	81.11
7) Thumb breadth	16.84	18.63	19.46	20.42	21.60
8) Middle finger breadth, proximal	16.38	17.51	18.35	19.04	20.18
9) Wrist circumference	142.10	150.53	155.89	162.92	174.34
10) Hand circumference	169.87	178.26	183.50	190.69	202.21

Table 7. Comparison of right hand measurements between Chinese males and females.

Hand dimensions	Male		Female		% diff.	t	P
	Mean	SD	Mean	SD			
1) Palm length	113.25	6.20	104.30	5.89	7.90	21.99	0.00
2) Hand thickness	30.50	1.92	27.05	1.79	11.31	27.73	0.00
3) Hand length	189.32	9.13	174.85	8.55	7.64	24.29	0.00
4) Hand breadth	83.58	3.89	75.57	3.57	9.58	31.91	0.00
5) Thumb length	58.50	4.02	54.54	3.42	6.77	15.71	0.00
6) Middle finger length	78.54	4.62	73.94	4.05	5.86	15.73	0.00
7) Thumb breadth	21.66	3.65	19.20	2.79	11.36	11.21	0.00
8) Middle finger breadth, proximal	19.99	3.28	18.05	2.54	9.70	9.84	0.00
9) Wrist circumference	174.30	9.72	156.94	9.65	9.96	26.48	0.00
10) Hand circumference	203.58	9.70	184.61	9.60	9.32	27.79	0.00

% diff. = (Left hand mean-Right hand mean)/Left hand mean.
Confidence interval percentage of statistically significant is 95%.

4 Discussion

In this study, ethnic did not be chosen as a criterion in participants recruitment. After 3D hand scanning and data collection, it was found that 98% of the participants are Han nationality. Han Nationality is the largest nationality among the 56 ethnic groups of China, accounting for 91.59% of China's population. So, the sample of this study could be thought to be in accordance with the ethnic group distribution of China.

A three-dimensional scanning method was adopted in this study. Duplicated hand models were obtained through 3D scanning, after which 10 hand dimensions were extracted. Consequently, the result of this study is expandable that more dimensions could be extracted and analyzed according in the future. It is worth noting that unlike conventional direct measurement, 3D scanning doesn't have skin deformation issues resulted from measurement tools, so the figure length dimensions of this study might be smaller than that of conventional direct measurement method, and the figures of width and thickness dimensions might be bigger [21]. With the development of computer-aided design (CAD), more and more products would be developed through CAD technology. Compared with conventional direct measurement method, three-dimension scanning method could match more with CAD, hence might gradually gain its popularity.

The result of this survey could be used to determine dimensions of hand related products and hand-held devices. When designing a dimension-adjustable product which covers 90% of Chinese population, product dimensions should range from the 5th to the 95th percentile. If a glove is developed for Chinese women, then it is not appropriate for the part of palm to be shorter than 94.7 mm (5th percentile value of Chinese female palm length). Besides, percentiles of finger breadth could be used to determine the diameter of rings, and percentiles of hand breadth could provide design reference to the breadth of mouses.

4.1   Left-Right Hand Comparison

Chinese males have significant differences ($p < 0.001$) between left and right hand in the measurement of hand thickness, hand breadth, wrist circumference, and hand circumference. Females have significant differences ($p < 0.001$) between left and right hand in the measurement of hand thickness, hand breadth, hand length, thumb length, thumb breadth, and hand circumference. Males and females both have considerable differences in the measurement of hand circumference, hand thickness and hand breadth. Moreover, for right hands, all length dimensions are shorter than left hand, and all breadth and width dimensions are bigger than left hand. This might be result from higher frequency of right-hand use.

It is also worth noting that although the p values of these measurements are below 0.001, the difference percentages of them only range from 0.1 to 4%. So, when producing products of both hands, whether to consider the differences between left and right hand should base on the specific scenery.

4.2   Male-Female Comparison

T-test results and percentage differences suggest a considerable differences ($p < 0.001$) between Chinese men and women. As expect, males have larger values in all dimensions, and the percentage differences are large (vary from 5.86 to 11.36%). This result indicates a strong necessity to design different product sizes for males and females respectively. For example, mouses for females should be shorter in length at about 7.5% (the percentage difference of hand length between males and females is 7.5%), be narrowed in breadth at about 11.5% (the percentage difference of hand breadth between males and females is 7.5%); straps of wrist-wearing products for females should have 10% shorter than males (the percentage difference of wrist circumference between males and females is 10%); rings for males and females should have an approximate 10% difference in diameter between them (the finger breadth of females are about 10% less than males).

5 Conclusion

In this study, 937 males and females from six representative cities of China were recruited and 3D scanned. Both hands of them were scanned as 3D models and 10 dimensions were measured and analyzed. The result shows basic hands features and percentiles of Chinese male and female. This is the first large-scale measurement of Chinese hands using 3D scanning, which could provide design references for various types of hand related products aimed for Chinese population.

This study compares the differences of hand dimensions between left and right hands. The result reveals that both male and female hands differ significantly in terms of hand thickness, hand breadth, middle finger middle phalanx length, and hand circumference. However, the percentage differences in these measurements are only between 0.1% and 4%, so it is worth considering whether to ignore the differences between the left and right hands when designing products.

In addition, a comparison of hand dimensions between male and female shows that all values are significantly larger for men compared with women. This suggests that in some hand product designs involving both male and female users, it is important to differentiate between them in separate designs. Furthermore, the hand characteristics of the Chinese differ significantly from those of European and American countries, but not so much from those of Asian countries such as Korea and Jordan. The results of this study can be utilized to design hand related products for other Asian countries.

References

1. León, B., Morales, A., Sancho-Bru, J.: From Robot to Human Grasping Simulation. vol. 19. Springer, Cham (2014). https://doi.org/10.1007/978-3-319-01833-1
2. Goonetilleke, R.S.: Designing to miminize discomfort. Ergon Design 6(3), 12–19 (1998)
3. Chang, S.R., Park, S., Freivalds, A.: Ergonomic evaluation of the effects of handle types on garden tools. Int. J. Ind. Ergon. 24(1), 99–105 (1999)
4. Kim, H.K., et al.: Does the hand anthropometric dimension influence touch interaction? J. Comput. Inf. Syst. 59(1), 85–96 (2019)
5. Li, K.W.: Ergonomic design and evaluation of wire-tying hand tools. Int. J. Ind. Ergon. 30(3), 149–161 (2002)
6. Andréu, J.-L., et al.: Hand pain other than carpal tunnel syndrome (CTS): the role of occupational factors. Best Pract. Res. Clin. Rheumatol. 25(1), 31–42 (2011)
7. Kong, Y.-K., Kim, D.-M.: The relationship between hand anthropometrics, total grip strength and individual finger force for various handle shapes. Int. J. Occup. Saf. Ergon. 21(2), 187–192 (2015)
8. Horgan, L., O'riordan, D., Doctor, N.: Neuropraxia following laparoscopic procedures: an occupational injury. Minim. Invasive Ther. Allied Technol. 6(1), 33–35 (1997)
9. Chang, J., et al.: Determination of bicycle handle diameters considering hand anthropometric data and user satisfaction. In: Proceedings of the Human Factors and Ergonomics Society Annual Meeting. SAGE Publications Sage CA: Los Angeles, CA (2010)

10. Reis, P.F., et al.: Influence of anthropometry on meat-packing plant workers: an approach to the shoulder joint. Work **41**(Supplement 1), 4612–4617 (2012)
11. Oviedo-Trespalacios, O., et al.: Hand anthropometric study in northern Colombia. Int. J. Occup. Saf. Ergon. **23**(4), 472–480 (2017)
12. Bures, M., Gorner, T., Sediva, B.: Hand anthropometry of Czech population. In: 2015 IEEE International Conference on Industrial Engineering and Engineering Management (IEEM). IEEE (2015)
13. Jee, S.-C., Yun, M.H.: An anthropometric survey of Korean hand and hand shape types. Int. J. Ind. Ergon. **53**, 10–18 (2016)
14. Mirmohammadi, S.J., et al.: Anthropometric hand dimensions in a population of Iranian male workers in 2012. Int. J. Occup. Saf. Ergon. **22**(1), 125–130 (2016)
15. Obi, O.F.: Hand anthropometry survey of rural farm workers in south-eastern Nigeria. Ergonomics **59**(4), 603–611 (2016)
16. Shahriar, M., Parvez, M., Lutfi, M.: A survey of hand anthropometry of Bangladeshi agricultural farm workers. Int. J. Ind. Ergon. **78**, 102978 (2020)
17. Vergara, M., Agost, M.J., Gracia-Ibáñez, V.: Dorsal and palmar aspect dimensions of hand anthropometry for designing hand tools and protections. Hum. Factors Ergon. Manuf. Serv. Ind. **28**(1), 17–28 (2018)
18. Rogers, M.S., et al.: A three-dimensional anthropometric solid model of the hand based on landmark measurements. Ergonomics **51**(4), 511–526 (2008)
19. Griffin, L., Sokolowski, S., Seifert, E.: Process considerations in 3D hand anthropometric data collection. In: Proceedings of 3DBODY. TECH, pp. 121–130 (2018)
20. Lin, C.H., Lin, P.T., Chao, Y.: Hand surface area variation analyzed by 3D laser scan measurement. In: Proceedings of the Second European Academic Research Conference on Global Business, Economics, Finance and Banking. Zurich-Switzerland (2015)
21. Lee, W., et al.: Comparison of a semiautomatic protocol using plastering and three-dimensional scanning techniques with the direct measurement protocol for hand anthropometry. Hum. Factors Ergon. Manuf. Serv. Ind. **27**(3), 138–146 (2017)
22. Chang, C.-C., et al.: Error control and calibration in three-dimensional anthropometric measurement of the hand by laser scanning with glass support. Measurement **40**(1), 21–27 (2007)
23. Lee, W.-S., Yoon, S.-H., You, H.-C.: Development of a 3D semi-automatic measurement protocol for hand anthropometric measurement. IE Interfaces **24**(2), 105–111 (2011)
24. Kim, M.-H., Nam, Y.-J.: Development of three dimensional scanner for anthropometric measurement. J. Ergon. Soc. Korea **20**(3), 77–88 (2001)
25. Li, Z., et al.: Validation of a three-dimensional hand scanning and dimension extraction method with dimension data. Ergonomics **51**(11), 1672–1692 (2008)
26. Zhao, Z., et al.: China's industrial policy in relation to electronics manufacturing. Chin. World. Econ. **15**(3), 33–51 (2007)
27. ISO, I., 15535: General requirements for establishing anthropometric databases. Int. Organ. Stand (2006). https://www.iso.org/standard/57179.html. Accessed on 5 April 2021
28. Choi, H., et al.: Development of hand measurement protocol for glove design. Seoul, South Korea: Size Korea (2006)
29. Hsiao, H., et al.: Firefighter hand anthropometry and structural glove sizing: a new perspective. Hum. Factors **57**(8), 1359–1377 (2015)
30. Mandahawi, N., et al.: Hand anthropometry survey for the Jordanian population. Int. J. Ind. Ergon. **38**(11–12), 966–976 (2008)
31. Cakit, E., et al.: A survey of hand anthropometry and biomechanical measurements of dentistry students in Turkey. Hum. Factors Ergon. Manuf. Serv. Ind. **24**(6), 739–753 (2014)
32. ISO, I.: 7250–1: 2017 Basic human body measurements for technological design—Part 1: body measurement definitions and landmarks. ISO: Geneva, Switzerland (2017)

33. China National Institute of Standardization et al.: Anthropometric project for technical design. General Administration of Quality Supervision, Inspection and Quarantine of the People's Republic of China; Standardization Administration of the People's Republic of China, p. 40 (2011)
34. Li, Z., et al.: An anthropometric study for the anthropomorphic design of tomato-harvesting robots. Comput. Electron. Agric. **163**, 104881 (2019)

Research on Peak Experience Design in Rural Cultural Tourism Service System: Take Diejiao Water Village of Foshan as an Example

Xiong Ding[✉], Jing Ning, and Zenan Pu

Guangzhou Academy of Fine Arts, Guangzhou 510006, China
dingxiong@gzarts.edu.cn

Abstract. This paper aims to discuss how to use the service design thinking and method to shape rural tourism services, that can better meet market demand and touch regional culture deeply. On the basis of Peak-end Rule and four peak experience factors of Behavioral Design, with the sense of experience, participation and ritual as the focus, through insight and analysis the needs of folk festivals, this paper deduced the "Moment-Goal" Model, and proposing "Four Peak Experience Moments" which including "Peak of Atmosphere", "Peak of Fun", "Peak of Emotion" and "Peak of Culture". Taking Foshan Diejiao Water Village as an example, according to the "Moment-Goal" Model of Peak Experience, "Drifting Dragon in Diejiao" cultural tourism brand and dragon boat cultural tourism service system are constructed. It has designed a full-time, multi-level and multi-route cultural travel service, as well as a series of touchpoints to help users achieve peak experience. The derivation of "Moment-Goal" Model of Peak Experience and its application in the cultural tourism service of "Drifting Dragon in Diejiao" have verified the important role of "Four Peak Experience Moments" in the innovation and optimization of rural cultural tourism service experience.

Keywords: Rural cultural tourism · Service design · Peak experience · "Moment-Goal" model · Four peak experience moments

1 Introduction

With the rapid development of China's social economy and industrialization, people have diversified consumption needs and their consumption concepts and needs are also changing. What's more, people pay more attention on services and experience. In recent years, cultural tourism that integrates leisure, entertainment and cultural experience has gained great popularity throughout the country. On the one hand, it is a manifestation of their spiritual and cultural needs after their basic needs have been fulfilled. The traditional culture with excellent and rich connotations has also quickly raised the public resonance. Compared with the "mark" tourism of just taking pictures at each spot, tourists hope to have an in-depth experience in terms of customs, folk customs, and dietary customs.

The rural revitalization strategic plan has mentioned that the implementation of the rural revitalization strategy is an effective way to inherit the excellent traditional Chinese culture. At the same time, a good combination of rural tourism and rural revitalization can also promote economic and cultural development. The development of local cultural tourism not only meets the needs of tourists for vacation and cultural experience, but also enhances local infrastructure and industrial development, unleashing the local value and diversifying its development. This paper will take Foshan Diejiao Water Village as an example, consciously design the peak moments of unique local folklore activities to re-adapt to modern life and explore the importance of creating "peak experience" in shaping rural tourism service experience with the service design thinking and method as well as the four factors theory of "Peak Experience" in Behavioral Design.

2 Rural Cultural Tourism Services and Development Trend Against the Backdrop of Experience Economy

James Gill pointed out in *The Experience Economy* that we are currently in a new era of "experience economy". When companies consciously use services as a stage, products and props to attract consumers, experience occurs [1]. China is currently undergoing a transition from an industrial society to a post-industrial society when the ecological civilization is taking shape. In the post-industrial society, design covers both lifestyles and services, which in turn derives new relationships between people and products, new design content, and new service systems [2]. Human-centered and Stakeholder-Centered [3] service design began to pay more attention to the experience of users in the service system, which, in addition to meeting functional needs, focus more on the psychological needs of users. Therefore, the development of the service economy has naturally spawned a wave of experience economy.

Most of the existing research focus on the revival of traditional folk culture and the development of cultural tourism from the perspective of experience economy, and take the specific historical and cultural venues as the carrier. Scholars have put forward different opinions and plans on how to develop experience tourism while protecting and embodying the authenticity of its culture. Dan Zhang proposed that in order to realize the sustainable development of historical and cultural places, it is necessary to fully explore and express cultural and emotional factors other than the material resources of the block, and reposition the role of the revived historical and cultural places in urban development [4]. Fang Lan believed that the spirit contained in historical and cultural places is mainly embodied in the four aspects of natural environment, artificial environment, human behavior factors and cultural environment, emphasizing that protection and development must have place awareness, and the combination of environment, space and human activities is the driving force for its sustainable development [5]. Jun Huo and Rong Han summarized three functional replacement modes which are continuous, replaceable and comprehensive for the cultural tourism transformation of historical districts. Based on the experience "4E Theory", they analyzed the supposed universality and particularity of the renewal of historical districts to combine the urban economy, cultural heritage, citizen memory and historical building protection as a whole [6]. The author of this paper has also discussed the combination of regional culture and entertainment atmosphere in the immersive travel experience based on the five senses of tourists, proposing that through the mutual support and repeated stimulation of synesthesia and five senses throughout the entire service, tourist's full role experience could be realized [7]. Ancient villages, historical districts and other places are one of the important carriers of local folk culture, and they are also experiential places. While achieving the rich levels and content of experiential places, it is necessary to fully explore local cultural resources, protect the original ecology of folk culture, and clarify the positions of venue's functions to avoid homogeneity.

The difference on people's experience demands between rural cultural tourism and the general sightseeing is that the former one emphasis on the in-depth experience of local culture. As a concentrated expression of regional cultural characteristics, folk rituals essentially have their corresponding cultural groups as the boundary of participants, and have certain participation thresholds for other cultural groups. This makes folk rituals a kind of self-identity and culture-identity. Through the interaction on folk rituals, abstract concepts are transformed into specific emotions, enabling people to understand, accept and practice culture in a perceptual and empirical way [8], so as to achieve the emotional communication. Modern young people's need for individuality is becoming more and more obvious. The traditional culture is inevitably subject to have collisions with multiple cultures coupled with the influence of globalization. This is also the main reason why "Nation Fashion" and cultural cross-border cooperation are popular. Although various changes have taken place in folklore activities, it is also the way that modern people express and inherit the value of traditional culture while enabling them to actively choose folklore cultural activities.

3 Four Factors for Shaping Peak Experience in Behavioral Design

In addition to the pleasant scenery, it is also necessary to realize culture promotion through the experience, knowledge and memory of the folk rituals with local character- istics for rural cultural tourism. The moments that can leave people with good memories are always during the peak experience. Psychologists have found that when people recall an experience, their impression usually depends on how they feel at the peak moment and at the end of the experience. This is the "Peak-end Rule" [9], which has been widely used in the field of business services, providing an important reference for user experience management and improving user satisfaction. On the theoretical basis of the "Peak-end Rule", the American behavioral designer Heath brothers conducted further research and exploration, and found that a pleasant peak-end experience often has one or more of the four elements, namely "happiness", "cognition", "glory" and "connection", and cited their requirements [10].

3.1 Elevation Moment

The "Elevation Moment" can be shaped by three ways: enhancing sensory perception, increasing the excitement of events, and breaking the routine [10]. "Seeing, hearing, smelling, tasting, touching" are the most direct ways for people to perceive things, amplifying people's different feelings in daily life, and creating a situational experience that is higher than that of daily life. Enhance the excitement means making the whole event more tenses by giving appropriate pressure and make participants feel uneasy about unknown results. Breaking the script can subvert people's expectations and create unexpected surprises.

3.2 Insight Moment

The "Insight Moment" is a change of people's original understanding. One is the self-knowledge of one's own abilities, social positioning, expectations and concepts, and the other is the knowledge of the external environment, things, and laws. Initiating a "Insight Moment" often requires practical action. The change of cognition comes from people's hearts. Through the transmission of concepts, it is difficult to change the original cognition of others. The key is to let users discover and form them by themselves. When facing new things, people need to try or challenge their own abilities to obtain accurate and profound cognitive changes.

3.3 Pride Moment

The "Pride Moment" refers to the moment when a sense of accomplishment and honor is obtained. Honor is the self-recognition which is closely related to the changes in people's cognition. The "Pride Moment" emphasizes affirmation given from outside, and it will be expressed as an external expression. Pride is worth remembering and sharing. Milestones can divide the final goal into multiple small targets and record each small achievement. Badges, trophies, prizes and other things can visualize glory which can also continuously trigger the glory experience in the future commemoration and sharing process.

3.4 Connection Moment

The "Connection Moment" can increase people's sense of belonging and draw closer relationships. The wonderful and glorious moments are always unforgettable precisely because of the participation, witness or comparison. French social psychologist Gustave Le Pen pointed out that when people gather together, their feelings and thoughts will develop in a same direction, thus forming a collective psychology [11], and it is easier for people in a group to feel happy in an "infection" or "synchronized" way. Anthropologists have found that the sense of mission is a more powerful driving force than passion as it is a group emotion, including a sense of responsibility to others. People with a high sense of mission are more efficient in completing tasks [12]. Another study found that group members who share adversity also have a stronger sense of connection [13].

4   Build the Peak Shaping Model of Rural Cultural Tourism

As an important part of rural cultural tourism, folk custom tourism experience is an important selling point of rural tourism economy [14]. Based on the characteristics of the demand for local folk cultural experience in rural cultural tourism, the author proposes the "Moment-Goal" Model of Peak Experience (which can be abbreviated as "M-G"PE Model), and points out the relationship between the four factors of peak experience and rural cultural tourism experience goals (Fig. 1).

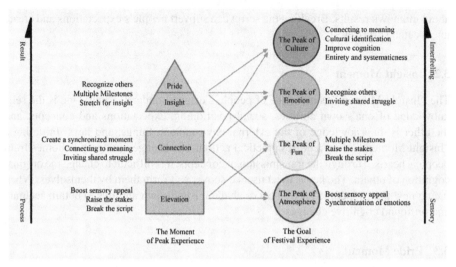

Fig. 1. "Moment-Goal" model of peak experience

The author surveyed on the experience needs of folk activities in rural tourism through questionnaire. Most of the respondents indicated that their needs for folk activities experience are mainly concentrated on the atmosphere, culture, and emotions, hoping that the folk activities can be rich and interesting in content, keep pace with the times and break routines. Tourism is a highly contextualized activity. The environmental atmosphere composed of people and objects in the tourism can easily affect people's psychology and make people feel happy and excited [15]. Atmosphere is the most intuitive expression of the scene and an important experience element to experience folk culture. Domestic tourists prefer to travel together, creating special memories during the journey, and enhancing the relationship between relatives and friends. In terms of cultural experience, the inheritance and development of local culture depends on the continuation of its cultural memory, and folk rituals is one of the main inheritance ways [16]. Through the interaction on rituals, abstract concepts are transformed into specific emotions, allowing people to understand, accept and practice culture in a perceptual way of experience [8].

Combining with people's four major needs of culture, atmosphere, emotion and fun of folklore experience in rural cultural tourism, and the inductive analysis of the four factors shaping the peak of behavioral design, we can add the Atmosphere Peak (for building atmosphere), Fun Peak (for adding entertainment), Emotion Peak (for enhance relations) and Culture Peak (for stressing rituals) into the folklore cultural experience activity process design to upgrade the sense of folk culture and meet people's psychological needs for rural cultural tourism experience. These four types of peaks can also be constructed by a four-factor method. If we sort out these four types according to the degree of difficulty, the Peak of Atmosphere triggered by Elevation Moment and Connection Moment is the easiest to obtain, and the Peak of Fun which also belongs to the external perception follows the Peak of Atmosphere. However, the Peak of Cultural and the Peak of Emotion that require deep internal perception are relatively more difficult to realize.

5 Peak Experience Design in the Cultural Tourism Service System of Diejiao Water Village

5.1 Historical & Cultural Resources and the Problems on Tourism Development of Diejiao Water Village

Diejiao is an ancient village in the city, located in the central area of Nanhai District, Foshan City, Guangdong Province, China. The village is surrounded by rivers, and the waterways are vertically and horizontally meandering, thus, it is called Dieshui (water overlapping) or Diexi (streams overlapping) since ancient times. According to local village history, the ancestors of Diejiao moved here in the south at the end of the Northern Song Dynasty. After the regional adjustment in the later years, the total area of Diejiao is now 393 districts where a lot of historical cultural buildings have been inherited. Temples, ancient roadways, and ancient dwellings all display the local cultural landscape. A lot of inherited folk traditional cultural events such as Dragon Lion Martial Arts, Chaji Shifan Gongs and Drums, Dragon Boat Race (what follows in the paper are abbreviated as DBR) have been added in to the intangible heritage name list.

DBR is an annual festival in Diejiao, and it also enjoys reputation in the surrounding areas. Because Diejiao's waterways are generally shallow and narrow with many twists and turns, the Dragon Boat Race is a time trial where a single dragon boat flows out of the race. The local people use "three turns passed only within one drum" to describe the sharp turns of Diejiao DBR. The competition is a test of people's skills and tacit understanding of the dragon boat team members as it requires them to control the boat to turn and avoid obstacles together. At present, there are 4 natural waterways of S-type, C-type, L-type and T-type in the area as the fixed track for the annual DBR. In recent years, with the promotion of traditional events by the media, Diejiao DBR has become more known as "Drifting Race" and "Curve Race". The Diejiao DBR has also become a spiritual and cultural symbol handed down by the locals from generation to generation. When it comes to dragon boats, the locals are very proud to talk about the mystery and fun of it.

Although the local DBR is enthusiastically sought after by the majority of tourists, it still faces four kinds of problems on the following aspects: 1) Physical space, lack of public facilities and space planning; 2) Activity process, few people can know the rich events and activities; 3) Culture promotion, non-sufficient cultural brands publicity and low participation of foreign tourists; 4) Public resources, lack of public space and supporting facilities. Thus, Diejiao Water Village face a lot of challenges in tourism development.

5.2 Build Peak Experience in Diejiao Water Village Cultural Tourism

As the DBR is a local annual festival, Diejiao Water Village has the most tourists through-out the year at this time, and has fewer tourists during the rest of the year. If we analyze it from the perspective of emotional experience curve, we can see that the peak of current year-round activities of Diejiao only happened during the Dragon Boat Festival. This research project hopes to turn Diejiao into a Dragon Boat Cultural Tourism Area, spreading the local water village culture and dragon boat culture, attracting tourists to travel throughout the year, so as to consciously design and arrange the experience peak from time and space perspectives and form a full-year peak experience system of the Diejiao Dragon Boat Cultural Activity.

After investigating the current situation of Diejiao tourism and analyzing the needs of users, we learned that the public expects a special experience other than sightseeing, and hopes to enhance cultural understanding and leave good memories during the journey. Formal, boring, and uninspiring activities should be avoided, and timely information on scenic activities and plenty of time for activities should be provided. Therefore, the "Drifting Dragon in Diejiao" (which is called "DDD" for short) cultural tourism brand will target at young people and families with children, focusing on people's needs for atmosphere, fun, emotion and culture in the folk activities. Build a full-time, multi-level, multi-route festival cultural tourism experience through four peak experience of festival activities, enhance the sense of experience, ritual and participation of traditional festivals, and create a year-round dragon boat cultural tourism service in Diejiao (Fig. 2).

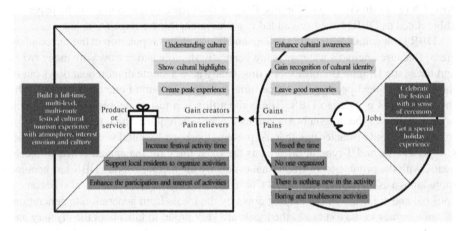

Fig. 2. Value proposition canvas of "DDD"

The development of rural cultural tourism not only provides leisure places for tourists, but is also the main place for local residents to spend their daily life and hold folk activities. Therefore, more stakeholders, who will participate in activities with tourists or provide related services for them, will be involved in the "DDD" dragon boat cultural tourism service system. With tourists as the main recipients of service, these stakeholders are the local government, local resources, cultural organizations, accommodation services, and suppliers. Besides, travel service staff, boatmen, and dragon boat race members, culture promoters, performers, intangible culture craftsmen from local cultural organizations are included. They are important service providers of local cultural tourism experience. The results of tourism development can better benefit local residents and promote the diversified development if a more authentic local culture can be provided for service providers.

Service System Map can clearly describe the various elements of the service, the structure and its purpose (Fig. 3), enabling to understand and present the interaction

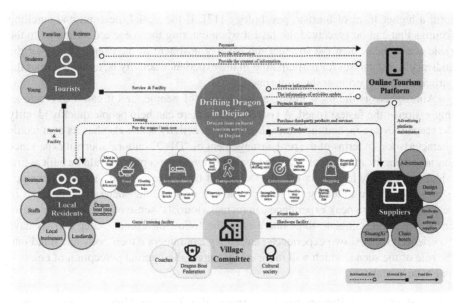

Fig. 3. Service system map of "DDD"

between service systems and elements. The "DDD" dragon boat cultural tourism service in Diejiao Water Village includes five major service sections related to tourism: food, accommodation, transportation, entertainment, and shopping, covering all aspects of tourists' travel in Diejiao. The "DDD" tourism brand operator closely cooperates with local residents to provide job opportunities and training for local residents, support local residents to operate inns and other consumption places, stimulating more local residents to become tourism service providers and enabling better integration of tourism development and residents' lives. Establish mutually beneficial relationships with the local village government, dragon boat clubs and cultural associations, and at the same time purchase products and services from suppliers, raise more funds and software and hardware sponsorships for dragon boat sports and other related cultural activities to promote dragon boat sports and cultural activities. Provide a mobile tourism service platform to facilitate tourists to get information services such as travel guidance, content reservations, and event information push at any time and any place.

Through the Service System Map, we can fully understand the service content of the dragon boat culture and tourism service section of "DDD", and its behavioral relationship with related stakeholders. Combine information flow, funds flow, and material flow in an organic way to build a circular service ecological network.

The Peak of Atmosphere: Quickly Integrate into the Scenario Experience. The atmosphere is obtained through five senses experience, among which the form as well as color, sound, and smell will be firstly transmitted, and then the taste and touch feelings are obtained in further experience. The five senses are also the way in which tourists feel various experiences during the travel. They consciously analyze and process the tourism products of food, accommodation, transportation and entertainment, and then form a higher level of tourism psychology [17]. If the visual, hearing, and smelling feelings that can be perceived the fastest when entering the scene are attributed to the basic atmosphere, then the stronger the basic atmosphere in the event, the higher the audience's enthusiasm for participating in the experience activity is, and the deeper the participation, the stronger the atmosphere is.

Atmosphere is the most intuitive first feeling of people, and it can also create an impression at the fastest speed. A specific atmosphere can help people quickly identify the scene they are in, and the atmosphere of each activity scene also has its own iconic characteristics. In terms of the peak arrangement of "DDD" cultural tourism experience journey, the atmosphere peak that are towards external perception should be built at first which can quickly lead users into the "stage" of the folklore scene. A good "opening" is more conducive to telling the "story" and can promote the shape of other kinds of peaks. Atmosphere peak experience can increase tourists' sense of role and enthusiasm on activity, and stimulate their interests in the following events. After tourists have experienced the first two experience peaks, they can integrate their body and mind into the role of the scene, which will more easily trigger the internal perception of emotion and culture peaks.

The Peak of Fun: A Personalized and Interesting Tourism Method. Fun peak may appear in multiple parts of the "DDD" experience. Create surprises by breaking the script to highlight the characteristics of Diejiao Water Village and the particularity and entertainment of the dragon boat culture. Setting up a competition or adventure game during the journey is moderately exciting, which is easier to bring excitement to the participants and make the activity more attractive. What's more, setting a mark milestone or achievement milestone in the event and provide visual rewards can create a sense of ritual and honor for the participants, and strengthen the memorial significance of the experience.

From a spatial perspective, the "DDD" tourism service area divides the central part into three functional sections according to the distribution of tourism resources and the amusement needs of different tourist groups. 1) "Discovery Zone of DDD" is positioned as a tourist experience zone mainly for young tourists. The waterways in this area are dense and changeable, with widely distributed scenic spots. The diverse spaces make it easier to set up adventure and sports activities. 2) "Parent-child Zone of DDD" is set as a tourist experience zone mainly for parent-child tourists. This area is centered on Chaji Village, with more concentrated attractions, simple and safe water network, and better space conditions for cultural education. 3) "Life and Business Service Zone of DDD" is between the above two areas with Diejiao area as the center, which is convenient for providing accommodation and catering and other tourism services for tourists in the whole region. The two amusement sections of "Discovery Zone of DDD" and "Parent-child Zone of DDD" have different amusement routes and activities based on the preferences of the main tourist groups, and the arrangement of the experience curve is also different. At the same time, both sections are completely open to everyone so that other tourist groups can also come here to play and participate in activities (Fig. 4).

At the same time, water-ways and land-ways can be offered as two choices for tourists. In addition to sightseeing, the two routes can also carry out the different theme activities based on the season. For example, water orienteering can be carried out in

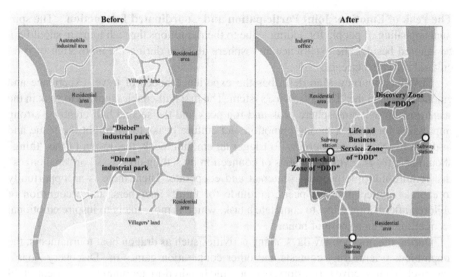

Fig. 4. Space planning of Diejiao

summer days and hiking along the river in winter. This can not only provide land and water transportation, but also enrich the content of Diejiao tourism and highlight the unique charm of water village.

From the time dimension, various limited theme activities can provide unique tourism experience in different periods. From the spatial dimension, the experience needs of different groups can be met in different sections. With the change of time and space, the activity content is constantly enriched, creating an endless tourism experience for tourists (Fig. 5).

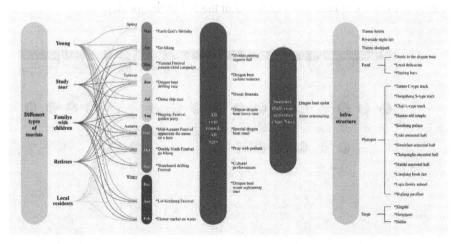

Fig. 5. All year-round activity planning of "DDD"

The Peak of Emotion: Joint Participation and Coordinated Interaction. The spiritual appealing of people for adding value to their emotions through tourism should not be ignored besides the experience atmosphere and fun during the innovation of rural cultural travel experience.

Customer Journey Map describes the experience nodes of travel experience and emotions peak in the "DDD" service system. The first half enables tourists to soak in the scenarios through atmosphere peak and fun peak and the second half creates a strong impression for tourists through emotion and culture peaks to highlight the value and in-depth insights of the journey. To trigger an emotion peak, the design of the "thing" should be a focus. Evoke moments of connection by setting up "tasks" or "challenges" that require multiple people to interact and cooperate. Then, there is an opportunity to express appreciation for peers, gratitude for family members, and recognition of children after a joint effort to complete a task, which is more likely to inspire emotional recognition, even a sense of honor.

During the non-holiday days, many activities such as dragon boat tournaments, the amphibious orienteering contests and other cooperation games in "Discovery Zone", parent-child interactive script story, parent-child hundred-meter running in "Parent-child Zone", are held to increase the cooperation and interaction among tourists whether they know each other before. In this way, they can meet new friends or strengthen their relationship. On the Dragon Boat Festival experience route, in addition to the interactive watching game and special dragon boat meal, tourists can also choose to join the short-term dragon boat training camp and participate in the dragon boat friendly competition held during the festival, enabling them to have deep understanding of the dragon boat culture of Diejiao, and experience the team spirit of dragon boat sports (Fig. 6). When leaving the spot, tourists can take a well-dressed dragon boat in a "Dragon Boat Chenjing" way to travel around the scenic spot along the waterway and take pictures. "Dragon Boat Chenjing" is a parade and display ceremony before the DBR, which delivers a good wish for everything to be amazing and smooth. A "leopard tail" peak can let tourists go back to their normal life in their best conditions at the end of the journey.

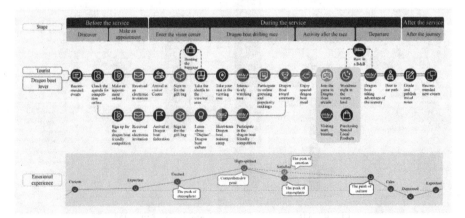

Fig. 6. Customer Journey Map of "DDD" during the Dragon Boat Festival

The Peak of Culture: A Display of Folk Custom Process throughout the Year. Festival folk custom activities are symbolic ceremonies of cultural groups. Strengthening the festival folk custom ritual experience can deepen people's understanding of culture, improve their cultural sense of belonging and cultural identity, and it is an important element to enhance the special cultural experience. The sense of ritual can be embedded into the whole process of cultural travel, which emphasizes the procedural process and symbolic behavior. If the whole activity process is regarded as a large ritual process, some symbolic behaviors can be regarded as small ritual events. The large-scale ritual process affects the atmosphere feeling and is a summative cultural experience after the process completed. Small-scale ceremony can provide an instant sense of cultural experience and trigger cultural experience peaks.

In the innovation of "DDD" cultural tourism experience, the author tries to use the Peak-end Rule to improve the cultural perception of cultural tourism in a longer time. In addition to the Dragon Boat Festival, there are many festivals and folk activities with regional characteristics and sweet connotations worth delivering and developing. After studying the traditional folk activities with local characteristics throughout the year in Diejiao village, the activities with strong regional cultural characteristics are selected as the theme activities in limited time. Continuing the custom of "New Year's Eve of Dragon Boat Festival" in Diejiao, the peak of cultural experience in a year is the Dragon Boat Festival with wonderful dragon boat drifting race, while the Spring Festival is the most solemn festival in China, symbolizing the end of the past year and the beginning of the next, which can be regarded as the "leopard tail" and "phoenix head" in the emotional experience curve of the whole year.

A year is divided into four parts based on the spring, summer, autumn and winter. Each quarter has two festival themed activities with a limited time, and the activities in the same quarter have different importance. The spring peak is in the Yuanzai Festival, which is also the local traditional children's day. There are special folk activities such as "Raking the Drought Dragon" and "Pray with Potluck", which are also the key activities of the parent-child tour throughout the year. The topic of the summer is the water activities dominated by the Dragon Boat Festival, and the Begging Festival indicts the end of summer activities. The peak of the autumn is the Mid-Autumn Festival, when there will be a grand autumn scenery parade. Combining the characteristics of the water village, appreciating the moon on a boat at night is also a unique experience. The peaks of the winter are New Year's Day and Spring Festival. Modern young people are keen on New Year's Eve activities, hoping to spend the time of ringing out the old year and ringing in the new year in a special way. The Spring Festival, according to the tradition of Canton, starts from the beginning of the flower market on water which is before the spring, until the fifteenth day of the Lantern Festival. During which time, a variety of festival activities will be held in order to meet people's needs that they can travel, but also keep the sense of festival ceremony of the Spring Festival.

Strengthening the sense of ceremony and realizing culture peak need a complete and systematic design and plan, and the transmission of the festival connotation in each link and the expression of symbolic meaning should also be considered. According to the characteristics of local traditional culture and environment, a variety of limited events with different themes should be designed based on the factors of seasons, festivals and so on, to attract tourists to travel here and provide them with more perspectives to experience Diejiao folk culture.

5.3   Touchpoint Design of "DDD"

In the book *This is Service Design Thinking*, Schneider Jakob and Mark Stickdorn puts forward five basic principles of service design, among which the principle of "evidencing" requires services to be tangible, so as to improve users' perception and deliver services through touchpoints [18].

The tangible touchpoints in the dragon boat cultural tourism service system of "DDD" mainly includes the design of IP image, physical contact points of peripheral products and event scenario, as well as the digital contact points of the online APP which named "Your Dragon Calendar" (Fig. 7). The IP image and script game are integrated into the scenic spot to enhance its charm, increase the atmosphere of cultural experience, enrich the tourism content, create more surprises, and thus set off one fun peak after another in the whole journey. The development of brand-related products are good souvenirs to carry people's memory. The online platform can provide more ways to participate in the activities, establishes an effective promotion channel of activity information, and better publicize the dragon boat culture in Diejiao water village. Through a series of products, spaces and digital touchpoints, visitors' service encounters can be extended for a longer time before and after services (Fig. 8).

Fig. 7. Touchpoints design of "DDD"

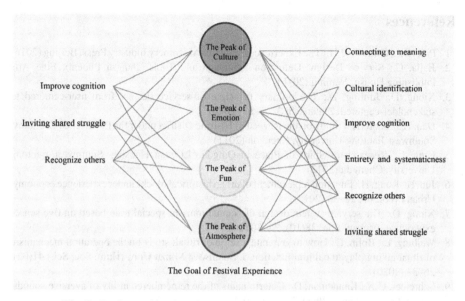

The Goal of Festival Experience

Fig. 8. Design verification about the "Goal Model" of festival experience

6 Conclusion

This paper discusses and analyzes how to organically combine the experience design of rural cultural tourism service with related theories of Peak-end Rule, and deduces the "M-G" PE Model. This model combines four kinds of moments which can trigger peak experience in Behavioral Design theory, and proposes four kinds of experience peaks, namely, "Atmosphere Peak" to establish lively atmosphere, "Fun Peak" to increase more interest, "Emotion Peak" to enhance good feelings, and "Culture Peak" to strengthen the sense of ritual based on the insight and analysis of mass cultural travel experience needs. And the "M-G" PE Model is used to build the dragon boat cultural tourism services which named "Drifting Dragon in Diejiao". From the time and space dimensions, the differentiated arrangement of experience peaks is carried out, and the annual peak experience system of the dragon boat cultural activities of Diejiao is also constructed. At present, the author only uses the cultural tourism experience design of Diejiao Water Village in Foshan as the practical verification of the theory, which may not represent the construction of cultural tourism in all rural areas due to the differences on regional culture or local resources. The guiding significance and universality of the theoretical model needs to be repeatedly proved by more practices in the future.

Acknowledgment. This paper is supported by the 2020 Co-construction Project of the 13th Five Year Plan for Philosophy and Social Sciences of Guangdong Province, which is "Research on the Integration Innovation Strategy of Cultural Tourism in Guangdong-Hong Kong-Macao Greater Bay Area from the Perspective of Service Design (GD20XYS16)".

References

1. Pine, B.J., Gilmore, J.H.: The Experience Economy. Machinery Industry Press, Beijing (2016)
2. Jiajia, C.: Service Design: Definition Language and Tools. Jiangsu Phoenix Fine Arts Publishing House, Nanjing (2016)
3. Xiong, D., Junling, D.: The primary principle of service design: from user-centered to stakeholder-centered. Zhuangshi **3**, 62–65 (2020)
4. Dan, Z.: Theoretical Study on the Revival in Historic District under the Experience Economy. Southwest Jiaotong University, Chengdu (2011)
5. Fang, L.: Research of Spirit of Place in Qingdao Li-yuan Housing. Southwest Jiaotong University, Chengdu (2012)
6. Jun, H., Rong, H.: Function replacement of urban historical blocks under experience economy. Urban Probl. **03**, 28–32 (2013)
7. Xiong, D.: The service system design of Nanhai tourism special train based on five senses experience. Packag. Eng. **38**(10), 24–30 (2017)
8. Weibing, L., Bolin, L.: How to generate a sense of ritual: study on the operation mechanism of ritual giving play to cultural function. J. Southwest Minzu Univ. (Hum. Soc. Sci.) **41**(02), 26–34 (2020)
9. Schreiber, C.A.: Kahneman, D.: Determinants of the remembered utility of aversive sounds. J. Exp. Psychol. Gen. **129**(1), 27–42 (2000)
10. Heath, C., Heath, D.: Behavioral Design: Why Certain Experiences Have Extraordinary Impact. China Citic Press, Beijing (2018)
11. Le Bon, G.: The Crowd: A Study of the Popular Mind. Guangxi Normal University Press, Guilin (2015)
12. Morten, T., Hansen.: Great at Work: How Top Performers Work Less and Achieve More. Simon & Schuster, New York (2018)
13. Fischer, R., Xygalatas, D.: Extreme rituals as social technologies. J. Cogn. Cult. **14**(5), 345–355 (2014)
14. Xiaoshuang, H., Jiayi, L.: research on the problems and strategies of Chinese traditional village tourism development from the perspective of experience economy: taking Shandong Shangjiushan ancient village as an example. Modern Business **29**, 109–110 (2020)
15. Yanjun, X.: Tourist field: the situational model of tourist experience. Res. Financ. Econ. Issue **12**, 64–69 (2005)
16. Xiaobing, W.: Words, rituals and cultural memory. Jiangxi Soc. Sci. **02**, 237–244 (2007)
17. Cuiling, X., Chen Qiuhua, S., Yuqing, X.T.: A study on the exploitation of rural creative tourism product by using the perspective of five senses: a case study of Qipan Stockaded village mulberry field. Issues Forestry Econ. **35**(1), 63–67 (2015)
18. Jakob, S., Stickdorn, M.: This is Service Design Thinking: Basics-Tools-Cases. Jiangxi Fine Arts Publishing House, Nanchang (2015)

Measuring Visual Attractiveness of Urban Commercial Street Using Wearable Cameras: A Case Study of Gubei Gold Street in Shanghai

Yi Hua Huang[(✉)] and Yuanquan Ouyang

Shanghai Academy of Fine Arts, Shanghai University, Shanghai, China
{yihua_huang,20723121}@shu.edu.cn

Abstract. Being a significant part of urban public spaces, streets are crucial to the organization of urban space. With the sustained progress of the construction of human spiritual civilization, streets with certain display attributes such as urban commercial streets have increasingly gained importance in displaying the city's history and cultural heritage. As an important indicator, visual appeal plays an indispensable role in promoting the vitality of streets. However, due to limitations by the existing evaluation tools, there is no consensus in the academic community on measuring the visual appeal of streets. With the constant development of science and technology, scholars have begun to explore the possibility of applying emerging technologies and equipment in the field of built environment research. New technologies make studies more scientifically sound, objective, and efficient than traditional methods. This study mostly adopts the collective perspective or studies the physical space of the built environment, and the research based on the individual perspective is relatively limited. The emergence of wearable cameras provides more margin in monitoring spatial behavior from a personal perspective. This paper takes Gubei Gold Street as the research area to explore the possibility of applying wearable cameras in the measurement of street space visual quality. The study set up 6 research groups consisting of two people each. All of them used wearable cameras to record information. They then performed image recognition on 11 pieces of video information and 1,174 pictures collected by researchers through manual recognition in a single day. Based on the results of manual identification, the study analyzes the characteristics of individual behavior, physical space elements of streets, and crowd perception characteristics. The study found that street furniture, shops, crowd vitality, and greening level are the visual elements intricately linked to the visual appeal of commercial streets and put forward four design principles: flexible furniture layout, reasonable greening level, conforming to business models and adhering to the cultural connotation. This series of efforts proves that it is feasible to study the attractiveness of commercial streets from the perspective of visual perception. Data collection using wearable cameras provides a novel research idea for the built environment from an individual perspective, preserving the site to the greatest extent possible. At the same time as spatiotemporal information, real-time monitoring of the investigators' behavior circumvents the issues regarding discontinuous data collection and single dimensions in previous studies. It is a research method with great potential.

M. M. Soares et al. (Eds.): HCII 2022, LNCS 13322, pp. 403–414, 2022.
https://doi.org/10.1007/978-3-031-05900-1_28

Keywords: Wearable camera · Commercial street · Visual appeal · Gubei Gold Street · Subjective perception

1 Introduction

With the transformation of the economic growth model, the city has gradually progressed from the stage of incremental expansion to the stage of stock renewal. The transition from "quantity" to "quality" reflects the popular demand for high-quality public activity spaces.

Spatial quality reflects comprehensive demands for urban spaces. It reflects the suitability of each element of the urban space to the urban population, urban-social and economic development in terms of "quantity" and "quality" [1]. From the perspective of discernment, the overall quality perception of a street can be divided into visual and non-visual perceptions. Non-visual perceptions (such as temperature, pollution, smell, etc.) vary, while visual perceptions are direct and relatively stable. It also laid a good foundation for street vision research.

In the era of the experiential economy, a high degree of visual appeal can trigger the economic and social vitality of public spaces, especially on commercial streets. However, in the traditional design analysis methods, which are limited by the evaluation tools, visual appeal is mostly overlooked in the evaluation of the street design. The emergence of new technologies has allowed a breakthrough in the study of visual appeal.

Wearable devices have been widely used in fields such as medical, environmental perception, and data analysis due to their singular advantages of being easy to wear, yielding instant feedback, flexible and compact. Presently, wearable devices can be roughly divided into two categories: one is mainly based on state monitoring, such as Peter Aspinar et al. using ECG sensors to monitor individual emotional changes [2]. The other is mainly based on behavioral recordings, such as Park Zhongxun used a pedometer to analyze the wearer's physical activity [3], and Georgina Brown et al. used a wearable camera, SenseCam, to help amnesia patients record their daily activities [4]. These attempts have yielded valuable experience for applying wearable devices in the built environment.

2 Literature Review

Compared with other senses, vision is the most stable and direct way for people to perceive the environment [5, 6]. In perceptual evaluation research, the biggest uncertainty factor is usually the influence of the subject's subjective screening on the evaluation results, and the visual perception image bridges the gap created by this defect. It can achieve indiscriminate recording of the spatial environment and encompass significant information such as time factors. Due to the characteristics of objectivity, stability, and comprehensiveness, image research based on visual perception has garnered widespread academic attention in recent years [5–11].

Based on the concept of human-computer interaction, Steve Mann developed the earliest wearable camera in the 1970s [12]. With the progress of microelectronics technology, wearable cameras ushered in several iterative updates, constantly developing towards smaller size, greater flexibility, and more comprehensive data recording.

Some scholars have also begun to use body-worn cameras to study the built environment. Amber L. Pearson et al. used a wearable camera to investigate the daily hydrophilicity of children. By analyzing the pixel ratio of the water body in each picture and other pictorial data, they have identified 23 waterfront activities and measured the wear and tear [13]. Timothy Chambers et al. invited 168 New Zealand children aged 11 to 13 to wear wearable cameras, supplemented by GPS devices to record their daily activities. They collected their distribution of activity points and activities [14]. Nonetheless, current research, including wearable cameras to explore the relationship between individuals and cities, is still limited.

3   Study Area

3.1   Gubei Gold Street

Taking the commercial pedestrian street of Gubei Gold Street (Fig. 1) as an example, this paper introduces a wearable camera as a test device and tries to exploit the advantages of wearable devices. The spatial environment, crowd behavior, and individual behavior of researchers are recorded to study the visual appeal of urban commercial streets.

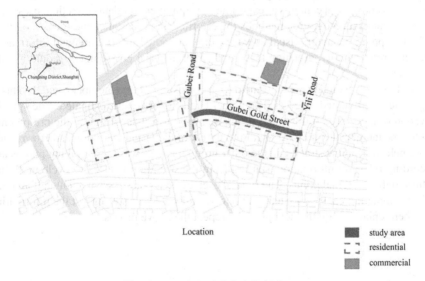

Fig. 1. Location of Gubei Gold Street

Gubei Gold Street was built in the early 21st century and is in the densely populated Gubei Phase II area. It was designed by the internationally renowned SWA Landscape Design Company and is an important urban public communication space in the region.

The total length of the street is about 1.8 km, and the width of the street is between 60–80 m. The project is based on building a landscaped pedestrian street, integrating the landscape with the surrounding buildings, providing people with various needs such as communication, recreation, shopping, etc. The design style advocates a soft, natural, and smooth form that represents a modern and free lifestyle. There are high-end international communities on both sides of the street. Most of the residents are foreigners, and most of them are from Southeast Asia. Koreans, Japanese, Hong Kong, and Taiwan compatriots also account for a large proportion. Such people have high-income levels and strong purchase power. Dao injected a steady stream of vitality.

To narrow the research scope, the research area selected starts from Gubei Road in the west to Yili South Road in the east, and the whole site stands at a distance of 650 m. The space is divided into three sections: the west section is the waterscape and the main entrance square. The middle section is an open area combined with sculptures and social squares. The east section is a leisure space with greenery as the mainstay.

4 Methods

4.1 Wearable Camera

To verify the possibility of applying body-worn cameras in the built environment, this study uses body-worn cameras as experimental equipment for data collection, uses high-accuracy manual recognition methods to perform data processing, and focuses on individual stopping behavior, visual attention, etc. Individual information and information such as crowd vitality, greening level, and street material environment should also be considered.

To this end, six teams were formed, each consisting of two members, and the shooting route was planned (Fig. 2). The Gubei Gold Street was investigated. The specific division of labor is as follows: the group members travel according to the pre-planned route, one member would wear a GoPro8 to record the visual attraction and crowd gathering behavior on the street, and the other group member was tasked taking photos and recording relevant information, starting from the starting point. It is a cycle until they return to their original points. The time of each cycle is controlled at about half an hour. After completing each cycle, half an hour was allocated for sorting out the information and then replaced with the next group to repeat the above process.

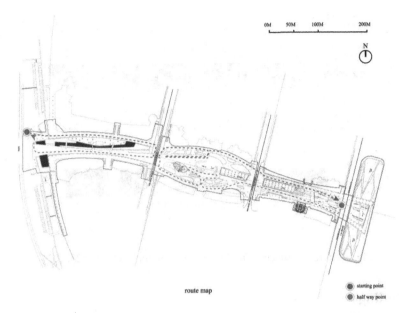

Fig. 2. The starting point, half-way point and research route map of Gubei Gold Street research

4.2 Manual Identification

Manual recognition refers to sorting out spatiotemporal information, human behavior, etc. The advantage is that the recognizer can make subjective judgments as per the experimental requirements, weed out obsolete information, thereby substantially boosting the accuracy and efficiency of information acquisition, and can supplement key information to a certain extent. The disadvantage is that the data scale is large and time-consuming. Since the sample size of this experiment is relatively small, manual recognition is deemed a more suitable data processing method in this experiment. The collected 11 videos and 1198 photos are analyzed, of which 11 were deemed valid videos and 1174 valid photos. In these data, we focus on the resident behaviors of researchers and people at the venue (including conversation, rest, entertainment, fitness, shopping, dining, etc.) because we believe that this is an important variable in the visual appeal of the commercial street (Fig. 3).

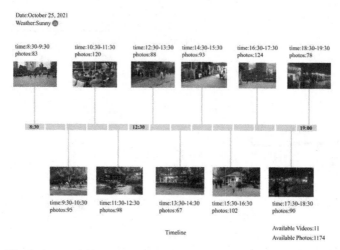

Fig. 3. Research timeline from 8:30am to 7:30pm on October 25, 2021

5   Findings

Through comprehensive analysis and comparison of the photographer's gaze behavior in the video, the crowd gathering phenomenon in the street, and the characteristics of the street material environment, we found some visual elements closely related to commercial streets' visual appeal streets. Generally, these visual elements can be divided into two categories: one is the street material elements based on street furniture and shop facades. The other is the pedestrian perception characteristics represented by the greening level and crowd vitality.

5.1   Street Furniture

People's complex behaviors in urban public spaces have given rise to street furniture. While meeting the basic functional needs of people to stop and rest, information retrieval, landscaping, leisure and entertainment, street furniture, as an important part of the street, is also increasingly responsible for the enhancement of the street space experience, creating a beautiful atmosphere, and reflect the level of street civilization.

Our survey results fully demonstrate the significance of street furniture in urban public spaces. In addition to the pedestrians, it was also concluded that most people tend to move towards street furniture. Different types of furniture fulfill different duties and meet various needs. Most of them are seats, compared to indoor furniture. In a closed space, people are more inclined to sit outdoors and connect with nature, which also impacts the behavior of researchers. Places where furniture is densely distributed are more likely to be visually attractive to researchers and are more likely to cause stopping the behavior (Fig. 4).

Fig. 4. Street furniture on Gubei Gold Street

5.2 Shop

The Gubei Gold Street is in the Gubei International Community, surrounded by over ten high-end communities such as Yucui Palace and Gubei International Garden. The gathering of multiple business formats brings a dazzling array of facade forms and meets people's differentiated needs for street functions and aesthetic attributes.

Through the observation and analysis of the storefronts of Gubei Gold Street stores, it was found that stores with high interface transparency, strong openness, and good ductility are more likely to spark attention and favor than in stores with weak integrity and poor decoration. This trend leads to the occurrence of commercial activities. Moreover, the visual appeal of the storefront with uniform color matching, stark contrast, and bright lights are also significantly stronger (Fig. 5).

Fig. 5. The impact of shop facades on visual appeal

5.3 Crowd Vitality

The level of a crowd gathering in a specific range can often represent the area's attractiveness to people to a certain extent, and the crowd gathering effect can form positive feedback, attracting more people to this area for activities, further fueling the street vitality.

By analyzing the staying behavior and visual attraction behavior of researchers in the video, it was found that crowd gathering behavior—that is, crowd vitality has a prominent effect on visual attraction. Areas with high crowd vitality usually have two characteristics: one characteristic is that there are many people, and the distribution is concentrated, which is easy to spark visual attraction. The other characteristic is that accompanied by crowd activities. The surrounding environmental sound environment would be affected, conducive to generating auditory attraction and thereby indirectly producing visual attention. After analyzing the behavior of researchers, it was also concluded that areas with high crowd vitality could induce researchers to stay longer and attract considerable visual atte. In contrast, areas with low crowd vitality do not exert any influence on the researchers. Moreover, the probability of attracting visual attention is also significantly lower.

In addition, we also observed significant differences in the age levels of the population gathered in different regions. Young and middle-aged people are mostly concentrated in the west and middle sections of the street. These two sections of space consist of a dazzling array of shops that can meet people's multi-faceted functional needs such as shopping, dining, and leisure. Children were mainly located in the middle section of the square, where they could play in an open and flat space. The elderly prefer the leisure square in the east of the street. The density of shops in this space is relatively low, and the level of greenery is higher. All kinds of street furniture are at the disposal of the elderly, where they can rest (Fig. 6).

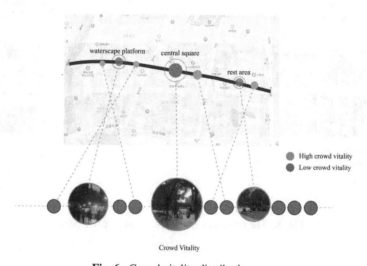

Fig. 6. Crowd vitality distribution map

5.4 Green Level

The variety of greening on Gubei Gold Street is rich, covering various types of trees, shrubs, and ground cover. With the combination of tree pools and seats, a reasonable distribution of greening has been realized. On the main axis of the street are ginkgo trees that bloom in autumn. Every year in the late autumn, they don the "golden new clothes" on the city road, which is also the origin of the name "Gubei Gold Street." The distribution of plant communities and the distribution of the middle and lower shrub ground cover is characterized by flowers and fragrance. Plants that are mainly used are American crape myrtle, North American crabapple, torch flower, golden bergamot, and the application of a series of new products to optimize the application of flowering shrubs substantially boosts the ornamental plant quality of Gubei Gold Street.

Current studies have proved that a reasonable level of greening is the key to improving environmental quality and ensuring environmental levels. In a prosperous commercial street, greening can act as a lubricant. From a spatial perspective, it can provide a sheltered place for people on the street and play a certain buffer and sound insulation effect on the noisy environment of the street. It can conclusively provide a more comfortable visual environment, thereby effectively alleviating visual fatigue.

By sorting out the experimental materials, it was concluded that the crowd vitality and crowd staying behavior in the areas with higher greening levels were significantly higher than those in the areas with lower greening levels. The researchers' gaze time for areas with high greening levels was significantly longer, showing a positive correlation between greenery levels and visual attraction (Fig. 7).

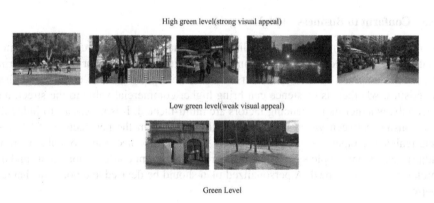

High green level(strong visual appeal)

Low green level(weak visual appeal)

Green Level

Fig. 7. The effect of greenery level on visual appeal

6   Design Principles

According to the visual attraction elements mentioned above, we cut in from two major perspectives: street material environment and people-oriented design. We highlighted several suggestions that will help to enhance the visual appeal of commercial streets.

6.1   Flexible and Diverse Furniture Arrangement

As an essential element in modern cities, urban street furniture is one way to perpetuate urban humanistic heritage. It makes the originally indifferent urban public space exude a strong humanistic atmosphere. People will inevitably put forward higher requirements and expectations for urban street furniture to further improve the environmental quality of urban public space. Therefore, under the premise of meeting the basic functional needs of people of different ages, arranging street furniture according to local conditions and enriching its cultural connotation is an important means to enhance the visual appeal, highlight the genes of the site, and demonstrate the charm of urban culture.

6.2   A Reasonable Level of Greenery

From the previous analysis, it can be concluded that the greening level has a significant positive effect on the overall quality of the street space and the visual appeal of the commercial street. Therefore, improving the greening level of the commercial street is to improve the visual environment of the street. However, there are also relevant studies that highlight that high greening levels are better. For example, Xu Leiqing highlighted in the article Healing-Oriented Street Design: An Exploration Based on VR Experiments that increasing the greenness rate of the street can improve the healing of the street; however, excessive green viewing rate will reduce the harmony of the street [15]. Therefore, on the premise of ensuring that the line of sight is not blocked, a reasonable increase in the greening level will effectively enhance the visual appeal of the commercial street.

6.3   Conform to Business Model

Commerce is vital in ensuring the vitality of a commercial street. The design of commercial streets often revolves around commercial activities. Therefore, prior to considering the visual elements of a street, the first consideration should be its commercial characteristics: whether its existence can bring higher commercial value to the street, and secondly, whether its influencing factors are multi-faceted. It is necessary to judge the relationship between visual elements and the street from the perspective of "things" and realize the ingenious integration of the two. It is also necessary to make adaptive adjustments from people's perspective according to current consumption habits and the preferences of the crowd. A personalized plan should be devised and not a mechanical copy.

6.4   Pay Attention to Cultural Connotation

With the continuous improvement of material living standards, people's needs gradually shift from satisfying basic functional requirements to higher-level and richer spiritual pursuits. Popular consumption patterns are developing towards diversification. An increasing number of consumers pursue cultural resonance while buying, which is an important way for them to reflect their own cultural values and satisfy their cultural tastes. To enhance the attractiveness of commercial streets, we need to respect the differences between different cultures, closely adhere to the cultural connotations, give them cultural values, and enhance their cultural attributes in the selection and design of visual elements. We must always consider "people-oriented" design principles from people's perspective, explore their cultural background, explore their cultural needs, and realize the profound expression of culture.

7 Discussion and Conclusion

With the development of big data and the continuous updating of measurement methods, there are an increasing number of studies on the large-scale quantification and evaluation of the physical space of the built environment using different data sources. However, there are still relatively few studies on the monitoring and interpretation of individual behaviors when experiencing the built environment regarding the microscopic level.

The application of wearable cameras provides favorable conditions for the research on the built environment based on individual perspectives. It addresses the issues of incomplete information recording, single dimension, and frequent interruption in previous studies. The greater significance is that its application entails the extension and popularization from the city level to the individual level, which is a good start to realize the digitization of individual subjective perception and more research based on the individual perspective in the future.

This study uses wearable cameras as experimental equipment to explore the factors affecting the visual appeal of the commercial pedestrian street of Gubei Gold Street, Changning District, Shanghai, by means of case analyses. Level and other four visual elements closely related to visual attractiveness put forward four design principles of flexibly arranging furniture, improving greening to a reasonable level, conforming to business models, and closely following cultural connotations. This study has also confirmed that wearable cameras are useful in the study of individual behavior and the potential for relationships in the built environment.

Acknowledgements. This work is supported by the Youth Foundation of Humanities and Social Sciences of the Ministry of Education in China under Grant 21YJC760031.

References

1. Zhou, J.: Planning control and guidance of urban public space construction: research on creating high quality urban public space. China Architecture & Building Press, Beijing (2005)
2. Aspinall, P., Mavros, P., Coyne, R.D., Roe, J.: The urban brain: analysing outdoor physical activity with mobile EEG. Br. J. Sports Med. **49**(4), 1–6 (2013). https://doi.org/10.1136/bjsports-2012-091877
3. Park, J., Shikawa-Takata, K., Tanaka, S., Mekata, Y., Tabata, I.: Effects of walking speed and step frequency on estimation of physical activity using accelerometers. Physiol. Anthropol. **30**(3), 119–127 (2011). https://doi.org/10.2114/jpa2.30.119
4. Browne, G., et al.: SenseCam improves memory for recent events and quality of life in a patient with memory retrieval difficulties. Memory **19**(7), 713–722 (2011)
5. Liu, Y.F., Li, X.: Review of city image study based on the uprising urban landscape iconology. Landscape Architect. **12**, 28–35 (2017)

6. Long, Y., Zhou, Y.: Pictorial urbanism: a new approach for human scale urban morphology study. Planner **33**(2), 54–60 (2017)
7. Liu, L.: Research on city image: from big data to learning era, planning of 60 years: achievement and challenges. In: Proceedings of Annual National Planning Conference 2016. Shenyang: Urban Planning Society of China (2016)
8. Li, Y., Zhao, M.X., Xu, Y., Chen, Y.L.: Space image of multi-scalar urban nightscape represented by photo landscape on the internet. Planner **33**(9), 105–112 (2017). https://doi.org/10. 3969/j.issn.1006-0022.2017.09.017
9. Tammet, T., Luberg, A., Järv, P.: Sightsmap: crowd-sourced popularity of the world places. In: Cantoni, L., Xiang, Z. (eds.) Information and Communication Technologies in Tourism 2013, pp. 314–325. Springer, Heidelberg (2013). https://doi.org/10.1007/978-3-642-36309-2_27
10. Liu, L., Zhou, B.L., Zhao, J.H., Ryan, B.D.: C-IMAGE: city cognitive mapping through geo-tagged photos. GeoJournal **81**(6), 817–861 (2016)
11. Cao, Y.H., Long, Y., Yang, P.F.: City image study based on online pictures: 24 cities case. Planners **33**(2), 61–67 (2017)
12. Mann, S.: An historical account of the "WearComp" and "WearCam" inventions developed for applications in "personal imaging." In: Proceedings of the First International Symposium on Wearable Computers, pp. 66–73 (1997)
13. Pearson, A.L., et al.: Measuring blue space visibility and "Blue Recreation" in the everyday lives of children in a capital city. Int. J. Environ. Res. Public Health **14**(6), 563 (2017). https:// doi.org/10.3390/ijerph14060563
14. Chambers, T., et al.: Kids in space: Measuring children's residential neighborhoods and other destinations using activity space GPS and wearable camera data. Soc. Sci. Med. **193**, 41–50 (2017). https://doi.org/10.1016/j.socscimed.2017.09.046
15. Xu, L.Q., Meng, R.X., Huang, S.Q., Chen, Z.: Healing oriented street design: experimental explorations via virtual reality. Urban Plann. Int. **34**(1), 38–45 (2019)

Pressure Sensitivity Mapping of the Head Region for Chinese Adults for AR Glasses Design

Yuxin Ju, Haining Wang[(✉)], Yujia Du, and Meng Qiu

School of Design, Hunan University, Changsha 410082, China
haining1872@qq.com

Abstract. With the increasingly competition in AR glasses industry, it is crucial to improve the ergonomics design to achieve good user experience, to which the pressure sensitivity distribution in the head region is directly related. Pressure threshold measurement has been widely used in medicine and product design for decades. In this study, the difference of pressure sensitivity in different head regions was obtained by measuring the pressure threshold of the contact area between the head and AR glasses using a hand-held electronic mechanical algometer. The relationship between pressure thresholds and demographic parameters was also analyzed. The average pressure thresholds of various compression levels obtained in the experiment were used to develop the pressure sensitivity maps to visualize the differences among pressure thresholds in head regions. This pressure distribution results in this study can be utilized as a design reference for AR glasses ergonomics design.

Keywords: Pressure threshold · Pressure sensitivity mapping · Augmented reality glasses · Head · Ergonomics

1 Introduction

Glasses-type wearable computer displays are now becoming popular and emerging technologies that enhance the perception of reality and provide the sensation of immersion [1]. They have changed the way people communicate information between the physical and digital worlds [2]. Augmented reality (AR) glasses are a representative class of glasses-type wearable computer displays. In recent years, AR glasses have been gradually applied to cultural heritage, environmental monitoring, medicine and so on [3], and proved to be a valuable solution in these scenarios. In order to reach mass-market usage, AR glasses will not only need to overcome the challenge of balancing functionality and wear resistance at an affordable price, ensuring a comfortable design will also be key to mass-adoption [4].

Head is the most crucial and vulnerable area of the human body. AR glasses normally require additional structures to perform smart functions [5], so they are more likely to cause discomfort to the head regions compared with traditional optical glasses. Uneven gravity distribution, excessive local pressure, and overweight are typical ergonomic issues that lead to discomfort. AR glasses usually apply constant pressure to soft tissues

M. M. Soares et al. (Eds.): HCII 2022, LNCS 13322, pp. 415–429, 2022.
https://doi.org/10.1007/978-3-031-05900-1_29

in areas like head sides and nose bridge to maintain stability. When the pressure excels the threshold of a specific head region, it would cause local discomfort or even pain. Therefore, understanding the pressure sensitivity of different head regions is important for designing AR glasses that are comfortable to use.

Pressure threshold is commonly used to quantify pressure sensitivity and is usually defined as the minimum pressure which induces pain or discomfort [6]. Pressure Algometry has been used to measure pressure thresholds to evaluate the assessment of pressure perception [7]. Various scholars have studied the pressure thresholds of different parts of the human body using this method. For example, it was found that long periods of standing and short walks resulted in increased sensitivity of workers' feet during the work day, which indicates the decreased pressure threshold [8]. Chinese adults were found to have lower sensitivity in the vertex region and higher sensitivity in the facial and nasal region [9]. The pressure sensitivity maps developed from the pressure threshold data can be used as references for product design [10]. Designers can intuitively understand the pressure sensitivity of various areas of the human body with the pressure threshold data visualization. Most of the previous studies focused on the pressure threshold measurement in a body part from the medical field, and few landmarks were used. There is a lack of pressure threshold measurement from product design perspective, especially for the AR glasses comfort design.

The aim of this study is to investigate the pressure sensitivity of the head and face for AR glasses design. By measuring the pressure thresholds under five oppression levels, the obtained data was statistically analysed and pressure sensitivity maps were generated to illustrate the difference among various head regions and demographic parameters. The pressure sensitivity distribution can be utilized as the design guideline for the improvement of AR glasses, so as to promote the wearing comfort.

2   Methods

2.1   Participants

198 healthy Chinese adult participants (mean age ± S.D. 31 ± 8 years), including 98 males and 100 females who had no facial soft tissue or skeletal deformities were recruited. The demographic information of the participants was shown in Table 1.

Table 1. Composition the the participants.

	Low body weight			Normal body weight			Overweight and obesity			Total
Male	18–25	26–35	36–45	18–25	26–35	36–45	18–25	26–35	36–45	98
	11	11	11	11	10	11	11	11	11	
Female	18–25	26–35	36–45	18–25	26–35	36–45	18–25	26–35	36–45	100
	11	10	11	12	12	11	11	11	11	
Total	65			67			66			198

According to the recommendation of Chinese adult BMI classification (Low body weight: BMI < 18.5, Normal body weight: 18.5 < BMI < 23.9, Overweight and obesity: BMI > 24) proposed by International Life Science Institute (ILSI) Focal Point in China [11], participants from all the BMI groups were included in this study. The height and weight of all participants were measured on-site, and body mass index (BMI) was calculated. The mean BMI of all participants was 22.23 kg/m2 (S.D. = 4.36).

2.2 Materials

The instrument for pressure threshold measurement is important and can affects the result accuracy directly. Previous studies used fixed indentation devices to measure pressure thresholds or soft tissue properties [12]. Such device has a limited range of motion and are not suitable for measurement toward different directions of the head. Some researchers utilized a hand-held electronic algometer or hand-held ultrasonic indentation devices to manually controlled the speed of force [9, 13, 14]. This method is more flexible compared with the fixed device, however, it is difficult to keep the force speed consistently merely by subjective judgment of the experimenters, and it is easy to cause a systematic error. A semi-automatic electronic force measuring device was designed and developed in this study, including an electronic mechanical algometer (YISIDA-DS2; Hong Kong, China), a set of stepper motor and console to control the speed of the force, a tripod and a slide rail to fix the algometer and adjust the direction of force. On one hand, the indentation speed can be the same for different trails using this device, on the other hand, the flexibility was greatly improved thanks to the adjustable height and direction. The schematic diagram of the experimental device is shown in Fig. 1.

Fig. 1. The experimental device.

Due to the narrow space of the supra-auricular region, two kinds of probes were designed and used in this experiment, a straight probe and a parallel probe, which were both made by aluminum alloy. It was ensured that the direction of force is parallel to the direction of algometer motion to avoid systematic errors. The end of the probe is 3 mm in diameter and was covered with a tip made of soft rubber to simulate the tactile sensation when wearing glasses. The tip dimensions are shown in Table 2. A schematic diagram of the probes and tips is shown in Fig. 2. During the experiment, the indentation speed and direction of the algometer were controlled by the stepper motor and console. According to Xiong et al., the range of indentation speed was recommended as 0–2 mm/s to avoid the premature sensation of discomfort or pain [10]. The indentation speed was kept at 1 mm/s in the experiment. By twisting the three knobs on the tripod, the algometer could be moved in six degrees of freedom, which allows the force to be applied vertically towards each landmarks. The experimental data was obtained through the software integrated to the algometer, and all participants were required to click the mouse to obtain the pressure data under different oppression levels.

Table 2. The tip dimensions.

	Diameter (mm)	Height of projection (mm)	Material
Side of head	9	2	Soft rubber
Nasal bridge	7	1	Soft rubber
Inferior orbital	7	1	Soft rubber
Supra-auricular	5	2	Soft rubber

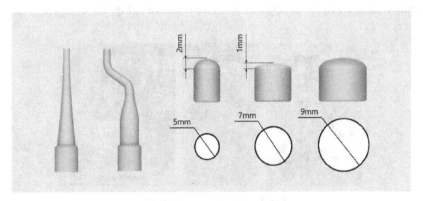

Fig. 2. The shapes and sizes of the probes and tips.

2.3 Landmarks

According to the possible contact position and anatomical characteristics, this study divided the measurement area into four regions: nasal bridge, inferior orbital, supra-auricular and the side of head. A total of 19 landmarks are shown in Fig. 3. There was one landmark on nasal bridge, inferior orbital and supra-auricular respectively, namely N1, O1, E1, and 16 landmarks (H1–H16) on the side of head.

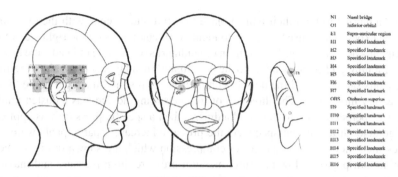

Fig. 3. 19 landmarks.

In order to determine the position of landmarks, researchers need to define a grid covering the region of interest [15]. Previous study used ear as an anatomical reference when measuring the pressure pain sensitivity of the temporalis muscle, and designed 10 mm * 15 mm grids to determine the position of 9 landmarks [16]. Due to the large contact area between glasses and the side of head, the grid was established with the otobasion superius OBS (H8) as a reference point in this experiment. The grid size was obtained by clustering the head shape eigenvalues of 1190 Chinese from the Chinese Headbase survey conducted by Haining Wang [17]. The two clustering characteristic values were head length (D), and the z-axis distance from the otobasion superius to the tragus in the head coordinate system (S). According to the clustering results, head sizes were divided into 9 categories: SS, SM, SL, MS, MM, ML, LS, LM, and LL. It was stipulated that the MM head type applied a unit grid of 10 mm * 10 mm, and other head types scaled the length and width of the grid in proportion to the size of MM. The corresponding relationship between head types and the size of unit grid is shown in Table 3.

To get an accurate pressure threshold, the experiment was repeated three times on each landmark. A counterbalanced approach was adopted to select landmarks in order to avoid any bias due to order and time effect.

Table 3. The relationship between head categories and unit grid size.

	SS	SM	SL	MS	MM	ML	LS	LM	LL
Length (mm)	9.1	9.1	9.1	10	10	10	11	11	11
Width (mm)	8.6	10	11.4	8.6	10	11.4	8.6	10	11.4

2.4 Procedure

First, all participants were asked to fill out a personal information form and a written informed consent. Basic dimensions like height (Ht), weight (Wt), head length (D) and the z-axis distance from the attachment point to the tragus (S) were measured by experimenters to calculate the BMI and decide head categories. Participants were required to wear a hairnet to hold their hair in place to avoid interference with the experiment. Then the experimenter used a crayon to identify 19 landmarks on the right side of each participant's head and face. The location of landmarks on the side of head were based on the positioning grid corresponding to the participant's head type. During the experiment, participants sat in front of the device with their heads resting on a fixed baffle to avoid unnecessary movement. The direction of the measuring device was adjusted until the probe was perpendicular to the first landmark, then a specific pressure was applied by the algometer at a constant speed. As the pressure increased, participants were asked to click their mouse at five degrees of compression which are shown in Fig. 4, including minimum pressure, low pressure, medium pressure, high pressure and maximum pressure. The maximum pressure refers to the highest pressure given by glasses while wearing glasses, rather than unbearable pressure in the sense of physiological limit. The algometer movement was stopped immediately right after the mouse was clicked 5 times. In order to maintain the consistence among the five compression levels for each participant, a pre-experiment was conducted before the formal experiment in each region for all participants. A rest break of approximately 30 s was provided between trials to minimize participant fatigue and any adaptation to the pressure stimulus [18]. The whole experiment lasted about two hours for each participant.

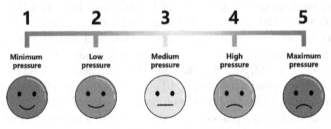

Fig. 4. Five oppression levels.

2.5 Data Processing

The entire data was exported to an excel sheet and checked for entry errors. The intraclass correlation efficient test was performed on the data obtained from the three repeated experiments. The mean values of the pressure thresholds for 19 landmarks at five degrees of compression were calculated. Outliers were screened for each group of data using the double standard difference method, and the abnormal data was removed.

2.6 Data Analysis

Statistical analysis of the mean values was performed using IBM SPSS Statistics for Windows, version 26.0 (IBM Corp., Armonk, N.Y., USA). Descriptive statistical analysis was performed on pressure thresholds to obtain the corresponding mean values, standard deviation and median. One-way ANOVA was used to investigate the relationship between age, BMI and pressure threshold. Gender difference was analyzed using independent-samples T test.

3 Results

3.1 Reliability Test

Table 4 listed the results of the intraclass correlation efficient test for the pressure thresholds of 19 landmarks at five degrees of compression. The experiment was considered to be poor reproducible if the ICC value < 0.4, while it was considered to have a excellent reproducibility if the ICC value > 0.75. The results showed that 17 landmarks showed excellent reproducibility across five degrees of compression. In addition, at 13 of the 19 landmarks, the maximum value of ICC appeared at the maximum degree of compression, indicating that the higher the degree of compression, the better the reproducibility of the experiment.

Table 4. Results of the intraclass correlation efficient test for the pressure thresholds.

Landmarks	Minimum pressure	Low pressure	Medium pressure	High pressure	Maximum pressure
N1	0.865	0.930	0.938	0.940	0.962
O1	0.828	0.833	0.912	0.941	0.950
E1	0.840	0.891	0.913	0.934	0.943
H1	0.920	0.889	0.888	0.894	0.913
H2	0.805	0.865	0.887	0.929	0.951
H3	0.913	0.886	0.902	0.933	0.956
H4	0.866	0.880	0.888	0.908	0.926
H5	0.885	0.864	0.868	0.886	0.928
H6	0.876	0.844	0.962	0.883	0.914
H7	0.853	0.883	0.889	0.915	0.934
OBS(H8)	0.950	0.925	0.926	0.930	0.929
H9	0.947	0.910	0.865	0.899	0.926
H10	0.906	0.868	0.859	0.023	0.910
H11	0.947	0.903	0.890	0.910	0.943
H12	0.956	0.932	0.925	0.925	0.940
H13	0.898	0.876	0.889	0.921	0.957
H14	0.888	0.878	0.884	0.920	0.945
H15	0.944	0.262	0.578	0.940	0.952
H16	0.941	0.911	0.911	0.927	0.942

3.2 Descriptive Statistics

Table 5 summarized the descriptive statistics for 198 participants at five oppression levels, including minimum pressure, low pressure, medium pressure, high pressure and maximum pressure, on a total of 19 regions on the head and face. Through one-way ANOVA, there were significant differences in the feelings of the five oppression levels among samples from different regions ($p < 0.05$). The results showed that H13, which was located on the side of the head, could handle higher pressure compared to other regions. And inferior orbital (O1) with the lowest pressure thresholds at all the five oppression levels was the most sensitive position to pressure.

Table 5. The descriptive statistics for the pressure thresholds of 198 participants.

Landmark	Minimum pressure		Low pressure		Medium Pressure		High pressure		Maximum pressure	
	Mean ± S.D.	Median	Mean ± S.D.	Median	Mean ± S.D.	Median	Mean ± S.D.	Median	Mean ± S.D.	Median
N1	0.20 ± 0.26	0.08	0.61 ± 0.63	0.38	1.01 ± 0.89	0.72	1.34 ± 1.04	1.00	1.73 ± 1.23	1.38
O1	0.08 ± 0.11	0.03	0.27 ± 0.38	0.07	0.49 ± 0.62	0.17	0.73 ± 0.81	0.34	1.03 ± 1.00	0.66
E1	0.42 ± 0.31	0.35	0.85 ± 0.52	0.80	1.18 ± 0.67	1.08	1.49 ± 0.85	1.42	1.80 ± 0.96	1.66
H1	0.22 ± 0.19	0.16	0.47 ± 0.34	0.37	0.76 ± 0.53	0.62	1.10 ± 0.71	0.92	1.53 ± 0.95	1.31
H2	0.12 ± 0.14	0.07	0.33 ± 0.30	0.24	0.64 ± 0.51	0.48	1.00 ± 0.74	0.84	1.48 ± 1.03	1.29
H3	0.14 ± 0.19	0.06	0.41 ± 0.41	0.28	0.83 ± 0.69	0.62	1.29 ± 0.96	1.05	1.81 ± 1.16	1.60
H4	0.25 ± 0.20	0.18	0.54 ± 0.40	0.44	0.86 ± 0.56	0.68	1.28 ± 0.79	1.16	1.80 ± 1.05	1.60
H5	0.17 ± 0.19	0.10	0.38 ± 0.32	0.25	0.72 ± 0.57	0.53	1.11 ± 0.83	0.84	1.57 ± 1.10	1.23
H6	0.14 ± 0.18	0.07	0.37 ± 0.35	0.26	0.77 ± 0.61	0.55	1.22 ± 0.84	0.95	1.76 ± 1.09	1.49
H7	0.20 ± 0.18	0.16	0.45 ± 0.33	0.37	0.77 ± 0.53	0.64	1.18 ± 0.75	1.01	1.73 ± 1.04	1.52
OBS(H8)	0.24 ± 0.27	0.15	0.47 ± 0.44	0.31	0.77 ± 0.67	0.55	1.08 ± 0.81	0.84	1.53 ± 1.09	1.26
H9	0.21 ± 0.20	0.16	0.48 ± 0.38	0.39	0.86 ± 0.64	0.67	1.33 ± 0.96	1.08	1.93 ± 1.33	1.50
H10	0.36 ± 0.27	0.30	0.70 ± 0.45	0.58	1.19 ± 0.75	0.97	1.91 ± 1.38	1.59	2.22 ± 1.17	2.06
H11	0.19 ± 0.16	0.15	0.43 ± 0.34	0.35	0.72 ± 0.53	0.58	1.13 ± 0.82	0.89	1.76 ± 1.23	1.45
H12	0.23 ± 0.21	0.17	0.53 ± 0.40	0.44	0.92 ± 0.64	0.74	1.38 ± 0.89	1.10	2.01 ± 1.27	1.60
H13	0.26 ± 0.23	0.20	0.67 ± 0.48	0.55	1.19 ± 0.79	0.99	1.79 ± 1.13	1.54	2.39 ± 1.40	2.14
H14	0.21 ± 0.17	0.17	0.46 ± 0.35	0.35	0.78 ± 0.57	0.59	1.22 ± 0.85	0.95	1.79 ± 1.19	1.41
H15	0.26 ± 0.22	0.21	0.54 ± 0.43	0.41	0.84 ± 0.58	0.69	1.18 ± 0.78	0.93	1.71 ± 1.12	1.38
H16	0.31 ± 0.26	0.23	0.60 ± 0.44	0.49	0.96 ± 0.70	0.75	1.36 ± 0.95	1.07	1.86 ± 1.24	1.58

Sample size(n) = 198. Mean and Standard Deviation (S.D.) values are in Newton.

3.3 Relationship Between Pressure Threshold and Demographic Parameters

Gender. The independent-samples T test for gender showed that there were significant differences between genders in the pressure threshold on 11 landmarks. In particular, at supra-auricular region (E1), there were gender differences in all five oppression levels, and the pressure thresholds for males were significantly higher than that for females. Table 6 showed detailed results of the independent-samples T test.

Table 6. Results of the independent-samples T test for pressure thresholds.

Landmark	Mean ± S.D.		t	p
	Female	Male		
N1 - Minimum pressure	0.20 ± 0.27	0.20 ± 0.25	0.02	0.98
N1 - Low pressure	0.60 ± 0.61	0.62 ± 0.65	−0.25	0.80
N1 - Medium pressure	0.96 ± 0.84	1.06 ± 0.96	−0.75	0.46
N1 - High pressure	1.27 ± 0.94	1.42 ± 1.15	−0.98	0.33
N1 - Maximum pressure	1.67 ± 1.12	1.80 ± 1.34	−0.72	0.47
O1 - Minimum pressure	0.07 ± 0.10	0.08 ± 0.13	−0.91	0.36
O1 - Low pressure	0.26 ± 0.37	0.28 ± 0.39	−0.39	0.70
O1 - Medium pressure	0.47 ± 0.61	0.51 ± 0.64	−0.46	0.64
O1 - High pressure	0.70 ± 0.80	0.76 ± 0.83	−0.56	0.57
O1 - Maximum pressure	0.96 ± 0.98	1.10 ± 1.03	−0.92	0.36
E1 - Minimum pressure	0.37 ± 0.28	0.47 ± 0.33	−2.37	0.02*
E1 - Low pressure	0.78 ± 0.52	0.93 ± 0.52	−2.10	0.04*
E1 - Medium pressure	1.07 ± 0.64	1.29 ± 0.68	−2.34	0.02*
E1 - High pressure	1.34 ± 0.79	1.66 ± 0.89	−2.67	0.01**
E1 - Maximum pressure	1.61 ± 0.88	2.00 ± 1.02	−2.77	0.01**
H1 - Minimum pressure	0.23 ± 0.21	0.21 ± 0.16	0.81	0.42
H1 - Low pressure	0.47 ± 0.38	0.46 ± 0.31	0.15	0.88
H1 - Medium pressure	0.77 ± 0.57	0.76 ± 0.48	0.20	0.84
H1 - High pressure	1.10 ± 0.76	1.09 ± 0.66	0.09	0.93
H1 - Maximum pressure	1.52 ± 1.00	1.54 ± 0.90	−0.16	0.88
H2 - Minimum pressure	0.11 ± 0.12	0.13 ± 0.14	−1.27	0.21
H2 - Low pressure	0.32 ± 0.30	0.35 ± 0.31	−0.85	0.40
H2 - Medium pressure	0.57 ± 0.47	0.70 ± 0.53	−1.79	0.08
H2 - High pressure	0.85 ± 0.62	1.15 ± 0.81	−2.83	0.01**
H2 - Maximum pressure	1.34 ± 0.98	1.63 ± 1.06	−1.95	0.05
H3 - Minimum pressure	0.13 ± 0.18	0.15 ± 0.19	−0.90	0.37
H3 - Low pressure	0.38 ± 0.41	0.45 ± 0.40	−1.25	0.21
H3 - Medium pressure	0.74 ± 0.67	0.91 ± 0.71	−1.66	0.10
H3 - High pressure	1.15 ± 0.88	1.45 ± 1.02	−2.24	0.03*
H3 - Maximum pressure	1.62 ± 1.07	2.00 ± 1.23	−2.33	0.02*
H4 - Minimum pressure	0.28 ± 0.22	0.21 ± 0.18	2.42	0.02*

(*continued*)

Table 6. (*continued*)

| Landmark | Mean ± S.D. | | t | p |
	Female	Male		
H4 - Low pressure	0.60 ± 0.42	0.49 ± 0.37	2.05	0.04*
H4 - Medium pressure	0.92 ± 0.57	0.80 ± 0.54	1.38	0.17
H4 - High pressure	1.31 ± 0.79	1.24 ± 0.79	0.64	0.52
H4 - Maximum pressure	1.81 ± 1.01	1.79 ± 1.09	0.17	0.86
H5 - Minimum pressure	0.18 ± 0.19	0.17 ± 0.19	0.27	0.79
H5 - Low pressure	0.37 ± 0.33	0.38 ± 0.30	−0.25	0.80
H5 - Medium pressure	0.67 ± 0.56	0.77 ± 0.59	−1.20	0.23
H5 - High pressure	1.03 ± 0.83	1.20 ± 0.83	−1.40	0.16
H5 - Maximum pressure	1.42 ± 1.06	1.73 ± 1.13	1.98	0.05*
H6 - Minimum pressure	0.13 ± 0.17	0.15 ± 0.18	−0.79	0.43
H6 - Low pressure	0.32 ± 0.30	0.42 ± 0.38	−2.06	0.04*
H6 - Medium pressure	0.68 ± 0.57	0.85 ± 0.65	−1.93	0.06
H6 - High pressure	1.09 ± 0.77	1.35 ± 0.89	−2.17	0.03*
H6 - Maximum pressure	1.60 ± 1.04	1.92 ± 1.13	−2.05	0.04*
H7 - Minimum pressure	0.24 ± 0.18	0.17 ± 0.16	2.92	0.00**
H7 - Low pressure	0.50 ± 0.33	0.39 ± 0.32	2.24	0.03*
H7 - Medium pressure	0.83 ± 0.51	0.71 ± 0.54	1.49	0.14
H7 - High pressure	1.24 ± 0.74	1.12 ± 0.77	1.12	0.27
H7 - Maximum pressure	1.79 ± 1.04	1.66 ± 1.03	0.87	0.39
OBS(H8) - Minimum pressure	0.27 ± 0.30	0.22 ± 0.23	1.31	0.19
OBS(H8) - Low pressure	0.49 ± 0.48	0.44 ± 0.41	0.72	0.47
OBS(H8) - Medium pressure	0.78 ± 0.71	0.75 ± 0.64	0.33	0.74
OBS(H8) - High pressure	1.09 ± 0.87	1.07 ± 0.75	0.17	0.86
OBS(H8) - Maximum pressure	1.50 ± 1.13	1.57 ± 1.04	−0.50	0.62
H9 - Minimum pressure	0.25 ± 0.19	0.17 ± 0.19	2.66	0.01**
H9 - Low pressure	0.52 ± 0.37	0.43 ± 0.38	1.63	0.10
H9 - Medium pressure	0.91 ± 0.64	0.80 ± 0.63	1.11	0.27
H9 - High pressure	1.31 ± 0.88	1.35 ± 1.04	−0.33	0.75
H9 - Maximum pressure	1.92 ± 1.28	1.94 ± 1.39	−0.14	0.89
H10 - Minimum pressure	0.36 ± 0.27	0.36 ± 0.28	0.20	0.84

(*continued*)

Table 6. (*continued*)

Landmark	Mean ± S.D.		t	p
	Female	Male		
H10 - Low pressure	0.71 ± 0.45	0.68 ± 0.44	0.42	0.67
H10 - Medium pressure	1.17 ± 0.75	1.20 ± 0.75	−0.30	0.76
H10 - High pressure	1.82 ± 1.28	2.01 ± 1.47	−0.96	0.34
H10 - Maximum pressure	2.12 ± 1.13	2.32 ± 1.21	−1.17	0.25
H11 - Minimum pressure	0.21 ± 0.14	0.17 ± 0.18	1.85	0.07
H11 - Low pressure	0.45 ± 0.29	0.42 ± 0.37	0.59	0.55
H11 - Medium pressure	0.72 ± 0.48	0.72 ± 0.57	−0.09	0.93
H11 - High pressure	1.07 ± 0.73	1.18 ± 0.90	−0.91	0.36
H11 - Maximum pressure	1.70 ± 1.20	1.83 ± 1.27	−0.70	0.49
H12 - Minimum pressure	0.27 ± 0.19	0.20 ± 0.22	2.41	0.02*
H12 - Low pressure	0.57 ± 0.35	0.49 ± 0.44	1.27	0.20
H12 - Medium pressure	0.95 ± 0.60	0.89 ± 0.67	0.64	0.52
H12 - High pressure	1.37 ± 0.85	1.39 ± 0.94	−0.15	0.88
H12 - Maximum pressure	1.93 ± 1.23	2.09 ± 1.32	−0.82	0.41
H13 - Minimum pressure	0.27 ± 0.23	0.25 ± 0.23	0.63	0.53
H13 - Low pressure	0.65 ± 0.46	0.69 ± 0.50	-0.64	0.52
H13 - Medium pressure	1.15 ± 0.79	1.23 ± 0.80	−0.69	0.49
H13 - High pressure	1.74 ± 1.15	1.84 ± 1.12	−0.62	0.53
H13 - Maximum pressure	2.30 ± 1.40	2.48 ± 1.41	−0.85	0.39
H14 - Minimum pressure	0.24 ± 0.17	0.18 ± 0.17	2.47	0.01*
H14 - Low pressure	0.49 ± 0.34	0.43 ± 0.37	1.25	0.21
H14 - Medium pressure	0.78 ± 0.49	0.79 ± 0.65	−0.17	0.87
H14 - High pressure	1.19 ± 0.77	1.25 ± 0.94	−0.46	0.65
H14 - Maximum pressure	1.73 ± 1.11	1.86 ± 1.27	−0.75	0.45
H15 - Minimum pressure	0.32 ± 0.23	0.20 ± 0.20	3.79	0.00**
H15 - Low pressure	0.60 ± 0.36	0.47 ± 0.48	2.23	0.03*
H15 - Medium pressure	0.91 ± 0.53	0.77 ± 0.63	1.71	0.09
H15 - High pressure	1.26 ± 0.75	1.11 ± 0.80	1.33	0.18
H15 - Maximum pressure	1.71 ± 1.05	1.71 ± 1.20	0.00	1.00
H16 - Minimum pressure	0.34 ± 0.23	0.28 ± 0.28	1.60	0.11

(*continued*)

Table 6. (*continued*)

Landmark	Mean ± S.D.		t	p
	Female	Male		
H16 - Low pressure	0.61 ± 0.38	0.59 ± 0.50	0.36	0.72
H16 - Medium pressure	0.95 ± 0.64	0.97 ± 0.76	−0.20	0.84
H16 - High pressure	1.31 ± 0.85	1.41 ± 1.04	−0.76	0.45
H16 - Maximum pressure	1.75 ± 1.05	1.98 ± 1.42	−1.27	0.21

Female sample size(n) = 100. Male sample size(n) = 98. Mean and Standard Deviation (S.D.) values are in N. * p < 0.05 ** p < 0.01.

Age. The results of one-way ANOVA for age showed that significant differences in pressure threshold among ages were only found on 3 landmarks. Similar to gender, supra-auricular region (E1) showed differences among ages in all the five oppression levels. The pressure thresholds for 18–25 group were significantly lower than those for the other two age groups.

BMI. The results of one-way ANOVA for BMI indicated that there were significant differences among BMI on 2 landmarks. The supra-auricular region (E1) also showed differences among BMI at all five oppression levels. The pressure thresholds for normal body weight on E1 were significantly lower than those for the other two groups.

To sum up, for head and facial areas that were in contact with AR glasses, except for the supra-auricular region, the pressure thresholds were basically not affected by the three demographic parameters including gender, age, and BMI.

3.4 Pressure Sensitivity Maps

Pressure sensitivity maps are maps covering the area between measurement landmarks created by interpolating pressure thresholds in order to create images of the deep structures sensitivity [19]. In this study, the inversed distance weighted interpolation method was adopted to develop pressure sensitivity maps using the pressure thresholds of the side of head through MATLAB (The Mathworks, Natick, MA, USA) [20]. The pressure sensitivity maps illustrated the pressure thresholds of different regions so as to distinguish the differences in the pressure sensitivity of various regions. Figure 5 showed the sensitivity maps of the head region on five oppression levels. As could be seen from the figures, the pressure thresholds of the H10, H13 and their surrounding areas were apparently higher than those of the other regions. The pressure thresholds around H1, H2, H5 and OBS were relatively low. And with the increase in the intensity of the oppression, this trend became more and more obvious.

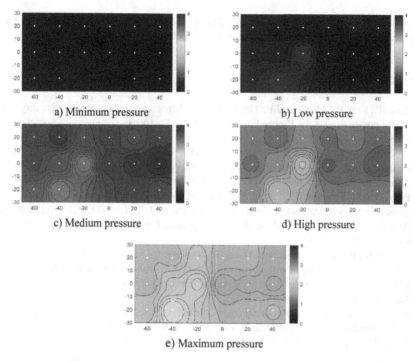

a) Minimum pressure

b) Low pressure

c) Medium pressure

d) High pressure

e) Maximum pressure

Fig. 5. Pressure sensitivity maps on five oppression levels.

4   Discussion

This study collected objective thresholds of 19 regions under five degrees of oppression by measuring pressure thresholds on the heads of 198 Chinese adults. It was found that the H13 region, which was located on the side of head, had the highest pressure thresholds and lowest pressure sensitivity which indicated that it could endure higher pressure without feeling uncomfortable. Therefore, in the design of glasses, this area can handle a greater holding force to ensure the stability of wearing. In contrast, the inferior orbital (O1) on the facial region had the highest pressure sensitivity which meant pressure should be avoided as much as possible in this area.

H13 is located behind the ear where the soft tissue thickness is low, and it exhibits less sensitive to pressure. The soft tissue in the inferior orbital is thicker and less rigid, and it may be responsible for the higher pressure sensitivity. Among the demographic parameters of gender, age and BMI, most regions don't show statistical differences on pressure thresholds. Significant effects are only found on the supra-auricular region which has more complicated sensitivity, and needs to be paid more attention for eyewear design.

The pressure sensitivity maps generated from the study can provide intuitive data support in the ergonomics design process of AR glasses. They can help designers to better understand the pressure sensitivity of different parts of the human body, so as to adjust the size, shape and material of the glasses accordingly, which will achieve a good balance among stability, functionality and comfort.

References

1. Rane, P., Kim, H., Marcano, J.L., Gabbard, J.L.: Virtual road signs: augmented reality driving aid for novice drivers. In: Proceedings of the Human Factors and Ergonomics Society Annual Meeting, pp. 1750–1754 (2016)
2. Zuidhof, N., Ben Allouch, S., Peters, O., Verbeek, P.-P.: Defining smart glasses: a rapid review of state-of-the-art perspectives and future challenges from a social sciences' perspective. Augmented Hum. Res. **6**(1), 1–18 (2021). https://doi.org/10.1007/s41133-021-00053-3
3. Pierdicca, R., Frontoni, E., Pollini, R., Trani, M., Verdini, L.: The use of augmented reality glasses for the application in industry 4.0. In: De Paolis, L.T., Bourdot, P., Mongelli, A. (eds.) AVR 2017. LNCS, vol. 10324, pp. 389–401. Springer, Cham (2017). https://doi.org/10.1007/978-3-319-60922-5_30
4. Surti, P.K., Pradnya, M.: Smart Glasses Technology, In: VIVA-IJRI, vol. 1(4), Article 161, pp. 1–7. Computer Engineering Department, VIVA Institute of Technology, Virar (2021)
5. Kim, Y.M., Bahn, S., Yun, M.H.: Wearing comfort and perceived heaviness of smart glasses. Hum. Factors Man. **31**, 484–495 (2021)
6. Fischer, A.A.: Pressure algometry over normal muscles. standard values, validity and reproducibility of pressure threshold. Pain **30**(1), 115–126 (1987)
7. Keele, K.D.: Pain-sensitivity tests: the pressure algometer. The Lancet **263**(6813), 636–639 (1954)
8. Messing, K., Kilbom, A.: Standing and very slow walking: foot pain-pressure threshold, subjective pain experience and work activity. Appl. Ergon. **32**(1), 81–90 (2001)
9. Shah, P., Luximon, Y.: Assessment of pressure sensitivity in the head region for Chinese adults. Appl. Ergon. **97**, 103548 (2021)
10. Xiong, S., Goonetilleke, R.S., Jiang, Z.: Pressure thresholds of the human foot: measurement reliability and effects of stimulus characteristics. Ergonomics **54**(3), 282–293 (2011)
11. Zhou, B.F.: Predictive values of body mass index and waist circumference for risk factors of certain related diseases in Chinese adults–study on optimal cut-off points of body mass index and waist circumference in Chinese adults. Biomed. Environ. Sci. **15**(1), 83–96 (2002)
12. Dohi, M., Mochimaru, M., Kouchi, M.: Distribution of tactile sensitivity and elasticity in Japanese foot sole. KANSEI Eng. Int. **5**(2), 9–14 (2004)
13. Knapstad, M.K., Nordahl, S.H.G., Naterstad, I.F., Ask, T., Skouen, J.S., Goplen, F.K.: Measuring pressure pain threshold in the cervical region of dizzy patients—the reliability of a pressure algometer. Physiother. Res. Int. **23**(4), e1736(2018)
14. Buso, A., Shitoot, N.: Sensitivity of the foot in the flat and toe off positions. Appl. Ergon. **76**, 57–63 (2019)
15. Alburquerque-Sendín, F., Madeleine, P., Fernández-de-Las-Peñas, C., Camargo, P.R., Salvini, T.F.: Spotlight on topographical pressure pain sensitivity maps: a review. J. Pain Res. **11**, 215–225 (2018)
16. Fernandez-de-las-Penas, C., Madeleine, P., Cuadrado, M.L., Ge, H.Y., Arendt-Nielsen, L., Pareja, J.A.: Pressure pain sensitivity mapping of the temporalis muscle revealed bilateral pressure hyperalgesia in patients with strictly unilateral migraine. Cephalalgia **29**(6), 670–676 (2009)
17. Wang, H., Yang, W., Yu, Y., Chen, W., Ball, R.: 3D digital anthropometric study on Chinese head and face. In: Proceedings of 3DBODY. TECH 2018–9th International Conference and Exhibition on 3D Body Scanning and Processing Technologies, pp. 287–295 (2018)

18. Le Johansson, L., Kjellberg, A., Kilbom, A., Hagg, G.M.: Perception of surface pressure applied to the hand. Ergonomics **42**(10), 1274–1282 (1999)
19. Binderup, A.T., Arendt-Nielsen, L., Madeleine, P.: Pressure pain threshold mapping-a new imaging modality of muscle sensitivity to pain. In: 2008 Annual IEEE Student Paper Conference, pp. 1–4. IEEE (2008)
20. Franke, R., Nielson, G.: Smooth interpolation of large sets of scattered data. Int. J. Numer. Methods Eng. **15**(11), 1691–1704 (1980)

Analysis on Aesthetic Turn and Social Factors of Beijing Jade Art in the Middle of the 20th Century

Xiangyang Li[1]([✉]) [iD] and Tian Cao[2] [iD]

[1] Higher Education Mega Center, Guangzhou Academy of Fine Arts, 168 Waihuan Xilu, Panyu District, Guangzhou 510006, China
369797043@qq.com
[2] Nanjing University of Science and Technology, Xiaolingwei.200, Nanjing 210094, Jiangsu, China

Abstract. The 20th century is a turning period for the development of Chinese traditional handicrafts that have a profound times brand made by political revolution and social instability. This paper attempts to analyze Beijing traditional handicrafts and jade art from the perspective of economy, handicrafts tools, social discourse and aesthetic trend of thought, and further explores the "design science" factors of our arts and crafts in the participation of social change by clarifying the relationship between traditional handicrafts and social factors.

Keywords: Handicrafts · Aesthetics · Social factors

1 Introduction

As one of the important carriers of Chinese traditional culture, jade culture not only has thousands of years of civilization accumulation, but also has a complete creation logic from concept to skill.

In the 20th century, China has been involved in the process of global modernization. The historical change brought by political revolution has made the overall cognition of society enter a new context which is different from agricultural civilization and explores modern industry. In the meantime, the function and cultural sequence of handicrafts in social life have changed quietly. For example, after the Revolution of 1911, the jade manufacturing skill that was renamed from "court art" to "special handicrafts" has made the jade changed from the original object appreciated by noble literati to a creative resource driving the national economy. Jade craftsmen also entered a new mixed state of consumption context, political context and cultural context to treat the creation of jade materials. At the same time, at the end of the 19th century and the beginning of the 20th century, the modern art education in China absorbed the contemporary art design consciousness of the west in the process of revitalizing the economy and saving the country, and was generating a knowledge system of modern art that integrated Chinese local culture and international art dialogue. The national policy on handicrafts has affected the creative logic of traditional handicrafts, while the production creation as an economic task has affected the technical logic of tool innovation in the context of the national industrial development. In such a special period, western art has become an international art discourse to enter China, and the new viewing method has formed an impact on the aesthetic cognition of traditional art, especially traditional handicrafts. For example, as a new and mainstream art form, sketch and oil painting have rapidly entered the Chinese art ecology. Moreover, the artistic expression in realistic context has developed rapidly in China and has a considerable mass base because of its intuitive visual expression and strong narrative characteristics. Therefore, refined and realistic visual expression has become a kind of evaluation standard to measure artistic expression and skills height. The accompanying knowledge, such as perspective and artistic anatomy, has further constructed a knowledge system expressed in realism. The knowledge has formed an impact on the traditional art, such as the aesthetic system formed by the tactile relationship between materials and body in jade carving art and the relationship between materials and Confucian culture.

This paper aims to discuss that the jade carving art may form a relationship between the new visual culture and tools under the new viewing method, its economic-oriented technical logic and policy-oriented artistic logic, which has brought great changes to the traditional craft aesthetics. On the one hand, the relationship between traditional jade and human body has been separated, while the related aesthetic value has also changed. On the other hand, it has also broadened the expression connotation and aesthetic taste of Chinese traditional jade to enter a richer contemporary expression, which is both an opportunity and a challenge for the modernization and development of traditional culture. In the latter half of the 20th century, the most direct expression of the modeling language and internal aesthetic logic of the mechanized jade carving creation was the transformation of the jade grinding machine by the sketch modeling. Consequently, we had to further think about what kind of value attitude and method we should adopt in the face of such a change to deal with the relationship between cultural genes and social change in the development of traditional art language, technical logic and arts and crafts.

2   Moving Towards the Market: Economic Task of Traditional Handicrafts in the New Era

The Republic of China has overthrown the monarchy. Conforming to the world trend, foreign capital flowed into China and national capitalists actively set up modern machinery industry, so active development of market and trade has become the main task of the whole country. The Revolution of 1911 overthrew the Qing Dynasty, which in fact overthrew the rule of feudal emperors for thousands of years in China. The court craftsmen who had specially served the feudal dynasty for thousands of years also "completely vanished". The "court" was overthrown, so the arts and crafts subordinated to the court accordingly lost their dependence of existence, but the original craftsmen monopolized by the court still existed. In order to make a living, these court craftsmen resumed their old business in the folk. However, the service object has changed from exclusively serving the emperor in the old days to facing the society. In the 1920s and 1930s, the arts and crafts market in Beijing was mainly composed of the following parts: "First, in order to show off the wealth and join the art, some newly-born nobles, warlords, officials and upstarts made their utmost efforts to snap up the court artworks to mark their identities; second, those who used to do their proud by the royal salary had no source of finance after the Revolution of 1911, but those survivals of bygone ages could not change their old way of life for a short while, so they had to make a living by selling the handicraft works left in their homes, and many people also engaged in making handicraft works in order to survive; third, it is believed that precious handicraft works could maintain and appreciate their value, and the original court artworks specially for emperors' enjoyment were scattered in the folk market. The struggles of warlords from all walks of life were back and forth, and the generals and important officials tried their best to plunder the articles used by the court before and even rushed to buy and order handicraft works for collection, or used "antiques" and treasured artworks as the "stepping stone" for promotion and profit, which have also become the gift of reciprocity; fourth, the imperialism coveted the rarity of craftsmen and handicrafts in Chinese feudal court, and the traditional handicraft works of the court were favored by foreign people. Foreign businessmen came in great numbers to buy in a predatory manner, so that the handicrafts in Beiping showed a temporary prosperity."[1] Thus it can be seen that before the founding of new China, as a model of court handicrafts, jade carving has completely moved towards various market-oriented explorations, and with a variety of market-oriented aspects, it started to have the change in artistic consciousness from the original single artistic form facing the court nobility.

On the other side, scholars who spoke of "saving the country by industry" advocated temporarily freezing the disputes of ideology, realizing industrialization with all strength, and forming "a up-and-coming spirit and habit" in society, and then issues related to politics, morality and social education would be readily solved. For example, Gu Chunfan put forward in the 1930s that "we can't immediately solve what kind of political system and moral standards China will adopt in the future, and whether we will embark on militarism, democracy or socialism, at least we can't completely solve it now. It can only be solved with industrialization."[2] In the middle of the 20th century, new China was established, and the production of traditional arts and crafts, which had been severely damaged during the War of Resistance against Japan, was gradually recovered under the national economic policy. In the early days of new China, the country restored the economy through a series of policies, such as respecting the independent choice of self-employed persons, allowing the existence of free markets and free competition, and allowing concurrence of diverse economic forms, etc. After three years of recovery, the handicraft industry was the first to recover quickly due to its characteristics. In 1953, our country entered the period of the First Five-Year Plan for the construction of national

---

[1] Written by Li Cangyan, *Beijing Arts and Crafts History*, Beijing Arts and Crafts Publishing House, Page 359.

[2] Gu Chunfan: General Theory of Industrialization in China, formerly known as Old Civilization and New Industry, Shanghai: Commercial Press, 36th year of the Republic of China, Page 1.

economic, and the general line of the transition period clearly took the socialist transformation of the handicraft industry as an important component. On December 17, 1953, Cheng Zihua made a report on Several Issues Concerning the Socialist Transformation of Handicraft Industry at the third national handicraft production cooperation conference of the All-China Federation of Cooperatives. Almost at the same time, the First National Folk Arts and Crafts Exhibition was held in Beijing under the direction of the Ministry of Culture and the Chinese Artists Association, displaying more than a thousand pieces of various folk arts and crafts. This exhibition showed the attention of the country on the arts and crafts industry, laying an important foundation for the subsequent socialist transformation of the handicraft industry. At that time, the country was in urgent need of a large amount of foreign exchange to support construction. Under the circumstance of completely backward technology and industry, the products of our light and heavy industries were in an unsalable state in the world. Only the exquisite craftsmanship and national characteristics of the handicraft industry were welcomed by Southeast Asia and even European and American countries, and became an important financial source for the country to earn foreign exchange at that time. One carving piece in the Beijing Ivory Carving Factory can be exchanged for a Volga car, and the total amount of the foreign exchange earned by the entire factory was equivalent to half the value of the first steel factory. Since then, the vigorous socialist transformation of handicraft industry has been rapidly carried out across the country. According to statistics, there were 1,300 handicraft cooperatives with 260,000 members in 1950, and the number of members soared to 6,039,000 by 1956, accounting for 91.7% of the workers in the handicraft industry. Later, Huaxun, a jade carving produced by Beijing Jade Factory sold for RMB 700,000 Yuan at the Spring Canton Fair of 1978, which was equivalent to exporting 25,000 domestic bicycles at that time. In the same year, Longfeng Chengxiang, a pair of high-green jade pendant created by Wang Shusen, an old craftsman from Beijing Jade Factory, which is about 3cm high, 7cm wide and 2cm thick and of which one side is the pattern of a swimming dragon and the other side is a soaring phoenix with two butterflies and a pair of words "Xi" (喜) on the top, was sold for RMB 1.8 million Yuan, which became a sensational news in Beijing, Hong Kong and Macau at that time.

Therefore, economic development was the overwhelming main task in the first thirty years after the founding of new China. At that time, it was just the traditional handicrafts representing traditional Chinese culture that may have differentiated competitiveness in the wave of global industrialization, especially jade carvings, ivory carvings, cloisonne, lacquer carvings and filigree inlays in the court handicrafts. On the one hand, complicated and exquisite craft characteristics had the value of art collection, and on the other hand, they represented that Chinese culture, especially Chinese imperial culture, has the cultural value that ordinary commodities cannot have in the formal style and semantic symbols. As a result, these artworks, which have served the imperial class in the past thousands of years, have been completely transformed into commodities in modern society and circulated for the first time, and their diverse flow channels and different production and manufacturing strategies based on market profits have dispelled the original interest and viewing relationship of these court handicrafts, thus giving them new object attributes (Figs. 1, 2 and 3).

Fig. 1. Technological *Reform is Everywhere*, cover of *China Pictorial* in 1958

Fig. 2. *Welcome the National Day with New Construction Achievements*, inner page of *China Pictorial* in 1954

Fig. 3. *Patriotic Production Competition*, inner page of *China Pictorial* in 1951

3 Reconstruction and Change: Handicraft Logic Under the Strategy of Pursuing

We can't deny that the 20th century is the era of global industrialization. The achievements of industrialization in the west, especially in the United States, have directly laid its leading edge and mainstream discourse in global development. Therefore, for new China, industrialization is the only way for the Chinese nation to get rid of poverty and backwardness. Zedong Mao, the state leader, pointed out that "we must realize the industrialization of the country so as to completely liberate the Chinese nation and people." In March 1956, Zedong Mao mentioned in *Accelerating the Socialist Transformation of Handicraft Industry* that "the handicraft industry should develop in the direction of semi-mechanization and mechanization, and labor productivity must be improved." After that, no matter in the machinery manufacturing industry or in the handicraft industry, the technical innovation movement and patriotic production competition were carried out vigorously. The main purpose of technical innovation was to improve production efficiency, which was carried out under the production movement of the "Great Leap Forward" at that time, hence, the production slogan of "more, faster, better, and less" has also become the direction standard of technical innovation. During the 1950s and 1980s, a number of classic traditional handicraft products were created, of which craft level, artistic level and culture level displayed have marked a peak in the modern development of the traditional handicraft industry. The traditions and methods of manual labor are difficult to support these achievements, which largely profit from the modernization of production tools. Practitioners of various categories have made tool innovations to different degrees, and electrical equipment has been introduced into the production of many categories, such as: the "all-purpose" jade grinding machine for making large jade carvings (1969), the jade grinding machine with infinitely variable speed for detailed processing (1978), and ultrasonic processing machine for bas-relief processing (1989); woodworking machine and grinding machine (1974); cloisonne polishing machine (1959), machine for making various brocade (1973), and wire rolling machine (1974); multifunctional trimming machine and plum blossom petal forming machine for filigree inlay production (1973), vine-breaking machine (1975); horizontal flat blanket machine and electric scissors for carpet production (1950s), etc., which has not only improved production efficiency, but also developed technical means to achieve efficiency and quality that cannot be achieved by traditional tools. The inventions of the rapid industrialization have transformed the craft logic of traditional handicrafts and incorporated traditional handicrafts into a "new" industrialization mechanism that conformed to China's national conditions, and the existence of traditional handicrafts has completely become a part of the economic tasks of the times (Figs. 4, 5 and 6).

Christopher Freeman once mentioned, "Technological and system changes are key variables for interpreting economic growth."[3] Derived from the Latin word "innovatus", "innovate" means "to reconstruct or change". Therefore, someone thinks that "to innovate is nothing but to find a new method to change things". In 1912, Joseph Schumpeter

---

[3] Erik, S, Reinert, Jia Genliang (editors-in-chief): *The Other Canon of Economics: A Selection on Essays of Evolutionary Development Economics (2)* (translated by Jia Genliang, etc.), Higher Education Press, 2007, pp. 166–167.

Fig. 4. Traditional pedal artificial jade-grinding bench, called "water bench". The pictures are from the internet.

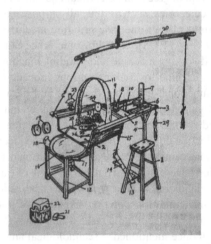

Fig. 5. Hand drawing of "water benches". The pictures are from *Local Chronicles of Beijing On Industrial Art*, Local Chronicles Compilation Committee of Beijing Municipality.

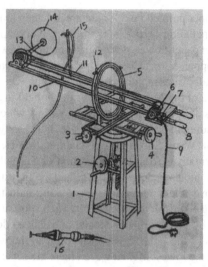

Fig. 6. Hand drawing of "Universal Jade-grinders". The pictures are from *Local Chronicles of Beijing - On Industrial Art*, Local Chronicles Compilation Committee of Beijing Municipality.

proposed the "innovation" theory to explain the agents for changes in the economy. He calls "innovation" as a new combination of production factors and production conditions realized by entrepreneurs, which will produce a new generation function after entering the enterprise production system.[4] In some sense, Schumpeter's "creative destruction" is almost as well-known as Adam Smith's "invisible hand".[5] From the mid-20th century, China's industry is under this development mechanism, bringing a historical opportunity of "reconstruction and change" for traditional handicraft under the strategy of pursuing.

4   Experts' Comment: Traditional Handicraft Becoming "Affinitive to the People"

After the peaceful liberation of Peiping in 1949, its handicraft industry was on the fringe of collapse. The People's Government decided to turn this consumer city into a production city. In March 1949, the municipal government organized relevant departments to perform an in-depth investigation about handicraft production of the city. On Apr. 16th, Peiping Municipal Party Committee pointed out in *Decision on Present Central Work of Peiping*: "To restore transformation and develop production is now a common central task of the Party, the government, the armed forces and the people of Peiping. All other work should be carried out based on and subject to this central task." On Apr. 24th, *People's Daily* published *Some Problems about Restoration and Development of the Special Handicraft Industry of Peiping* written by its journalist Feng Zhong after making

---

[4] Joseph Schumpeter: *Theory of Economic Development* (translated by He Wei, Yi Jiaxiang, etc.), Commercial Press, 1991, pp. 70–71.

[5] Stuart Crainer, Des Dearlove: *Essence of Innovation* (translated by Li Yue, etc.), China Renmin University Press, 2017, page 4 and page 8.

an investigation. The paper pointed out, "There are nineteen kinds of special handicraft industries in Peiping, including carpet, bone artifact, ivory, applique, carved lacquerware, embroidery, velvet paper flower, porcelain, enamel, jade ware, inlay, enamel ware, filament, glassware, copper & tin ware, toy, palace lantern, jade tree and iron openwork." Special handicrafts were major exports of Peiping. On Aug 31st, the Industrial and Commercial Bureau of the Municipal Government held in Jiefang Hotel "Seminar on Production and Sales of Special Handicrafts of Peiping, which was attended by more than thirty people including experts and scholars such as Liang Sicheng, Xu Beihong, Lin Huiyin, Wu Zuoren, Wang Shixiang, Fei Xiaotong/Ma Heng, Han Shouxuan and Ma Dayou, and representatives from the Federation of Special Handicrafts, import & export industries, the Women's Federation, banks and the Industrial Laboratory of Peiping. They deliberated over the strategy for rejuvenating industrial art of Peiping. The sociologist Fei Xiaotong expressed his viewpoint: The export and market of handicrafts in Peiping are affected by the complicated state, unbalanced development and significant quality differences of the industry. In terms of cost, the workers' wages are only enough for maintaining the lowest life. However, there are several layers of exploitation from producers to consumers. To reduce the cost, this problem must be solved. President Xu Beihong suggested: Special handicrafts should be closely related to artists in the future for improving the patterns of the present products. He said unequivocally to representatives from the jade ware industry attending the seminar that if they had any problems about patterns, they could directly seek help from him. Liang Sicheng and Lin Huiyin stressed in their speeches the great significance of maintaining and improving product quality and reported how they studied special handicrafts for the past few months and their understandings, pointing out that the artistry of a product is consistent with its market. Therefore, we should know the good traditions of Chinese fine arts and exhibit the spirit of new China. Through researches and experiments, handicrafts can be improved in form and pattern. Representatives from the import & export industry expected designers to know about changes in production technologies and domestic and overseas demands. Representatives from the Industrial Laboratory expected special handicrafts to be combined with modern science for reducing costs and improving quality. Experts and professors such as Ma Heng, Han Shouxuan and Wang Shixiang delivered a speech successively, suggesting that special handicrafts should strengthen a tie with museums. After the seminar, units such as Department of Architecture of Tsinghua University, Cultural Relics Display Museum, Society for the Study of Chinese Architecture, the Federation of Special Handicrafts and Renli Textile Company jointly established "Research Association for Improving Design of Special Handicrafts of Peiping City".

With jade ware making in feudal society as an example. Whether in the imperial court or in a folk workshop, jade ware making tended to follow a "customized" operation method. Jade ware making in the imperial court would follow the "reverent style". For example, after the southern and northern parts of Xinjiang were surveyed in the 24th Year of Emperor Qianlong (1795), jade material from Xinjiang would be under unified management and exploitation of feudal officials and be contributed to the imperial court. The emperor would take a personal interest in and participate in the whole process about material, design and production of jade sculptures. For example, No. 3442 of *Archives of*

Handicrafts of the Workshop of the Imperial Household Department of the Qing Court recorded:

Ruyi House, August, the 18th Year of Emperor Qianlong.

On the 12th day, the assistant department director Bai Shixiu reported that the eunuch Hu Shijie would contribute a white jade cicada with three rubies of different sizes, and a white marble celestial being. The emperor issued a decree: "Hand them to Yao Zongren for removing the color of the celestial being and changing the white jade cicada into another thing as he likes. That's all."

Imperial artistic creations include jade ware affected by the emperor's culture, knowledge and taste exhibit a "reverent style of the imperial court", which is different from folk art and assumes an imperial bearing. However, of the experts attending "Seminar on Production and Sales of Special Handicrafts of Peiping" and offering suggestions, Xu Beihong, a painter studying oil painting in France; Liang Sicheng, an architect born in Tokyo, Japan; and Lin Huiyin, an architect, poet & writer graduating from University of Pennsylvania of the US, and traditional Chinese painters, cultural relic scientists and representatives from all walks of life all expressed their opinions about traditional handicrafts of Beijing based on their knowledge and experience and their social divisions. The "social discourse" formed from identity assembly embodies that traditional handicrafts are becoming "affinitive to the people".

5 Aesthetic Changes of Viewing: Modern Fine Art Trend

At the beginning of the 20th century, Liang Qichao advocated the concepts of "painting school reform", "poetry circle revolution" and "novel circle revolution". The "poetry circle revolution" must meet three basic standards from contents to form: new artistic conception, new sentences and ancient style, while the true spirit and thought imported from Europe are its ultimate purpose. The "poetry circle revolution" and "novel circle revolution" he advocated was a part of socio-political revolutionary movements, stressing that revolution is to change the spirit rather than the form. The "painting circle revolution" can be regarded as an extension of the "poetry circle revolution" in logic. At the early 1920s, he even pointed out straightforwardly in *Introduction to Academics of the Qing Dynasty*, "The academic atmosphere of the former Qing Dynasty was quite different from that of renaissance Europe. The biggest difference is that its fine art and literature was not well-developed. Though the fine art (painting) of the Qing Dynasty cannot be said to be far worse than that of previous dynasties, it had never attempted to develop in new aspects. This problem will not be discussed in detail."[6] (Figs. 7, 8, 9 and 10)

It can be seen that from the beginning of the 20th century, the Western learning trend had been spread from the whole circle of literature and art. Li Bosheng, a Beijing jade carver born in 1941, recalled that when he started to work in Beijing Jade Ware Factory (about late 1950s), the factory had set a special reading room, which was filled with

---

[6] Written by Liang Qichao, checked and annotated by Zhu Weizheng: Liang Qichao's Two Explanations about the Academic History of the Qing Dynasty, Fudan University Press, 1986, pp. 82–83.

Fig. 7. 1925, *Representative Works of Renaissance: Full Figure of the Last Judgment, Picture Times.*

Fig. 8. 1979, *Beijing Industrial Art*, Beijing Special Handicraft Industrial Company.

Fig. 9. Work of Jade Carver Li Bosheng *Man at Birth*

Fig. 10. Work of Jade Carver Li Bosheng *Creation of the World*

all kinds of albums of jade ware patterns and drawings. Of them, what obsessed him most was a collection of sculptures of Michelangelo, an Italian Renaissance sculptor. In addition, there were oil paintings of Botticelli and Titian. These works made Li Bosheng concentrate his efforts on studying the body structure and different dynamic states under the body structure. Benefiting from the knowledge of Western perspective science and human anatomy, he created many classic jade wares of character images.

The Western learning trend of the 20th century should be an overall reflection from economic area to social reform. In the perspective of handicraft industry, Beijing jade sculpture art should naturally be in the pace of social reform of the whole 20th century. From trend changes at social consciousness level to aesthetic changes about the work viewing structure formed from renewal of embodiment knowledge, the traditional jade culture was injected with a connotation of the era.

6 Conclusion

There is a widely-spread saying among people, "The wonderfulness of jade caving is in the imperial court, while court jade wares are in Beijing", reveals the relationship between the jade carving tradition of Beijing and the imperial court culture. However, going through situation turbulence of the 20th century and modernized rebirth of traditional skills, the social soil that traditional skills rely for existence has changed. Jade sculpture art of Beijing has come from the imperial court to the market. Imperial court handicraft no longer serves a single social division but has an opportunity to be combined with the era and the people in life. Handicraft transformation under socialist system had saved traditional handicraft from the verge of collapse, making it be restored and developed. Under the pursuing strategy of the post-industrial age, the involvement of experts' discourse, collision with Western artistic cultures and integration of knowledge have transformed and remodeled traditional handicraft structurally so that it presents the appearance features today. Viewed from special historical nodes, the relationship between aesthetic changes and social factors of industrial art has also revealed "design science" factors about traditional handicraft getting involved in social reform.

Acknowledgement. Phased achievements of the academic promotion plan for Guangzhou Academy of Fine Arts's school-level project "Research on Beijing Jade Carving Skills" (No. 21XSC58).

Research on Touchpoint Management in the Catering Industry——Taking Haidilao as an Example

Xuanjie Lu[✉], Zhichao Liu, and Chen Yang

Guangzhou City University of Technology, GuangZhou 51000, China
sophiedear@qq.com

Abstract. Touchpoint management is an important management tool for the service industry. In the Internet era, the interaction between enterprises and consumers is stimulated to create more channels and touchpoints. Haidilao has established its own reputation in the catering industry through its excellent service and has become an excellent example of touchpoint management. Therefore, from the perspective of consumers, this article digs deeply into Haidilao's touchpoint management to understand the stage division and key touchpoint of touchpoints in the catering industry. Observe the interaction between waiters and consumers through the on-site observation method and invite consumers to conduct interviews. This paper finds that the touchpoint stages in the catering industry can be divided into pre-consumption, in-consumption and post-consumption. Among the many touchpoints, it is necessary to pay attention to the key touchpoint moments of personalization and emotion, which is the key for consumers to recognize the consumption experience. The design and management of touchpoints are not the more the better, the more complex the better. Based on the social and cultural background and the characteristics of the target population, we need to find a balance to obtain a good input-output ratio. This study provides a practical reference for the management of touchpoints in the catering industry.

Keywords: Consumer · Touchpoint management · Haidilao · Experience · Personality · Emotion

1 Introduction

A good company is always as close to its customers as possible. The goal of work communication in different periods and in different fields is to reach out to customers. The core goal of effective contact between enterprises and customers is to maximize customer satisfaction and ultimately maximize marketing effects. This is the core of touchpoint management research, and therefore touchpoint management is a hot topic of discussion in modern marketing. In the fields of business, communication, education, finance, transportation, industrial design and medical services, all involve the research and discussion of touchpoint management. Different industries have different perspectives and directions of analysis. Hence the formation of scattered and fragmented viewpoints.

M. M. Soares et al. (Eds.): HCII 2022, LNCS 13322, pp. 443–454, 2022.
https://doi.org/10.1007/978-3-031-05900-1_31

This research takes the catering industry as the direction and takes Haidilao as a case to discuss the touchpoint management. From the perspective of consumers, this paper explores the stage division of touchpoint management in the catering service industry and the view of key touchpoints. This research analyzes and discusses the division of touchpoint management stages and the distinction of key touchpoints through on-site observation and case interviews.

Through the discussion of the above problems, we can provide some experience in case study for the research and development of touchpoint management theory in the catering industry. The catering industry is an industry with more real-time and human-to-human interaction. The case study in this study can bring some new thinking or inspiration to the management and customer relationship processing of similar enterprises.

Through the discussion of this research, we found that the touchpoint stage in the catering industry can be divided into three stages: pre-consumption, in-consumption and post-consumption, and subdivided into multiple touchpoints within the three stages. Among the many touchpoints, it is necessary to pay attention to the key touchpoint moments of personalization and emotional experience. Touchpoints in these categories are key for consumers to recognize the consumer experience. The design and management of touchpoints are not the more the better, the more complex the better. Based on the social and cultural background and the characteristics of the target population, we all need to find a balance to obtain a good input-output ratio.

2 Literature Review

The touchpoint management and business combination proposed in the early stage are based on the need for service brands to guide customer behaviors, understand the relationship between brands and customers, and ultimately obtain more customer value [1]. Touchpoint management is also key to brand success [12]. Industrial design always pays attention to user experience, and constantly deduces the scope of user experience perception from the experience model [2]. This does not appear to be related to touchpoint management. However, belonging to a certain type of product characteristics, after the final product reaches the user, the touchpoints between the brand and the user will continue to interact, and the positive and negative brand impressions will also build their own brand impressions in consumers' cognition. The industrial design industry provides the object itself, and both objects and services will have touchpoints with consumers. Identify your business' customer touchpoints and treat them differently by industry and product. Then filter out key touchpoint. Many industries and brands have used brainstorming, questionnaires and other methods to explore their own consumer touchpoints [3, 5].

Regardless of industrial design or service, the moment of contact with customers is generated. We call these moments "real moments". It is a collection of information that stimulates the senses, ultimately and emotionally. Each contact produces three possibilities. Lost customers, satisfied customers, loyal customers [4]. This reminds us that the selection process of touchpoint management is not purely from a business perspective, a management perspective. In order to pursue satisfied and loyal customers, enterprises can reduce costs and improve management efficiency. But the key point that cannot be ignored is that touchpoints should be observed from the perspective of consumers. They are the key to experiencing the "real moment". Some people think that touchpoint management is an all-round and full-cycle concept. Compared with 360°, touchpoint management is not only a dynamic process, but also a key to consider the effect between market cultivation and return on investment. Therefore, the links of touchpoint management optimization include product design and development, marketing channels, sales services, competitors in the market, customers, their own subsidiaries and so on. Among many complex factors, the purpose is to maximize the return on investment. The level of return is guided by customer experience [6].

From an enterprise perspective to a consumer perspective, from individual touchpoints to a system-wide perspective. CTP management (Customer Touchpoint Management) is not the same as traditional customer relationship management. CRM design is holistic, but CTP is customer oriented. To really play a role, CTP management not only becomes part of the corporate strategy, but also needs to be shaped as a corporate philosophy. CTP is functionally differentiated, one is used to inform customers, the other is to sell to customers, and the third is to provide services. The design of CTP also depends on the nature of the product itself and the characteristics of the target customers. Taking new media marketing as an example, there is a big gap between the acceptance speed and response speed of new media between the younger generation and the older generation [7]. It can be seen that the design of CTP needs to recognize the overlapping area between the target customer group and the product nature itself from the very beginning. Managerial approval is not enough for CTP to be implemented and to have a real effect. I think CTP needs to rely on corporate culture to be effective. The recognition of corporate culture at the employee level, especially the employees who directly communicate and interact with customers. Their recognition of CTP in the integration and corporate culture is the key to make CTP take effect. Another scholar looks at touchpoint management more from a consumer-focused perspective. While touchpoint management design is particularly important, consumer's own expectations affect the ultimate result of interaction with employees. Consumer's personal expectations, positive and negative tendencies of emotional level, greatly affect the satisfaction itself. Another hidden problem is the cultural background of consumers themselves. If the cultural background of the enterprise itself, the products and services itself, the employees themselves and the customers are very different and the compatibility is low, there is a lack of consideration for the cultural integration and understanding of the touchpoint management design. It must be difficult to obtain customer satisfaction. In addition, among many employees, in the process of direct-to-consumer face-to-face employees, service completion and the status quo of touchpoint characteristics are the key, but a natural, sincere smile and attitude can always improve satisfaction. Even if there are occasional service errors, we can obtain the understanding of consumers with a positive and sincere attitude. To study the restaurant service part of hotel services, it involves the management of touchpoints and key touchpoints [8].

This shows how much satisfaction the design of touchpoint management can ultimately generate. Satisfaction needs to depend on the interaction between employees and consumers. Some scholars mentioned that the sincere attitude and smile of employees could play a positive evaluation. Therefore, it can be summed up as the happiness of employees, which directly affects the interaction with consumers. The interactive experience between people also responds to the views of the aforementioned scholars, the "instant real" experience. In the research from the perspective of touchpoints of construction enterprises, the effect of touchpoint management is also emphasized, and it is necessary to integrate evaluation from the perspective of consumers and enterprises to achieve better results [9, 11]. Since the beginning of the millennial generation, offline retail has transformed into a powerful "digital retail". The new retail form of "digital retail" relies on electronic products and electronic media to attract consumers and provides them with an efficient shopping experience. From the perspective of touchpoint management, to achieve this goal, consumers' cognition and enterprise's cognition need to have consistent direction and recognition of effective touchpoints. However, there are still multiple levels of employees and departments with different functions within the enterprise. Do they have the same understanding and recognition of contact management? According to the research data of a fashion retailer, there are indeed differences in the perception of touchpoints and differences in the direction of action between different management levels and departments. This difference is also particularly important for digital retail [10]. At present, the concept of omni-channel management is rising, and the concept of consumer touchpoint management is becoming more and more important [13]. When referring to touchpoint management, there are also many academics or business people who refer to the customer journey. The customer journey also assumes that all consumers experience some of the same touchpoints and that these touchpoints are equally important. But this equally important assumption is wrong. The difference of consumers, the experience of consumers must filter out those touchpoints is crucial [14]. From the perspective of commercial interests and efficiency, we often hope to seize an important touchpoint for comprehensive design, so as to make the consumer experience better. But themes are clear, consistent, and not just a single point of contact can be effective. Enabling consumers to have a great experience and build customer loyalty requires a comprehensive and consistent touchpoint management design. Of course, the differences between industries cannot be ignored [15].

When we look at touchpoint management from the perspective of the restaurant industry. In Chinese culture, the idea that "the people take food as the sky" is deeply rooted in the hearts of the people, and the competition among various types of restaurants is quite fierce. As a traditional diet, hot pot is highly competitive in the catering industry and has a high elimination rate. Haidilao established its head office in Sichuan in 1994, and opened its first branch in 1999, and has been expanding its business since then. As of June 30, 2021, Haidilao has opened 1,597 directly-operated restaurants around the world, of which 1,491 stores are located in mainland China, and 106 stores are located in Hong Kong, Macau, Taiwan and overseas, including Singapore, South Korea, Japan, and the United States., Canada, the United Kingdom, Vietnam, Malaysia, Indonesia and Australia [16]. Affected by the new crown epidemic in 2020, its annual revenue was 28.614 billion yuan, a year-on-year increase of 7.75%. In November 2021, Haidilao announced on Weibo that due to the rapid expansion strategy formulated in 2019, a series of management and operation problems were caused. Managers were overwhelmed by their own organizational structure, insufficient number of excellent store managers, and so on. Therefore, before December 31, 2021, 300 stores that did not meet expectations would be closed. However, the closure of stores would not lay off employees, and relevant employees and management would be properly settled. For Haidilao's experience management, this is undoubtedly a huge setback. But from this announcement, we can also find Haidilao's sincerity and efforts towards its own strategic mistakes. The corporate culture conveys the belief that employees and managers, who should not be affected by high-level decision-making mistakes, should be properly accommodated. Since the announcement, the enthusiasm of consumers who were keen on Haidilao had not diminished, and there were no complaints from employees who complained on the Internet.

For a long time, Haidilao has been deeply cultivating the Chinese catering market, and its excellent to "perverted" service is very popular among consumers. Compared to similar hot pot meals. The positioning of Haidilao's business model is very clear. Excellent service, excellent product, and price acceptable to consumers, service is the primary positioning, product is the secondary positioning, and the overall level is better than its peers [17]. In an empirical study, perceived service quality and perceived product quality affect customer satisfaction, and customer satisfaction has a significant impact on consumer retention. Among them, service empathy has the greatest impact on customer satisfaction and retention, followed by response speed, featured products, service tangibility and basic products [18]. The success of catering enterprises is inseparable from the management of human resources. What makes Haidilao outstanding is its innovation in the catering industry. There is no doubt that Haidilao's excellence is closely related to the selection, employment and training of employees. Since the establishment of Haidilao, in China's catering industry, the long-term reputation of consumers and the satisfaction of employees are inseparable from the company's understanding and emphasis on people [19, 20]. For a long time, "the customer is always right" and "the customer is God" are the beliefs and slogans that many companies use when training their employees and publicizing their business philosophy. This concept is actually "customer first". However, in order to achieve "customer first", quite a lot of companies ignore this premise, the premise is that employees are regarded as "employee first" by the company. The catering industry is a service industry. In the process of contacting consumers in large numbers, it not only consumes the physical strength of employees, but also consumes the spirit, emotions, and psychological energy of employees to a greater extent. The empowerment of employees must come from the enterprise, and the enterprise needs to create greater value and empower employees with positive emotions and spiritual strength [21].

The pricing of Haidilao is not advantageous for products in the same category. Excellent service is not smooth sailing in the whole crowd, and some customers are troubled. After all, being too enthusiastic is also a burden. Although the service is still praised by consumers, the voice of "too enthusiastic" cannot be ignored [22]. Looking at Haidilao's hospitality style from a cultural and anthropological point of view, it is a way to break the "high context" Chinese traditional catering culture and create a service experience that exceeds consumers' expectations with smiling service. Making individual consumers feel "excessive enthusiasm and discomfort" also comes from differences with traditional culture. The consumer experience is like a journey. Before they enter a store and come into contact with the actual product, there is already overwhelming publicity that makes them have expectations or impressions of the start of the journey. When you really set foot in an offline store or an online store, the actual experience of the journey will form more touchpoints. The construction of touchpoint management is also the consumer journey construction [14]. For the construction of touchpoints, it comes from both consumers and frontline workers. The cognitive consistency and emotional consistency of the two dimensions to touchpoints are directly related to the effectiveness of touchpoint management [15]. The restaurant industry is highly dependent on design itself in the nature of touchpoint management. Catering service touchpoints are highly interactive, low in intangibility, and the service process is relatively discrete. Consumers seek satisfaction in catering services based on hedonic motivation [23].

Haidilao is a company that has done a good job in service marketing in the catering industry, with high user satisfaction and good reputation. If the analysis is conducted from the perspective of customer touchpoint management, what is the success of Haidilao, what problems exist, and how to rebuild it? This is what this article will seriously discuss. Taking Haidilao, a benchmark enterprise in the catering industry as an example, this paper discusses the analysis of its touchpoints, the design of services and its effects. Through interviews and observation methods, it is sorted out that Haidilao consumers are divided into three major stages of touchpoint management: before consumption, during consumption, and after consumption. Pre-consumption touchpoints include advertising, reception at the front desk, and waiting services; In-consumption touchpoints include consumer-employee exclusive matching, ordering, serving meals, accompanying catering, personalized service, and payment; Post-consumption touchpoints are classified as sending off customers, Post-meal evaluation.

3   Methodology

The goal of this research is to explore and explore Haidilao consumers from the perspective of consumers to divide the touchpoint management into three major stages: before consumption, during consumption, and after consumption. The methods of interviewing and observation are suitable. According to the research topic, the criteria for selecting participants for case interviews should have the following characteristics: first, they have been to Haidilao for consumption; second, they have visited Haidilao for consumption within the past year; third, they are willing to be interviewed for this academic discussion. In addition, the author went to Haidilao stores several times to obtain information by observation method. Therefore, this study relies on primary data and secondary data for data collection and data analysis. The primary data comes from the interviewees and the author's observations. Secondary data information is obtained from relevant literature reviews.

Both the observation method and the interview method are divided into three stages: before consumption, during consumption, and after consumption. Pre-consumption touchpoints include advertising, reception at the front desk, and waiting services; In-consumption touchpoints include consumer-employee exclusive matching, ordering, serving, accompanying catering, personalized service, and payment; Post-consumption touchpoints are classified as sending off customers, Post-meal evaluation. The time, place, period and brief introduction of the interview are shown in Table 1.

Table 1. Collection paths of the first-hand data

Time	Place	Objects
December 2021 to January 2022	Guangzhou Haidilao Restaurant (Haizhu Wanda Store; Haizhu Kecun Store; Tianhe Sports West Road Store; Yuexiu Liuhua Trade Center Store)	We observed waiters interacting with consumers in four restaurants in Guangzhou for 12 h; we invited consumers to conduct interviews with a total of 23 people, and actually completed all the interviews with 8 people for a total of 11 h

4   Results

The author observed the interaction between waiters and consumers in four Haidilao restaurants in Guangzhou for 12 h; and invited a number of consumers to participate in interviews. There were 23 consumers who knew the purpose of this interview and agreed. However, some consumers terminated the interview for personal reasons during the interview. In the end, 8 consumers actually completed the whole process of interviews, with a total of 11 h of interviews. Consumer experience was based on the three stages of pre-consumption, in-consumption and post-consumption. Information is represented through Tables 2 and 3.

Table 2. Information of interviewing customers

Serial number	Gender	Age	Frequency of dining at Haidilao within half a year	Main form of dining
1	F	20	4	Personal dining
2	F	42	2	Family dining
3	M	28	1	Couple dating
4	F	32	3	Friends dining
5	M	19	2	Personal dining
6	F	27	3	Personal dining
7	M	37	3	Family dining
8	M	38	5	Family dining

In the pre-consumption stage of Haidilao, the author's observations and interviews with consumers identified the touchpoints as advertising, seating arrangements, food entertainment while waiting, board game entertainment while waiting, manicure service while waiting, and discount service when waiting for overtime. As a touchpoint in consumption, it can be divided into exclusive matching between consumers and employees, being informed of the location of the hot pot seasoning station, providing mobile phone protection and stand services, providing aprons to protect clothing, ordering assistance, and free for the elderly and children. Meals or items, waiters warmly accompany and

Table 3. Research results of Haidilao consumer touchpoint management at different stages

Before consumption	During consumption	After consumption
1) Advertising impact 2) Seat arrangement 3) Food reception while waiting 4) Board game entertainment while waiting 5) Nail service while waiting 6) Waiting for Timeout Discount Service	1) Consumer and employee exclusive matching 2) Hot pot seasoning station location notification 3) Mobile phone protection and stand provided 4) Provide aprons to protect clothing 5) Order assistance 6) Meals and items for the elderly and children 7) The waiter warmly accompanies the chat 8) The waiter finds bright spots and praises from consumers 9)Quickly organize the table 10) Festive or special discount handling 11) Personalized service or care according to the consumer	1) Giving of small gifts 2) Dining Satisfaction and Questions 3) Sharing of personal consumption experience

chat, waiters excavate the characteristics of consumers and sincerely praise, quickly arrange tables, holiday or special discounts, and provide personalized services according to consumers. Post-consumption touchpoints include gift giving, inquiries about meal satisfaction, and consumer sharing of consumer experience.

From the many touchpoints in the three consumption stages summarized above, the touchpoints in the pre-consumption stage are already an important part of Haidilao's services, and it is also a place that effectively distinguishes it from other catering brands. In this process, although the actual consumption has not yet been generated. In general, the touchpoint of the catering industry at this stage is mainly advertising. But this advertisement is mainly for the brand side to take the initiative as publicity. However, in the interviews with Haidilao consumer groups, we found that advertising is actually divided into users' online and offline word-of-mouth communication and brand propaganda, but the former occupies the main position. Haidilao's stores often have to wait for a long time for a seat. Food hospitality while waiting, board game entertainment while waiting, manicure service while waiting, and overtime discount service mentioned before consumption are all important means to effectively reduce consumer anxiety and improve consumer satisfaction. The consumers in the interview are still quite satisfied with these services. Although they also find it a bit annoying to wait in line, after all, there are entertainment and entertainment in the process, which is acceptable.

The touchpoints in the consumption process are richer and more diverse. Haidilao's services already have a set of standardized service processes. At this stage of consumption, consumers actually accept a standard service process. That is to say, whether you are dining in South China, Central China or North China, the touchpoints in the consumption process are standard design and standard development. But beyond the standard, the moment when employees and consumers actually come into contact will still bring some unexpected surprises to consumers. Eating out, in the past, we were mainly in the form of confidants, colleagues and friends, family banquets and so on. But today in 2022, what we can focus on is the "dining alone" group, which is a ubiquitous group in more and more countries and is or will be a mainstream consumer group.

A female college student from Generation Z and post-00s talked about a Haidilao moment that moved her the most. "I came to eat alone, and the waiter immediately took the big doll over. I asked the doll to accompany me to eat hot pot, and they also provided various considerate services. They might think that something had happened to me when I came to eat alone. Are you in a bad mood?, so it's a different way to accompany me. It's really touching."

The post-00s male college student who is also a generation Z said, "I felt very happy. I could drink all kinds of juice freely, and I could challenge the cheapest price to eat all kinds of Haidilao hot pot. I shot short videos and the waiters still warmly entertained me. They also shared with me some tricks that I didn't know about. I didn't pay a lot to pay the bill, but they also gave me gifts. I like to eat alone, especially in Haidilao".

Another touching moment to share the consumer service in the special era of the epidemic. "My work is often reversed day and night, but working alone in Guangzhou, I am often too tired to cook. Haidilao's business hours match mine, and their waiters are always full of energy. The waiters saw that I was tired and caring. Prepare some small things for me, spoke kindly and softly. Now that the Chinese New Year is approaching, they also gave me a pack of bacon, which was really like family." From the moment when the three consumers who dined alone touched them, you will find that this touchpoint has been Not a standardized service process, but "personalized service or care according to the consumer" that belongs to the touchpoint in consumption. It's a touchpoint management full of personalization and emotion. This requires a high level of observation, empathy, responsiveness, and empathy for employees themselves. In the catering process, consumers do not just want to be full, but the hedonic motive is the main factor in the catering process. Consumers with similar motivation, but each person's definition of pleasure is very different, so the service they need is very different. We cannot say that Haidilao is perfect in the service process, but what can be said is that they have indeed made a lot of efforts to retain loyal customers, and have produced many real moving, loyal and effective moments.

Among the post-consumer touchpoints, the most critical is whether consumers share a positive dining experience online or offline. This is the embodiment and nurturing of loyal customers and can also inspire a new round of interactions at pre-consumer touchpoints. During the interview process, we found that in the pre-consumption and mid-consumption stages, the interaction with the waiters is high and can inspire real moments of personalization and emotional resonance, and for the post-consumption stage online or offline to share a positive dining experience have an important role.

5 General Discussion

Haidilao's excellent service has been recognized and praised by many consumers, but the background of these recognitions is not easy and smooth. The times are changing and the needs of consumers are changing with each passing day. The innovation and improvement of enterprises also need to learn quickly. In this research and discussion, we dig deep into the inner thoughts behind consumers' consumption behavior. The language, expressions, and behaviors displayed by consumers actually involve personal motivation, personality, characteristics of life stages, and social and cultural influences.

5.1 Management of Pre-consumer, In-consumer and Post-consumer Touchpoints that Cannot be Ignored

The catering service industry can be divided into three stages: pre-consumption, in-consumption and post-consumption under the touchpoint management theory. The touchpoints of each stage in the Haidilao case can also be clearly distinguished. Induction before consumption often comes from online and offline word-of-mouth communication, which is worthy of attention in today's catering industry. The "personalized service or care provided by the consumer" in the mid-consumption stage is a key touchpoint to inspire high consumer recognition and retention of loyal customers. Sharing a positive dining experience online or offline in the post-consumer stage is to verify the mining and cultivation of loyal customers.

5.2 Pay Attention to Personalized and Emotional Key Touchpoint Moments

The touchpoints in the middle stage of consumption "according to the personalized service or care provided by consumers" are very worthy of our attention and consideration. Companies need to rely on the real, effective moments generated by the actual interaction between employees and consumers, and this process is not easy. Only with high emotions and high attention of employees can we quickly capture the needs of consumers and the moment they resonate with consumers. The daily skill training of employees is often not enough to solve this problem. Employees need "soft" training to understand consumers' psychology, understand consumers' behavior and make appropriate responses. This is a process that requires repeated learning and practice.

5.3 The More Touchpoints Are not the Better

Is touchpoint management the more the better, the richer the better? This is also a question we have repeatedly thought about when discussing Haidilao as a case. During on-site observations and interviews, we paid more attention. In the process we noticed a keyword "too enthusiastic". Consumers still like the service of Haidilao, and they can also feel the enthusiasm and thoughtfulness of Haidilao employees. When standardized touchpoints repeat similar actions like assembly line workers, will employees bring some fatigue, and will consumers feel it? Mr. Zhang Yong, the founder of Haidilao, is also aware of this problem. In the process of Haidilao's excellent service becoming increasingly standardized, consumers have complained about the overly enthusiastic service, and even hope to give some space for consumption. Enthusiastic and appropriately beneficial service is the most difficult degree to control in touchpoint management.

5.4 Reflections from the Touchpoint Management Institute

The touchpoint management theory can be applied to different fields, and the theory itself is combined with the development and characteristics of the industry field, bringing us different inspirations. In this study, the touchpoint management of the catering industry is the hotpot category in the catering subdivision, which is of reference significance for the catering management of the same category. However, it remains to be considered whether there is a corresponding reference for other categories in catering. It is undeniable that the catering industry, as one of the industries with the most frequent interactions between people, is a positive aspect of management as a research touchpoint. On the other hand, since the catering industry is highly dependent on the contact between front-line waiters and consumers, the effectiveness of touchpoint management is highly dependent on the effectiveness and perfection of the training of front-line waiters. In addition, based on different social and cultural backgrounds, the discussion in this study may not be applicable to the catering industry with large social and cultural differences.

References

1. Pan, Y.: Research on the management of service brand touchpoint based on customer value. Thesis (2004)
2. Bo, O., Yun, H.: User research and user experience design. J. Jiangsu Univ. (Nat. Sci. Edn.) **27**(5A), 55–57, 77 (2006)
3. Li, Z.: Management path for customer touchpoints. Enterp. Reform Manag. **12**, 72–73 (2006)
4. Rao, J.: Grasp the real moment - talk about customer touchpoint management. Enterp. Res. **8**, 69–71 (2004)
5. Luo, S., Zhu, S., Ying, F., Zhang, J.: Context-based user experience design in mobile interfaces. Comput. Integrat. Manuf. Syst. **16**, 239–248 (2010)
6. Spengler, C., Wirth, W., Sigrist, R.: 360-grad-touchpoint-management — Muss unsere Marke jetzt twittern? Market. Rev. St. Gallen **27**(2), 14–20 (2010)
7. Eva-maria Hefner, F.: Mit dem Kunden zum Erfolg – customer touchpoint management als strategie. Mark. Rev. St. Gallen **27**(2), 27–31 (2010)
8. Liu, Y.: Research on front-line staff management in hotel service contact. Thesis(2007)
9. Yin, F.: Employee happiness management model based on customer satisfaction——Experimental research on customer contact point management. Thesis (2012)
10. Zimmermann, R., Auinger, A.: Managerial and departmental differences in the perceived influence of brand-owned touchpoints on brand perception - case study. Procedia Comput. Sci. **181**, 157–165 (2021)
11. Dhebar, A.: Toward a compelling customer touchpoint architecture. Bus. Horiz. **56**, 199–205 (2013)
12. Esch, F.-R., Kochann, D., Schneider, J.: Customer Touchpoint Management: Kontaktpunktemarken-undkundenspezifischdeklinieren (2019)
13. Barann, B., Hermann, A., Heuchert, M., Becker, J.: Can't touch this? Conceptualizing the customer touchpoint in the context of omni-channel retailing. J. Retail. Consum. Serv. **10**, 1–11 (2020)

14. Rosenbauma, M.S., Otalorab, M.L., Ramırezb, G.C.: How to create a realistic customer journeymap. Bus. Horiz. **9**, 1–8 (2016)
15. Kuehnl, C., Jozic, D., Homburg, C.: Effective customer journey design: consumers' conception, measurement, and consequences. J. Acad. Market. Sci. **47**, 551–568 (2019)
16. Haidilao. https://www.haidilao.com/. Accessed 17 Jan 2021
17. Li, F., Li, D., Ma, Y.: The formation mechanism of good service positioning points for service brands——a double case study of Haidilao and Fat Donglai. J. Manag. Case Stud. **6**, 594–605 (2017)
18. Cheng, L., Wang, J.: Different effects of perceived quality on customer satisfaction and customer retention: an empirical study based on Haidilao restaurants. Indust. Eng. J. **5**, 125–132 (2013)
19. Liu, X., Xu, X.: Upgrading and innovation of catering industry——taking Haidilao as an example. J. Indust. Technol. Econ. **3**, 3–13 (2014)
20. Yu, J., Yang, B., Wang, M.: The successful way of human resource management in catering enterprises——take little sheep and Haidilao as examples. East China Econ. Manag. **11**, 115–122 (2014)
21. Meng, L., Xian, Q.: Say goodbye to emotional burnout: from "customer first" to "employee first." Tsinghua Bus. Rev. **9**, 52–57 (2020)
22. Han, S., Fan, J., Cheng, Y.: Analysis of the causes and problems of Haidilao customer satisfaction. Inner Mongolia Sci. Technol. Econ. **1**, 56–61 (2021)
23. Lee, K., Chung, K., Nam, K.: Orchestrating designable touchpoints for service businesses. DMI (Fall), 14–21 (2013)

From "Fire Pit" to "Hall": Spiritual Space Design in Chinese Family Life

Qian Lu[✉] [iD]

China Central Academy of Fine Arts, No. 8 Hua Jia Di Nan St., Chao Yang District, Beijing, People's Republic of China
136794311@qq.com

Abstract. The dual structure design of material and spiritual spaces in traditional Chinese family life is an important condition for family stabilization, family continuation and cultural inheritance. However, the qualitative change of modern social life has not only destroyed the order of material space structure but also nearly collapsed the spiritual space structure. From the perspective of design culture, this paper has analyzed the spiritual space of traditional Chinese families represented by "fire pit" and "hall", reflected upon the modern changes of Chinese family life after modern technology getting involved in daily life, stressed the important value of the dual structure design of traditional family life space, and discussed the practical significance of restructuring or amending the dual structure of material and spiritual spaces in modern family life and the responsibility of design.

Keywords: Family life · Material space · Spiritual space · Modernity · Technology · Design innovation

1 Dual Structure of Material and Spiritual Spaces in Chinese Family Life

The traditional Chinese family life is rich in spiritual space. The spiritual space and material space support each other and constitute a dual structure design in family life. The dual structure exists along with human evolution and ethnic multiplication, and keeps on adjusting its forms with the development of patriarchal families and the accumulation of family life experience. The dual structure constituted by material and spiritual spaces guarantees the order of traditional Chinese families and so has important influence on daily life and family members.

Mr. Zhu Qiling, the founder of Society for the Study of Chinese Architecture mentioned in the founding speech in the 1930s, "Room is a living representation and a concentrated reflection of the builder's social outlook and mental attitude... It is not merely a dwelling place. In a yard whose size and wall height are stipulated, in a room for social interaction, in a temple for worshiping divinities and ancestors and holding various rites, or in a private bedroom, concepts and etiquette are gradually established." Any house elevated to the height of "home" is not merely a shelter for dodging from

M. M. Soares et al. (Eds.): HCII 2022, LNCS 13322, pp. 455–465, 2022.
https://doi.org/10.1007/978-3-031-05900-1_32

inconstant bad weather and maintaining life security. As a foundation of family life, residence space can provide family members with material conditions required for their daily life. However, mankind's family life is not just for satisfying the needs of material life. From the day when a house is built, the owner has blended his nice expectation and wish about the family into his residence. When a "family house" is completed, the family members will live in a common material space, maintaining family solidarity and continuing family cultures. The intangible spiritual space and detailed material space gradually roll into one and constitute a complete life. In Chinese family life, there has always been a dual structure design, which is a foundation for the proper operation of the Chinese family organizational form and the continuation of family cultures.

2   Evolution of Family Spiritual Space Design from "Fire Pit" to "Hall"

In traditional Chinese life, "fire pit" and "hall" are not all contents of family spiritual space, but are the most important constituent and structural center in different historical periods.

2.1   Earlier Human Family Spiritual Structure Centered on "Fire"

Before "family" in a real sense came into being, "fire" had widely existed in human life. Subsequently, with the improvement of survival conditions and lifestyles, "fire" was involved in the forming of "families" and entered human family space as a matter of course. People built a house centered on "fire" and kept on improving it. For a very long period, "fire" had remained the center of family material space and a place for aggregation of family members. The most important rites in family life would be held there. The most important things would be decided there. A family spiritual structure centered on fire was gradually constituted. In the West, the spirit of "fire" in a family is embodied in the fireplace, which is the center of a dwelling space. In China, there is a tradition of family members gathering around a furnace. Even now, traditional fire pits can still be seen in the center of family space in some primitive minority areas (Fig. 1). "Fire pit" or a certain "family fires" having the same nature as "fire pit", had remained the center of material and spiritual spaces in Chinese family life for a long time, and so is of special and great significance to family life.

As human history kept on moving forward, changes in lifestyle would inevitably lead to new requirements about the dwelling environment. In the process of residence transformation, the spatial position of "fire" in a Chinese family had changed. The "fire", which had remained the absolute center of family material space for a long time had been moved to the inconspicuous kitchen with the "cooking hearth". The adjustment of residence material space shook the central status of "fire" in a family spiritual structure to some extent. Though kitchen god worship based on "cooking hearth" still reflects the continuation of "fire" in family spirit from primitive society, the cooking hearth is no longer the center of family material space.

In modern times, social development had greater influence on lifestyle than in any other previous eras. After the Industrial Revolution, renewal of technologies and fuels

Fig. 1. Fire Pit in a Residential Building of the Miao Nationality in the Southeast of Guizhou Province, Shot in a Basha Miao Village of Congjiang County, Guizhou Province in April 2015

and changes in ideology had impact on the stable functional space and material structure of a traditional kitchen. The modern technological revolution first changed the appearance of kitchens in the West and then rapidly spread to other areas of the world. The kitchen space in a home became a "combination of miniature workshop and laboratory". The kitchen is one of the areas making the most rapid response to technological progress. Modern kitchen design based on technological development has solved problems about fuel, fume, pollution, food storage, storage method and sanitary system that may occur in a traditional kitchen, effectively improved the kitchen environment, and largely facilitated people's daily life. In modern times, China has been exploring on the path of learning from the West, with the daily lifestyle and residence space form gradually westernized. The modern kitchen culture of the West had been grafted to Chinese families and gradually replaced the traditional Chinese kitchen form centered on "cooking hearth". The kitchen has been transformed from a traditional functional space to a beautiful, comfortable, pleasant and even entertaining space. In the fast-paced life of modern society, the kitchen has become a stage for fashion and technology displaying their abilities, and at the same time, bears complicated signal significance associated with traditions.

2.2 Hall - Center of Material and Spiritual Spaces of Traditional Residential Building

After "fire" occurred in human life, people began to live with "fire" as the center. Whether in a cavern or in a palace building, "family fire" is unceasingly passed on in the dwelling space. As the center of family life, "fire" bears important material functions and abundant spiritual cultural connotations. With the development of human society, the "family house", as a carrier of "family fire", has gradually evolved to a more and more complicated and mature material space structure. Moreover, there is a complete family spiritual space structure synchronously developing with the material structure.

As an organic system with comprehensive functions and complete structures in family life, "family house" has been steadily revolving around an important structural center. In earlier period, the center of human family life was "fire". When productivity developed to a certain stage and the level of material life was improved, "fire" was moved to the kitchen along with the cooking hearth, gradually deviated from the center of family material and spiritual spaces. At the same time, the hall, as another center of material and spiritual spaces in family life, gradually emerged. Once, the number of households in a residence was counted according to the number of fire pits, and the founding of a new family was defined as "setting up another cooking stove". Later, after brothers live apart, they must set a "central room" in the new residence to show that they have truly established independent small families.

The traditional Chinese architectural culture attaches importance to uprightness, rigorousness and symmetry. Traditional Chinese residential buildings with a certain scale are always arranged in a form of axial symmetry. As the most important living space in a traditional Chinese residential building, "hall" is usually located at the center of a residence's symmetric layout and serves as a place for ancestor worship, guest reception, weddings and funerals. The hall occupies an important central position in the overall layout of residence material space. The arrangement of its interior furniture is also particular, just like a miniature of the overall large structure of the residential building. Hall furniture usually has a north-south layout and extends westward and eastward respectively, following the same principle of uprightness, impressiveness, symmetry and balance as residence buildings and creating a solemn atmosphere. In a hall facing south, the furniture, accompaniments and ornaments at the center of the north wall (or called "Taishi Wall") are usually used for family sacrifice. It is the center of the hall and is usually placed with shrines and ancestors' memorial tablets. On the wall behind the ancestors' memorial tablets is usually hanged with a central scroll with a couplet at each side, usually bearing maxims or verses related to moral cultivation and family management. In front of the shrines or memorial tablets is usually placed with an altar table slightly higher than an ordinary one. It is usually used for placing sacrificial offerings, or articles for entertainment or with a good meaning such as desk clock, table screen, porcelain bottle and cap container. In front of the altar table is usually placed with a "square table for eight people", with a group of Taishi chairs (an old-fashioned wooden armchair) at each side, or with officer's cap chairs or round-backed armchairs sometimes. At ordinary times, fruit trays and tea sets will be placed on the table. At a time of worship, foods and sacrificial offerings will be placed there. In some families, they will dine together; entertain relatives and friends or holding family meetings there at ordinary times. If the shrine and memorial tablet can be deemed as the center of spiritual ballast of family members, the square table for eight people is the center of the mundane life.

Chengzhi Hall (Fig. 2) located in Hongcun, Anhui Province was built in the fifth year of Xianfeng Emperor of the Qing Dynasty (1855 AD) and was the residence of Wang Dinggui, a great salt merchant in the late Qing Dynasty. On the central section of the altar table in the hall is placed with a chime clock, with cap containers at both sides. An ancient porcelain bottle and a delicate wooden-bottom mirror are placed at the east and west side of the cap container respectively, which means "clock sound and bottle mirror", or homophonous pun of "tranquility all one's life". The owner hoped that both his business career and family life would be peaceful. It embodies the desire and expectation of the then Huizhou merchants about their survival environment. Chengzhi Hall was not a particular case in Hongcun. As to local residential buildings, no matter what the property scale is, a building with a yard must have a hall, and the hall must have basically the same layout of altar table. The design of "clock sound and bottle mirror (tranquility all one's life)" can be deemed as a "theme" in the local room pattern.

With social changes, in the layout of residence material space, "hall" gradually replaced "fire pit" and "cooking range" to become an important living space of central status. The transfer of the spatial center has influenced the family spiritual structure. In a more mature human family life, "hall" has constituted a center of family spiritual space, which is more complicated and systematic than "fire pit". In a traditional Chinese family, the hall associates the family and its members with moral standards universally accepted by the society. In some sense, the hall has become the most sacred core of a family in some aspects, while the outlook on life and values represented by ornaments and ceremonies reflecting family beliefs are always connected to the sacred core in the process of social changes. The hall is the most important public space in traditional Chinese family life and embodies a concentrated reflection of family etiquette. It is not only a material space for daily life, but also a spiritual space for worshiping ancestors and deities, educating descendants and inheriting family learning and cultures.

However, in modern times, significant social changes have fundamentally changed people's material life and ideology, and also the family lifestyle. People have a different understanding and expectation about family from what is before, and naturally requires corresponding adjustment in different aspects of production and life. "Hall" may be a family space greatest influenced in the tremendous social changes.

In modern family space, what corresponds to the traditional hall is a drawing room, which is still the most open space in a family. Communications between family members previously carried out in the hall have been retained in a drawing room in the modern family to a large extent. However, interactions between family members become more relaxed than in the past, the seriousness of the hall has been weakened and the drawing room undertakes more family amusement functions. This change is caused by the modern social environment, and has a complicated and far-reaching impact on the family life and the family spiritual space structure.

Fig. 2. Chengzhi Hall, Shot in Hongcun, Anhui Province in February 2018

3   Characteristics of Spiritual Space Design in Chinese Family Life

3.1   Complete Spiritual Structure Based on Highly-Stable Material Space

An important precondition for the dual structure of material and spiritual spaces supporting each other in traditional Chinese family life is long-term stability of material space. Traditional Chinese family lifestyles have not changed much for thousands of years. This highly stable physical environment is the foundation for the formation of spiritual structure.

A Chinese residence is an organic integrity rather than a simple combination of different spaces. Affected by factors such as natural environment, productivity and social attributes of the dwellers, the appearance of a residence is a central embodiment of daily material life and family humanistic spirit. As this residence mode restricted by many forces was finalized, it would produce powerful cultural inertia. The uniformity of the living space makes family members living together form recognition and inertial reliance on family space, thus constituting a relatively stable relation mode, behavioral pattern and unified family recognition. This dwelling culture accepted by the society and family members has become a stable "tradition", accompanying the Chinese family life. The more stable the "traditional" family lifestyle is, the more secure the family spiritual structure bases on it will be.

With the development of human society, the level of family material life is keeping on improving and the dwelling form has changed correspondingly. The family spiritual structure corresponding to material life is become more and more sophisticated. Just like an intangible net, the spiritual structure of the Chinese family life shrouds the whole family and maintains its stability and completeness.

3.2 Aggregation of Spiritual Space Structural Center in Traditional Families

In the early period of human family life, "fire", at the center of family material space, is also the center of the family spiritual structure. The peculiarity of "warmth" and "security" it contains is self-evident to aggregation of family members. The family life space centered on "fire" occurred in the early period of human society. When the residential buildings were relatively simple and people's life was relatively unsophisticated, its central status in the design of family spiritual structure was relatively absolute. When a lifestyle with "hall" as a major family spiritual space came into being, residential buildings in China had become rather complicated and mature, and the residence space had become more diversified. Through a long time, the Chinese have formed complete and systematic family material space, and correspondingly more diversified family spiritual space. All concentrated and scattered spiritual spaces in a residence have jointly constituted a complete and systematic family spiritual structure.

However, not all elements associated with thought, emotion and mentality can constitute a family spiritual space, and not all spiritual spaces have the same structural effect on family spirit. Most minor details of residential building decorations and numerous daily articles in family life, even having some symbolic meanings or spiritual metaphors, can only be deemed as elements in family spiritual space rather than independently constitute a complete spiritual space. Residential elements that can constitute an independent spiritual space of aggregation such as hall, kitchen, bedroom and yard have different levels of importance in the overall family spiritual structure. As the most typical concentrated spiritual space, "hall" is the center of the overall family spiritual structure as well as the spiritual ballast of the whole family. The Chinese family spiritual structure is radiating with "hall" as the core. In a collective orderly organization based on etiquette, each individual will strictly observe common codes of conduct and submit to the restraints of parents, thus forming a centrality, which is progressive and aggregated from the outside inward. The management center of this orderly organization is set in the hall. Without this center, family spiritual spaces scattered in different places of "family house" would be in a state of disunity, and there would be no overall family spiritual structure design. The traditional family spiritual structure design centered on "hall" is a living, natural and non-rational cultural construction method, and this cultural mode has exhibited startling rationality and effectiveness in traditional Chinese family life.

For spiritual structure design in traditional Chinese family life, "fire pit" and "hall" are two typical material space symbols. The traditional family space represented by "fire pit" and "hall" embodies a concentrated reflection of the dual structure of material and spiritual spaces supporting each other in Chinese family life. Whether viewed from "fire pit" or "hall", there is no exception that the spiritual structure design in Chinese family life has an evident center. This structural center plays an important role in aggregating family members and makes the overall spiritual structure system more stable. Therefore, it is the soul of family spiritual structure design.

4   Modern Evolution of Chinese Family Spiritual Space

Ever since the 1980s, stimulated by the accelerated development of the economy, the Chinese family life is changing at an amazing speed. Benefiting from technological development, transportation has become more convenient, and means of communication has become more diversified. There is a possibility of "time-space" extension in modern society. Modern social changes have constituted a new daily life organizational form for families. Family life has been separated from residence to some extent. It is one of the reasons why modern people feel barren spiritually and "homeless".

Since ancient times, the Chinese have spared no effort to build houses, hoping that not only the residence as means of subsistence but also abstract family spiritual cultures can be passed down from generation to generation. For traditional Chinese, "it is not an old home if there are no calligraphy and painting in the hall." What matters is not "calligraphy and painting" but the "old" state. It vividly shows the recognition and even admiration of the Chinese towards an accumulated sense of history. As a medium, architectures can establish a tie and exchange between offspring and ancestors, thus creating happiness of "home".

Material space can be renewed rapidly yet the spiritual space structure is a stable cultural state formed through a very long time and cannot be changed within a short period. Maybe it can explain why modern residences always reveal a lack of connotations while old houses are loaded with implications. People like to call architecture "frozen notes"; however, residence has never been in a static state in a real sense. Residence has a life and will make gradual internal self-adjustment with the development of families. Traditional Chinese residential buildings have witnessed the development and vicissitude of families. The history and memories of families have left a mark in the yards.

The spiritual and material spaces of traditional Chinese residences are highly unified and harmonious. Moreover, through a long history of human life, a rather mature and complete dual structure has been formed. It is a hierarchical structure respecting order and having very powerful central aggregation. Articles in family space, daily activities and regular rites have added rich connotations to space and architectures. Therefore, the

Chinese residence is a "family house" filled with "memories". In modern life affected by the industrial spirit, people are attaching more and more importance to individual consciousness, right of privacy and freedom, while the traditional Chinese family life organizational form stressing ethic and order is criticized as a compelling, development-restrictive and backward thing. The lazy, comfort, amusing and interesting tendency of modern family life has gradually disorganized the traditional family spiritual structure.

Residence space is not only a material structure but also a social and cultural structure. Space division of residence embodies the underlying fundamental principles for handling interpersonal relationship and managing daily life. As a continuation of "hall", the drawing room is the center of modern family material space. The material structure of the traditional hall has been retained in the drawing room to a large extent. The position of the TV wall in a modern drawing room usually coincides with the "Taishi wall" for ancestral worship in a traditional hall. The altar table for placing offerings and important memorials before the "Taishi wall" continues to exist in the form of TV cabinet or low cabinet with almost no changes in function. What's different is that the square table and Taishi chair placed from the angle of ancestors have been replaced by sofa and tea table centered on TV or other observation objects and placed from the angle of dwellers. The modern drawing room is still a public space for family members discussing things and sharing life together. It is one of the most important spiritual spaces in a modern family but reveals no rituality and discipline like in a "hall". As compared with the serious traditional "hall" space, the modern drawing room has presented an evidently relaxing and amusing tendency. In a modern family, the orderly and stable traditional family spiritual structure with strong central aggregation has been replaced by a scattered and weak-correlated family spiritual space, which is more diversified and individualized and at the same time, lacks structural integrity and effectiveness.

5 Exploration of New Possibilities of Spiritual Space Design in Modern Chinese Family Life

The dual structure design of "material space" and "spiritual space" coexisting in traditional Chinese family life has provided us with a sense of security required for life and strengthened the cohesive force of "home". Based on this highly completed and stable "material - spirit" dual structure, family lifestyles of the Chinese did not change too much for a long time. After the Industrial Revolution, with the rapid development of technologies, revolutionary changes have taken place in our daily life. The world-wide vigorous social changes inevitably affected the traditional Chinese family life, ranging from family scale, lifestyle and faith culture to residence structure and daily articles. Technologies have shortened the spatial distance. While industrial civilization has brought in a more convenient and comfortable modern life, it has made us fall into a void of implement reason and material survival. Qualitative changes of social life have led to a deficiency of complete and reasonable space structures and life connotations in family life and made people suffer from psychological disorder in life. As the enthusiasm about capital accumulation and wealth occupation keeping on being raised from the Industrial Revolution gradually fades or cools to some extent, someone begins to perceive that the craze about technology, cult for implement reason and infatuation about commercial society have not brought in a "perfect life". Through reflection, they find that only based on a traditional and stable space structure and living order can the house become a warm and safe "home". The traditional dual structure of material and spiritual spaces supporting each other is a stable structure supporting the normal order of Chinese family life throughout the history.

Modern design came into being along with the development of industrial capitalism after the Industrial Revolution. For the short two hundred years, the development of modern design is always accompanied by contradictions and arguments between form and function, or between tradition and technology. The "function first" principle of modernist architecture design and Mies' architectural philosophy "less is more" has laid a keynote for modern architectures. Residential buildings with a modernist style have brought people's "homes" to a forest of reinforced concrete. With the maturity of commercial society, popularity of consumerism and rapid rise of furniture decoration and design, standardized and industrialized material design has been introduced to families. Traditional residences representing the owner's view of life and family ideals have been replaced by mass-produced and stereotyped products. Just like mass-produced products, mass-produced residences also lack warmth and cannot give people a sense of security. Occupation of commodities can never replace the pleasure and inspirations from nice life, which cannot be realized only through material prosperity. Therefore, people began to pursue for "warm" design, hoping to find the most essential core of a family - providing a warm harbor and emotional belonging. Through introspection, it is found that those aspects associated with traditions and being abandoned seem to be none other than the source for security and warmth of a "home". The dual structure of "material" and "spirit" synchronously developing in family life is a guarantee for nice life. A spiritual center accepted by all family members and used for activities plays an important role in stabilizing the family structure. People cannot live together harmoniously unless having some common values and spiritual pursuits. It is the very sense of a traditional family spiritual space.

One of the features of modernist design is to solve general social demands with industrial technologies. In a specific historical environment, behaviors and activities guided by "implement reason" can effectively solve practical problems in life. Therefore, people have gradually neglected the important significance of "value rationality". To discuss "how to live" in a modern design context taking "industrial rationality" as behavioral orientation is the reason for forming the appearance of modern family space. It cannot be said that there are no spiritual spaces in the life of modern people, but most of them are scattered and individualized. Moreover, with the great increase of entertainment, the great decrease of aggregation and nearly disappearance of sacredness and disciplines, they cannot constitute a complete family spiritual structure. To make function and design innovation of modern family space, find a suitable existing form of the traditional family spiritual structure in modern families and reconstitute a dual structure design of material and spiritual spaces supporting each other as the core of modern family life, maybe we can restore a home to its original warmth rather than gradually alienate it in material life and consumer society. At the same time, to explore the function and design innovations of the two space structures can provide us with broader development perspectives and innovation thoughts for future design.

The paper will stress that any design practice cannot be separated from social and cultural backgrounds. Behind the design of any detailed thing lies a gigantic and complicated material system and cultural network. In this highly-integrated and closely-related world, any detailed design activity should treat problems from a systematic and structural perspective. As modern design develops in China to the present, the stage of handling design problems merely in an aesthetic or functional principle has gone by, and so practitioners in the design industry should have a broader thinking pattern. The spiritual structure in traditional Chinese family life is a basis and important reference for reconstituting modern family spiritual space. At the same time, its structural integrity, systematicness and effectiveness, and its remarkable role in coordinating and constituting relations between man and space or between man and man have important reference values and practical significance to any design activities.

References

1. Chen, Z., Li, Q.: Local Treasure: Residence. SDX Joint Publishing Company, Beijing (2007)
2. Pan, L.: Residential Buildings and Courtyards. Shandong Fine Arts Publishing House, Jinan (2005)
3. Sun, D.: Research on Chinese Residential Buildings. China Building Industry Press, Beijing (2004)
4. Tang, J., Sun, L.: Chinese Auspicious Decorations. Guangxi Fine Arts Publishing House, Nanning (2000)
5. Cai, H.: History of Social Evolution. Oriental Press, Beijing (1996)
6. Fei, X.: Rural China. People's Publishing House, Beijing (2008)
7. [America] Knapp, R., Luo, Q. (Editors-in-Chief): Home: Residential Culture of the Chinese. New Star Press, Beijing (2011)

Dissemination of São Tomé and Príncipe Culture Through Virtual Reality: Comparative UX Study Between Potential Tourists from Portugal and Santomean Inhabitants

Yanick Trindade[1]([✉]), Francisco Rebelo[1,2], and Paulo Noriega[1,2]

[1] CIAUD, ergoUX, Faculdade de Arquitetura, Universidade de Lisboa, Rua Sá Nogueira, Pólo Universitário, Alto da Ajuda, 1349-063 Lisboa, Portugal
lamberttrindade@hotmail.com

[2] ITI/LARSyS Universidade de Lisboa, Rua Sá Nogueira, Pólo Universitário, Alto da Ajuda, 1349-055 Lisbon, Portugal

Abstract. Context analysis is an essential condition in the development of a product or service. Understanding the context in which the system is used (characteristics of users, tasks, technical and physical environment), but also the cultural context (physical environment, historical, social, and cultural factors), are part of the activities of the Human-Centered Design process. Nowadays, due to the accessibility and improvement of technology, experience based on virtual reality, can be used to provide immersive experiences that absorbs and awakens the user's interest in cultural aspects in a playful but also didactic way. In this context, the present study sought to assess and compare the user experience through the development of an immersive virtual reality game experience. The goal of this study is to evaluate the user experience of participants from Portugal (13 potential tourists) and from São Tomé Island (18 local inhabitants) in a 3D VR environment prototype of a traditional hostel, with a beach landscape view. For interaction in VR, we measure participants through a presence questionnaire. For emotional responses, we used a scale of valence and arousal from Self-Assessment Manikin (SAM). The compared results reveal that the VR prototype provided a high level of immersion in both samples. However, the data from control factors reveal that the sample from São Tomé had more interaction problems. Regarding the emotional reactions (SAM), the compare results reveal that the user experience was emotionally positive with high values of pleasure for both samples. The data from arousal, indicate that the participants from Portugal were calm, and from São Tomé are very excited (Arousal average Portugal = 4.5; Arousal average São Tomé = 7.3) In conclusion, the 3D VR environment prototype was able to engage the participants with high levels of pleasure and provide interactive experiences. However, the control factor and arousal data reveal differences between the two samples that should be considered and analyzed to provide a better experience in future studies.

Keywords: UX · Virtual Reality · Tourism · Culture · Design

M. M. Soares et al. (Eds.): HCII 2022, LNCS 13322, pp. 466–476, 2022.
https://doi.org/10.1007/978-3-031-05900-1_33

1 Introduction

When developing a new product, service, or experience that is related to the cultural aspect of a region, it's important to include people from this community. In this context, this study compares how two groups of people (inhabitants of São Tomé and potential tourists from Portugal) react to an immersive VR experience that was built with the intention of making people aware of the culture and geography of São Tomé and Príncipe (STP). Using concepts like stakeholders can be helpful to create value for users and other stakeholders. Stakeholders are any group or individuals that may affect or be affected by the goals of a corporation [1]. It's important to include in the projects all stakeholders related, and the impact on them, and not restrict just to those considered as users. In the present study, we developed communication and interactive strategy aiming to share the culture of São Tomé and Príncipe, through interactive experiences based on Virtual Reality game. But why is this study relevant? Regarding the island of São Tomé and Príncipe, the justification is in: (1) Valuing São Tomé and Príncipe culture internally; (2) General lack of knowledge about São Tomé and Príncipe externally [2]. Regarding design, the justification lies in developing strategies to: (1) Offer a better user experience; and (2) Increase user engagement. The culture of STP is linked to mutual acculturation between Africans of the African coast to the south of Sahara, and the Europeans from Portugal [3]. Understanding cultural and geographic aspects through the exhaustive analysis of factors inherent to geographic [4], demographic [4], economic [4], and access to information [4], as well as historical [5–7], social [8], and cultural [3, 9], will allow understanding its context. This is the cultural context. However, it is also necessary to look at the context in which the system is used, namely the characteristics of the stakeholders, challenges and tasks, and the system environment [10], and apply a Human-Centered Design (HCD) perspective. HCD, it is "an approach to interactive systems development that aims to make systems usable and useful by focusing on the users, their needs and requirements and by applying human factors/ergonomics, and usability knowledge and technique" [10, 11]. Every product intended for human beings has a user, and each time a product is used, it offers an experience [12]. Human-Computer Interaction (HCI) is concerned with how human beings interact with technology and how the computer system can be designed to facilitate their interaction [13]. Traditionally, usability emphasizes ease of use, learning, and effectiveness. Norman [14] questioned this traditional perspective and emphasized the importance of aesthetics in user interfaces and emotional responses. When designing something related to HCI, the emphasis on understanding and designing the subjective aspects of technology is an increasingly essential need [15]. Therefore, it is essential that technology providers not only design systems, but rather engaging experiences [15]. The effectiveness of virtual reality systems is directly related to the quality of presence [16]. For Schuemie [13], presence indicates the level at which human beings can respond to a given virtual environment as if it were real.

1.1 Goals

The goal of this study is to compare the User Experience (UX) of Portuguese potential tourists and Santomean inhabitants in a VR game experience, that was built with the aim to share the São Tomé and Príncipe culture and geographic aspects.

2 Method

2.1 Participants

Thirty-one (31) students participated in this study, 13 from Portugal and 18 from São Tomé and Príncipe, being divided into two phases. In the first, university students from Portugal participated, whose age range was between 26 and 45 years old. Of these, 7 were male and 6 were female. In the second phase, high school students from São Tomé and Príncipe participated. Their age range was between 15 and 18 years old. The most relevant fact to highlight in this second group, concerns with non-use of virtual reality devices previously. The justification for extending the data collection to include participants from the island of São Tomé, is linked to the fact that we want to add and evaluate an endogenous view of the content we want to offer to potential tourists. Do the local inhabitants of the island of São Tomé and Príncipe like the experience we want to provide and disseminate? The data collected in this study, will allow defining strategies in future projects.

2.2 Game Apparatus

A Virtual Reality (VR) device was used to evaluate 3D virtual reality environment prototype. Participants interact with a "mystery game" SOIA, which was created using the UNITY® game engine.

To perform VR experience, the user will use the Virtual Reality device HTC VIVE® with, one Head-Mounted Display (HMD), two controllers and two motion sensors. This game experience was divided into two parts: The training room, and Hostel. The 3D objects and environment were developed in Autodesk Maya®, and later attached to the UNITY® game engine. The UI and some images and texture were developed using Inkscape®. Actions and movements of the gameplay inside the virtual environment, was made using VR tools developed in our laboratory - ergoUX, as well as the VRTK tool and SteamVR®. The game was run on an ASUS® computer, with Intel® Core ™ i7 processors, 16 GB RAM and NVIDIA® GeForce® GTX 1080 graphics for the first group from Portugal, and with an MSI® computer, with Intel® Core ™ i5 processors, 8 GB RAM and NVIDIA® GeForce® GTX 1050 graphics for the second group from São Tomé Island.

2.3 Virtual Environment Prototype

In the beginning, the tutorial room is revealed, and participants need to perform some tasks, allowing participants to become familiar with the virtual environment and all interactions inside this virtual world. The tasks participants need to perform were as follows:

The Head-Mounted Display: Move and Rotate the Head (Up and Down, Left, and Right). Also, we gave instructions to move their body too, so they can explore the VR world and not be static.

Movement, Bounds, and Safety Procedures. Move in the virtual world using the teleporting feature, knowing places he can go or not using the HTC VIVE controllers. Also, we gave sound and visual instructions so he can avoid colliding with objects and walls in the real world.

Grab/Touch. Manipulate objects and interact with the 3D environment in the virtual world through the HTC VIVE controller. These interactions can be by grabbing a 3D object and moving it from point A to point B, or simply touching the controller on a 3D object.

After finishing the tutorial interactive sequence, the user is virtually teleported from the training room to a Hostel bedroom located in the São Tomé Island. Inside this place, the user will hear the narrator's voice first, with some instruction related to the place that he is inside, so the user can get a sense of the place where he is (see Fig. 1). The user will have to perform the following tasks:

Finding the Golden Key. The user needs to find a golden key, to be able to open the door of the balcony. After touching the key, the key will fly magicking for the lock of the balcony door that is closed at the beginning and will open it.

Go to the Balcony Zone. On the balcony, the user will hear sound information related to the landscape.

Find the Cell Phone. Still, on the balcony, the user will have to find the cell phone, that is placed on top of a little bamboo table. After grabbing the cell phone, the user will need to go back into the bedroom and find a painting.

Take a Picture. Inside the bedroom, the user will have to take a picture of a painting made by a Santomean artist. After taking the picture, a hologram of information related to the artist will be displayed, like augmented reality (AR) inside virtual reality (VR).

End of the Experience.

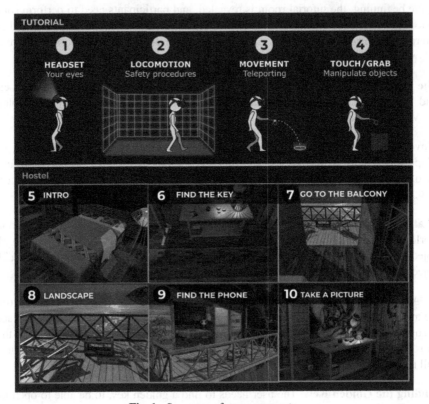

Fig. 1. Sequence of game moments.

2.4 Measures

To assess and analyze user experience, behavioral and subjective tools was applied, to assess user subjective perceptions about their interaction with the virtual environment. To achieve the evaluation goal, the following tools were applied:

Self-Assessment Manikin (SAM). A non-verbal pictorial assessment technique to measures the pleasure and arousal, associated with the participants affective reaction to a wide variety of stimuli [17] in the tutorial zone, hostel bedroom and the balcony.

The Presence Questionnaire (PQ). This questionnaire, was applied to evaluate how much the participants felt present inside the Virtual Environment [18] and was used to control the Presence level of the participants in both scenarios. Participants were asked to score the quality of their Virtual Environment, according to their sense of presence, and factors related to the Virtual Environment characteristics, namely: sensory; level of realism; interaction; distraction; and display image quality. Each question was ranked using a 7-point scale, where participants indicated the strength of their agreement with the questions' statements.

Some questions on the Presence questionnaire, are related to control factors (moving in the virtual world and how natural this moving in this environment was), that are something related to his performance. Performance is related to usability. In this sense, those questions can be useful for usability analyses.

2.5 Procedure

All participants filled in a written consent and were informed of the goals of the study. In Portugal, the experiment was performed in a room using a desktop computer and Virtual Reality equipment. Moments before the game experience, each participant received essential information about the game. Then, each participant performed a pre-test using SAM to measure the emotional reaction, through generic examples to become familiar with the methods that will be applied at the end of the VR experience. Each participant will complete the gaming experience in approximately 20 min. After finishing the game experience, the participant answered the SAM questionnaire, where we use two scales: affective valence scale (Pleasure/Displeasure) and activation scale (Calm/Excited). Then, the participants answered the PRESENCE Questionnaire.

In São Tomé Island, the experiment was performed in a library belonging to the Portuguese school of São Tomé and Príncipe, using a desktop computer and Virtual Reality equipment. Likewise, the SAM and QP was applied under the terms mentioned above (in Portugal). Another fact to be highlighted during the experiment in São Tomé, is the fact that the participants are not familiar with the Virtual Reality equipment. Due to this detail, it was necessary to intervene during the tutorial, mainly to make them move without fear or constraints in the Virtual Reality environment (Fig. 2).

Fig. 2. VR experience - Participant from Portugal (left), and São Tomé and Príncipe (right).

3 Results and Discussion

When comparing the results regarding the data collected in the two countries using SAM (see Fig. 3), the São Tomé participants reported a high level of Pleasure compared to the Portuguese sample (average Pleasure in São Tomé = 8.8 and average of pleasure in Portugal = 7.7). The excitement in using the Virtual Reality device for the first time in line with the fact that they interact with something that is directly related to their cultural reality, through this type of interaction medium (VR/game), perhaps justifies the high values of Pleasure and Arousal, as well the fact that they like the VR game experience (average Arousal in São Tomé = 7.3; average Arousal in Portugal = 4.5). Some participants after finishing the VR experience and, fill out the questionnaires in São Tomé, questioned where they can find the game or the date of release. Another factor that we can relate to the data recorded, particularly in the variable arousal for participants from São Tomé, is their age (between 15 and 18 years old). In Portugal, after finishing the VR experience and, fill out the questionnaires, some participants question about the author of the painting that they saw in the bedroom (inside VR experience), and where they can find more about other paintings of the artist or other artist related.

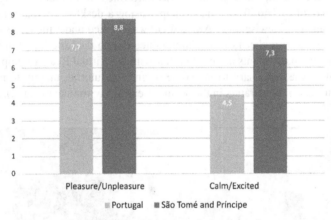

Fig. 3. SAM: participants emotional reaction.

Concerning Presence questionnaire, when comparing the results related to sensory quality/level of immersion (score from 1 to 7, where 1 is never and 7 is always), we registered a greater sense of immersion from both samples. If we looked at the first question related to the immersion level, "During the simulation, did you feel that you were" inside "the virtual environment?" we found that the responses tended to "always" with the percentage of responses at 80% for the São Tomé sample and 46% for the Portuguese sample, for score 7 (see Fig. 4). However, this difference can be small if we consider that in both cases, the score was concentrated between 7 and 6.

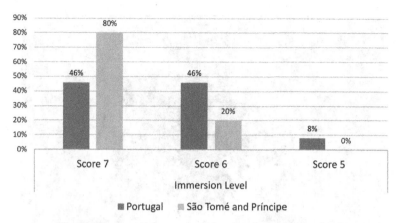

Fig. 4. Presence: first question related to the immersion level.

As for the control factors, the question "How well were you able to navigate or move in the virtual world (go to a certain point in the VR environment)" reveals differences. Comparing the results (see Fig. 5), the highest scores were 7 for Portugal (score 7 = 54% for Portugal and 11% for São Tomé) and 5 for São Tomé and Príncipe (score 5 = 67% for São Tomé and 8% for Portugal). These data reinforce the idea that participants from the island of São Tomé faced some difficulty in interacting in the virtual environment compared to participants from Portugal, thus demonstrating a lower sense of control over the experience compared to the Portuguese sample.

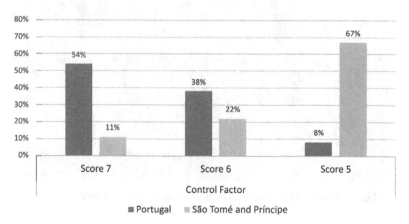

Fig. 5. Presence: first question related to the control-factor.

Briefly, Fig. 6 shows the comparison between the two samples (Portugal and São Tomé) regarding emotional reaction (level of pleasure and arousal), as well as immersion (if participants felt that they are inside the virtual environment), and control factors (interaction in the virtual environment).

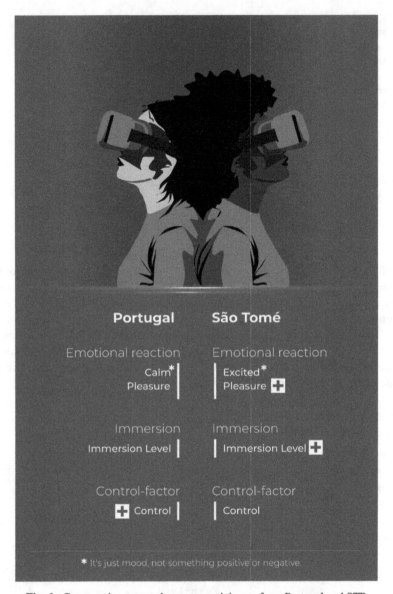

Fig. 6. Comparative aspects between participants from Portugal and STP.

As other studies have reported [19, 20], there is a tendency for VR experience to increase emotional responses [19], and as well as the ability of the VR system to make users feel physically present in the virtual environment and consequently contribute to positive emotional reactions, which can also contribute positively to the user behavior in relation to touristic products and services [20].

4 Conclusions

This paper emerged as part of the constructive process of a methodology that allows us to create an experience in virtual reality to share cultural and geographic aspects of São Tomé and Príncipe. As for the goal we proposed for this study, the data collected was rich and varied. The results were very positive regarding emotional data collection through SAM, in specific for the variable pleasure (São Tomé average Pleasure = 8.8 and average pleasure in Portugal = 7.7). The arousal data collected with the same method, reveals that the Portuguese sample was calm, and the São Tomé sample was very excited (average Arousal in São Tomé = 7.3; average Arousal in Portugal = 4.5). If we look at the goal of this virtual game experience (in the bedroom and balcony with beach landscape), it was to provide a calm feeling for the potential tourist that want to visit São Tomé, and that was successfully achieved. However, data from local inhabitants (sample from São Tomé) reveals that people from within the community can be very enthusiastic about content that is related to their cultural and geographic reality, and the arousal can rise, even if the game experience was to produce a relaxed. Regarding the immersion, both samples reveal a great sense of immersion (score 7 = 80% for the São Tomé sample and 46% for the Portuguese sample; score 6 = 46% for the Portuguese sample and 20% for the São Tomé sample). The data from the control-factor, show that people that are not familiar with VR devices, can face some struggle interacting with the VR content inside the virtual environment (score 7 = 54% for Portugal and 11% for São Tomé; score 5 = 67% for São Tomé and 8% for Portugal). Perhaps some shame in relation to their movements in the real world, lack of confidence with this equipment, can justify this difficulty, as some did not even move at first, even with the visual and sound indication. Sometimes we had to move them by turning them and trying to give them the confidence to move at the beginner. Another point that we can relate to these results, is the fact that they act on the virtual environment as if they were watching TV, that is, passive. But they became more comfortable over time, and when the game experience ends, they ask for more. The data from both samples show that they liked the VR game experience, with a high level of pleasure, and want to see more things related to the content inside the VR environment, as some reported informally after the end of the experience and after answering the questionnaires. And this is important because all stakeholders present in the project must be positively involved and give feedback.

The use of codes of communication and interaction, contemporary of the new generations, will allow that, through a media used by them, we can spread the cultural aspects for those who do not know the cultural aspects of a particular sociocultural group.

Acknowledgements. This work is financed by national funds through FCT - Fundação para a Ciência e a Tecnologia, I.P., under the Strategic Project with the reference UIDB/04008/2020.

References

1. Kivits, R., Sawang, S.: Stakeholder theory. In: The Dynamism of Stakeholder Engagement. Contributions to Management Science. Springer, Cham (2021). https://doi.org/10.1007/978-3-030-70428-5_1

2. Smith, J.: Why you should go to the world's least-visited countries. CNN Travel (2019)
3. Seibert, G.: Camaradas, Clientes e Compadres: Colonialismo, Socialismo e Democratização em São Tomé e Príncipe. 2nd edn. Vega Editora, Lisboa (2002)
4. Central Intelligence Agency - São Tomé and Príncipe. The world factbook (2020)
5. Negreiros, A.: Historia Ethnographica da Ilha de S. Thomé. Lisboa: Antiga Casa Bertrand - José Bastos (1895)
6. Seibert, G.: Os angolares da ilha de São Tome: Náufragos, Autóctones ou Quilombolas? Revista Do Programa De Pós-graduação Em História. Vol. 12, N° 1/2 pp. 43–64 (2004)
7. Lima, J.: Ensaio sobre a statistica das ilhas de S. Thomé e Principe no Golfo da Guiné, e sua dependencia Forte de S. João Baptista d'Ajuda na Costa de Léste chamada dos Popós Além da Mina. Ensaios sobre a statistica das possessões portuguezas na Africa Occidental e Oriental, na Asia Occidental, na China e na Oceania: escriptos de ordem do Governo de Sua Magestade Fidelissima a Senhora D. Maria II. Lisboa: Imprensa Nacional, Livro II, Parte I, (1844)
8. Seibert, G.: Colonialismo em São Tomé e Príncipe: Hierarquização, classificação e segregação da vida social. Anuário Antropológico. In: Brasília: Programa de Pós-Graduação em Antropologia Social, Vol. 49, no. 2, pp. 99–120 (2015)
9. Hagemeijer, T.: As línguas de S. Tomé e Príncipe. Revista de Crioulos de Base Lexical Portuguesa e Espanhola, Vol. 1.1. Lisboa: ACBLPE - Faculdade de Letras da Universidade de Lisboa (2009)
10. ISO 9241–210 - Ergonomics of human–system interaction — Part 210: Human-centred design for interactive systems (2010)
11. ISO 13407 - Human-centred design processes for interactive systems (1999)
12. Garrett, J.: The Elements of User Experience: User-Centered Design for the Web and Beyond. Second Edition: New Riders (2011)
13. Schuemie, M.: Human-computer Interaction and Presence in Virtual Reality Exposure Therapy. Delft, SIKS Dissertations Series (2003)
14. Norman, D.: Emotional design: why we love (or hate) everyday things. New York, Basic Books (2004)
15. Atfield, S., Kazay, G., Lalmas, M., Piwowarski, B.: Towards a science of user engagement. In: WSDM Workshop on User Modelling for Web Applications, pp. 09–12 (2011)
16. Wiederhold, B., Wiederhold, M.: The effect of presence on virtual reality treatment. In: Wiederhold, B.K., Wiederhold, M.D. (eds.) Virtual Reality Therapy for Anxiety Disorders: Advances in Evaluation and Treatment. American Psychological Association, pp. 77–86 (2005)
17. Bradley, M., Lang, P.: Measuring emotion: the self-assessment manikin and the semantic differential. J. Behav. Ther. Exp. Psychiat **25**(1), 49–59 (1994)
18. Reis, L., Duarte, E., Rebelo, F.: Older workers and virtual environments: usability evaluation of a prototype for safety sign research. In: Soares, M. (Ed.), Rebelo, F. (Ed.). Ergonomics in Design, Boca Raton, CRC Press, pp. 279–295 (2016)
19. Estupiñán, S., Rebelo, F., Noriega, P., Ferreira, C., Duarte, E.: Can virtual reality increase emotional responses (arousal and valence)? a pilot study. In: Marcus, A. (ed.) DUXU 2014. LNCS, vol. 8518, pp. 541–549. Springer, Cham (2014). https://doi.org/10.1007/978-3-319-07626-3_51
20. Melo, M., et al.: Immersive multisensory virtual reality technologies for virtual tourism. Multimedia Systems (2022)

Shenzhen Maker Culture with Innovation and Entrepreneurship Policy in the Context of Belt and Road Initiatives

Xinyue Wang[1]([✉]) [iD] and Xiangyang Li[2] [iD]

[1] Beijing Normal University, Jinfeng Road 18, Zhuhai 519087, Guangdong, China
wangxy@bnu.edu.cn
[2] Guangzhou Academy of Fine Arts, 168 Waihuan Xilu, Panyu District,
Guangzhou 510006, China

Abstract. From 2013, when the Belt and Road Initiative was formally proposed, the Maker Culture has entered China and developed simultaneously: the relevant support policies "mass entrepreneurship and innovation" were introduced to support creative industries. This article compares the different stages of Maker Culture in Shenzhen that how the government supports the innovation and entrepreneurship from various levels, and how the Maker Culture in Shenzhen has given a new meaning to the promotion of collaborative innovation under international cooperation. Connecting "technology" and "culture" at the level of design interventions, Maker Culture should be considered as the condensation point of cultural mobility and local cultural innovation in Shenzhen along with the development of Belt and Road Initiative.

Keywords: Maker culture · Design policy · Belt and Road Initiative · Cultural creativity · International cooperation

1 Introduction

Maker culture, as an exotic product of Western culture, has entered China for more than ten years. In this special land of Shenzhen, thanks to the coincidence of entrepreneurs' characteristic of "being bold of vision and courageous in action" with the independent spirit in maker culture, makers in this land are springing up like mushrooms, thus expediting a complete industrial chain and attracting more innovative talents in digital industry and manufacturing industry. Despite the fact that the maker space has developed incrementally in recent six years, and has formed a broad position with the support of policies, and the maker culture is also in the gradual development with the government's investment in space construction, activities and education, its appearance is still less clear. In this paper, such status quo will be analyzed firstly.

Shenzhen, as a window oriented to the world and the future, the geographical location of its seaport and the advantages of emerging industry are undoubtedly a powerful fulcrum to inject new connotations to Culture of the Silk Road. Maker culture, as an aspect, also provides an opportunity for Shenzhen to promote the new situation of mutual understanding and cooperation among human beings in the new era. In this paper, it is illustrated that maker culture should be regarded as the coagulation point of cultural flow and gathering and the starting point of local cultural innovation in Shenzhen, and how to reconnect the cultural and creative industry policy with the entrepreneurship and innovation policies through design intervention, and transform from simply spreading cultural content to the innovation of "content + mode", so as to make the maker culture comprehensive in its connotations.

2 The Growth of Shenzhen Maker Culture (2015–2021)

2.1 The First Stage: Interest Fosters Spontaneous Design

The Maker Movement sprouted in China, which was introduced from developed countries and regions in Asia, Europe and America as a foreign culture. By gathering scattered manual and mechanical enthusiasts as the subject, it formed a maker community by exchanging DIY production experience and sharing technical knowledge. At this stage, the meaning of "Maker" is still "Maker". Dale Dougherty, the founder of American Maker Faire and *Make* magazine, once said that the essence of Maker Movement is a DIY culture created by oneself based on their own interest, and their original intention is to influence the mainstream mass culture by creating a subculture from maker. He said, "We connect many different groups of people who are actually making things, but each thinks they are doing something different from others. Artists see themselves as a different group of people than those who develop robots or make electronic products. From a certain point of view, calling them "artisans" brings people from different groups together so that they can see what they have in common."[1] In this field, everyone is unconsciously taking on the role of designer/craftsman. Nevertheless, as a place to bear these spontaneous community activities, Maker Space is mainly a physical space where maker resources gather, and its existence is the embodiment of specific maker culture.

What lie behind the self-makers of Shenzhen are the nutrients for the innovation culture provided from the copycat products, which account for 80% of the long tail effect of the market, namely, the grounding informal economy beyond the advanced mainstream business. The most prominent design gene of innovation at this stage lies in improvisation and heterogeneity: the unrelated product modeling is combined with electronic components to form fancy mix-and-match results. With the gradually standardized market, measures of "de-copycat" rendered the fading tide of copycat culture, and the spontaneously formed electronic industry chain and spontaneous innovation spirit have become the heritage of copycat culture. Just as IDEO, a design consulting company, commented, "copycat can become an open platform for creativity". Names of Huaqiangbei such as "China's First Electronic Street" and "China's Silicon Valley" also grew up in this soil and the copycat wave it experienced (Fig. 1).

Fig. 1. The copycat mobile phone models once sold in Huaqiangbei Market

2.2 The Second Stage: The Policy Stimulates the Vitality of Mass Entrepreneurship and Innovation

The Shenzhen Action Plan on Made in China 2025 issued by Shenzhen Municipal Government in 2015 aims to initially form an industrial system characterized by active innovation, optimized structure, leading scale, complete supporting facilities, developed services and world-class level in 2025 through "two steps" in two five-year plans, so as to build an international maker center and venture capital. After visiting the Chaihuo Makers Space originally established in Shenzhen at the end of 2015, Premier Li Keqiang officially wrote "mass entrepreneurship and innovation" into the government work report, thus supporting innovation and entrepreneurship as a major national strategy. Subsequently, the Shenzhen Municipal Government launched a series of support policies successively. Stimulated by a number of favorable conditions, various maker spaces, co-working spaces and business incubators serving makers emerged constantly, and exhibitions, competitions and activities related to innovation and entrepreneurship also flourished. According to the Three-year Action Plan for Promoting Maker Development in Shenzhen (2015–2017), Shenzhen's annual maker space, maker service platform and maker number will increase substantially starting from 2015; Moreover, the municipal and district governments of Shenzhen also provide special funds to support maker projects and maker spaces from individuals, enterprises, students and society at different levels every year.[1] It can be seen that the Maker Movement began to develop into the one officially organized in China, which was promoted step by step in a planned way and popularized in a top-down manner, with the aim of boosting the construction of digital industry and sustainable smart city oriented to the future.

When the Maker Movement first appeared in America, the typical types can be divided into Community Space, Fab Lab and For-profit Space. However, the operation mode in China was transformed from the imitation of the developed countries from the beginning, and the gradual derivation of a mechanism more suitable for the national conditions. At present, there are five modes of operation for maker space in China:

---

[1] Notice on Applying for Supporting Funding of Maker Project of Shenzhen Longgang Talents Program in Longgang District in 2020[EB/OL]. http://sz.shenkexin.com/project/notice-3969. html. 2020-08-28.

community maker space, business incubation space, children's education space, open access university laboratory, and innovative R&D department of enterprises.

In addition, it can be seen through the overall classification and the observation of its business format of Shenzhen's policy guidance, the current maker spaces in Shenzhen International Block can be mainly divided into innovative business incubators, accelerators, Fab Lab certified by the state, province and city as well as other uncertified for-profit experience spaces, while each district carries out specific construction by further refining the requirements of implementing policies.

2.3 The Third Stage: Management and Support with Emphasis on Science and Technology

With the gradual implementation of the policy of promoting the maker development, the upsurge of mass innovation began to cool down. Many community-style maker spaces and co-working spaces disappear due to unsustainable business direction and modes. From this period, the Maker Movement began to try to shed its spontaneous original state in China, emphasizing the "hard" results and paying more heed to the improvement of its professional skills and innovation ability.

In February 2019, Shenzhen has set up a special science and technology innovation committee, which was designed for the management and support of "entrepreneurship and innovation". Specifically, 6 research centers of different professional fields and 11 departments were established for administration, policy and examination and approval, resource allocation management, science and technology supervision, basic research and platform building, electronic information technology, biotechnology and social development technology, intelligent equipment manufacturing, high and new technology, regional innovation and achievement transformation, and services of foreign experts and scientific and technological talents. In the *Measures for the Administration of Shenzhen Science and Technology Business Incubators and Maker Space* issued in 2020, it further clarifies the business incubators and maker spaces in Shenzhen, and standardizes the definition of "maker space" as "innovation and entrepreneurship support platforms with low cost, convenience, complete production factors and open operation by providing workspace, cyberspace, social space and resource sharing space, and by means of 'crowdfunding, public support and crowdsourcing' for the main service objects such as technology-based entrepreneurial teams and start-ups." Generally speaking, the services provided by maker spaces, which begun to take shape in Shenzhen, cover the whole process from production to sales, including the services of industrial design, IDH (technical scheme), rapid proofing, cross-border e-commerce, logistics services, PCB production, supply chain finance, mold making, parts production, assembly plant and so on.[2]

Taking the most representative Huaqiangbei International Maker Center as an example, it has developed from the spontaneous copycat cultural center in the early stage to the national maker space supported by the government; From parts assembly and processing to the spontaneous design imitation and manufacturing, and to product research and

---

[2] Shenzhen Maker Map Information Statistics Table of Longgang District Science and Technology Innovation Bureau [EB/OL]. http://www.lg.gov.cn/bmzz/kjj/xzzx/qt/content/post_1362058.html. 2015-01-30.

development based on core technologies, the realization of 5G intelligent upgrade, technological progress and industrial structure upgrade have promoted Huaiangbei to realize core product transformation in several stages. Their core competitiveness lies in the establishment of a new model combining maker and cross-border e-commerce. By building a comprehensive ecology integrating innovation, research, production and marketing, as driven by market demand, maker centers export products to customers at different levels (cross-border e-commerce parks, designer shops or experience stores, industrial towns). The products include not only basic supply of goods, but also the products and project sources in practice, which indicates that such innovation ecology relies heavily on market data and reflects a direct and pragmatic innovation attitude. Such squeezed high-density supply chain greatly improves the efficiency of maker and makes Huaqiangbei an innovative energy center. The reason why foreign makers regard Huaqiangbei as a paradise for makers is that they take a fancy to the inexhaustible resources of electronic components and the distance advantage from production to supply (Fig. 2).

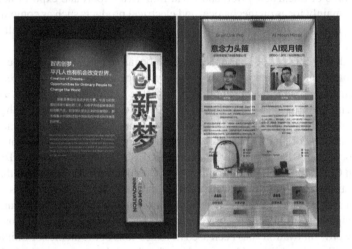

Fig. 2. Exhibition of Maker Culture in Huaqiangbei Museum

It can be seen that under the guidance of policies, Guangdong-Hong Kong-Macau Greater Bay Area has gradually formed the main advantages of the region: industrial chain and innovation chain. However, as a result of the strong requirements of technological and economic development, the original cultural outlook of Maker Movement is far from clear.

3   New Connotations to Maker Culture from Belt and Road Initiative Policy

In addition, the Belt and Road Initiative is also conducive to the development of Shenzhen Maker culture. However, in the policy of the "Belt and Road Initiative", culture and technology are two independent parts, namely, cultural and creative industries and technological innovation industries; The essence of maker culture means the intersecting part of these two fields, which reflects the culture reflexivity: scientific and technological culture. It is mainly manifested in the cultural education of young makers, exhibition activities, humanistic innovation construction of international blocks and so on.

Since 2013, the "Belt and Road Initiative" was formally put forward in the form of "Silk Road Economic Belt". Furthermore, the economic and trade cooperation as well as the bilateral and multilateral interconnection with relevant developing countries were gradually established within this framework, and the Belt and Road Initiative cooperation document was signed with New Zealand, a western developed country, for the first time in 2017. Hence, the connotation of the Silk Road from the narrow sense is constantly expanding and enriching with the needs of the times and industrial development. Since 2018, China's continuous holding of international import fairs functions as a signal, which means "firmly supporting trade liberalization and actively opening market to the world" and "building a new platform for all parties to enter the Chinese market".[3] As the main force of Shenzhen's Belt and Road Initiative import and export trade, private enterprises mainly focus on mechanical and electrical products such as computers, LCD panels, smart phones and so on, which are favored by countries along the "Belt and Road Initiative".

It was during this period that maker culture began to enter China and developed at the same pace, and the opportunities of policy happened to benefit culture. With the rise of cultural exchange events and forum activities such as Maker Space and Maker Carnival, another broader window has been opened for the construction of the Belt and Road Initiative. Examples include the Belt and Road China-Singapore Innovation & Entrepreneurship Forum (2016), the Belt and Road Cultural and Creative Entrepreneurship Competition (2019), the Belt & Road and BRICS Skills Development & Technology Innovation Competition (BRICS Youth Maker Competition, 2019)… With the integration of instructors at multiple levels such as industry development, skills guidance, innovation and invention, Chinese and foreign exchanges, teaching and training and so on, it attempted to stimulate the awakening of innovative talents in the industry. Since 1999, the word "innovation" has been used in 15 sessions of the themes of China Hi-Tech Fair held in Shenzhen initiated by a number of national departments, which shows that innovation has always been the core of high-tech industry. In 2021, the maker exhibition area and "the Belt and Road Initiative" special pavilion were set up. On the one hand, they gathered innovative and entrepreneurial projects, personal inventions and educational achievements of young makers from the entrepreneurship and innovation platform, college and university students and industry-university-research cooperation, and the achievements of emerging makers are displayed through roadshows and release activities; On the other hand, advanced technologies from all over the world and important international scientific and technological cooperation and exchange projects were demonstrated, focusing on the industries including electronic information, artificial intelligence, smart cities, energy conservation and environmental protection, new materials, new energy, high-end manufacturing, aerospace and so on. As two parallel exhibition

---

[3] Xi Jinping. Keeping Abreast of the Trend of the Times to Achieve Common Development-Speech at the BRICS Business Forum. [EB/OL]. Xinhuanet. 2018-7-26.

areas, we can see the basic significance for the development of high-tech industries by young makers or young innovative talents.

In terms of the creative design industry, Shenzhen, as the core leading city in Guangdong- Hong Kong -Macau Greater Bay Area, shall take the lead of building its own brand of "Design Capital" and becoming the spokesperson of Chinese innovative cultural city serving the world. In April, 2019, Shenzhen issued Opinions on Promoting the High-quality Development of Creative Design in Shenzhen[4], proposing "focusing on promoting the high-quality development of creative design industry", and taking the "going global" of creative design industry as an important path to expand the national culture and be geared to international standards. Specifically, it is manifested in selecting key enterprise projects for national cultural export, encouraging overseas investment cooperation, setting up industrial parks and institutions, and exploring overseas markets, especially the construction of industrial cooperation circles with the Belt and Road Initiative countries and regions and Guangdong-Hong Kong-Macau Greater Bay Area. Moreover, in "focusing on consolidating the creative design infrastructure in Shenzhen", the construction of new creative design space and design park, including maker spaces, is the key of optimizing the development environment of creative design, which will serve as a publicity window for external display and convey the signal of national policy support for design industries. These requirements for the development of creative design in Shenzhen are consistent with the Belt and Road Initiative Cultural Development Action Plan (2016–2020) issued by the Ministry of Culture in January 2017, with the special emphasis on effectively promoting the innovative development of cultural exchange, cultural communication and cultural trade. Specifically, by improving the cultural exchange and cooperation mechanism, establishing the cultural exchange and cooperation platform, and building cultural exchange and cooperation brands, the scale of cultural industry and foreign cultural trade can be formed.

Taking Shenzhen Culture, Creativity & Design Association (SCCDA)[5] as an example, as a professional, local and non-profit social organization voluntarily initiated by the relevant cultural creativity and design institutions, enterprises, designers and other cultural and creative workers in Shenzhen, it has absorbed nearly 160 members. There are four core tasks of SCCDA: (1) to provide professional consultation and suggestions for the government, and to standardize the management cultural creativity and design industries; (2) to optimize the resource allocation of cultural creativity and design industry in Shenzhen, and promote the exchange and cooperation of creative design; (3) to build a public service platform for cultural creativity and design industry, and provide relevant training, education and exchange activities; (4) to organize and plan promotion and exchange activities both at home and abroad, and publicize the brand image of Shenzhen as the "Design Capital". Among them, the first three points are carried out under

---

[4] *Several Opinions* Issued by the General Office of the Municipal Party Committee and the General Office of the Municipal Government to Promote the High-quality Development of Creative Design in Shenzhen. Shenzhen Special Zone Daily [EB/OL]. http://www.sz.gov.cn/cn/xxgk/zfxxgj/zwdt/content/post_1428869.html. 2019-07-22.

[5] The Shenzhen Design Capital Promotion Association, which runs and manages Shenzhen's design capital brand, changed its name in August 2021.

the intrinsic requirements additionally under "mass entrepreneurship and innovation", especially for the emerging cultural creativity and design makers.

In addition, international talents are also an important force led by the government to stimulate cultural flows, and the Belt and Road Initiative has also given new cultural connotations to maker culture in China. In June 2019, the Shenzhen Municipal Government issued the Implementation Opinions on Promoting the Construction of International Blocks and Improving the Internationalization Level of Cities, proposing that the first batch of 20 international blocks will be built in the next three years, covering 10 districts of the city, and at least 15 international blocks are to be completed in 2022. iMakerbase, which was first selected as a national maker space in Shenzhen, is located in a bright international block. The maker services it provides mainly include providing the global technology maker teams with intellectual property protection, brand design, industrial design, software design, hardware design, handboard production, 3D printing, mold manufacturing, SMT, small batch production, mass production, monitoring and certification, product crowdfunding, traditional e-commerce, livestream marketing, offline channels, cross-border trade, venture capital, banking finance, etc.; The whole process of hardware supply chain in-depth services includes all aspects of the process - product start-up design-production-marketing-financing. In supporting to promote the exchange and cooperation of design innovation between Greater Bay Area's industrial supply chain and countries along the route of the "Belt and Road Initiative", examples include the holding of "2020 International Innovation Design and GBA Hardware Supply Chain Cloud Forum" hosted by iMakerbase in Shenzhen Design Week in 2020. With the theme of "Industrial Chain Design, Innovation for the Future", innovative design representatives from the Belt and Road Initiative countries (Japan, Korea, Malaysia and Canada) and cities of Guangdong-Hong Kong-Macau Greater Bay Area were invited to jointly discuss how to deeply integrate innovative design and supply chain through activities such as forums, workshops, exhibitions, etc. However, the operation structure and discussion problems of iMakerbase reflect that the design does not reflect the innovation advantage as the basic link at the front end of innovation chain in the maker space services, which further indicates that the potential possibility of its soft power still needs to be deeply explored.

When more and more foreigners choose to settle in Shenzhen, and an increasing number of overseas creative companies are looking forward to setting up branches in Shenzhen and seeking development, it also proves that under the context of the Belt and Road Initiative and the industrial upgrading of the domestic Maker Movement, the guiding connotation of "bringing in and going global" is undergoing innovation: it is no longer simply focusing on introducing foreign capital, but focusing on bringing resources together in Guangdong-Hong Kong-Macau Greater Bay Area with talents as the core; The output is no longer low-end products, but innovative industrial services and achievements oriented to the future.

In addition to attracting external talents by incubating enterprises in maker spaces, keeping up the construction of public services in international blocks is an essential grass-roots work to ensure that talents live and work in peace and happiness. Shenzhen Foundation for International Exchange and Cooperation (SFIEC), a non-public welfare foundation established in 2014, is a diversified international exchange platform committed to integrating social resources such as government and social organizations, enterprises and think tanks, and continuously developing international exchange and cooperation brand activities and funded projects, so as to jointly promote foreign exchanges and cooperation of cities and the construction of international cities. It has established links with 35 cities in 26 countries. As a public window, the "CityPlus" project under the foundation provides various information to foreign makers who settle in Shenzhen. The presents such as *@755 Series City Guide, Diagram of Shenzhen International Block, Poster of Shenzhen International Block* and *Hand-painted Map of Shenzhen International Block*, etc. enable immigrants to quickly understand the resource distribution in Shenzhen and facilitate their living and work (Fig. 3).

Fig. 3. "@755" Series of City Guide

Located in Guanlan, Longhua District, a comprehensive public service platform with international first-class blocks as its construction goal, has built up its reputation as the "hometown of overseas Chinese". The first youth maker center in Guangdong-Hong Kong-Macau Greater Bay Area with "New Cultural Creativity" as its core is Guanlan International Block Service Center. The service center mainly provides online and offline shared services for international friends, young people from Hong Kong and Macao, high-end talents, street residents and social organizations. With Guangdong-Hong Kong-Macau Greater Bay Area "New Cultural Creativity" entrepreneurial youth or team as the main part, it provides one-stop services such as workplace, entrepreneurship policy interpretation, entrepreneurship counseling, practical support, resource link, intellectual property application and protection, etc. Nevertheless, as far as resource links are concerned, the current main services are concentrated in administrative resources in the entrepreneurial application stage including industrial and commercial registration, financial management, legal consultation, policy declaration, marketing, intellectual property planning and so on. If foreign makers hope to get further information on industry trends or professional guidance to design or cultural and creative industries, but they are lack of related resource links, which will bring great uncertainty to the construction of a creative and sustainable cultural block. In the long run, community services will lose reputation and influence, for lack of content and characteristics (Fig. 4).

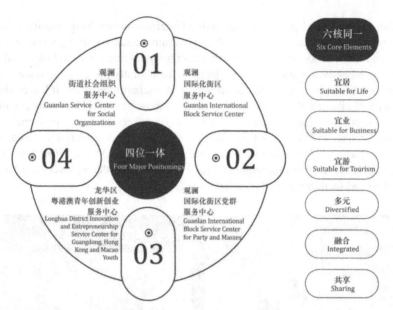

Fig. 4. Building a comprehensive public service platform centering "Four Major Positionings and Six Core Elements" in Guanlan International Block Service Center

4 Conclusions and Suggestions

With nearly seven years of exploration and the guidance of the entrepreneurship and innovation policies policy, the Maker Movement has formed a top-down innovation and entrepreneurship model in China. Development of innovative industries is the original purpose, exploration and introduction of innovative talents, and the support and invest-ment of funds and service platforms are the conditions, while the exhibition activities, grand prize competitions and maker education are the paths. However, due to the rapid process of promoting technological development and industrial transformation, the basic research and communication of the Maker Movement in the integration of science and technology and design culture are far from adequate, which makes Greater Bay Area fail to form a relatively stable cultural outlook based on the genes of Chinese maker cul-ture, which also deviates from the original purpose of the Maker Movement. While the Belt and Road Initiative encourages and promotes "soft innovation", the contemporary connotation of "bringing in and going global" has changed: it is no longer to introduce technology and export products, but to introduce talents and export culture so as to realize the endogenous development. With the intervention of design, the innovation factors in the spontaneous stage of culture can be fully explored, the path of industrial transformation can be expanded, and information dissemination can be accelerated, so that the genes of maker culture can bring much more potential possibilities.

Culture flows not only geographically, but also among different groups of people. The most important is to break the barriers between high-tech industries and cultural and creative industries by means of design, connecting "technology" and "culture" at the level of design intervention. For example, setting up design departments in innovation committees, public technology service platforms and industrial promotion centers to promote the integration of technology and culture, so as to emphasize the value of design in science and technology culture in specific industrial requirements, and enrich the dimensions and transmission channels of "culture" from different levels, and expand the publicity of design in enhancing the cultural value of makers. Therefore, our view of maker culture in Shenzhen shall be established on the basic cognition of cultural flow. Maker spaces are not only the business incubators linking industries, but should be more regarded as the carriers for gestating scientific and technological culture, exchanging and sharing technical knowledge and cultural experience.

References

1. Shenzhen Finance Committee, Shenzhen Science and Technology Innovation Committee. Interim Measures for the Administration of Special Funds for Makers in Shenzhen (2015). http://www.sz.gov.cn/zwgk/zfxxgk/zfwj/bmgfxwj/content/post_6573208.html
2. Interview Record. Current Situation and Future of Maker Market in the Eyes of ROHM and "Chaihuo Makers" Part 1. R Class. https://techclass.rohm.com.cn/knowledge/tech-info/inspire/events/7775. Accessed 05 Oct 2020
3. Shenzhen Science and Technology Innovation Committee, Policy Interpretation of Measures of Shenzhen Municipality on the Administration of Science and Technology Business Incubators and Maker Spaces [EB/OL]. http://www.sz.gov.cn/zfgb/zcjd/content/post_6735231.html. Accessed 09 Feb 2020
4. Shenzhen Culture, Creativity & Design Association (SCCDA). Shenzhen Design Capital Report 2019 [R/OL]. SCCDA. https://szcod.org/codsz
5. Shenzhen Cultural Innovation and Development 2020 (Implementation Plan) [EB/OL]. Shenkexin. http://sz.shenkexin.com/news/info-policy-2515.html. Accessed 05 June 2018

Research on the Experience of Beautiful Rural Spatial Morphology in Shaoguan Area of Northern Guangdong Province Based on Space Syntax: A Case Study of Bailou Village, Shatian Town, Xinfeng County

Luyao Zhang[ID] and Mingjie Liang[(✉)][ID]

School of Design, South China University of Technology,
Guangzhou 510006, People's Republic of China
lmj1700@163.com

Abstract. Shaoguan area in northern Guangdong, as a broad branch of Lingnan regional culture, is rich in traditional villages. With the in-depth development of the Rural Revitalization Strategy, Shaoguan has advantage of backwardness. Taking the Hakka traditional village in Shatian Town, Xinfeng County, Shaoguan City, Guangdong Province as an example, this paper uses the Space Syntax theory and method, uses DepthMap software to establish the axial model and visual model, quantitatively analyzes its spatial morphological characteristics and internal texture through relevant indicators, summarizes the optimization countermeasures of beautiful rural experience, and refines the scientific method of renewing and transforming the spatial vitality of traditional village streets, in order to provide reference for the experience of beautiful rural spatial form.

Keywords: Shaoguan region of Northern Guangdong · Traditional villages · Space Syntax · DepthMap software · Spatial Morphology experience

1 Introduction

The Rural Revitalization Strategy (2018–2022), the 14th Five-Year Plan (2021–2025) for economic and social development and the long-range objectives through the year 2035 put forward higher requirements for rural revitalization, adhere to the priority development of agriculture and rural areas, and comprehensively promote rural revitalization.

As a strategic ecological development zone in Guangdong Province, northern Guangdong has great ecological value within the scope of the province and even a larger geographical space. Shaoguan area in northern Guangdong is a broad branch of Hakka culture in Lingnan regional culture (Guangfu culture, Chaoshan culture and Hakka Culture), which has strong uniqueness.

M. M. Soares et al. (Eds.): HCII 2022, LNCS 13322, pp. 488–501, 2022.
https://doi.org/10.1007/978-3-031-05900-1_35

In the past, the construction of beautiful villages in China mainly consisted of the top-down construction method led by the government and the bottom-up construction method led by the villagers. The former is easy to cause one sidedness in the construction content, rapidity and closeness in the construction process, subjectivity in the landscape pattern and neglect of villagers in the interest pattern; the latter has single content, destroyed landscape pattern, arbitrariness of construction process and sacrifice of public interests [1].

Space Syntax theory is used to study social logic problems in spatial structures and the spatial laws within them. Since the 1970s, Space Syntax theory has been widely used in the research fields of cities, settlements, architecture, gardens and other fields. Space Syntax gives three classical space segmentation methods, namely convex space method, axial method and visual method. The convex space method is applicable to static internal space of buildings, public space of cities and settlements, the axial method is applicable to dynamic linear space such as cities and streets, and the visual method is applicable to static nonlinear space [2]. This paper will use the axial model and the visual model from both dynamic and static aspects, and select the corresponding theory for topological relationship analysis according to the characteristics of spatial analysis.

2   Current Situation of Traditional Villages in Shatian Town, Xinfeng County, Shaoguan, Northern Guangdong

2.1   Village Architecture

The Macro Level. The building complex is built according to the mountainous terrain, with scattered roofs, undulating contours and a sense of tranquility from a distance. However, the architectural style is diverse, the color of the facade is not unified, and presents a pattern of obvious separation between the new residential area and the old residential area.

The Meso Level. Some Hakka traditional ancient buildings in the village have strong regional style characteristics, which is of far-reaching significance for continuing Hakka historical context and retaining Hakka nostalgic memory. But at the same time, some mud brick houses with a long history are in disrepair for a long time, which has a certain potential residential safety hazard. The newly-built or renovated residential houses around blindly follow the urban architectural model, resulting in a strong contrast between the old and new architectural styles.

The Micro Level. Some of the traditional Hakka buildings with a long history are rich in details in roof shape, eaves painting, wood carvings on beams, etc., which are the treasures of Hakka history and culture. However, due to the lack of protection, some decorations have been damaged. New or renovated buildings also have problems such as private wires and untidy walls, which affect the overall building environmental quality.

2.2 Village Landscape

The landscape of Bailou village level can be divided into habitat landscape, production landscape and living landscape. After field investigation and survey, the author sorted out the overall landscape pattern, landscape elements and element types of the village (see Table 1).

Table 1. Landscape elements to be considered at village level.

Village landscape	Overall landscape pattern	Landscape elements	Element type
Habitat landscape	Node - Street - production cluster - living cluster	Terrain	Basin
		Botany	Camphor, crape myrtle, yellow locust, mango, loquat, papaya, Tsui Luli, red pompon, Hairy Cuckoo, Safflower sorrel, Bidens pilosa, Lantana camara, etc.
		Water	Wenluo River and Meikeng River
Production landscape		Production room	The processing plant of local agricultural products such as sugar orange and passion fruit
		Water conservancy facilities	Dam on the west side of Bailou Village
		Drying site	Most of them are village squares, idle space in front of and behind houses, and roofs
		Small production area	Passion fruit base and agro-ecological park, Bailou Tabebuia chrysantha nursery garden and rape flower planting site
Living landscape		Street network	X851 and X262 county roads constitute the main road skeleton of the town
		Housing cluster	Wenluo River bank-X851-Bailou main Road residential group
		Public activity scenario	Bailou village square, Bailou village ancestral hall, Tabebuia chrysantha nursery garden clip Road

3   Data Sources and Research Methods

This study mainly used the field survey data of Bailou Traditional Village in Shatian Town, Xinfeng County, Shaoguan City, Guangdong Province (Fig. 1), combined with aerial photos (Fig. 2) as the base map, to draw its convex space plan, street and lane network axial map, etc., and to establish a spatial model and database.

Based on the spatial survey data, this study selects the axial method and visual method of Space Syntax to analyze the spatial morphology and internal texture of the village, imports the road network axial map and convex spatial plan into the Space Syntax software DepthMap, draws the axial and visual model required for spatial analysis, and further select the axial integration, axial synergy, visual integration, visual clustering coefficient, visual control and so on from many spatial measurement indicators. Through analysis and arrangement, the morphological characteristics of its inner street space and visual space are obtained.

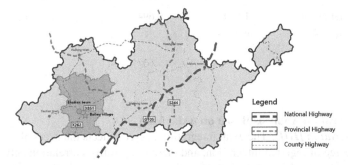

Fig. 1. Location map of Bailou Village, Shatian Town, Xinfeng County, Shaoguan City.

Fig. 2. Aerial map of Bailou Village, Shatian Town, Xinfeng County, Shaoguan City.

4 Analysis of Spatial Morphological Features of Beautiful Countryside Based on Space Syntax

4.1 Axial Analysis

The axial model analyzes the road space and square space around the plot of Bailou village, puts the street network at the center of the research, and analyzes its different forms [3]. In the analysis of axial model, two important indicators of axial integration and axial synergy are selected to analyze the spatial morphological characteristics of village dynamic street space. The axial model of Bailou village contains 79 axes in total, and the specific axial analysis and related measurement indicators are shown in Table 2.

Table 2. Relevant measurement indicators of axial analysis.

Name	Maximum	Minimum value	Average value
Axial integration [HH]	1.519	0.694	1.154
Intelligibility (R^2)	0.833		
Count	79		

Axial Integration Analysis Based on Axial Map

Axial Integration [HH]. The axial integration degree reflects the accessibility of space and the degree of regional integration, and there is a positive correlation between them, the greater the axial integration degree, the higher the accessibility, and vice versa. According to the analysis of the axial graph of the axial integration degree of Bailou traditional village (see Fig. 3), the axial integration degree of the village gradually decreases from three roads to the interior of the village, showing typical linear and core characteristics. The lowest axial integration is in the axis where the road to a villager's house is located at the end of Bailou Village, with a value of 0.694. Combined with the current situation, the road leads directly to the old residence of the villager with a sloping roof, which is open circuit and unreachable. The average value of the axial integration degree of Bailou Village is 1.154, and the number of axes greater than 1.154 accounts for 29.11% of the total, indicating that the axial integration degree is not high and the accessibility is general, which is mainly due to the relatively independent internal courtyard enclosure and ancestral hall layout of the village, resulting in low axial integration and poor traffic accessibility.

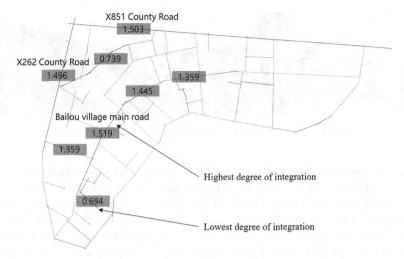

Fig. 3. Integration [HH] diagram based on axial map.

Axial Integration Core. The axial integration core (the 10% most integrated lines) refers to the collection of elements with the highest integration value, that is, the collection of streets with the highest accessibility [3]. Among them, the integration of Bailou Village Main Street (the section from the Villagers' Square to the ancestral hall), X851 County Road and X262 county road is greater than 1.305, and the accessibility is very high. According to the field investigation, there is the only basketball court and fitness activity area in the central main street of Bailou Village (as shown in Fig. 4). In addition to public activities, the square is also the villagers' grain drying field and the core functional area of the village. Opposite the square is the old ancestral hall of Bailou Village (Fig. 5), the walls of the ancestral hall are relatively well preserved, and the main building inside the ancestral hall has fallen into disrepair and the utilization rate is low. The intersection of two county roads at the periphery of the village is close to 90°, which is an important road connecting Bailou village to the outside world. X262 county road is the only channel connecting Bailou village, Xianshui village and Shatin Town, and its traffic accessibility is very high.

Fig. 4. Bailou village basketball court (Photo by the author).

Fig. 5. Ancestral hall of Bailou Village (Photo by the author).

Axial Synergy Analysis Based on Axial Map. Different integration radii reflect urban systems of different scales, and the key to understanding parts and wholes is to understand the relationship between different radii of integration [3]. Space Syntax theory leads to the concept of synergy, that is, the synergy between local and global accessibility is judged by the correlation between local integration and global integration. Limited to the three topological steps of Bailou village, after intercepting a small area near the central space, the scatter diagram of the relative position of each axial in the axial graph of the whole village is shown in Fig. 6, in which the horizontal axis represents the axial integration degree (radius n) and the vertical axis represents the local integration degree (radius 3). If the two are linearly related, the local and global traffic accessibility synergy is good. In addition, most of the axes with high local integration value are the axes starting from the edge and passing through the center. The scatter diagram composed of the axial integration value of these axes determines the slope of the fitted trend line [3].

According to the Rn-R3 scatter diagram of Bailou Village (Fig. 6), the local integration degree and global integration degree of the village basically have a linear distribution, and the correlation coefficient is 0.833 > 0.7. There is a high positive correlation between the two, with good synergy, namely, after reducing the analysis scope and remapping, the area with the highest local integration degree of the village is roughly the same as the area with the highest global integration degree of the whole village. The slope of the fitted trend line is 1.857, indicating that the local integration value of the axial with the highest integration degree in Bailou village is higher than its global integration value. After comparing the data, it is found that the maximum value of local integration is 2.283, which is 0.764 higher than that of 1.519, and the average value of local integration is 0.206 higher than the average value of global integration, illustrating that there are characteristics in the areas where the integration core is located, and it shows high accessibility in the systems of villages with different measurement scales, it can attract more people. In addition, most of the scatters coincide with the linear regression line of the local-global integration fit scatter map of the whole village, which means that Bailou Village as a whole is more of a smaller space connected to the main network of villages and towns, and the number of local characteristic areas outside the trunk grid is smaller. On the other hand, there are three areas in the village (a homestead tunnel road at the end of the village, an ancestral garden road and a homestead in the southwest of the village) with extremely low global and local integration. In the axial analysis, they can be regarded as an isolated space and do not exist as a secondary area [4].

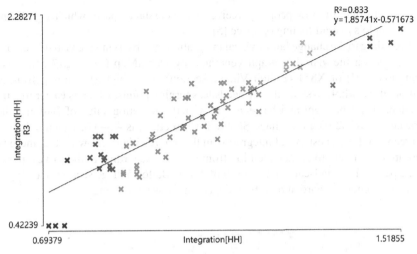

Fig. 6. Rn-R3 scatter diagram.

4.2 Visibility Graph Analysis

Visibility graph analysis mainly selects three representative indicators: visual integration [HH], visual clustering coefficient and control values to analyze the spatial morphological characteristics of static visual field. The visual model of Bailou village contains 36033 elements involved in operation, and its specific relevant measurement indicators are shown in Table 3.

Table 3. Relevant measurement indicators of visual analysis.

Name	Maximum	Minimum value
Visual integration [HH]	10.376	2.035
Visual clustering coefficient	1.000	0.306
Visual control	1.926	0.007
Visual controllability	0.680	0.006

Visual Integration Analysis. In the analysis of visual integration, the village is divided into topological structure based on square grid. In the actual calculation, DepthMap software abstracts the square grid into topological elements, calculates the total visual depth of each square grid, and then forms the visual integration degree value after mathematical calculation. Visual integration [HH] means that the global visual depth is the shallowest after eliminating all influencing factors in topology. Visual integration has a direct effect on how people perceive and understand space, which significantly affects people's overall feeling of space [5].

According to the change law of visual integration, by observing the visual integration [HH] based on the visibility graph generated by DepthMap (see Fig. 7), the visual integration [HH] of X851 (Bailou Village section) is the highest. Starting from any position of the whole system, it only needs less turning points, which is easier to attract the attention of the sight and be seen; The visual integration value of Bailou village entrance and X262 (Bailou village Shatin Town section) is 4.5–5.0, which belongs to the area with the highest visual integration in the whole village, showing that these two areas are most likely to attract attention from the eye; According to the survey, there is a large paddy field landscape in the north of X851 (Bailou Village section) (see Fig. 8), and a large vegetable garden built by villagers in the west of X262.

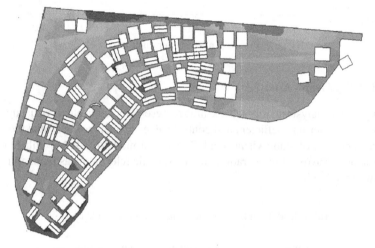

Fig. 7. Visual integration based on visibility graph [HH].

Fig. 8. Landscape of paddy field in the north of X851.

Visual Clustering Coefficient Analysis. Visual clustering coefficient refers to the strength of the visual limiting effect of spatial boundary (the spatial boundary is assumed to be an opaque entity interface in DepthMap software). The higher the value, the stronger the effect of the restriction. The value of visual clustering coefficient can better predict the degree of spatial privacy and openness. In terms of specific spatial function distribution, it can better predict the display effect of space. For example, some religious and ritual spaces require high spatial function privacy.

According to the analysis chart of visual clustering coefficient (see Fig. 9), on the whole, in Bailou village, the value of visual clustering coefficient in the periphery of the village is low, and gradually increases in the interior of the village. The village presents a good sense of encirclement and extends outward with a transparent line of sight. Due to the large number of self-built houses along the main road of the village, the spatial boundary composed of the building facade has a great visual restriction, and the sight is obscured to a high extent. On the one hand, the ancestral hall area is closely connected with the surrounding buildings, and the sight on both sides is limited; On the other hand, the entrance of the ancestral hall is close to the main road, which is opposite to the Bailou village square, and the value of visual clustering coefficient decreases rapidly. In the actual investigation, the entrance to the ancestral hall courtyard looks out of the sight, and the facade of the surrounding buildings in the ancestral hall courtyard is tall, which effectively reduces the field of view and better focuses people's eyes on the ancestral hall building itself.

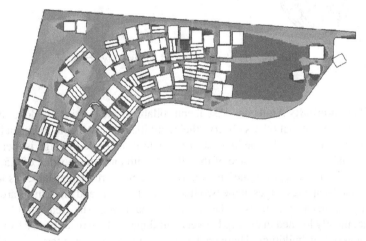

Fig. 9. Visual clustering efficiency based on visibility graph.

Visual Control Analysis. Visual control refers to the visually dominant area, which is easily to see people's activities without difficulty being seen by the observer. According to the analysis chart of visual control (see Fig. 10), the place with the largest visual control range in the village is located in the center of Bailou village square, with a value of 1.785, which is the place with the highest sight span in the whole village. For one thing, the area is the only activity square in the village, with a good sight. There are many historical buildings around, and it is enclosed, reflecting the core position. And the area is an important traffic road and a core distribution center. Most of the places with small visual control range are located in the areas close to the villagers' self-built houses. Some of the "handshake buildings" have weak accessibility and insufficient importance between the sides or backs of the building. Some villagers' old houses are closely connected with the new homestead, the protection of the old houses is poor, and there are few other core landscapes. They are in marginal areas, and their social status will decline significantly, visual control ability is at a disadvantage.

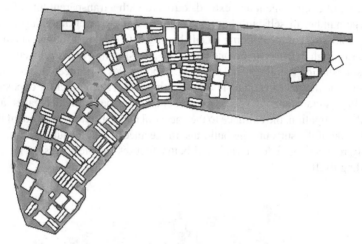

Fig. 10. Visual control based on visibility graph.

Visual Controllability Analysis. Visual controllability means visually dominant area, people are not aware that others observe their activities. According to the visual control analysis chart (see Fig. 11), the highest visual control of Bailou village is located in a large farmland area at the entrance of the village, with an average value of 0.5. It is an area with high visual depth in the village. There are more rural landscape resources in sight, less landscape resources at the two line of sight depths, and more turns are needed in other areas, this area belongs to the visual dominant area. The areas with low visual control are mostly located in the gap between buildings and the road formed by the close arrangement of row buildings. There are less landscape resources in the scope of vision, and there are more landscape resources from the two sight depths, the visual dominance is low.

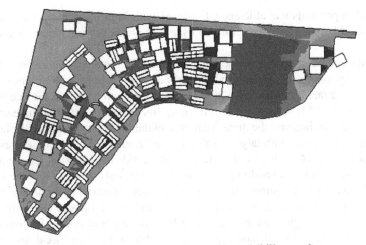

Fig. 11. Visual controllability based on visibility graph.

5   Discussion and Conclusion

Spatial form is the form and significance of each spatial element after forming a whole through structural relationship. Spatial form contains two meanings: one is spatial element, which refers to the real form that people can see with the naked eye, which is a tangible and objective spatial form; Second is the form and significance of the spatial elements after they constitute the whole, including the spatial characteristics and significance formed by the construction mode, lifestyle and cultural concept, as well as people's cognition and psychological feeling of space, which forms a subjective and invisible spatial form [6].

5.1   Spatial Syntactic Optimization Strategy

In terms of dynamic street space function experience optimization starting from the axial model, Bailou village can improve the road network structure as a whole, sort out some unreachable areas, add garden roads behind the village, open up the inside and outside of the village, and make the village boundary more transparent and enrich the internal experience of the village; The area of integration core can increase public facilities, such as table tennis table, billboard and cultural stage, so as to make the core position of the area more obvious; At the same time, fully excavate the areas with good synergy and accessibility in the village, and add characteristic areas, such as small garden demonstration sites and viewing platform behind the village. For the areas with poor accessibility, targeted functional points can be added according to the current characteristics, such as improving the poultry captive shed behind the village. The overall idea of experience optimization of beautiful rural spatial form is to optimize the spatial structure near the core of integration to the greatest extent and in the most detail. The traditional village experience design can take the public space as the core point, distribute dispersed, strengthen the vitality of the traditional village public square space and improve its use efficiency. For areas with high integration, the streets and alleys should be open and open from all over the village, full of changes and increase interest.

The static street space form experience based on the visual model can provide a way to deeply experience the agricultural interests of rice fields by adding viewing plank roads and other facilities for areas with high visual integration, such as the rice field area in the north of X851; A large area with strong line of sight control at the entrance of Bailou village can increase the theme sculpture of the village and enhance the landmark of the portal; For areas with large visual clustering coefficient, we can make use of the comparison of visual limiting effects inside and outside the ancestral temple to better repair the ancestral temple buildings and enrich the cultural connotation of the ancestral temple. Visual control ensures a degree of relaxation and enriches the focus of vision. The area with a wide range of visual control in traditional villages has nothing to do with the building height. Control the height limit of self-built houses in rural areas to ensure a wide view of rural landscape. The "handshake building" weakens the visual control, in the design process, we should take cultural development as the starting point, fully investigate the needs of relevant stakeholders (local residents, tourists, government, etc.), and improve the visual experience of traditional villages.

5.2   Spatial Element Level Optimization Strategy

Reconstruct the landmark historical buildings and improve the architectural experience of ancestral halls in Bailou village. Repair the ancestral hall building, and transform the key buildings and enclosed space in the village into a unified facade. Other buildings in the ancestral hall courtyard can be transformed into an elderly activity center or cultural activity room according to the actual functional needs, so as to improve the integration and control value of the region and further enhance the regional social status and influence.

Maintain the natural ecological landscape and create a harmonious, interactive and sustainable rural ecological experience. Bailou village has rich natural conditions and distinctive rural landscape. On the basis of respecting the local natural environment, it will be regarded as an ecological whole to create a beautiful ecological environment of mountains, rivers, forests and fields.

Highlight the historical and cultural connotation of Hakka region and create a red tourism cultural experience. As a village in northern Guangdong Hakka area, it forms a cultural background with the historical landscape of northern Guangdong Hakka culture and red revolutionary culture, and creates an external environmental image with Hakka cultural symbols.

5.3   Subjective Perception Level Optimization Strategy

Respect the original culture of the site, develop the village form, and tap the local advantages of Shatian town's fruit industry. The Fruit cultural tourism brand, which focuses on the passion fruit industry, converts the advantages of the village's historical resources and industrial resources into rural tourism cards, carries out local leisure activities, promotes tourism development, and makes Bailou village a place to carry nostalgia, establish a career, settle down and rest.

Give full play to the local advantages of each village in Shatian Town, create different natural space experiences, combine the different needs of stakeholders, create a livable rural landscape in northern Guangdong, create rich and diverse leisure activity space and characteristic tour lines, and promote industrial upgrading, spatial vitality and ecological improvement.

Acknowledgements. This research is supported by Guangdong Philosophy and Social Science Planning Project "Research on the Logic of Painting and Gardening in Jiangnan, Ming and Qing Dynasties" (X2sjN4210430).

References

1. Weiwei, S.: Research on the Integrated Method of Rural Landscape Construction of Zhejiang Region, 1st edn. Southeast University Press, Nanjing (2016)
2. Xiaorui, Z., Zhigang, C., Yan, B.: Progress and prospects of spatial syntax research. Geogr. Geo-Inf. Sci. **30**(3), 82–87 (2014)
3. Hillier, B.: Space is the Machine: A Configurational Theory of Architecture, 3rd edn. Space Syntax Press, London (2007)
4. Yixi, L., Ning, W., Yana, W., Zhiyao, M.: Research on the optimization strategy of traditional village protection and inheritance based on spatial syntax: taking Furong Village in Yongjia as an example. J. Tianjin Univ. Soc. Sci. Edn. **22**(3), 275–281 (2020)
5. Xiaoqin, W., Chunqing, L., Jianhua, J.: Research on the morphological characteristics and influencing factors of public space around Hakka Villages in Southern Jiangxi Province: case study of Li Yuen Wai in Jiangxi Province. Decoration **7**, 108–111 (2019)
6. Xuemei, Z.: Traditional Village Forms and Architectural and Cultural Characteristics in Northern Guangdong, 1st edn. China Construction Industry Press, Beijing (2015)

Author Index

Printed in the United States
by Baker & Taylor Publisher Services

Printed in the United States
by Baker & Taylor Publisher Services